# Excel 2.1 Made Easy:
# IBM PC Version

# Excel 2.1 Made Easy
# IBM PC Version

Martin S. Matthews

**Osborne McGraw-Hill**
Berkeley  New York  St. Louis  San Francisco
Auckland  Bogotá  Hamburg  London  Madrid
Mexico City  Milan  Montreal  New Delhi  Panama City
Paris  São Paulo  Singapore  Sydney
Tokyo  Toronto

Osborne **McGraw-Hill**
2600 Tenth Street
Berkeley, California 94710
U.S.A.

Osborne/McGraw-Hill offers software for sale. For information on software, translations, or book distributors outside of the U.S.A., please write to Osborne **McGraw-Hill** at the above address.

This book is printed on recycled paper.
This book was produced using Ventura Publisher Version 2.0.

### Excel 2.1 Made Easy: IBM PC Version

Copyright © 1990 by Martin S. Matthews and Carole Boggs Matthews. All rights reserved. Printed in the United States of America. Except as permitted under the Copyright Act of 1976, no part of this publication may be reproduced or distributed in any form or by any means, or stored in a database or retrieval system, without the prior written permission of the publisher, with the exception that the program listings may be entered, stored, and executed in a computer system, but they may not be reproduced for publication.

1234567890 DOC 99876543210

ISBN 0-07-881677-7

Acquisitions Editor: Jeff Pepper
Technical Reviewer: Dan Fingerman
Copy Editor: Barbara Conway
Word Processors: Lynda Higham, Judy Koplan, Stefany Otis
Composition: Bonnie Bozorg
Proofreaders: Julie Anjos, Jeff Green
Cover Design: Bay Graphics Design, Inc.
Production Supervisor: Kevin Shafer

Information has been obtained by Osborne **McGraw-Hill** from sources believed to be reliable. However, because of the possibility of human or mechanical error by our sources, Osborne **McGraw-Hill**, or others, Osborne **McGraw-Hill** does not guarantee the accuracy, adequacy, or completeness of any information and is not responsible for any errors or omissions or the results obtained from the use of such information.

# CONTENTS AT A GLANCE

|   | I   | Introducing Windows and Excel |   |
|---|-----|-------------------------------|---|
| 1 |     | The Windows Environment       | 5 |
| 2 |     | The Components of Excel       | 51 |
| 3 |     | The Excel Environment         | 77 |
| 4 |     | Entering and Editing Information | 103 |
|   | II  | The Fundamentals of Excel     |   |
| 5 |     | Creating a Worksheet          | 135 |
| 6 |     | Enhancing a Worksheet         | 183 |
| 7 |     | Producing Charts              | 229 |
| 8 |     | Building a Database           | 283 |
|   | III | Advanced Uses of Excel        |   |
| 9 |     | Linking Worksheets and Using External Files | 331 |
| 10|     | Dates, Functions, and Macros  | 369 |
| 11|     | Automating a Worksheet        | 419 |
|   | IV  | Command Reference             |   |
| 12|     | Menu Commands                 | 473 |

| 13 | Functions | 565 |
|----|-----------|-----|
| 14 | Macro Functions | 627 |
| A  | Installing Windows and Excel | 705 |
|    | Index | 727 |

# TABLE OF CONTENTS

Introduction   xvii
Why This Book Is for You   1

## I   Introducing Windows and Excel

### 1   The Windows Environment ..................................... 5

Introducing Windows   6
The Windows Screen   8
Using the Mouse   10
    Mousing Around   10
Using Windows   14
    Using Scroll Bars   18
    Starting Applications   20
Using Menus   25
    Using Dialog Boxes   28
Using the Keyboard   31
    Using the Control Menu   33
Using the Main Group Applications   37
    Setting Defaults with the Control Panel   38
    Creating a Directory with the File Manager   41
Getting Help   45
Leaving Windows   49

### 2   The Components of Excel ..................................... 51

Worksheets   52
    Worksheets and Files   52

   Rows and Columns 53
   Addresses, Cells, and Ranges 54
   Formulas and Functions 57
   Commands 60
   Worksheet Windows 65
   Multiple Files and File Linking 66
   Help 68
  Databases 70
   Rows and Records 71
   Columns and Fields 71
   Using Databases 71
  Charts 73

**3 The Excel Environment ............................................. 77**

  Getting Started 77
  Excel's Screen and Menus 78
   The Worksheet Window 79
   The Excel Window 80
  Excel's Use of the Keyboard 91
   Direction Keys 92
   Function Keys 96
  Quitting Excel 102

**4 Entering and Editing Information ......................... 103**

  Typing on the Worksheet 104
   Entering Text Versus Numbers 104
   Completing an Entry and Moving to the Next Cell 113
  Making Changes 113
   Editing During Entry 114
   Using Undo 115
   Editing After Entry 115
   Editing with the Mouse 118
  Using Menus 120
  Using Files 124
   Naming Files 125

      Saving Files   126
      Using Directories   127
      Retrieving Files   128
Quitting Excel   129

## II   The Fundamentals of Excel

## 5   Creating a Worksheet .......................................... 135

Planning for a Worksheet   136
Placing Labels, Headings, and Titles   138
      Entering a Column of Labels   139
      Centering a Title   141
      Entering a Row of Headings   142
Placing a Border   143
Saving the Worksheet   146
Entering Numbers and Formulas   147
      Entering a Column of Numbers   148
      Building Formulas   150
      Copying Formulas   155
      Using Assumptions   157
      Using Absolute Addressing   159
      Editing Formulas   161
      Copying a Column of Formulas   166
Copying   167
Completing the Worksheet   169
      Producing a Total   169
      Calculating a Percentage   170
      Copying a Row of Formulas   170
      Clearing a Range of Cells   172
      Inserting a Row   174
      Deleting a Row   175
      Inserting and Deleting   176
      Making Corrections   177
      Saving and Quitting Excel   178

**6  Enhancing a Workshhet .......................................... 183**

    Loading a Worksheet   184
    Formatting   185
        Overall Number Format   186
        Formatting Alternatives   189
        Overall Column Width Format   195
    Detail Formatting   196
        Creating a Percentage Format   197
        Adding Dollar Signs   200
        Centering Headings   201
    Changing the Layout   202
        Moving Formulas   203
        Deleting a Column   204
        Adjusting Individual Column Width   204
        Recentering the Title   206
        Adding Notes to Cells   207
        Erasing a Range   208
        Using Undo   209
    Printing the Worksheet   211
        Setting the Parameters   211
        Doing the Printing   217
        Trial and Error   222
        Saving the Worksheet   224
    Making a Template   224
        Changing Titles   224
        Copying Values—Paste Special   225
        Other Modifications   226
        Saving and Quitting   227

**7  Producing Charts ...................................................... 229**

    How a Chart Is Built   230
        Standard Charts   230
        Customizing Charts   231
    Deciding What to Chart   237

Selecting the Type of Chart
- Area Charts 238
- Bar Charts 239
- Column Charts 242
- Combination Charts 243
- Line Charts 244
- Pie Charts 246
- Scatter Charts 248

Creating a Line Chart 251
- Selecting the Ranges to Plot 251
- Creating a New Chart 253
- Changing the Chart Type 254
- Adding Annotation 256
- Saving and Printing the Chart 267
- Closing a Chart 268

Building a Pie Chart 269
- Selecting a Pie Chart 269
- Adding a Title from the Worksheet 271
- Adding Refinements 273
- Saving, Printing, and Closing 276

Generating a Stacked Column Chart 278
- Building the Chart 278
- Saving, Printing, and Closing 279

Leaving Excel 281

## 8   Building a Database ............................................. 283

Building a Database 284
- Entering Field Names 284
- Numbering with a Data Series 285
- Entering Records 288

Sorting a Database 289
- Selecting the Sort Range 290
- Identifying a Sort Key 292
- Doing the Sort 294
- Changing and Resorting 294

...ation from a Database   296
　　Selecting a Second Database   296
　　　Bg the Database   301
　　　zing Information from a Database   312
　　Using Database Statistical Functions   313
　　Creating a Data Table   319
　　Working with Two-Input Data Tables   322
Using Lookup Functions   324

## III   Advanced Uses of Excel

### 9   Linking Worksheets and Using External Files .................................................. 331

Linking Worksheets   332
　　Creating Multiple Worksheets   334
　　Copying Across Worksheets   337
　　Creating Linking Formulas   342
　　Saving Multiple Worksheets   346
Combining Files   349
Saving a Worksheet as a Text File   353
Importing ASCII Text Files   359
　　Opening ASCII Delimited Text Files   361
　　Opening Nondelimited Text Files   362
　　Parsing Nondelimited Text Files   364

### 10   Dates, Functions, and Macros .............................. 369

Using Dates and Times   369
　　Dates and Excel   370
　　Times and Excel   372
　　Formatting Dates and Times   374
　　Date and Time Functions   375
　　Entering and Generating Dates and Times   378
　　Date and Time Arithmetic   385
Functions   387
　　Using Functions   388

        Additional Functions   392
    Macros   397
        Macro Basics   398
        Creating Additional Macros   403
        Entering Macros   411
        Function Macros   414

## 11  Automating a Worksheet ......................................... 419

    Planning an Application   420
        What Is It Going to Do   421
        How It Will Be Laid Out   422
    Building the Worksheet   423
        Building Screens   423
        Preparing for the Database   425
    Building the Macros   427
        Preparing and Controlling the Worksheet   429
        Building the Data Entry Tools   436
        Using Data Form for Editing   453
        Printing, Saving, and Quitting   455
        Building and Using a Menu   459
    Testing and Correcting the Macros   463
        Working Through the Application   463
    Future Enhancements   470

## IV  Command Reference

## 12  Menu Commands ....................................................... 473

## 13  Functions .................................................................. 565

## 14  Macro Functions........................................................ 627

## A  Installing Windows and Excel ................................. 705

    What Equipment Do You Need?   706
    What Equipment Do You Have?   708
        Memory   710

    Disk Drives 711
    Disk Directories 711
    Displays 713
    Printers 713
    Changing CONFIG.SYS 714
    Changing AUTOEXEC.BAT 715
Preparing to Store Data 716
    Creating Directories on a Hard Disk 717
Running Setup 718
Starting Windows and Excel 720
Leaving Excel and Windows 724

**Index** ............................................................................ **727**

# ACKNOWLEDGMENTS

Part IV of this book is a complete command reference section explaining every menu option, every worksheet function, and every macro function in Excel. The yeoman effort to produce this section came from Stephanie Thomson. She not only did this in a short period of time, but while she was completing her Junior year in Computer Science at the University of Washington. Her work is a very material part of the book and is greatly appreciated.

Dan Fingerman performed the technical review of the book and definitely improved its accuracy and readability. His efforts are appreciated.

Osborne/McGraw-Hill, as always, assembled an excellent team to produce this book. Thanks to Jeff Pepper, Editor in Chief, and all the others on the team.

    Selecting the Type of Chart   238
        Area Charts   238
        Bar Charts   239
        Column Charts   242
        Combination Charts   243
        Line Charts   244
        Pie Charts   246
        Scatter Charts   248
    Creating a Line Chart   251
        Selecting the Ranges to Plot   251
        Creating a New Chart   253
        Changing the Chart Type   254
        Adding Annotation   256
        Saving and Printing the Chart   267
        Closing a Chart   268
    Building a Pie Chart   269
        Selecting a Pie Chart   269
        Adding a Title from the Worksheet   271
        Adding Refinements   273
        Saving, Printing, and Closing   276
    Generating a Stacked Column Chart   278
        Building the Chart   278
        Saving, Printing, and Closing   279
    Leaving Excel   281

## 8   Building a Database .................................................. **283**

Building a Database   284
    Entering Field Names   284
    Numbering with a Data Series   285
    Entering Records   288
Sorting a Database   289
    Selecting the Sort Range   290
    Identifying a Sort Key   292
    Doing the Sort   294
    Changing and Resorting   294

Selecting Information from a Database   296
    Building a Second Database   296
    Using the Database   301
Analyzing Information from a Database   312
    Using Database Statistical Functions   313
    Creating a Data Table   319
    Working with Two-Input Data Tables   322
Using Lookup Functions   324

## III   Advanced Uses of Excel

### 9   Linking Worksheets and Using External Files ............ 331

Linking Worksheets   332
    Creating Multiple Worksheets   334
    Copying Across Worksheets   337
    Creating Linking Formulas   342
    Saving Multiple Worksheets   346
Combining Files   349
Saving a Worksheet as a Text File   353
Importing ASCII Text Files   359
    Opening ASCII Delimited Text Files   361
    Opening Nondelimited Text Files   362
    Parsing Nondelimited Text Files   364

### 10   Dates, Functions, and Macros ............ 369

Using Dates and Times   369
    Dates and Excel   370
    Times and Excel   372
    Formatting Dates and Times   374
    Date and Time Functions   375
    Entering and Generating Dates and Times   378
    Date and Time Arithmetic   385
Functions   387
    Using Functions   388

        Additional Functions   392  
   Macros   397  
        Macro Basics   398  
        Creating Additional Macros   403  
        Entering Macros   411  
        Function Macros   414  

## 11   Automating a Worksheet ......................................... 419

   Planning an Application   420  
        What Is It Going to Do   421  
        How It Will Be Laid Out   422  
   Building the Worksheet   423  
        Building Screens   423  
        Preparing for the Database   425  
   Building the Macros   427  
        Preparing and Controlling the Worksheet   429  
        Building the Data Entry Tools   436  
        Using Data Form for Editing   453  
        Printing, Saving, and Quitting   455  
        Building and Using a Menu   459  
   Testing and Correcting the Macros   463  
        Working Through the Application   463  
   Future Enhancements   470  

## IV    Command Reference

## 12   Menu Commands ....................................................... 473

## 13   Functions .................................................................. 565

## 14   Macro Functions ....................................................... 627

## A   Installing Windows and Excel ................................. 705

   What Equipment Do You Need?   706  
   What Equipment Do You Have?   708  
        Memory   710

　　　　Disk Drives   711
　　　　Disk Directories   711
　　　　Displays   713
　　　　Printers   713
　　　　Changing CONFIG.SYS   714
　　　　Changing AUTOEXEC.BAT   715
　Preparing to Store Data   716
　　　　Creating Directories on a Hard Disk   717
　Running Setup   718
　Starting Windows and Excel   720
　Leaving Excel and Windows   724

**Index** ............................................................................... **727**

# ACKNOWLEDGMENTS

Part IV of this book is a complete command reference section explaining every menu option, every worksheet function, and every macro function in Excel. The yeoman effort to produce this section came from Stephanie Thomson. She not only did this in a short period of time, but while she was completing her Junior year in Computer Science at the University of Washington. Her work is a very material part of the book and is greatly appreciated.

Dan Fingerman performed the technical review of the book and definitely improved its accuracy and readability. His efforts are appreciated.

Osborne/McGraw-Hill, as always, assembled an excellent team to produce this book. Thanks to Jeff Pepper, Editor in Chief, and all the others on the team.

# INTRODUCTION

Microsoft Excel, which runs in the Windows graphical environment, is an integrated business software package for producing worksheets, databases, and charts. Each of these products contribute to your ability to increase productivity and make better decisions in your business or profession. By doing this in a graphical environment, Excel adds real ease of use to a high degree of capability allowing you to easily do the tasks you need.

## ABOUT THIS BOOK

*Excel 2.1 Made Easy: IBM PC Version* supplements Microsoft's own documentation, the *Microsoft Excel Reference Guide*, by continuing where that documentation leaves off. Whereas the Microsoft documentation presents you with short and simple explanations designed to help you find answers to immediate questions, *Excel 2.1 Made Easy: IBM PC Version* provides more substantial examples designed not only to get you started, but also to guide you in building your skills so that you can perform more advanced business tasks—all with clear, step-by-step instructions.

# HOW THIS BOOK IS ORGANIZED

*Excel 2.1 Made Easy: IBM PC Version* was written the way most people learn Excel. The book starts by reviewing the basic concepts. It then uses a learn-by-doing method to demonstrate the major features of the product. Next, the book provides examples and clear explanation of many advanced features. Finally, it incorporates a complete reference section that documents every menu option, worksheet function, and macro function in Excel.

## Part I, Introducing Windows and Excel

Part I introduces Windows and Excel and provides the basic concepts needed to use them. It includes four chapters. The first explains the features and functions of Windows and the mouse that are needed to use Excel. Included are all parts of the screen, windowing, menus, the mouse buttons and moves, and using the keyboard. The second chapter describes each of the three components of Excel, worksheets, databases, and charts, with particular attention to worksheets. It also quickly introduces cells, ranges, formulas, functions, commands, and macros. The third chapter looks at how Excel uses the Windows graphical environment and the mouse to build and maintain worksheets. Each of the menus is described as are the keystrokes and mouse moves necessary to utilize them. Chapter 4 focuses on how to create and modify a worksheet, including using the menus, mouse, and keyboard to enter and edit information, save the worksheet, and leave Excel.

Part I provides the foundation concepts upon which all else in this book is based. This section will be slower paced than the rest of the book due to the importance of building a firm foundation. If you are a new user of Excel, Part I is vital to your success. If you have some experience with Excel you need Part I to a lessor extent. At the very least, you should skim Part I to assure that you have an understanding of the terms and concepts.

## Part II, The Fundamentals of Excel

Part II provides the fundamentals of Excel—creating and manipulating worksheets, producing charts, and using a database. It includes four chapters.

Chapters 5 and 6 are companions. Chapter 5 creates a worksheet. Included are planning, placing texts and headings, entering numbers and formulas, copying formulas, inserting and deleting rows, and saving the worksheet. Chapter 6 formats, changes, and prints the worksheet. Included are loading the worksheet, formatting numbers and headings, moving, deleting, erasing, and setting parameters for and printing the worksheet.

Chapter 7 looks at producing charts. It covers line charts, pie charts, and bar charts and includes selecting the type of chart, determining the worksheet ranges to plot, adding legends and titles, viewing, and printing.

Chapter 8 builds and uses a database. The chapter includes sorting a database and selecting and analyzing information from a database. In analyzing information, you are shown how statistical functions and data tables are used.

Part II should be read by all levels of users. For new users it provides the experience with which they can create their own worksheets, charts, and databases. For intermediate and advanced users, Part II provides a refresher course that also provides considerable insight into Excel.

## Part III, Advanced Uses of Excel

Part III contains three chapters that discuss the advanced features of Excel. The pace of presentation will quicken in Part III; the focus will almost entirely be on the advanced topics, with little or no time spent on the building of the worksheets used to demonstrate the topics. You may, if you wish, continue to follow along on your computer. The detailed steps for building the underlying worksheets, however, are left up to you.

Chapter 9 describes linking worksheets and using external files. Included are setting up links and transferring information among worksheets as well as combining worksheets, exporting and importing text files, and dividing or parsing a text file. Linking worksheets is one of the most powerful features of Excel.

Chapter 10 looks at worksheet functions and macro functions. The section on worksheet functions ties together the work already done on functions in previous chapters. It provides a general discussion on using them as well as discussion and examples of the types of functions not previously discussed. Most important here are date and time functions and text functions. The macro section looks at macro functions in general, discusses how they are built, used, and debugged, and provides a number of examples.

Chapter 11 provides the *pièce de résistance*—all of the features needed to automate a sophisticated worksheet. Included are automatic loading, custom menus, and updating of a database from a custom data entry dialog box, all operated by a set of macro commands. Chapter 11 shows you the full power of Excel.

It is not necessary for all readers to immediately read Part III. New users may want to wait until they have completed several spreadsheets of their own and know they want more of the capability of the product before reading Part III. Intermediate users probably will want to continue on immediately; it is the next logical step in their Excel education. This section is what advanced users have been waiting for! At some point, all readers are encouraged to go through Part III. The "booster rockets" of Excel are discussed in this part. Such things as linking worksheets, functions, and macros are not as hard to use as you might think, and they significantly increase the power of Excel.

## Part IV, Command Reference

Part IV provides a complete command reference for Excel. It lists in alphabetical order, and provides a description for every menu option, worksheet function, and macro function. Part IV is not meant to be read. Rather it is a quick and handy reference for looking up how a particular menu option or function works.

### Appendix, Installing Windows and Excel

The Appendix provides both the background and detail steps to install Windows and Excel. It describes what equipment you need, how to determine what equipment you have, and how to start and use both the Windows and the Excel Setup programs. In addition, it discusses how you prepare to store the data you will create with Excel and how to leave Windows and Excel.

## CONVENTIONS USED IN THIS BOOK

*Excel 2.1 Made Easy: IBM PC Version* uses several conventions designed to make the book easier for you to use. These are as follows:

- **Bold** type is used for text you are instructed to type from the keyboard.
- Keys on the keyboard that are commands are presented in key shaped boxes; for example, RIGHT ARROW and ENTER.
- When you are expected to enter a command, you will be told to *press* the key(s). If you are to enter text or numbers, you will be told to *type* them.

## ADDITIONAL HELP FROM OSBORNE/McGRAW-HILL

Osborne/McGraw-Hill provides top-quality books for computer users at every level of computing experience. To help you build your skills, we suggest that you look for the books in the following Osborne/McGraw-Hill series that best address your needs.

The "Teach Yourself" series is perfect for beginners who have never used a computer before or who want to gain confidence in using program basics. These books provide a simple, slow-paced introduction to the fundamental usage of popular software packages and programming languages. The "Mastery Skill Check" format ensures that concepts are learned thoroughly before progressing to new material. Plenty of exercises and examples are used throughout the text, and answers are at the back of the book.

The "Made Easy" series is also for beginners or users who may need a refresher on the new features of an upgraded product. These in-depth introductions guide users step-by-step from the program basics to intermediate-level usage. Plenty of hands-on exercises and examples are used in every chapter.

The "Using" series presents fast-paced guides that quickly cover beginning concepts and move on to intermediate-level techniques, and even some advanced topics. These books are written for users who already are familiar with computers and software and who want to get up to speed quickly with a certain product.

The "Advanced" series assumes that the reader is already an experienced user who has reached at least an intermediate skill level and is ready to learn more sophisticated techniques and refinements.

The "Complete Reference" series of handy desktop references list every command, feature, and function of popular software and programming languages, along with brief, detailed descriptions of how they are used. Books are fully indexed and often include tear-out command cards. This series is ideal for all users—beginners and pros.

The "Pocket Reference" is a pocket-sized, shorter version of the "Complete Reference" series and provides only the essential commands, features, and functions of software and programming languages for users who need a quick reminder of the most important commands. This series also is written for all users and every level of computing ability.

The "Secrets, Solutions, Shortcuts" series is written for beginning users who are already somewhat familiar with the software and for experienced users at intermediate and advanced levels. This series gives clever tips and points out shortcuts for using the software to greater advantage. Traps to avoid are also mentioned.

Osborne/McGraw-Hill also publishes many fine books that are not included in the series described above. If you have questions about which Osborne book is right for you, ask the salesperson at your local book or computer store.

# OTHER OSBORNE/MCGRAW-HILL BOOKS OF INTEREST TO YOU

We hope that *Excel 2.1 Made Easy: IBM PC Version* will assist you in mastering this fine product, and will also peak your interest in learning more about other ways to better use your computer.

If you're interested in expanding your skills so you can be even more "computer efficient", be sure to take advantage of Osborne/McGraw-Hill's large selection of top-quality computer books that cover all varieties of popular hardware, software, programming languages, and operating systems. While we cannot list every title here that may relate to Excel and to your special computing needs, here are just a few books that complement *Excel 2.1 Made Easy: IBM PC Version.*

Handle Microsoft's newest version of Windows effectively and creatively with the skills you learn from *Windows 3 Made Easy* by Tom Sheldon. If you're just beginning to use Windows, Tom Sheldon takes you through all the fundamentals step-by-step, including how to install it and get a fast start. If you're already using Windows, you'll learn all the newest features of the recently released version 3 and how to apply these capabilities through customizing Windows, transferring information between Windows, and Windows accessories like Write and Paintbrush. *Win-*

*dows 3 Made Easy* is loaded with short examples, hands-on projects, screen illustrations, and plenty of tips for everyday use.

## ABOUT THE AUTHOR

Martin Matthews is a partner in Matthews Technology, a company providing consulting and programming to large and small firms. He assists companies and individuals in selecting and installing computer systems and advises in the design and development of software. Martin combines expertise in computing with solid business experience. He has been president, vice president, as well as systems designer and software developer for a variety of companies. Martin has more than 30 years of computer experience. Martin Matthews and his wife Carole Boggs Matthews have authored thirteen other computer books including *AppleWorks Made Easy, Using PageMaker for the PC, AppleWorks: The Pocket Reference, WordStar Professional: The Complete Reference, Using WordStar Professional, Using 1-2-3 Release 3, Microsoft Works for the PC Made Easy, PageMaker 4 for the Macintosh Made Easy,* and *Q & A Made Easy.*

# DISK ORDER FORM

The worksheets, databases, and charts produced in this book are available on disk. The disk is not required to use the book, but by using the disk you can save the time and effort of typing the input and also eliminate the possibility of introducing errors.

The files are available on 360 KB 5 1/4" diskettes for the IBM PC or AT or 720 KB 3 1/2" diskettes for the IBM PS/2 and 100% compatible computers.

Be sure that your input is accurate and avoid the inconvenience of typing the detail by purchasing this disk. Save time and explore Excel now.

To order, complete the following form and return it to Matthews Technology with your payment. Please allow four to six weeks for delivery.

TO:          Matthews Technology
               P.O. Box 967
               Freeland, WA 98249

Please send me the disk indicated for *Excel 2.1 Made Easy: IBM PC Version*. My check for $15.00 in U.S. funds and drawn on a U.S. bank is enclosed. (Washington state residents add 7.8% sales tax for a total of $16.17.)

_____ 360 KB 5 1/4" disk     _____ 720 KB 3 1/2" disk

SEND TO:
Name: _____
Company: _____
Street: _____
City: _____ State: _____ ZIP: _____
Phone: _____

RETURN POLICY: Returns are accepted only if a disk is defective. In that case, return the disk within 15 days and you will be sent a replacement disk immediately.

*Osborne/McGraw-Hill assumes no responsibility for this offer. This is solely an offer of Matthews Technology and not of Osborne/McGraw-Hill.*

# WHY THIS BOOK IS FOR YOU

If you have purchased Excel or are contemplating buying it to use in your business, *Excel 2.1 Made Easy: IBM PC Version* was written for you. It will help you learn how to use Excel effectively in solving business problems and also to define the types of problems Excel can address. *Excel 2.1 Made Easy: IBM PC Version* will help you whether you're a new user of Excel or a somewhat experienced user who now wants to develop more advanced skills or get some new ideas on how you might apply the program.

Because the book is written for you, the business professional or small-business operator, the examples and exercises are designed to address real-life business problems, which you may find useful in and of themselves.

The book is a tutorial in which you learn by performing exercises. It instructs you in a step-by-step manner, explaining not only what you should do, but also why, and what the implications of each procedure are. As you work with the examples, you will be able to compare the screens on your monitor with reproductions of the screen throughout the book, so that you will always be firmly anchored in the program.

## LEARN MORE ABOUT EXCEL AND OTHER SOFTWARE YOU CAN USE WITH EXCEL

Here is an excellent selection of other Osborne/McGraw-Hill books on Excel and software you can use with Microsoft Excel that will help you build your skills and maximize your computer power.

*Excel Made Easy for the Macintosh*, by Edward Jones, helps you quickly learn Macintosh Excel Versions 1.5 and 2.2, even if you've never used a spreadsheet before. Jones covers designing, building, editing, and printing spreadsheets and discusses ways to create charts and build databases. There are also chapters on Excel's built-in functions and more advanced features.

*Using Microsoft Word for Windows*, by David Dean, shows you how to take full advantage of all the Windows graphical user interface features including clipboard and dynamic data exchange hot links. Dean covers in detail all the basic and advanced features of the program and how to best apply them.

# INTRODUCING WINDOWS AND EXCEL

Part I introduces Windows and Excel and provides the basic concepts needed to use Excel. It includes four chapters. Chapter 1 explains the features and functions of Windows and the mouse that you need to use Excel. It also discusses all parts of the screen, windowing, menus, the mouse buttons and moves, and using the keyboard. Chapter 2 describes the three components of Excel—worksheets, databases, and charts—with particular attention to worksheets. It also quickly introduces cells, ranges, formulas, functions, commands, and macros. Chapter 3 looks at how Excel uses the Windows graphical environment and the mouse to build and maintain worksheets. It describes each of the menus, as well as the keystrokes and mouse moves necessary to utilize them. Chapter 4 focuses on how to create and modify a worksheet, including using the menus, mouse, and keyboard to enter and edit information, save the worksheet, and leave Excel.

Part I covers concepts that form the foundation for the rest of this book. This section will be slower paced than other parts of the book due to the importance of building a firm foundation. If you are a new Excel user, Part I is vital to your success. If you have some experience with Excel, you need Part I to a lesser extent; however, you should at least skim it to assure that you have an understanding of the terms and concepts.

# 1

# THE WINDOWS ENVIRONMENT

Introducing Windows
The Windows Screen
Using the Mouse
Using Windows
Using Menus
Using the Keyboard
Using the Main Group Applications
Getting Help
Leaving Windows

Excel is a Windows application. This means that Excel requires Microsoft Windows for it to run. Windows provides the interface between you and Excel—the way Excel tells you on the screen what it is doing, and the way you tell Excel what to do. This chapter introduces you to some of the essentials of Microsoft Windows 3. You may never use all of the capabilities and tools available in Windows, but when you become acquainted with them, you will appreciate the additional power in the Excel environment.

This chapter is more of a tutorial than the rest of the book. It proceeds more slowly in order to establish a common ground for using this book and Excel. If you are already familiar with Windows and using a mouse, simply scan the chapter to verify that you know the vocabulary used here and the basic operating procedures used in Windows 3.

If you have installed the runtime version of Windows supplied with Excel rather than the full system, you cannot perform the exercises in this chapter. If you do not have Windows as a separate application, read this chapter anyway to see how Windows has influenced Excel. The runtime version of Windows is an older version (Microsoft does not produce a runtime version of Windows 3). Windows 3 has a different, much improved on-screen look and several different, improved commands. Therefore, it is recommended that you use the full Windows 3 in place of the runtime version.

## INTRODUCING WINDOWS

Excel is designed to run "under" Microsoft Windows, an extension of the MS-DOS operating system. This is desirable for several reasons, but primarily because Windows offers a standard environment for all of the programs, or *applications,* that run under it. This environment consists chiefly of a standard screen display, or *visual interface,* that you use to communicate with Windows applications. Once you learn to use Windows, you will find that working with the various applications, including Excel, that run under Windows is very similar.

Windows also provides a way to transfer information among applications, such as from Excel to Word for Windows or to PageMaker. Through this feature, called the Clipboard, you can easily move a portion of an Excel worksheet or an Excel chart to a word processing document.

Windows 3 also allows you to load more than one application into memory at once and to switch between them with minimal effort. You can work with a word processor, a graphics application, and Excel all at the same time. Of course, the degree to which this can be done depends on the amount of memory in your computer.

Finally, Windows provides a set of applications that are handy tools. These include the following:

| | |
|---|---|
| Calculator | A calculator program for adding, subtracting, dividing, and multiplying numbers |
| Calendar | A scheduling program for jotting down your appointments and commitments |
| Cardfile | A list-management program |
| Clock | A clock that can be displayed on the screen at all times |
| Notepad | A program that lets you keep notes, reminders, and other memos handy |
| Paintbrush | A graphics program |
| PIF Editor | A special editor for PIF files |
| Recorder | A means of recording and playing back sets of keystrokes (macros) |
| Terminal | A communications program that lets you connect via a modem and telephone lines to another computer |
| Write | A word processing program |

As a result of operating under Windows, Excel has all these tools available to it on demand.

The quickest way to learn about Windows is to start using it. If you have not already done so, turn on your computer now and start Windows. If you have not already installed Windows, refer to

Appendix A, "Installing Windows and Excel." When you complete the installation and your mouse is connected, return to this chapter.

Starting Windows depends on how you installed it. If you followed the instructions in Appendix A and the suggestions in the Windows Setup program, you put the Windows directory in the path statement of your AUTOEXEC.BAT file along with the program name, WIN. This automatically starts Windows when you start or boot your computer. If you did not change your AUTOEXEC.BAT for Windows, you must tell DOS which directory contains Windows. See Appendix A for the specific instructions needed to do this.

## THE WINDOWS SCREEN

When Windows 3 is started, you first see a screen similar to the one shown in Figure 1-1, if you installed Windows with the instructions in Appendix A. Depending on how you installed Windows and if you have more or fewer Windows applications, your screen may look different. The screen in Figure 1-1 shows two windows, both with several standard features that appear in most windows of Windows 3. The top line, or *Title bar,* of a window contains its title. The two windows in the figure are the Program Manager and Windows Applications. On the left end of the Title bar is the *Control-menu box.* You use this box to access the *Control menu,* which contains window options that allow you to perform such operations as moving, sizing, or closing a window.

On the right end of the Title bar are the *Minimize* and *Maximize* buttons, which are used for changing the size of the window.

Below the Title bar in the Program Manager window is the *Menu bar.* The menus available (File, Options, Window, and Help) apply only to the Program Manager. The menus displayed in the Menu bar change as the window changes.

Below the Menu bar is the *workspace,* which contains the document or information currently being worked on. At the bottom

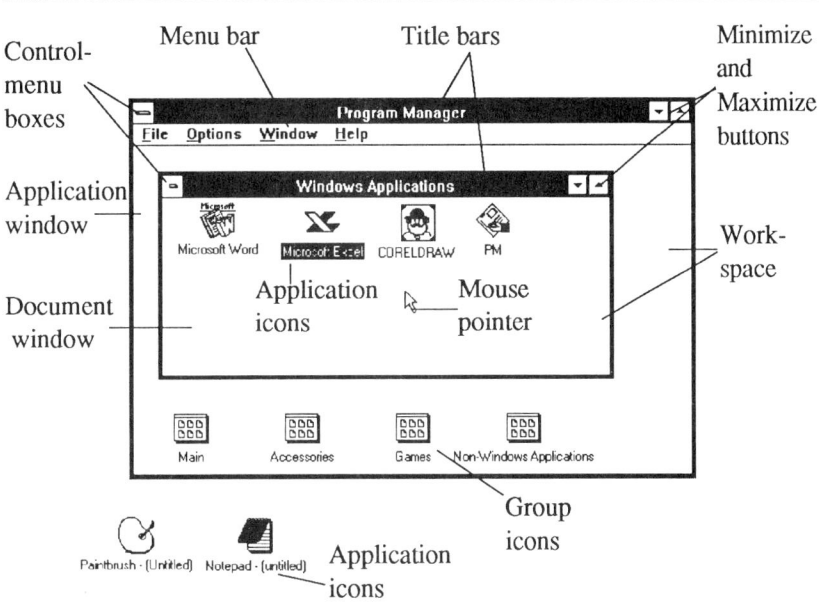

**FIGURE 1-1** Windows 3 startup screen

of the workspace, as shown in Figure 1-1, are graphic symbols, called *icons,* that represent four groups of programs you can use.

At the bottom of the screen, below the Program Manager window, is an area called the *Icon area.* It currently contains two icons, for the Notebook and Paintbrush applications. When you start an application such as Notebook or Excel, and then temporarily set it aside while you do something else, the application becomes an icon. You can activate a program, move it, or deactivate it with the icon. When an application is inactive, its icon is stored in the Icon area.

Several indicators show where you are on the screen. First, the *active window*—the one you are currently working in—is indicated by a Title bar and border that are filled in and normally a dark color with light letters. Both the Program Manager and Window Applications windows are active in Figure 1-1. Second, the *selected object* or objects—what your next action will effect—is highlighted. In Figure 1-1 the Microsoft Excel program icon is the selected object, and the program name is reversed with white or light-colored letters on a black or dark-colored background. The third indicator is the *mouse pointer,* which is an arrow that tells you where the mouse is pointing. In Figure 1-1 the arrow is in the Windows Applications window. All three indicators change as you work, and the varying symbols tell you something about the task being done. You'll see examples later.

## USING THE MOUSE

Although Windows allows you to use either the mouse or the keyboard to enter commands, it is strongly recommended that you use a mouse because it greatly increases the power of Windows. Most instructions in this book assume such use. The keyboard occasionally does offer shortcuts, so these shortcuts and some general rules for using the keyboard are covered later in this chapter.

The mouse is used to move the pointer on the screen. You can select an object by moving the mouse until the pointer is on top of it (pointing *on* it) and then pressing the mouse button. Using the mouse in this way allows you to choose, for example, an option on a menu. A mouse can have one, two, or three buttons. Normally, Windows and Excel use only one button, called *the mouse button* in this book. By default the left button is used, but you can change the default to another button, which you may want to do if you are left-handed.

### Mousing Around

If you move the mouse across a flat surface such as a table or desk, the mouse pointer (the arrow on the screen) also moves. Practice moving the mouse as follows:

1. Place your hand on the mouse. The button(s) should be under your fingers with the cord leading away from you.

2. Move the mouse now, without pressing the mouse button, and watch the pointer move on the screen.

If you run out of room while moving the mouse, simply pick it up and place it where there is more room. Try experimenting with this now.

3. Move the mouse to the edge of your work surface; then pick it up and place it in the middle of your work surface, and move it again.

Watch how the pointer continues from where the mouse was picked up. When you point on the border of the window, the arrow changes to a double-headed arrow. This tells you that the pointer is on the border. If you press the mouse button here, you can size the window, as you will see shortly.

This book uses the following standard Windows terminology to describe your actions with the mouse:

| Term | Action |
| --- | --- |
| Press | Hold down the mouse button |
| Release | Quit pressing the mouse button |
| Point on | Move the mouse until the tip of the pointer is on top of the item you want |
| Click | Quickly press and release the mouse button once |
| Double-click | Press and release the mouse button twice in rapid succession |
| Drag | Press and hold the mouse button while you move the mouse (to move the highlight bar within a menu to the desired option, to move an |

| | |
|---|---|
| | object in the work area, and to highlight contiguous text you want to delete, move, or copy) |
| Select | Point on an item and click the mouse button; also called "click on" |
| Choose | Drag the pointer (and the corresponding highlight bar) to a menu option and release the mouse button |

This book assumes that you know this terminology. For example, the instruction "Select the File menu and choose the Run option" indicates that you should point on the word File in the Menu bar, press and hold the mouse button while moving the mouse toward you to drag the highlight bar down to the Run option, and then release the mouse button. Practice using the mouse to perform some of these actions:

1. *Point on* the Excel icon by moving the mouse (and the corresponding pointer) until the pointer is resting on it.

2. *Select* the Excel icon by *clicking*—quickly pressing and releasing the mouse button while pointing—on it. The Title bar beneath the icon is highlighted, indicating it is selected.

3. *Drag* the Excel icon to the lower-right corner of the Window Applications window: point on the icon, and press and hold the mouse button while you move the mouse until the pointer and the icon move to the lower-right corner of the window, as shown in Figure 1-2.

4. *Drag* the Excel icon back to its original position.

5. *Click* on the Minimize button—the downward pointing arrow in the upper-right corner of the Windows Applications window. The window closes and becomes another group icon, as shown in Figure 1-3.

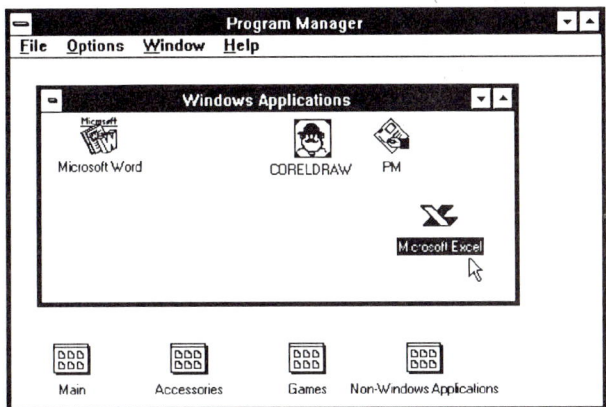

**FIGURE 1-2** Excel icon moved to the lower-right corner of the window

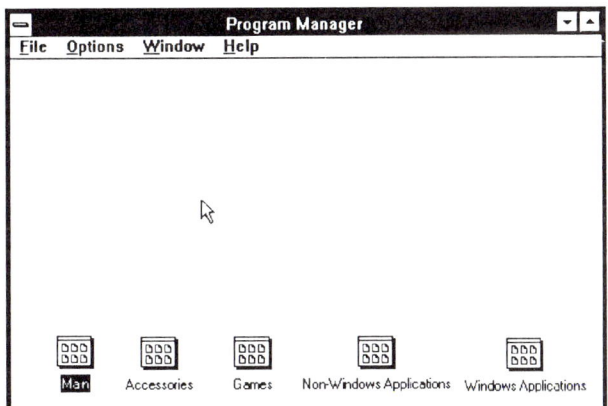
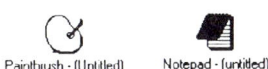

**FIGURE 1-3** Windows Applications window closed to a group icon

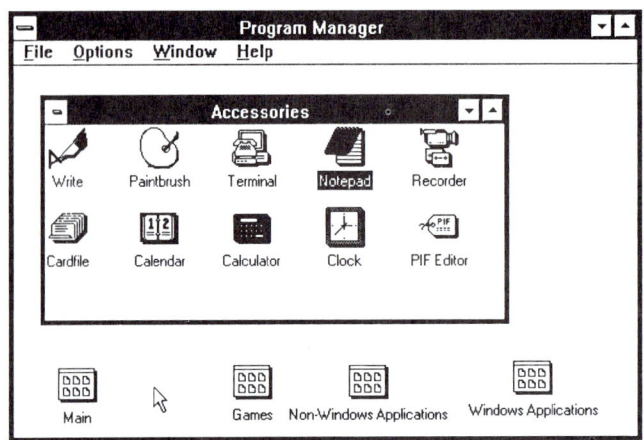

**FIGURE 1-4** Accessories window opened

6. *Double-click* on the Accessories group icon in the Program Manager window. The Accessories window opens, as shown in Figure 1-4.

It sometimes takes a couple of tries to get the rhythm of double-clicking. A frequent problem is double-clicking too slowly. You will see later in this chapter how to adjust the speed of double-clicking.

## USING WINDOWS

A *window* is an area of the screen that is assigned a specific purpose. There are two types of windows: *applications windows,* which contain running programs or applications such as Excel, and *document windows,* which contain documents used with applications, such as an Excel worksheet. An application window may contain one or more document windows. The Accessories and Windows Applications windows that you have been looking at on your screen and in the above figures are document windows, whereas the Program Manager window is an application window. An application window has a Menu bar while a document window does not. Either type of window has a Title bar with the window title in the middle, the Control-menu box on the left, and the Minimize and Maximize buttons on the right.

Windows can be quite small (about 1 × 2 inches minimum), they can fill the screen, or they can be any size in between. You click on the Maximize button to make a window fill the screen. When you maximize a window, a new button—the *Restore button*—appears in place of the Maximize button. You click on the Restore button to return the window to its size just before you clicked the Maximize button. As you have already seen, if you click on the Minimize button, the window shrinks to an icon at the bottom of the screen. Then by double-clicking on that icon you can return it to an open window that is the size it was before you minimized it.

An open window can be sized to any intermediated size by dragging on the border of the window. When you place the mouse pointer on top of the border around the window, the mouse pointer becomes a double-headed arrow. While you see the double-headed arrow, press the mouse button and drag the border to change the window size. Drag on any one side to change the size of the window in one dimension, and drag on a corner to change the size of the window in two dimensions.

Both an open application window and an application icon can be dragged anywhere on the screen. A document window can be dragged only within its application window. To drag an open window, point on the Title bar of the window (anywhere except on the Control-menu box or the Minimize or Maximize buttons) and drag it where you want. To drag an icon, point anywhere on the icon and drag it.

Practice using some of the window-sizing features with these instructions:

1. Click on the Maximize button in the upper-right corner of the Accessories window. The Accessories window expands to fill the Program Manager window.

   Notice that the Title bar has changed. The title is now Program Manager - [Accessories], which tells you that the Accessories window has filled the Program Manager window. Also note that the Control-menu box in the Title bar is for the Program Manager, while the Control-menu box in the Menu bar is for the Accessories window.

2. Click on the Restore button that now appears just under the Program Manager's Maximize button. The Accessories window returns to its former size.

3. Click on the Maximize button of the Program Manager window. It expands to fill the screen.

4. Click on the Restore button of the Program Manager window, and the window shrinks to its former size.

5. Point on the lower-right corner border of the Accessories window. A double-headed arrow appears if you are precisely on the border.

6. Drag the lower-right corner toward the lower right until the Accessories window is about one and a half times its former size.

7. Drag the lower-right corner toward the upper left until the Accessories window is about half its former size before it was enlarged, as shown in Figure 1-5.

The Windows Environment 17

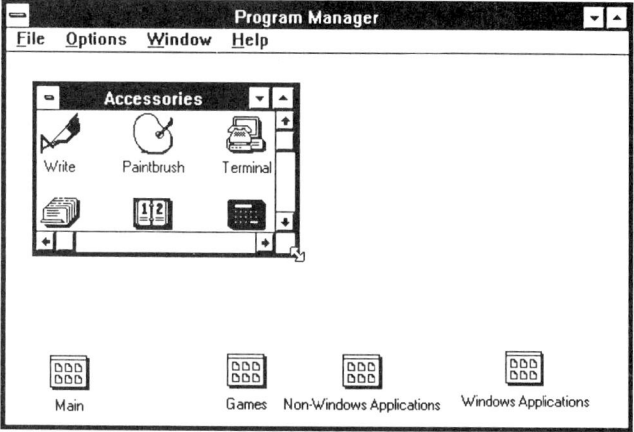

 FIGURE 1-5  Shrunken Accessories window

8. Point on the Title bar of the Accessories menu, anywhere but the Control-menu bar and the Minimize and Maximize buttons.

9. Drag the Accessories window to the lower-right corner of the Program Manager window. Notice that you cannot get out of the Program Manager window.

10. By pointing on the Program Manager's title bar, drag it around the screen.

11. Click on the Minimize button of the Program Manager window. It closes to an icon at the bottom of the screen.

12. Double-click on the Program Manager icon. Notice how the Program Manager and Accessories windows open in the same location in which they closed.

13. Drag both the Accessories window and the Program Manager window back to their original positions, as shown in Figure 1-5.

## Using Scroll Bars

A window on the screen is just that—an opening through which you can see something displayed. If what is displayed is very small, a small window adequately displays it all. If what is displayed is very large, the largest window you can create (one that covers the entire screen) is not large enough to display it all. In that case, you can horizontally or vertically move, or *scroll,* what the window contains.

Imagine that you are reading a billboard by looking through a stationary knothole in a high fence close to the billboard. You must move the billboard from left to right to read a full line on it, and you must move the billboard from top to bottom to read all of the lines. The scroll bars perform the same function for a Windows window. The scroll bars move the *area being displayed* (not the window itself) up or down (that is, vertically) or left or right (horizontally).

Each of the two scroll bars has three mechanisms for moving the area being displayed. First, there are four *scroll arrows* at the ends of each scroll bar. When you click on one of the scroll arrows, you move the display area in the direction of the arrow by a small increment—one line vertically. Second, there are the two square *scroll boxes* in the middle of the scroll bars. Drag a scroll box to move the display area by a corresponding, proportional amount. Third, there are the scroll bars themselves. When you click on the scroll bars (in areas other than the scroll arrows and scroll boxes), you can move the display area in the direction corresponding to where you clicked and by the height or width of one window.

Use the reduced Accessories window and the following instructions to try out the scroll bars:

1. Click on the down scroll arrow at the bottom of the vertical scroll bar. Notice that the display area moved up to display the information below that previously shown. Notice also that the scroll box has moved down in the scroll bar.

The position of the scroll box in the scroll bar represents the approximate position of the area displayed within the overall area. When the vertical scroll box is at the top of its scroll bar, you are looking at the top of the overall area. When the horizontal scroll bar is at the left end of its scroll bar, you are looking at the left edge of the overall area. When both scroll boxes are in the middle of their scroll bars, you are looking at the middle of the overall area.

2. Click on the right scroll arrow several times until the scroll box is at the far right of the horizontal scroll bar. Your screen should look like Figure 1-6.

3. Click on the horizontal scroll bar, on the left of the scroll box, until the scroll box is at the far left of the scroll bar. Notice how it takes fewer clicks to move over the length of the scroll bar.

4. Drag the vertical scroll box a small amount toward the middle of the scroll bar. Note how this allows you to move the display area in very precise increments.

The three scrolling mechanisms give you three levels of control. Clicking on the scroll bar moves the display area the furthest; dragging the scroll box can move the display area in the smallest and most precise increments; and clicking on the scroll arrows moves the display area a small to intermediate amount.

Now that you can scroll the Accessories window, your next step is to do so to select an application.

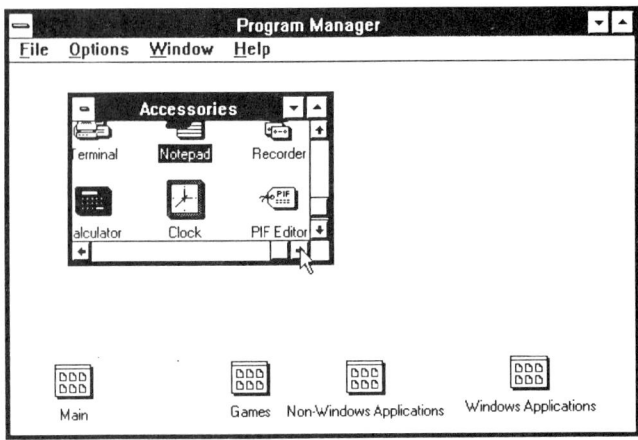

FIGURE 1-6   Accessories window scrolled to the lower-right corner

## Starting Applications

The Accessories window contains the icons for the various accessories available in Windows 3. Each of these accessories is an application that runs under Windows just like Excel. To start an application you simply double-click on its icon. Do that now, and then you can work with several application windows.

1. Scroll the Accessories window until you can see the Clock icon.

2. Double-click on the Clock icon. The Clock application starts and opens a window entitled Clock, as shown in Figure 1-7.

Notice how the Clock window's Title bar and border are dark with light letters while the Program Manager's Title bar and border

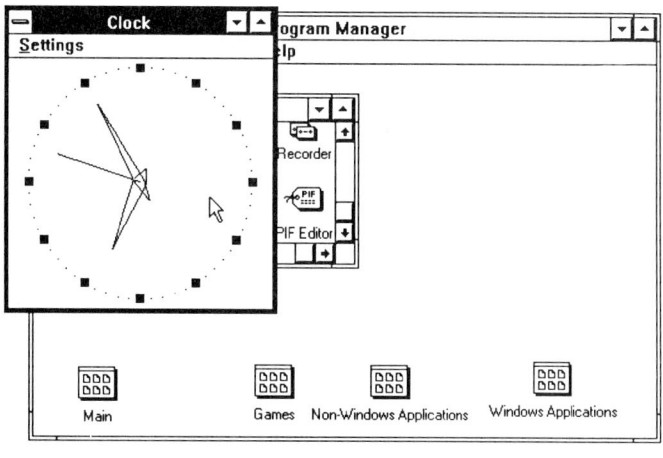

**FIGURE 1-7** Clock window open

has become light with dark letters. This means that the Clock is now the active application while the Program Manager is inactive.

(There may be some differences between your screen and the figures and illustrations shown in this book. That is due to the differences in displays, display adapters, and in the options you selected during Windows installation.)

3. Click on the Clock's Maximize button. The Clock window expands to fill the screen.

4. Click on the Restore button, and the Clock window returns to its original size.

5. Drag the Clock window (by dragging on the Clock window's Title bar anywhere except the buttons or the Control-menu box) to the lower-right corner of the screen.

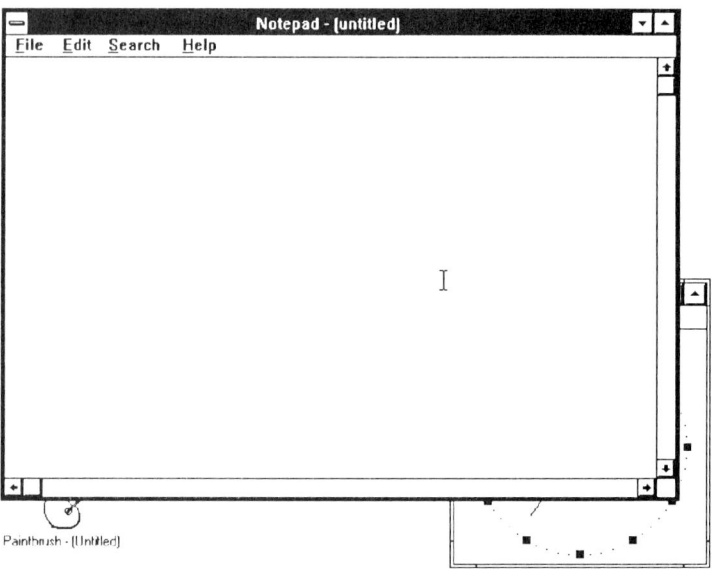

**FIGURE 1-8** Notepad window open

6. Click on the Accessories window to activate the Program Manager, scroll the Accessories window until you can see the Notepad icon, and then double-click on it. The Notepad application starts, and its window opens and becomes the active window, as shown in Figure 1-8.

7. Drag the Notepad window until it overlaps but does not completely cover the Clock, if it was not that way originally.

8. Click on the Clock to activate it. Notice how it now overlaps the Notepad.

9. Click on the Notepad window to reactivate it, and then drag on the upper-left corner to reduce the size of the Notepad to about half its original size so you can see the Accessories window.

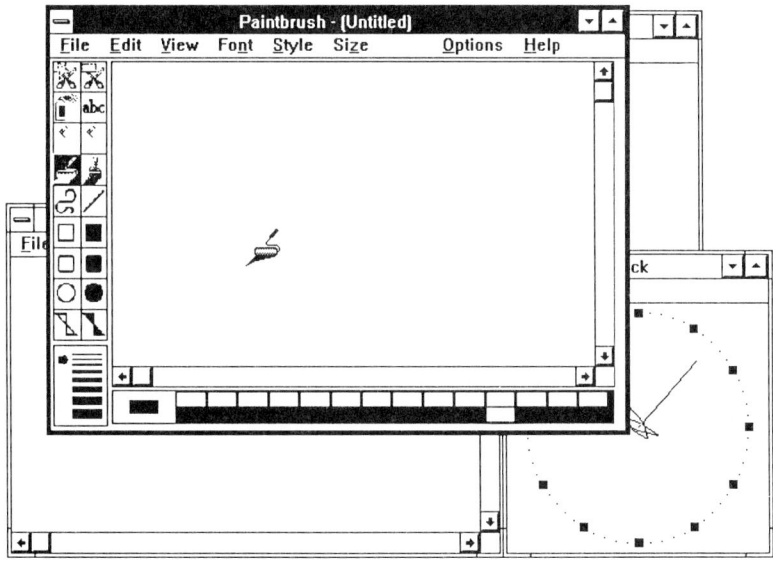

**FIGURE 1-9**  Paintbrush window added

10. Click on the Accessories window to activate the Program Manager, scroll the Accessories window until you can see the Paintbrush icon, and then double-click on it. The Paintbrush application starts and its window opens and becomes the active window.

11. Size the Paintbrush window so you can see the Clock, the Notepad, and the Program Manager windows, as shown in Figure 1-9.

You now have four applications running in Windows: the Program Manager, the Clock, the Notepad, and Paintbrush. Move them around, size them in various ways, and activate first one and then another. Continue this until you are comfortable working with these windows.

Notice that as you move the mouse among these windows that the mouse pointer changes. In the Paintbrush window the mouse pointer can be a paint roller, a dot, a crosshair, or several other shapes; in the Notepad window the pointer is an *I-beam;* and in the Clock and Program Manager windows the pointer is the familiar arrow. The pointer is telling you what can be done when it is in the various windows. With the dot in Paintbrush you can draw, while the crosshairs are for cutting away a part of a drawing. The I-beam is used with text; its skinny nature allows you to insert it between characters. When you click an I-beam you are establishing an *insertion point,* which determines where text you type is placed.

12. Click on the Minimize button of the Notepad, Clock, Paintbrush, and Accessories windows. The first three become application icons at the bottom of the screen while the Accessories window becomes the now familiar group icon at the bottom of the Program Manager window, as shown in Figure 1-10.

Notice how the clock still tells time even though it has turned into an icon. This is generally true about application icons—they are running programs that are just temporarily inactive. The only difference between an inactive window and an application icon is the amount of the screen they use and that you must double-click on an icon to activate it while you need only click on an inactive window.

13. Drag the three applications icons to reorder them, and place them in other locations on the screen just to see how you can do it. When you are done, drag them back to their original location and order, as shown in Figure 1-10.

Manipulating windows and their icons—by selecting, dragging, maximizing, minimizing, sizing, and scrolling—is one of the

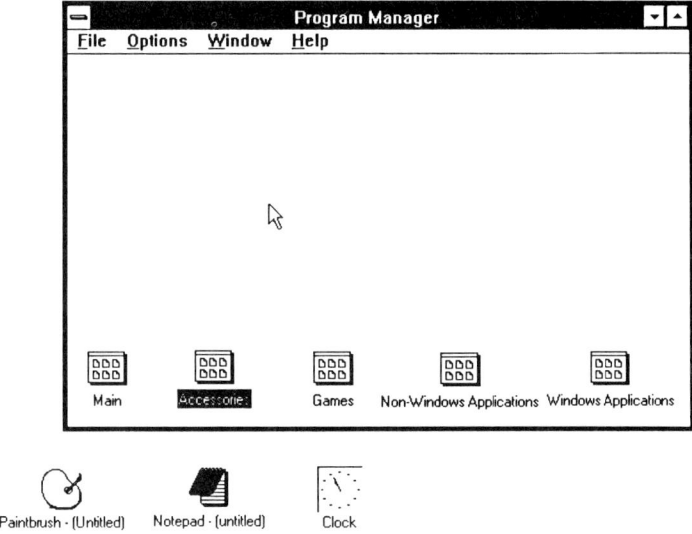

**FIGURE 1-10**   Application windows turned into icons

primary functions of the Windows environment. Practice these techniques until they are second nature. You will use them often. Another primary function of the Windows environment is the use of menus.

# USING MENUS

Menus are the primary device you use to give instructions to Windows and its applications. MS-DOS, by itself, is command orientated—you type commands at a system prompt. Within Windows, you give a command by making a choice on a menu. The menus available to you at any given time are shown in the Menu bar. By clicking on a menu name—*selecting* a menu—you open the menu. When you click on a menu option—*choose* an option—the option performs its function.

Menu options can represent several different functions. Often when you choose a menu option you are telling the application to carry out a command, such as saving a file or copying something. Other menu options allow you to set parameters or defaults for the items you are working on, like selecting the size of a page to be printed or the color of an object. Still other menu options are themselves menus—in other words, selecting a menu option opens another menu. This is called *cascading menus*.

Look at several menus now and get a feel for how they operate.

1. Click on the Program Manager's File menu. It opens as shown here:

The Program Manager's File menu has eight options. Notice that several of the options (Move and Copy, for example) are dimmed while others are not (not in the above illustration, but on your screen). Dimmed options are not available in the context of what you are doing. For example, if you do not have an open file in the current window's workspace, you cannot save a file from that window; therefore, the Save option is dim. Many of the options, such as New, Copy, and Run, have an ellipsis (...) after them. This means that if you select that option, a *dialog box* opens. A dialog box is a place for you to provide further information or answer questions about the option you selected. For example, if you ask to save a file but you never provided the application with a filename, a dialog box opens asking you for the filename.

2. Click on New in the File menu.

A dialog box opens asking if you want to add a new group or a new application to a group and what to name the group or application.

3. Click on Cancel to close the dialog box.

4. Click on the File menu again. Then click on Properties and then Run to look at their dialog boxes. Click on Cancel in each case to close the dialog boxes.

5. Click on the Options, Window, and Help menus in succession to look at each of them.

Notice in the Window menu that one of the lists of windows has a check mark to the left of it. This means that window is currently active. One or more of the options of the Window menu allows you to choose the active window. When you click on your choice, a check mark is placed beside it so that the next time you open the menu you can tell which is active.

Notice also that a menu option may have a series of keystrokes to the right of the option name. These are *shortcut keys*. By pressing these keys you can choose the menu option directly without first opening the menu.

## Using Dialog Boxes

As you have seen, dialog boxes are a means of providing information about an option you have chosen. The dialog boxes you have looked at are rather simple, with only a couple of items. Dialog boxes can be very complex, with many different components. Windows uses several types of components to gather different types of information. These components are shown in the dialog boxes displayed in Figures 1-11, 1-12, and 1-13. These dialog boxes are used in Excel for opening files, setting up a printer, and placing a border around a section of the worksheet.

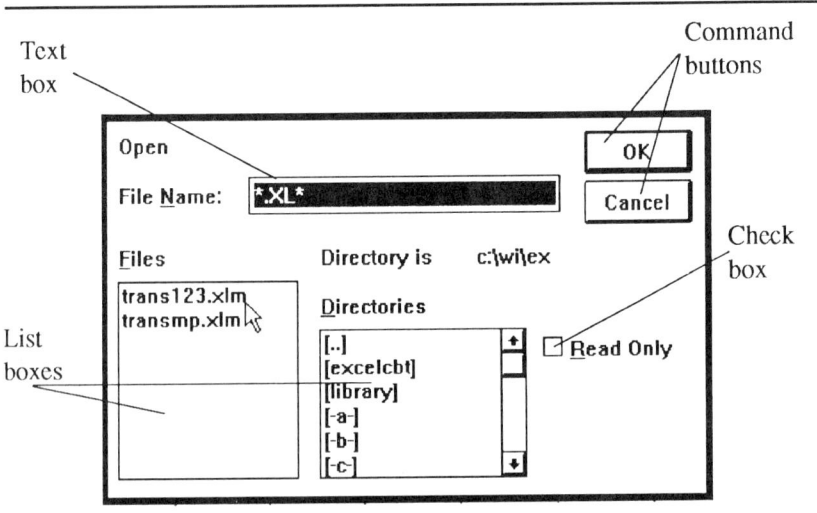

**FIGURE 1-11**   The File Open dialog box

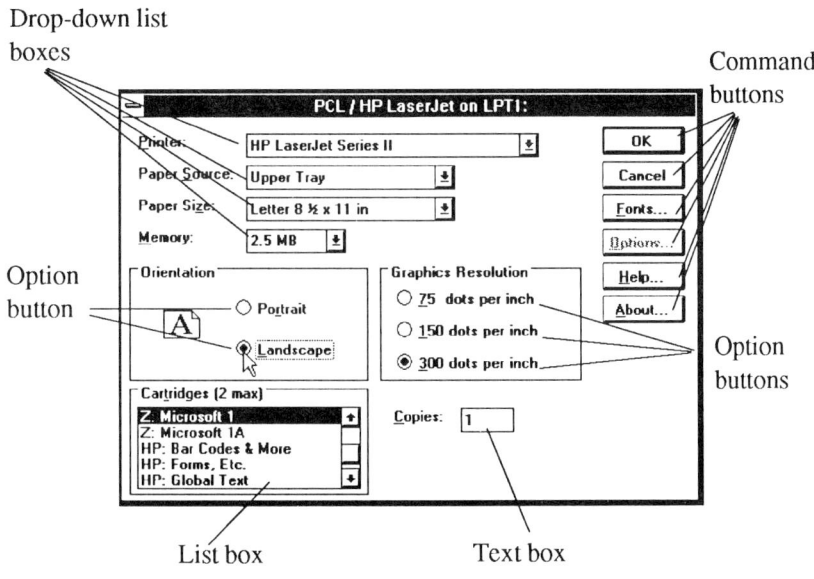

**FIGURE 1-12**  The Printer Setup dialog box

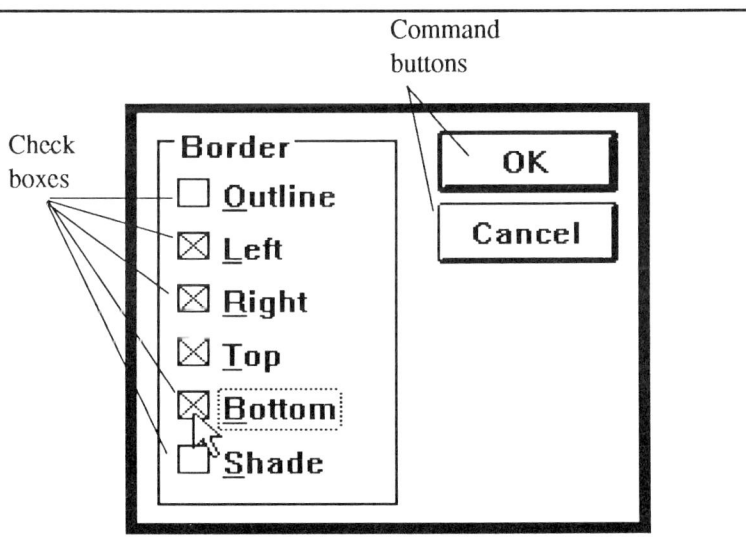

**FIGURE 1-13**  The Border dialog box

The various dialog box components, as well as their uses, are as follows:

| Component | Usage |
|---|---|
| Check box | To select several items from among a series of options. Click on as many check boxes as desired to select those options. When selected, a check box contains an "X;" otherwise the box is empty. |
| Command button | To take immediate action; for example, to close a dialog box, to cancel a command, to open another dialog box, or to expand the current dialog box. Clicking on a command button activates it. OK, the most common command button, is used to close a dialog box. An ellipsis (...) indicates that a command button opens another dialog box, and two greater-than symbols (>>) indicate a command button expands the current dialog box. |
| Drop-down list box | To select normally one item from a list in a constrained space. The current selection is shown. Clicking on the arrow to the right opens the drop-down list box. Click on the option desired, possibly using the scroll bar first. |
| List box | To select normally one item from a list. The current selection is highlighted. Click on the option desired, possibly using the scroll bar first. |
| Option button | To select one item from a set of mutually exclusive options. A selection is changed by clicking on another option. |

Text box    To enter text, such as a filename. The mouse pointer turns into an I-beam in a text box. Clicking the mouse in a text box places an insertion point, and any text typed will follow the insertion point. Without clicking an insertion point, any existing text in a selected text box is replaced by anything typed. The (DEL) key removes existing selected text in a text box.

Dialog boxes provide a very powerful and fast means of communicating with Windows and its applications. It is important that you know these terms and are comfortable using dialog boxes.

## USING THE KEYBOARD

You can do almost everything (except enter text) with a mouse, but the keyboard provides a shortcut in a number of instances. You have seen how several of the menu options have direct shortcut keys. You can also choose any of the other menu options with a general keyboard procedure. You can open a menu by pressing (ALT) (you do not have to hold it down) followed by the underlined letter in the menu name. After pressing (ALT) you can also use (LEFT ARROW) and (RIGHT ARROW) to highlight a menu name, and then use (DOWN ARROW) to open the menu and highlight an option. After a menu is open you can choose an option by typing the underlined letter in the option name or highlighting the option with the direction keys and pressing (ENTER). (ENTER) can also be used to open a menu once you have highlighted the menu name, and the (F10) function key can be used in place of (ALT) to initiate the process. To cancel a menu selection and return to the workspace, press (ALT) or (F10) a second time. To cancel a menu selection but stay in the Menu bar so that another menu selection can be made, press (ESC).

Give the mouse a rest for a moment and access several menu options using the keyboard.

1. Press (ALT+F) to open the Program Manager's File menu.

2. Type **R** to select the Run option. The Run dialog box opens.

3. Press (TAB) to move among the various fields in the dialog box, and then press (ESC) to cancel the dialog box, close the File menu, and deactivate the Menu bar.

In general, to move around in a dialog box you first press (TAB) to move through the major groups of options, normally from left to right and top to bottom, or use (SHIFT+TAB) to reverse the direction; alternatively, press *and hold* (ALT) while pressing the underlined letter in the option or group name to move directly to that option or group. Then use the direction keys to highlight an option within a group, and use (SPACEBAR) to make the final selection of the option. Finally, press (ENTER) to complete and close the dialog box.

4. Press (F10) to reactivate the Menu bar.

5. Press (LEFT ARROW) twice to move to the Window menu.

6. Press (ENTER) to open the Window menu, and then press (DOWN ARROW) four times to highlight the second group of applications.

7. Press (ENTER) to select the highlighted menu item, close the menu, return to the workspace, and open the selected group window.

8. Click on the Minimize button of the open group window to shrink it once again to an icon.

## Using the Control Menu

The Control menu in the upper-left corner of most windows and icons and some dialog boxes allows you to perform many other Windows functions with the keyboard that you have previously learned to perform with the mouse. There is some difference among Control menus but, for the most part, the options are the same.

1. Click on the Control-menu box or press (ALT+SPACEBAR) to open the Program Manager's Control menu shown here:

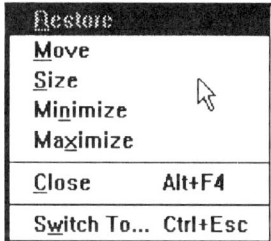

The options available in this Control menu and their function are as follows:

| Option | Function |
| --- | --- |
| Restore | Restores the window to the size it was prior to being minimized or maximized |
| Move | Allows moving the window with the keyboard |
| Size | Allows sizing the window with the keyboard |
| Minimize | Minimizes the window size to an icon |
| Maximize | Maximizes the window size, normally, to fill the screen |
| Close | Closes the window |

Switch To        Switches among the currently running applications and allows rearrangement of their icons and windows

The following additional options are available on other Control menus:

Edit            Opens an Edit menu with four options (non-Windows applications in 386 enhanced mode only): *Mark* allows selection of text to be copied to the Clipboard, *Copy* copies text to the Clipboard, *Paste* copies the contents of the Clipboard to the insertion point in the active document window, and *Scroll* scrolls the active document window

Next            Switches to the next open document window or document icon (on document windows only)

Paste           Copies the contents of the Clipboard to the insertion point in the active document window (real and standard mode only)

Settings        Allows entering settings for multitasking (non-Windows applications in 386 enhanced mode only)

Now try several of the Control menu options using the keyboard.

2. Press (DOWN ARROW) to highlight Move and press (ENTER) to choose it. The pointer becomes a four-headed arrow.

3. Press one or more of the direction keys to move the window in the direction you choose. An outline shows you where you are going.

4. When the outline of the window is where you want it, press (ENTER). Should you want to cancel the move, press (ESC) before pressing (ENTER).

5. Press (ALT+SPACEBAR) to reopen the Program Manager's (the active window) Control menu.

6. Press (DOWN ARROW) twice to highlight Size, and press (ENTER) to choose it. The pointer becomes a four-headed arrow.

7. Press one arrow key to select one side whose size you want to change, or press two direction keys simultaneously to select two sides whose sizes you want to change. (Pressing two direction keys simultaneously is the same as selecting a corner with the mouse.)

8. Press one or two arrows until the window is the size you want it. Then press (ENTER). If you want to cancel the sizing, press (ESC) before pressing (ENTER).

9. Press (ALT+SPACEBAR) to reopen the Program Manager's Control menu.

10. Type **X** to choose Maximize. The Program Manager window expands to fill the screen.

11. Press (ALT+SPACEBAR) to open the Program Manager's Control menu, and press (ENTER) to choose Restore. The Program Manager window returns to its original size.

12. Press (ALT+SPACEBAR) again, and type **N** to choose Minimize. The Program Manager window shrinks to an icon.

13. Press (ALT+ESC) to cycle through the various application icons (or windows if any were open). When you have reached the Program Manager again, press (ALT+SPACEBAR) to open the Control menu.

14. Press (ENTER) to choose Restore. The Program Manager window reopens at its last size and location.

15. Press (CTRL+F6) or (CTRL+TAB) to cycle through the various document (group) icons (or windows if any were open).

16. When you reach Main, press (ALT+-) (hyphen) to open the Main group's Control menu.

17. Choose Restore by pressing (ENTER), since Restore is already highlighted. Your screen should look like that shown in Figure 1-14.

Notice that for applications windows and document windows you use different key combinations to open their Control menus

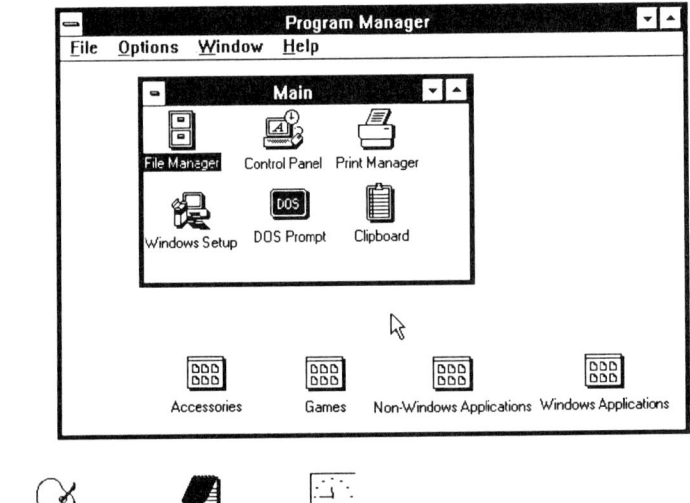

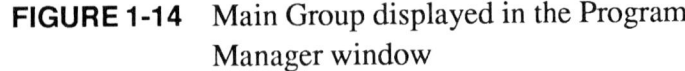 FIGURE 1-14  Main Group displayed in the Program Manager window

and to cycle through windows and icons. Use `ALT+SPACEBAR` to open an applications window Control menu, and use `ALT+ESC` to cycle through the application windows and icons that are running (on the screen). Use `ALT+-` (hyphen) to open a document window Control menu, and use `CTRL+F6` or `CTRL+TAB` to cycle through the document windows and icons in the active application window.

One important Control menu option you have not tried yet is Close. In most windows, Close simply closes the window. With the Program Manager, Close closes Windows and returns you to DOS. You will do that later in the chapter. Once the Control menu is open, you can choose Close in the normal ways: by clicking on it, by highlighting it and pressing `ENTER`, or by typing C. You can choose Close with the Control menu closed by double-clicking on the Control-menu box or by pressing `ALT+F4`. The other Control menu commands (Switch To, Edit, Next, Paste, and Settings) are not relevant to Excel and are thus beyond the scope of this book.

The keyboard and the Control menu are important adjuncts to the mouse. But they should be viewed as that and not the other way around. With Windows and Excel the mouse is by far the most effective and expeditious way to do most things. For that reason, this book usually has instructions for the mouse. Keyboard instructions normally are given only for shortcut keys when you are already typing on the keyboard.

## USING THE MAIN GROUP APPLICATIONS

The Main application group, which should currently be displayed on your screen, includes six applications that have the following functions:

| Application | Function |
|---|---|
| File Manager | To view and manipulate files (replaces MS-DOS Executive in previous versions of Windows). |
| Control Panel | To set defaults such as color, double-click speed, and date and time. |
| Print Manager | To manage the queuing and printing of files. |
| Clipboard | To display the contents of the Clipboard. |
| DOS Prompt | To provide a DOS command-line prompt at which any DOS command can be entered. Type **exit** to return to Windows. |
| Windows Setup | To make changes to the hardware and software configuration you are using with Windows. |

Two of these applications are of value with Excel: the Control Panel and the File Manager.

## Setting Defaults with the Control Panel

The Control Panel is the primary place in Windows where you set the parameters or defaults that tell Windows how you want a number of different functions handled. Open the Control Panel now and look at the options.

1. Double-click on the Control Panel icon. The Control Panel opens as shown here:

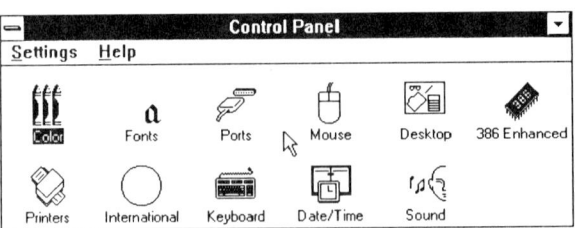

The Control Panel consists of the following functions, each with its own icon, for which you can set defaults.

| Icon | Function Set |
|---|---|
| Color | Colors associated with the various parts of the screen |
| Fonts | Fonts available for both screen and printer(s) |
| Ports | Communications parameters used with serial ports |
| Mouse | Behavior of the mouse, including the double-click rate, the speed the pointer moves across the screen, and whether the left or right mouse button is primary |
| Desktop | Characteristics of the screen or "desktop," including the cursor blink rate, the presence or absence of a "magnetic" grid to better align objects, and the patterns used for various areas |
| Network | Parameters applicable to your network (available only if you are using a network) |
| Printers | Parameters applicable to your printer(s), including ports assigned, paper size and orientation, graphics resolution, and the identification of the default printer |
| International | Formats for numbers, currency, dates, and times |
| Keyboard | Keyboard repeat rate |
| Date/Time | System date and time |
| Sound | Presence or absence of the warning sound or beep |
| 386 Enhanced | Sharing of peripheral devices and system resources in multitasking environment (available only if you are using 386 enhanced mode) |

Setting any of the functions is done in the same way: selection of the icon (by double-clicking on it) opens a dialog box in which you enter the necessary parameters. Try that now by setting the double-click rate of the mouse.

2. Double-click on the Mouse icon in the Control Panel. The Mouse dialog box opens as shown here:

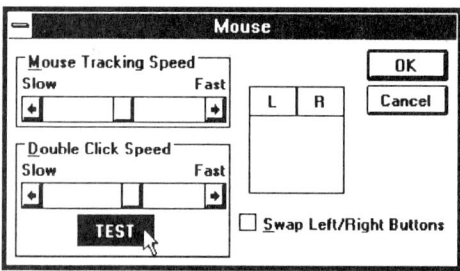

3. If you are left handed and want to make the right mouse button the primary mouse button, click on the Swap Left/Right Buttons check box at the bottom middle of the screen.

4. Double-click on the Test command button. If the button darkens, the double-click speed is set correctly.

5. If the Test button does not darken, you need to change the speed. Click on the Slow or Fast scroll arrow, whichever is correct for you, and try double-clicking again.

6. Repeat steps 4 and 5 until the double-clicking speed is set correctly.

7. When you are done with the mouse settings, click OK to close the dialog box and return to the Control Panel window.

On your own, look at the other Control Panel functions. You'll find you can do a lot to tailor Windows to your tastes. Unless you want to change something, click on Cancel in each dialog box so you won't change anything inadvertently.

8. When you are done with the Control Panel, double-click on the Control Panel's Control-menu box in the upper-left corner. This closes the Control Panel and returns you to the Main group window of the Program Manager.

## Creating a Directory With the File Manager

The File Manager provides all of the customary DOS file-handling commands, such as COPY, DELETE, and RENAME, as well as a number of file-manipulation tools that have only been available with such packages as Xtree and PC Tools. Open the File Manager now by double-clicking on the File Manager icon in the Main group window of the Program Manager. The File Manager window opens, and a directory tree window for your root directory also opens, as shown in Figure 1-15.

The directory tree provides a very powerful way of viewing and working with your directories and their files. In the initial view of your directories, you see an alphabetical list of all of the subdirectories under your root directory. Each of the directories are represented by a file folder. The root directory's file folder has a minus sign in it. This means that when you click on the root directory's file folder, you collapse all of the subdirectories into the root directory. Some of the other file folders have a plus sign

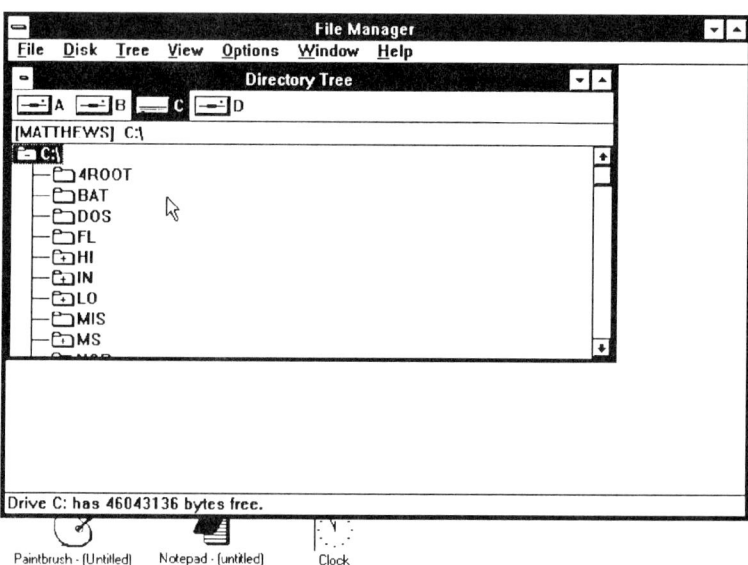

FIGURE 1-15   File Manager and root directory tree

in them, which means they have subdirectories, and when you click on them the subdirectories open, as shown here:

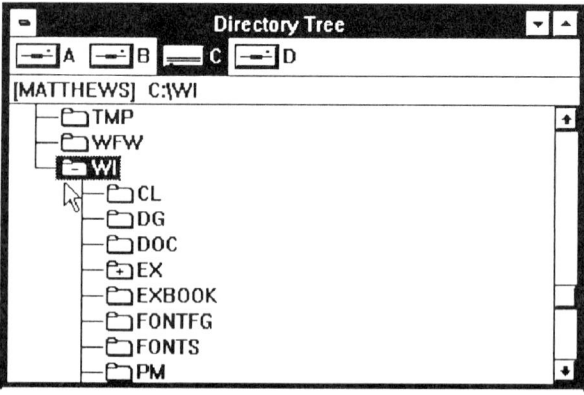

Other directory file folders are empty. This means they do not have subdirectories under them. You may open and list the files and subdirectories in any directory by double-clicking on the folder icon. If you were to double-click on the Excel directory folder you would get this directory window:

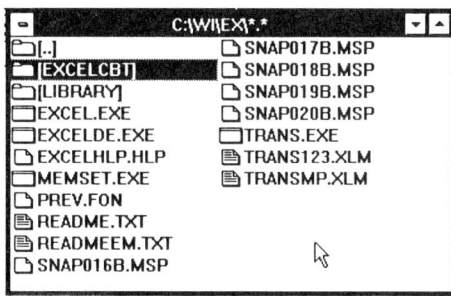

You can have as many directory windows as you like. In a directory window you can select or highlight files you want to move, copy, rename, or delete. For moving and copying, have both the source and destination directories open and visible. Then, to move a file, press and hold (ALT) while you drag the file icon from the source directory to the destination directory. To copy a file, press and hold (CTRL) while you drag the file icon. If you wish to move, copy, rename, or delete several files at one time and the files are listed sequentially, click on the first filename, and then press and hold (SHIFT) while you click on the last filename in the sequence. If you want to select several files and they are not in sequence, press and hold (CTRL) while you click on each of the items. To cancel a selected item, press and hold (CTRL) while you click on the item. To delete or rename files, select the files and then choose the appropriate command from the File menu.

The File menu provides access to several other file functions, as you can see in Figure 1-16. Among these is creating a directory.

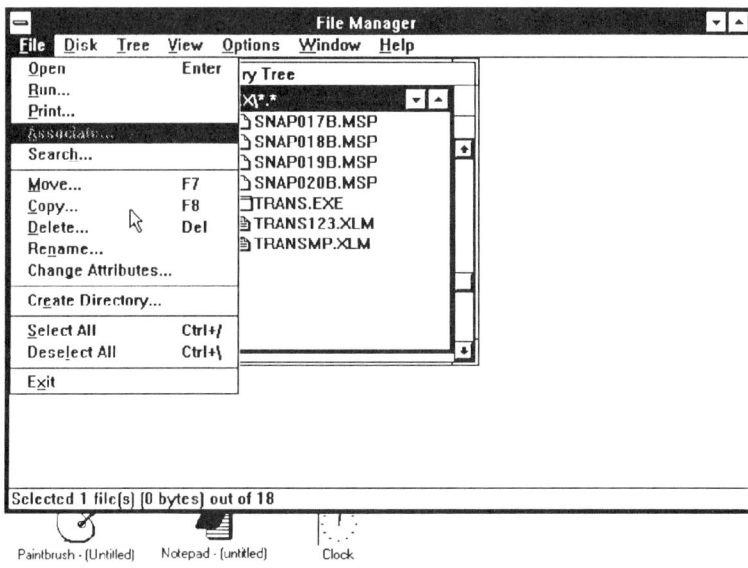

FIGURE 1-16   File Manager's File menu

Use that command now to create a directory called SHEETS to store your Excel worksheets if you did not do this in Appendix A.

1. Click on the File Manager's File menu to open it.

2. Click on Create Directory to choose that option. The Create Directory dialog box opens, as shown here:

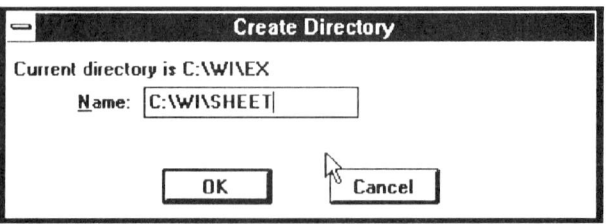

If you had correctly selected the directory under which you wish to create a new subdirectory, all you would need to enter is the new directory's name. Otherwise you need to type the full pathname of the new directory.

3. Type **sheet** or, if necessary, precede it with the pathname you want to use, for example typing **C:\WI\SHEET**, as shown in the illustration.

4. Press (ENTER) to close the dialog box, create the directory, and return you to the File Manager window.

5. When you are done with the File Manager, double-click on its Control-menu box to close it and return you to the Main group window of the Program Manager.

## GETTING HELP

Windows 3 on-line help is very extensive and context sensitive—it tries to provide specific help about what you are doing. You can get help by several methods. The fastest and most context-sensitive method is to press (F1). If you highlight a command or option before pressing (F1), you will get specific help about that command or option. The second and most general-purpose method of getting help is to use the Help menu on most application windows. You can access the Help menu by either clicking on it or pressing (ALT+H). Do that next and look at the Program Manager's Help facility with these instructions:

1. Click on Help in the menu bar. The Program Manager's Help menu opens, as shown here:

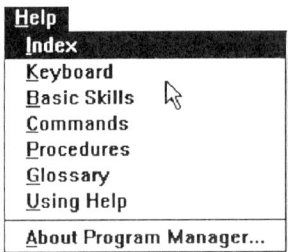

Most Help menus within Windows 3 have the same set of options. These options with the information they provide are as follows:

| Option | Information Provided |
|---|---|
| Index | Topics covered in alphabetical order |
| Keyboard | Keys used to perform various functions |

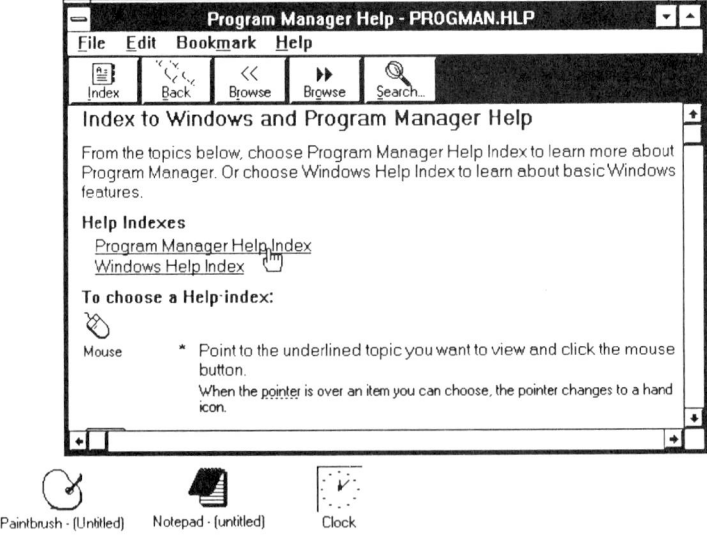

**FIGURE 1-17** Index to Windows and Program Manager Help

| | |
|---|---|
| Commands | Explanation of all commands |
| Procedures | Description of procedures to accomplish various functions |
| Using Help | Tutorial on how to use Help |
| About | Information about the application and your system resources |

If you want information about the keys used with menus you would proceed with these steps:

2. Click on Index. A window appears, as shown in Figure 1-17, asking you to choose between the Program Manager's help index and Windows' help index. In the help window you make a choice by clicking on an underlined topic. When the pointer is pointing on a topic that can be chosen, it becomes a hand.

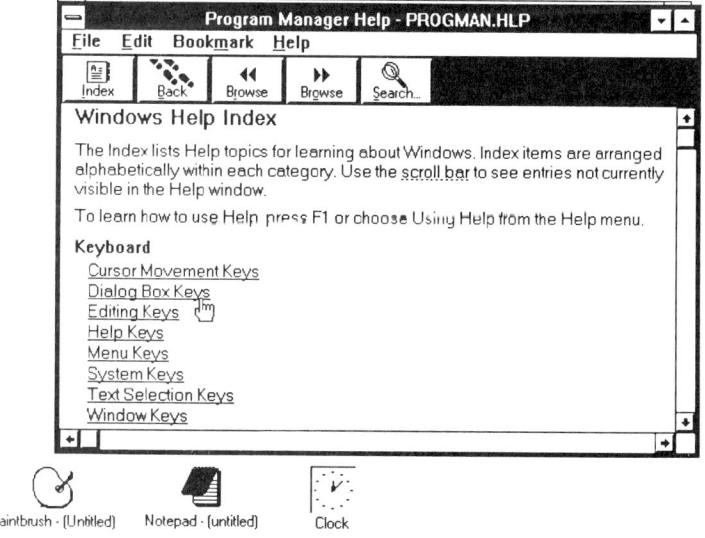

FIGURE 1-18  Windows Help Index window

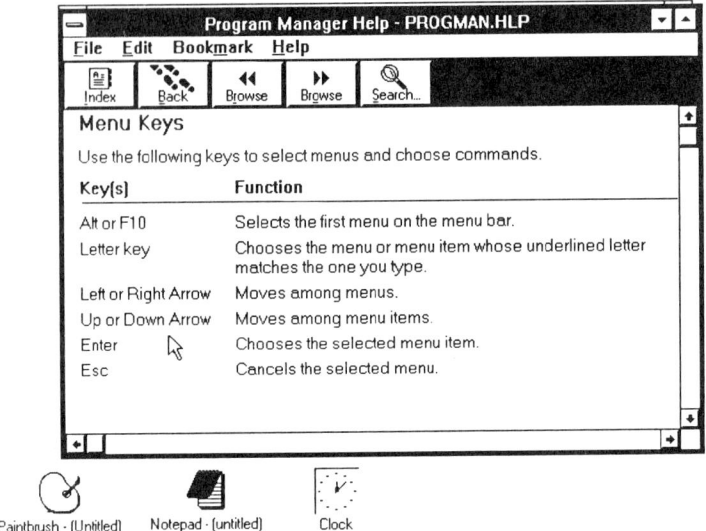

**FIGURE 1-19** Menu Keys help window

3. Click on Windows Help Index. The Windows Help Index window opens, as shown in Figure 1-18.

4. Click on Menu Keys. The Menu Keys Help window opens, as shown in Figure 1-19.

The command buttons at the top of a help window return you to the index, retrace the path you have taken to get to the current help window, allow you to browse through related topics either before or after the current topic, or allow you to search for a topic.

5. Use the Help command buttons on your own to review the Windows 3 Help facility.

6. When you are done reviewing Help, double-click on the Control-menu box to close Help. You will be returned to the Main group window of the Program Manager.

## LEAVING WINDOWS

Windows 3 and many of the applications, like Excel, that run under Windows use temporary files to store intermediate information as the program is running. If you leave the applications and Windows in the correct manner, not only are these temporary files erased, but you are reminded to save any files you have not saved. The

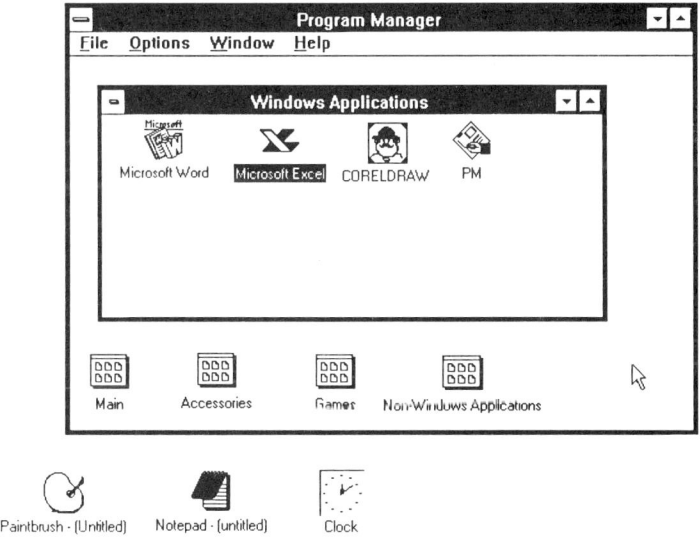

FIGURE 1-20  Program Manager and Windows Applications windows in final position

correct manner to leave any window is to double-click on its Control-menu box. Simply do this until you are out to the DOS prompt and you have correctly left Windows. Then, and only then, can you safely turn off your computer.

Arrange your Program Manager window the way you want it to be when you next use Windows—with the Windows Applications group open—and then leave Windows with these instructions:

1. Double-click on the Control-menu box of the Main group window to close it.

2. Double-click on the Windows Applications group icon to open it.

3. Size and position the two windows and icons in those windows (not the icons at the bottom of the screen) so they look approximately like Figure 1-20.

4. Double-click on the Program Manager's Control-menu box. You are asked to confirm you want to leave Windows. Click OK to leave Windows. You are returned to the DOS prompt.

This chapter has laid a foundation on which you can now begin to add specific knowledge of Excel. Windows is not a simple subject, but it provides a very powerful framework that is fully utilized by Excel. You now have enough knowledge of that framework to use it in Excel, as you will do in Chapter 2, "The Components of Excel."

# 2

# THE COMPONENTS OF EXCEL

Worksheets
Databases
Charts

This chapter explains the three components of Excel—worksheets, databases, and charts—with particular attention to worksheets. It also quickly introduces cells, ranges, formulas, functions, commands, and macros.

Excel is considered a worksheet program, yet it really has three components that perform three different tasks: the *worksheet* component displays and analyzes text and numbers in rows and columns; the *chart* component produces charts; and the *database* component manipulates lists of information.

Each component is really just a different way of looking at and interacting with data that has a common structure based on rows and columns. This common structure is really the worksheet. It may contain data from one or more of the three components, but underlying the different components, all data is contained in the same row and column structure. It is this common data structure that makes Excel *integrated*—able to transfer and manipulate data easily among the three components.

# WORKSHEETS

The easiest way to think of a worksheet is to consider an accountant's multicolumn paper worksheet—a piece of paper that is divided into rows and columns. Generally there is a wide column on the left for text labels that describe what is in each row. To the right of the label column are several columns for entering numbers. Paper worksheets are used for manually listing sales or expenses, for preparing budgets or financial plans, or any other similar task.

The worksheet component of Excel, shown in Figure 2-1, is an electronic multicolumn worksheet far more flexible than its paper namesake. Excel provides 256 columns and 16,384 rows. Each column can be between 0 and 255 characters wide, and words and numbers can be intermixed as needed. Excel allows many types of calculations over rows and columns, and copying and moving information from one column or row to another is easy with Excel.

## Worksheets and Files

Both the paper worksheet and Excel's are a means of analyzing data by organizing it into rows and columns. Excel's worksheets, however, are stored on your computer's hard disk in *files*. When you build a worksheet, you do so in your computer's temporary memory, called *RAM,* for random access memory. When you load another program, or turn off your computer, what is in RAM is lost. You must save your worksheet in a file on disk for it to be permanent. A file that has been stored on disk can be read back into Excel, reviewed, altered, and saved again. Also, a worksheet

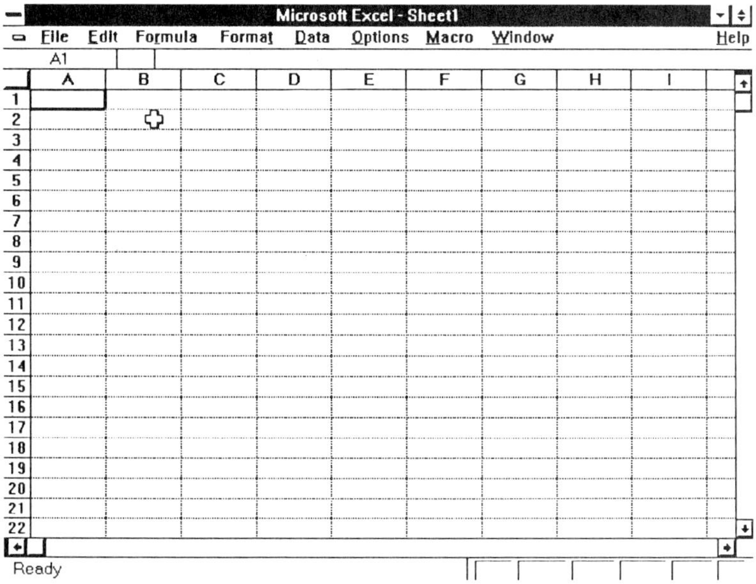

**FIGURE 2-1** Excel's worksheet

file on disk can be run on another computer running Excel, which means you can share your work. The only outwardly distinguishing feature of an Excel file is the name you give it. Like a manila file folder, an Excel file is just a collection of information with a name.

## Rows and Columns

The row and column structure of the Excel worksheet provides a powerful framework for financial analysis. Consider a company's financial plan or budget, as shown in Figure 2-2. Each row is an account—an element of revenue or expense. Each column is a period of time—months, quarters, or years. Summing across columns you get the total for an account, and summing down rows you get the total for a time period.

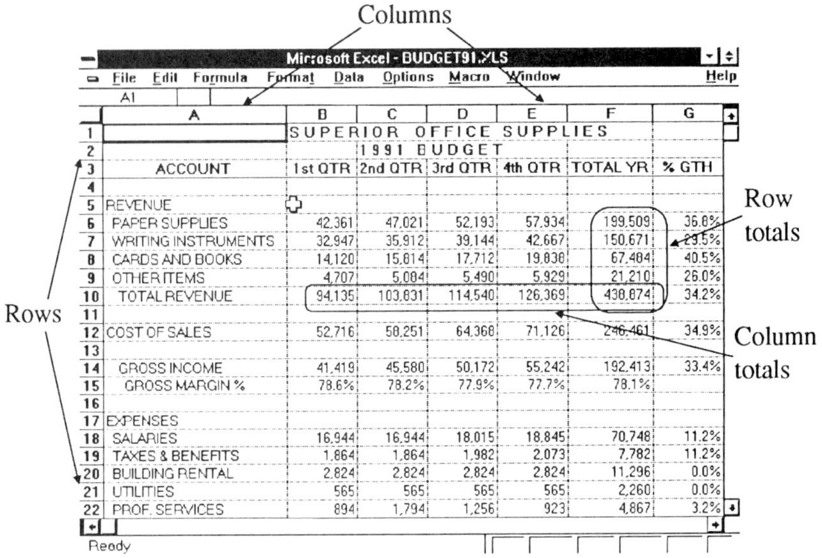

**FIGURE 2-2** Financial plan

The horizontal rows and vertical columns make a two-dimensional grid. The rows are numbered 1 through 16,384, while the 256 possible columns are labeled A through IV (A through Z, then AA through AZ, BA through BZ, and so on through IV). With this grid, you could build a formula that, for example, adds column C from row 24 through row 32, or you can graph row 15 from column AC through column AH.

## Addresses, Cells, and Ranges

When information is entered into a worksheet, it is stored in a specific location. You know what that location is by the row and column the information is in. Using Excel's row and column grid, you can give the information you stored an *address;* for example, column D, row 7. Excel addresses are written with the column reference first, followed by the row. Using this convention, you can write the example address as D7.

A single address, the intersection of a row and a column, is called a *cell*. You can think of a worksheet as a collection of over four million cells. These are addressed from A1 for the cell in the upper-left corner to IV16384 for the cell in lower-right corner. Of course, the amount of memory you have in your computer limits the number of these you can use at a time.

**NUMBERS AND TEXT** A cell may contain either numbers or text. Numbers, which include formulas that evaluate to numbers, can be formatted in many ways, including dollars, percentages, dates, or time. Text can include numbers and can be used as titles, row and column labels, and notes on a worksheet.

The primary difference between numbers and text is that you can do arithmetic on numbers but not on text. Think of numbers as arithmetic values and text as everything else.

Based on what you type, Excel determines whether your entry is a number or text. If you type only numbers (0 through 9) or the numeric symbols

+ - ( ) . , : $ %

Excel considers your entry a number. If you enter a date or time value in one of Excel's built-in formats, it is considered a number. Finally, a recognizable formula that results in a number is treated as a number. Everything else is text.

You can enter numbers that range from $2.225E^{-307}$ to $1.789E^{305}$ and format them in several ways. For example, you can enter **3.25**, **3.25%**, **$3.25**, **32.5E-1**, or **3,250,325.25**. In other words, you can include commas, dollar signs, and percents in numbers and Excel will interpret it correctly. The entry of formulas, which are also numbers, is discussed below, as is more about entering, formatting, and aligning text and numbers.

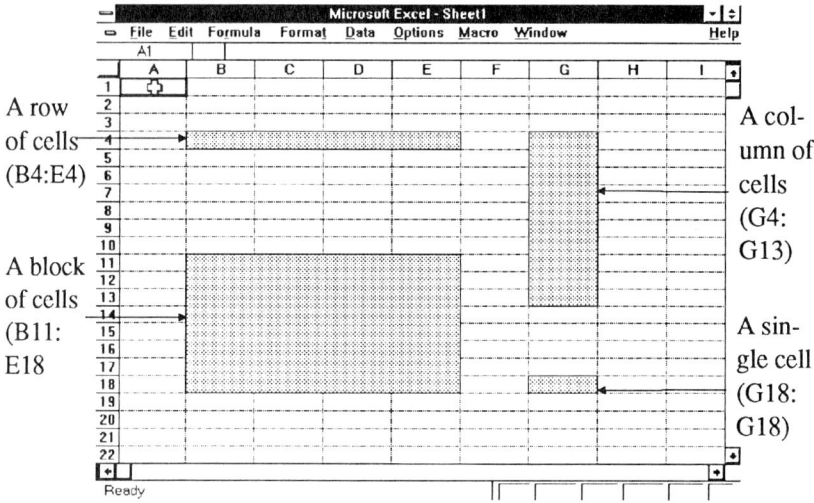

**FIGURE 2-3**   Types of ranges

**RANGES AND RANGE NAMES**   A rectangular group of adjacent cells is called a *range*. Figure 2-3 shows four kinds of ranges that can exist on a worksheet: a row of cells, a column of cells, a rectangular block of cells, or a single cell. A range cannot be an L-shaped or otherwise nonrectangular arrangement of cells; it must be a complete rectangle.

Ranges are used in many Excel commands to specify a group of cells you want Excel to work on. To specify a range in a command, you may use the pair of addresses representing the first and last cells in the range (the upper-left and lower-right corners, respectively) separated by a colon, as in B11:G18. Alternatively, you may highlight the range on the screen or you may use a *range name* that you have previously given to that range of cells.

A range name is a text string that begins with a letter and can be as long as 255 characters. A range name such as Salaries is often used because it is easier to remember and more meaningful than a range address, such as G16:T16. Many of Excel's arithmetic functions use ranges as arguments and, when a range name is substituted for the address, they become very descriptive. For example, to add a group of salaries you would use the Excel function =SUM(Salaries) if you had previously defined the range name Salaries.

## Formulas and Functions

The ability to enter text and numbers is not very useful unless you can do something with them. You need to be able to add columns of numbers, calculate percentages, and perform numerous other mathematical operations. Formulas are the means of doing this. Formulas may operate on numbers, other formulas, or text. When a formula uses text it is called a *text formula* and may contain the text operator (&) for concatenation (combining two text strings). Formulas that contain the arithmetic operators

+ - * / ^ %

are *numeric formulas,* and formulas that contain the comparison operators

= < > <= >= <>

are *logical formulas,* which produce the logical values True or False.

Formulas use standard algebraic notation with nested parentheses, if necessary, and they always begin with an equal sign (=). Formulas may be up to 255 characters long but may not contain spaces, except within a *literal*—a set of letters, numbers, or symbols enclosed in quotation marks. Formulas usually use data in other locations on a worksheet by referencing either a cell address, a range of cells, or a range name.

Examples of formulas are shown here,

| Formula | Contents of the Cell Containing the Formula |
|---|---|
| =B5 | The contents of B5. |
| =C6-C7 | The result of subtracting the contents of C7 from the contents of C6. |
| =.45*1590 | The product of 0.45 times 1590. |
| =subtotal*tax | The product of the ranges named Subtotal and Tax. |
| ="Dear "&D5 | The combination of the literal string "Dear " with the contents of D5. (Quotation marks define a literal string, character for character.) |
| =date<=today | The logical value True (which is also the numeric value 1) if a range named Date is less than or equal to a range named Today; otherwise the logical value False (which is also the numeric value 0). |

**ORDER OF CALCULATION** Excel calculates or evaluates a formula in a particular order determined by the precedence number of the operators being used and the parentheses placed in the formula. The following table describes each operator and gives its precedence number. Operators with a lower precedence number are performed earlier in the calculation. When two operators in a formula have the same precedence number, Excel evaluates them sequentially from left to right.

| Operator | Description | Precedence |
|---|---|---|
| : | Range of cells | 1 |
| (a space) | Intersection of cells | 1 |
| , | Union of cells | 1 |
| - | Negation | 2 |
| % | Percentage (/100) | 3 |
| ^ | Exponentiation | 4 |
| * | Multiplication | 5 |
| / | Division | 5 |
| + | Addition | 6 |
| - | Subtraction | 6 |
| & | Concatenation | 7 |
| = | Equal to | 8 |
| < | Less than | 8 |
| > | Greater than | 8 |
| <= | Less than or equal to | 8 |
| >= | Greater than or equal to | 8 |
| <> | Not equal to | 8 |

Parentheses in a formula change the order of calculation. For example, to add two amounts before multiplying them by a third, you cannot use the formula =A+B*C because the multiplication is performed before the addition, in accordance with the order of calculation. When you put parentheses around the addition operation, the formula becomes =(A+B)*C, and the addition is performed first. Excel performs the calculation within the innermost parentheses first. Parentheses must always be added in pairs and may be nested up to eight levels deep.

**FUNCTIONS**  Excel has a number of built-in formulas, called *functions,* that can be used within other formulas or can be used alone. Functions always begin with an equal sign and include mathematical, logical, database, text, financial, and statistical calculations. A function can be either text or a number depending on whether it is operating on text or numbers. Here are some examples of functions and their uses:

| | |
|---|---|
| =SUM(A4:A7,A9) | Adds A4, A5, A6, A7 and A9 |
| =NOW( ) | Produces the current date and time |
| =PI( )*G3^2 | Calculates the area of a circle whose radius is in G3 |
| =PV(C4,F6,B1) | Calculates the present value of a series of equal payments at an interest rate contained in C4, for the number of periods in F6, and with the payment amount contained in B1 |
| =RIGHT(T22,5) | Displays the rightmost five characters of a text string contained in T22 |

Functions are discussed throughout this book, but they get an in-depth treatment in Chapter 10. Chapter 13 provides an alphabetical listing and summary description.

## Commands

You can give Excel commands in four ways: by selecting options from a menu presented on the screen, by clicking or dragging the mouse on the worksheet, by pressing particular keys on the keyboard, and by activating a set of commands you have stored on a special worksheet. In this book, *command* refers to one of the first three methods: those implemented either with the mouse by itself or with a menu, and those implemented by pressing keys on your keyboard. Commands stored on a worksheet are called *macro functions* or *macros*.

**COMMANDS FROM A MENU** The primary means of giving Excel a command is by choosing an option from a menu presented to you on the screen. When you use menus to choose an option, you sometimes are asked for additional information with a dialog box, or you may be presented with a secondary menu. As you saw in Chapter 1, you can begin menu selection in several ways: by clicking with the mouse on the name of the menu you want to use or by pressing (ALT), (F10), or / (slash). This book assumes that you usually use the mouse, but you should become familiar with all of the menu selection techniques. For the most part, the instructions in this book state "Select the File menu" or "From the File menu." Whether you use the mouse or the keyboard is up to you.

If you use the keyboard, the (ALT), (F10), or / key only gets you to the Menu bar; you must still select the menu you want to use (which is one of many good reasons why using the mouse is preferable). There are two methods to select a menu with the keyboard: you can type the underlined letter in the menu name you want, or you can use the direction keys to highlight the menu name and then press either (DOWN ARROW) or (ENTER) to open the menu.

Once a menu is open, you can choose a menu option in one of three ways: click on the menu option with the mouse, type the underlined letter in the option name, or use the direction keys to highlight the option and press (ENTER) to choose it. Examples of the three methods follow, in which you select the Options menu and choose the Calculate Now option, as shown in Figure 2-4. The message area on the left side of the Status bar at the bottom of the Excel window displays an explanation of the highlighted menu or menu option. No other change appears on the screen as a result of these steps.

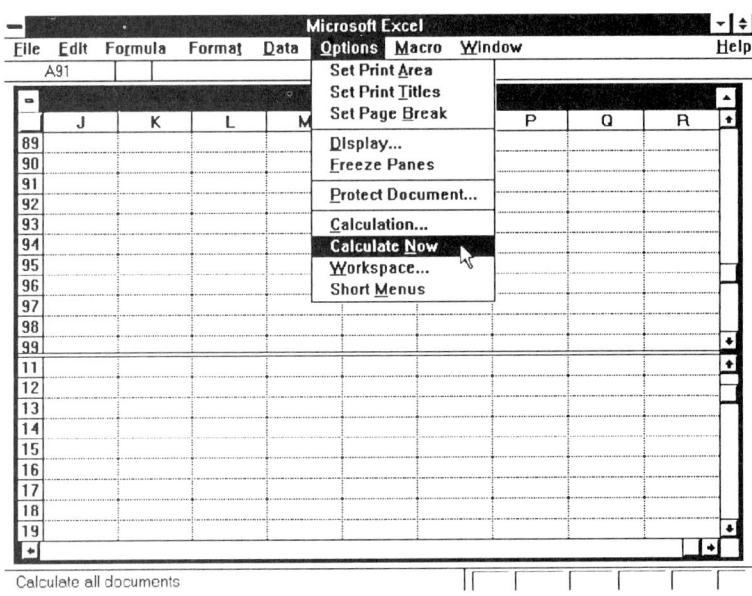

**FIGURE 2-4** Choosing Calculate Now from the Options menu

*Mouse Method*

1. Click on the Options menu.

2. Click on the Calculate Now option.

*Keyboard Method 1*

1. Press (ALT), (F10), or /.

2. Type **o**, (you can use upper- or lowercase), the underlined letter in Options.

3. Type **n**, the underlined letter in Calculate Now.

*Keyboard Method 2*

1. Press (ALT), or (F10), or /.

2. Press (RIGHT ARROW) five times.

3. Press (DOWN ARROW) eight times.

4. Press (ENTER).

Because you will be using the menuing system extensively as you work with Excel, menu commands are a primary subject of this book. Chapter 3 introduces each Excel menu, and Chapter 12 provides an alphabetical summary of all menu options.

**DIRECT MOUSE COMMANDS** Beside its function in choosing commands from menus, the mouse can also be used directly on the worksheet. Most importantly you can use the mouse to highlight a range of cells on which you want to operate—copy, move, or format, for example. You do this by pointing on a cell in one corner of the range, pressing the mouse button, and dragging the mouse (pressing and holding the mouse button while moving the mouse) to the opposite corner. For example, the highlighted range in Figure 2-5 was created by pointing the mouse on C7 and dragging the mouse to E13.

Other direct mouse commands within Excel include placing an insertion point in a formula or text string, selecting an entire row or column by clicking on the row or column headings, widening a column or heightening a row by dragging on the intersection of two columns or two row headings, and dividing the window into panes by dragging the horizontal or vertical split bar. (The parts of the Excel window are discussed in Chapter 3.) Of course, you can also use the mouse with the scroll bars to change what is being

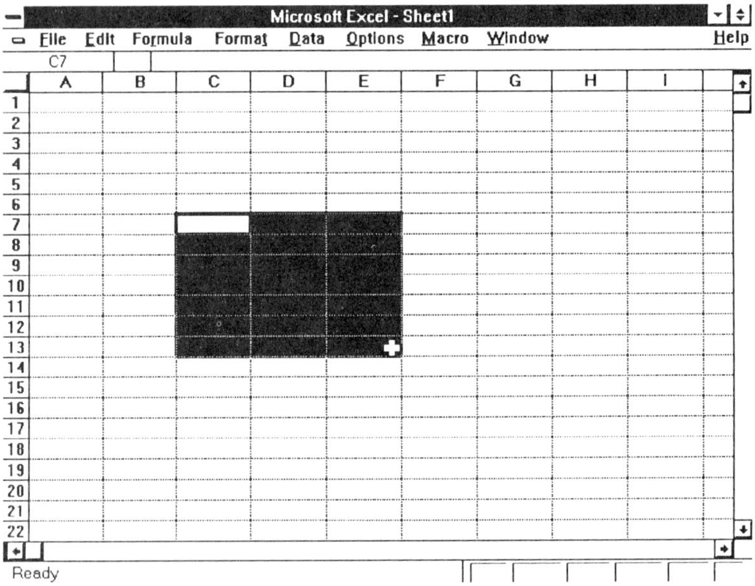

**FIGURE 2-5** Highlighted range

displayed and to size and move the window, as you learned in Chapter 1.

A large portion of this book focuses on using the mouse. Therefore, you will see many examples of using the mouse directly on the worksheet and have ample opportunity to practice such maneuvers.

**COMMANDS FROM THE KEYBOARD** Most of the keys on the keyboard that are not standard typewriter keys can be used to give Excel commands. Microsoft provides a keyboard template that lists many of these keys.

Many of the keyboard commands are implemented with the *function keys* ((F1) through (F10) or (F12)) on the top or left of most keyboards. On the right of most keyboards are the *direction keys*—the keys marked with the four arrows and (HOME), (END),

(PGUP), and (PGDN). Use these keys to move around the screen, from cell to cell, or through a menu.

Some Excel commands are implemented through the use of two or more keys. Just as the (SHIFT) key is used with the normal typewriter keyboard to produce alternate characters, the (CTRL) and (ALT) keys are used with other keys to produce alternative commands.

Chapter 3 describes these keys in more detail. Also there is a card in the back of the book that lists keys that are shortcuts for menu options—called *shortcut keys*.

**MACRO FUNCTIONS**  A macro function is one or more commands, stored on a *macro sheet,* that behave like automatic menu, mouse, and keyboard commands when executed. You can have Excel execute a macro function, or macro, by pressing two keys. For example, you can format a number with a macro that accomplishes six or more keystrokes with two. Macros are used to automate or speed up repetitive procedures.

Almost all commands that you can perform with a menu, the mouse, or the keyboard can be stored on a macro sheet in a macro function and can be activated as you choose. In addition to menu, mouse, and keyboard commands, a set of macro functions can be used to perform built-in programming functions, such as repeating a sequence or accepting input from the keyboard. With these additional macro functions you can build custom menus and automate a worksheet. Chapter 10 discusses macros in depth, Chapter 11 demonstrates worksheet automation with macros, and Chapter 14 provides an alphabetical summary.

## Worksheet Windows

The Excel worksheet window, as it appears in Figure 2-5, uses as much of the screen as possible to display a single portion of one worksheet. With the scroll bars or direction keys you can change

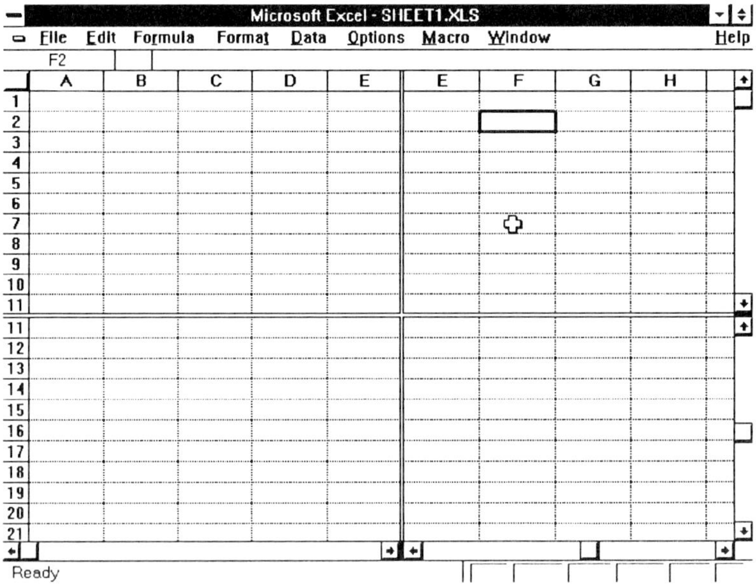

**FIGURE 2-6** Single worksheet window split into four panes

the rows and columns being displayed, but the view is similar. In addition to this basic view, Windows 3 and Excel provide several other views that give you a different look at one or more worksheets.

By splitting the window into *panes,* vertically, horizontally, or both, you can look at two or four parts of the same worksheet at the same time, as shown in Figure 2-6. With multiple windows, you can look at several worksheets simultaneously, either tiled, as shown in Figure 2-7, or overlapping, as shown in Figure 2-8.

## Multiple Files and File Linking

As implied by Figures 2-7 and 2-8, Excel allows you to have more than one worksheet open at one time. That means that you can compare, copy, or move information between open worksheets.

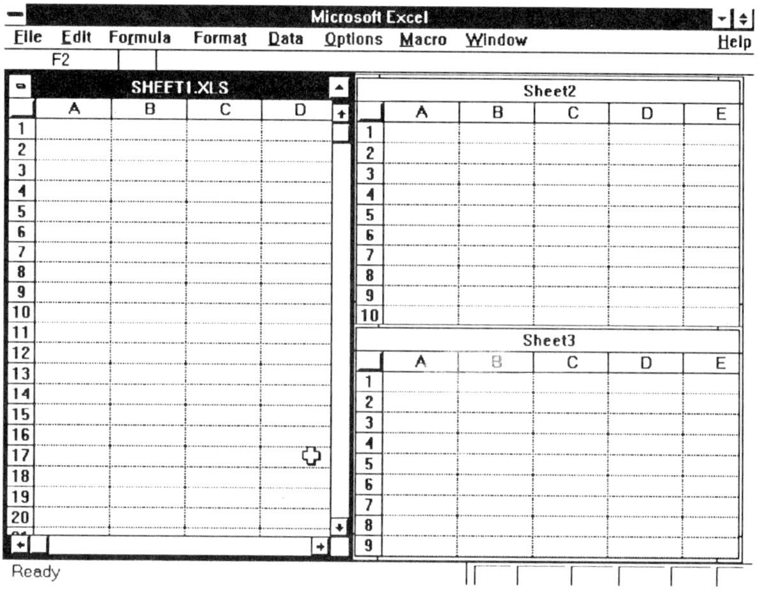

**FIGURE 2-7** Three worksheet windows, tiled

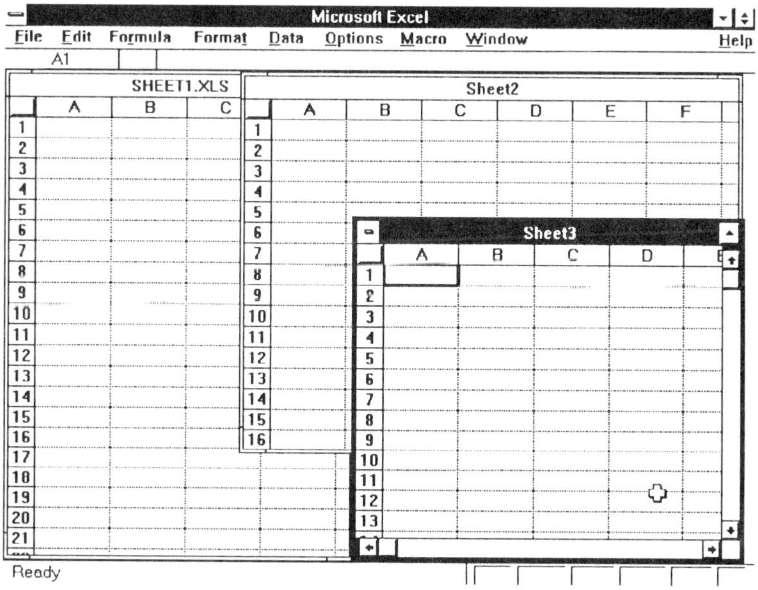

**FIGURE 2-8** Three worksheet windows, overlapping

Excel also allows you to refer to cells or ranges contained in one worksheet file in a formula contained in a second worksheet file. This is called *file linking*. The files may both be open in memory, or one may be closed on the disk. As a result you can easily combine information contained in separate files. A change in one linked file automatically is reflected in the second file. If the second file is on the disk, it must be loaded and recalculated before the change is apparent.

To refer to another file in a formula, the formula must contain the filename. This is accomplished by appending the filename, followed by an ! (exclamation point), to the front of an address or range name. For example, QTR3BUD!SALARIES refers to a range named Salaries in a file named QTR3BUD.

## Help

As you are learning Excel, and possibly even after you know it fairly well, you may forget how a command works or what the arguments are for a function or macro. To assist you in these instances, Microsoft has provided a context-sensitive help system in Excel. It is activated by pressing (SHIFT+F1). Because it is context sensitive, what message you see after asking for help depends on what you were doing when you asked for it. For example, if you were looking at the Edit Copy option when you pressed (SHIFT+F1), you will get a help window describing the Edit Copy options, as shown in Figure 2-9. Also, when you get an alert or error message, you can press (SHIFT+F1) and get a help window describing the message.

Most help topics have cross-references, or *jump terms,* to other help topics that cover related areas. You can easily identify the jump terms because they are underlined. If you place the mouse pointer on them, the pointer turns into a *grabber hand.* To look at the jump term, place the mouse pointer on it and press the mouse button (click on them). Also, many help topics have *glossary terms,* which are highlighted terms. The mouse pointer again

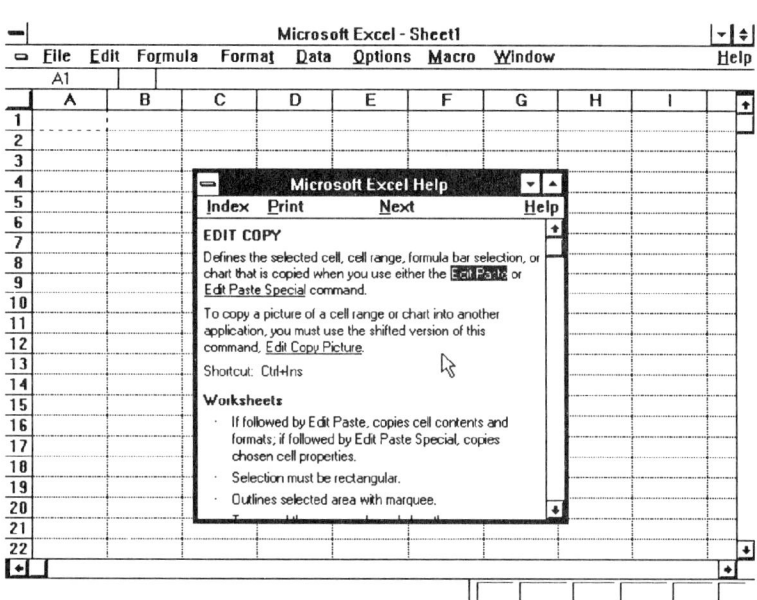

**FIGURE 2-9** Help window for the Edit Copy command

becomes a grabber hand if you point on them, and when you click on the term you get its definition. Each help window has a small menu that allows you to go to the help index, print the current help statement, and go backward or forward through a series of help statements.

In addition to the context-sensitive help you can get by pressing (SHIFT+F1), you can go right to the help index or several major categories of help, as well as the tutorial, by using the Help menu on the far right of the Menu bar or by pressing (F1), as shown here:

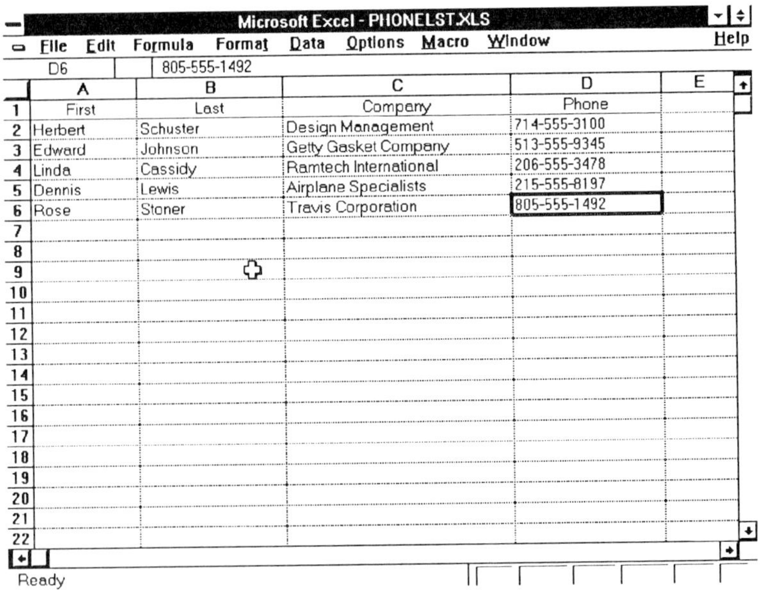

FIGURE 2-10  Phone list on a worksheet

## DATABASES

The row and column structure of a worksheet is excellent for storing lists of information. Consider the phone list shown in Figure 2-10. Each entry in the list is called a *record* and is stored in a single row of the worksheet. Each part of an entry—the name, company, or phone number in Figure 2-10—is called a *field* and is stored in a column. You therefore have a natural and common relationship between records and fields in a list and rows and columns in a worksheet.

A list of related information organized in a consistent, logical manner is called a *database*. A database must be completely contained on a single worksheet, but a single worksheet can contain more than one database.

## Rows and Records

Each row of a database, other than the first row, is a record representing a single entry. The first row of a database must contain the names of each field, one per column. These *field names* are used to identify the fields in commands and functions. All rows after the first in a database are data records. They can be blank or contain a divider line, for example, but they are still considered data records. A database can contain a maximum of 16,383 records (one less than the number of rows in a worksheet).

## Columns and Fields

Each column of a database is a field representing a common data element in all records. For example, the company name in Figure 2-11 is a field. Each field can contain a number, text, or a formula. A database can contain a maximum of 256 fields, one for every column in a worksheet, but you cannot have two fields with the same field name in one database.

The parts of a database are shown in Figure 2-11.

## Using Databases

You can use a database any time you need a list of items. Examples of databases, in addition to the phone list, are stocks in a portfolio with dates and prices, parts of a machine with the part number and supplier, salesmen with their quotas and commissions, and products with their prices and margins.

72  Excel 2.1 Made Easy

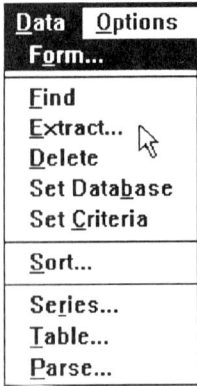

FIGURE 2-11   Parts of a database

Within Excel there is a set of commands that let you manipulate databases. These commands are called *data commands* because they are all accessed through the Data menu shown here:

The primary functions of these commands are sorting databases, extracting information from them, and analyzing them. For example, you can sort the phone list by company, extract stocks that are performing below your expectations, find the parts of a machine that are from a given supplier, and analyze the change in sales commissions that would result from changes in quotas. Database-related commands and functions are explored in Chapters 7 and 8.

## CHARTS

If a picture is worth a thousand words, a chart is worth at least a thousand numbers. A chart allows you to give visual meaning to a set of numbers, to show the difference or sameness between them,

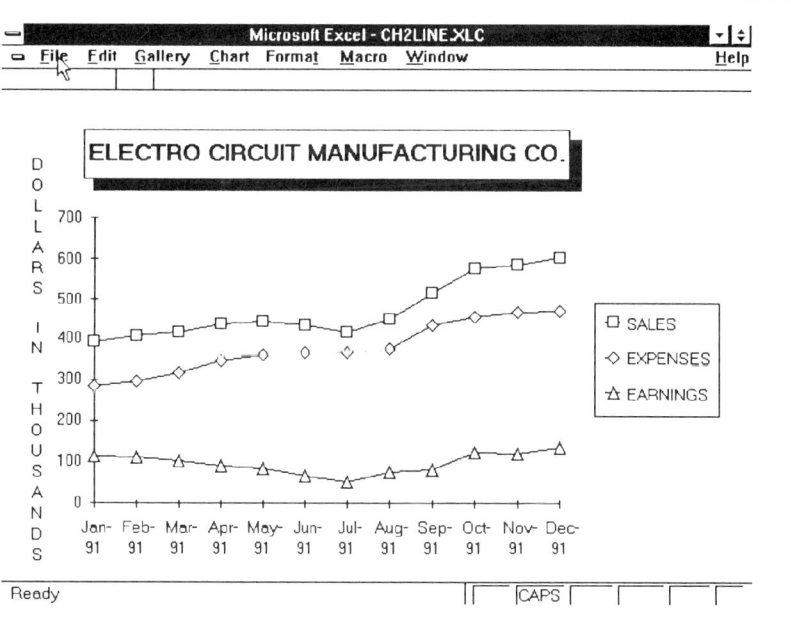

FIGURE 2-12  Line chart of sales, expenses, and earnings

and to show the patterns that they are producing. Many people find that they get information faster and easier from charts, or even that they see things in charts that they do not see in the numbers that produce the charts.

An Excel chart is a pictorial representation of one or more ranges on a worksheet. If you have a range on a worksheet that contains company sales by month, you can produce a line chart that would make it easy to show fluctuations in monthly sales. Given ranges for expenses and earnings by month, you can produce additional lines on the same chart and tell not only if they are going up or down, but also how they are trending in relation to each other. Figure 2-12 shows such a line chart.

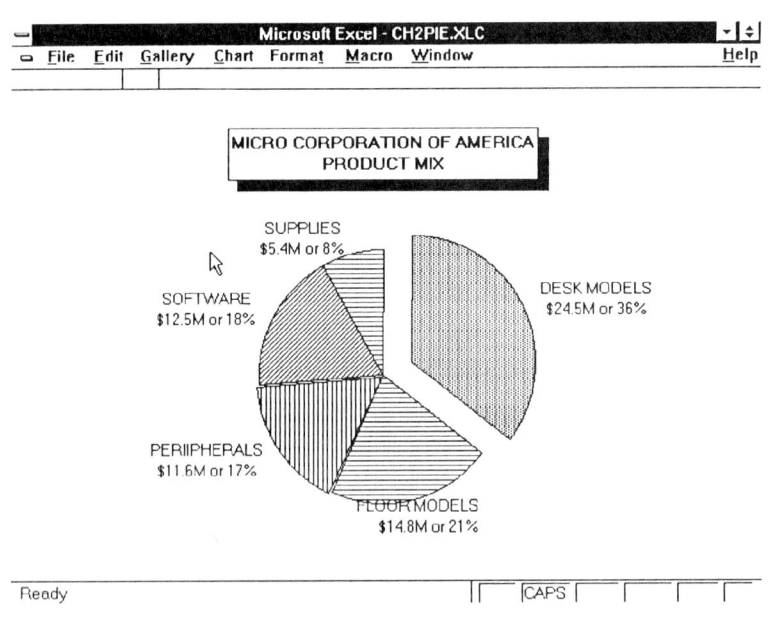

**FIGURE 2-13** Pie chart showing product contribution to sales

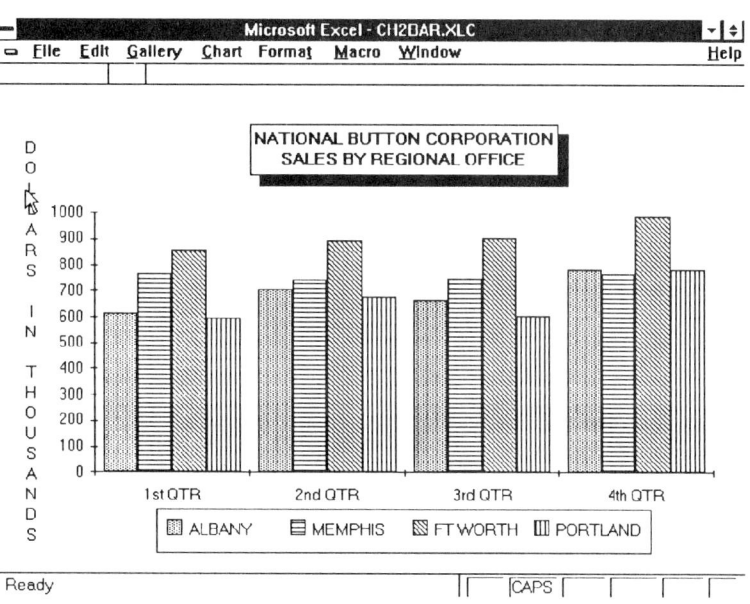

**FIGURE 2-14** Bar chart of plant sales by quarter

The pie chart shown in Figure 2-13 shows the proportion each of four product lines contributes to total company sales by charting a range containing the sales by product. Given ranges containing sales by quarter for each of three regions, the bar chart shown in Figure 2-14 can be produced.

Excel provides seven primary types of charts—Area, Bar, Column, Combination, Line, Pie, and Scatter—plus several alternatives for each type. As a result you have many ways to chart information on a worksheet.

To produce these charts, Excel provides a unique set of menus in the chart window opened with a new chart. Through these menus you select the type of chart you want to produce and identify the ranges on the worksheet that will generate it. You can add titles and annotations, as well as specify the color and fonts to be used. Charts can be named, saved, and printed on most printers. The production of charts is discussed in detail in Chapter 7.

# THE EXCEL ENVIRONMENT

Getting Started
Excel's Screen and Menus
Excel's Use of the Keyboard
Quitting Excel

## GETTING STARTED

This chapter and the remainder of this book were written with the assumption that you would follow along on your computer as you read. This allows you to see for yourself what a keystroke does and how the screen looks as a result. Most people find that they learn much faster by doing while reading than by reading alone.

To use Excel on your computer, you must first install Windows and then Excel. This process is discussed in Appendix A. If you have not installed Windows or Excel yet, turn to Appendix A and complete the installation, including the startup procedure. When you are done, you can return to this chapter.

If you have already installed Windows and Excel, start them now, following the procedure described in Appendix A.

## EXCEL'S SCREEN AND MENUS

When you first start Excel, after briefly seeing the Microsoft copyright message, you see a blank worksheet on your screen like the one shown in Figure 3-1. This screen contains two windows. On the outer perimeter of the screen is the Excel application window. This contains Excel's menus, the address of the currently active cell, the Formula bar, and the Status bar. Within the Excel window is a single worksheet document window. The worksheet window is the primary working area in Excel. The Excel application window may contain several worksheet windows as well as one or more chart, macro, and information document windows.

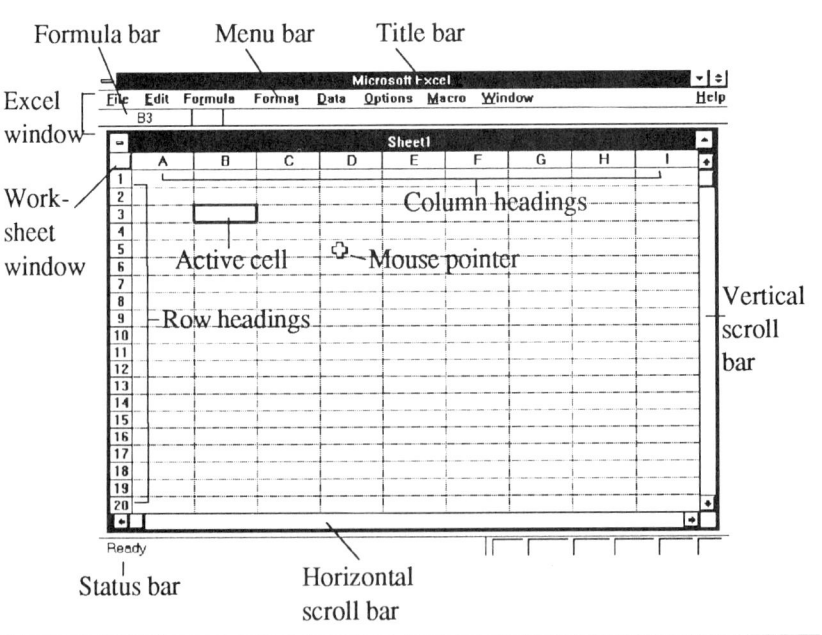

**FIGURE 3-1** Blank worksheet screen

The two primary windows, Excel and worksheet, are discussed in the following sections.

## The Worksheet Window

Initially, Excel opens a single worksheet window. As you saw in Chapter 2, you can open additional worksheet windows as well as chart and other types of windows. You use a single worksheet window most often and open other windows only for special purposes.

The worksheet window in which you are currently working is called the *active window*. You may have other worksheets open, but they are not active until you click the mouse on them or choose a different window from the Window menu. You can tell which worksheet is active because its Title bar and an active cell are highlighted. In Figure 3-2, Sheet2 is the active window.

A worksheet window provides the area for you to enter numbers, text, and formulas to build what you want. The worksheet's inherent structure—its rows and columns—allows you to enter and organize your work easily.

**ROWS AND COLUMNS** The blank worksheets in Figures 3-1 and 3-2 show the row and column nature of the worksheet: the row and column headings are across the top and down the left side and the two-dimensional grid forms individual cells. The intersection of one row and one column is a cell in which you can enter numbers, text, or a formula. One cell at a time is active and available for entry or editing. You know which cell is active because it has a heavy border around it. In Figure 3-1, cell B3 is active. This is the cell formed by the intersection of column B and row 3. Cell B3 of Sheet2 is active in Figure 3-2.

You can make a different cell active by either clicking on it with the mouse (moving the mouse pointer to the new cell and pressing the mouse button) or by using the direction keys on the right of

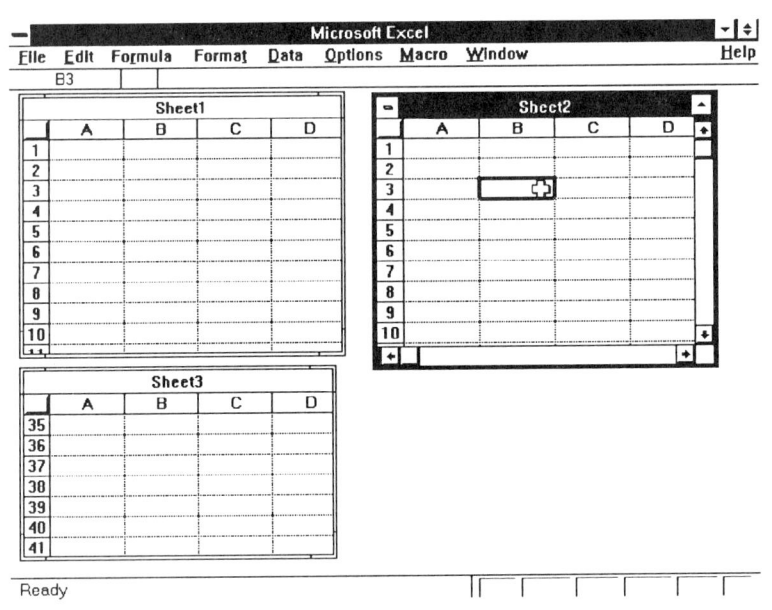

**FIGURE 3-2** Sheet2 is the active window

your keyboard to move the active cell border to the new cell. You will do that shortly.

By using the scroll bars on the right and bottom of the worksheet window or by using the direction keys, you can look at and work on other areas of the active worksheet. Compared to Excel's total potential area, the area actually displayed on your screen is quite small—20 out of 16,384 rows and 9 out of 256 columns. Of course most applications in Excel also use only a small amount of the total area but often are larger than what you initially see on the screen.

## The Excel Window

The Excel window contains four bars—three at the top and one at the bottom. The top two bars, the Title bar and the Menu bar, are common to all Windows applications. The other two bars, the Formula bar and the Status bar, are unique to Excel. The Title bar is standard in Windows, with nothing but the name it contains to set it apart. The Menu bar, while consistent in layout to other Windows applications, has a unique set of menus.

**THE MENU BAR**   The Excel menu set includes eight Excel menus and two standard Windows menus, Control and Help. Since you looked at Control and Help in Chapter 1, only the eight Excel menus are reviewed here.

Remember that to open a menu you can click on the menu name with the mouse. Also, you can press (ALT) or (F10) or type / to activate the Menu bar, and then type the underlined letter in the menu name or move the highlight to the menu name with the direction keys and press (ENTER). With a menu open you can look at another menu by either clicking on the menu name or using the direction keys to move to the other menu. If you want to close a menu without choosing an option, you press (ESC).

Excel has two menu levels: short and long. The only difference is that long menus include several infrequently used options that are not on short menus. Since there is no reason for not having the full long menus always available, this book assumes you are using long menus. To set that option, which remains set until you change it back, follow these steps:

1. Click on the Options menu in the Menu bar (or press (ALT) and type **o**) to open the Options menu.

2. Click on Long Menus (or type **m**) to choose the Long Menu option.

Use these menu-handling techniques now to look at each of the Excel menus as they are discussed.

*File Menu*   The File menu provides the means of creating new worksheets, charts, and macro sheets; opening existing worksheets, charts, and macro sheets stored on disk; and closing, saving, and deleting worksheets, charts, and macro sheets. It also allows you to set up the page you will print, set up your printer, print a worksheet or chart, and exit Excel. The File menu is shown here:

*Edit Menu*   You use the Edit menu to copy, move, and clear the contents of a cell or range of cells, to undo or repeat the last thing you did, and to insert and delete rows and columns. The Edit menu is shown here:

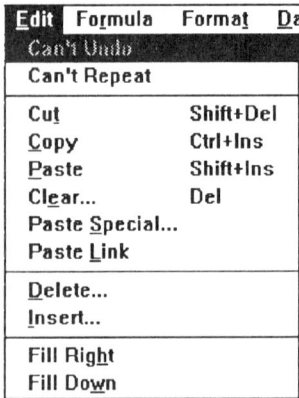

***Formula Menu*** The Formula menu is used to build and maintain formulas. This includes creating, using, and deleting range names, adding functions, and switching between absolute and relative references. Also, through the Formula menu you can add notes to cells, go to a particular cell, select cells based on their contents, search and replace text, and select cells of a specified type. The Formula menu is shown here:

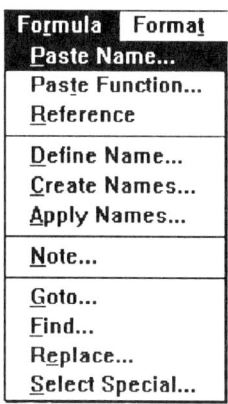

***Format Menu*** Through the Format menu you determine how a cell entry looks. If it contains a number, you can format it as dollars or percents, with or without commas, and set the number of decimal places. For both text and numbers you can left, right, or center align them; place a border around or shade them; protect a cell from being overwritten; and determine a cell's width and height. Finally, you can justify text in a range of cells. The Format menu is shown here:

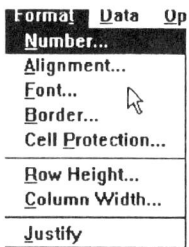

*Data Menu* The Data menu is used with databases to define them; to determine selection criteria; to find, extract, or delete selected records based on the criteria; to view and maintain them as a form instead of a table; and to sort them. The Data menu is also used to fill a range of cells with a series of numbers or dates, to create a table, and to divide a text string into individual cells (that is, to parse). The Data menu is shown here:

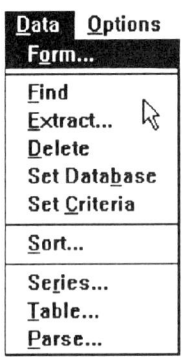

*Options Menu* The Options menu is the catch-all menu for options that do not fit in any other menu. It provides the means of specifying the area of the worksheet to be printed and to identify repeated titles on a printout. The Options menu also allows you to set manual page breaks, to determine how your screen will look, to freeze columns on the left and rows on the top of a worksheet, and to protect a document (worksheet, chart, or macro sheet) or window from being overwritten. Additionally, you can set how Excel calculates a worksheet; force the recalculation of a worksheet at any time; change overall defaults, like the display of the Status bar, scroll bars, and Formula bar; and change the type of menu. The Options menu is shown here:

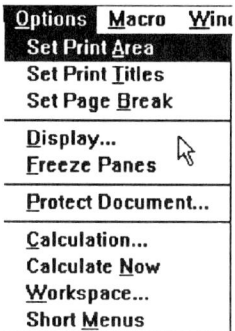

***Macro Menu***   The Macro menu is used to record and run macro functions. Macro functions, you remember, are Excel commands that have been stored on a macro sheet. The Macro menu allows you to record functions on the macro sheet as you carry out the related commands on a regular worksheet, to run a macro once it has been recorded, and to set several options for recording macros. The Macro menu is shown here:

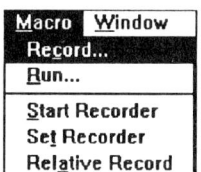

***Window Menu***   The Window menu allows you to open another window on the same worksheet, to look at information behind the current active cell, to arrange all open windows so they can be seen on the screen, to hide or unhide a window, and to choose among open windows. The Window menu is shown here:

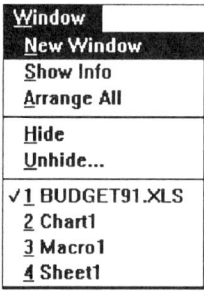

***Dialog Boxes*** Menu options with an ellipsis (...) after them require that you enter additional information or choose from among additional options. For example, you may have to enter the name of a file to save or choose the type of cell alignment you want. When this occurs, a dialog box is opened for this purpose. As you saw in Chapter 1, a dialog box employs one or more devices for collecting information. Many of the devices are illustrated in the Save Worksheet as dialog box shown here and the Fonts dialog box shown in Figure 3-3.

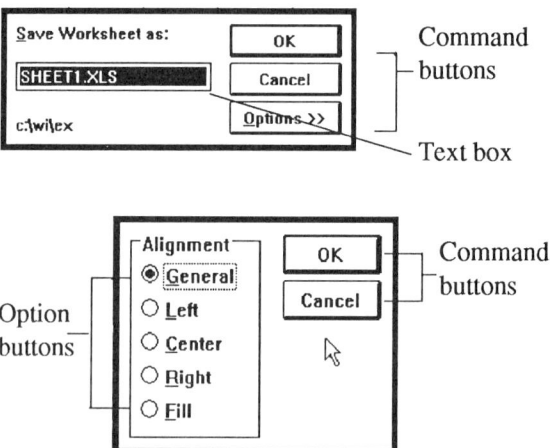

You will have many opportunities in the chapters that follow to become more familiar with Excel's menus and their related dialog boxes.

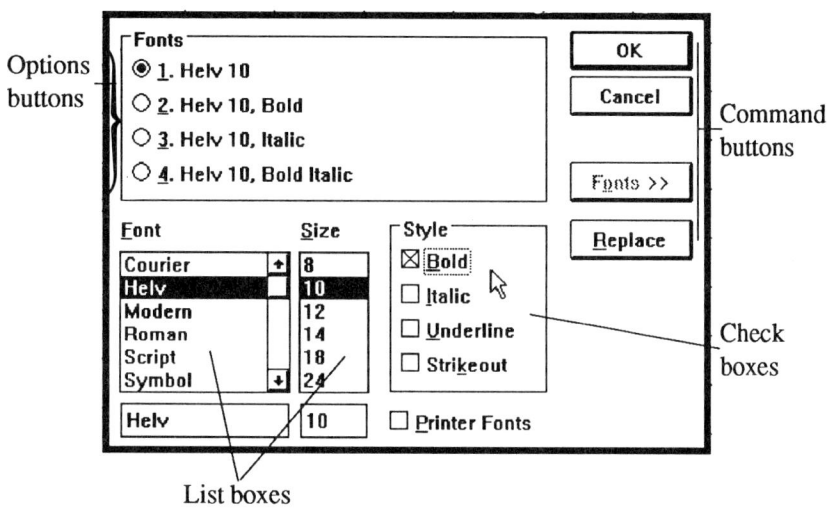

**FIGURE 3-3** Fonts dialog box

**THE FORMULA BAR** Beneath Excel's Menu bar is the Formula bar, as shown in Figure 3-4. On the left side of the Formula bar is the *reference area,* which contains the address of the currently active cell on the worksheet. For example, when the cell address of C6 is displayed, this tells you that the currently active cell is in the third column (column C) and the sixth row. While you are in the process of selecting a range of cells—C3:E4, for exam-

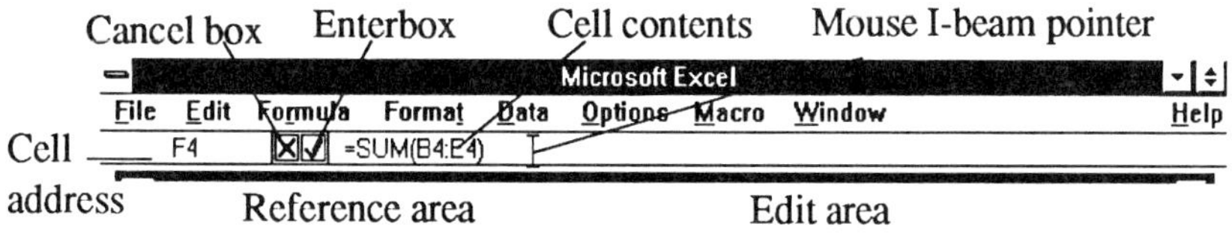

**FIGURE 3-4** Elements of the Formula bar

ple—the reference area tells you the number of rows and columns selected—2RX3C in the example, for 2 rows by 3 columns. The reference area also has some specialized uses with charts and during several operations. These are discussed later in this book with the related topics.

On the right side of the Formula bar is the *edit area,* where you enter and edit text, numbers, and formulas for the active cell. If you are entering or editing a cell's contents, two boxes appear to the right of the reference area: the Cancel box with an "X" in it and the Enter box with a check mark in it. Clicking on the Cancel box cancels any changes you made in the edit area and returns a cell's original contents. The Cancel box is similar to pressing (ESC). Clicking on the Enter box is like pressing (ENTER). It transfers the edited contents of the edit area to the active cell.

When you begin typing in an empty cell, the letters or numbers that you type go into both the cell itself and the edit area of the Formula bar. In many instances the cell is not wide enough to display all of what you type, but the edit area expands to the 255 maximum characters a cell can hold. After completing the entry and pressing (ENTER), the edit area still displays the cell's contents. If you move to another cell and then come back, the edit area again displays the cell's contents.

If you want to change or edit the contents of a cell, you do so in the edit area of the Formula bar. First make the cell you want to edit active by clicking on it or by using the direction keys. You then click on the Formula bar, or you can press the (F2) function key to activate the edit area. While you are entering or editing a cell's contents, a vertical line appears in the edit area. This line is called the insertion point. Characters you type are added to the immediate left of the insertion point. When the mouse pointer is in the edit area, it becomes an I-beam, as shown in Figure 3-4. The I-beam is thin enough to be inserted between characters in the edit area. By placing the I-beam between two characters and clicking, you move the insertion point to where you clicked. This allows you to insert new characters between existing characters.

While you are making an entry, what you see in the edit area and what you see in the cell are the same up to the cell width. Once you complete a formula entry, the formula is displayed in the edit area, while the cell displays the value resulting from the formula. If the entry is a number or text, it is displayed in both the Formula bar and the cell. Figure 3-4 shows a formula in the edit area.

**STATUS BAR** The Status bar, at the bottom of the Excel window, displays messages on the left and up to six keyboard indicators on the right, as shown here:

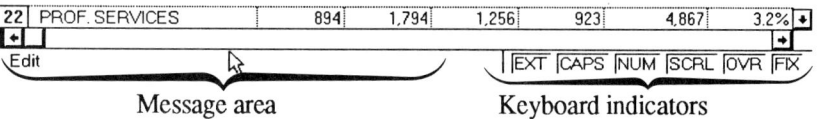

*Message Area* The message area has several uses depending on what you are doing. If you highlight a menu name or a menu option, the message area displays a brief description of the menu or option. When you are using a dialog box or have an alert message on the screen, the message area tells you how to get help. At other times the message area serves as a mode indicator that tells you what Excel is doing. The most common mode is Ready, meaning that Excel is ready for you to make an entry or use a menu. There are 13 other modes, as shown with their meanings in the following table:

| Mode | Meaning |
|---|---|
| Calculate | With manual calculation, this indicates that a change has been made to the worksheet and it needs to be recalculated. |
| Circular | A circular reference has been detected where, through whatever route, a cell is referencing |

|   |   |
|---|---|
|   | itself. One of the cells in the circular path will be identified. |
| Copy | A copy operation has started, and a destination needs to be selected. |
| Cut | A cut operation has started, and a destination needs to be selected. |
| Edit | An entry is being edited in the Formula bar. |
| Entry | Data is being entered into the active cell. |
| Find | A database record matching the stated criteria has been found and is being highlighted. |
| Help | A help window is being displayed. |
| Move | A window or chart item is being moved. Use the direction keys to complete it. |
| Point | You are being asked to highlight a cell or range for use in a formula. |
| Ready | Excel is ready for a command or entry. |
| Recording | The macro recorder is recording what you are doing with Excel. |
| Size | A window or chart item is being sized. Use the direction keys to complete it. |
| Split | A window is being split. Use the direction keys to complete it. |

*Keyboard Indicators*  The keyboard indicators on the right of the Status bar tell you that a certain key has been pressed or that a certain condition exists. The status indicators and their meaning are as follows:

| Indicator | Meaning |
|---|---|
| ADD | The Add key, (SHIFT+F8), has been pressed to make multiple selections. |
| CAPS | (CAPS LOCK) has been pressed for uppercase letters. |

EXT        The Extend key, (F8), has been pressed to extend a selection.

FIX        The Fixed Decimal option has been chosen from Options Workspace. This adds a fixed number of decimal places on all numeric entries, similar to an adding machine.

NUM        The (NUM LOCK) key has been pressed, enabling the numeric keypad to type numbers.

OVR        The (INSERT) key has been pressed while a cell is being edited, turning on overtype mode instead of the normal insert mode.

SCRL       The (SCROLL LOCK) key has been pressed, causing the direction keys to move the entire worksheet instead of just the active cell.

# EXCEL'S USE OF THE KEYBOARD

You may find looking at the screen interesting, but to accomplish anything you must use the mouse and the keyboard. Excel's use of the mouse is fairly straightforward and is adequately covered in Chapter 2. This section covers how Excel uses the special-purpose keys surrounding the typewriter keyboard.

Most keyboards can be divided into three areas. On the left or along the top are a set of function keys, (F1) through (F10) or (F12). You use these keys to give Excel commands, such as to recalculate the worksheet or display a help screen. In the center of all keyboards are the normal typewriter keys, and on the far right of most keyboards is a set of direction keys, either superimposed on or separate from the numerical keypad. The direction keys can move the active cell around the worksheet and the highlight bar down a menu. These three regions of the keyboard are discussed in the following sections.

## Direction Keys

Eight keys comprise the direction keys: the four arrow keys (DOWN ARROW, LEFT ARROW, RIGHT ARROW, and UP ARROW) plus HOME, END, PGUP, and PGDN. These keys, either alone or in combination with CTRL and SHIFT on the typewriter keyboard, can move you quickly and easily anywhere on the worksheet. Also, the same keys can move you within the menus and dialog boxes and within the Formula bar for cell editing. With the mouse, the use of the direction keys is not as important as it might otherwise be. Nevertheless it is important to understand how the direction keys can be used.

The direction keys have a two-dimensional task in moving the active cell vertically (up or down a column) and horizontally (left or right along a row). Excel has ways to do this one cell at a time, one screen at a time, to the beginning or ending of contiguously occupied cells, or to the first or last cell in an active worksheet.

**USING DIRECTION KEYS ON A WORKSHEET**  The easiest way to learn about the direction keys is to use them. Try them now with the following instructions. Your computer should be turned on, Excel should be loaded (see Appendix A if not), and you should be looking at the blank worksheet screen shown in Figure 3-1, with cell A1 selected as the active cell. If your Scroll Lock light is on, press SCROLL LOCK to turn it off.

*Moving One Cell at a Time*

1. Press RIGHT ARROW. The active cell moves one cell to the right, to cell B1.

2. Press DOWN ARROW. The active cell moves down one cell, to cell B2.

3. Press (LEFT ARROW). The active cell moves one cell to the left, to cell A2.

4. Press (UP ARROW). The active cell moves up one cell, to cell A1—where you started from.

The four arrow keys are the most heavily used of the direction keys. Their function is to move you one cell in any direction, as you just saw in the one-cell square you just made.

***Moving One Screen at a Time***   Moving one cell at a time can be slow if you have very far to go. The next set of direction keys move you a screen at a time. Make a larger square now with these keys.

1. Press (PGDN). The active cell and the portion of the worksheet shown in the window moves down one window height to the first cell in column A beyond that originally shown—cell A21.

2. Press (CTRL+PGDN) (press and hold (CTRL) while pressing (PGDN)). The active cell and the portion of the worksheet shown in the window moves to the right one window width to the first cell in row 21 beyond that originally shown—cell J21.

3. Press (PGUP). The active cell and the portion of the worksheet shown in the window moves up one window height to cell I1.

4. Press (CTRL+PGUP) (press and hold (CTRL) while pressing (PGUP)). The active cell and the portion of the worksheet shown in the window moves to the left one window width to cell A1.

You have completed another square, one window on a side. (PGDN) and (PGUP) are used frequently, but (CTRL+PGDN) and (CTRL+PGUP) are forgotten by many people.

*Moving Around the Periphery of the Worksheet* The set of keystrokes used to move around the periphery of the worksheet require that you first enter some information on the worksheet. Simply type the information in one cell using the typewriter keyboard, and then press one of the arrow keys to go to the next cell. You can then use a set of direction keys to move around the periphery of the worksheet. Try that now.

1. Type **a** and press (RIGHT ARROW). The letter "a" is placed in cell A1, and the active cell moves to B1.

2. Do the combination of typing **a** and pressing (RIGHT ARROW) six more times. The final active cell is H1.

3. Type **a** and press (DOWN ARROW). The letter "a" is placed in cell H1, and the active cell moves to H2.

4. Do the combination of typing **a** and pressing (DOWN ARROW) nine more times. The final active cell is H11. Your screen should look like Figure 3-5. Now use the direction keys to jump around the information you just entered.

5. Press (HOME). The active cell jumps to cell A11.

6. Press (END). The active cell jumps back to cell H11.

7. Press (UP ARROW) and (CTRL+UP ARROW). The active cell jumps to cell H1.

8. Press (CTRL+LEFT ARROW). The active cell jumps to cell A1.

9. Press (CTRL+RIGHT ARROW). The active cell jumps to cell H1.

10. Press (CTRL+DOWN ARROW). The active cell jumps to cell H10.

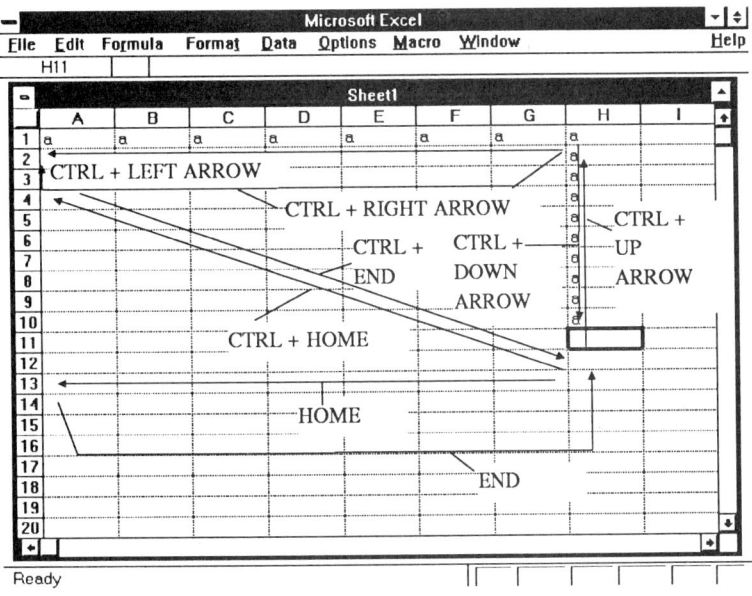

**FIGURE 3-5** Screen after entries

11. Press (CTRL+HOME). The active cell jumps to cell A1.

12. Press (CTRL+END). The active cell jumps to cell H10.

13. Press (CTRL+HOME). The active cell returns to cell A1.

The (CTRL) plus direction key combinations are not only very powerful but also extremely useful. You use them often if you do not have a mouse.

**DIRECTION KEY SUMMARY** The following table summarizes the direction keys:

| Key | Moves the Active Cell |
|---|---|
| [RIGHT ARROW] or [LEFT ARROW] | Right or left one column |
| [UP ARROW] or [DOWN ARROW] | Up or down one row |
| [PGUP] or [PGDN] | Up or down one window height |
| [CTRL+PGDN] or [CTRL+PGUP] | Right or left one window width |
| [CTRL+UP ARROW] or [CTRL+DOWN ARROW] | Up or down to the first intersection of blank and nonblank cells |
| [CTRL+RIGHT ARROW] or [CTRL+LEFT ARROW] | Right or left to the first intersection of blank and nonblank cells |
| [HOME] | Left to column A in the row with the active cell |
| [END] | Right to the last occupied column in the row with the active cell |
| [CTRL+HOME] | Up and/or to the left to cell A1 |
| [CTRL+END] | Down and/or to the right to the lowest and rightmost occupied cell |

## Function Keys

The function keys [F1] through [F10] or [F12] are located on the top or left of most keyboards. With function keys you can give Excel special commands using one or several keystrokes (when you press the key itself, or press and hold [SHIFT], [CTRL], or [ALT] while pressing a function key). Many of the commands performed by the function keys are used only in certain circumstances and are not easy to demonstrate here. Try several that can be easily demonstrated now with the instructions that follow. You will use the others later in the book. Following the instructions is a table that summarizes each function key.

**USING FUNCTION KEYS** The following instructions assume that you are picking up where you left off in the previous section. The active cell is A1, and the worksheet is the one in which you entered the "a"s. Excel is in ready mode. Also, from your previous work, cell A1 should contain the letter "a." If you do not have an "a" in A1, type it now and press (ENTER).

1. Press (F1) (Help). If you have not used Help since you most recently started Excel, the Index of Help Topics screen shown in Figure 3-6 appears. From this window you can select subjects on which to get help. If you have used Help during this Excel session, the most recent help screen you looked at is displayed.

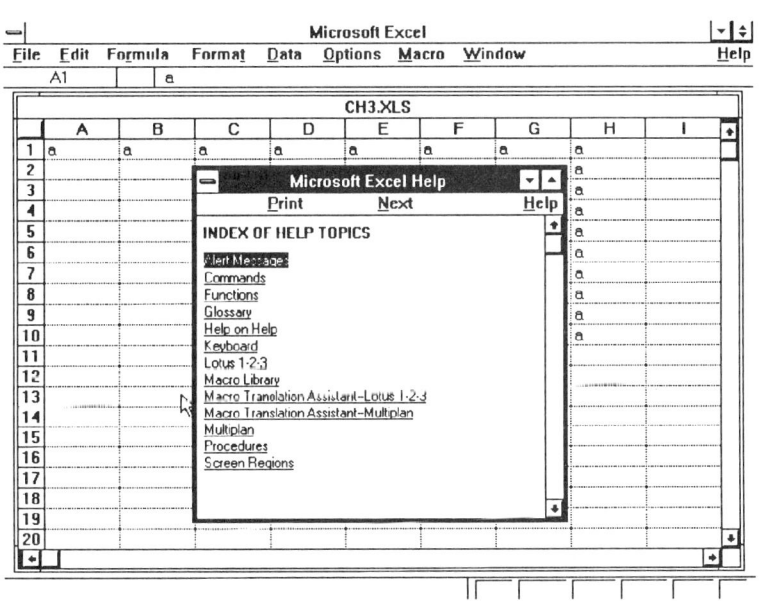

**FIGURE 3-6** Index of help topics

2. Press (ESC). Excel returns to ready mode, and A1 is still the active cell.

3. Press (F2) (Edit). The letter "a" appears in the edit area of the Formula bar, with the insertion point just to the right of the letter.

4. Press (BACKSPACE). The "a" is removed.

5. Type **b** and press (ENTER). Excel is returned to ready mode, and "b" replaces "a" in cell A1.

6. Press (ALT+BACKSPACE) (Undo). The contents of cell A1 are again "a."

7. Press (F5) (Goto). A dialog box appears, asking for the address to jump to.

8. Type **e14** and press (ENTER). The active cell jumps to cell E14.

9. Press (CTRL+HOME). The active cell returns to cell A1.

10. Press (F12) (Save As) or (ALT+F2) if you have only 10 function keys. The Save Worksheet as dialog box opens.

11. Type **ch3** (for Chapter 3) and press (ENTER) to save the active worksheet with the filename CH3.XLS (the XLS extension is automatically added by Excel).

12. Press (SHIFT+F11) (New Worksheet) or (ALT+SHFT+F1) if you have only 10 function keys. A new worksheet opens, probably entitled Sheet2.

Both (F2) (Edit) and (F5) (Goto) will get increasingly heavy use as you learn Excel. Also useful, although not a function key, is (ALT+BACKSPACE) (Undo). The Undo command reverses many commands if they were the last thing you did. You can even undo an undo. It does *not* undo File commands, especially File Deletes, Data Deletes, or Data Extracts.

Several function keys are shortcut keys for menu options. For example, F3 is the Formula menu Paste Name option, F4 is the Formula menu Reference option, and F12 is the File menu Save As option.

**FUNCTION-KEY SUMMARY** The following table provides a summary of the function performed by each function key. The keys are discussed in depth with the particular subject to which they apply. For example, F11 (New Chart) is discussed in Chapter 7 with charting.

| Key | Name | Function Performed |
| --- | --- | --- |
| F1 | Help | Opens a help window |
| SHIFT+F1 | | Displays context-sensitive help |
| ALT+F1 | New | Creates a new chart window |
| ALT+SHIFT+F1 | | Creates a new worksheet window |
| ALT+CTRL+F1 | | Creates a new macro sheet window |
| F2 | Edit | Activates the Formula bar for editing |
| SHIFT+F2 | Note | Allows entering, editing, or deleting a note that is to be attached to the active cell |
| CTRL+F2 | Info | Displays a window containing information about the active cell |
| ALT+F2 | Save | Opens the File Save As dialog box |
| ALT+SHIFT+F2 | | Saves the active document |
| ALT+CTRL+F2 | | Opens the File Open dialog box |
| ALT+CTRL+SHIFT+F2 | | Opens the File Print dialog box |

| Key | Name | Description |
|---|---|---|
| F3 | Name | Opens the Formula Paste Name dialog box |
| SHIFT+F3 | | Opens the Formula Paste Function dialog box |
| CTRL+F3 | | Opens the Formula Define Name dialog box |
| CTRL+SHIFT+F3 | | Opens the Formula Create Name dialog box |
| F4 | Absolute | Makes a cell address or range name absolute, mixed, or relative |
| CTRL+F4 | Close | Closes the active document window |
| ALT+F4 | | Closes the application window |
| F5 | Goto | Moves the active cell to the cell address, range name, or file entered |
| SHIFT+F5 | Find | Opens the Formula Find dialog box |
| CTRL+F5 | Restore | Restores the size of the active document window |
| ALT+F5 | | Restores the size of the application window |
| F6 | Pane | Moves the active cell clockwise to the next pane |
| SHIFT+F6 | | Moves the active cell counterclockwise to the previous pane |
| CTRL+F6 | Window | Moves the active cell to the next document window |
| CTRL+SHIFT+F6 | | Moves the active cell to the previous document window |
| F7 | Next | Finds the next cell matching the specified contents |
| SHIFT+F7 | Previous | Finds the previous cell matching the specified contents |

| | | |
|---|---|---|
| `CTRL+F7` | Move | Sets up the active document window to be moved with the direction keys |
| `ALT+F7` | | Sets up the active application window to be moved with the direction keys |
| `F8` | Extend | Toggles the extension of the current selection |
| `SHIFT+F8` | Add | Allows adding to the current selection |
| `CTRL+F8` | Size | Sets up the active document window to be sized with the direction keys |
| `ALT+F8` | | Sets up the active application window to be sized with the direction keys |
| `F9` | Calculate | Recalculates all open documents |
| `SHIFT+F9` | | Recalculates the active document |
| `ALT+F9` | Minimize | Minimizes the application window |
| `F10` | Menu | Activates the menu bar |
| `CTRL+F10` | Maximize | Maximizes the active document window |
| `ALT+F10` | | Maximizes the active application window |
| `F11` | New | Creates a new chart window |
| `SHIFT+F11` | | Creates a new worksheet window |
| `CTRL+F11` | | Creates a new macro sheet window |
| `F12` | Save | Opens the File Save As dialog box |
| `SHIFT+F12` | | Saves the active document |

| CTRL+F12 | Open | Opens the File Open dialog box |
| CTRL+SHIFT+F12 | Print | Opens the File Print dialog box |

## QUITTING EXCEL

You are done with Excel for this chapter. Use the following instructions to leave it:

1. Double-click (click twice in rapid succession) on the Excel Control-menu box in the upper-left corner of the Excel application window. (From the keyboard, press ALT+SPACEBAR+C.)

2. Click on No (or type **N**) to not save the worksheet again. You return to the Windows Program Manager window.

3. Double-click on the Program Manager's Control-menu box, and click OK to end the Windows session. You return to DOS.

4. If you desire, you can now shut off your computer following your normal shutdown procedure.

# 4

# ENTERING AND EDITING INFORMATION

Typing on the Worksheet
Making Changes
Using Menus
Using Files
Quitting Excel

In several examples in Chapter 3, you practiced entering and editing information. Entering text and numbers is a simple matter of typing what you want in each cell. You can edit as you type or, after you have completed the entry, you can come back and edit it. These operations are more subtle than they first appear, however, and their considerable power demands further study.

## TYPING ON THE WORKSHEET

All information that you type on a worksheet is stored in cells. While there are a lot of cells, each cell can hold only 255 characters. The normal practice is to place only a single number or a short text string (usually much smaller than 255 characters) in a cell and spread most of the information over many cells, using the row and column structure to organize it.

A cell on a worksheet can hold either a number or text, but not both. You therefore must decide what a cell will contain before you make an entry. If you decide an entry is text, you must then decide if it will be left, right, or center aligned in the cell. If an entry is a number, you must decide on alignment as well as formatting, such as dollars, percents, and dates. Finally, when you complete an entry, you must determine what you want to do next so you can move the active cell to support that.

### Entering Text Versus Numbers

Entering numbers (including formulas) or text (letters as well as numbers) depends on what you type. If your entry contains only numbers or these numeric symbols.

+ - = . , ( ) % $

then the entry is a number. If the entry contains anything other than a number or numeric symbol, the entry is text.

**GENERAL ALIGNMENT** When Excel recognizes that text is being typed, it automatically left aligns the text in the cell (meaning that it pushes text up against the left side of the cell). When you enter a number, Excel automatically right aligns it in the cell (pushes it up against the right side). This default alignment—left-aligned text and right-aligned numbers—is called *General Align-*

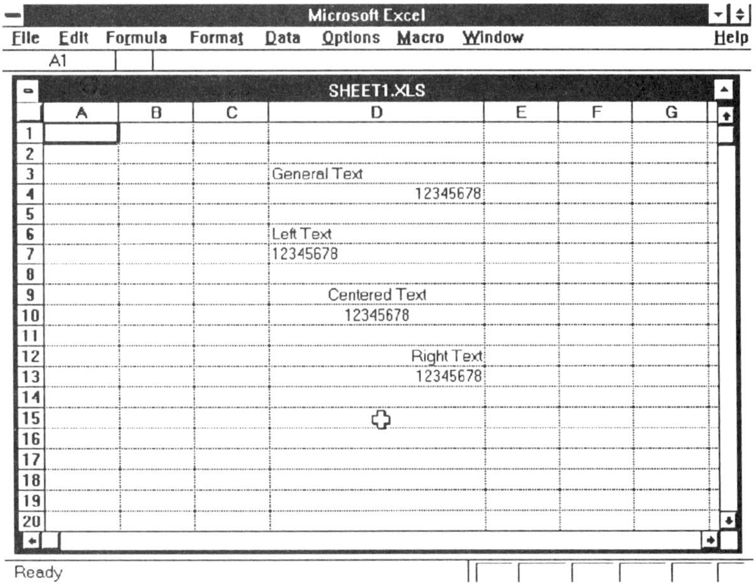

**FIGURE 4-1** Types of alignment

*ment*. General alignment also aligns logical values (TRUE or FALSE) and error values (#NUM!, for example) in the center of a cell. With the Format menu Alignment option you can align text, numbers, and logical or error values on the left, in the center, or on the right as you choose.

Figure 4 1 shows the various types of alignment.

**TYPING TEXT** Try entering some text now, following these instructions:

1. Load Windows and Excel as discussed in Appendix A. A blank worksheet should appear on the screen. (If you still have the work you did in Chapter 3 on your screen, double-click on the worksheet's (not Excel's) Control-menu box to close the work-

sheet. Then from the File menu choose New and click on OK to create a new worksheet.)

2. Type **This is some text**. As you type you will see the letters go into the edit area of the Formula bar as well as into cell A1. If you make a mistake, press (BACKSPACE) to correct it. The top of your screen should look like this:

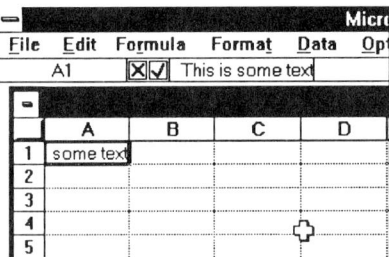

Notice that the text is in both the edit area and cell A1. You can see only the last two words in the cell. Also notice the blinking line in the edit area. This is the insertion point.

3. Press (ENTER). The edit area is deactivated (the insertion point, Cancel box, and Enter box disappear). Also, the text in A1 adjusts itself so you can see it all, although it does not fit completely in a single cell. The active cell remains in A1.

4. Press (DOWN ARROW) on the right side of your keyboard. The active cell moves to A2.

5. Type **left** and press (RIGHT ARROW). The word "left" is left aligned in cell A2, and the active cell moves to B2.

6. Type **right** and press (ENTER). The word "right" also is left aligned in B2.

7. Click on Format in the Menu bar to open the Format menu.

8. Click on the Alignment option and the Alignment dialog box opens, as shown here:

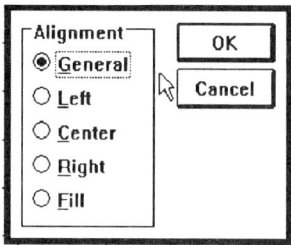

9. Click on Right in the dialog box and then click on OK to close the dialog box. The word "right" in cell B2 is right aligned. Press (RIGHT ARROW) to move to C2.

10. Type **center** and press (ENTER). Again click on Format, Alignment, Center, and then OK. The word "center" is centered in C2. Press (RIGHT ARROW) to move the active cell to D2.

11. Type = and press (ENTER). Click Format, Alignment, Fill, and OK. The = is repeated to fill D2, less one space. Press (RIGHT ARROW).

12. Type **555-1234** and press (RIGHT ARROW). Cell E2 contains a left-aligned text string in the format of a phone number.

13. Type **=555-1234** and press (ENTER). The equal sign turns this into a formula, and the cell contains the number -679 (the results of 555 minus 1234). In other words, to make this a number you must tell Excel it is a formula.

Your screen should now look like Figure 4-2. The contents of F2 looks different in the edit area and in the cell. Unless you or someone else changed the default, the text in A1 is left aligned, as shown in the figure. You did not align it; it is left aligned because of Excel's General Alignment default.

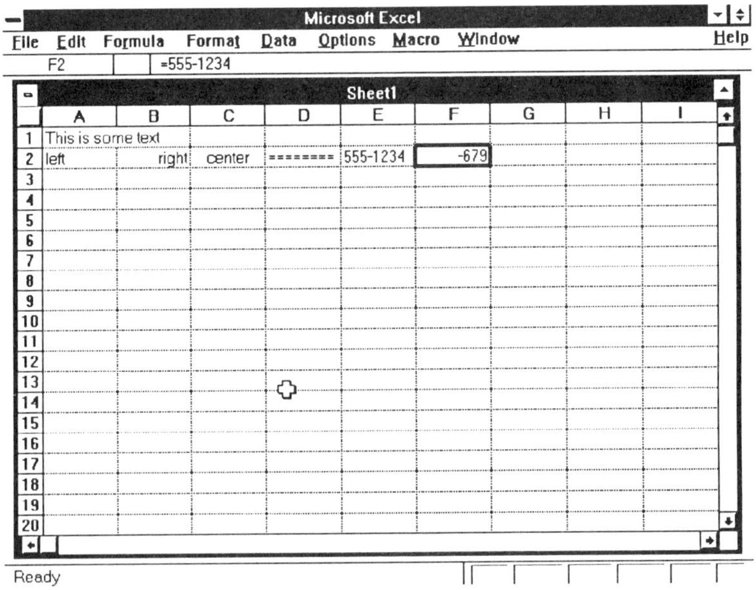

**FIGURE 4-2** Text entries

You may have noticed that the Format Alignment option is cumbersome. It is often found that way. To get around this you can align a larger range of text by highlighting the range before selecting Format Alignment.

**COLUMN WIDTH VERSUS CONTENTS WIDTH** The first entry you typed in the previous exercise, shown in cell A1 in Figure 4-2, is wider than the cell—it hangs over into cell B1. Because there is nothing in B1, the full text from A1 is displayed. If you enter something in B1, the text in A1 would appear truncated, based on the width of column A. Try that now:

1. Press (CTRL+HOME), (RIGHT ARROW). The active cell moves to B1.

2. Type **new text** and press (**ENTER**). The words "new text" fill B1 and, on the screen, truncate the text from A1. The full original entry is still in A1; you just can't see it all.

The top portion of your screen should look like this:

|   | A | B | C | D | E | F | G |
|---|---|---|---|---|---|---|---|
| 1 | This is so | new text |  |  |  |  |  |
| 2 | left |  | right | center | ======== | 555-1234 | -679 |
| 3 |  |  |  |  |  |  |  |

The width of a worksheet area is considered in terms of column width, not cell width. You cannot adjust the width of an individual cell, only the width of the column that contains the cell. In Chapter 5 you will see how to change the width of both individual columns and a range of columns.

**ENTERING NUMBERS** Excel gives you a lot of flexibility in entering numbers. You can enter numbers with commas, dollar signs, percents, and scientific notation. Excel converts your entry into a number between $2.225E^{-307}$ and $1.789E^{305}$ with up to 15 significant places. You can then format the cell to display the number in any way you choose, no matter how you entered it.

Try entering several numbers now:

1. Press (**HOME**) and then press (**DOWN ARROW**) four times. The active cell moves to A5.

2. Type **1,234,567.89**. The number appears as typed in the edit area, but only part of the number shows in the cell.

3. Press (**DOWN ARROW**). The number disappears from the edit area, and 1234568 appears in A5. The full number is too wide to fit

in the standard column width, so it is rounded to fit within the column.

4. Type **3.25** and press (RIGHT ARROW). The number 3.25 appears in A6 as entered.

5. Type **$3.25** and press (RIGHT ARROW). The number $3.25 appears in B6.

6. Type **3.25%** and press (RIGHT ARROW). The number 3.25% appears in C6.

7. Type **3 1/4** and press (RIGHT ARROW). The text string 3 1/4 appears in D6. You know it is a text string because it is left aligned in the cell. Excel knew it was a text string because you entered a space after the 3.

8. Type **32.5E-1** and press (RIGHT ARROW). The number 3.25 appears in E6.

9. Type **=e6** and press (ENTER). The number 3.25 appears in F6. You entered a formula by placing = in front of a cell reference, and you used it to pick up the contents of cell E6 in cell F6.

Figure 4-3 shows how your screen should look when you have completed these entries.

Even though there is nothing in B5, the number in A5 was rounded to fit the column width. Unlike text, numbers do not hang over the adjacent cell when they are too big for the column they are in. The column must be widened for the number to show without being rounded.

Being able to enter commas, dollar signs, and percents is an important capability, even if you must change them later. When you enter numbers that you are copying from a source that has dollar signs, commas, and so on, without thinking you may type the symbols as well as the numbers. In some worksheet packages

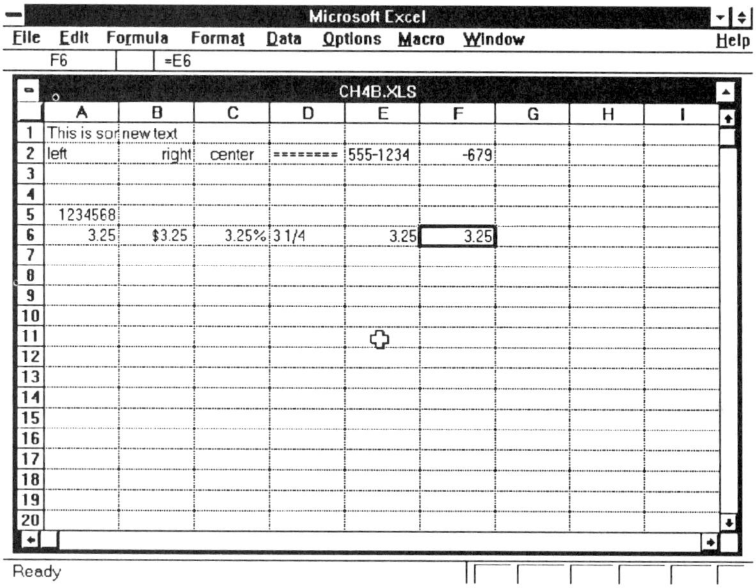

**FIGURE 4-3** Text and numbers on the worksheet

you would get an error with such entry. Excel gives you the flexibility to enter numbers with or without symbols.

**USING THE NUMERIC KEYPAD** While you were not given directions to that effect, it is likely that you entered the above numbers in the previous exercise using the numeric keys at the top of the typewriter keyboard. Unless you are using a laptop computer, you also have a numeric keypad on the right of your keyboard. The numeric keypad performs two functions: movement of the active cell when (NUM LOCK) is off and numeric entry when (NUM LOCK) is on. The (NUM LOCK) key is at the top of the numeric keypad. Most keyboards have a light to tell you if it is on or off, and Excel has a status indicator, NUM, that appears at the bottom of the window to tell you when (NUM LOCK) is on.

When (NUM LOCK) is on, the numeric keypad can be used for numeric entry like a 10-key adding machine. The direction keys on the numeric keypad are no longer available when (NUM LOCK) is on, unless you press and hold down (SHIFT) while pressing a direction key. Enhanced keyboards have a set of direction keys, separate from the numeric keypad, that can be used at any time. Throughout your work with Excel, you may use either set of keys for numeric entry without affecting the results.

**FIXING THE NUMBER OF DECIMAL DIGITS** If you are experienced using a 10-key adding machine or calculator and like the ability to enter numbers with a fixed number of decimal digits without typing the decimal point, you can do that with Excel. To set up a fixed number of decimal digits, follow these steps:

1. Select the Options menu and choose Workspace.

2. Click on the Fixed Decimal check box. An "X" appears in the box.

3. If you want to change the number of decimal digits, press (TAB) to move the highlight to the Places text box and type the number you want to use. Your Workspace dialog box should look like that shown here:

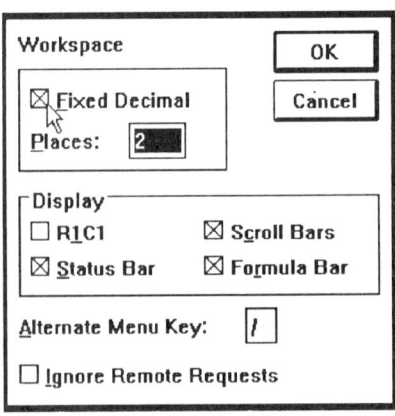

4. Click on OK to close the dialog box and return to the worksheet.

Remember that when you change this setting you have a fixed number of decimal digits in every number you type. Typing **6** gives you .06, and typing **3500** gives you 35 with two decimal places. Excel remembers this the next time you start it up—it is a permanent setting until you turn it off.

## Completing an Entry And Moving to the Next Cell

As you saw in the previous examples, you can complete an entry either by pressing (ENTER) or by pressing one of the direction keys, depending on where you want to go next. If you use (ENTER), the active cell remains the cell in which you made the entry. After using (ENTER) you can then use one of the direction keys to move where you wish. If you want to go directly to another cell, you can save one keystroke by pressing a direction key to complete the entry.

You are not limited to the arrow keys. You can complete an entry using (HOME), (END), or even (PGUP), (PGDN), (CTRL+PGUP), or (CTRL+PGDN)—it just depends on where you want to go next.

# MAKING CHANGES

Making changes to the information you are entering or have entered into Excel is a task at least equal to making the initial entry. One of the beauties of an electronic worksheet is that changes can be made easily and often. You can make changes in four ways. First, you can replace a completed entry in a cell by typing over the original entry. The original entry disappears and the new entry takes it place. Second, you can edit an entry as you are entering it. Third, immediately after completing an entry you can remove it and restore the previous contents of the cell by pressing the Undo key, (ALT+BACKSPACE), or by choosing Undo from the Edit menu. Fourth, you can edit a completed entry. The next several sections explore the last three of these methods.

## Editing During Entry

Editing during entry has a simple mode that uses the (BACKSPACE) or (ESC) key and an edit mode using the (F2) (Edit) key. In the simple mode you press (BACKSPACE) to erase one or more characters to the left of the insertion point, or you press (ESC) to erase the entire entry. After pressing one of these keys, you can continue to type the corrected or new entry. When you press (F2) (Edit) the mode indicator in the Status bar becomes EDIT, and you have full use of the edit keys. The edit mode of editing is the same during and after entry, so it is explained in the "Editing After Entry" section. Now try simple mode editing:

1. Select the File menu, choose New, and click on OK to create a new worksheet.

2. Type **Spring 91**. Spring 91 appears in the edit area.

3. Press (BACKSPACE) and type **2**. Spring 91 changes to Spring 92 in the edit area.

4. Press (ESC) and type **Fall 91**. Spring 92 changes to Fall 91 in the edit area.

5. Press (ENTER). The edit area closes and Fall 91 is the final contents of cell A1.

Simple mode editing is just that, simple. It is used constantly by all mortals to correct the many small errors constantly made during data entry.

## Using Undo

The Undo option from either the Edit menu or its shortcut keys (`ALT+BACKSPACE`) is a great life saver. It lets you remove the last thing you did and restore the worksheet to the way it was before you did it. The definition of "the last thing you did" is usually whatever happened between two ready modes, but there are exceptions. Two important things you cannot undo are File Delete and Data Delete. Also, you cannot undo a file operation, and you cannot undo the effect of recalculating the worksheet. You can undo an Undo. When you are editing, you can use Undo to reverse the last change you made to a cell. Try that now:

1. Make sure the active cell is still the cell in which you last entered Fall 91.

2. Type **Spring 92** and press `ENTER`. Spring 92 replaces Fall 91 in A1.

3. Press `ALT+BACKSPACE` (Undo). Fall 91 is restored in A1.

When you make a mistake that requires retyping, immediately choose Undo from the Edit menu, or press `ALT+BACKSPACE` (Undo) and see if it restores the worksheet to its condition before the mistake. It cannot make the situation worse.

## Editing After Entry

To edit a cell entry after it is completed, highlight the cell and press `F2` (Edit). The Edit mode indicator is displayed, and the cell entry is moved to the edit area with the insertion point blinking on the right of the entry. The `LEFT ARROW`, `RIGHT ARROW`, `HOME`, and `END` keys all move the pointer within the entry so that individual characters can be changed. `BACKSPACE` removes the character to the left of the insertion point, and `DEL` removes the character to the right of the insertion point. Also, you can press (INS) to switch from *insert mode,* which pushes existing characters to the right of new characters, to *overtype mode,* which replaces existing characters with new ones at the insertion point. Try editing now:

1. Make sure the active cell still contains Fall 91.

2. Press (F2) (Edit). The edit area is activated (the Cancel box, Enter box, and insertion point appear) with the insertion point to the right of 91.

3. Press (HOME). The insertion point moves to the left of Fall.

4. Type **Summer/**. The entry becomes Summer/Fall 91.

5. Press (LEFT ARROW) four times. The insertion point is between the two "m"s in Summer.

6. Press (INS). The OVR mode indicator is displayed in the Status bar.

7. Type . (period). The . replaces the second "m" in Summer.

8. Press (DEL) twice. The "e" and "r" are removed from Summer.

9. Press (END) and then (LEFT ARROW) three times. The insertion point moves to the right of the second "l" in Fall.

10. Press (INS). The OVR mode indicator is removed, and Excel returns to insert mode.

11. Type **/Win..** The entry now reads Sum./Fall/Win. 91.

12. Press (END). The insertion point moves to the right end of the entry.

13. Type **/92**. /92 is added to the right end of the entry. The top part of your screen should look like this:

14. Press (ENTER). The edit area closes and A1 reflects the final entry.

**EDIT KEYS** The functions of the keys you can use while editing are summarized here:

| Key | Function |
| --- | --- |
| (BACKSPACE) | Deletes the character to the left of the insertion point |
| (CTRL+DEL) | Deletes text from the insertion point to the end of the current line |
| (CTRL+END) | Moves the insertion point to the right of the last character in the edit area |
| (CTRL+HOME) | Moves the insertion point to the left of the first character in the edit area |
| (CTRL+') | Inserts the formula in the cell above the active cell at the insertion point |
| (CTRL+") | Inserts the value in the cell above the active cell at the insertion point |
| (CTRL+;) | Inserts the current date in your computer at the insertion point |
| (CTRL+:) | Inserts the current time in your computer at the insertion point |
| (DEL) | Deletes the character to the right of the insertion point |

| | |
|---|---|
| (END) | Moves the insertion point to the right end of the current line of the entry |
| (ENTER) | Completes editing, closing the edit area and leaving the active cell where it was originally |
| (F2) | Activates the edit area so you can do a character-by-character edit on the active cell |
| (ESC) | Cancels any changes made during editing, closes the edit area, and returns the original contents to the active cell |
| (HOME) | Moves the insertion point to the left end of the current line of the entry |
| (INS) | Switches between insert mode, in which newly typed characters push existing characters to the right, and overtype mode, in which newly typed characters replace existing characters |
| (LEFT ARROW) or (RIGHT ARROW) | Moves the insertion point one character to the left or right in the entry |
| (UP ARROW) or (DOWN ARROW) | Moves the insertion point between lines in the edit area if the entry occupies more than one line; otherwise does nothing |

## Editing with the Mouse

Editing with the keyboard is effective and often preferred if you are doing a lot of typing. However, the mouse has two benefits: you can jump immediately to the characters you want to change by clicking on the spot, and you can easily highlight characters to be deleted or otherwise changed by dragging across them. These benefits often make it worthwhile taking your hands off the keyboard to use the mouse. Try it now:

1. The worksheet you have on your screen should have Sum./Fall/Win. 91/92 in cell A1.

2. Click on E12. The active cell moves to E12.

   Assume that you want to edit cell A1. If it were not in the home position, it would take at least two keystrokes to get there. With the mouse all you must do is

3. Click on A1. The active cell moves to A1.

4. Drag across Sum./ in the edit area. (Place the mouse pointer on the "S" in Sum in the edit area, not cell A1. Press and hold the mouse button while dragging the mouse pointer across um./, then release the mouse button.) Sum./ in the edit area is highlighted.

   Notice that the mouse pointer becomes an I-beam when you move it into the edit area. This allows you to click between characters to place the insertion point. Notice, also, that you activated the edit area as soon as you pressed the mouse button while pointing anywhere in the edit area.

5. Press (DEL). The edit area contains Fall/Win. 91/92.

6. Drag across the period following Win. Press (DEL) and type **ter**. The edit area now reads Fall/Winter 91/92, as shown here:

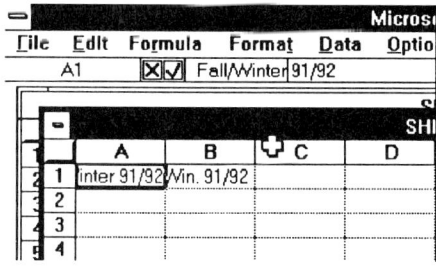

7. Click on E12 to carry on where you started.

The ability to jump quickly to a cell, make a change by clicking and dragging in the edit area, and then jump back to where you started is powerful. Use it for a while and you will agree.

## USING MENUS

Menus are the primary means of having Excel perform tasks such as opening a file, copying a range, printing a worksheet, or creating a chart. All menu operations begin in one of two ways:

- Clicking on a menu name

- Pressing **ALT** or **F10** or typing / (slash) and then either highlighting the menu name with the direction keys and pressing **ENTER** or typing the underlined letter in the menu name.

Either of these methods cause the selected menu to be displayed. Once a menu is displayed, you again have two ways to choose an option:

- Clicking on an option name

- Using the direction keys to highlight an option and pressing **ENTER**, or typing the underlined letter in the option name.

Once you have selected a menu and chosen an option, either the command immediately executes (as does Save in the File menu or Copy in the Edit menu, for example) or a dialog box opens. When you choose a menu option with an ellipsis (...) after it, a dialog box opens. Excel (and all Windows applications) uses a dialog box to get further information. Dialog boxes give you additional choices and provide the means for you to type in a name or some other information.

Take a look now at how the menu system works. In the following instructions the keyboard and mouse methods are intermixed to give you experience with both.

1. Press **ALT**. The File menu name in the Menu bar is highlighted. Notice that the Status bar at the bottom of the window gives you a brief description of the File menu.

2. Press **ENTER**. The File menu opens.

3. Press **DOWN ARROW**, and then press it several more times. Notice that the Status bar provides a description of each option as you highlight it.

4. Press **RIGHT ARROW**. The File menu closes and the Edit menu opens.

Some of the options in the Edit menu are light gray or dimmer than the other options. These options are not available because they are not applicable to the current situation. The gray options in the current Edit menu all deal with pasting (copying something from the Clipboard to the worksheet). To paste you must first cut or copy, both of which place something from the worksheet onto the Clipboard.

5. Press **RIGHT ARROW** slowly seven more times. Look at each of the menus in succession. Use **DOWN ARROW** to explore some of the options that interest you. Look at the Status bar to see the description of the option.

6. Press **RIGHT ARROW** three more times. The highlight wraps around and opens first the Excel Control menu and then the worksheet Control menu and finally returns to the File menu where you started.

If you continue to press (RIGHT ARROW), you continue to move around the set of menus. If you press (LEFT ARROW) you move the other way. If you press (UP ARROW) or (DOWN ARROW), you move up or down through the options in the menu that is currently open. The direction keys provide a sure way to move through the menu system.

7. Press (ESC). The Menu bar is deactivated and you return to the worksheet.

8. Click on A1, and it becomes the active cell. A1 should still contain Fall/Winter 91/92. If it doesn't, type anything in it (your first name, for example) so you have something to work with in the next set of instructions.

9. Click on Edit in the Menu bar. The Edit menu opens.

10. Click on Copy in the Edit menu. The Edit menu closes, and a blinking marquee appears around the active cell, A1, telling you that a copy of the contents of A1 has been placed on the Clipboard and is ready to be copied to some other cell on the worksheet.

11. Click on C5 to select it as the destination of the copy. Press (ENTER) to complete the copy. C5 now contains a copy of A1's contents.

12. Press (F10) to activate the Menu bar.

13. Type **e** to open the Edit menu.

14. Type **t** to choose the Cut option. The Edit menu closes and again a blinking marquee forms around the active cell, in this case C5. The contents of C5 is placed on the Clipboard.

15. Click on E9 and press (**ENTER**). The contents of C5 is moved to E9. In other words, the contents of C5 is removed (cut) and placed (pasted) in E9.

16. Drag on the Edit menu until Undo is highlighted (point on the Edit menu name in the Menu bar, press and hold the mouse button while dragging the highlight bar down to the Undo option, and then release the mouse button). The contents of E9 is restored to C5 and a blinking marquee reappears. With Edit Undo you have completely undone step 15 and you are back where you were when you completed step 14, except that E9 is the active cell.

17. Drag to highlight cells C5, C6, C7, and C8 (place the mouse pointer on C5, press and hold the mouse button while dragging the mouse pointer over C6, C7, and C8, and then release the mouse button). Cells C5 through C8 are highlighted.

18. Click on the Edit menu to select it, and then click on Fill Down to choose it. The contents of C5 are replicated in cells C6 through C8, as shown in Figure 4-4.

The majority of menu options are discussed in later chapters of this book. The same procedures are used throughout the book to open a menu and choose an option. The ease and flexibility with

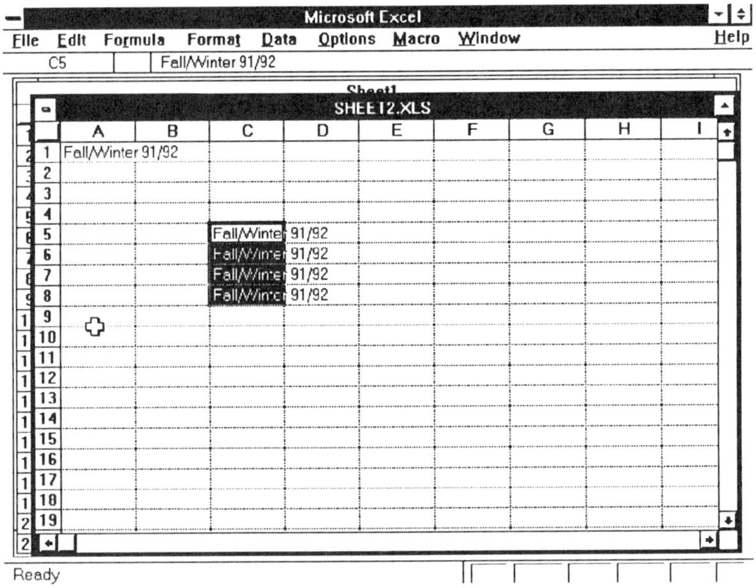

**FIGURE 4-4** Results of choosing Fill Down from the Edit menu

which you can make a menu selection and choose an option is one of Excel's and Windows' greatest strengths. Most instructions in this book do not tell you to use one method or the other when using the menus; you can choose the method you prefer.

## USING FILES

Files provide a permanent record of the worksheets you build. To create a file you must save the worksheet on a disk. If a worksheet is not saved, it is lost when you leave Excel or turn off the computer (although you receive a warning if you try to leave Excel without saving an open worksheet).

## Naming Files

When you save a file you must give it a name. The full name of a file has three components: a path, a filename, and an extension. The path is made up of the drive letter—for example, C: or A:—and one or more directory names—for example, \WI\ or \EXCEL\PLAN\. The drive letter is a single letter followed by a colon and a directory name is one to eight characters enclosed in backslashes. In a tree structure set of directories several directory (or subdirectory) names make up the path, as in \PLAN\SALES\1991\.

A filename is one to eight characters long. A filename can consist of any combination of letters, numbers, and the following special characters:

~ ' ! @ # $ % ^ & ( ) - _ { } '

but may not include blanks. Also the two *wildcard characters*, ? and *, can be used to replace a single character in the case of ? or any number of consecutive characters for *. For example, ?QTRPLAN.XLS refers to 1QTRPLAN.XLS, 2QTRPLAN.XLS, 3QTRPLAN.XLS, and so on, while *.XLS refers to all files with an .XLS extension.

The filename extension is optional but highly recommended. It begins with a period and can be up to three characters long. Unless you override it, Excel automatically adds an extension to all files. The extensions and the types of files they are applied to are as follows:

| Extension | File Types |
|---|---|
| .BAK | Backup |
| .CSV | Comma-separated values |
| .DBF | dBASE II/III |
| .TMP | Temporary |
| .WKS or .WK1 | Lotus 1-2-3 |
| .XLC | Chart |
| .XLM | Macro sheet |
| .XLS | Worksheet |
| .XLW | Workspace |

## Saving Files

You have already saved a file when you worked through some steps in Chapter 3. That example included minimal explanation, so use the following instructions to save another file now (even though there is not much on the worksheet to save):

1. Click on File. The File menu opens, as shown here:

2. Click on Save As. The Save Worksheet as dialog box opens, asking for the name of the file you want to save, as seen here:

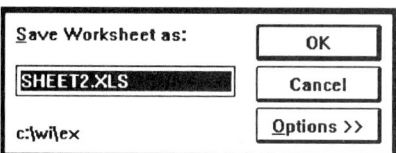

3. Type **ch4**. The name CH4 goes into the filename text box of the Save Worksheet as dialog box. Excel automatically adds the extension .XLS, and for now you are using the current drive and directory (see the next section, "Using Directories").

4. Click on OK. The worksheet is saved in a file named CH4.XLS, and Excel returns to ready mode.

## Using Directories

In the previous example, as well as the one in Chapter 2, you saved a file without specifying a drive or directory. When you do that, Excel uses the current drive and directory. Unless you or someone else changes your default drive and directory, the current drive and directory on your computer is the one in which you installed Excel. In other words, you store your worksheet files in the same directory as your programs are stored.

While there is nothing inherently wrong with using the program directory to store data files, it is not a good idea for files that are important. You should not keep data and program files together because you can end up erasing the data files along with all the program files you want to erase when you get a new release of the program. Also, the number of Excel program files in the directory make it hard to find your data files.

It is recommended that you create one or more separate directories to hold your data files. You can then specify one of these directories when saving files. Appendix A describes creating a subdirectory named \SHEET\ under your Windows directory in which you can store the sample files created in this book. If you have not done that, it is recommended that you turn to Appendix A now and do it. For the rest of this book, it is assumed that you are using a path of \WI\SHEET\ for your files.

## Retrieving Files

Retrieving files is similar to saving files. You select the File menu and then choose Open. A dialog box opens that asks you for the filename, and a list of files in the current directory is displayed. You can use the direction keys to highlight the file you want in the list, and press (ENTER) to have Excel retrieve that file from disk. Try that now with the following instructions:

1. Click on the File menu. The File menu opens.

2. Click on Open. The Open dialog box opens, as shown here:

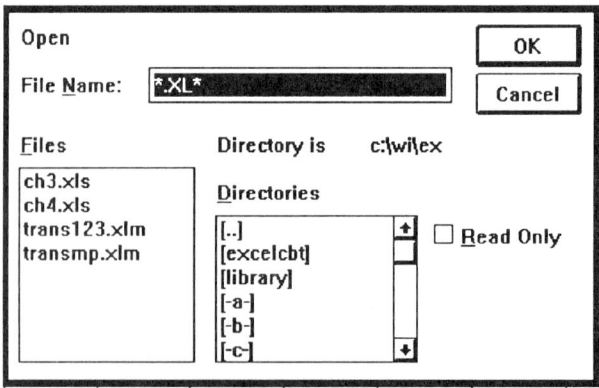

3. Double-click on ch3.xls in the Files list box. The file CH3.XLS opens.

It is important to note that when Excel opens a file, it creates a new worksheet window that is added to the other worksheet or document windows you have open. You can find out what document windows are open by opening the Window menu, as shown here:

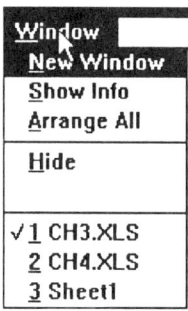

You can see that you currently have three windows open. If you want to go to another window, choose that window from the Window menu or click on the window if you can see it on the screen. To display all windows currently open, choose Arrange All from the Window menu. With the current windows available, this will produce a screen that looks like Figure 4-5.

## QUITTING EXCEL

When you are done using Excel you should formally leave it with the Close option from Excel's Control menu, rather than just turning off your computer. The main reason is that if you have forgotten to save a file, Excel's Close option reminds you as part

**FIGURE 4-5**  Effect of choosing Arrange All from the Window menu

of the quitting process. Also, with the Close option, Excel erases any temporary files it has written, thus keeping your hard disk from getting filled with them. Use the following steps to leave Excel:

1. Double-click on Excel's Control-menu box. A Save changes dialog box opens, as shown here:

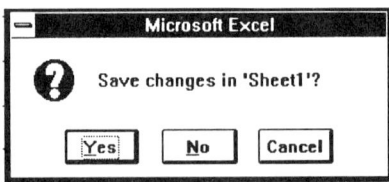

The dialog box asks if you want to save changes in Sheet1 and gives you three command buttons to choose from: Yes, No, and Cancel. Choosing Yes saves Sheet1 in a file named Sheet1.XLS in the current directory. Choosing No exits Excel without saving Sheet1—in essence throwing away Sheet1. Choosing Cancel interrupts the quitting process and puts you back in ready mode. You can then look at Sheet1 and determine if you want to save it. In this case you want to throw away Sheet1, so choose No.

2. Click on No to leave Excel without saving Sheet1.

3. Double-click on the Program Manager's Control-menu box to leave Windows and return to DOS.

4. Click on OK to end your Windows session.

Excel and Windows shut themselves down, erasing any temporary files and returning you to the DOS prompt.

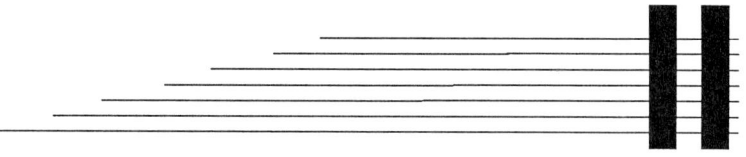

# THE FUNDAMENTALS OF EXCEL

The four chapters included in Part II provide the fundamentals of Excel—creating and manipulating worksheets, producing charts, and using a database.

Chapters 5 and 6 are companions. In Chapter 5 you create a worksheet: you plan it, place text and headings, enter numbers and formulas, copy formulas, insert and delete rows, and save the worksheet. Chapter 6 covers formatting, changing, and printing the worksheet. Included are instructions on loading the worksheet, formatting numbers and headings, moving, deleting, erasing, and setting parameters for and printing the worksheet.

Chapter 7 looks at producing charts. It describes line charts, pie charts, and bar charts and includes instructions on selecting the type of chart, determining the worksheet ranges to plot, adding legends and titles, viewing, and printing.

In Chapter 8 you build and use a database. The chapter covers sorting a database and selecting and analyzing information from a database. You practice using frequency distributions, statistical functions, and data tables.

Part II should be read by all levels of users. If you are a new user, it provides the experience you need to create your own worksheets, charts, and databases. For intermediate and advanced users, Part II provides a refresher course as well as considerable insight into Excel.

# 5

# CREATING A WORKSHEET

Planning a Worksheet
Placing Labels, Headings, and Titles
Placing a Border
Saving the Worksheet
Entering Numbers and Formulas
Copying
Completing the Worksheet

Creating a worksheet is the central focus of Excel—its reason for being—and it is the one thing every user of Excel does. The importance of learning how to do this well, and becoming familiar with as many tricks and shortcuts as possible, cannot be overemphasized. This chapter provides the foundation for that learning process by taking you through the actual construction of a worksheet to demonstrate how it is done. Chapter 6 builds upon this foundation to demonstrate additional worksheet capabilities in Excel.

You will benefit from following along on your computer as you read this chapter. It is not absolutely necessary to do this—there are plenty of figures and illustrations to show you what is going on—but you will learn far more by actually seeing for yourself what is happening as the worksheet progresses. More importantly, you will learn how to untangle yourself from the many small mistakes that everyone makes but are impossible to predict in a book.

Creating a worksheet has a number of steps. This chapter covers the planning phase: placing headings and titles, entering numbers and formulas, copying formulas, and completing and saving.

## PLANNING FOR A WORKSHEET

You could start building a worksheet by simply entering the necessary headings, labels, and numbers or formulas. If you need an extra row or column, you could just insert it and delete those you do not need. A great number of worksheets—probably the majority—are built that way. As with most things, however, a little planning up front saves considerable time as you go along. Planning involves simply visualizing what the worksheet will look like and sketching it out so you have a layout to follow as you build the worksheet. It takes only a few minutes.

Figure 5-1 shows a completed layout for a third-quarter budget worksheet that you will build in this chapter. This layout was done using Excel, but most are simply sketched on a scrap of paper. To construct this layout required the answers to three questions: How many revenue, cost of sales, and expense accounts are to be

|   | A | B | C | D | E | F | G | H |
|---|---|---|---|---|---|---|---|---|
| 1 | | | | TITLE - 2 ROWS | | | | |
| 2 | | | | (1 TITLE ROW PLUS 1 BLANK) | | | | |
| 3 | | | | | | | | |
| 4 | | | | ASSUMPTIONS - 4 ROWS | | | | |
| 5 | | | | (3 ASSUMP. ROWS PLUS 1 BLANK) | | | | |
| 6 | | | | | | | | |
| 7 | | | | | | | | |
| 8 | | | | COLUMN HEADINGS - 3 ROWS | | | | |
| 9 | | | | (2 HEADING ROWS PLUS 1 BLANK) | | | | |
| 10 | | | | | | | | |
| 11 | ROW HEADINGS | | DATA AREA - 6 COLUMNS C - H | | | | | |
| 12 | 17 ROWS 10-26 | | (2 QUARTERS, 3 MONTHS, & PERCENT GROWTH) | | | | | |
| 13 | | | | | | | | |
| 14 | (5 REVENUE, | | | | | | | |
| 15 | 4 COS, | | | | | | | |
| 16 | 6 EXPENSE, & | | | | | | | |
| 17 | 2 NET INCOME) | | | | | | | |
| 18 | | | | | | | | |
| 19 | | | | | | | | |
| 20 | | | | | | | | |
| 21 | | | | | | | | |
| 22 | | | | | | | | |
| 23 | | | | | | | | |
| 24 | | | | | | | | |
| 25 | | | | | | | | |
| 26 | | | | | | | | |

**FIGURE 5-1** Layout for Third Quarter Budget worksheet

included? How many time periods are covered? What assumptions are involved?

The answers to these questions allow you to make the following decisions regarding the layout in Figure 5-1:

- A title will appear at the top of the worksheet with a blank line under it.

- There will be three assumptions, one each for the growth of revenue, cost of sales, and expenses. Each requires a row, and there will be a blank line under each.

- Each column heading will take 2 rows and have a blank line below it.

- The row headings will be in columns A and B and take 17 rows, 10 through 26 (5 for revenue, 4 for cost of sales and gross income, 6 for expense, and 2 for net income).

- The data area will occupy 6 columns: C through H (2 for quarters, 3 for months, and 1 for the percent growth).

If you cannot visualize the worksheet from the layout in Figure 5-1 and the above decisions, don't feel bad. Sneak a look at the finished product in Figures 5-18 and 5-19 at the end of the chapter. As you build more worksheets you will be able to visualize them better.

That's all there is to the planning process: constructing a rough layout of what will go where on the worksheet after making a series of decisions about what is to be included and how much room it will take. Use the plan to begin building the worksheet by placing headings and other elements where you have decided they belong.

# PLACING LABELS, HEADINGS, AND TITLES

Where you begin a worksheet probably has as much to do with how you visualize or create it in your mind as anything else. It is important to minimize the number of keystrokes and therefore the traveling you must do around the worksheet, but trying to reach the absolute minimum path is more trouble than it's worth and does not allow for errors that may be made. Therefore, start where you would like to and don't worry about it. Here you will start with the row labels, knowing that you will have to go back and enter the title and assumptions.

## Entering a Column of Labels

If it is not on already, turn on your computer and load Windows and Excel. With a blank worksheet on your screen, use the following instructions to enter a column of labels:

1. Click on A10 to move the active cell to A10.

2. Type **REVENUE** and press (DOWN ARROW). The all caps style is used to set off an account title. If you make a mistake in typing before pressing (DOWN ARROW), use (BACKSPACE) or (ESC) to correct it. If you notice a mistake after pressing (DOWN ARROW), ignore it. You can come back later and edit the labels.

3. Press (SPACEBAR) four times. This indents a detail account.

4. Type **Forms** and press (DOWN ARROW).

5. Indent (press (SPACEBAR) four times), type **Supplies**, and press (DOWN ARROW).

6. Type **Total Revenue** and press (DOWN ARROW) twice. When you complete this instruction you should be in A15.

Using this process, type the remaining row labels as shown in Figure 5-2. Use (BACKSPACE) to correct any errors you notice prior to completing an entry, but ignore errors you notice after the fact. Leave the space between P/R Taxes and Other Expenses to allow for its use later. Press (ENTER) when you complete Net Income since it is the last account.

**EDITING COMPLETED ENTRIES** Read over the row labels carefully for any typing errors. If there are none, read through the

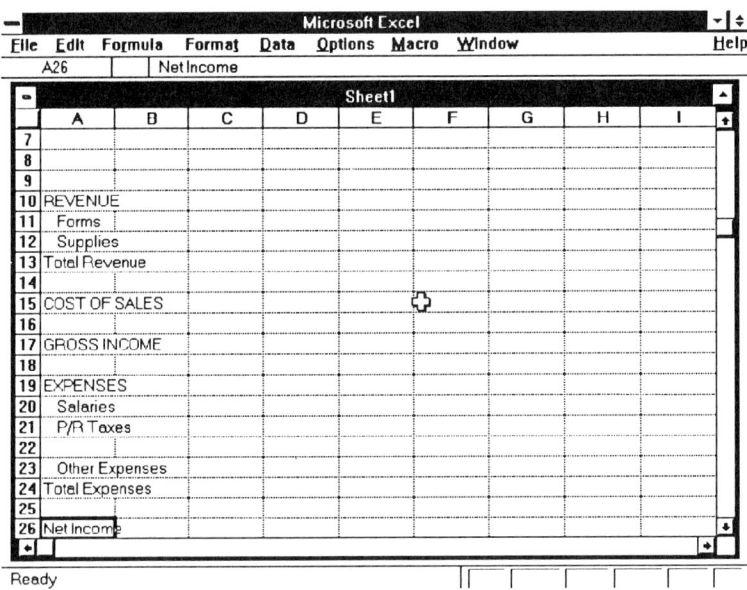

FIGURE 5-2   Row labels completed

following steps to see how you would correct errors in the future. Otherwise, use these steps to correct your errors. (For the sake of example, it is assumed that the second "a" in Salaries has been left out.)

1. Click on the entry to be corrected (A20 for Salaries).

2. Move the mouse pointer to the edit area, place the I-beam at or to the right of the error (between the "l" and "r" if the second "a" is missing in Salaries), and click to place the insertion point. Excel enters edit mode.

3. Correct the error. If you need to delete an incorrect character, press (DEL) to delete a character to the right of the insertion

point, or use (BACKSPACE) to delete a character to the left. Then type the correction. In the case of Salaries, type the missing "a."

4. Press (ENTER). Excel returns to ready mode.

Correct all of the errors you see in the row labels in a similar manner: move the active cell to the incorrect label, go into edit mode (you can press (F2) as well as click in the edit area), get to the incorrect character, use (BACKSPACE) or (DEL) to remove characters you do not want, type characters that need to be added, and press (ENTER) to complete the editing.

**LONG LABELS** As you look at the row labels, notice that many are longer than the width of column A. They hang over into the next column. This works fine while there is nothing in the next column. As you saw in Chapter 4, if you place a label or number in the cell to the right of the long label, you truncate the label at the edge of the column. This worksheet was laid out with that in mind, providing a blank column B. In Chapter 6 you will see how columns can be widened to accommodate long labels and numbers, eliminating the need for a blank column beside them.

## Centering a Title

The second step is to add a title to the worksheet: Third Quarter Budget. You want to center it across the width of the worksheet. Excel has no multicolumn centering command, so you must use trial and error to place the title so that it appears to be centered. For this example, place it in column C with 13 leading spaces. The title fills columns D and E and part of F, leaving G and H on the right balanced against A and B on the left.

Follow these steps to add the title:

1. Click at the top of the vertical scroll bar just under the scroll arrow. The worksheet moves down so you can see the top rows.

2. Click on C1. The active cell moves to C1.

3. Press (CAPS LOCK) for uppercase letters.

4. Type 13 spaces and then **THIRD QUARTER BUDGET**. Before pressing (ENTER), check your entry for mistakes. If you have made any, either press (BACKSPACE) or click in the edit area to correct it.

5. Press (ENTER). The upper-left corner of your screen should look like this:

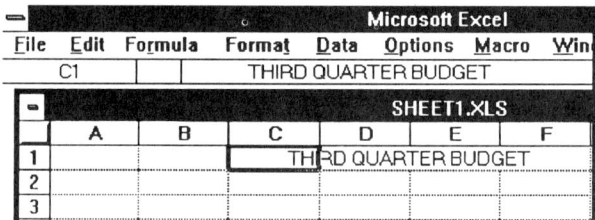

6. Press (CAPS LOCK) to return to lowercase letters.

## Entering a Row of Headings

Each column of data on this worksheet needs a heading. Two rows have been left for this purpose, plus one row for a double line under the headings. Enter these now.

1. Click on C7 to make that the active cell.

2. Type **Second** and press (DOWN ARROW).

3. Type **Quarter** and press (RIGHT ARROW).

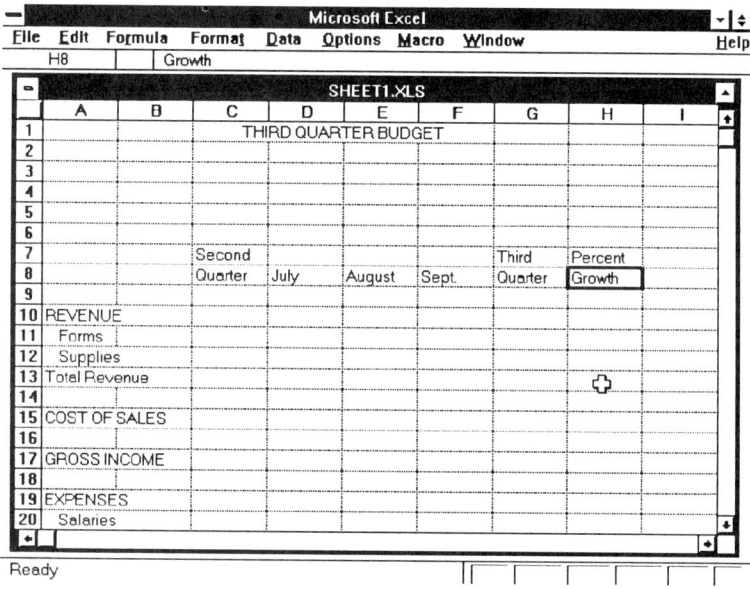

**FIGURE 5-3**  Completed column headings

4. Type **July** and press (RIGHT ARROW).

5. Type **August** and press (RIGHT ARROW).

Use Figure 5-3 as a guide to finish the remaining column headings.

## PLACING A BORDER

For this exercise you want to separate your row labels and column headings by a border. With Excel you can format a cell or range of cells to have a border on any or all of its four sides. This is different from using a string of hyphens, equal signs, or vertical lines to produce a border. It is actual formatting of a cell to include a line on one or more of its sides while keeping its text or number intact. The border is placed on the grid lines, so adjoining cells share a border.

If you want a double line, you must dedicate a row or column for that purpose. For example, if you want a horizontal double line, you must place a top and bottom border on a row and then reduce the height of the row to the space you want between the lines. You would not be able to read anything else contained in the row.

Add a double-line border across row 9 and then a single line between columns B and C with the following instructions:

1. Drag across row 9 from column A through column H. (Move the mouse pointer to A9, press and hold the mouse button while moving the mouse to H9, and then release the mouse button.) Row 9 cells A through H are highlighted.

2. Click on the Format menu and the Border option. The Border dialog box opens.

3. Click on Top and Bottom in the Border dialog box, as shown in Figure 5-4.

4. Click OK. The dialog box closes and a top and bottom border is placed across row 9.

5. Point on the row numbers on the left of the window at the intersection of rows 9 and 10. The mouse pointer becomes a two-headed arrow with a bar in the middle. This allows you to change the height of a row.

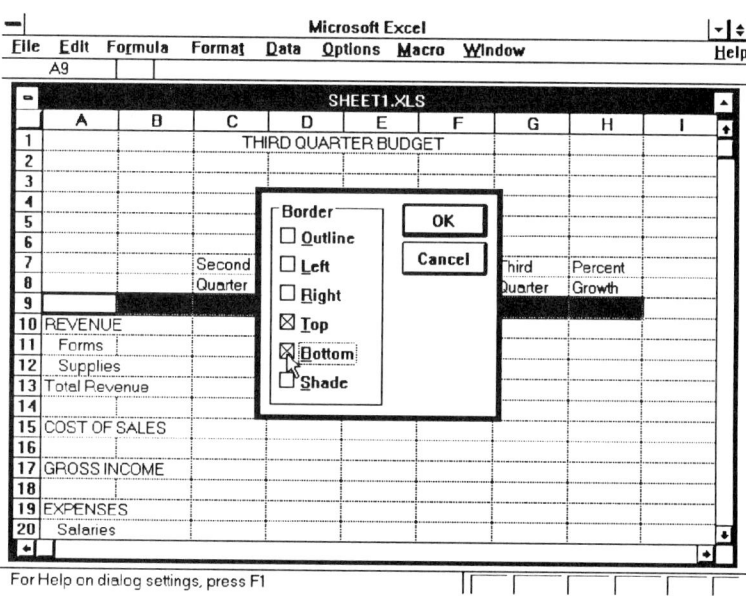

**FIGURE 5-4**   Creating a double-line border

6. Press and hold the mouse button while dragging the mouse upward to reduce the height of row 9 to roughly 1/16 inch, as shown here:

7. Drag column B from row 10 through row 26. B10 through B26 are highlighted.

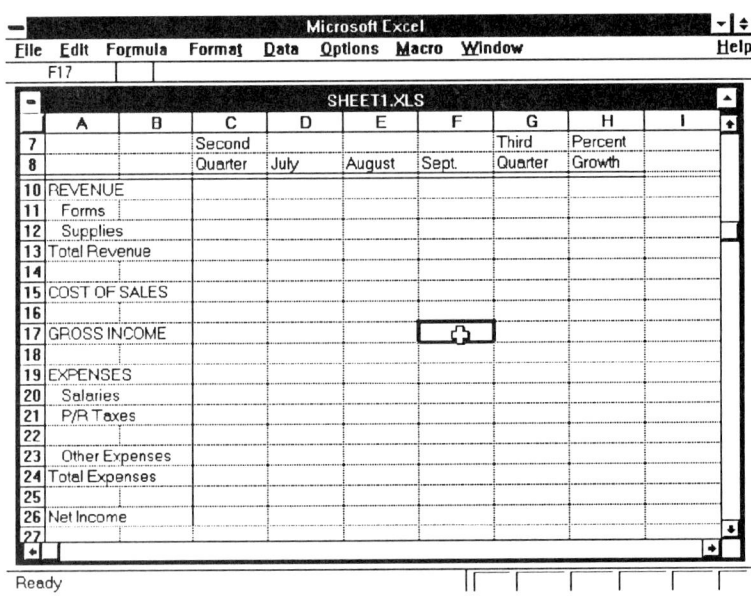

**FIGURE 5-5** Horizontal and vertical borders in place

8. Click on the Format menu and the Border option to again open the Border dialog box.

9. Click on Right and OK to close the dialog box and add a single line border down the right side of B10 through B26. Figure 5-5 shows the results.

You can also add shading with the Format Border command. Figure 5-1 is an example of how such shading is used.

## SAVING THE WORKSHEET

You have now done a fair amount of work on the worksheet that you probably would not want to redo. It is a good idea to save your worksheets early and often, so save this worksheet now.

1. Click on the File menu and Save As option. The Save Worksheet as dialog box opens.

2. Type **c:\wi\sheet\qtr3bud**. (The path C:\WI\SHEET\ is the example path discussed in Appendix A. If your path is different, use your path.) The Save Worksheet as dialog box looks like this:

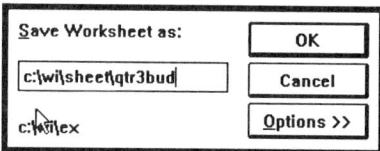

3. Click OK. The worksheet is saved on your hard disk, and Excel returns to ready mode.

Saving a file is simple and should be done often to prevent losing your work from a power failure or human error. As you will see later in this chapter, once you have saved a file, you can resave it with the File Save command without reentering the filename.

## ENTERING NUMBERS AND FORMULAS

Your next task is to enter the body of the worksheet—the numbers and formulas that make up the budget proper. Most budgets are projections based on actual sets of numbers. In this example you start with an actual second quarter to project the third quarter. In other words, the second quarter is an actual set of numbers, while each month of the third quarter contains a formula that calculates its value based on the second quarter. You start by entering the second quarter actuals.

## Entering a Column of Numbers

You enter a column of numbers just as you entered the column of labels earlier: You type one number and press (DOWN ARROW) to move to the next one. You can enter the numbers with or without commas as you choose, but the commas disappear when you complete the entry. Follow these steps to enter the column of numbers:

1. Click on C11. The active cell moves to C11.

2. Type **87,000** and press (DOWN ARROW). If you make a mistake while typing, use (BACKSPACE) or (ESC) to correct it. If you see a mistake after completing an entry, wait until you are done with the column to correct it.

3. Type **147,300** and press (DOWN ARROW).

4. Type **234,300** and press (DOWN ARROW) twice.

In a similar manner complete the column of numbers shown in Figure 5-6. When you reach Net Income, cell C26, press (ENTER) instead of (DOWN ARROW).

**EDITING AND COMPLETING THE COLUMN** When you finish entering the numbers, look back over them and compare what you see to Figure 5-6. It is important that the numbers be accurate because the rest of the worksheet is based on them. If you see an error, use the following instructions to correct it. (For the sake of example, assume that Other Expenses was entered as 14,660 instead of 14,760.)

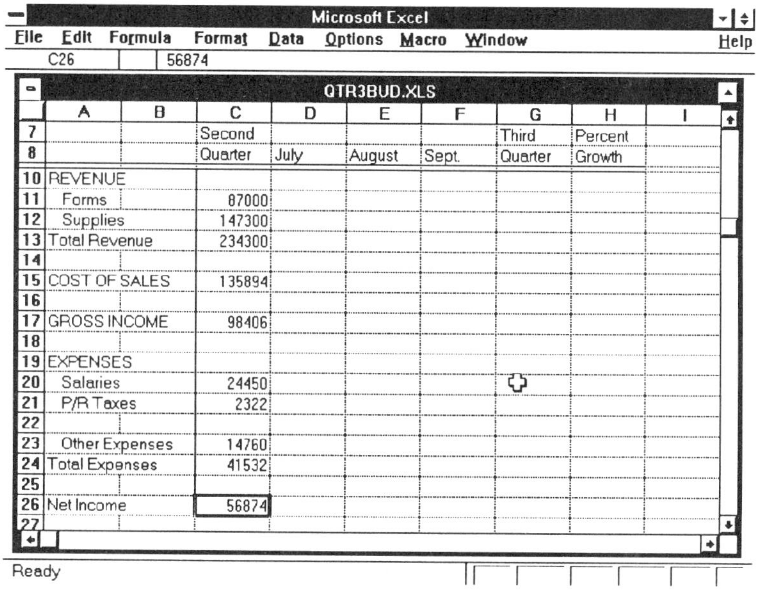

**FIGURE 5-6** Completed column of numbers

1. Click on the cell in error (for example, C23 for Other Expenses).

2. Click or drag on the edit area to highlight the error. The mode indicator changes to EDIT. In this example you would drag across the left 6 in 14,660.

3. If you dragged over number(s) to be replaced, type the replacement numbers. For this example, type **7**. In other cases use (BACKSPACE) or (DEL) to remove unwanted characters and type correct ones.

4. Press (ENTER). The correct number is placed on the worksheet, and Excel returns to ready mode.

Use this procedure to correct as many errors as you have, moving up the list as you go. In the next section you must be near the top of the list.

## Building Formulas

The next three columns (D, E, and F) represent the projected amounts for July, August, and September. Each month is totally derived, using formulas based on the actual second quarter. There are 11 figures per month (including one for the blank after P/R Taxes) and three months. This means you have 33 formulas, which is a lot if you had to enter them all. Thankfully, the copying facility for formulas is very powerful in Excel, so most of the work is done for you.

If you look down a month and think about the formulas, you will notice that four of the formulas are based on other numbers in the same column—columnar formulas: Total Revenue, Gross Income, Total Expense, and Net Income. They are the same formula for all three months. It would be worthwhile doing them first in July so they can be copied to the other months.

In building the formulas, you can use + and -, either above the typewriter keyboard or on the right of the numerical keypad, and you can use either upper- or lowercase letters. As you are building the formulas, check them carefully. It is easier to catch an error and correct it as formulas are being built rather than after the fact. The following steps build the first formula:

1. Click on D13, Total Revenue for July.

2. Type **=d11+d12**. The formula appears in the edit area and in D13. The formula adds Forms (D11) to Supplies (D12) to get Total Revenue.

3. Press (ENTER). Excel returns to ready mode.

On the worksheet you see only a 0 in D13, but in the edit area you see the formula. When numbers are available in D11 and 12, D13 will reflect them.

**POINTING VERSUS TYPING** When entering the first formula, you directly typed it as you would text or a number. This works fine when you can see on the screen the cell addresses that you want to use in the formula. Excel has another method of entering formulas that works even if the cell is not on the screen. The process is to start a formula with an equal sign (=), use the mouse or direction keys to point to the first cell in the formula, type one of the following arithmetic symbols:

+ - * / ^ % & : , ( )

and then point to the second cell, and so on to complete the formula. The following instructions demonstrate this:

1. Click on D17, Gross Income for July.

2. Type =. An = appears in the edit area, and the mode indicator changes to ENTER.

3. Click on D13. A blinking dotted line appears around D13. D13 is displayed in the formula under construction in the edit area, and the mode indicator changes to POINT.

4. Type -. A - appears in the edit area after D13, and the blinking dotted line disappears from D13.

5. Click on D15. A blinking dotted line appears around D15, and D15 goes into the formula in the edit area. Your screen looks like that shown in Figure 5-7.

6. Press (ENTER). The formula is completed, and Excel returns to ready mode.

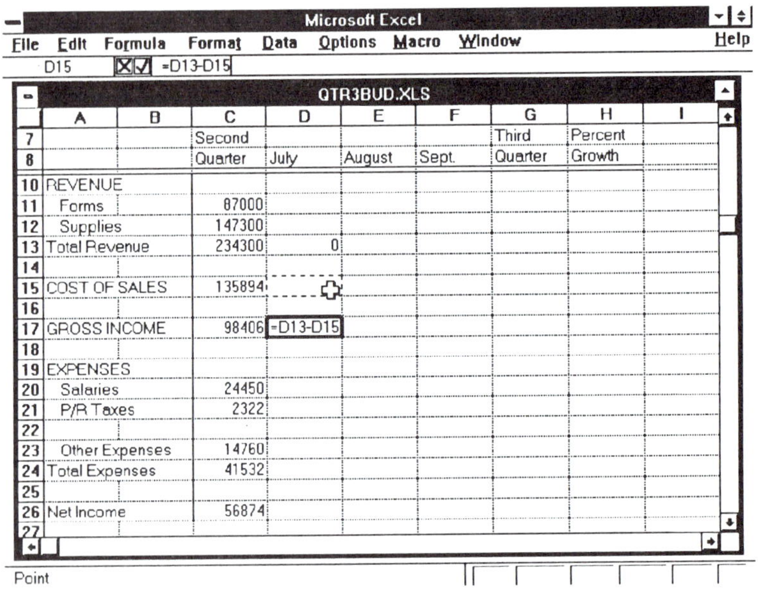

**FIGURE 5-7** Formula under construction in the edit area

Again you see only a 0 in the worksheet, but the formula appears in the Edit area. The process of entering an arithmetic symbol and pointing at a cell can go on as long as you want up to a maximum of 255 characters in a formula. Also, there are shortcuts for formulas, as you are about to see.

**FUNCTIONS VERSUS FORMULAS** The next formula is for total expenses in D24. This is the sum: D20+D21+D22+D23. You can type in such a formula; with an = in front it is 16 keystrokes. You also can point to the four cells and type + four times. Alternatively, you can use the SUM function that Excel uses for summing. Instead of identifying each cell, you identify (type or point to) the range encompassing the cells to be summed. Here is how it is done.

1. Click on D24. The active cell moves to D24, Total Expenses for July.

2. Type **=sum(**, which appears in the edit area. The ENTER indicator comes on.

3. Click on D20. The blinking dotted line appears around D20. D20 is displayed in the formula under construction in the edit area, and the mode indicator changes to POINT.

4. Type **:**. The starting address of a range is anchored at D20.

5. Click on D23. The blinking dotted line appears around D23, and the formula in the edit area includes the range D20:D23, as shown in Figure 5-8.

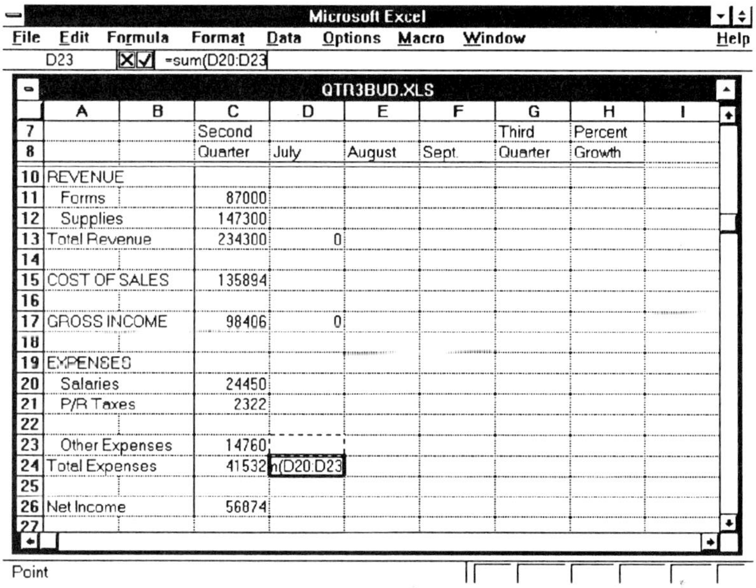

**FIGURE 5-8** SUM formula under construction

6. Type ) and press (ENTER). The completed formula is placed in D24, and you can see it in the edit area.

The SUM function is the most heavily used Excel function. You will find it very useful. A rule of thumb is to use SUM if you are summing three or more cells, and individually add two cells. Depending on how big the cell addresses are, you may not save keystrokes with SUM on three cells, but it provides another benefit—it is expandable.

When you insert a row or column in the middle of a normal summation, the summation adjusts so you are still summing the same cells you originally identified, but you do not add the new cell in between. For example, if your original formula is =C4+C5+C6 and you insert a new row between rows 4 and 5, the formula adjusts to become =C4+C6+C7. The formula is still the way you specified it—the old C5 has become C6 and is so recognized in the formula. The problem is that the new C5 is not included. That may be the way you want it. Normally, however, when you insert a new cell in a range, you want that cell included in the summation. If you use SUM the new cell is included. In the previous example, the original formula is =SUM(C4:C6). After inserting the new row, the formula becomes =SUM(C4:C7) and includes the new C5.

**FINISHING COLUMNAR FORMULAS** One columnar formula is left—net income in D26. Use these instructions to enter it:

1. Click on D26. The active cell moves to D26.

2. Type =. The mode indicator changes to ENTER, and the = goes into the edit area.

3. Click on D17. The blinking dotted line appears around D17, Gross Income. D17 is reflected in the edit area, and the mode indicator changes to POINT.

4. Type -. The blinking dotted line disappears from D17.

5. Click on D24. The blinking dotted line appears around D24, Total Expense, and D24 is reflected in the edit area.

6. Press (ENTER). The formula is completed, and Excel returns to ready mode.

## Copying Formulas

You have now completed the four columnar formulas and are ready to copy them to the other two months. You could copy the same formulas to the Third Quarter total in column G, but you will handle that differently. Also, you will be copying other formulas from August to September and you can include the totals in that copy. Therefore, the copying you do here is from July to August, column D to E.

You might wonder how you can copy a formula from column D—for example, =D11+D12—to column E and have it work. It would need to be changed to =E11+E12. Excel knows that and, unless you tell it otherwise, it automatically changes the formula relative to the location to which it is copied. Follow these steps to copy one formula, and look at it for yourself (the active cell should be D26):

1. Click on the Edit menu and the Copy option. A blinking marquee appears around D26, indicating that it is the source of the copy.

2. Click on E26. The active cell moves to E26, indicating that E26 is the destination of the copy.

3. Press (ENTER). The copy completes by placing the copied formula in E26.

Look now at the formula in E26. It is =E17-E24 as you can see in the edit area:

```
                                          Micr
File  Edit  Formula  Format  Data  Op
   E26         |   =E17-E24
```

In the process of copying from D26 to E26, the formula automatically changes from =D17-D24 to =E17-E24.

**RELATIVE ADDRESSING**  This ability to adjust a formula from one location to another, as you just did, is called *relative addressing*. The formula is always adjusted relative to its location. This means that the net income formula within Excel is

="the cell 9 cells up"-"the cell 2 cells up"

Such a formula will work anywhere on the worksheet. Of course, sometimes you want to fix one or more parts of an address. If the entire address is fixed—locked on to a particular cell no matter where you copy it—the addressing scheme is called *absolute addressing*. If some parts of the address are fixed and some are not, the addressing scheme is called *mixed addressing*. Mixed and absolute addressing will be discussed shortly.

**COPYING THE REST OF THE COLUMNAR FORMULAS**
You have seen how to copy formulas, so now you can easily copy the rest of the columnar formulas, following these instructions:

1. Drag on D13 through D24 (point on D13, and then press and hold the mouse button while dragging the mouse down to D24). The range D13:D24 is highlighted.

2. Drag on the Edit menu to highlight Copy. The blinking marquee appears around D13:D24.

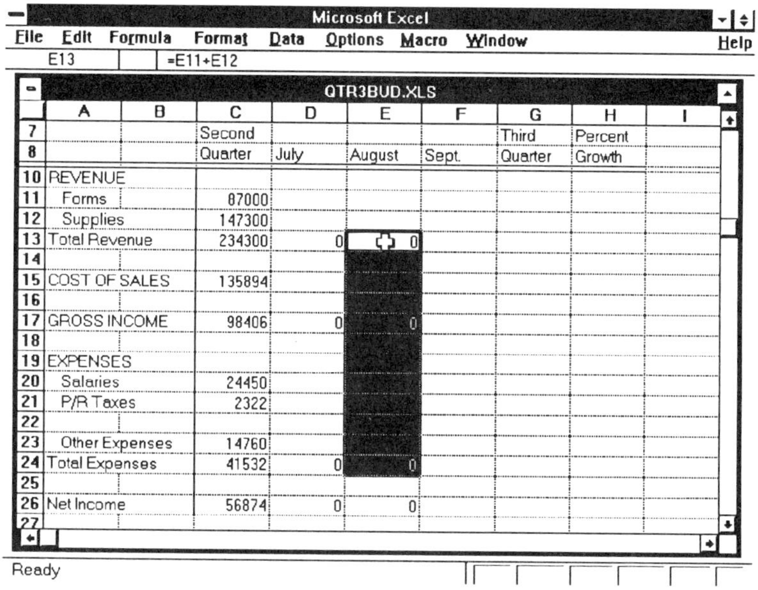

**FIGURE 5-9** Copying a column of formulas

3. Click on E13. The active cell moves to E13.

4. Press (ENTER). The copy process is completed, as shown in Figure 5-9.

The three remaining columnar formulas are thus copied from column D to E and adjusted relative to their new location. You can now calculate all of the totals for July and August.

## Using Assumptions

The formulas used for projection in this model are simple growth formulas that use an assumption for the rate of growth. This assumption can be built into the formula, but if you want to change it, you must edit each formula that uses the assumption. Even in this small budget, that is a lot of formulas. Also, when an assumption is buried in a formula, you cannot see it without moving the active cell to the formula. A better technique is to have all assumptions in a separate table that you can see and easily change. Then the formulas that use these assumptions can reference the table.

The next step, then, is to build a table of assumptions. It consists of three growth factors, one each for revenue, cost of sales, and expenses. Enter these assumptions now with the following instructions:

1. Press (CTRL+HOME) and (DOWN ARROW) twice. The active cell moves to A3.

2. Type **Revenue Growth/Mo.** and press (DOWN ARROW).

3. Type **C O S Growth/Mo.** and press (DOWN ARROW).

4. Type **Expense Growth/Mo.** and press (ENTER).

5. Click on C3. The active cell moves to C3.

6. Type **.012** and press (DOWN ARROW).

7. Type **.013** and press (DOWN ARROW).

8. Type **.01** and press (ENTER).

When you finish the last assumption, the upper-left corner of your screen should look like this:

```
                                    Microsoft Exce
File   Edit  Formula  Format  Data  Options  Ma
       C5           0.01
                                             QTR3BUD.XL
       A        B           C         D        E
  1                              THIRD QUARTER BUDG
  2
  3  Revenue Growth/Mo.     0.012
  4  C O S Growth/Mo.       0.013
  5  Expense Growth/Mo.     0.01
  6
```

## Using Absolute Addressing

The formula that you use to project July from the second quarter divides the quarter by 3 (to get months) and then multiplies by 1 plus the growth rate. It is the same formula for all accounts: revenue, cost of sales, and expense. The only difference is in the growth rate you use. For the two revenue accounts, the growth rate is the same. Therefore when you copy the formula from D11 to D12, if you do not use absolute addressing for the growth rate, it is changed by the copy and points to the growth rate for Cost of Sales. The growth rate in the formula, then, must use an absolute address. Use the following instructions to build a formula for projecting July's forms revenue with an absolute address for the growth rate and then copy it for use in projecting July supplies revenue.

1. Click on D11, Forms revenue for July.

2. Type = and press (LEFT ARROW). The mode indicator changes to POINT, and =C11 is placed in the edit area.

3. Type **/3\*(1+**, which is added to the formula under construction in the edit area.

4. Click on C3. The blinking dotted line appears around C3, the revenue growth rate, and C3 is added to the formula in the edit area.

5. Press **(F4)** (Absolute). The address C3 in the edit area is changed to $C$3, an absolute address. The upper-left corner of your screen should look like this:

|   | Microsoft Excel |
|---|---|
| File Edit Formula Format Data Options Ma |
| C3 | ☒☑ =C11/3*(1+$C$3) |

| | | | | QTR3BUD.XL |
|---|---|---|---|---|
| | A | B | C | D | E |
| 1 | | | | THIRD QUARTER BUDG |
| 2 | | | | | |
| 3 | Revenue Growth/Mo. | | 0.012 | | |
| 4 | C O S Growth/Mo. | | 0.013 | | |
| 5 | Expense Growth/Mo. | | 0.01 | | |
| 6 | | | | | |
| 7 | | | Second | | |
| 8 | | | Quarter | July | August |
| 10 | REVENUE | | | | |
| 11 | | Forms | 87000 | 3*(1+$C$3) | |
| 12 | | Supplies | 147300 | | |

6. Type **)** and press **(ENTER)**. The formula is completed and placed in D11, which becomes the active cell. Note that the totals immediately reflect the number.

7. Drag the Edit menu to highlight Copy. The blinking marquee appears around D11.

8. Click on D12 and press **(ENTER)**. The copy operation is completed; the formula in D11 is copied to D12 and the active cell moves to D12 so you can see the resulting formula in the edit area. It should look like this:

```
 ─                                    Micr
 File  Edit  Formula  Format  Data  Op
         D12         |  =C12/3*(1+$C$3)
```

In the formula in D12, the reference to the second quarter has changed from C11 to C12 but the reference to the growth rate has remained C3. The $ in front of each part of the growth rate address means that it is an absolute reference and it remains the same no matter where it is copied.

**TYPES OF MIXED ADDRESSES** When you make an address absolute each part of the address—the column and the row—is fixed. You also can have various combinations of fixed and relative. These are called mixed addresses. To get a mixed address you must keep pushing (F4) (Absolute), which cycles through all four possible combinations as follows:

| Start with: | Press (F4) to get: | Type = of address |
|---|---|---|
| C3 | $C$3 | Absolute address |
| $C$3 | C$3 | Mixed (fixed row) |
| C$3 | $C3 | Mixed (fixed column) |
| $C3 | C3 | Relative |

(F4) (Absolute) always cycles through the alternatives in the same order independent of where you start.

## Editing Formulas

The formulas for projecting cost of sales and expenses are relatively the same as the formulas for projecting revenue, except for the growth rate. You can easily copy the revenue formula to cost of sales and expense and then edit the formula. Once the first expense account is corrected, it can be copied to the other expense accounts. Use these steps to do the copying and editing of July's formulas. Your active cell should be D12.

1. Drag the Edit menu to highlight the Copy command.

2. Click on D15 and press (ENTER). The active cell moves to D15, which is selected as the copy destination, and the copy operation is complete.

3. Drag the Edit menu to highlight the Copy command.

4. Click on D20 and press (ENTER). The active cell moves to D20, which is selected as the copy destination, and the copy operation is complete.

5. Drag across the rightmost 3 in the formula in the edit area. Excel goes into edit mode, and the row reference to the growth rate is highlighted.

6. Type **5**. The formula reference, previously referring to the growth rate in C3, is changed to C5, as shown here:

7. Press (ENTER). The correct formula is placed in D20, and Excel returns to ready mode.

8. Drag D20 through D23. The range D20:D23 is highlighted.

9. Click on the Edit menu and then click on Fill Down. The formula in D20 is copied to D21, D22, and D23, as shown in Figure 5-10.

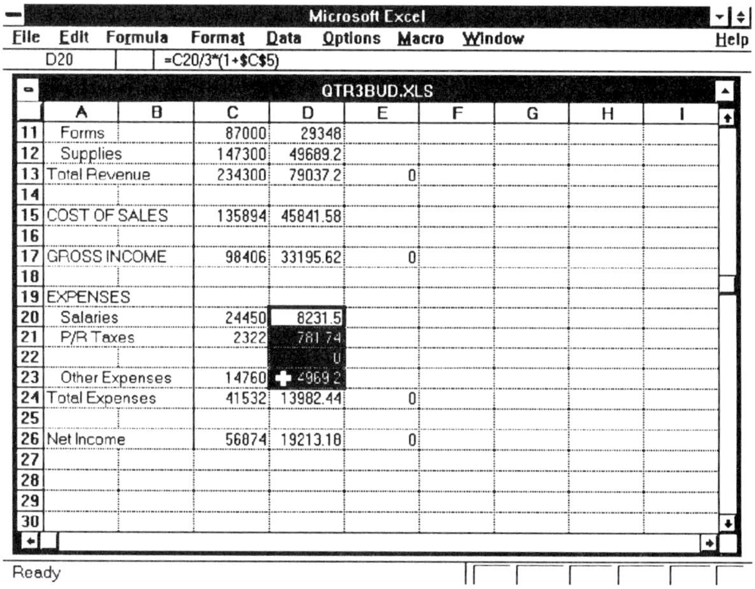

[A screenshot of a Microsoft Excel worksheet titled QTR3BUD.XLS, showing cell D20 selected with formula =C20/3*(1+$C$5). The worksheet displays budget data with rows for Forms, Supplies, Total Revenue, COST OF SALES, GROSS INCOME, EXPENSES (Salaries, P/R Taxes, Other Expenses, Total Expenses), and Net Income, in columns C and D.]

**FIGURE 5-10** Copying expense formulas

As you can see, Fill Down and its partner Fill Right are fast forms of copying when you have a range immediately above or to the left of the area to which you want to copy. By pressing (SHIFT) when you select the Edit menu, you also get Fill Up and Fill Left, which do the same thing in those directions.

10. Click on D15 and drag across the rightmost 3 in the formula in the edit area.

11. Type **4**. The formula reference to the growth rate in C3 is changed to C4.

12. Press (ENTER). The correct formula is placed in D15, and Excel returns to ready mode.

A similar situation exists between the formulas that project July and those that project August. In formulas used in July, the second-quarter amounts (in the cell to the left) were divided by 3 to get a monthly amount and then multiplied by the growth factor. In formulas for August, you multiply the July amounts (in the cell to the left) by the same growth factor. The only difference is that in July you divide the cell to the left by 3 and in August you do not. You can copy the July formulas to August and edit out the /3. Follow these steps to build the projection formulas for August:

13. Click on D11.

14. Drag the Edit menu to highlight Copy. The active cell (D11) is selected as the source of the copy.

15. Click on E11 and press (ENTER). The active cell moves to E11, which is selected as the copy destination, and the copy operation is complete.

16. Drag across /3 in the formula in the edit area, press (DEL), and press (ENTER). The formula for projecting August Forms revenue in E11 is modified to remove the division by 3, as shown here:

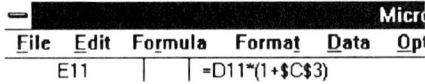

17. Drag the Edit menu to highlight Copy. E11 becomes the source of the copy.

18. Click on E12 and press (ENTER). E11 is copied to E12.

19. Click on D15. Drag the Edit menu to highlight Copy. D15 becomes the source of the copy.

20. Click on E15 and press (ENTER). D15 is copied to E15.

21. Drag across /3 in the formula in the edit area, press (DEL), and press (ENTER). August Cost of Sales in E15 is modified to remove the division by 3.

22. Click on D20. Drag the Edit menu to highlight Copy. D20 becomes the source of the copy.

23. Click on E20 and press (ENTER). D20 is copied to E20.

24. Drag across /3 in the formula in the edit area, press (DEL), and press (ENTER). E20 is modified to remove the division by 3.

25. Drag E20 through E23. The range E20:E23 is highlighted.

26. Click on the Edit menu and then click on Fill Down. E20 is copied to E21, E22, and E23.

Your screen should look like the one shown in Figure 5-11.

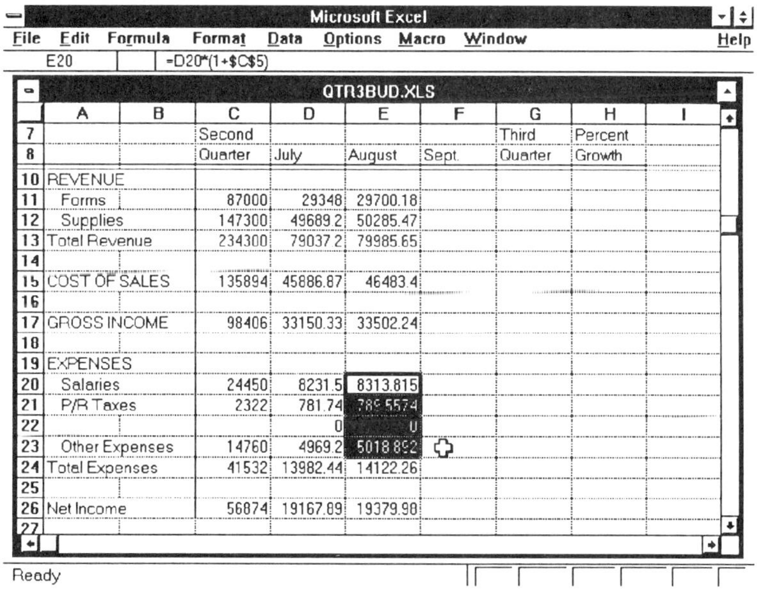

**FIGURE 5-11** Completed August projection

## Copying a Column of Formulas

With August completed, you can copy it to September. There are no differences between the relative formulas as they are now constructed in August and what is needed for September. Use the following instructions to produce September:

1. Drag from E11 through E26. The entire range of Revenue, Cost of Sales, and Expense (E11:E26) is highlighted.

2. Drag on the Edit menu to highlight Copy. The blinking marquee appears around E11:E26 to indicate it has been selected as the source of the copy.

3. Click on F11 and press **ENTER**. F11 is selected as the destination of the copy. E11:E26 is copied to F11:F26, as shown in Figure 5-12.

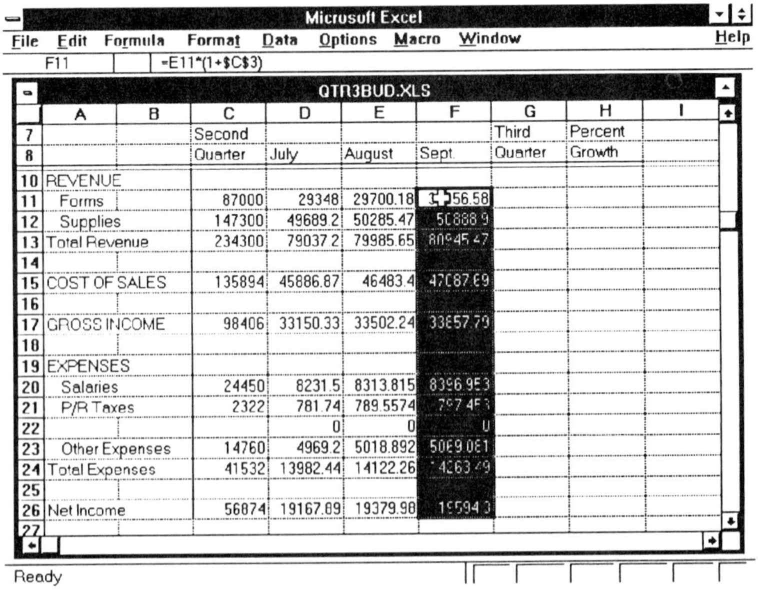

**FIGURE 5-12** September, as a result of copying

Here again you see the power of the Copy command. If you want to build an annual budget by month, all you have to do is build one month and copy it to the other eleven.

# COPYING

The copying capability is extremely valuable and quite simple. As you have seen, there are two types of copying. With the Copy option, you identify a range you want to copy from—the source range—choose the Copy option from the Edit menu, and then specify the range you want to copy to—the destination range. With the Fill Down or Fill Right option (or Fill Up or Fill Left, which you get by pressing (SHIFT) when you select the Edit menu), you identify both the source and destination ranges and then choose the command from the Edit menu. The Copy option can do the same type of copying as the Fill options, but the Fill options do it faster with one less step.

For either type of copying, the mouse is by far the easiest means of identifying both the source and destination ranges. The keyboard can be used, however. Using the direction keys, you first move the active cell to one of the corners of the range, and then press and hold (SHIFT) while using the direction keys to expand the highlight to the other cells in the range.

There are four copy range combinations that work:

- Copying a single column to a range spanning several columns. The destination is a single row.

- Copying a single row to a range spanning several rows. The destination is a single column.

- Copying a single cell to another single cell, to a row of cells, to a column of cells, or to a block of cells. The destination is another cell, a row, a column, or a block.

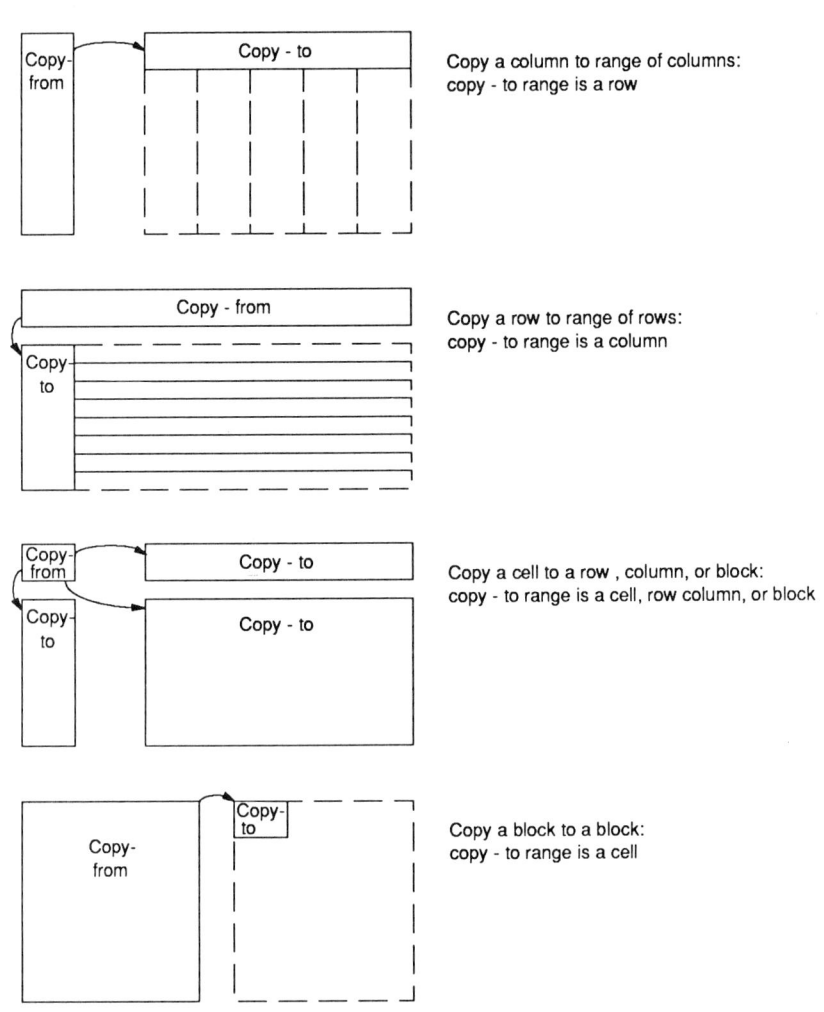

**FIGURE 5-13** Four copy range combinations

- Copying a block to a second block. The destination is a single cell—the upper-left corner of the receiving range.

Figure 5-13 shows these four copy range combinations.

## COMPLETING THE WORKSHEET

The basic three-month projection is now complete. Still to be added, however, are the quarterly total and percentage growth columns. Also, you will spruce up the worksheet a bit before this chapter ends.

### Producing a Total

The quarterly total is just the sum of the three months. Use the SUM function again to produce a quarterly total:

1. Click on G11. The active cell moves to G11.

2. Type **=sum(** and click on D11. The edit area contains =sum(D11.

3. Type **:** and click on F11. The summation range is D11 through F11, as shown here:

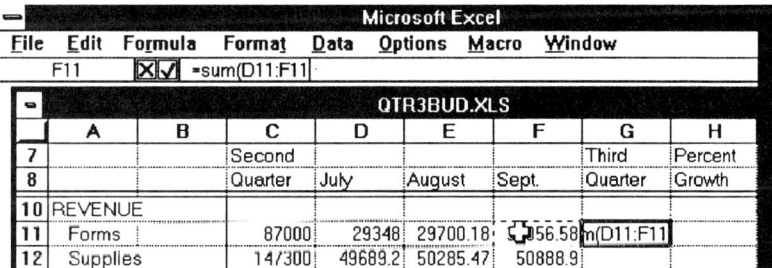

4. Type **)** and press (**ENTER**). The summation formula is completed, and Excel returns to ready mode.

The summation formula is copied down the third-quarter summary with the percentage growth in a moment.

## Calculating a Percentage

The percentage growth formula is the difference between the second and third quarters divided by the second quarter. Build that formula by following these instructions:

1. Click on H11.

2. Type =( and click on G11. The mode indicator changes to ENTER and then to POINT, and =(G11 is placed into the edit area.

3. Type - and click on C11. -C11 is added to the edit area.

4. Type )/ and click on C11 again. The edit area now looks like this:

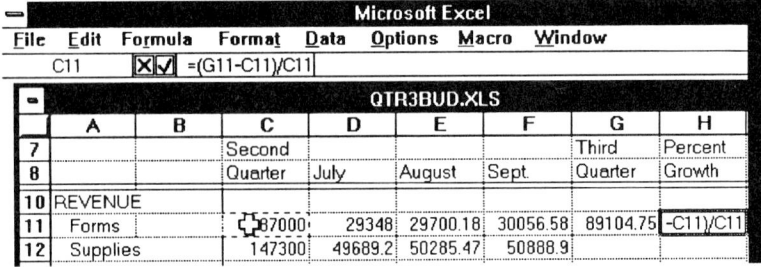

5. Press (ENTER) to complete the percentage growth formula.

## Copying a Row of Formulas

The quarterly summation and percentage growth formulas now must be copied down their columns. There are two ways to do this. One way is to copy the formulas in five operations to the five segments that need it (Revenue accounts, Cost of Sales, Gross Income, Expense accounts, and Net Income). The other method is to copy the formulas to the entire column at one time and then erase

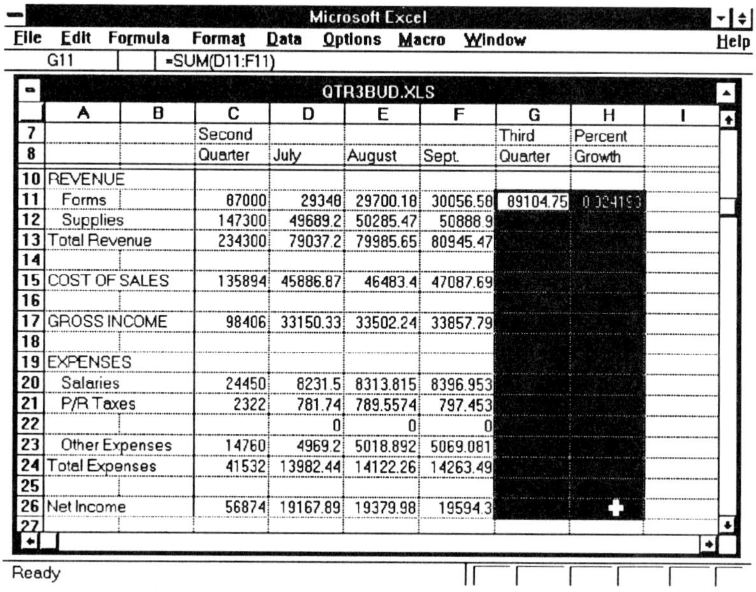

**FIGURE 5-14** Range for copying totals and percents

the four blank lines that divide the segments. There is no reason for choosing one method over the other, although the copy/erase method may be a little faster. Use it in the following exercise:

1. Drag across G11 and H11 and, while still holding the mouse button, drag down to H26. You have highlighted the range G11:H26, as shown in Figure 5-14.

2. Click on the Edit menu and click on Fill Down. Columns G and H are filled with figures, as shown in Figure 5-15.

On the unused rows, like 14, you get the message #DIV/0!. This is an error message stating you are dividing by zero. Don't let it bother you. You are going to erase or clear these next.

**FIGURE 5-15** Completed totals and percents

## Clearing a Range of Cells

Clearing a range (which, you remember, can be a cell, a column, a row, or a block) is very easy: highlight the range, press (DEL), and click OK. Do that next for row 14:

1. Drag across G14 and H14. The range G14:H14 is highlighted.

2. Press (DEL) or choose Clear from the Edit menu. The Clear dialog box opens, as shown here:

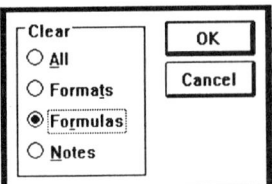

The options that are available in the Clear dialog box and their meaning are as follows:

| Option | Result |
|---|---|
| All | Erases everything (contents, formats, and notes) from the cell and returns it to the General format. |
| Formats | Erases only the formats, leaving the contents and notes. The cell is returned to the General format. |
| Formulas | Erases only the contents, leaving the formats and notes. |
| Notes | Erases only the notes, leaving the contents and formats. |

Formulas is the default and the one most generally used. Since your Third Quarter Budget worksheet does not have any formatting or notes, Formulas is just fine here. (Notes, which are discussed in Chapter 6, are blocks of text that you can attach to a cell.)

3. Click OK to accept clearing only the contents of the cells G14 and H14, as shown here:

| | A | B | C | D | E | F | G | H | I |
|---|---|---|---|---|---|---|---|---|---|
| 7 | | | Second | | | | Third | Percent | |
| 8 | | | Quarter | July | August | Sept. | Quarter | Growth | |
| 10 | REVENUE | | | | | | | | |
| 11 | Forms | | 87000 | 29348 | 29700.18 | 30056.58 | 89104.75 | 0.024193 | |
| 12 | Supplies | | 147300 | 49689.2 | 50285.47 | 50888.9 | 150863.6 | 0.024193 | |
| 13 | Total Revenue | | 234300 | 79037.2 | 79985.65 | 80945.47 | 239968.3 | 0.024193 | |
| 14 | | | | | | | | | |
| 15 | COST OF SALES | | 135894 | 45886.87 | 46483.4 | 47087.69 | 139458 | 0.026226 | |
| 16 | | | | | | | | 0 | #DIV/0! | |

4. Drag across G16 and H16.

5. Press (DEL) and click OK to clear G16 and H16.

Use similar steps to erase rows 18, 19 (which can be done together), and 25. Leave row 22 for the moment.

## Inserting a Row

To make the worksheet easier to read, you will now insert a line between the expense and revenue totals and the detail accounts above them. To do this, you must insert a blank row and then copy a line across it.

1. Drag across A13 through H13.

2. Click on the Edit menu and on the Insert option. The Insert dialog box opens, as shown here:

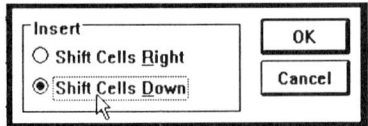

The Insert dialog box gives you two options: shifting cells right, which is the same as inserting columns, or shifting cells down, which is the same as inserting rows and is what you want here. Since Shift Cells Down is the default, you only need click OK.

3. Click OK. A new, blank row 13 is inserted, and all the cells below A13:H13 are shifted down.

4. Click on C13, type - (hyphen), and press (ENTER). C13 contains a single hyphen.

5. Click on the Format menu and the Alignment option. The Alignment dialog box opens.

6. Click on Fill and OK. The dialog box closes, and C13 fills with hyphens.

7. Drag C13 through H13. Click on the Edit menu and the Fill Right option. The line in C13 is copied across the range D13:H13, as shown here:

| REVENUE | | | | | | | |
|---|---|---|---|---|---|---|---|
| Forms | | 87000 | 29348 | 29700.18 | 30056.58 | 89104.75 | 0.024193 |
| Supplies | | 147300 | 49689.2 | 50285.47 | 50888.9 | 150863.6 | 0.024193 |
| | | ▬▬▬▬▬ | ▬▬▬▬▬ | ▬▬▬▬▬ | ▬▬▬▬▬ | ▬▬▬▬▬ | ▬▬▬▬▬ |
| Total Revenue | | 234300 | 79037.2 | 79985.65 | 80945.47 | 239968.3 | 0.024193 |

Go down to A25 and, following the previous instructions, insert a new row and copy a line across columns C through H. Note that in both cases the total formulas remain unaffected by the new rows.

## Deleting a Row

You have been hanging on to what is now row 23 with the idea that you will do something with it. You will, you'll delete it. Row 23 was added to demonstrate deleting a row in a SUM range. Do that now by following these instructions:

1. Drag across A23 through H23.

2. Click on the Edit menu and the Delete option. The Delete dialog box opens with the options Shift Cells Left (to delete columns) or Shift Cells Up (to delete rows), as shown in Figure 5-16. The default, Shift Cells Up, is what you want. Therefore, you need only click OK.

3. Click OK. The range A23:H23 is deleted and all the cells below that row shift up. Note that the row deletion did not change the Total Expenses or Net Income amounts.

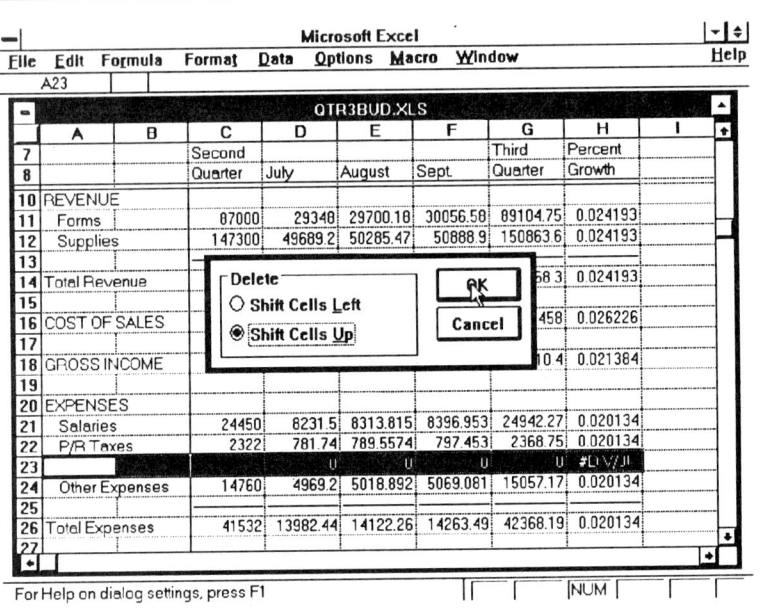

**FIGURE 5-16** Row deletion in progress

## Inserting and Deleting

Inserting and deleting rows and columns are both very powerful and potentially dangerous operations. They are powerful because they allow you to easily change the structure of a worksheet after it is built; for example, adding new or forgotten accounts or deleting unwanted elements. Inserting and especially deleting can be dangerous because, under certain circumstances, you can cause a formula to become incorrect.

Excel has many safeguards against causing a formula error with an insertion or a deletion. You have seen how both cell-by-cell addition and SUM formulas are not affected by inserting rows. Even an absolute range is correctly adjusted if an inserted row changes its position. For example, if a row is inserted between rows

2 and 3, pushing the assumptions in C3 through C5 down a row, the absolute references to those cells are corrected automatically.

One safeguard is that both inserts and deletes can be undone if you choose Undo from the Edit menu or press [ALT+BACKSPACE] before you carry out another operation that takes Excel out of ready mode. You can look at a formula, but do not try to edit it. A good habit to get into is to pause after doing an insert or delete and look around the worksheet. Highlight several formulas to see if they have been correctly changed and thereby give yourself a chance to use Undo if necessary.

Excel's formulas are extremely flexible, especially SUM. Not only can you insert or delete cells in the middle of a summation range, but also you can delete the named first and last cells in a summation and the formula will be correctly adjusted.

When you do an insert or delete, it is handy to think of it as inserting or deleting rows or columns. However, there is good reason for Excel's not using this terminology in their dialog boxes: you insert or delete only the specific cells you previously highlighted. You do not insert or delete a row or column across or down the entire worksheet.

While it may be obvious that to delete three rows, you need to highlight three rows, it is not so obvious that to insert three rows, you need to highlight that number. The number of rows highlighted are inserted immediately above the top row highlighted. For columns, the number of columns highlighted are inserted immediately to the left of the leftmost column highlighted.

## Making Corrections

This completes all of the work you will do on the worksheet in this chapter. Your screen should now look like the one shown in Figure 5-17. If your numbers are different, you may have an error in one of your formulas. Although it is a bit of a pain, you might want to

|  | A | B | C | D | E | F | G | H | I |
|---|---|---|---|---|---|---|---|---|---|
| 7 |  |  | Second |  |  |  | Third | Percent |  |
| 8 |  |  | Quarter | July | August | Sept. | Quarter | Growth |  |
| 10 | REVENUE |  |  |  |  |  |  |  |  |
| 11 | Forms |  | 87000 | 29348 | 29700.18 | 30056.58 | 89104.75 | 0.024193 |  |
| 12 | Supplies |  | 147300 | 49689.2 | 50285.47 | 50888.9 | 150863.6 | 0.024193 |  |
| 13 |  |  |  |  |  |  |  |  |  |
| 14 | Total Revenue |  | 234300 | 79037.2 | 79985.65 | 80945.47 | 239968.3 | 0.024193 |  |
| 15 |  |  |  |  |  |  |  |  |  |
| 16 | COST OF SALES |  | 135894 | 45886.87 | 46483.4 | 47087.69 | 139458 | 0.026226 |  |
| 17 |  |  |  |  |  |  |  |  |  |
| 18 | GROSS INCOME |  | 98406 | 33150.33 | 33502.24 | 33857.79 | 100510.4 | 0.021384 |  |
| 19 |  |  |  |  |  |  |  |  |  |
| 20 | EXPENSES |  |  |  |  |  |  |  |  |
| 21 | Salaries |  | 24450 | 8231.5 | 8313.815 | 8396.953 | 24942.27 | 0.020134 |  |
| 22 | P/R Taxes |  | 2322 | 781.74 | 789.5574 | 797.453 | 2368.75 | 0.020134 |  |
| 23 | Other Expenses |  | 14760 | 4969.2 | 5018.892 | 5069.081 | 15057.17 | 0.020134 |  |
| 24 |  |  |  |  |  |  |  |  |  |
| 25 | Total Expenses |  | 41532 | 13982.44 | 14122.26 | 14263.49 | 42368.19 | 0.020134 |  |
| 26 |  |  |  |  |  |  |  |  |  |
| 27 | Net Income |  | 56874 | 19167.89 | 19379.98 | 19594.3 | 58142.16 | 0.022298 |  |

**FIGURE 5-17** Finished worksheet

look for it just to see how a search is done. Go down columns D and E highlighting each cell. Also, look at cells G11 and H11. Compare the cell contents in the edit area with various figures and descriptions in this chapter. It should not take long to find it. A good rule is to thoroughly check formulas as you are building them to prevent having to go back and correct them later.

## Saving and Quitting Excel

The only task remaining is to save the worksheet and leave Excel. Use these instructions for that purpose:

1. Drag on the File menu and highlight Save. The file is saved under the name you originally gave it: QTR3BUD.

As a default, when Excel saves a file it simply copies over the last copy of the same file on disk. The save you just completed copied over the file that you created by saving the worksheet early in the chapter. You can have Excel make a new file each time you save a file. Since you can have only one file with a given name, Excel automatically renames the old file by changing its extension to .BAK. The third time you save a file, the first copy is deleted and the second copy is given the .BAK extension. This is called making a *backup*.

To have Excel make a backup, use the Options button in the Save Worksheet as dialog box, as shown in the following steps:

2. Click on the File menu and click on Save As. The Save Worksheet as dialog box opens.

3. Click on the Options button in the Save Worksheet as dialog box. An enlarged dialog box opens, as shown here:

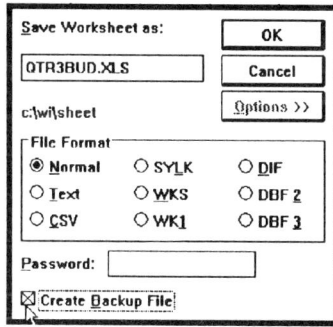

4. Click on the Create Backup File check box, and then click on OK. The Save Worksheet as dialog box closes, and another dialog box opens asking if you want to replace the existing QTR3BUD.XLS file.

5. Click on OK.

|   | A | B | C | D | E | F | G | H |
|---|---|---|---|---|---|---|---|---|
| 1 |   |   |   | THIRD QUARTER BUDGET |   |   |   |   |
| 2 |   |   |   |   |   |   |   |   |
| 3 | Revenue Growth/Mo. |   | 0.012 |   |   |   |   |   |
| 4 | C O S Growth/Mo. |   | 0.013 |   |   |   |   |   |
| 5 | Expense Growth/Mo. |   | 0.01 |   |   |   |   |   |
| 6 |   |   |   |   |   |   |   |   |
| 7 |   |   | Second |   |   |   | Third | Percent |
| 8 |   |   | Quarter | July | August | Sept. | Quarter | Growth |
| 9 |   |   |   |   |   |   |   |   |
| 10 | REVENUE |   |   |   |   |   |   |   |
| 11 |   | Forms | 87000 | 29348 | 29700.18 | 30056.58 | 89104.75 | 0.024193 |
| 12 |   | Supplies | 147300 | 49689.2 | 50285.47 | 50888.9 | 150863.6 | 0.024193 |
| 13 |   |   | ---------- | ---------- | ---------- | ---------- | ---------- | ---------- |
| 14 | Total Revenue |   | 234300 | 79037.2 | 79985.65 | 80945.47 | 239968.3 | 0.024193 |
| 15 |   |   |   |   |   |   |   |   |
| 16 | COST OF SALES |   | 135894 | 45886.87 | 46483.4 | 47087.69 | 139458 | 0.026226 |
| 17 |   |   |   |   |   |   |   |   |
| 18 | GROSS INCOME |   | 98406 | 33150.33 | 33502.24 | 33857.79 | 100510.4 | 0.021384 |
| 19 |   |   |   |   |   |   |   |   |
| 20 | EXPENSES |   |   |   |   |   |   |   |
| 21 |   | Salaries | 24450 | 8231.5 | 8313.815 | 8396.953 | 24942.27 | 0.020134 |
| 22 |   | P/R Taxes | 2322 | 781.74 | 789.5574 | 797.453 | 2368.75 | 0.020134 |
| 23 |   | Other Expenses | 14760 | 4969.2 | 5018.892 | 5069.081 | 15057.17 | 0.020134 |
| 24 |   |   | ---------- | ---------- | ---------- | ---------- | ---------- | ---------- |
| 25 | Total Expenses |   | 41532 | 13982.44 | 14122.26 | 14263.49 | 42368.19 | 0.020134 |
| 26 |   |   |   |   |   |   |   |   |
| 27 | Net Income |   | 56874 | 19167.89 | 19379.98 | 19594.3 | 58142.16 | 0.022298 |

**FIGURE 5-18** Printed worksheet with grid

THIRD QUARTER BUDGET

| | | |
|---|---|---|
| Revenue Growth/Mo. | 0.012 | |
| C O S Growth/Mo. | 0.013 | |
| Expense Growth/Mo. | 0.01 | |

|   | Second Quarter | July | August | Sept. | Third Quarter | Percent Growth |
|---|---|---|---|---|---|---|
| REVENUE |   |   |   |   |   |   |
| Forms | 87000 | 29348 | 29700.18 | 30056.58 | 89104.75 | 0.024193 |
| Supplies | 147300 | 49689.2 | 50285.47 | 50888.9 | 150863.6 | 0.024193 |
| Total Revenue | 234300 | 79037.2 | 79985.65 | 80945.47 | 239968.3 | 0.024193 |
| COST OF SALES | 135894 | 45886.87 | 46483.4 | 47087.69 | 139458 | 0.026226 |
| GROSS INCOME | 98406 | 33150.33 | 33502.24 | 33857.79 | 100510.4 | 0.021384 |
| EXPENSES |   |   |   |   |   |   |
| Salaries | 24450 | 8231.5 | 8313.815 | 8396.953 | 24942.27 | 0.020134 |
| P/R Taxes | 2322 | 781.74 | 789.5574 | 797.453 | 2368.75 | 0.020134 |
| Other Expenses | 14760 | 4969.2 | 5018.892 | 5069.081 | 15057.17 | 0.020134 |
| Total Expenses | 41532 | 13982.44 | 14122.26 | 14263.49 | 42368.19 | 0.020134 |
| Net Income | 56874 | 19167.89 | 19379.98 | 19594.3 | 58142.16 | 0.022298 |

**FIGURE 5-19** Printed worksheet without grid

The previous file, which was QTR3BUD.XLS, is now renamed QTR3BUD.BAK, and a new file named QTR3BUD.XLS will be created. You now have two files on disk. The file backup capability is handy should you need to reuse the earlier file for any reason.

You are done with Excel and Windows for this chapter. Therefore shut them both down now.

5. Double-click on Excel's Control-menu box and then on Windows' Control-menu box. Click OK to end your Windows session.

At this point, the worksheet in printed form is not particularly pretty, as shown in Figure 5-18 with the grid and in Figure 5-19 without the grid. The formatting of the numbers is messy and the columns seem to run together. Making it look better in a number of ways, as well as printing it, are the subjects of Chapter 6.

# 6

# ENHANCING A WORKSHHET

Loading a Worksheet
Formatting
Detail Formatting
Changing the Layout
Printing the Worksheet
Making a Template

In Chapter 5 you created a worksheet for preparing a third quarter budget. The results were usable, but they were not particularly attractive and they were difficult to read. In this chapter you use a number of techniques to make the budget easier to read and more attractive. This includes changing the formatting of numbers and headings and moving, deleting, and erasing sections of the worksheet. You also set the parameters for and print the worksheet. You conclude by changing the Third Quarter Budget worksheet into a template for any quarterly budget.

## LOADING A WORKSHEET

To begin working on the budget worksheet, you must load the file that holds it on the disk. Remember that the last thing you did in Chapter 5 before leaving Excel was to save the file. You must now load that file back into memory so you can work on it. Use the following instructions:

1. Click on the File menu and the Open option. The File menu opens, followed by the File Open dialog box, which asks for the name of the file to open. A list of files is shown in the list box similar to what is seen here:

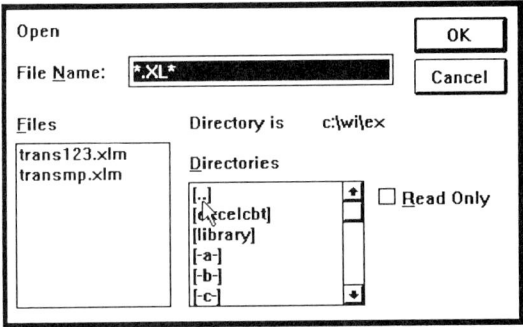

If you came directly here from Chapter 5 without leaving Excel, you are probably looking at the correct directory and can skip the next two steps. However, if you closed Excel and Windows as suggested in Chapter 5 and restarted both here, the directory you are looking at in the File Open dialog box is the Excel program directory, not the \WI\SHEET directory where you stored QTR3BUD. Your first task, then, is to change directories. Make the necessary changes in the following steps:

2. Double-click on [..] in the Directories list box. A new Directories list box is shown. (If you need to use the keyboard, press (ALT+D) and (DOWN ARROW) to highlight [..], and then press (ENTER).)

3. Double-click on [sheet] in the Directories list box. If you do not see [sheet], use the vertical scroll bar (click on the down arrow scroll box) to find it. QTR3BUD.XLS should appear in the Files list box, as shown here:

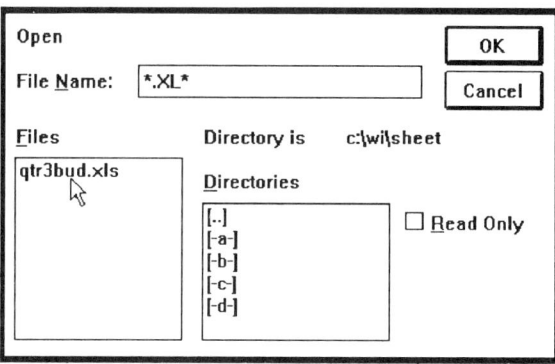

4. Double-click on QTR3BUD.XLS in the Files list box.

The third quarter budget opens on your screen, as shown in Figure 6-1. You can now begin working on it.

## FORMATTING

Excel lets you format individual cells as well as groups or ranges of cells. After formatting a range with the most common format in that range, you can come back and change specific cells that you

| | A | B | C | D | E | F | G | H | I |
|---|---|---|---|---|---|---|---|---|---|
| 7 | | | Second | | | | Third | Percent | |
| 8 | | | Quarter | July | August | Sept. | Quarter | Growth | |
| 10 | REVENUE | | | | | | | | |
| 11 | Forms | | 87000 | 29348 | 29700.18 | 30056.58 | 89104.75 | 0.024193 | |
| 12 | Supplies | | 147300 | 49689.2 | 50285.47 | 50888.9 | 150863.6 | 0.024193 | |
| 13 | | | | | | | | | |
| 14 | Total Revenue | | 234300 | 79037.2 | 79985.65 | 80945.47 | 239968.3 | 0.024193 | |
| 15 | | | | | | | | | |
| 16 | COST OF SALES | | 135894 | 45886.87 | 46483.4 | 47087.69 | 139458 | 0.026226 | |
| 17 | | | | | | | | | |
| 18 | GROSS INCOME | | 98406 | 33150.33 | 33502.24 | 33857.79 | 100510.4 | 0.021384 | |
| 19 | | | | | | | | | |
| 20 | EXPENSES | | | | | | | | |
| 21 | Salaries | | 24450 | 8231.5 | 8313.815 | 8396.953 | 24942.27 | 0.020134 | |
| 22 | P/R Taxes | | 2322 | 781.74 | 789.5574 | 797.453 | 2368.75 | 0.020134 | |
| 23 | Other Expenses | | 14760 | 4969.2 | 5018.892 | 5069.081 | 15057.17 | 0.020134 | |
| 24 | | | | | | | | | |
| 25 | Total Expenses | | 41532 | 13982.44 | 14122.26 | 14263.49 | 42368.19 | 0.020134 | |
| 26 | | | | | | | | | |
| 27 | Net Income | | 56874 | 19167.89 | 19379.98 | 19594.3 | 58142.16 | 0.022298 | |

**FIGURE 6-1** Third quarter budget as initially loaded

want to be different from the overall format. You can set overall formats for several aspects of the worksheet, but here you will set the overall format just for numbers and for the width of columns.

## Overall Number Format

The overall number format determines how numbers appear on a worksheet, both on the screen and when printed. The numbers in Figure 6-1 are formatted with the General format, which is the format Excel starts with. It is the most versatile format in terms of

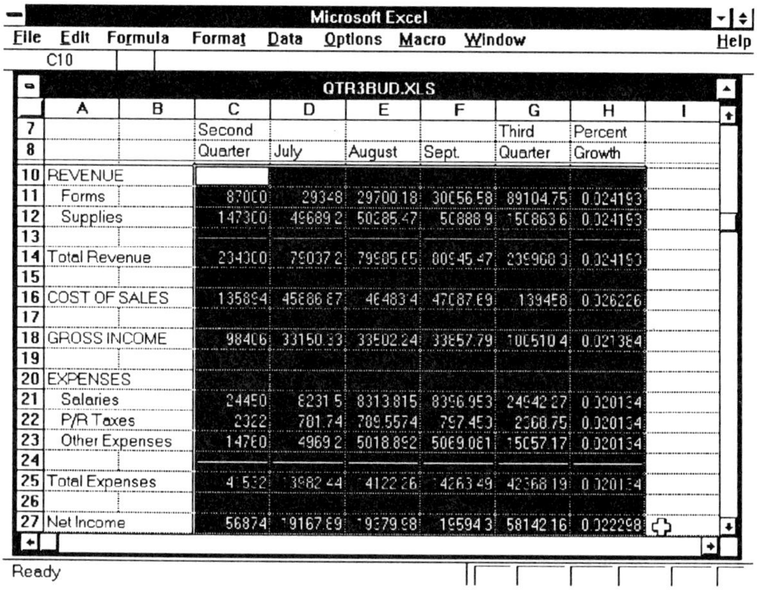

**FIGURE 6-2** Range to be formatted

the variety of numbers it can display, but it is also the least appealing. Let's first look at how to change the number format and then at some of the formatting alternatives. Start out by highlighting the area to be formatted.

1. Drag the mouse from C10 through H27 to highlight that area, as shown in Figure 6-2.

2. Click on the Format menu and the Number option. The Format Number dialog box opens, as shown here:

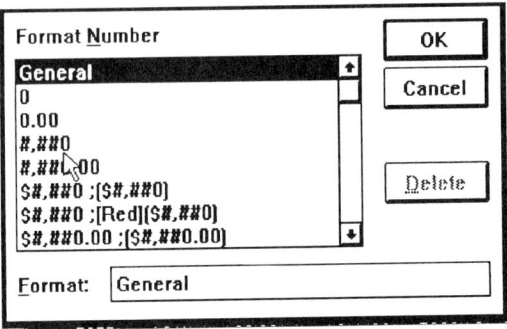

3. Double-click on the fourth alternative (#,##0). The Format command completes, and the worksheet is redisplayed in the new format.

Your screen should now look like the one in Figure 6-3. Don't be concerned that all of the percentages went away. When you

**FIGURE 6-3** After setting the overall format

selected #,##0 from the Format Number dialog box, you told Excel to format the numbers without decimal places (you'll see how this works in a moment). Excel took you literally and displayed zero decimal places even when decimals are all you have. You will come back soon to override the overall format with a specific percentages format for column H.

You might wonder why you use the format chosen when the majority of numbers on the worksheet are currency. If you use a currency format, the worksheet becomes cluttered with dollar signs. Later in this chapter you will format the total lines as currency. That sets the totals off from the rest of the worksheet and doesn't clutter the worksheet with dollar signs.

## Formatting Alternatives

The Format Number dialog box offers many formatting alternatives from which you can select. You can also construct your own format. This chapter discusses both the built-in formats and how you construct a format of your own.

In Excel, numbers can be displayed with up to 15 decimal places. Of course, the column must be wide enough. For all formats except the General format, the column must be wide enough to display all of the whole digits to the left of the decimal point, the number of decimal digits specified, and any other characters such as dollar signs, commas, or periods. If the column is not wide enough, it is filled with # symbols.

**FORMAT SYMBOLS** You communicate to Excel the type of format you want to use with a picture. The picture uses symbols to describe such things as the number of decimal places; whether or not a dollar sign, percent sign, or comma should be used; and how to handle negative numbers, zero values, and text. There are 11 picture formats for numbers and another 9 formats for dates and times that are built into Excel and listed in the Format Number option. Each of these built-in formats, plus any that you build, use the following symbols to communicate their formats:

| Symbol | Usage |
|---|---|
| 0 | Specifies the number of decimal places to the right of the decimal point and the minimum digits to the left of the decimal point. For example, with the built-in format 0.00 you always have two decimal places to the right of the decimal point and at least one digit to the left of the decimal point. The following numbers are formatted as shown: |

| Entry | Display |
|---|---|
| .456 | 0.46 |
| 45 | 45.00 |

| Symbol | Usage |
|---|---|
| # | Specifies the number of optional digits on either side of the decimal point. For example, in the built-in format #,##0 the # provides the optional digits surrounding the comma, which is used as a thousands separator. These will be blank if there are not enough digits to fill the number of places. You want the first place to be a 0 and not a #, so you will get at least a 0 printed if you have a fraction too small to round to 1. With the #,##0 format, the following entries are formatted as shown: |

| Entry | Display |
|---|---|
| 46.67 | 47 |
| 12345 | 12,345 |

| Symbol | Usage |
|---|---|
| . | Specifies where the decimal point is. |
| , | Specifies that the thousands separator is a comma if a comma is surrounded by zeros or # symbols. |
| ; | Separates sections of a format. You can have up to four sections. The first, or leftmost, specifies how to format positive numbers, the second section specifies how to format negative numbers, the third specifies how to format zero, and the fourth section specifies how to handle text. All numbers are handled the same if there is only one section. With two sections, positive and zero values are formatted with the first, and negative numbers are formatted with the second. Text is not given special treatment with only three sections. An example of using a semicolon is shown with the next set of symbols. |
| $ + - () : space | Specify a literal character to be displayed. For example, the built-in format $#,##0;($#,##0) places a $ to the left of the leftmost number and ( ) around negative numbers. With the $#,##0;($#,##0) format, the following numbers are formatted as shown: |

| Entry | Display |
|---|---|
| -45.67 | ($46) |
| 1234 | $1,234 |

If ( ) are specified for negative numbers, positive numbers are shifted one position to the left so that negative numbers line up.

| Symbol | Usage |
|---|---|
| "text" | Specifies that whatever is between the " " is displayed. As an example, $#,##0"DB" ;$#15##0"CR";0 places DB after positive numbers, CR after negative numbers, and 0 for zero values. |
| \ | Specifies that the character following the \ is displayed. This is the same as enclosing a single character in " ". |
| @ | Specifies where any text in a cell is placed in a format. For example, 0.00 ;@ formats all numbers with 0.00 and displays any text appearing in the cell. (0.00 by itself does the same thing.) |
| * | Specifies that the character following the * is repeated to fill any unused space in the cell. For example, S**#,##0 places a $ in the leftmost position in a cell, fills any intervening space with *, and right aligns the number in the cell as usual. With the $**#,##0 format, the following numbers are formatted as shown: |

| Entry | Display |
|---|---|
| 45 | $*******45 |
| 1234 | $***1,234 |

| | |
|---|---|
| % | Specifies that a number is multiplied by 100 and a % placed to the right. For example, the built-in format 0.00% multiplies the number by 100 and places a % after it. With the 0.00% format, the following numbers are formatted as shown: |

| Symbol | Usage | |
|---|---|---|
| | **Entry** | **Display** |
| | .07 | 7.00% |
| | .4575 | 45.75% |
| | -0.067 | -6.7% |

E+ E- e+ e-     Specifies that the scientific format is used with either E or e. If a - is specified, only negative numbers have a sign. With + both positive and negative numbers have a sign. For example, the built-in format 0.00E+00 uses a capital E and both plus and minus signs for the scientific format. With the 0.00E+00 format, the following numbers are formatted as shown:

| | **Entry** | **Display** |
|---|---|---|
| | 4567 | 4.57E+03 |
| | -12345 | -1.23E+04 |
| | .0045 | 4.50E-03 |

m mm mmm mmmm     Specifies that a month is displayed as a number without a leading zero (m) or with a leading zero (mm), as a three letter abbreviation (Apr or Sep), or as a full name. If m or mm follows h or hh it specifies minutes rather than a month.

d dd ddd dddd     Specifies that a day is displayed as a number without a leading zero (d) or with a leading zero (dd), as a three-letter abbreviation (Tue or Thu), or as a full name.

yy yyyy     Specifies that a year is displayed as either a two- (91) or four-digit number (1991).

| Symbol | Usage |
|---|---|
| h hh | Specifies that an hour is displayed as a number either without a leading zero (4) or with a leading zero (04). |
| m mm | Specifies that a minute is displayed as a number either without a leading zero (5) or with a leading zero (05). If the m or mm do not appear after an h or hh, the month is displayed. |
| s ss | Specifies that a second is displayed as a number either without a leading zero (6) or with a leading zero (06). |
| AM/PM am/pm A/P a/p | Specifies that time is displayed using a 12-hour clock with AM, am, A, or a before noon and PM, pm, P, or p from noon to midnight. |
| [color] | Specifies that the characters in the cell should be displayed in a color. The colors available are black, white, red, green, blue, yellow, magenta, and cyan. |

When you have a fixed number of decimal places, the decimal digits are rounded to fit the format. Also, if you have blank format sections (semicolons with nothing between them), that type of number is not displayed. For example, 0.00;;;@ displays and formats positive numbers and text, but does not display negative numbers and zero values.

**GENERAL FORMAT** Every time you create a new worksheet, all cells are automatically formatted with the General format. The General format displays numbers with a variable number of decimal places, no thousands separators, a minus sign if the number is negative, and a leading zero if the number is less than 1. If the column is not wide enough to display all of the decimal digits, they are rounded to the nearest digit that can be displayed. If the column is not wide enough to display all of the whole digits to the left of the decimal point, the number is converted to scientific notation.

Here are some examples of General formatting with the standard column width of 8.43 characters:

| Entry | Display |
|---|---|
| 1234567.89 | 1234568 |
| 1234567890 | 1.23E+09 |
| -4567.89 | -4567.89 |
| .8956 | 0.8956 |

## Overall Column Width Format

Excel starts with a standard column width of 8.43 characters. This allows you to display eight or nine text characters or a number with eight characters in it. Every number has at least one blank character placed on its right. A column's width can be set from 0 to 255 characters.

To set the width of a column in a worksheet, you can either drag the intersection between two column headings, to the right of the column whose width you want to change, or you can use the Format Column Width dialog box. The dragging method is fine for changing individual columns, but to change a range of columns, as you want to do here, you want to use the dialog box. Do that now with the following steps:

1. If columns C through H are not currently highlighted (it doesn't matter what rows), drag across C11 through H11.

2. Click on the Format menu and the Column Width option. The Format Column Width dialog box opens, as shown here:

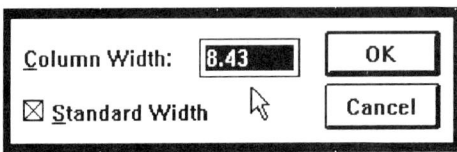

3. Type **10** and press **ENTER**. All columns in the C through H range are widened to 10 characters, as shown in Figure 6-4.

# DETAIL FORMATTING

You have now set the overall format and column width. Now you can tailor specific areas with the formatting that makes them look best. In the following sections your formatting tasks include recovering the percentages that disappeared, formatting the summary lines in the budget as currency, and centering the column headings in their columns.

**FIGURE 6-4** Effect of widening columns C through H to 10

## Creating a Percentage Format

The percentages disappeared when the overall format was set with no decimal places. With the General format the percentages were not easy to read. A format with the % symbol, which multiplies a number by 100 and adds a percent sign, is a better way to display percentages. Two areas or ranges on the worksheet require this kind of format: the percent growth in column H and the assumptions in the upper part of column C. First you must create your own format.

Excel comes with two built-in formats for percentages: one with zero decimals and one with two decimals. If you want a percentage format with one decimal place, you must create it because it does not exist. The easiest way to create a format that is only slightly different from a built-in format is to start with the built-in format. Do that now.

1. Drag down column H from H11 through H27 to highlight the first area to be formatted.

2. Click on the Format menu and the Number option.

3. Click on the downward pointing vertical scroll arrow until you can see the 0.00% format, and then click on that format. Your Format Number dialog box should look this:

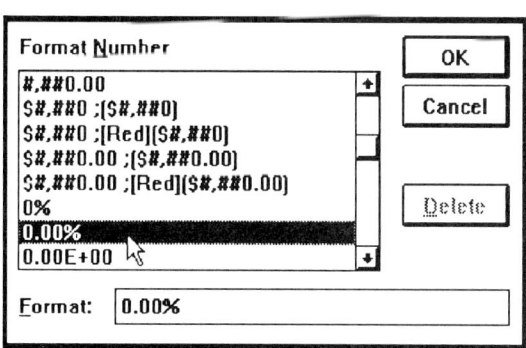

4. Drag across one of the decimal zeros and press (DEL). You have created a new format, as shown here:

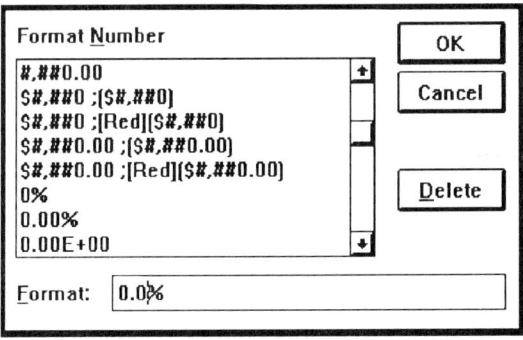

5. Click on OK. The Format Number dialog box closes and the percent growth numbers in column H are formatted as shown in Figure 6-5.

**FIGURE 6-5** Growth percentages formatted with a single decimal place

The new percent format you created is an additional format that is available on this worksheet. It does not replace the original format you used to create the new one.

6. Click just under the upward pointing vertical scroll arrow and then drag down column C from C3 through C5. The upper-left corner of your screen should look like this:

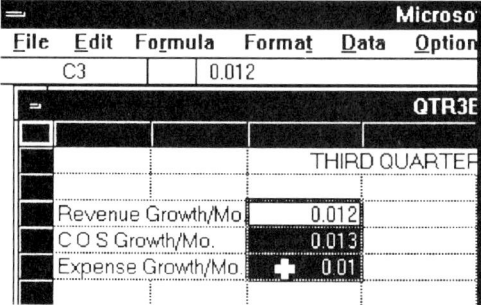

7. Click on the Format menu and the Number option. The Format Number dialog box opens.

8. Click twice on the vertical scroll bar just above the downward pointing scroll arrow. The new single decimal place percent format should appear.

9. Double-click on the new format. The three growth assumptions are formatted, as shown here:

## Adding Dollar Signs

To set off the total lines from the rest of the budget, you can format them as currency, which places a dollar sign in front of each number. There are four total lines: Total Revenue, Gross Income, Total Expenses, and Net Income. Use these instructions to format the first of the lines:

1. Drag across C14 through G14. The two quarterly and three monthly totals are highlighted.

2. Click on the Format menu and the Number option. The Format Number dialog box opens.

3. Double-click on the sixth format, the first with a dollar sign, as shown here:

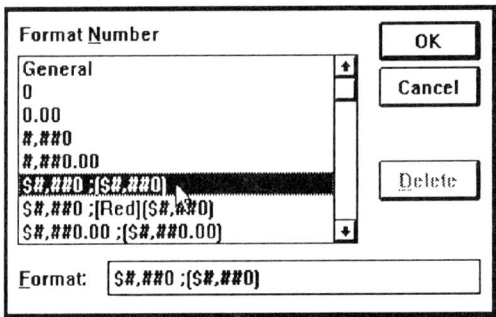

The Total Revenue amounts are now formatted with dollar signs. Use a similar procedure to format the Gross Income amounts in row 18, Total Expense amounts in row 25, and Net Income amounts in row 27 (rows 25 and 27 can be done together by dragging C25:G27, since row 26 is blank). When you are done your screen should look like the one in Figure 6-6.

|   | A | B | C | D | E | F | G | H |
|---|---|---|---|---|---|---|---|---|
| 7 |   |   | Second |   |   |   | Third | Percent |
| 8 |   |   | Quarter | July | August | Sept. | Quarter | Growth |
| 10 | REVENUE |   |   |   |   |   |   |   |
| 11 |   | Forms |   | 87,000 | 29,348 | 29,700 | 30,057 | 89,105 | 2.4% |
| 12 |   | Supplies | 147,300 | 49,689 | 50,285 | 50,899 | 150,864 | 2.4% |
| 13 |   |   |   |   |   |   |   |   |
| 14 | Total Revenue |   | $234,300 | $79,037 | $79,986 | $80,945 | $239,968 | 2.4% |
| 15 |   |   |   |   |   |   |   |   |
| 16 | COST OF SALES |   | 135,894 | 45,887 | 46,483 | 47,088 | 139,458 | 2.6% |
| 17 |   |   |   |   |   |   |   |   |
| 18 | GROSS INCOME |   | $98,406 | $33,150 | $33,502 | $33,858 | $100,510 | 2.1% |
| 19 |   |   |   |   |   |   |   |   |
| 20 | EXPENSES |   |   |   |   |   |   |   |
| 21 |   | Salaries |   | 24,450 | 8,232 | 8,314 | 8,397 | 24,942 | 2.0% |
| 22 |   | P/R Taxes | 2,322 | 782 | 790 | 797 | 2,369 | 2.0% |
| 23 |   | Other Expenses | 14,760 | 4,969 | 5,019 | 5,069 | 15,057 | 2.0% |
| 24 |   |   |   |   |   |   |   |   |
| 25 | Total Expenses |   | $41,532 | $13,382 | $14,122 | $14,263 | $42,368 | 2.0% |
| 26 |   |   |   |   |   |   |   |   |
| 27 | Net Income |   | $56,874 | $19,168 | $19,380 | $19,594 | $58,142 | 2.2% |

**FIGURE 6-6** Totals formatted as currency

## Centering Headings

The final item of detail formatting that you need to do is to center each of the column headings within their columns. Remember from Chapter 3 that Excel automatically left aligns text. Unless you or someone else changed your third quarter budget, all of the headings are left aligned.

Centering the column headings makes them look better and is easy to do with the Format Alignment option. Use it now to center the column headings:

1. Drag across C7 through H8.

2. Click on the Format menu and the Alignment option. The Format Alignment dialog box opens, as shown here:

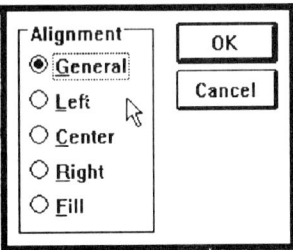

3. Double-click on the Center option. The dialog box closes and the headings are centered, as shown here:

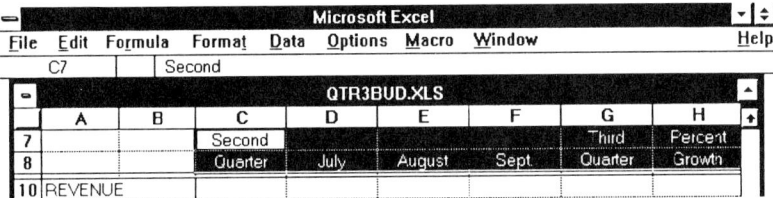

## CHANGING THE LAYOUT

Now you can make some changes to the worksheet. The largest change is deleting column B. To facilitate that, you move the assumptions over one column. Then you widen column A, narrow column H, and recenter the title. To make the formulas more understandable, you add some notes to them. Finally, you erase the previous month in preparation for the next quarter, and then remembering that you have not printed the worksheet yet, you undo the erasure.

## Moving Formulas

You need to move the growth assumptions from column C to column D so the assumption labels still have enough room when column B is deleted. When the contents of a cell are moved, any formula that refers to that cell is changed to reflect the move, even if it has an absolute reference. This gives you significant flexibility.

1. Click on the vertical scroll bar below the upward pointing arrow and drag C3 through C5. The assumptions are highlighted.

2. Click on the Edit menu and the Cut option. A blinking marquee appears around C3:C5.

3. Click on D3 and press (ENTER). The assumptions are moved.

4. Click on D11 to look at the formula.

The reference to the assumption in the formula in D11 used to be $C$3. It has now changed to $D$3, as shown here:

## Deleting a Column

Column B of the third quarter budget was used to provide room for the row labels without changing the column width. Now that you can change the column width, there is no longer a reason to keep column B. Using these instructions, delete column B:

1. Drag down column B from B1 through B27.

2. Click on the Edit menu and the Delete option. The Edit Delete dialog box opens and gives you the choice of shifting cells either left (the default) or up, as shown here:

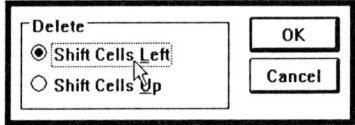

3. Click on OK since the default, Shift Cells Left, has the effect of deleting a column.

As a result of the column being deleted, the remaining columns to the right of the deleted column are relettered, as shown in Figure 6-7. Also, all formulas are revised accordingly. Look at several formulas that used to refer to the old column C, and you see they now refer to column B.

## Adjusting Individual Column Width

Now that column B is gone, you need to widen column A so you can read the row labels. Do that by following these steps:

1. Place the mouse pointer in the column heading, just underneath the worksheet title bar, at the intersection of columns A and B.

The mouse pointer turns into a two-headed arrow with a line in the middle, as shown here:

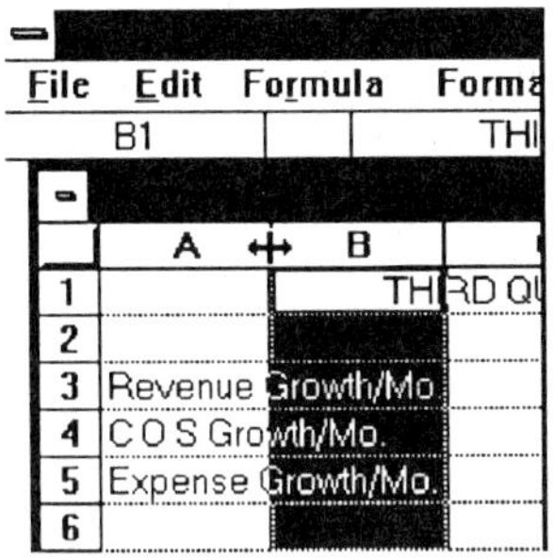

2. Drag the column intersection to the right until you are over the intersection of columns B and C. In other words, you are making column A about equal to the sum of the old columns A

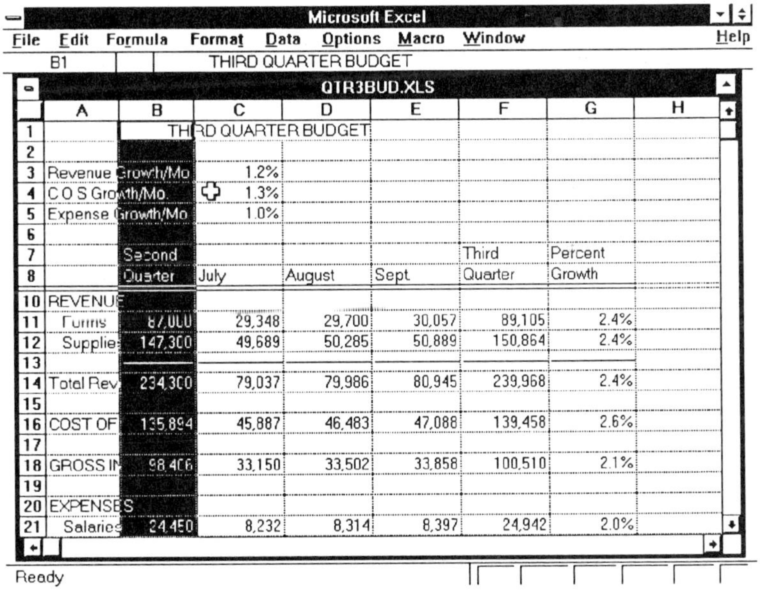

**FIGURE 6-7** Effects of deleting the original column B

and B. (If you do this via the Format Column Width dialog box, this is a width of 17.57.)

The second column sizing you want to do is narrowing the percentage growth column to about seven characters.

3. Place the mouse pointer in the column heading at the intersection of columns G and H.

4. Drag the column intersection to the left until you are in the middle of the "n" in "Percent."

If you wish, click on column G and then open the Column Width dialog box from the Format menu and look at the column width. It should be about 7. Your worksheet should look like that shown in Figure 6-8.

## Recentering the Title

As a result of the deletion of column B and the column width adjustments, the title is no longer centered on the worksheet. Do that next with these instructions:

1. Click on B1. The active cell moves to B1.

2. Click in the edit area, to the left of the word "THIRD."

3. Press (SPACEBAR) six times and then press (ENTER). The title moves to the right enough to approximately center it.

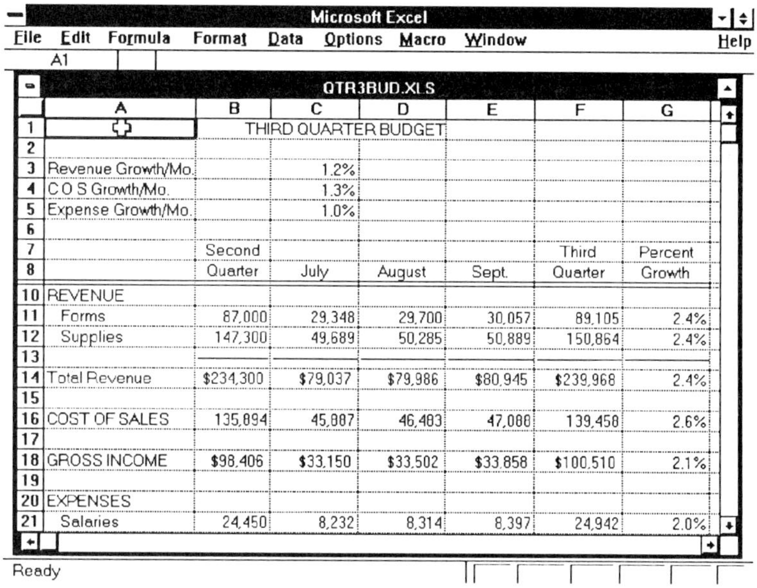

**FIGURE 6-8** Completed column resizing

## Adding Notes to Cells

After a period of time, it is sometimes difficult to remember why you built a formula the way you did or who gave you a certain figure. This problem becomes doubly difficult if you give your worksheet to someone else to use. Excel has a feature that allows you to add notes to cells to explain their contents. Use this feature with the following steps to add several notes to your worksheet:

1. Click on C11. The active cell moves to C11.

2. Click on the Formula menu and the Note option. The Cell Note dialog box opens, as shown here:

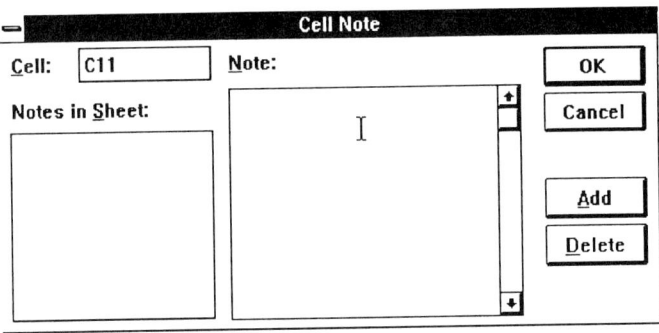

3. Type **Previous Quarter / 3 * ( 1 + Growth Rate )** and press (ENTER). This note is added to cell C11.

4. Click on C3. The active cell moves to C3.

5. Click on the Formula menu and the Note option. The Cell Note dialog box opens.

6. Type **From George Brown** and press (ENTER). This note is added to cell C3.

You can read a note by moving the active cell to a cell with a note and opening the Cell Note dialog box from the Formula menu or opening the Information window from the Window menu. You can also print notes by selecting the appropriate option in the Page Setup dialog box from the File menu.

## Erasing a Range

The third quarter budget is now complete. You can turn it into another quarter's budget by changing the previous quarter's actuals and growth rates. All the formulas are based on those two sets of numbers. A simple way to change the actuals is to erase them and enter new ones. Use the following steps to save the worksheet twice, once under its current name and once under a name for the new quarter. Then erase the second quarter actuals.

1. Click on the File menu and the Save option. The worksheet is saved under its current name, QTR3BUD.XLS.

2. Click on the File menu and the Save As option, type **qtrbud**, and press (ENTER). The worksheet is saved again under the name QTRBUD.XLS.

3. Drag down column B from B11 through B27. The second quarter actuals are highlighted.

4. Press (DEL). The Edit Clear dialog box opens and the Formulas option is selected. This, remember, is synonymous with the cell contents, which is what you want to erase or clear.

5. Click on OK. The second quarter actuals disappear, as shown in Figure 6-9.

Notice that most of the formulas that depended on the second quarter actuals have changed to 0. The exception is the percentage growth amounts, which changed to #DIV/0!, indicating you are trying to divide by zero. All of the formulas, including the percents, will change back to legitimate values as soon as you enter a new set of actuals. However, don't do that yet.

# Using Undo

We forgot to print the worksheet before erasing column B. Luckily, Excel has a feature that can restore the column, as long as you have done nothing since you erased it.

1. Press (ALT+BACKSPACE) (Undo) now. Your worksheet should be restored to the way it was before you erased column B.

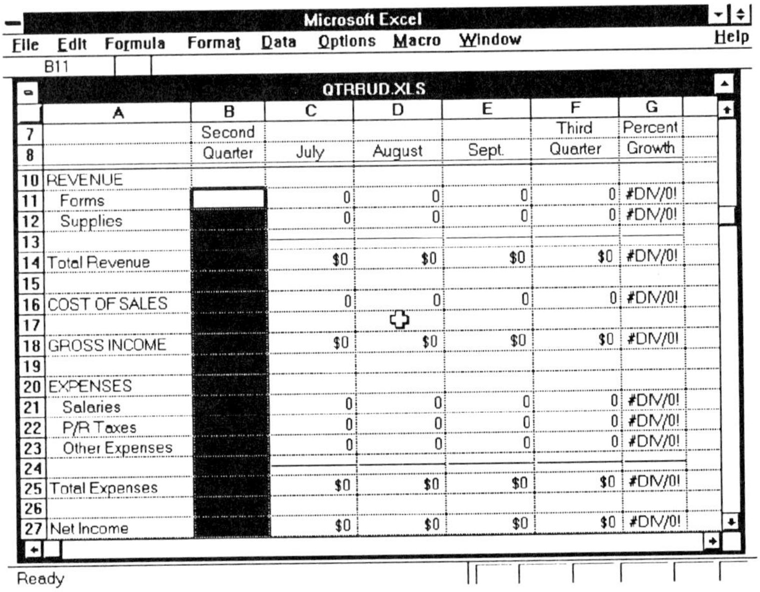

**FIGURE 6-9** Second quarter actuals erased

Undo is a life-saver, as you can see. It even restores a full worksheet erase. The key is to use it immediately after making a mistake. If you do anything that causes Excel to leave ready mode, Undo undoes only to that point. Note that you can choose Undo from the Edit menu as well as use the shortcut (ALT+BACKSPACE).

If, for some reason, your worksheet is not restored, restore it from disk with this instruction.

2. Click on the File menu and the Open option, type **qtr3bud**, and press (ENTER). Your worksheet is now restored to its original condition.

# PRINTING THE WORKSHEET

So far you have only seen your budget results on the screen. That may give you the information you need, but it does not allow you to share it easily with others—for that you must print the budget. To print you must give Excel some information about what and how to print. In other words, you must set some parameters for Excel to use while printing. Once you have set the parameters, you can do the actual printing. The options for both setting parameters and doing the printing are contained on a couple of menus and several dialog boxes, which are discussed in the next several sections. Begin the printing process by determining the area to be printed and by entering the settings on the Page Setup dialog box.

## Setting the Parameters

If you specified your printer correctly when you installed Excel, the only required parameter for printing is the range on the worksheet that you want to print. To give the printed output the same polish you did to the screen image you can add a heading and check the page margins and length. Excel has a number of other parameters that can be set, but these are the ones most people use.

**IDENTIFYING THE PRINT RANGE** The most important information that Excel needs is what to print. What range on the worksheet do you wish printed? In the current example you want to print the entire worksheet— everything you have done on the third quarter budget. Use these steps to specify the range representing the current worksheet:

1. Click on the vertical scroll bar to see the top of the worksheet.

2. Drag from A1 through G27 to highlight the entire worksheet.

3. Drag on the Options menu to highlight Set Print Area option. Your screen should look like Figure 6-10 while the Options menu is open.

**SETTING UP A PRINTED PAGE** Use the Page Setup dialog box to specify the major facets of the page to be printed. Through this dialog box you can enter a header and/or footer to be printed on the page, set the page margins, and turn the row and column headings and gridlines on or off. Open that dialog box now by

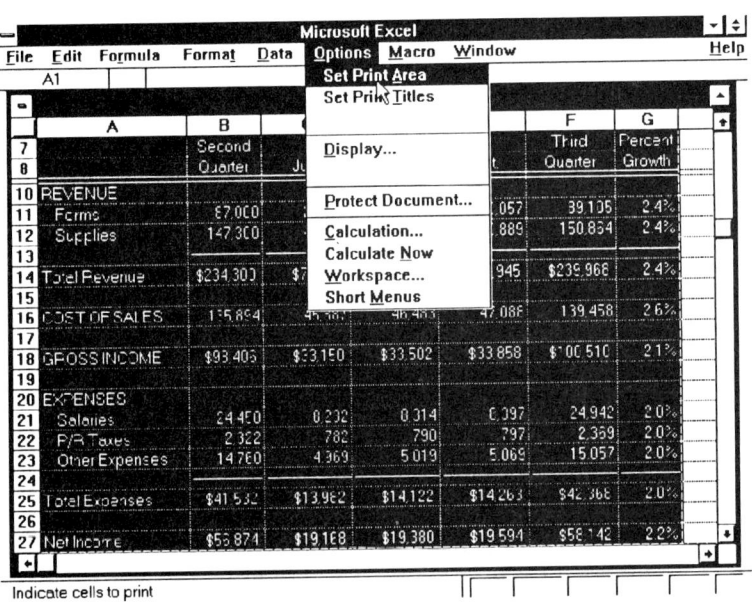

**FIGURE 6-10** Highlighting the print range

clicking on the File menu and the Page Setup option. The Page Setup dialog box opens, as shown here:

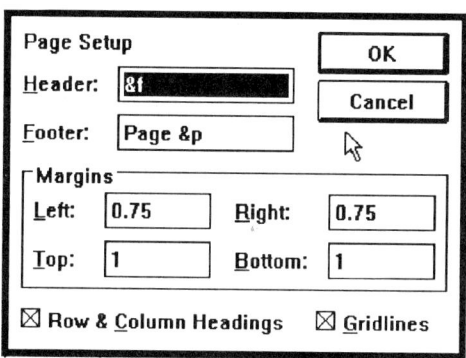

The next two sections examine the areas of this dialog box.

***Entering a Heading*** A *header* or heading is a line of text that is added to the top of every printed page. It often contains a page number, the date of printing, and a descriptive line of text (like a company name). A *footer* is a line of text added to the bottom of every printed page. Excel provides several codes that you can include in either a header or footer to specify the alignment, use of bold or italic fonts, and inclusion of such things as the date and page number. These codes and their function are listed here:

| Codes | Function |
|---|---|
| &b | Emboldens the header or footer segment |
| &c | Centers a header or footer segment |
| &d | Prints the date maintained in your computer |
| &f | Prints the filename of the worksheet, chart, or macro sheet |
| &l | Left aligns a header or footer segment |
| &p | Prints the current page number |

| Codes | Function |
|---|---|
| &p+*number* | Prints the page number after adding *number* to it. |
| &p-*number* | Prints the page number after subtracting *number* from it. |
| &r | Right aligns a header or footer segment |
| &t | Prints the time maintained in your computer |
| && | Prints a single & |

A header or footer can have up to three segments: a left-aligned segment, a centered segment, and a right-aligned segment. Each of these segments is identified by the codes to the left of the segment, and any formatting (bold or italic) applies only to that segment. A header or footer can be up to 255 characters long, but all of it prints on a single line. If you have only one segment and do not specify its alignment, it is centered. A header always prints on the first line of a page, approximately a half inch from the top, independent of the top margin. A footer always prints on the last line of a page, approximately a half inch above the bottom, independent of the bottom margin. Headers and footers also have a fixed 0.75-inch margin on the left and right, independent of the left and right margin you set in the Page Setup dialog box.

Add a header containing the date, company name, and page number to the printout of the Third Quarter Budget worksheet with the following steps:

1. Press (DEL) to delete the standard header, which contains only the code for the filename.

2. Type **&l&d&c&bMORNINGSIDE SPECIALITIES&r Page &p**. This generates a heading with the current date left aligned, a bold company name centered, and a page number right aligned:

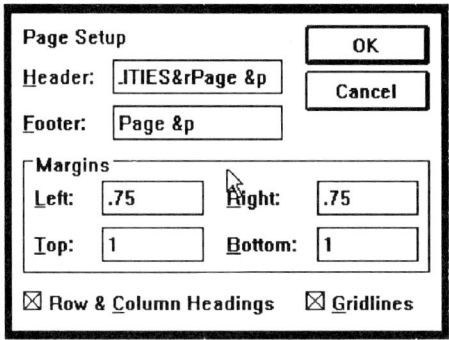

3. Press (TAB) and press (DEL). The standard footer, which contains the page number, is deleted.

***Setting the Margins*** Margins are the distances in inches from the edge of the page to the printed data or graph on four sides: top, bottom, left, and right. Figure 6-11 shows the four margins and their relationship to the header, footer, and page length.

The maximum width of a printed line or a graph is determined by subtracting the left margin and right margin from the page width. For example, using the default margins of 0.75-inch for the left margin and 0.75-inch for the right margin, you can print a line or graph that is 7 inches wide on a normal 8.5 x 11-inch page.

Set the margins now for the third quarter budget with the following steps:

1. Press (TAB). The Left margin text box is highlighted.

2. Type **1.1** and press (TAB). The left margin is set to 1.1 inches, and the highlight moves to the Right margin text box.

3. Type **1.1** and press (TAB). The right margin is set to 1.1 inches, and the highlight moves to the Top margin text box.

4. Type **2.5** and press (TAB). The top margin is set to 2.5 inches, and the highlight moves to the Bottom margin text box.

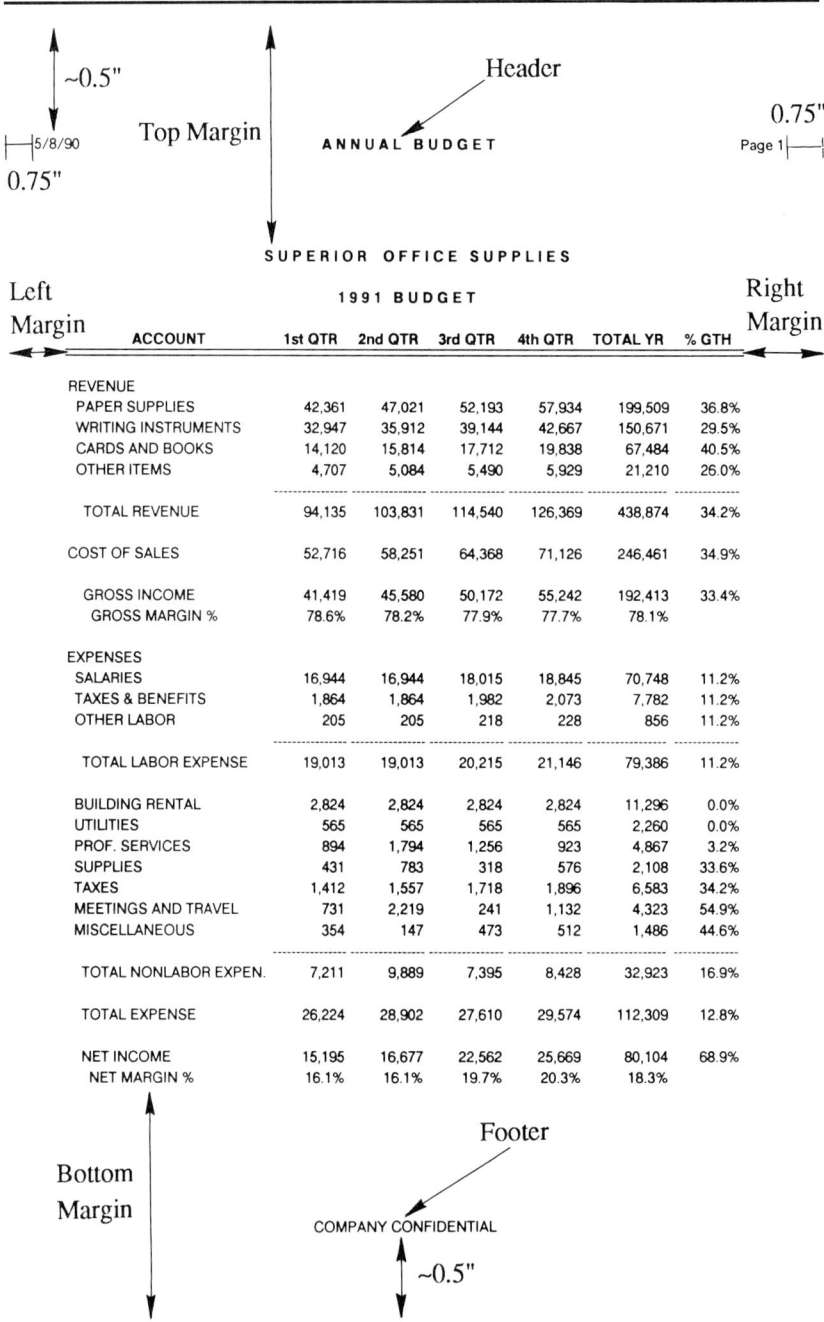

**FIGURE 6-11** Margins and a printed page

5. Type **2.5**. The bottom margin is set to 2.5 inches. Your Page Setup dialog box should look like this:

```
Page Setup
Header:  &l&d&c&bMORNI           OK
Footer:                          Cancel
┌Margins─────────────────────────────┐
│ Left:  1.1      Right:  1.1        │
│ Top:   2.5      Bottom: 2.5        │
└────────────────────────────────────┘
  ☒ Row & Column Headings    ☒ Gridlines
```

At the bottom of the dialog box are two check boxes, currently checked, that control whether the row and column headings (A, B, C, and so on across the columns and 1, 2, 3, and so on down the rows) or the gridlines are printed. If you do not want them on your output, click on the check boxes to turn them off.

6. Press (**ENTER**) to close the dialog box and return to the worksheet.

The determination of where to set the margins is almost always a guess the first time you print a worksheet. As soon as you print the worksheet you can tell how to correct them, so it is not worth much effort on the first pass. Just make a quick guess and then come back and correct the margins after seeing the results.

## Doing the Printing

The actual printing is anticlimactic after setting up the page, but you still must perform several steps, such as readying your printer, setting some final printing parameters, and finally telling Excel to print.

The steps to prepare your printer depend on the printer you are using. All printers must be turned on and placed on-line. In most printers the paper must be aligned so the upper-left corner is correctly positioned. Also, your printer must be correctly cabled to your computer. Finally, you should have installed your printer with the Windows Setup program or by using the Windows Control Panel. (If you do not know whether your printer is installed correctly, try printing. If it works, you have an affirmative answer.) If your printer is not installed, see the section on installing it in Appendix A. Take whatever other steps are necessary to ensure that your printer is ready to print.

Once your printer is ready, you start printing with the Print option from the File menu. The Print option does not begin the printing directly but rather opens another dialog box that asks you several more questions. Look at that dialog box next and then actually do the printing.

1. Click on the File menu and the Print option. The Print dialog box opens, as shown in Figure 6-12.

Figure 6-12 shows the Print dialog box for the HP LaserJet printer. If you are using a different printer, your dialog box may be slightly different but should have most of the options shown. Among these are the ability to specify the number of copies you want, to print all or only selected pages, to preview the output on your screen, and to print just the worksheet, just notes, or both. Look at the last two of these options.

2. Click on the Preview check box, click on the Both option button, and click on OK. The worksheet and dialog box clear

Enhancing A Worksheet 219

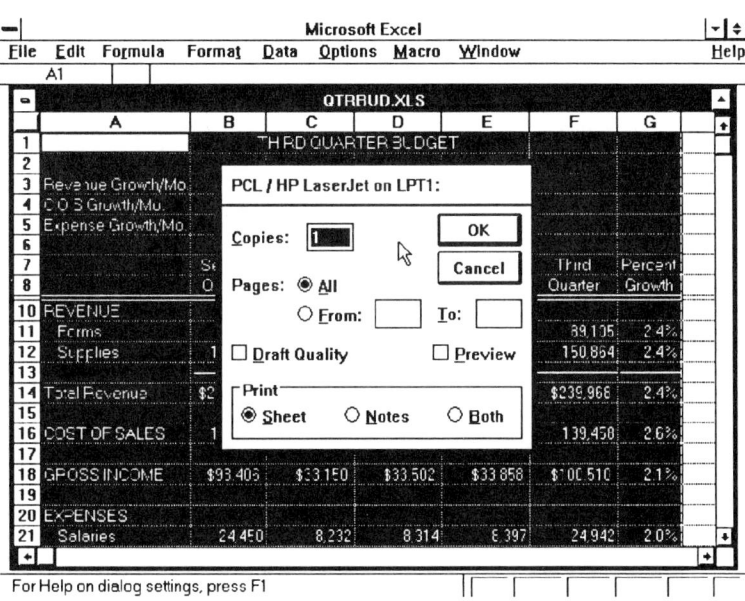

**FIGURE 6-12** Print dialog box

from your screen and a small representation of the printed worksheet appears, as shown in Figure 6-13.

On most displays you cannot easily read the image on the preview screen, but you can tell a lot about placement on the page and how good a guess you made on the margins. You can also zoom in and see a particular area. Do that next.

3. Move the mouse pointer, which you notice has become a magnifying glass, to the approximate center of the worksheet

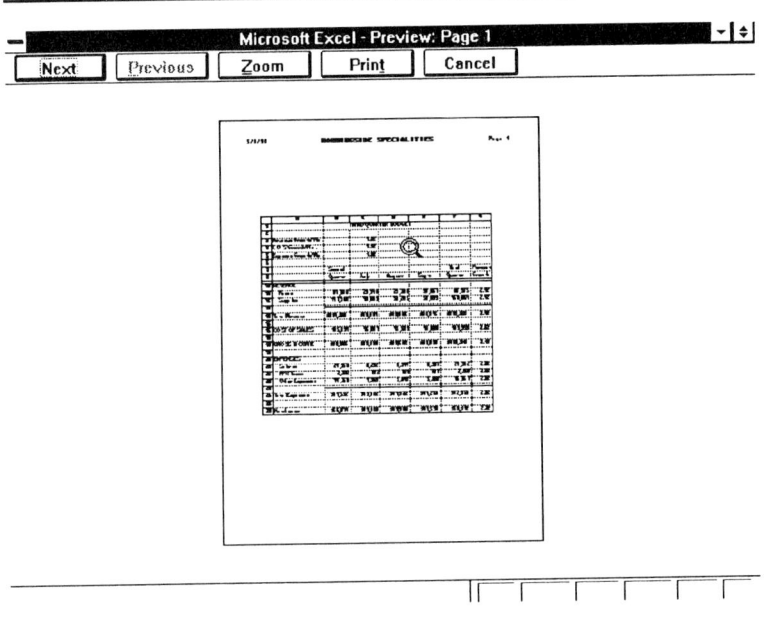

**FIGURE 6-13**  Preview of the printed worksheet

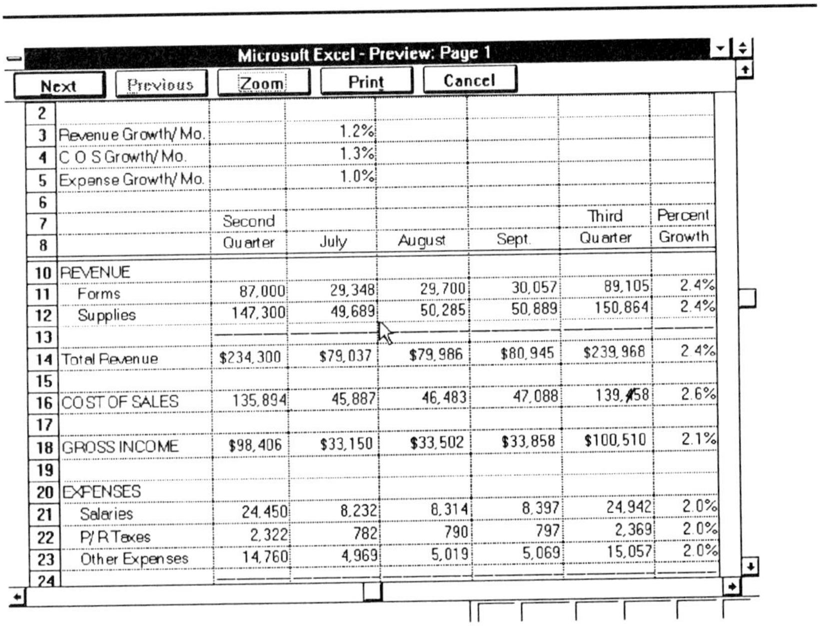

**FIGURE 6-14**  Preview zoomed in on the center

and click. The image expands to clearly show the center of the worksheet, as you can see in Figure 6-14.

4. Use the horizontal and vertical scroll bars to look around the worksheet and the header.

5. Click on the Next command button at the top of the window. The two notes you entered appear, as shown here:

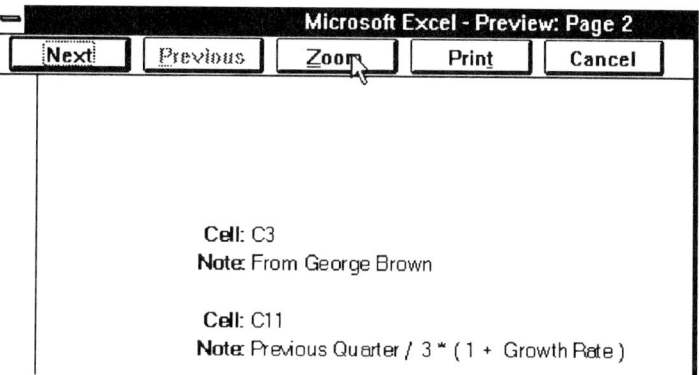

6. Finally, click on the Print command button to do the actual printing. Your final printed output should look like Figure 6-15.

7. If you want to stop printing once you have started, click on the Cancel button in the Printing information box, as shown here:

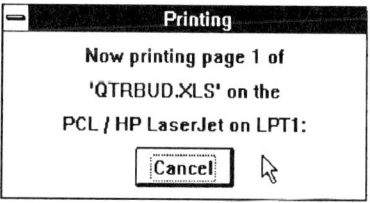

When you tell Excel to print, it creates a print job in memory, containing all of the information to be printed, and sends it to the Windows Print Manager. You can then go back to work while, in the background, the Print Manager is actually doing the printing.

|   | A | B | C | D | E | F | G |
|---|---|---|---|---|---|---|---|
| 1 |   |   | THIRD QUARTER BUDGET |   |   |   |   |
| 2 |   |   |   |   |   |   |   |
| 3 | Revenue Growth/Mo. |   | 1.2% |   |   |   |   |
| 4 | C O S Growth/Mo. |   | 1.3% |   |   |   |   |
| 5 | Expense Growth/Mo. |   | 1.0% |   |   |   |   |
| 6 |   |   |   |   |   |   |   |
| 7 |   |   | Second |   |   |   | Third | Percent |
| 8 |   |   | Quarter | July | August | Sept. | Quarter | Growth |
| 10 | REVENUE |   |   |   |   |   |   |
| 11 | Forms | 87,000 | 29,348 | 29,700 | 30,057 | 89,105 | 2.4% |
| 12 | Supplies | 147,300 | 49,689 | 50,285 | 50,889 | 150,864 | 2.4% |
| 13 |   | ---------- | ---------- | ---------- | ---------- | ---------- |   |
| 14 | Total Revenue | $234,300 | $79,037 | $79,986 | $80,945 | $239,968 | 2.4% |
| 15 |   |   |   |   |   |   |   |
| 16 | COST OF SALES | 135,894 | 45,887 | 46,483 | 47,088 | 139,458 | 2.6% |
| 17 |   |   |   |   |   |   |   |
| 18 | GROSS INCOME | $98,406 | $33,150 | $33,502 | $33,858 | $100,510 | 2.1% |
| 19 |   |   |   |   |   |   |   |
| 20 | EXPENSES |   |   |   |   |   |   |
| 21 | Salaries | 24,450 | 8,232 | 8,314 | 8,397 | 24,942 | 2.0% |
| 22 | P/R Taxes | 2,322 | 782 | 790 | 797 | 2,369 | 2.0% |
| 23 | Other Expenses | 14,760 | 4,969 | 5,019 | 5,069 | 15,057 | 2.0% |
| 24 |   | ---------- | ---------- | ---------- | ---------- | ---------- |   |
| 25 | Total Expenses | $41,532 | $13,982 | $14,122 | $14,263 | $42,368 | 2.0% |
| 26 |   |   |   |   |   |   |   |
| 27 | Net Income | $56,874 | $19,168 | $19,380 | $19,594 | $58,142 | 2.2% |

**FIGURE 6-15** Printed worksheet

You can have several print jobs in memory waiting to be printed. The Print Manager gives you the ability to cancel a job after it has left Excel and to rearrange the priority of the jobs waiting to be printed. For a small worksheet like the one you built here, the advantage of the Print Manager is not very evident, but with a large multipage print job it is a significant benefit.

## Trial and Error

Your printout probably did not come out exactly the way you wanted it—or maybe it did not come out at all. Using a printer is almost always a trial-and-error process. Be persistent, and you should get it to work. To cure several types of problems, try the following ideas. (If you leave Excel, choose Save from the File menu to save the worksheet on disk before leaving.)

If you could not print at all, try these steps:

1. Start at the printer end. Is the printer plugged in, turned on, and set on-line? Does it have adequate paper and a ribbon? Is there a cable connecting the printer to the computer?

2. Look at the computer. To which port is the printer connected (LPT1, COM1, COM2)? Do you need a MODE command in your AUTOEXEC.BAT file (see your operating system manuals)? Are any other devices interfering with the printer port (for example, are both a printer and a modem connected to the same port)?

3. Open the Windows Control Panel in the Main group. Double-click on Printers, and make sure your printer name is correctly specified and that the port to which it is connected is also correct.

4. Look at the print settings you have specified. Go through the steps of setting the parameters again, checking each against the figures and illustrations in this book.

If the budget printed but it is not the way you want it, try these steps:

5. Adjust the print settings to fit your particular situation. For example, if the margins are not right, change them until the worksheet is located on the page as shown in Figure 6-15.

6. Make sure your printer is not set through its console for some particular type of printing (for example, compressed printing when you want to print at full size).

## Saving the Worksheet

When you are satisfied with your printout, you need to resave the worksheet to capture the print settings you entered.

1. Click on the File menu and the Save option.

## MAKING A TEMPLATE

After building the third quarter budget, you can use it for the fourth quarter and other future quarters. None of the formulas need to be changed. You must change only the titles and the previous quarter actuals. When you make this worksheet more general-purpose, it becomes a *template* for use in any quarter. The remainder of the chapter discusses how this is done.

## Changing Titles

To make the titles general-purpose, you need to remove the references to the third quarter. Use the following instructions to edit the titles to make them generic:

Click on B1. The active cell moves to the worksheet title.

2. Drag across the word "THIRD" in the edit area and press (DEL). The word "THIRD" is removed.

3. Press the spacebar four times to recenter the title.

4. Click immediately after the word "QUARTER."

5. Type **LY** and press (ENTER). "QUARTER" becomes "QUARTERLY," and the corrected title is returned to the worksheet.

6. Click on B7. The active cell moves to the first column heading.

7. Type **Previous** and press (ENTER). "Second" is changed to "Previous," which is centered in the column.

8. Press (DOWN ARROW) and (RIGHT ARROW). The active cell moves to the July column heading.

9. Type **Month 1** and press (ENTER). "July" is changed to "Month 1" and centered in the column.

In a similar manner, change the second and third month and the third quarter total, so the column headings are as shown here:

|   | A | B | C | D | E | F | G |
|---|---|---|---|---|---|---|---|
| 1 |   |   | QUARTERLY BUDGET |   |   |   |   |
| 2 |   |   |   |   |   |   |   |
| 3 | Revenue Growth/Mo. |   | 1.2% |   |   |   |   |
| 4 | C O S Growth/Mo. |   | 1.3% |   |   |   |   |
| 5 | Expense Growth/Mo. |   | 1.0% |   |   |   |   |
| 6 |   |   |   |   |   |   |   |
| 7 |   | Previous |   |   |   | Current | Percent |
| 8 |   | Quarter | Month 1 | Month 2 | Month 3 | Quarter | Growth |
| 10 | REVENUE |   |   |   |   |   |   |

## Copying Values—Paste Special

There are several ways to change the previous quarter's actual values. One way is to erase the column and reenter the new numbers. Another way is to either edit or type over the current numbers. A third way is to copy the current quarter's numbers to the previous quarter. These are not actuals *per se*. If you literally copy column F to column B, you would get a set of formulas that did not have meaning. What you want to do is to copy the *values* produced by the formulas in F, but not the formulas themselves. To do this, use Excel's Paste Special command. Follow these steps to see how Paste Special works.

1. Drag on F11 through F27.

2. Click on the Edit menu and the Copy option. A blinking marquee appears around the highlighted cells in column F.

3. Click on the vertical scroll bar above the scroll box, and then click on B11, which you want to be the recipient of the copy.

4. Click on the Edit menu and the Paste Special option. The Paste Special dialog box opens, as shown here:

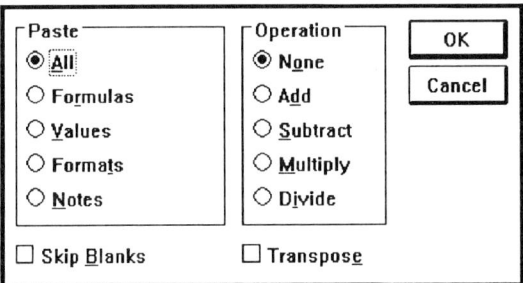

5. Click on Values and OK in the Paste Special dialog box. The dialog box closes. Now only the values in column F are copied to column B. See Figure 6-16 for the result. Note the number in B11.

## Other Modifications

You could make many other changes to this worksheet. You could add an assumption for every account by inserting a new column to the left of column A with the assumptions in it. You could also add more accounts and subtotals of accounts, or you could add more months and quarterly totals for a year. Try these on your own if you like.

|   | A | B | C | D | E | F | G |
|---|---|---|---|---|---|---|---|
| 7 |   | Previous |   |   |   | Current | Percent |
| 8 |   | Quarter | Month 1 | Month 2 | Month 3 | Quarter | Growth |
| 10 | REVENUE |   |   |   |   |   |   |
| 11 | Forms | 89,105 | 30,058 | 30,419 | 30,784 | 91,260 | 2.4% |
| 12 | Supplies | 150,864 | 50,891 | 51,502 | 52,120 | 154,513 | 2.4% |
| 13 |   |   |   |   |   |   |   |
| 14 | Total Revenue | $239,969 | $80,949 | $81,921 | $82,904 | $245,774 | 2.4% |
| 15 |   |   |   |   |   |   |   |
| 16 | COST OF SALES | 139,458 | 47,090 | 47,702 | 48,323 | 143,115 | 2.6% |
| 17 |   |   |   |   |   |   |   |
| 18 | GROSS INCOME | $100,510 | $33,859 | $34,218 | $34,581 | $102,658 | 2.1% |
| 19 |   |   |   |   |   |   |   |
| 20 | EXPENSES |   |   |   |   |   |   |
| 21 | Salaries | 24,942 | 8,397 | 8,481 | 8,566 | 25,444 | 2.0% |
| 22 | P/R Taxes | 2,309 | 797 | 805 | 814 | 2,416 | 2.0% |
| 23 | Other Expenses | 15,057 | 5,069 | 5,120 | 5,171 | 15,360 | 2.0% |
| 24 |   |   |   |   |   |   |   |
| 25 | Total Expenses | $42,363 | $14,264 | $14,407 | $14,551 | $43,221 | 2.0% |
| 26 |   |   |   |   |   |   |   |
| 27 | Net Income | $58,142 | $19,595 | $19,812 | $20,030 | $59,437 | 2.2% |

**FIGURE 6-16** Results of copying values

## Saving and Quitting

The last step prior to leaving Excel is to save your work, even if you just did it a few moments earlier. In this case you want to save the generalized version of the budget. Use these instructions to do that and then leave Excel:

1. Click on the File menu and the Save As option. The Save As dialog box opens and asks you for a filename.

2. Type **qtrbud**, press (ENTER), and click OK. The current worksheet is saved under the name QTRBUD.WK3, replacing the worksheet you saved under that name earlier.

3. Double-click on the Excel and Windows Control-menu boxes and click OK. You leave Excel and Windows and return to the operating system.

# 7

# PRODUCING CHARTS

How a Chart Is Built
Deciding What to Chart
Selecting the Type of Chart
Creating a Line Chart
Building a Pie Chart
Generating a Stacked Column Chart
Leaving Excel

In this chapter you work with the second of Excel's three components: charts. First you look at creating charts in Excel. Then you go over the types of charts that are available and their variations and peculiarities. Finally, you build three types of charts using the data from Chapter 6.

Many people find information in a pictorial form easier to understand than the numbers that generated the picture. Excel charts are pictorial representations of data on the worksheet. They are another way of displaying the results a worksheet produces.

# HOW A CHART IS BUILT

Producing charts in Excel is very simple: You create a range on a worksheet, highlight that range, and tell Excel to create a new chart. This produces a standard chart based on the defaults built into Excel. You can then change any of these defaults and add many special features to customize the chart. Look first at a standard chart and then how to customize it.

## Standard Charts

A standard chart lets you see quickly how data looks when it is plotted and provides a starting point for a customized chart. It is not meant to be a final, presentation-quality chart.

A standard chart is based on a range of data on the worksheet. For Excel to turn this data into a chart, the range must adhere to the following guidelines:

- The highlighted range must be a rectangle, with text labels on the topmost row and/or leftmost column. Otherwise, the range may contain numbers or text, but text is interpreted as zeros.

- Excel defines the first *data series*—a range of numbers on the worksheet that are related *data points* to be plotted—as beginning with the first cell in the upper-left corner of the highlighted range containing a number not formatted as a date and continuing across the rows and columns that are highlighted.

- Excel determines whether more rows or more columns are highlighted and, with the assumption that there will be more data points than data series, makes the larger of the two the data points. So if you highlight six columns and three rows, each column will be a data point (a single number to be plotted) and each row a data series.

- Additional data series can be included in the range by highlighting additional rows or columns, depending on whether you are building a columnwise or rowwise chart. You can have 10 or more data series, but the resulting chart may not be readable.

- If the first column or row of the highlighted range contains labels or date-formatted numbers and/or the cell in the upper-left corner is blank, the first column or row—depending on whether data series are down columns (columnwise) or across rows (rowwise)—is used for the X- or *category axis*.

- The numbers on the Y- or *value axis* are formatted with the same format that has been used with the data points on the worksheet.

- The initial default is to produce a Column or vertical Bar chart. This and other options can be easily changed.

Figure 7-1 contains a range of rowwise data series that fit the guidelines for a standard chart. The topmost row contains date-formatted numbers that are used for the X- or category axis; the next two rows are two data series, each containing four numeric data points used to produce the Column chart shown in the lower part of the figure.

## Customizing Charts

Once you have a standard chart, you can customize it using three special chart menus: Gallery, Chart, and Format, as shown in the menu bar in Figure 7-1. Using these menus you can change the type of chart by choosing from among seven chart types in the Gallery menu; adding titles, arrows, legends, and gridlines from the Chart menu; and applying many formatting features from the Format menu. Almost all charts, both "quick and dirty" charts and presentation-quality charts, require some amount of customiza-

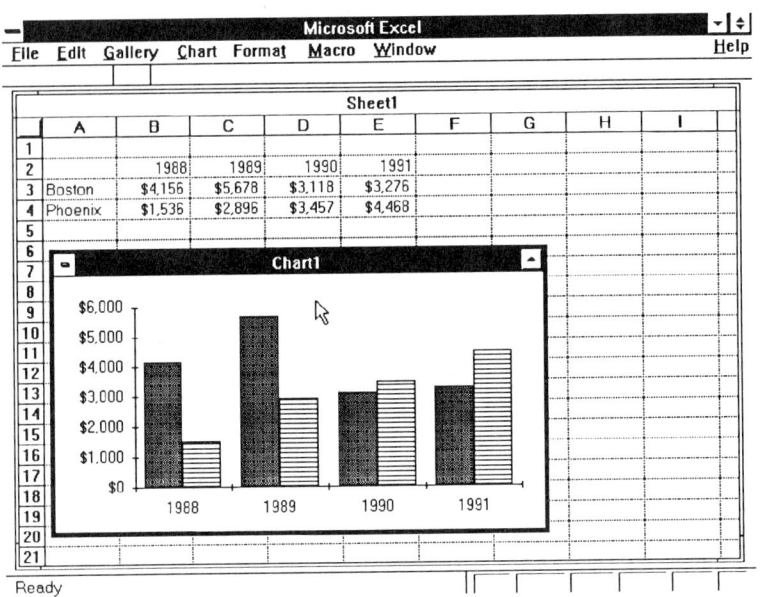

**FIGURE 7-1** Data range and its resulting chart

tion. The rest of this chapter is devoted to the topic of customizing charts.

**THE CHART MENUS** When you create a new chart or load an existing chart from disk, you get a set of chart menus in the Menu bar. Of the eight menus, five—File, Edit, Macro, Window, and Help—are virtually the same as the worksheet menus. The other three—Gallery, Chart, and Format—are either unique or considerably different from the worksheet menus. Briefly look at each of the three different chart menus.

*Gallery Menu* The Gallery menu, shown here, allows you to choose from among seven types of charts and then from between five and eight alternatives of each type.

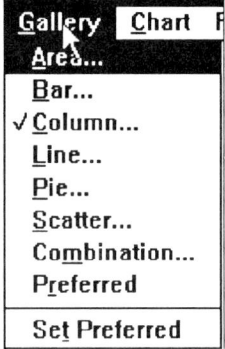

The seven chart types—Area, Bar, Column, Line, Pie, Scatter, and Combination—are discussed in sections that follow. When you select a chart type from the Gallery menu, you get a pictorial dialog box, or gallery, that offers up to eight alternatives of the chart type you picked, as shown here:

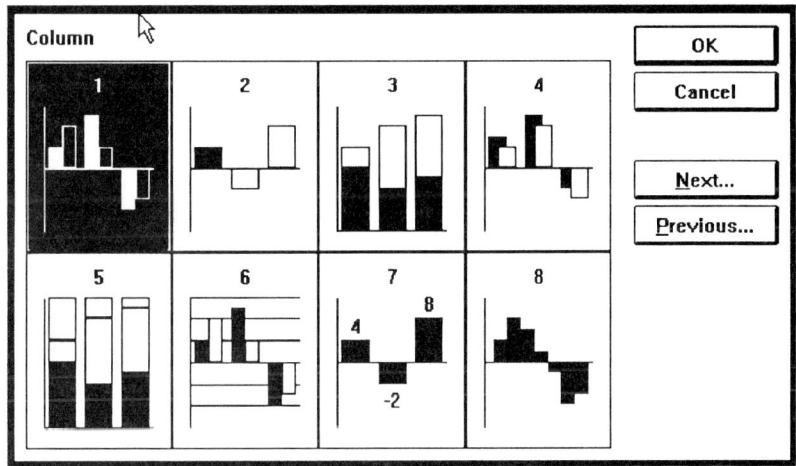

One of the alternatives in the gallery (chart type dialog box) is highlighted (the first alternative in the illustration). This is known as the *preferred alternative,* and the column type of chart is the *preferred type.* From the Gallery menu you can return to the preferred type and alternative with the Preferred option. Also, you can set the preferred type and alternative. This setting, however, is lost when you leave Excel.

*Chart Menu*   The Chart menu, shown here, allows you to make a number of changes and additions to a chart you have created.

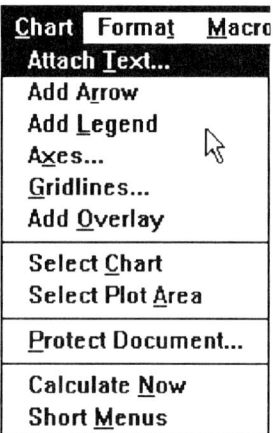

The additions include adding text and titles to many chart elements, adding arrows and gridlines, and adding legends. The changes include turning one or both of the axes on or off, changing the type of gridlines used, and changing the chart into a combination chart by placing half of the data series in an overlay that can be a different chart type. Figure 7-2 shows the addition of a title, arrow, unattached text, gridlines, and legend to the chart shown in Figure 7-1.

From the Chart menu you can also select the active chart or the plot area on the active chart for various formatting functions. You also can protect the chart with a password, recalculate the underlying worksheet and redraw the chart, and change to short or long menus.

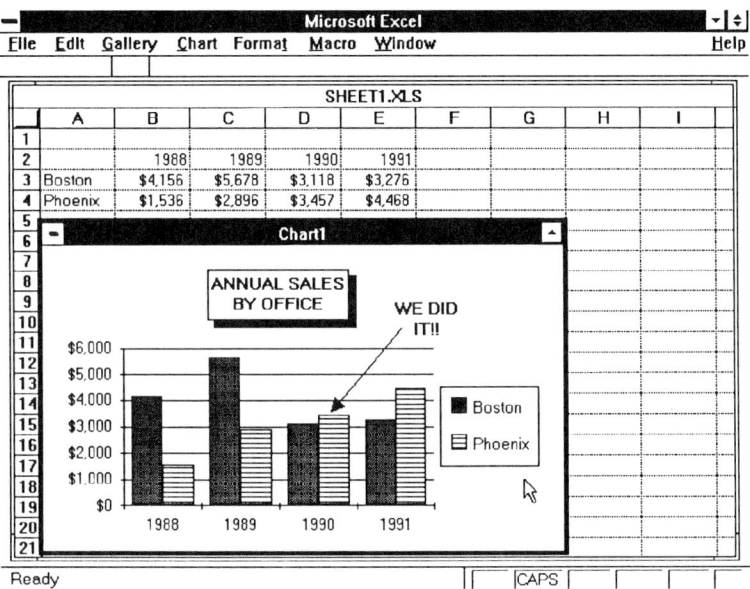

**FIGURE 7-2**   Enhanced chart

*Format Menu*   The Format menu, shown here, allows you to change the patterns, font, color, shading, line width, size, and position of many of the chart elements.

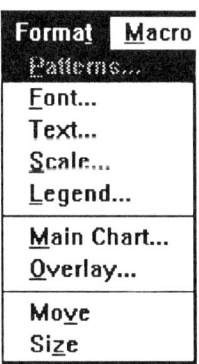

Before using the Format menu, you need to select a chart element that you want to format. Elements include the various titles and text, either of the two scales, any of the data series, legends, the whole chart, and just the plot area. You can select most elements by simply clicking on them (with the keyboard press (SHIFT) and a direction key and cycle through the elements). To select the whole chart or the plot area, you must use the Chart menu or cycle through the elements using (SHIFT) and a direction key until you select them.

When you select a chart element, selection boxes appear around or on either end of the element. For most elements, such as titles, gridlines, and axes, the selection boxes are white or empty. For other elements, such as arrows and unattached text, the selection boxes are black and indicate that the element can be moved and sized with the mouse or the keyboard.

When you select a chart element and open the Format menu, certain options become available, but others do not. What options are available depends on the element. For example, the Patterns, Font, and Text options are available for text elements such as titles. Patterns allows you to change the border line width, style, and color as well as the foreground and background pattern and color. Font allows you to select the typeface, size, style, and color, while Text allows you to adjust the alignment and position of text.

The Scale option allows you to set the minimum, maximum, and major and minor increments as well as the type of scale. The Legend option allows you to position the legend, and the Main Chart and Overlay options allow you to choose the type of chart and some of its characteristics. The Move and Size options are used with those chart elements that can be moved and sized, such as arrows and unattached text, to allow the direction keys to do the work in place of the mouse.

|  | A | B | C | D | E | F | G |
|---|---|---|---|---|---|---|---|
| 7 |  | Second |  |  |  | Third | Percent |
| 8 |  | Quarter | July | August | Sept. | Quarter | Growth |
| 10 | REVENUE |  |  |  |  |  |  |
| 11 | Forms | 87,000 | 29,348 | 29,700 | 30,057 | 89,105 | 2.4% |
| 12 | Supplies | 147,300 | 49,689 | 50,285 | 50,889 | 150,864 | 2.4% |
| 13 |  |  |  |  |  |  |  |
| 14 | Total Revenue | $234,300 | $79,037 | $79,986 | $80,945 | $239,968 | 2.4% |
| 15 |  |  |  |  |  |  |  |
| 16 | COST OF SALES | 135,894 | 45,887 | 46,483 | 47,088 | 139,458 | 2.6% |
| 17 |  |  |  |  |  |  |  |
| 18 | GROSS INCOME | $98,406 | $33,150 | $33,502 | $33,858 | $100,510 | 2.1% |
| 19 |  |  |  |  |  |  |  |
| 20 | EXPENSES |  |  |  |  |  |  |
| 21 | Salaries | 24,450 | 8,232 | 8,314 | 8,397 | 24,942 | 2.0% |
| 22 | P/R Taxes | 2,322 | 782 | 790 | 797 | 2,369 | 2.0% |
| 23 | Other Expenses | 14,760 | 4,969 | 5,019 | 5,069 | 15,057 | 2.0% |
| 24 |  |  |  |  |  |  |  |
| 25 | Total Expenses | $41,532 | $13,982 | $14,122 | $14,263 | $42,368 | 2.0% |
| 26 |  |  |  |  |  |  |  |
| 27 | Net Income | $56,874 | $19,168 | $19,380 | $19,594 | $58,142 | 2.2% |

**FIGURE 7-3**  Third quarter budget from Chapter 6

# DECIDING WHAT TO CHART

The first step in creating a chart is deciding what to chart. This step may also be one of the hardest. It is easy to pick a range of numbers to put on a chart, but does that range or comparison of several ranges tell the story that you believe is in the numbers? Consider the third quarter budget from Chapter 6, shown in Figure 7-3. It has lots of numbers, but which are the most important and which best lend themselves to a chart?

These questions are not easy to answer, and there are probably several substantially different opinions. The best answer comes from asking yourself if the chart tells the story you are trying to tell. In later sections of this chapter, you will build charts based on the third quarter budget. For each, you can decide how well the chart tells the story that is in the numbers.

## SELECTING THE TYPE OF CHART

The type of chart to use is as much a subjective decision as what to chart. The choice depends primarily on what you like, but there are some rules of thumb. The next several sections discuss each of Excel's chart types and when to use them. You also learn what variations are available for each type of chart and how each uses particular options in the chart menus.

### Area Charts

An Area chart shows the magnitude of change over time. It is particularly useful when several components are changing and you are interested in the sum of those components. You can see the change in the individual components as well as the change in the total. For example, in the Area chart shown Figure 7-4, you can see the change in the sales of three products as well as the change in total sales, which is the sum of the three products.

An Area chart is a *Stacked Line chart,* with the area between the lines filled in with color or shading. An Area chart plots one data series above another. For example, if you have two data series in an Area chart, and the first data point of the first series is 50 and the first data point of the second series is 60, the data points would be plotted at 50 and 110. In a normal Line chart, the points would be plotted at 50 and 60. In Figure 7-4, floor units are added to desktop units and laptop units are added to the sum of the first two. The top line on the chart represents total sales, and each layer is that product's share of those sales.

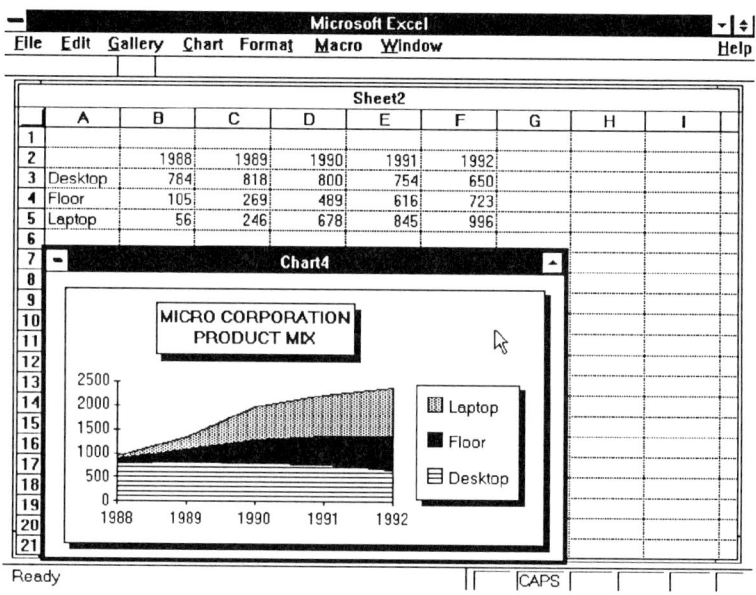

**FIGURE 7-4** Area chart of product sales

## Bar Charts

A Bar chart consists of a series of horizontal bars that allow comparison of the relative size of two or more items generally at one point in time. For example, the Bar chart shown in Figure 7-5 compares sales among offices for one year by presenting a bar for each office's sales. Each bar in a Bar chart is a single data point or number on the worksheet. The set of numbers for a single set of bars is a data series. For example, the Bar chart in Figure 7-5 contains a single data series representing the sales figures for the five offices.

**BAR CHART VARIATIONS** The Bar chart has three primary variations: the Stacked Bar chart, the Clustered Bar chart, and the

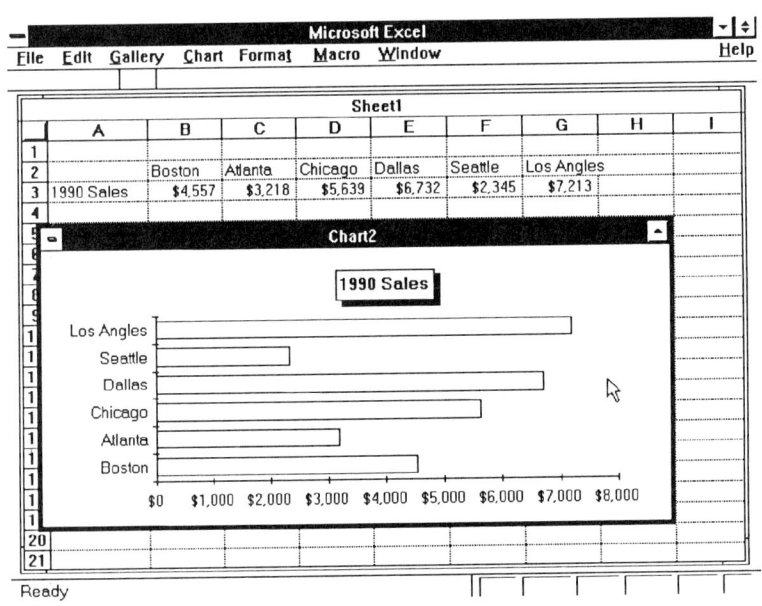

**FIGURE 7-5**  Bar chart of sales by sales office

100% Bar Chart. The Stacked and Clustered Bar charts are similar: In both you use additional data series for either the multiple bars or multiple segments. With three data series and the first or preferred alternative in the Bar chart gallery, you get the Clustered Bar chart shown in Figure 7-6. The same multiple ranges with the third gallery alternative produce the Stacked Bar shown in Figure 7-7. In both cases each of the three regions or offices is contained in a separate data series.

In the Stacked Bar chart, the total length of the bar is the sum of the segments (total company sales, in the example). Therefore, the size of each segment is relative to both the total and to the other segments. In a Clustered Bar chart you can only visually compare the bars; you do not see the total of the bars added together. There are places for both types of charts, but for the example the Stacked Bar is more informative.

Producing Charts 241

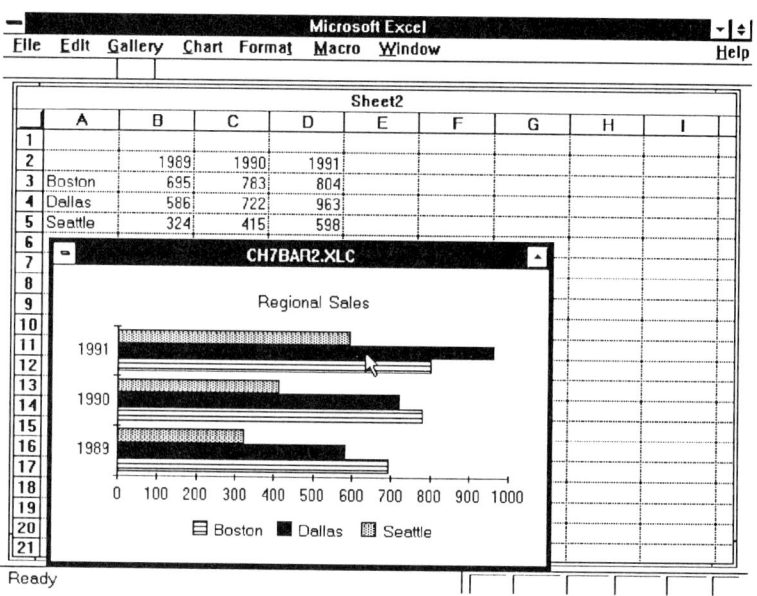

**FIGURE 7-6** Clustered Bar chart of regional sales

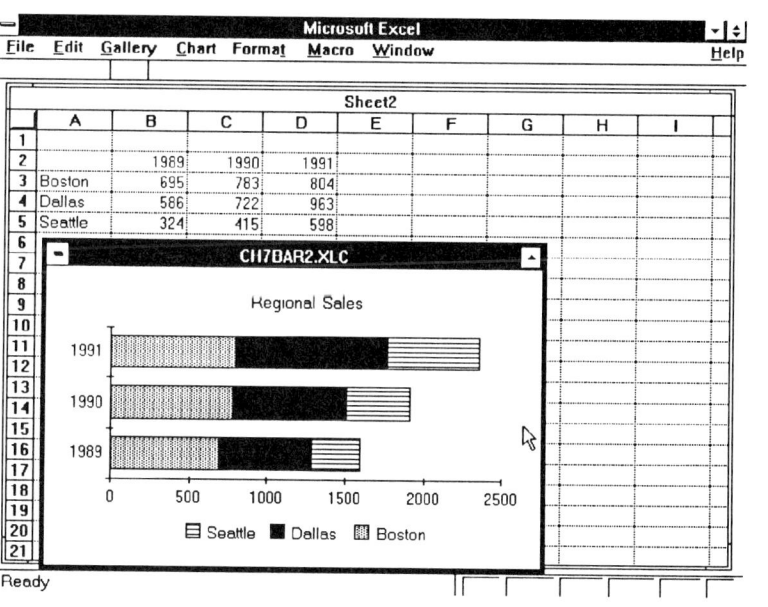

**FIGURE 7-7** Stacked Bar chart of regional sales

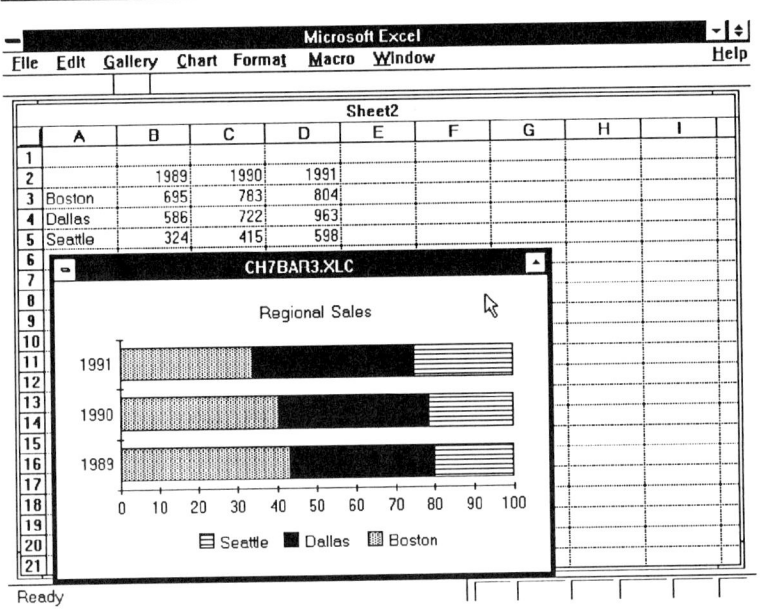

**FIGURE 7-8**   100% Bar chart of regional sales

In the 100% Bar chart, all bars become the same height, representing 100%. The segments then become their percentage of the total instead of their numerical number, as shown in Figure 7-8.

## Column Charts

A Column chart consists of a series of vertical columns that allow comparison of the relative size of two or more items, often over time. For example, the column chart shown in Figure 7-9 compares quarterly sales by presenting a column for each quarter's sales. Each column in a Column chart is a single data point or number on the worksheet. The set of numbers for a single set of columns is a data series. For example, the Column chart in Figure 7-9 contains three data series, each showing the quarterly sales for one office.

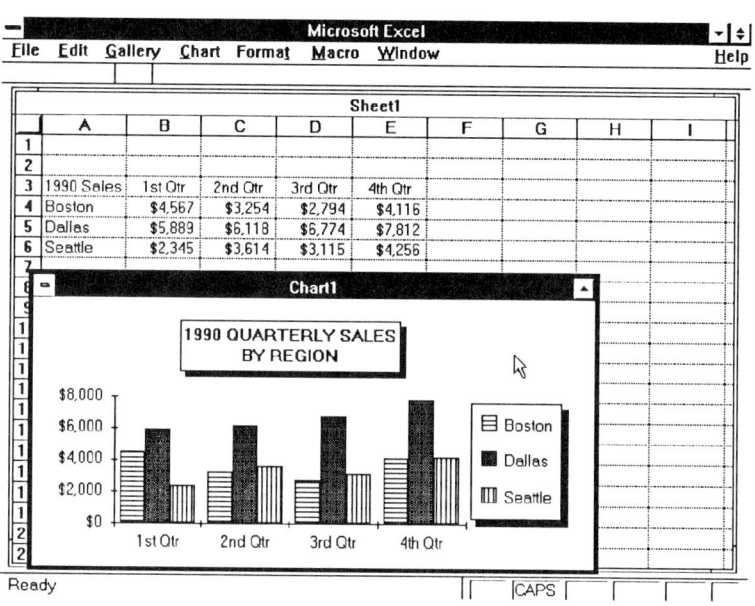

**FIGURE 7-9** Column chart of quarterly sales

Column charts have the same variations as bar charts.

## Combination Charts

A Combination chart, shown in Figure 7-10, combines a Column chart with a Line chart. It is used to compare two types of data. Examples are stock prices versus the volume of stock sold, advertising expenditures versus sales dollars, or maintenance expenditures versus production volume.

A Combination chart is one chart type overlaid on another chart type. The Combination chart gallery includes several variations of Line charts overlying Column charts, Line charts overlying Line charts, and Column charts overlying Area charts. You can create several other combination charts using the Add Overlay option from the Chart menu. In all cases the data series are divided evenly

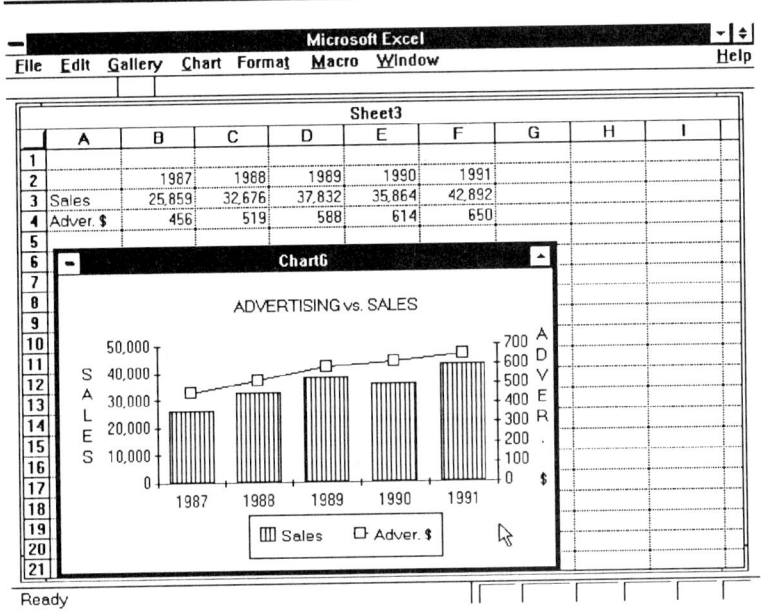

FIGURE 7-10   Combination chart of sales versus advertising

between the two types of charts. If the number of data series are uneven, an extra series is placed on the base chart giving the overlay one less.

## Line Charts

A Line chart is used to show trends over time. For example, the Line chart in Figure 7-11 shows that sales are trending upward while expenses are fairly flat, allowing earnings to follow revenue. With Line charts the eye can make a projection into the future.

In a Line chart, each of the data series is used to produce a line on the chart, with each number in the range producing a data point. There are three data series in Figure 7-11—Sales, Expenses, and Earnings—with 12 data points in each series.

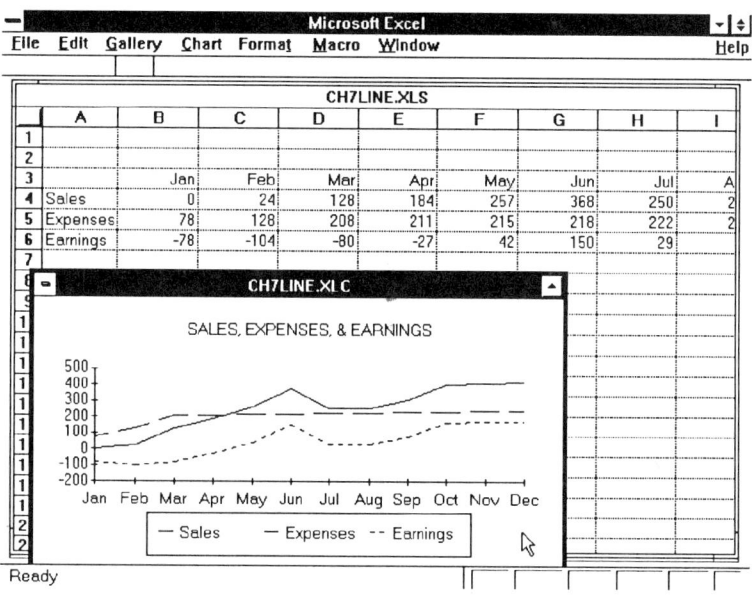

**FIGURE 7-11** Line chart of sales

One of the Line chart gallery alternatives deserves further discussion. This is the Stock Market or High-Low-Close chart.

**STOCK MARKET CHARTS** A Stock Market or High-Low-Close chart is a Line chart with three data series used to display a stock's high, low, and closing prices for a given time period. High-Low-Close charts also work well for commodity prices, currency exchange rates, and temperature and pressure measurements.

Figure 7-12 shows a High-Low-Close chart for stock prices. It contains three data series for the high, low, and closing prices of a stock issue on a given day. The vertical lines are formed by drawing a line between the high and the low data points while the tick mark is the closing price.

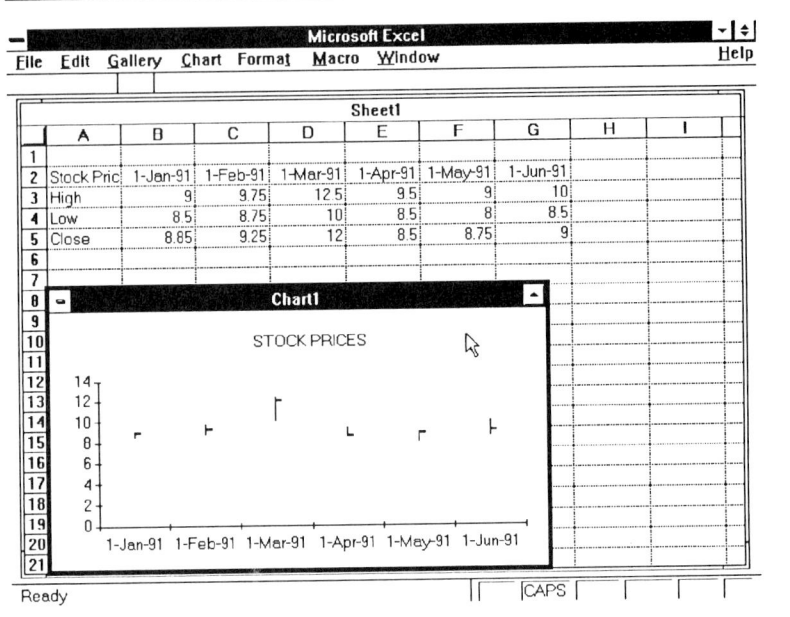

**FIGURE 7-12** Stock Market or High-Low-Close chart

## Pie Charts

A Pie chart is best used for comparing the percentages of a sum that several numbers represent. The full pie is the sum, and each number is represented by a wedge or slice. Figure 7-13 shows an example of a Pie chart. Each slice represents the percentage of total sales for a given product category. There is only one data series in a Pie chart. In the example in Figure 7-13, five numbers are in the data series, one for each product category, that represent the sales of each category. Excel automatically adds the numbers together and calculates the percentages to produce the chart.

Figure 7-13 was created by selecting alternative 6 from the Pie chart gallery, which provided the percentages for each slice. This saves you from calculating the percentages. If you want to do away with the legend and add the product types to each slice, you can

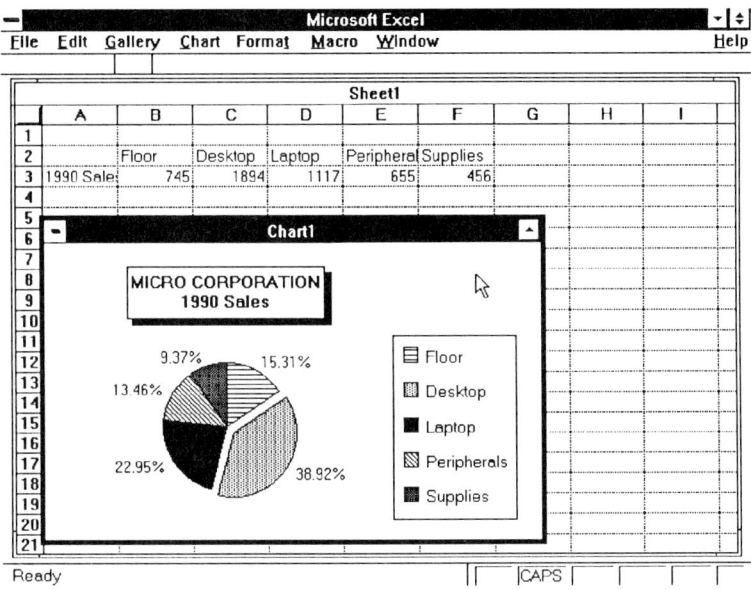

**FIGURE 7-13** Pie chart for product comparison

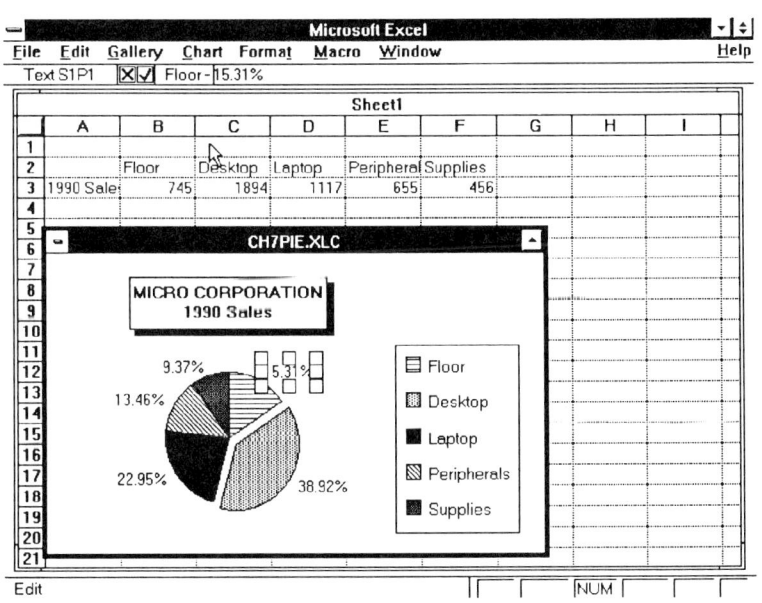

**FIGURE 7-14** Editing Pie chart labels

do that by selecting each percentage label and editing it in the edit area, as shown in Figure 7-14.

You may notice that the Pie chart gallery alternative with the percentage labels is exploded. That is, one of the slices is separated from the other slices. This is very easy to do without using the gallery alternatives. You simply click on the slice and drag it away from the others. When you click on a slice, notice that black selection boxes appear around it, meaning it can be moved, as shown here:

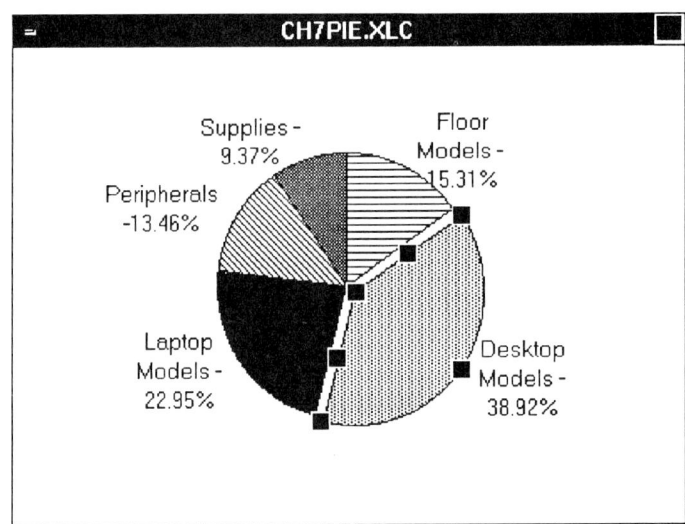

## Scatter Charts

Scatter or XY charts show the relationship between pairs of numbers and the trends they present. For each pair, one of the numbers is plotted on the X- or category axis and the other number is plotted on the Y- or value axis. Where the two meet, a symbol is placed on the chart. When a number of such pairs is plotted, a pattern may emerge, as shown in Figure 7-15.

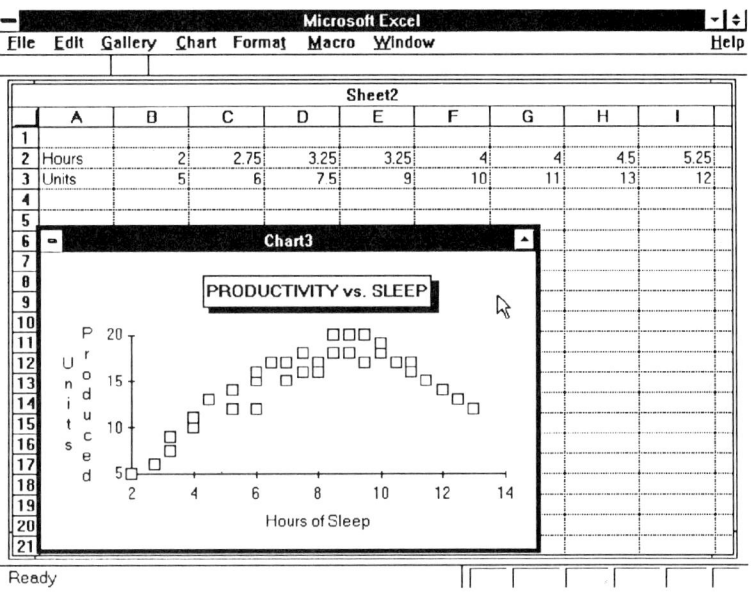

**FIGURE 7-15**   Scatter or XY chart

If you were to try to produce a Scatter chart in the same manner as you produce other charts you would not get the result you would expect. If you use the standard steps of highlighting a range on the worksheet, creating a new chart, and changing the chart type to Scatter, using the data in Figure 7-15, you get the chart shown here:

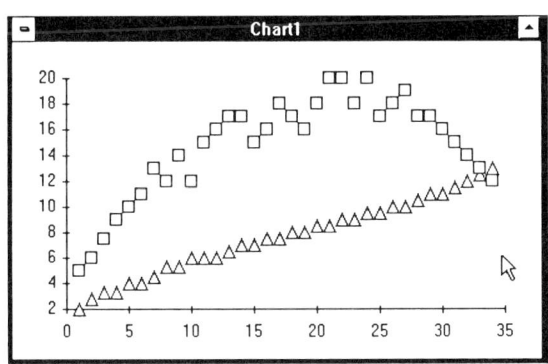

In a Scatter chart, the X-axis labels are one of the data series. When Excel builds a scatter chart with the normal procedure, both data series are plotted, and the X-axis labels are a default set of plot numbers because Excel thinks there were no X-axis labels. (The triangular markers in the previous illustration are supposed to be the X-axis labels.) To correct this you must copy the worksheet range to the Clipboard, create a new chart, and then use Paste Special to copy the data to the chart. See how that is done with these steps:

1. Highlight a range consisting of two or more rows or columns. The top row or left column contains the numbers you want to appear on the X-axis.

2. From the Edit menu, choose Copy. The blinking marquee appears around the worksheet range.

3. From the File menu, choose New, click on Chart, and click on OK. A blank chart is produced.

4. From the Edit menu choose Paste Special (you must be using Full menus). The Paste Special dialog box is displayed, as shown here:

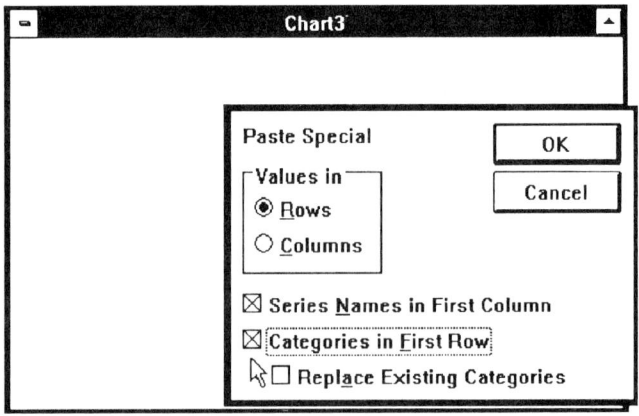

Excel has detected that the data series are in rows, so it automatically selected that option from the Values in field. Further, it has detected that the series names are in the first column. Excel has not identified that the categories or X-axes labels are in the first row, but they are, so you need to check that.

5. Click on Categories in First Row and click on OK. You get the standard Column chart that you need to change to a Scatter chart. The X-axis, however, has the first data series (row) as labels.

6. From the Gallery menu choose Scatter and select the first alternative from the Scatter chart gallery. The result is the scatter chart shown in Figure 7-15.

The Scatter chart in Figure 7-15 shows the hypothetical correlation between hours of sleep on the X-axis and units of production on the Y-axis. This is typical of how a Scatter chart is used.

# CREATING A LINE CHART

Remember that a Line chart is best at showing trends. In the third quarter budget completed in Chapter 6, Total Revenue, Cost of Sales (COS), and Total Expenses are among the items whose trends are important. Therefore, for your first chart, build a Line chart of Total Revenue, COS, and Total Expenses data from the Third Quarter Budget.

## Selecting the Ranges to Plot

Your first step in building a chart is to select the ranges on the worksheet that you want to plot. Load the third quarter budget, position the screen, and select the ranges. For this Line chart you want to identify four data series. The data series for the X-axis or category labels is the three months of July, August, and September in C8 through E8. The other three data series are Total Revenue, COS, and Total Expenses, respectively, in rows 14, 16, and 25.

Unlike the other charts you have seen so far in this chapter, the data series ranges on the worksheet are not a contiguous rectangular range, they are separated from one another by several intervening rows. This is called a *multiple selection*—you must select multiple independent ranges on the worksheet. To make a multiple selection you select (highlight) the first range, press (SHIFT+F8) (Add Selection), and then select the remaining ranges. Open the Third Quarter Budget worksheet and select the ranges with the following steps. Your computer should be turned on and Excel loaded.

1. From the File menu, choose Open.

2. If necessary, make the \WI\SHEET\ directory current (or the directory you are using for the files from this book).

3. Double-click on the QTR3BUD file.

4. Click on the downward scroll arrow until you can see the range A7 through G26.

5. Select or highlight C8 through E8.

6. Press and release (SHIFT+F8) (Add Selection). The ADD indicator comes on in the Status bar.

7. Select C14 through E14, C16 through E16, and C25 through E25.

When you are done selecting the four ranges, your screen should look something like Figure 7-16.

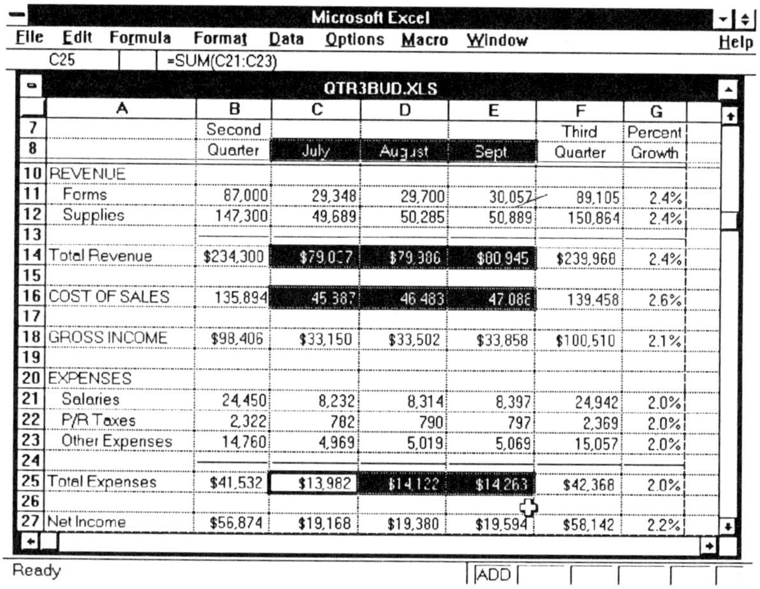


| | A | B | C | D | E | F | G |
|---|---|---|---|---|---|---|---|
| 7 | | Second | | | | Third | Percent |
| 8 | | Quarter | July | August | Sept | Quarter | Growth |
| 10 | REVENUE | | | | | | |
| 11 | Forms | 87,000 | 29,348 | 29,700 | 30,057 | 89,105 | 2.4% |
| 12 | Supplies | 147,300 | 49,689 | 50,285 | 50,889 | 150,864 | 2.4% |
| 13 | | | | | | | |
| 14 | Total Revenue | $234,300 | $79,0[illegible]7 | $79,386 | $80,945 | $239,968 | 2.4% |
| 15 | | | | | | | |
| 16 | COST OF SALES | 135,894 | 45,387 | 46,483 | 47,088 | 139,458 | 2.6% |
| 17 | | | | | | | |
| 18 | GROSS INCOME | $98,406 | $33,150 | $33,502 | $33,858 | $100,510 | 2.1% |
| 19 | | | | | | | |
| 20 | EXPENSES | | | | | | |
| 21 | Salaries | 24,450 | 8,232 | 8,314 | 8,397 | 24,942 | 2.0% |
| 22 | P/R Taxes | 2,322 | 782 | 790 | 797 | 2,369 | 2.0% |
| 23 | Other Expenses | 14,760 | 4,969 | 5,019 | 5,069 | 15,057 | 2.0% |
| 24 | | | | | | | |
| 25 | Total Expenses | $41,532 | $13,982 | $14,122 | $14,263 | $42,368 | 2.0% |
| 26 | | | | | | | |
| 27 | Net Income | $56,874 | $19,168 | $19,380 | $19,594 | $58,142 | 2.2% |

**FIGURE 7-16** Ranges selected for the Line chart

## Creating a New Chart

The second step in building a chart is to create a new chart that you can then modify. Use the following instructions to create a chart:

1. From the File menu, choose New. The New dialog box opens.
2. Click on Chart and on OK. A new column chart is created, as shown in Figure 7-17.

Your bars may be colored if you have a color display, or they may have a different shading if you have a monochrome display. The color or shading does not matter at this point.

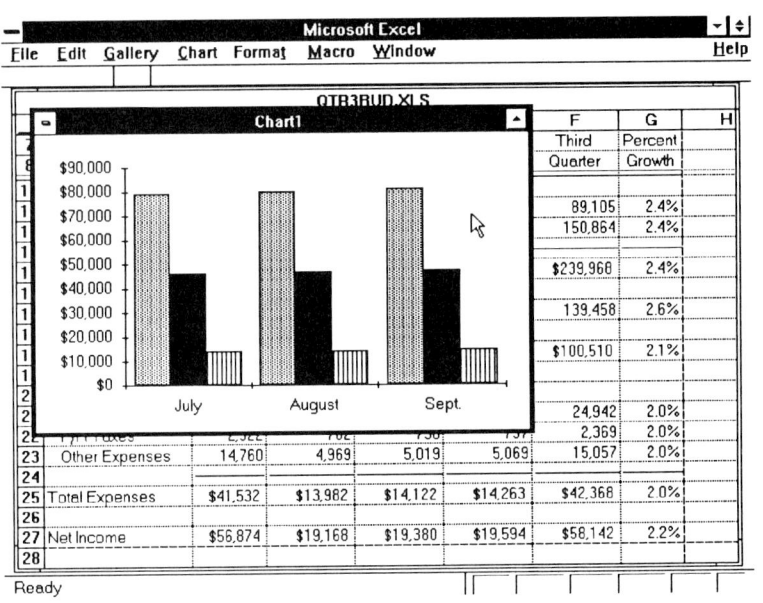

FIGURE 7-17    Initial Column chart of third quarter data

## Changing the Chart Type

You now have the standard Column chart—one that appears every time you create a new chart—so your next task is to change it to a Line chart. The Chart Gallery menu serves that purpose. Use it with these instructions and see the results on your screen:

1. From the Gallery menu, choose Line. The Line chart gallery opens, as shown here:

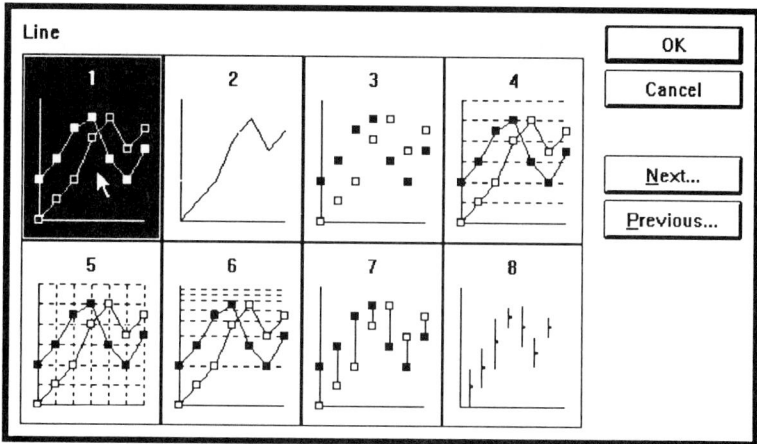

2. You want the first alternative, which is already selected, so just click on OK. The following Line chart appears on your screen (the markers or symbols on your screen may be different than what is shown here):

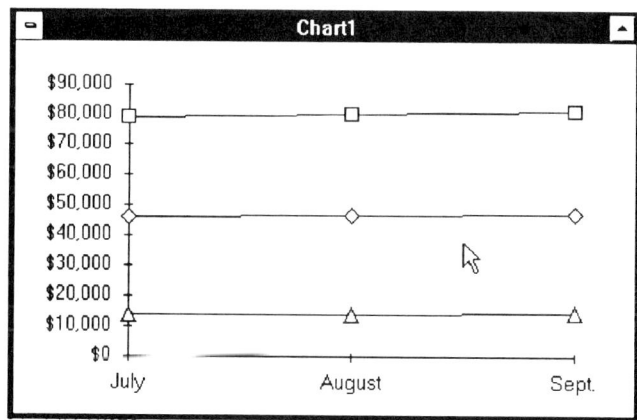

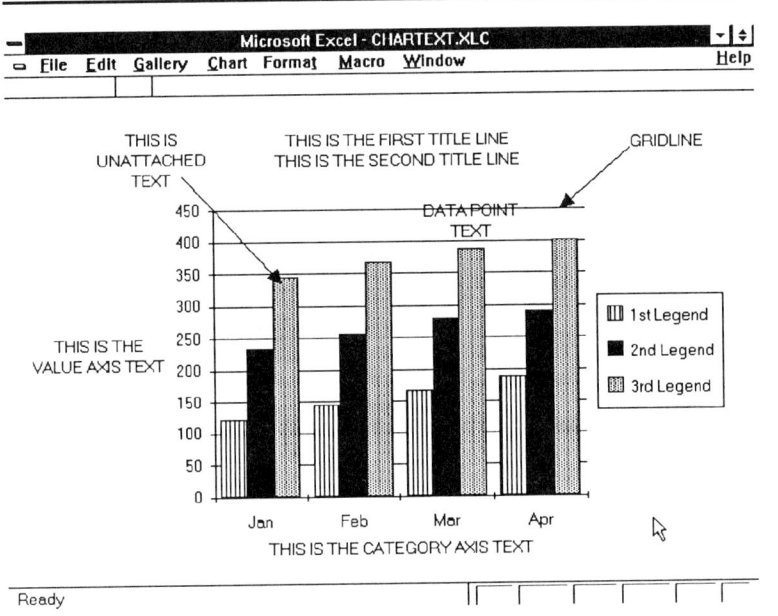

**FIGURE 7-18** Titles, legends, and notes

What you see on your screen is the barest rudiments of a chart. You can see the three-month labels along the X-axis at the bottom and three lines across the chart representing Total Revenue, COS, and Total Expenses. Only by knowing that Total Revenue is greater than COS, which is greater than Total Expenses, do you know which line is which. Also, from looking at the chart there is no way of knowing that the chart has anything to do with Morningside Specialities' Third Quarter Budget.

## Adding Annotation

The next step in building the Line chart is to add annotation. This includes titles in several locations, legends for the lines on the chart, and possibly some notes. All of these items are handled with options on the Chart menu.

Excel allows you to add a number of titles, legends, and notes to a chart, as shown in Figure 7-18. At the top of the chart is the first title and below it the second title. On the left side is the Y-axis or value text. At the bottom of the chart is the X-axis or category text, to the right are the legends, and in the upper-left and upper-right corners are two notes, also called *unattached text*. For your Line chart, you want to add a legend to identify the three lines and add text in several places.

**BUILDING A LEGEND** A legend is a set of labels or short descriptions, one for each data series or range that is plotted. These descriptions are attached to a symbol, to a color, or to crosshatching that is associated with the plotted data series and placed on the chart (initially to the right, but you can move it). For your Line chart, you need a legend consisting of three descriptions, one each for the Total Revenue, COS, and Total Expense data series. To add a legend to the chart, choose Add Legend from the Chart menu. A legend box is created on the Line chart, as you can see here:

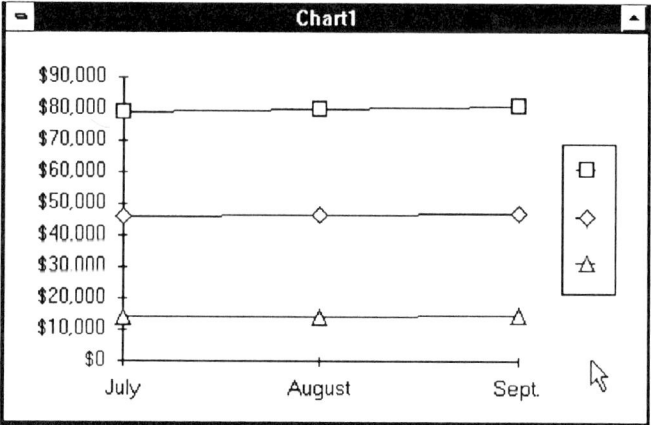

The legend box that appears on the Line chart gives you a reference to each line, but it does not tell you what they are because in highlighting the data series you did not highlight a name for each. The names are the row labels in column A and are therefore not contiguous to the data series in columns C through E. Without including column B there was no way to connect the series name with the data series. In a neat, contiguous set of ranges, the series name is immediately above or to the left of the data series. Excel can then create a legend containing the series names with only the steps you just followed.

In this case you must go to considerable more effort to get the series names, but in the process you will learn a lot about how Excel does its plotting.

**EDITING THE SERIES FORMULA** Each line, bar, column, or pie wedge on an Excel chart is created with a *series formula*. A series formula contains the SERIES function as well as up to four elements or arguments needed to plot a line, bar, column, or wedge. The four arguments are the series name or a reference to it, a reference to the categories against which you are plotting, a reference to the values that are to be plotted, and the order in which you want a line, bar, column, or wedge plotted.

When Excel builds a new chart with File New Chart, a set of series formulas are automatically built based on the ranges that have been selected on the worksheet. The Line chart currently on your screen has three such formulas, one for each line. Use the following instructions to first look at the series formulas and then edit them:

1. Click on the center marker on the top line of your Line chart. (If you are using the keyboard, press and hold (SHIFT) while pressing (DOWN ARROW). You cycle through several chart elements and eventually get to the top line.) The series formula appears in the edit area of the Formula bar, as shown here:

The series formula always starts out with =SERIES(. It then contains up to four arguments separated by commas and a closing parenthesis. In the series formula just shown, the first argument, for the series name, is missing. The other three arguments are

Category range:     QTR3BUD.XLS!$C$8:$E$8
Values range:       QTR3BUD.XLS!$C$14:$E$14
Plot order:         1

Both the category argument and the values argument are references to absolute ranges on the worksheet QTR3BUD. When you refer to a range on another worksheet, whether from a chart or a second worksheet, you use the complete worksheet name and extension (and path if it is stored in another directory), followed by an exclamation mark (!) and the absolute reference or range name. So the category range is the set of three column headings—July, August, and September—contained in C8:E8 of the QTR3BUD worksheet. The values range is the Total Revenue dollars in C14:E14 of the same worksheet.

In the current series formulas for the lines on your Line chart, there is a comma immediately after the opening parenthesis. This tells you that the first argument for the series name is missing. When you add that reference, you must insert it between the opening parenthesis and the comma. The series name can be either its name in quotation marks or a reference to a worksheet cell. Try both of these techniques in these steps:

2. Click the insertion point between the opening parenthesis and the first comma.

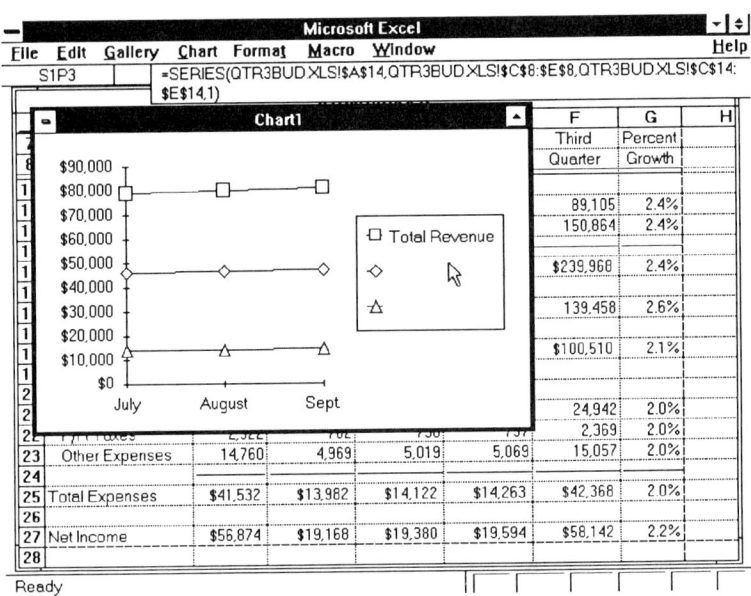

**FIGURE 7-19** Series name for the first legend marker

3. Type **qtr3bud.xls!$a$14** and press (**ENTER**). You return to ready mode, and the first legend marker has a series name to go with it, as shown in Figure 7-19.

4. Click on the middle marker of the middle line (or press (**SHIFT+UP ARROW**)). The series formula for the middle line appears in your edit area.

5. Click the insertion point before the first comma, type **"Cost of Sales"** (be sure to include the quotation marks), and press (**ENTER**).

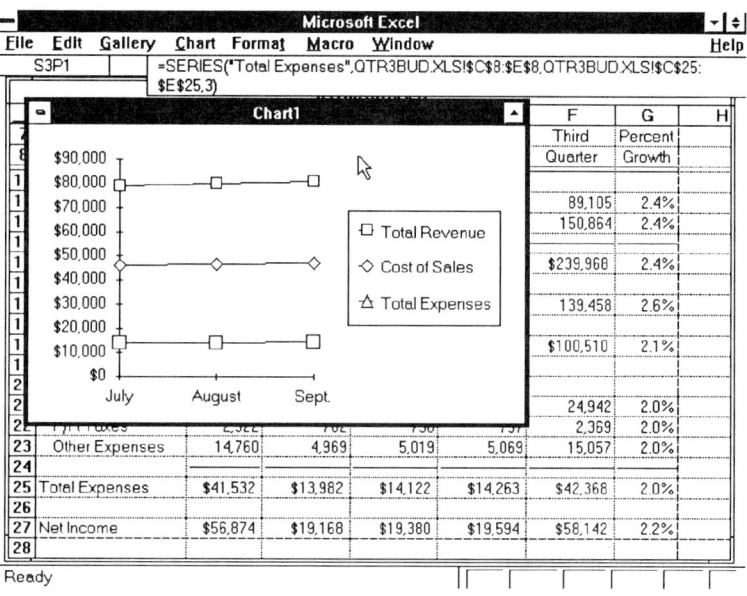

**FIGURE 7-20** Completed legend

6. Use either of the above techniques to add the series name Total Expenses from A25 of QTR3BUD to the series formula for the bottom line of the Line chart. This completes the legend, as shown in Figure 7-20.

**PLACING TITLES AND TEXT** The next step is to add two title lines to the top of the chart and some text on the Y- or value axis. To go to the second title line, you press (CTRL+ENTER) at the end of the first line. Type each piece of text directly with these instructions:

1. From the Chart menu, choose Attach Text. The Attach Text To dialog box opens, as shown here:

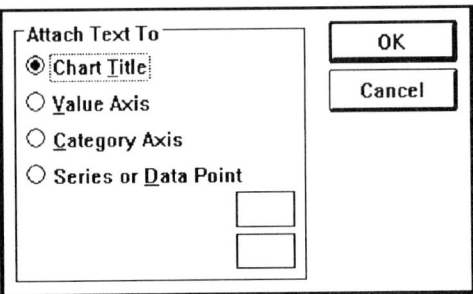

2. Click OK since Chart Title, the option you want, is already selected.

3. Type **MORNINGSIDE SPECIALITIES**. Since this is just the first line of the title, do not press (ENTER).

4. Press (CTRL+ENTER) to move to the second line, type **THIRD QUARTER BUDGET**, and then press (ENTER). Both lines of the title are placed on the worksheet, as shown in Figure 7-21.

5. From the Chart menu, choose Attach text, click on the Value Axis, and click on OK. A "Y" will be placed on the Y-axis and in the edit area.

6. Type **Thousands**, and press (ENTER). Thousands becomes the Y-axis title.

   The word "Thousands" on the Y-axis squeezes the chart so it is too tight. If you turned the word vertically, it would look much better. Do that as a final step. The word "Thousands" should still have the selection boxes around it.

Producing Charts   263

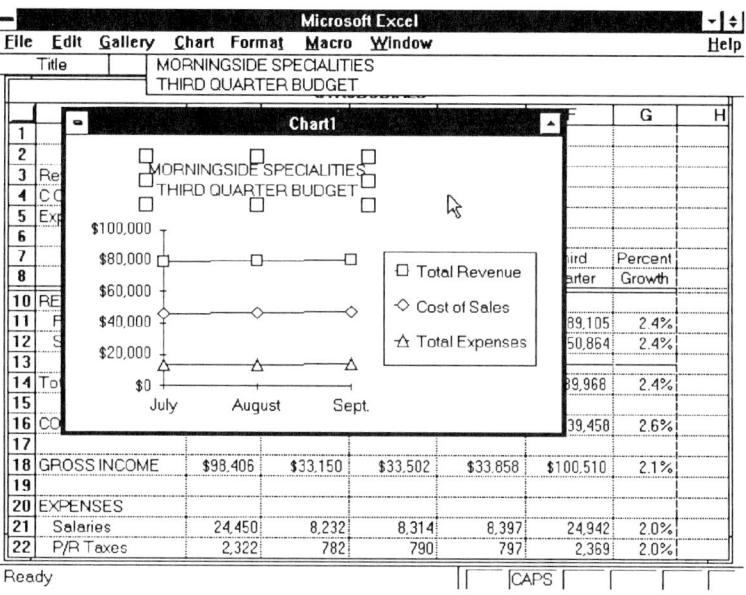

**FIGURE 7-21**   Title placed on the worksheet

7. From the Format menu, choose Text. The Text Alignment dialog box opens, as shown here:

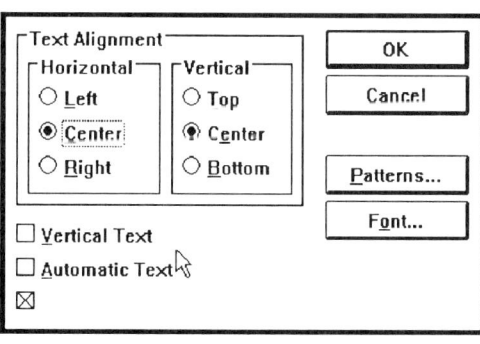

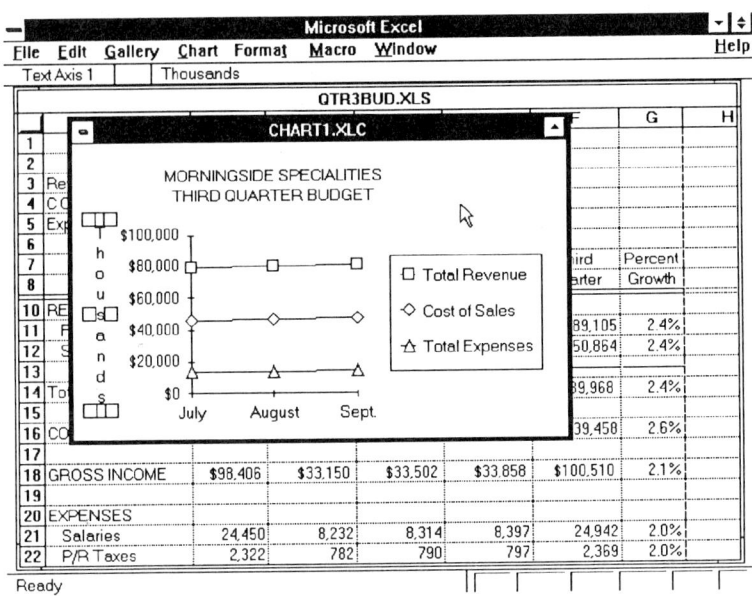

**FIGURE 7-22** All chart text in place

8. Click on the Vertical Text check box in the lower part of the dialog box and click on OK. The Y-axis text is turned vertical, as shown in Figure 7-22.

**FORMATTING TEXT** You probably noticed that all chart text is the same size, typeface, and style. You can change these to give the correct weight to the various parts of the chart. The Y-axis text should still be selected.

1. From the Format menu, choose Font. The Font dialog box opens, as shown here:

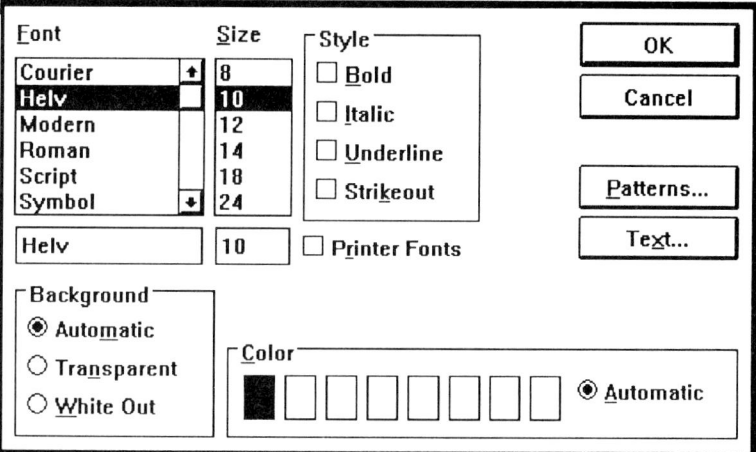

2. Click on 8 for the text size (press (ALT+S) and type **8** from the keyboard), and click on OK. The Y-axis text becomes smaller.

3. Click on the legend, choose Font from the Format menu, again click on 8 for the text size, and click on OK. The legend text becomes smaller.

4. Click on the chart title, choose Font from the Format menu, click on Bold Style, and click on OK. The title becomes bold.

5. With the chart title still selected, choose Patterns from the Format menu. The Patterns dialog box opens, as shown in Figure 7-23.

The Patterns dialog box for the chart title lets you place a border around the title, select among a number of alternatives for that border, and select from among a number of colors and patterns for the area behind the title. What you want to do with the Line chart

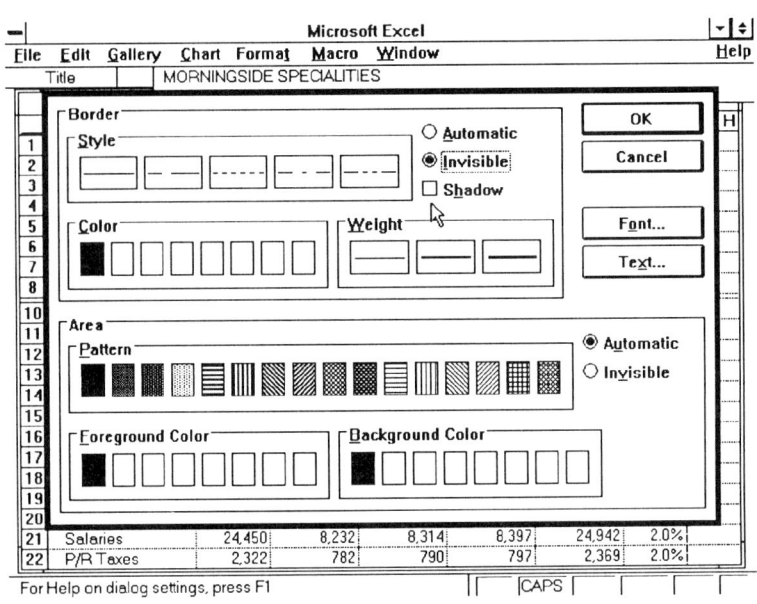

**FIGURE 7-23** Patterns dialog box

is place a shadow border around the title. Do that next and you will see its effect.

6. Click on Shadow in the Border area of the dialog box, and then click on OK.

7. Click somewhere else on the chart to remove the selection boxes from the title. The results are shown in Figure 7-24.

In a similar manner you could place a shadow border behind the legend and the chart itself. Now you simply save and print the chart.

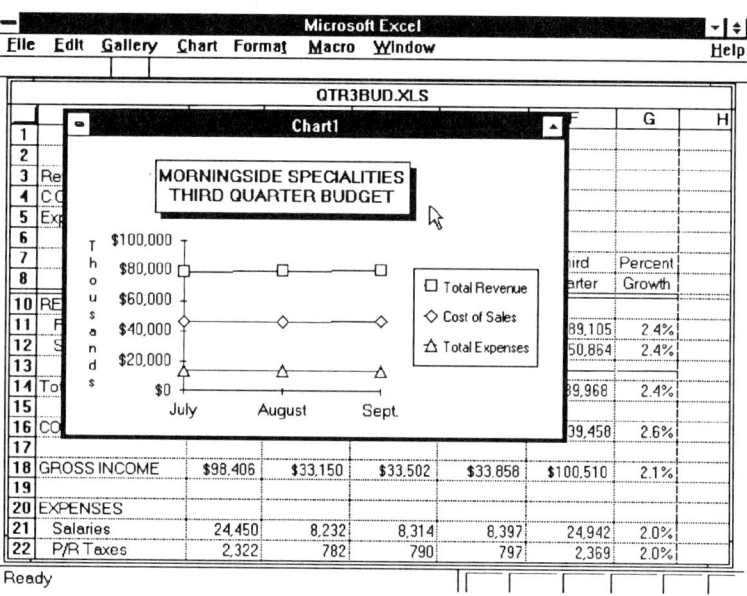

**FIGURE 7-24** Shadow border around the chart title

## Saving and Printing the Chart

You are now done with the Line chart, so you need to save it and then print it. Follow these instructions:

1. From the File menu choose Save As. The Save as dialog box opens.

2. Type **QTR3LINE** and click on OK. The chart is saved with the name QTR3LINE.XLC.

3. Choose Page Setup from the File menu. The Page Setup dialog box opens.

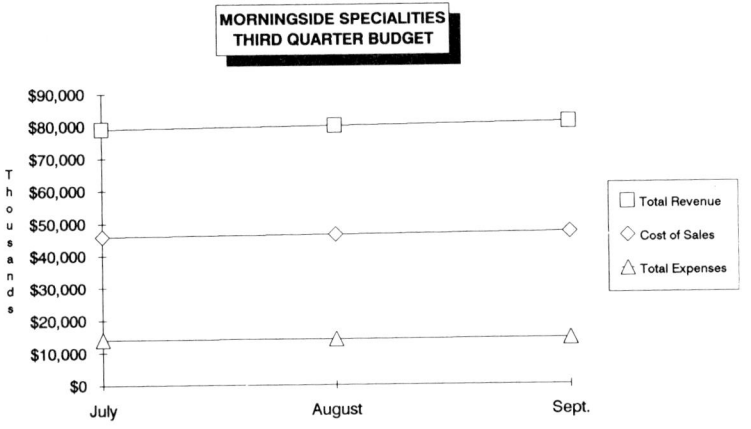

**FIGURE 7-25**   Printed Line chart

4. Type **&l&d&rPage &p**, press (TAB), press (DEL), and click on OK. A left-aligned date and a right-aligned page number are placed in the header text box, while the footer text box is cleared.

5. Choose Print from the File menu and click on OK. The Line chart is printed, as shown in Figure 7-25.

## Closing a Chart

You are now done with the Line chart. While you can leave it open on the desktop, it serves no real purpose to do so. Close it by double-clicking on the Line chart's Control-menu box. When the line chart closes, the chart menu bar is replaced with the worksheet menu bar.

# BUILDING A PIE CHART

The Pie chart you will build displays the percentage of contribution to third quarter expense from each of the expense accounts (the Salaries, P/R Taxes, and Other Expenses fields). The first steps are to select or highlight the third quarter expenses and create a new chart.

1. Select F21 through F23.

2. From the File menu, choose New, click on Chart, and then on OK. A standard column chart is produced, as shown here:

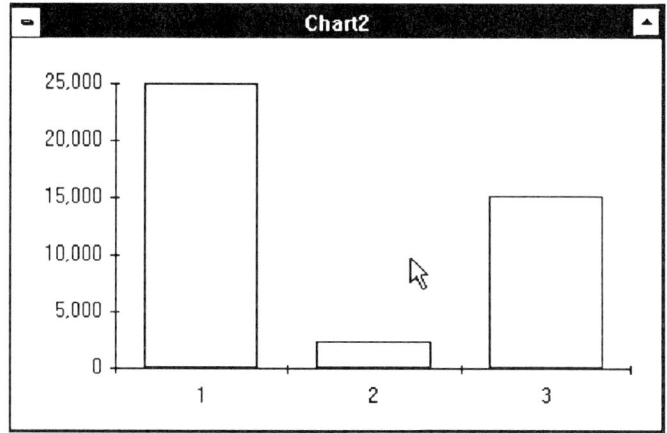

## Selecting a Pie Chart

The Pie chart to be created is an exploded Pie chart (one of the wedges separated from the rest) with both a description and a percentage on each wedge. The Pie chart gallery, shown in Figure 7-26, provides six alternatives, but none of them provides all of the features you want. From the gallery you can choose a Pie chart with any one of the three features (exploded, description, or percentage), but not all three. Remember from the earlier Pie chart

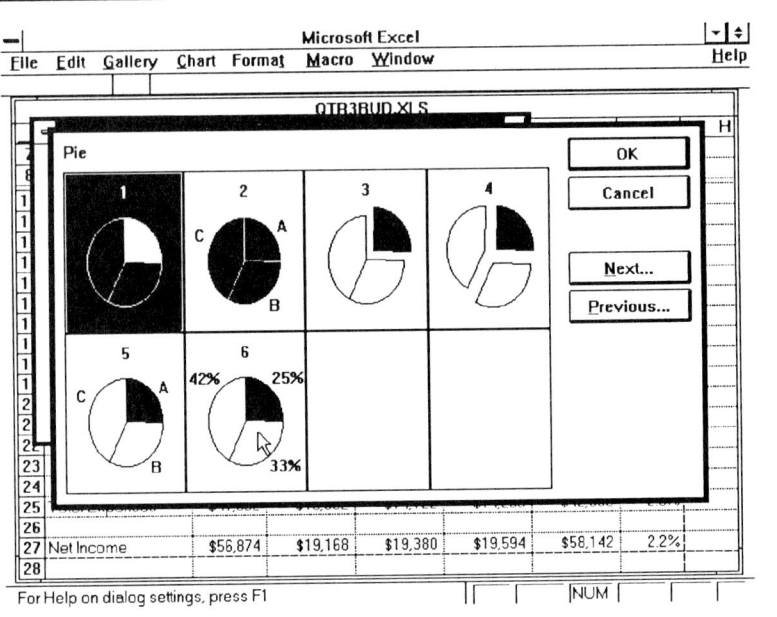

**FIGURE 7-26**  Gallery of Pie charts

discussion, moving a wedge to explode it is very easy, as is adding a description to a percentage. Adding a percentage, however, requires manual calculation. Therefore, you want alternative 6 with the percentages, and you can add the other two features after creating the chart. Change the chart type to a Pie with percentages with these instructions:

1. From the Gallery menu choose Pie. The Pie chart gallery opens.

2. Click on alternative 6 and click on OK. The Pie chart shown in Figure 7-27 appears.

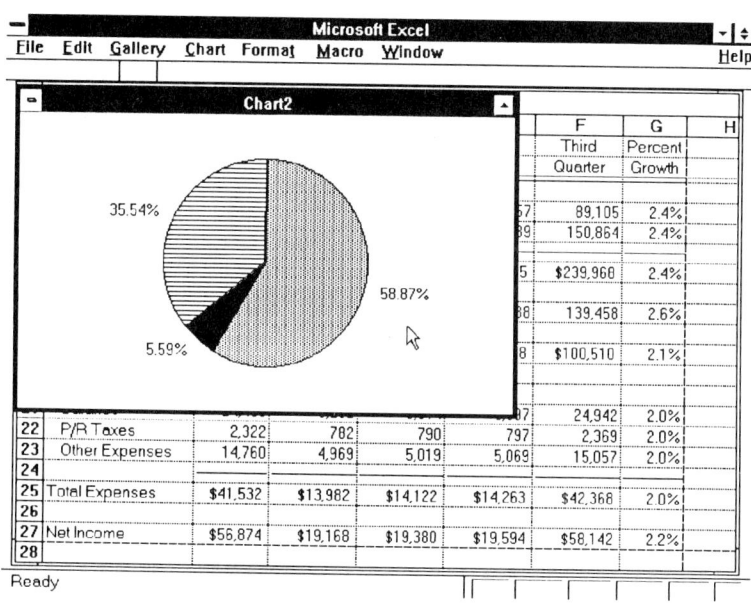

**FIGURE 7-27** Initial Pie chart

## Adding a Title from the Worksheet

Text on a chart can be typed in as you did for the Line chart, or you can pick up text already on the worksheet by entering a formula instead of the text. For the Pie chart, pick up the Third Quarter Budget title from the QTR3BUD worksheet instead of typing the title. Use these instructions:

1. From the Chart menu, choose Attach Text. The Attach Text To dialog box opens with Chart Title, the option you want, already selected. You need only to click on OK.

2. When you click on OK, the word "Title" appears at the top of the chart with selection boxes around it. You can enter a new title by simply typing.

3. Drag the Title bar of the chart down so you can see B1 on the worksheet.

4. Type = and click twice (do not double-click) on B1 on the worksheet and click on the check box or type **=qtr3bud.xls!$b$1** and press (ENTER). The worksheet reference B1 on the QTR3BUD worksheet (which contains the Third Quarter Budget title) is used for the title, as shown here:

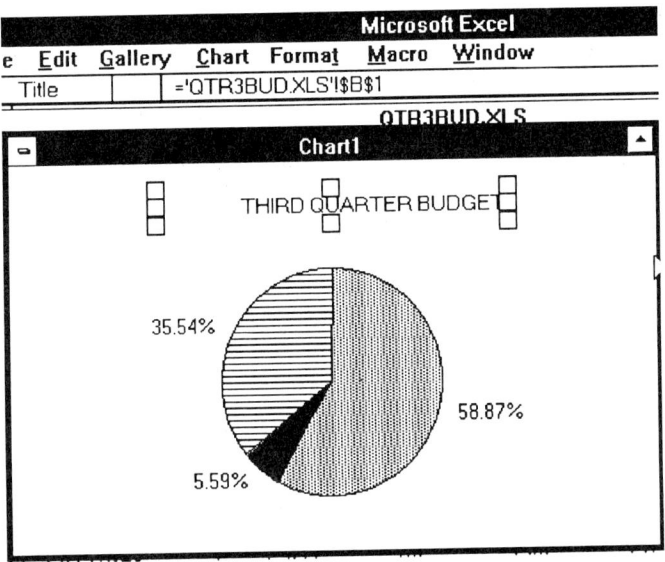

To pick up text off a worksheet for any text field on a chart, enter a formula with an absolute external reference to the worksheet filename and cell. In this case the title is off-center due to the leading spaces you entered to center the title on the worksheet. Accept that for what you are doing here.

## Adding Refinements

Now you can make several refinements to improve the appearance of the Pie chart. First, change the labels on the slices to include the expense title. Second, change the color or pattern of the slices. Finally, separate the slice that represents salaries since it is the largest.

**ADDING TITLES TO WEDGES** The wedges currently have the percentages they represent. To these percentages you want to add the expense title. You do this simply by editing the percentages and typing in the title. Follow these steps:

1. Drag on the Title bar to move the chart so you can see the three expense titles (Salaries, P/R Taxes, and Other Expenses).

2. Click on the 58.87% (or press (SHIFT+RIGHT ARROW) and cycle through the chart elements until you get to 58.87%).

3. Click the insertion point to the left of the 58.87% in the edit area.

4. Type **Salaries-** and press (ENTER). The expense title Salaries is added to the right-hand wedge of the Pie chart.

5. In a similar manner type **P/R Taxes-** to the left of 5.59% and **Other Expenses-** to the left of 35.54%. The completed wedge titles look like this:

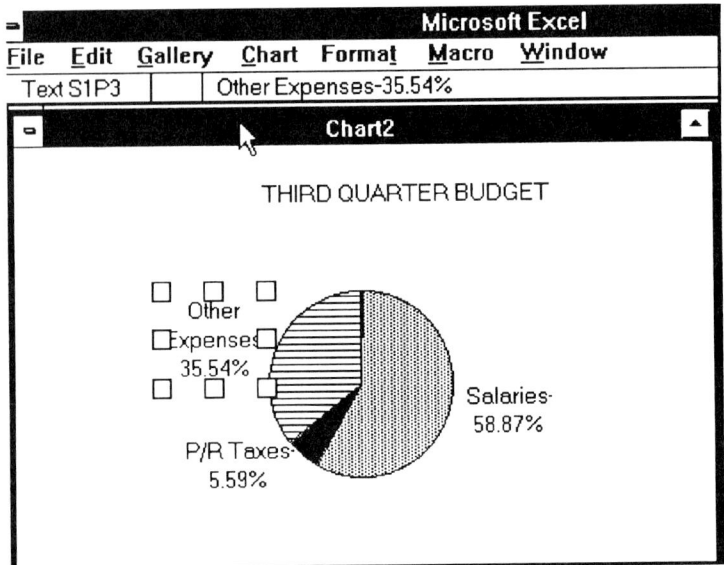

## CHANGING THE COLOR OR PATTERN OF A WEDGE

If you have a color display, each wedge in the Pie chart is in a different color. If you have a monochrome display, each wedge has a different pattern. You may or may not like the colors or patterns that you automatically get, so Excel provides a way to change them. Use the following instructions to see how that is done:

1. Click on the Salaries wedge. Selection boxes appear around the wedge.

2. From the Format menu, choose Patterns. The Patterns dialog box opens, as shown in Figure 7-28.

This Patterns dialog box is slightly different from the one you got for the Line chart title. Like the title Patterns dialog box, this one has two major areas: one for the border around the wedge, and one for the area within the wedge. Both of these should have the

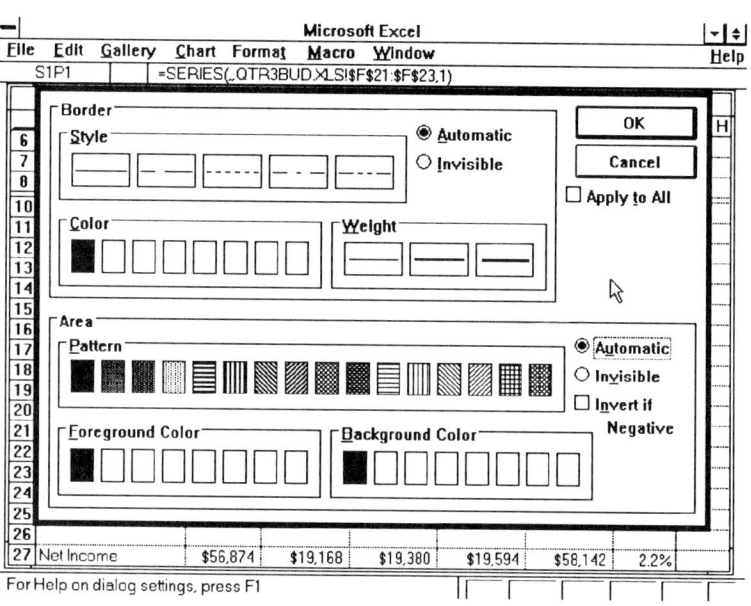

**FIGURE 7-28** Patterns dialog box

Automatic option button selected. The wedge Patterns dialog box does not have the Shadow option that is on the title Patterns, and some of the other options and command buttons are different. You want to change either or both the pattern and color of the area within the wedge.

3. Click on a pattern and/or color in the Area section of the Patterns dialog box, and click on OK. The Pie chart is redisplayed with the new pattern or color.

4. Click on the other two segments, and change their patterns and/or colors in a like manner. If you have a color display, experiment with combinations of color and pattern.

**EXPLODING A WEDGE**  The final bit of refinement is to explode or move the Salaries wedge away from the other wedges. See how easy that is with these steps:

1. Click on the Salaries wedge. Selection boxes appear around the wedge.

2. Drag the Salaries wedge about a 1/16 inch away from the other wedges.

3. Click on a blank area of the chart to remove the selection boxes from the Salaries wedge. Your Pie chart should look like the one shown here:

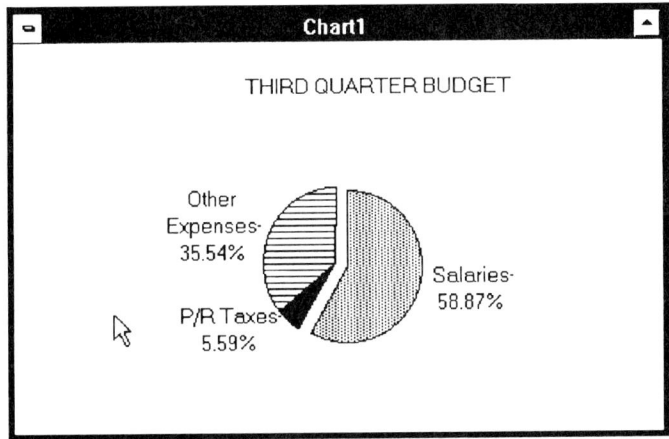

## Saving, Printing, and Closing

You have now completed the Pie chart. Print it, and then save and close it:

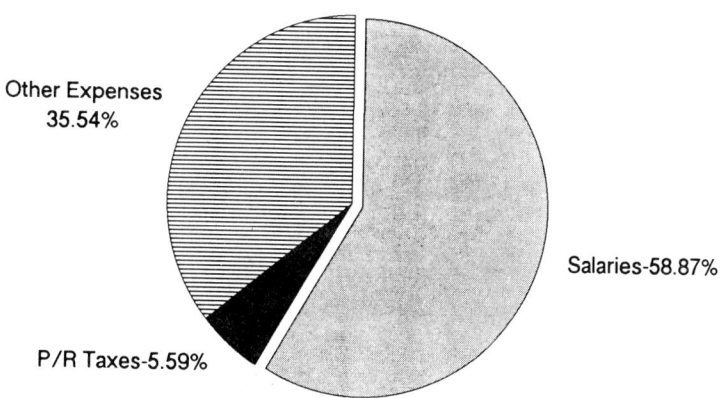

**FIGURE 7-29**   Printed Pie chart

1. From the File menu, choose Print and then click on OK in the Print dialog box. (If you want to change the standard header or footer, do so in the Page Setup dialog box first.)

When your Pie chart is printed it should look something like Figure 7-29. If you used different crosshatch patterns or color, your chart will differ.

2. From the File menu, choose Save As, type **qtr3pie**, and click on OK.

3. Double-click on the pie chart's Control-menu box to close the chart.

# GENERATING A STACKED COLUMN CHART

The third chart to be created is a Stacked Column chart in which each of the three columns is one month's total expenses, and each layer is one type of expense (salaries, payroll taxes, and other expenses). The layers, therefore, show a type of expense in proportion to the total expense for a given month. Since you have done two charts already, this chart can be done quickly.

## Building the Chart

The now familiar steps to building a chart are highlight the appropriate ranges on the worksheet, create a new chart, change its type as necessary from the Gallery menu, and add titles, text, and formatting as desired. Use these instructions to do that:

1. Select the range C8:E8, press (SHIFT+F8) (Add Selection), and select the range C21:E23.

2. From the File menu, choose New, click on Chart, and click on OK to create a new chart.

3. From the Gallery menu, choose Column, click on alternative 3, and click on OK to change the chart type to a Stacked Column chart.

4. From the Chart menu, choose Attach Text, and click on OK to select Chart Title.

5. Type **THIRD QUARTER EXPENSES** and press (ENTER) for the title.

6. Click on one of the bottom layers and click the insertion point after the left parenthesis in the series formula. Type **"Salaries"** and press (ENTER).

7. Similarly type **"P/R Taxes"** for the middle layer and **"Other"** for the top layer.

8. From the Chart menu, choose Add Legend.

9. Click on the legend to select it, and then from the Format menu choose Legend. The Legend dialog box opens, as shown here:

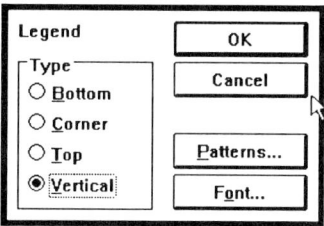

10. Click on Bottom and OK to move the legend to the bottom of the chart. Your Stacked Column chart should look like that shown in Figure 7-30.

## Saving, Printing, and Closing

You have completed the Stacked Column chart. Print, save, and close it now.

1. From the File menu choose Print, and then click on OK on the Print dialog box.

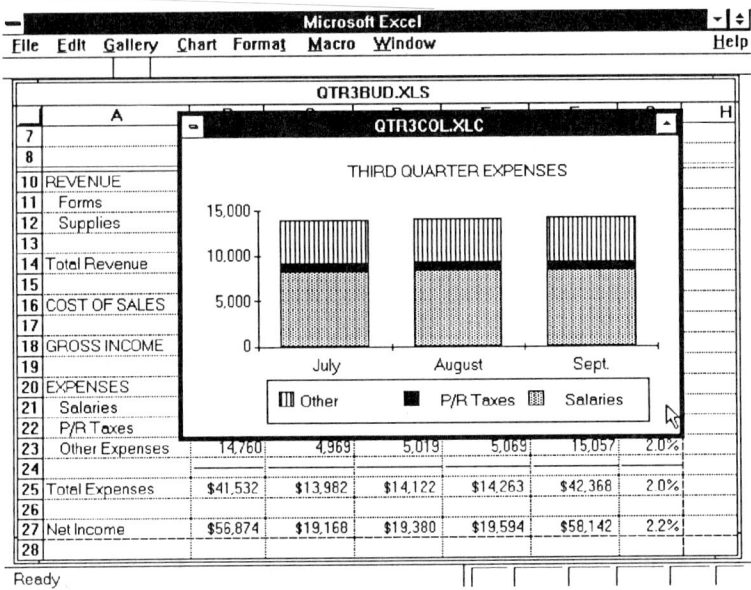

**FIGURE 7-30**   Stacked Column chart

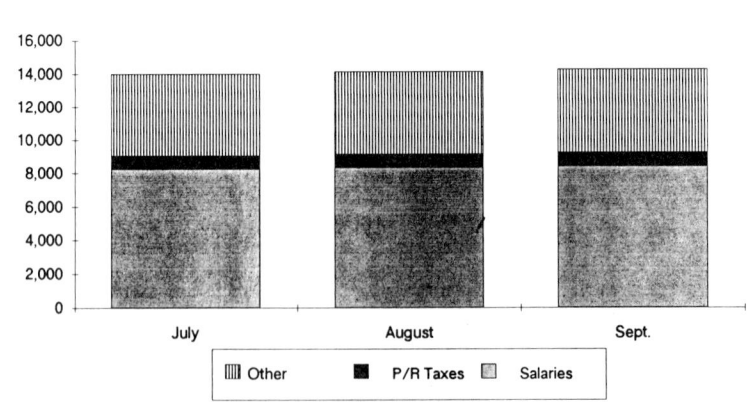

**FIGURE 7-31**   Printed Stacked Column chart

When the chart is printed it should look something like Figure 7-31. Again, different crosshatch patterns or colors may make your chart different than the one shown here.

2. From the File menu, choose Save As, type **qtr3col**, and click on OK.

3. Double-click on the chart's Control-menu box to close the chart.

## LEAVING EXCEL

Since you have not made any changes to the QTR3BUD worksheet in this chapter, it does not need to be resaved. You need only leave Excel and Windows. Do that now with these steps:

1. Double-click on Excel's Control-menu box to close Excel.

2. Double-click on the Program Manager's Control-menu box and click OK to close Windows.

# 8

# BUILDING A DATABASE

Building a Database
Sorting a Database
Selecting Information from a Database
Analyzing Information from a Database
Using Lookup Functions

A database is a list—a phone list, a list of products, a list of parts, a list of cities—a set of related information organized into the row-and-column structure of Excel. In this chapter you build two databases. You then sort the tables, extract information from them, and analyze the information.

Databases are the third of Excel's three components (worksheets and charts are the other two). A database is a natural adjunct to Excel because Excel's row-and-column structure lends itself to containing information in a database. One entry in the database, called a record, is placed across a row. For example, in a phone list containing names and phone numbers, a record is a single name and phone number combination. Each part of a record (for example, the name or the phone number) is called a field and is entered in a column. Thus, a direct relationship exists between rows and columns on a worksheet and records and fields in a database.

A database must be contained on a single worksheet. A single worksheet can contain many databases, but only one of them may be designated "the database" that allows you to do several predefined operations on that database. The first row of a database must contain *field names*—the labels in each column of a database that name the field in that column. The maximum size of a database in Excel is 256 fields in 16,383 records (the maximum number of columns in a worksheet, and one less than the maximum number of rows to accommodate the field names).

A database can contain any information you want to organize into fields and records. However, it is a good idea to have at least one blank row at the bottom of the database to allow for expansion. (You can insert a new record above the last record and the database range will automatically expand to include the new record.) All of the field names in a database must be unique—they cannot be duplicated—and field names cannot be numbers, logical values, error values, blank cells, or formulas.

## BUILDING A DATABASE

Building a database involves little more than typing. You must enter a set of field names and then enter the records, and that's all there is to it. Later you will learn some tricks to speed up the entry, but otherwise the process is simply typing.

### Entering Field Names

The first database for you to build is a list of six sales offices. The record for each office contains an office number, a location, a manager's name, a quota, and a commission rate. The first step in building the database is entering the field names. Your computer should be on and Excel loaded, and you should have a blank worksheet on your screen with A1 as the active cell.

1. Type **Number** and press (RIGHT ARROW). "Number" is entered in A1, and the active cell moves to B1.

2. Type **Office** and press (RIGHT ARROW). "Office" is entered in B1, and the active cell moves to C1.

Complete the remaining field names as shown here, using a similar procedure. In column E press (ENTER) instead of (RIGHT ARROW).

|   | A | B | C | D | E | F |
|---|---|---|---|---|---|---|
| 1 | Number | Office | Manager | Quota | Commission | |
| 2 | | | | | | |
| 3 | | | | | | |

E1: Commission

## Numbering with a Data Series

When you have to enter almost any sort of consecutive numbers or dates, you can get help from Excel's Data Series option. To use this option you must specify the range you want to fill and then enter a start number, an increment or step number, and, optionally, a stop number. For example, if you want a list of numbers from 1 to 10 in column A, beginning in A1, you enter **1** as the start number, highlight the range, and enter (or accept the default of) **1** as the step number. You get 1 in A1, 2 in A2, 3 in A3, and so on to 10 in cell A10.

The start number must be entered on the worksheet in the first cell of the row or column you want to fill. Excel uses 1 and the remaining rows or columns selected as the defaults for the step and stop numbers if you do not enter them. You can enter any number as the start number, including dates (in a recognizable format), negative numbers, or formulas that evaluate to one of those. The step or stop value must be a recognizable number, not a formula or range name. You can use fractional numbers for the step and stop values, and the stop number may be a date (in a recognizable format).

Either the stop number or the end of the range can stop the series operation. If the stop number stops the series, it does so before the stop number is exceeded. There are special considerations for series with dates. These are discussed later in this chapter.

Even though you have only six numbers to enter, the Data Series option makes it short work. Try it with these steps:

1. Click on A2. The active cell moves to A2.

2. Type **250** and press (ENTER). 250 is entered in A2 as the start value.

3. Highlight the range A2 through A7.

4. From the Data menu, choose Series (you must be using the long menus). The Data Series dialog box opens, as shown here:

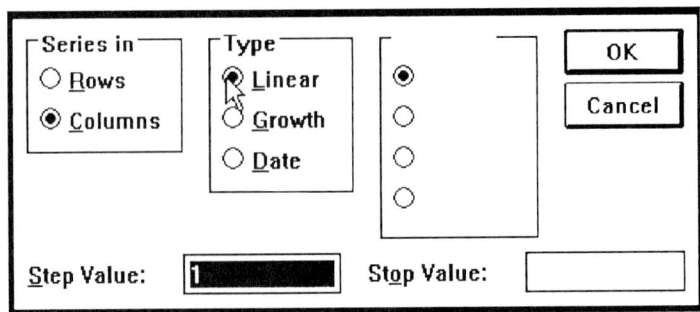

You can see in the Data Series dialog box that Excel has detected you want the series to go down a column. The default Type setting is Linear, which is what you want. The other Type options are Growth, which multiplies the last cell times the step value, and Date, which produces a series of date values. If you choose Date, the Date Unit option becomes available (in the illustrated dialog box this option is blank) and allows you to choose whether the date increment is Day, Weekday, Month, or Year.

5. Type **5** for the step value and press (ENTER). The dialog box closes and the series of numbers appears in column A, as shown in Figure 8-1. Notice that the range size was used to stop the fill operation.

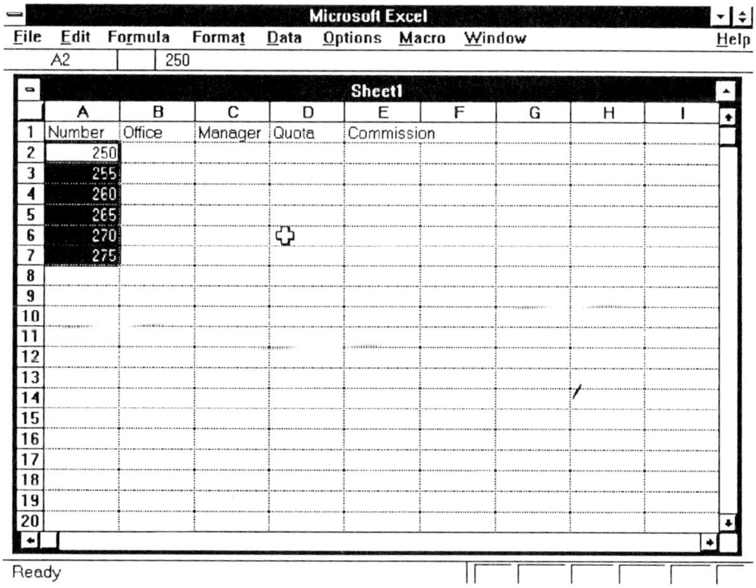

**FIGURE 8-1** Numbers produced with the Data Series option

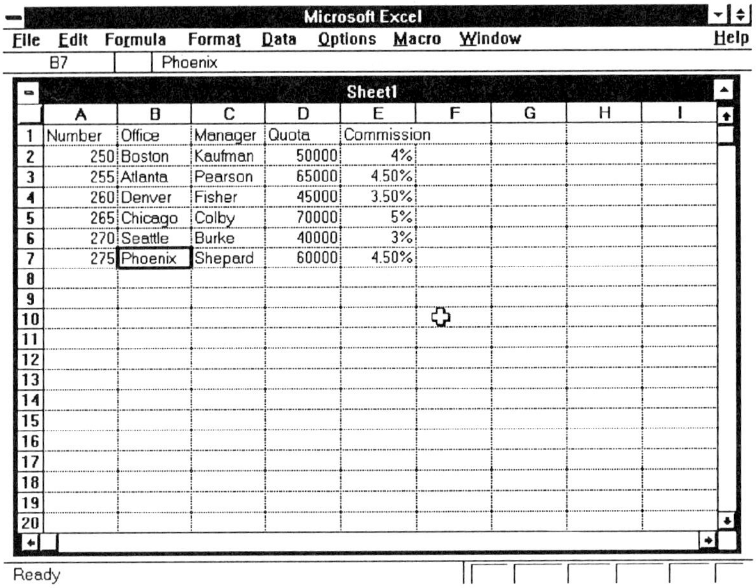

```
                    Microsoft Excel
 File  Edit  Formula  Format  Data  Options  Macro  Window          Help
       B7            Phoenix
                          Sheet1
       A        B         C         D         E       F      G      H      I
 1  Number   Office    Manager   Quota    Commission
 2     250   Boston    Kaufman    50000       4%
 3     255   Atlanta   Pearson    65000    4.50%
 4     260   Denver    Fisher     45000    3.50%
 5     265   Chicago   Colby      70000       5%
 6     270   Seattle   Burke      40000       3%
 7     275   Phoenix   Shepard    60000    4.50%
```

**FIGURE 8-2** Completed sales office database

## Entering Records

Entering the remaining parts of the records is just rote typing. You can either type down a column or across a row, whichever is easier for you. Do that now, entering all of the information shown in Figure 8-2. If it is easier for you, you may enter the commissions as decimals instead of percents, for example, entering **.04** instead of **4%**. If you do enter decimal percents, they appear that way on the screen.

**MAKING THE DATABASE EASIER TO READ** The rightmost pair of columns could stand some formatting, so do that now with these steps:

1. Drag on D2 through D7.

2. From the Format menu, choose Number. The Format Number dialog box opens.

3. Click on #,##0 and OK. The quotas in column D are formatted with a comma.

4. Drag on E2 through E7 and choose Number from the Format menu.

5. Click on the Format text box at the bottom of the Format Number dialog box, type **0.0%** to create a single decimal percent, and press (ENTER). The percents in column E are formatted with a single decimal.

The result of formatting the right pair of columns is shown in Figure 8-3.

## SORTING A DATABASE

Sorting a database rearranges the records in the database to produce a specific order to the records. You must identify the range or database you want sorted and then specify the key or keys you want to sort on. The keys are one or more fields that you want ordered. Unlike many of the other Data commands, Data Sort does not require the field names, and they should *not* be included in the data range. That means you can sort anything on an Excel worksheet, not just a database. When you use Data Sort, each row or each column within the range you specify is reordered along with the key fields in that row or column.

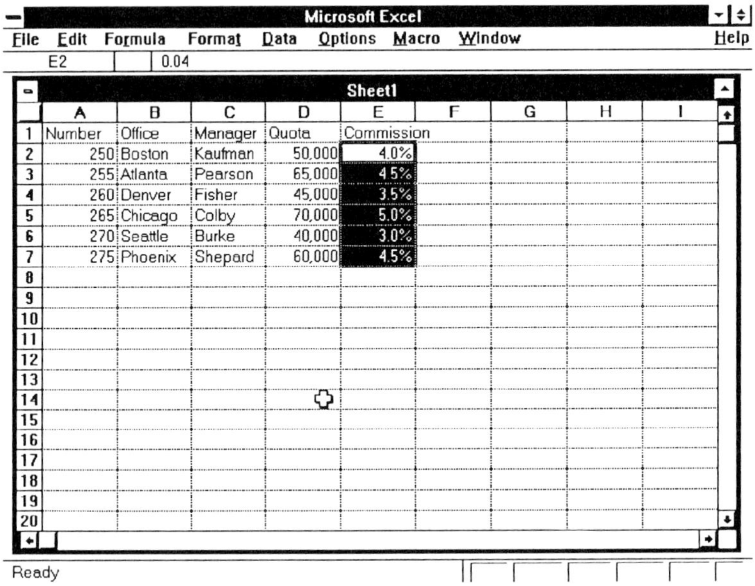

**FIGURE 8-3** Columns D and E formatted

## Selecting the Sort Range

There are several ways to sort the database you just built; alphabetically by either office or manager are two ways you consider here. Start by sorting the table by office. The basic procedure is to highlight a range of records to be sorted, choose Sort from the Data menu, enter the keys on which to sort, and start the sort by clicking on OK. Begin that procedure with these instructions:

1. Select the range A2 through E7, as shown here:

## Building a Database

|   | A | B | C | D | E | F |
|---|---|---|---|---|---|---|
| 1 | Number | Office | Manager | Quota | Commission | |
| 2 | 250 | Boston | Kaufman | 50,000 | 4.0% | |
| 3 | 255 | Atlanta | Pearson | 65,000 | 4.5% | |
| 4 | 260 | Denver | Fisher | 45,000 | 3.5% | |
| 5 | 265 | Chicago | Colby | 70,000 | 5.0% | |
| 6 | 270 | Seattle | Burke | 40,000 | 3.0% | |
| 7 | 275 | Phoenix | Shepard | 60,000 | 4.5% | |
| 8 | | | | | | |

2. Choose Sort from the Data menu. The following Data Sort dialog box opens:

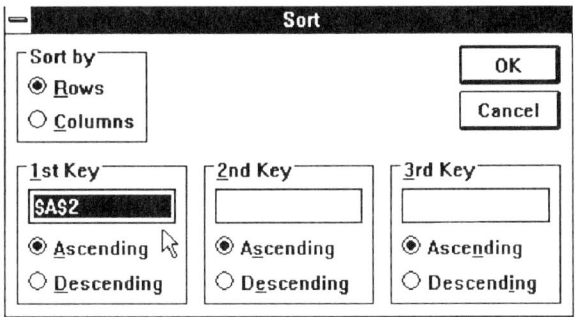

The Data Sort dialog box shows that Excel has guessed correctly that you want to sort by rows. This means that all the cells in one row within the highlight are moved together as the sort is carried out. This makes sense in terms of the database because one row is a single record and, while you want to rearrange the records, you want any given record to remain intact. You can also sort by columns, which has the opposite implication.

## Identifying a Sort Key

The sort key, when sorting by rows, is the column containing the field you want sorted. In this example, you want the records sorted by offices, so column B is the sort key. It does not matter what row you specify. You can type in the cell address or you can click on the worksheet. If necessary you can move the dialog box to see the worksheet.

Click on B2 to select the column you want to sort on. A blinking marquee appears around B2, and $B$2 appears in the 1st Key text box. Figure 8-4 shows how your screen should look.

You have entered the first sort key, which is all you want to sort on in this example. You might wonder what happens in a larger database when you have duplicates in the key you are sorting on.

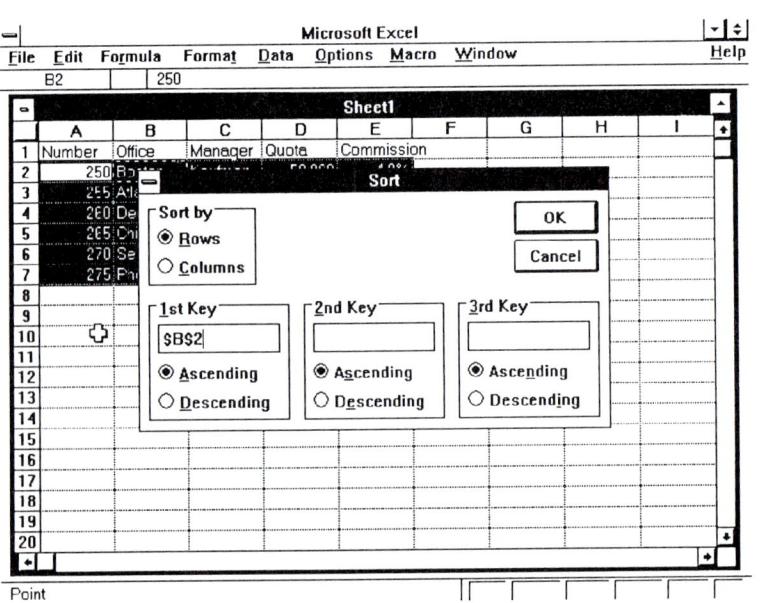

**FIGURE 8-4** Sort key selected for sorting by office

If you specify only one key, duplicates are left in the same order in which they started. But you can specify a second key to sort records with duplicate first keys, and even a third key to sort duplicate second keys. You even can sort on more than three keys by doing more than one sort, using the lowest priority keys first and the highest priority keys last.

**ASCENDING VERSUS DESCENDING** Once you have specified the sort key, you can specify the sort order—ascending or descending. You indicate whether you want to sort in normal ascending alphabetical order (A first, Z last) or the reverse of that, descending order.

The normal alphabetic sequence (A,B,C,...Z) has been extended to include numbers, blanks, symbols, and logical and error values. Microsoft has established a specific sort order that is followed in all cases. The ascending sequence of this sort order is as follows:

1. Numbers from the largest negative number to the largest positive number

2. Text, ignoring capitalization and including numbers entered as text, in this sequence:

   Space ! " # $ % & ' ( ) * + , - . / 0 1 2 3 4 5 6 7 8 9 : ; < = > ? @ a b c d e f g h i j k l m n o p q r s t u v w x y z [ \ ] ^ _ ' { | } ~ ¢ ¥ ±

3. Logical values, False first and then True

4. Error values

5. Blank cells

The descending order is the reverse of the order just shown, except that blank cells are always sorted last.

In this example you are dealing with simple alphabetic letters. You want to sort from A to Z, which is ascending order and the default already selected. If you wanted to change the sort order you would click on Descending.

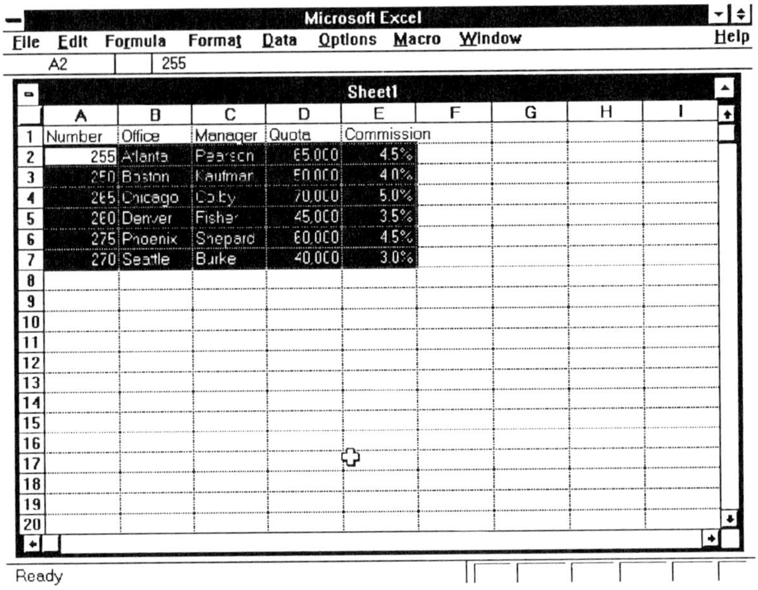

**FIGURE 8-5**  Database sorted by office

## Doing the Sort

The actual sorting is anticlimactic.

Click on OK.

The dialog box closes, and the database is sorted alphabetically by office, as shown in Figure 8-5. Excel is returned to ready mode.

## Changing and Resorting

Once sorted, the database can be resorted on a different sort key in a few quick steps. One reason to have a numbered column in the database is you can resort the list on the numbers and return the database to the original order in which it was entered. You could do that with this database, but instead follow these steps to change the sort key to carry out the sort on the office manager. You should be in ready mode with the database still selected.

1. Choose Sort from the Data menu. The Data Sort dialog box opens.

2. Click on C1 as the sort key, and click on OK to close the dialog box and do the sort. (You can click on either C1 or C2, but C1 is more visible.)

The database is sorted alphabetically by manager, as shown in Figure 8-6.

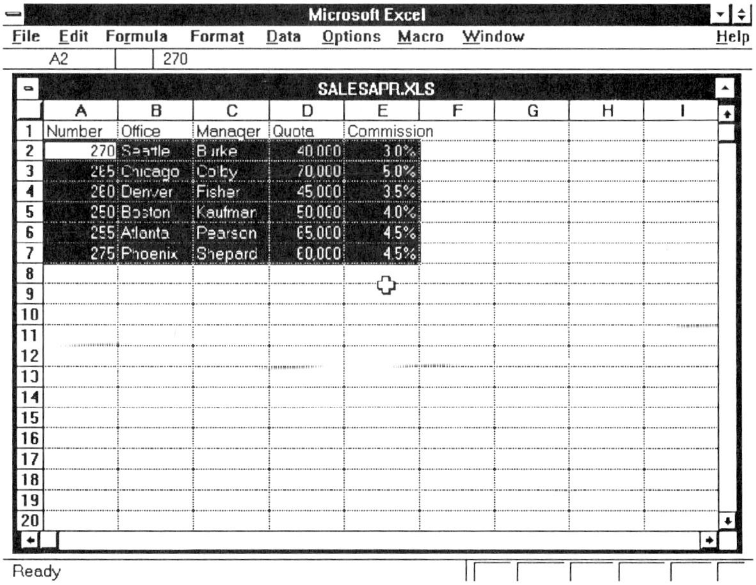

**FIGURE 8-6** Database sorted by manager

# SELECTING INFORMATION FROM A DATABASE

A database is primarily an ordered storage place for information. You place information in a database so you can get to it more easily, either to select particular records or to analyze it. After building a second database, you will spend the remainder of this chapter selecting or analyzing information in one or both of the databases.

## Building a Second Database

The second database contains the weekly sales amounts for three of the offices for the month of April. The fields will be the office number and name, the week the figures are for, the number of sales, and the total dollar amount of sales. Enter the field names for this table with these instructions:

1. Click on the vertical scroll bar below the scroll box, and click on A21 to move your active cell to A21.

2. Type the five field names shown here:

|    | A | B | C | D | E | F |
|----|---|---|---|---|---|---|
| 21 | Number | Office | Week | Sales | Amount | |
| 22 | | | | | | |
| 23 | | | | | | |

**ENTERING DATES AS A DATA SERIES** One of the fields is an identifier for the week of the month for each record. Instead of typing this sequence of dates, you can use the Data Series option to enter them automatically. For the start number you enter the starting date, for the step number you enter a calendar increment (day, weekday, month, or year), and for the stop number you enter the ending date. The starting and ending dates can be in any recognizable Excel date format. The step number can be a decimal—1.5, for instance. Its units depend on the date units you select: days, weekdays, months, or years. Since you cannot display fractional days without also displaying the time (which you can do), the entries for this database are rounded to the closest whole day.

For the April sales database, you want to enter the weeks in column C, beginning with April 1, 1991, and ending May 1, 1991. Do that with these steps:

1. Click on C22, type **4/1/91**, and press (ENTER).

2. Choose Series from the Data menu, type **7** for a step value of seven days, press (TAB) to move to the Stop Value field, type **5/1/91**, and click on Columns for the direction of the series. The Data Series dialog box looks like this when you are done:

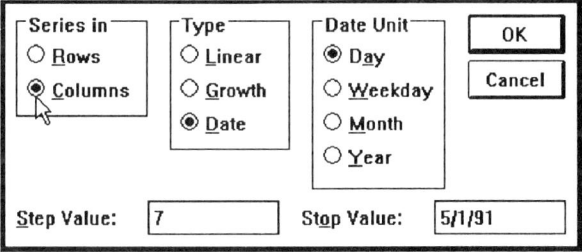

3. Click OK. The dialog box closes and the dates appear on your worksheet as shown in Figure 8 7.

The dates could use a little formatting, so do that next.

4. Select the range C22 through C26.

5. From the Format menu choose Number. The Format Number dialog box opens.

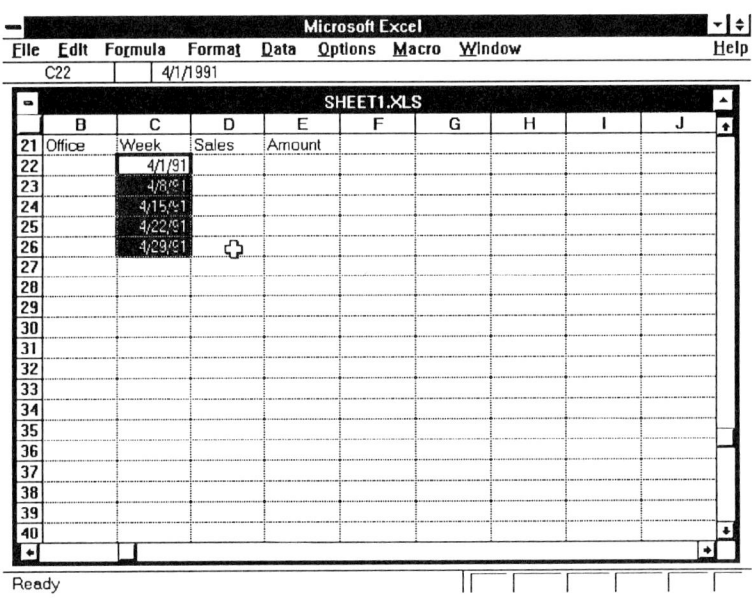

**FIGURE 8-7** Date series displayed

6. Press (TAB) to highlight the contents of the Format text box, and type **mmm dd**. Your dialog box should look like this:

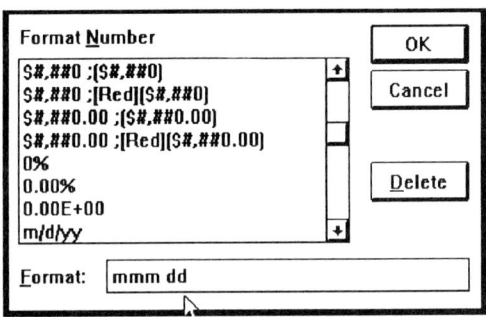

7. Click on OK. The date sequence is formatted as demonstrated in Figure 8-8.

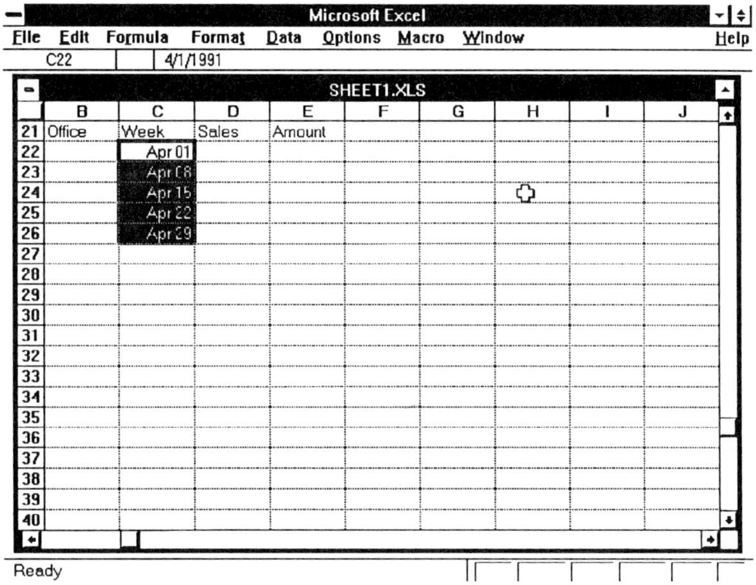

**FIGURE 8-8** Dates reformatted

**COMPLETING DATA ENTRY** The table of sales amounts that you must enter is for five weeks and three sales offices—a total of fifteen entries. The dates you just entered are for one sales office and therefore need to be copied twice more down column C. Each sales office (Boston, Denver, and Seattle) and corresponding number must be entered five times, once for each week in the month. The Edit Copy option makes short work of this. Finally, you must enter the sales quantities and amounts. Perform these tasks with the following steps. The week beginning dates still should be highlighted. Begin by copying the dates twice.

1. From the Edit menu, choose Copy. The blinking marquee appears around the dates.

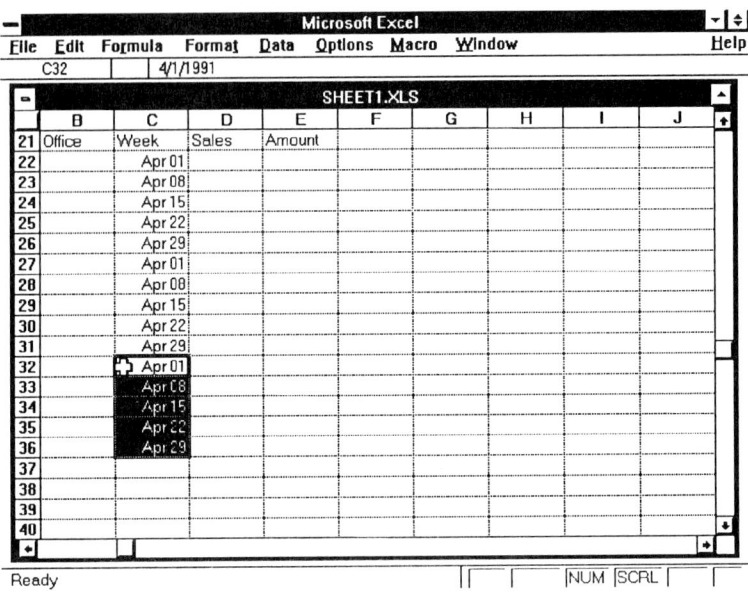

**FIGURE 8-9**   Dates as copied

2. Click on C27 and press (ENTER). The dates are copied to C27:C31. (C27:C31 is highlighted.)

3. Again choose Copy, click on C32, and press (ENTER). The dates are copied a second time, as shown in Figure 8-9.

Next copy the sales office number and name.

4. Click on the vertical scroll bar above the scroll box and drag across the two cells containing "250 Boston."

5. From the Edit menu choose Copy.

6. Again click on the vertical scroll bar, this time below the scroll box, drag A22 through B26, and press (ENTER). "250 Boston" is copied five times, as shown here:

|    | A      | B      | C      |
|----|--------|--------|--------|
| 21 | Number | Office | Week   |
| 22 | 250    | Boston | Apr 01 |
| 23 | 250    | Boston | Apr 08 |
| 24 | 250    | Boston | Apr 15 |
| 25 | 250    | Boston | Apr 22 |
| 26 | 250    | Boston | Apr 29 |
| 27 |        |        | Apr 01 |

7. Repeat steps 4 through 6 to copy "260 Denver" to A27:B31 and "270 Seattle" to A32:B36.

As the third step enter and copy a formula to calculate the sales amount from the sale units, and then enter those units to complete the database.

8. Click on E22, type **=D22*145.95**, press (**ENTER**), and with Format Number, format E22 with a comma and no decimals (#,##0). (145.95 is the average value of a sale, so you can derive the total sales amount by multiplying the number of sales by this average.)

9. Highlight E22 through E36, and from the Edit menu choose Fill Down.

10. Type the sales figures in D22 through D36 as shown in Figure 8-10, which shows the finished database.

Carefully check your work against Figure 8-10. This April sales database is used for the remainder of the chapter. Entry errors could cause considerable confusion in subsequent sections.

## Using the Database

The selection or modification of data within an Excel database requires that you identify two or three ranges for use in these operations. The first range is the database itself and is required by

|    | A      | B      | C     | D     | E      |
|----|--------|--------|-------|-------|--------|
| 21 | Number | Office | Week  | Sales | Amount |
| 22 | 250    | Boston | Apr 01| 46    | 6,714  |
| 23 | 250    | Boston | Apr 08| 31    | 4,524  |
| 24 | 250    | Boston | Apr 15| 68    | 9,925  |
| 25 | 250    | Boston | Apr 22| 55    | 8,027  |
| 26 | 250    | Boston | Apr 29| 42    | 6,130  |
| 27 | 260    | Denver | Apr 01| 61    | 8,903  |
| 28 | 260    | Denver | Apr 08| 48    | 7,006  |
| 29 | 260    | Denver | Apr 15| 43    | 6,276  |
| 30 | 260    | Denver | Apr 22| 78    | 11,384 |
| 31 | 260    | Denver | Apr 29| 36    | 5,254  |
| 32 | 270    | Seattle| Apr 01| 38    | 5,546  |
| 33 | 270    | Seattle| Apr 08| 51    | 7,443  |
| 34 | 270    | Seattle| Apr 15| 78    | 11,384 |
| 35 | 270    | Seattle| Apr 22| 46    | 6,714  |
| 36 | 270    | Seattle| Apr 29| 81    | 11,822 |

**FIGURE 8-10** Completed April Sales database

all operations other than sorting. The *database range* is the source for selecting records on which you will operate. The second range, the *criteria range*, also is required by all operations other than sorting. The criteria range contains the criteria by which the selections are made. The third range, the *extract range*, is required only by the Extract option. The extract range is a separate database that is filled by the Extract option.

**DEFINING THE DATABASE** To define the database from which you want to select records, you must select or highlight it and choose the Data Set Database option. The database range must contain the full set of records from which you want to select, as well as the field names for those records. When you choose the Set Database option, Excel attaches the name Database to the range you have highlighted. This range name is the same as range names

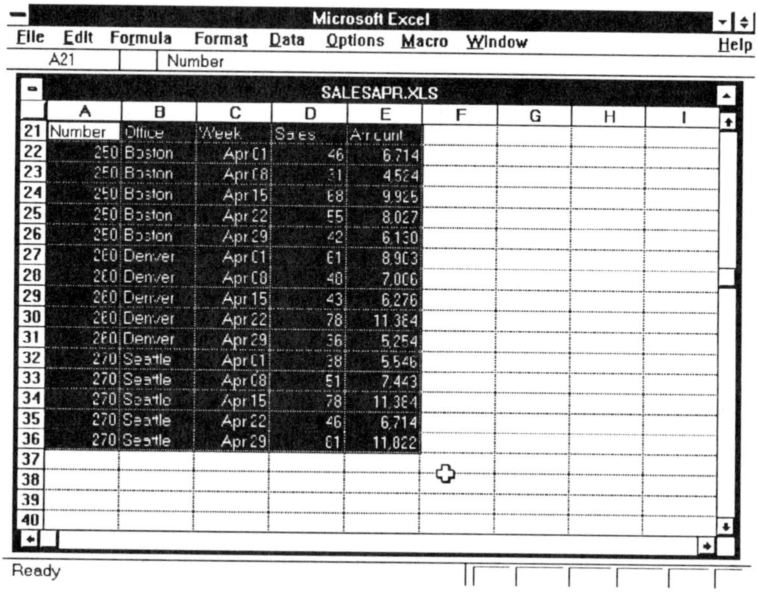

**FIGURE 8-11** April Sales database highlighted

you can create yourself with the Formula Define Name option. Define the database range for the April sales database with these steps:

1. Drag from A21 through E36. The database is highlighted as shown in Figure 8-11.

2. From the Data menu choose Set Database.

The highlighted range is accepted as the database, and you are returned to ready mode.

**ESTABLISHING THE SELECTION CRITERIA** Establishing the selection criteria requires that you identify a criteria range with the Set Criteria option. The criteria range is a small database.

The first row of the criteria range must contain some or all of the field names from the database you just defined. The rest of the criteria range contains the criteria that will be the basis of your selection.

You can build the criteria range in any blank area of the worksheet, but it is usually best not to build it directly below the database so there is room for expansion. The field names in the criteria range must be exact copies of the field names in the input range. Frequently the full set of field names is copied from the input range with the Copy option.

The criteria directly relate to the field name under which they are entered. For example, if you want to select all of the records for the Boston sales office in the April sales database, you build a two-cell criteria range. The top cell has the field name Office; the bottom cell contains "Boston." The selection process searches for "Boston" in the Office field. This process gives you the matches between the criterion and the records in the input range. A criterion of "Boston" also gives you a match with "Bostonian." If you want just "Boston" you must enter the formula =" =**Boston**", including the quote marks. You can use text, numbers, or formulas as criteria for matching.

You can also use text, numbers, or formulas that cause Excel to search for records that are not matches. For example, if you want all records from the April Sales database that have more than 60 sales, you build a criteria range with Sales as the field name and >60 as the criterion. Do that now, and identify it as the criteria range with the following instructions. Since you want the field name in the criterion to be exactly the same as the field name in the database, you copy the database field name.

1. Click on D21, choose Copy from the Edit menu, click on G21, and press (ENTER). The word "Sales" is copied from D21 to G21.

2. Click on G22, type **>60**, and press (ENTER). The field name and criterion are entered as shown here:

|   | B | C | D | E | F | G | H |
|---|---|---|---|---|---|---|---|
|   | \multicolumn{7}{c}{SHEET1.XLS} |
|   | Office | Week | Sales | Amount |   | Sales |   |
|   | Boston | Apr 01 | 46 | 6,714 |   | >60 |   |
|   | Boston | Apr 08 | 31 | 4,524 |   |   |   |

3. Drag on G21 through G22 and choose Set Criteria from the Data menu. The criterion is identified.

The >60 criterion entered in the example is just one of many ways to specify criteria. Some rules on specifying criteria are as follows:

- Use relational operators (< for less than, > for greater than, = for equal to, < > for not equal to, < = for less than or equal to, and > = for greater than or equal to) with both text and numbers, either alone or in a formula.

- Use wildcard characters (? for any single character and * for any group of characters) in text that will not be exact matches. For example, entering **pea?** as the criterion selects "peak", "peal", and "pear", while entering **for*** selects "for", "foray", "forecast", and "forest". You can combine wildcard characters. For example, AM??DC* might be used with part numbers in an inventory system to select all parts from a given manufacturer (the AM) for a particular machine (the DC).

- Numbers are matched without regard to their format. For example, the number 54 matches $54, 5400%, 5.40E+01, and 54.00.

- Formulas that refer to fields in the database range should use relative addresses. Formulas that refer to fields outside the database range should use absolute addresses. For example, =SALES>=AMOUNT/150 is the same as =D22>=E22/150 and uses relative addressing to refer to fields within the database range of the April sales database. On the other hand,

=SALES>=$H$23 uses absolute addressing to refer to an address outside the database range.

- Usually a criterion refers to the field name under which it has been entered. If the criterion is a formula that relates to the total record instead of a specific field (as an example, =SALES>= AMOUNT/150), then you need to use a field name in the criteria not used in the database. For example, Formula might be such a field name.

- You can use the database field names in a criterion formula (=SALES>=AMOUNT/150 for example) without defining them with the Formula Define Names option. You will get the error message #NAME? in the criterion cell, but the formula is utilized correctly for database selection. An example of the error message resulting from a field name formula is shown here:

| F | G | H |
|---|---|---|
|   | Formula |   |
|   | #NAME? |   |
|   |   |   |

- If you put criteria in multiple columns but only one row of a criteria range, all of the criteria must be satisfied for a record in the database range to be selected. It is as if you had put a logical And between the fields. For example, if you create a criteria range with field names of Sales and Amount and enter **>60** under Sales and **>8000** under Amount, only records that have both greater than 60 sales and greater than $8,000 in the amount are selected. If either of those conditions are not met, the record is not selected. This is an And criteria range:

| F | G | H | I |
|---|---|---|---|
|   | Sales | Amount |   |
|   | >60 | >8000 |   |
|   |   |   |   |

- If you put criteria in multiple rows of a criteria range, satisfying either of the criterion causes a record in the database range to be selected. It is as if you had put a logical Or between the fields. For example, if you enter **>60** under Sales in row 1 and **>8000** under Amount in row 2, records that satisfy either criterion are selected. This is an Or criteria range:

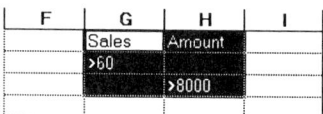

- If you have a blank row in a criteria range, you select all of the records in the database. You can combine as many rows and as many columns as necessary to specify the criteria you need, but do not include a blank row unless you want to select all records.

- You can select records that fall within a range for a given field. For example, select all records that have greater than 60 sales and less than 70 sales by creating two criteria columns, both with the same field name, and entering the **>60** in one column and **<70** in the other, as shown here:

**FINDING SELECTED RECORDS**  Once you have specified both the database range and the criteria range, you can identify selected records in the database range with the Data Find option. When you choose the option, Excel highlights the first record in the database range that satisfies the criteria, the mode changes to find, and the scroll bars become striped. The striping tells you that the scroll bars have changed their use—they now take you from one selected record to another. You can find (select) additional records by clicking on the down scroll arrow or return to a record selected earlier by clicking on the up scroll arrow. By clicking on the scroll bar itself, you move to a selected record in the next or previous screen. If you want to return to ready mode you can select Exit Find from the Data menu or click anywhere on the worksheet outside of the database.

You can also use the following keys to continue to select records or to end the process:

| Key | Action |
| --- | --- |
| (DOWN ARROW) | Highlights the next record that satisfies the criteria |
| (UP ARROW) | Highlights the previous record that satisfies the criteria |
| (ENTER) | Moves the active cell within the selected record |
| (ESC) | Ends Data Find and returns you to ready mode |
| (LEFT ARROW) or (RIGHT ARROW) | Scrolls the worksheet left or right one column at a time without affecting the selected record |

Try the Data Find option with the following instructions:

1. From the Data menu, choose Find. The Data Find option changes the mode indicator to FIND and highlights the first record that satisfies the criteria, as shown in Figure 8-12.

2. Click on the down scroll arrow or press (DOWN ARROW). The second record that satisfies the criteria is highlighted.

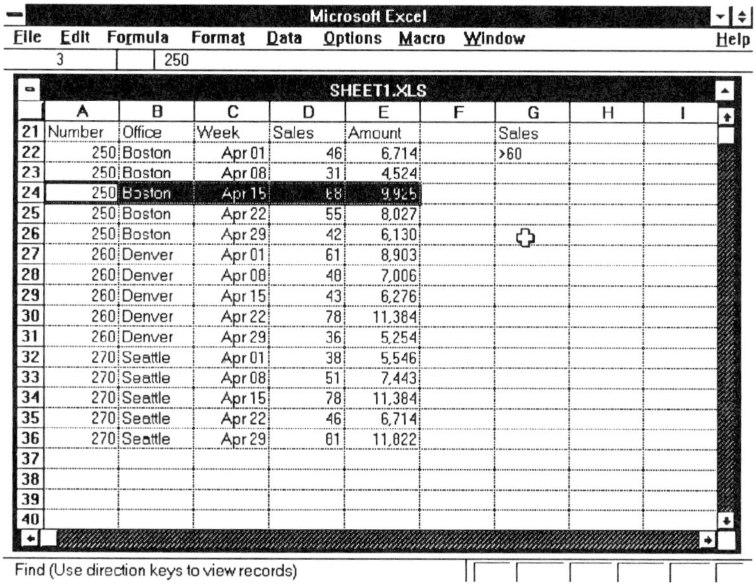

**FIGURE 8-12** First record found with Data Find

3. Click on the scroll bar and up scroll arrow, and try the other keys to become familiar with how they work.

4. Click on the worksheet outside of the database or press (ESC) to return to ready mode.

**DEFINING AN EXTRACT RANGE** The Data Extract option needs a place to put the records selected from the database range. The extract range is that place. It is defined by the Data Extract option. The extract range, like the criteria range, must have a row containing one or more field names that exactly match the field names in the database range. If you want to limit the number of rows that Excel can fill with selected records, then you need to highlight that number of rows in addition to the row of field names when you define the extract range. If you want Excel to define the number of rows it needs, then highlight only the row of field names when you define the extract range. Define an extract range with these steps:

1. Click on G26, type **Office**, press (RIGHT ARROW), type **Week**, and press (ENTER). The labels "Office" and "Week" will be placed in G26 and H26, respectively.

2. Drag G26 through H40 to highlight the range to be used as the extract range, as shown in Figure 8-13.

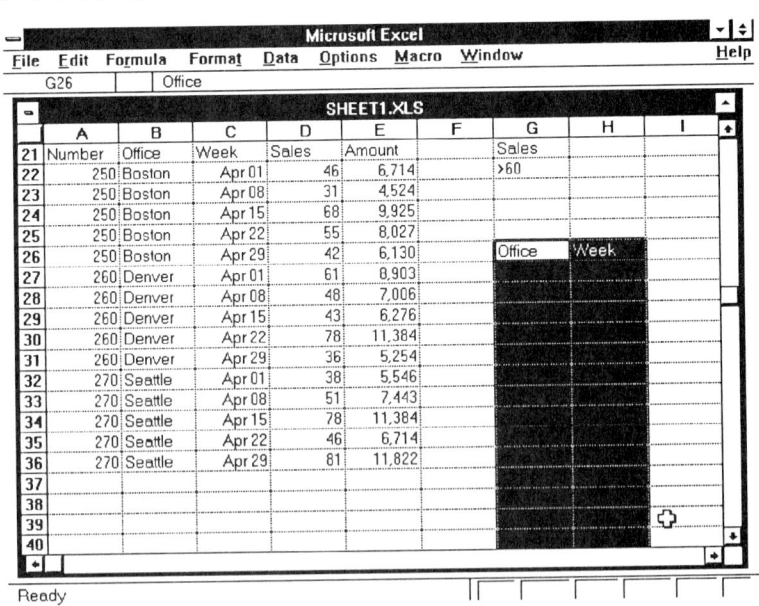

**FIGURE 8-13**   Extract range selected

**EXTRACTING SELECTED RECORDS** The Data Extract option copies the selected records in the database range to the extract range. The selection is based on the selection criteria. Try it now.

1. Choose Extract from the Data menu. The Data Extract dialog box opens, as shown here:

The Data Extract dialog box allows you to select all records that match the criteria or only unique records, thus eliminating duplicates. Here you select all records.

2. Click OK. Data Extract executes, filling a part of the extract range with the selected records, as shown in Figure 8-14.

If Data Extract selects more records than can fit in the extract range, you get an error message to that effect. Enlarge the area or highlight only the field names and repeat the extract.

 If you specify only a one-row extract range and thereby allow Excel to use as much room as it needs for selected records, any other information in the rows under the field names of the extract range are written over. All rows below the extract range are cleared, whether or not they are used for extracted data. You cannot undo Data Extract.

You have done quite a bit of work on this worksheet, so this is a good time to save it before going on.

|   | A | B | C | D | E | F | G | H | I |
|---|---|---|---|---|---|---|---|---|---|
| 21 | Number | Office | Week | Sales | Amount |  | Sales |  |  |
| 22 | 250 | Boston | Apr 01 | 46 | 6,714 |  | >60 |  |  |
| 23 | 250 | Boston | Apr 08 | 31 | 4,524 |  |  |  |  |
| 24 | 250 | Boston | Apr 15 | 68 | 9,925 |  |  |  |  |
| 25 | 250 | Boston | Apr 22 | 55 | 8,027 |  |  |  |  |
| 26 | 250 | Boston | Apr 29 | 42 | 6,130 |  | Office | Week |  |
| 27 | 260 | Denver | Apr 01 | 61 | 8,903 |  | Boston | Apr 15 |  |
| 28 | 260 | Denver | Apr 08 | 48 | 7,006 |  | Denver | Apr 01 |  |
| 29 | 260 | Denver | Apr 15 | 43 | 6,276 |  | Denver | Apr 22 |  |
| 30 | 260 | Denver | Apr 22 | 78 | 11,384 |  | Seattle | Apr 15 |  |
| 31 | 260 | Denver | Apr 29 | 36 | 5,254 |  | Seattle | Apr 29 |  |
| 32 | 270 | Seattle | Apr 01 | 38 | 5,546 |  |  |  |  |
| 33 | 270 | Seattle | Apr 08 | 51 | 7,443 |  |  |  |  |
| 34 | 270 | Seattle | Apr 15 | 78 | 11,384 |  |  |  |  |
| 35 | 270 | Seattle | Apr 22 | 46 | 6,714 |  |  |  |  |
| 36 | 270 | Seattle | Apr 29 | 61 | 11,822 |  |  |  |  |

**FIGURE 8-14** Results of the Data Extract

3. Choose Save As from the File menu, type **c:\wi\sheet\salesapr**, and press (ENTER). The file is saved. If you are using a different directory, make the appropriate changes.

# ANALYZING INFORMATION FROM A DATABASE

In addition to extracting or selecting information, the other primary reason for building a database is to analyze the information it contains. Analyzing includes summarizing, averaging, counting, grouping, and calculating the standard deviation and variance. The next few sections cover several functions and options within Excel that are used for analyzing information in databases.

## Using Database Statistical Functions

In previous chapters you used the SUM function to add a set of numbers in a range. SUM has the general form, or syntax, of

SUM(*range*)

where *range* is any set of range names or addresses. Other functions include AVERAGE, which calculates the average of a range; COUNT, which counts the number of items in a range; and MIN and MAX, which identify the minimum and maximum numbers in a range. They have similar syntaxes:

AVERAGE(*range*)
COUNT (*range*)
MAX(*range*)
MIN (*range*)

Excel has another set of functions called *database statistical functions*. Among them are DSUM, DAVERAGE, and DCOUNT. They have the same general purposes as statistical functions: they sum, average, and count. Database statistical functions, however, are meant to operate on specific fields in a database and to perform only on records that match criteria. Each database statistical function has a syntax similar to

DSUM(*database, field,criteria*)

where *database* is a range on the worksheet containing the field, *field* identifies a field name or column in the database on which you want to operate (sum, average, count), and *criteria* is a criteria range used to select the particular records you want to use.

The primary differences between SUM and DSUM or between statistical and database statistical functions is that statistical functions operate on a range without any selection. Database statistical functions select both a particular column (field) within a larger range and particular records (cells in the column) on which to operate. DSUM is the same as SUM if the database is a single column you want to sum and the criteria is blank.

All of the information you have learned about database ranges and criteria ranges as they apply to Data options applies to database statistical functions. The *database* can be the addresses of a range on the worksheet (A21:E36, for example), the name of a range you have defined with Formula Define Name, or the name Database if you have defined a range with the Data Set Database option.

The *field* can be a field name, a field number, or the address of a cell that contains a field name or number. If a field name is used, it should be in quotation marks and match the field name in the database range exactly. The number determines the column within the database table beginning with the leftmost column as 1. The number for the second column is 2, the number for the third column is 3, and so on.

The *criteria* can be the addresses of a range on the worksheet (G21:G22, for example), a name you have defined with Formula Define Name, or the name Criteria if you have defined a range with the Data Set Criteria option.

All of the following formulas do the same thing: sum the selected sales units in the April Sales database you entered into A21:E36 using the criteria you entered into G21:G22.

=DSUM(A21:E36,4,G21:G22)
=DSUM(Database,"Sales",Criteria)
=DSUM(sales,D21,top) if you have defined the names "sales" as A21:E36
  and "top" as G21:G22.

**CREATING RANGE NAMES** You have already named the database and criteria ranges of the April Sales database using the Set Database and Set Criteria options on the Data menu. These options name the ranges Database and Criteria, respectively. Once you have used the options to set the names, you can use them in any Excel function, as if they were any other range name. As you probably guessed, a range name is a name, like Sales, that you define to represent a range of cells on the worksheet. You can have only one range with a given range name, so you can have only one range named Database and one range named Criteria. As you work with database statistical functions, you are going to want to use ranges other than those defined as Database and Criteria. For these other ranges you can use either range addresses or range names.

There are two and possibly three reasons to use range names over range addresses. First, and most compelling, is that a range name always accurately reflects changes you make to a worksheet. When you use a range name in several functions, all those functions are updated when you change the range referred to by the name. Secondly, range names are often easier to remember and almost always more recognizable than the range addresses they represent. Third, in some cases a short range name is easier to enter than a long set of range addresses. Since you will be building several database statistical functions with the same database and criteria ranges, get some practice naming a couple of ranges even though you could use the name already attached to one of those ranges. Use these instructions for that purpose:

1. Highlight the range A21:E36 (the database) and choose Define Name from the Formula menu. The Define Name dialog box opens, as shown here:

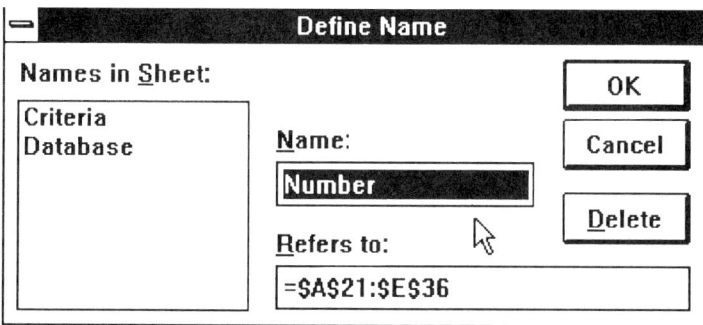

Notice that Criteria and Database are listed as names already existing on the worksheet. Also the range that you highlighted is shown as the range to which the new name you will enter will be attached. Number, which came from the first cell of the highlighted range, is shown as a default name, but you want a different name for the range.

2. Type **Sales** and press (ENTER). The database is now named Sales as well as Database. This does not conflict with the field named Sales.

3. Highlight the range A38:A-39, which you will use as a second criteria range, choose Define Name, type **Loc** (short for location), and press (ENTER) to name the range.

Next, prepare an area on the worksheet for entering database statistical functions by entering several titles.

4. Click on A38, type **Office**, press (RIGHT ARROW) twice to C38, type **Number**, press (RIGHT ARROW), type **Total #**, press (RIGHT ARROW), type **Total $**, press (RIGHT ARROW), type **Average #**, press (RIGHT ARROW), type **Average $**, and then press (ENTER).

The bottom few lines of your screen should look like this:

|    |        |   |        |         |         |           |           |
|----|--------|---|--------|---------|---------|-----------|-----------|
| 37 |        |   |        |         |         |           |           |
| 38 | Office |   |        | Number  | Total # | Total $   | Average # Average $ |
| 39 |        |   |        |         |         |           |           |
| 40 |        |   |        |         |         |           |           |

**BUILDING THE FORMULAS** Under each of the titles (Number, Total #, and so on) you can enter a database statistical function. (Use Office as a criteria range field, not a title for a database statistical function.) The titles are not necessary for the database statistical functions, but they are informative; after the formulas are entered, their result is all that is displayed. The formulas you enter are DCOUNT, to count the number of nonblank cells in a field in the records in the database range that match the criteria; DSUM, to sum a field in the records of the database range that match the criteria; and DAVERAGE, to average a field in the records of the database range that match the criteria. Initially you leave the criteria blank to select all of the records in the database range.

When you enter a function, do not include spaces anywhere except in a literal enclosed in quotation marks. Also, be sure to include the = symbol and both parentheses. With these rules in mind, enter several database statistical functions with the following steps.

1. Click on C39. The active cell moves to C39.

2. Type **=dcount(sales,"number",loc)** and press (ENTER). The result appears in C39, as shown in Figure 8-15. The DCOUNT function counts the number of nonblank cells in the Number field of the Sales database that match the criteria in Loc.

When typing a function, it is a good idea to use lowercase letters. That way you can tell if Excel recognizes what you are typing. If it does, the functions automatically change to all uppercase, and range names change to leading caps. Excel acts like a spelling checker.

3. Click on D39, type **=dsum(sales,"sales",loc)**, and press (RIGHT ARROW). The result, 802, appears in D39. This DSUM function adds all the numbers in the Sales field of the Sales database that match the criteria in Loc.

4. In the next three cells type the following formulas. Press (RIGHT ARROW) after the first two and (ENTER) after the last.

|    | A      | B       | C      | D     | E      | F | G     | H      | I |
|----|--------|---------|--------|-------|--------|---|-------|--------|---|
| 21 | Number | Office  | Week   | Sales | Amount |   | Sales |        |   |
| 22 | 250    | Boston  | Apr 01 | 46    | 6,714  |   | >60   |        |   |
| 23 | 250    | Boston  | Apr 08 | 31    | 4,524  |   |       |        |   |
| 24 | 250    | Boston  | Apr 15 | 68    | 9,925  |   |       |        |   |
| 25 | 250    | Boston  | Apr 22 | 55    | 8,027  |   |       |        |   |
| 26 | 250    | Boston  | Apr 29 | 42    | 6,130  |   | Office | Week  |   |
| 27 | 260    | Denver  | Apr 01 | 61    | 8,903  |   | Boston | Apr 15 |  |
| 28 | 260    | Denver  | Apr 08 | 48    | 7,006  |   | Denver | Apr 01 |  |
| 29 | 260    | Denver  | Apr 15 | 43    | 6,276  |   | Denver | Apr 22 |  |
| 30 | 260    | Denver  | Apr 22 | 78    | 11,384 |   | Seattle | Apr 15 | |
| 31 | 260    | Denver  | Apr 29 | 36    | 5,254  |   | Seattle | Apr 29 | |
| 32 | 270    | Seattle | Apr 01 | 38    | 5,546  |   |       |        |   |
| 33 | 270    | Seattle | Apr 08 | 51    | 7,443  |   |       |        |   |
| 34 | 270    | Seattle | Apr 15 | 78    | 11,384 |   |       |        |   |
| 35 | 270    | Seattle | Apr 22 | 46    | 6,714  |   |       |        |   |
| 36 | 270    | Seattle | Apr 29 | 81    | 11,822 |   |       |        |   |
| 37 |        |         |        |       |        |   |       |        |   |
| 38 | Office |         | Number | Total # | Total $ | Average # | Average $ | | |
| 39 |        |         | 15     |       |        |   |       |        |   |
| 40 |        |         |        |       |        |   |       |        |   |

**FIGURE 8-15**   =DCOUNT completed

```
=dsum(sales,"amount",loc)
=daverage(sales,"sales",loc)
=daverage(sales,"amount",loc)
```

5. Drag C39:G39, choose Number from the Format menu, click on #,##0, and click on OK. The row of database statistical functions is formatted with the comma format and no decimal places. Figure 8-16 shows the results.

You are now in a position to change the criteria and immediately see the result—called a what-if situation. The formulas in C39:G39 reflect the criterion in A39. Enter a new criteria, and the formulas reflect the result. Currently, the blank criteria means that the formulas are utilizing the entire database range. If you enter

|    | A      | B       | C      | D      | E       | F | G        | H       | I |
|----|--------|---------|--------|--------|---------|---|----------|---------|---|
| 21 | Number | Office  | Week   | Sales  | Amount  |   | Sales    |         |   |
| 22 |    250 | Boston  | Apr 01 |     46 |   6,714 |   | >60      |         |   |
| 23 |    250 | Boston  | Apr 08 |     31 |   4,524 |   |          |         |   |
| 24 |    250 | Boston  | Apr 15 |     68 |   9,925 |   |          |         |   |
| 25 |    250 | Boston  | Apr 22 |     55 |   8,027 |   |          |         |   |
| 26 |    250 | Boston  | Apr 29 |     42 |   6,130 |   | Office   | Week    |   |
| 27 |    260 | Denver  | Apr 01 |     61 |   8,903 |   | Boston   | Apr 15  |   |
| 28 |    260 | Denver  | Apr 08 |     48 |   7,006 |   | Denver   | Apr 01  |   |
| 29 |    260 | Denver  | Apr 15 |     43 |   6,276 |   | Denver   | Apr 22  |   |
| 30 |    260 | Denver  | Apr 22 |     78 |  11,384 |   | Seattle  | Apr 15  |   |
| 31 |    260 | Denver  | Apr 29 |     36 |   5,254 |   | Seattle  | Apr 29  |   |
| 32 |    270 | Seattle | Apr 01 |     38 |   5,546 |   |          |         |   |
| 33 |    270 | Seattle | Apr 08 |     51 |   7,443 |   |          |         |   |
| 34 |    270 | Seattle | Apr 15 |     78 |  11,384 |   |          |         |   |
| 35 |    270 | Seattle | Apr 22 |     46 |   6,714 |   |          |         |   |
| 36 |    270 | Seattle | Apr 29 |     81 |  11,822 |   |          |         |   |
| 37 |        |         |        |        |         |   |          |         |   |
| 38 | Office |         | Number | Total # | Total $ | Average # | Average $ |   |   |
| 39 |        |         |     15 |    802 | 117,052 | 53 | 7,803 |         |   |

**FIGURE 8-16** Database statistical functions entered and formatted

**Boston** in the criteria range, the formulas utilize only records with Boston in the Office field. Try that next with these instructions:

6. Click on A39, type **Boston**, and press (ENTER). "Boston" is entered in the criteria range, and the formulas recalculate to reflect that, as shown in Figure 8-17. Note that the criteria is not case sensitive. You could enter **boston** or **BOSTON** with equal results.

## Creating a Data Table

As powerful as the criteria-and-formula combination is, Excel has a better way to handle it—a *data table*. A data table shows the results of one or more formulas when one or two variables in the formulas are varied. As an example, a data table can show the

```
                          Microsoft Excel
File  Edit  Formula  Format  Data  Options  Macro  Window            Help
      A39              Boston
                          SALESAPR.XLS
     A        B         C        D        E       F       G        H        I
21 Number  Office     Week    Sales   Amount         Sales
22         250 Boston  Apr 01    46     6,714         >60
23         250 Boston  Apr 08    31     4,524
24         250 Boston  Apr 15    68     9,925
25         250 Boston  Apr 22    55     8,027
26         250 Boston  Apr 29    42     6,130         Office   Week
27         260 Denver  Apr 01    61     8,903         Boston   Apr 15
28         260 Denver  Apr 08    48     7,006         Denver   Apr 01
29         260 Denver  Apr 15    43     6,276         Denver   Apr 22
30         260 Denver  Apr 22    78    11,384         Seattle  Apr 15
31         260 Denver  Apr 29    36     5,254         Seattle  Apr 29
32         270 Seattle Apr 01    38     5,546
33         270 Seattle Apr 08    51     7,443
34         270 Seattle Apr 15    78    11,384
35         270 Seattle Apr 22    46     6,714
36         270 Seattle Apr 29    81    11,822
37
38 Office              Number  Total #  Total $  Average # Average $
39 Boston                  5     242    35,320       48     7,064
40
Ready                                                      NUM
```

**FIGURE 8-17**   Effects of changing the criterion to Boston

results of the five database statistical functions entered in the last section for all of the three sales offices at one time. The variable in this case is the criteria, and the three offices are the variations. This is known as a *one-input data table*.

A one-input data table is a specially configured rectangular range on a worksheet. It can be configured in rows or columns, but rows are most common. For the row configuration, the top row contains as many formulas as you want to use. C39:G39 would be such a row. Then, in the column to the left of the first formula and beginning one row beneath it, you enter as many variables as you want applied to those formulas. Here you will enter the three cities **Boston**, **Denver**, and **Seattle**. Each formula needs to refer to one cell where the variable is substituted. This is known as the *input cell* and is A39 in this example. Build this data table now, and observe how it works. A39 should still be the active cell.

1. Press (DEL) and then (ENTER). The criterion (Boston) is erased, and the database statistical functions once again show the totals in the database range.

2. Click on B40, type **Boston, Denver,** and **Seattle**, pressing (DOWN ARROW) after the first two and (ENTER) after the last.

3. Highlight B39 through G42 as your data table range, which is shown here:

4. Choose Table from the Data menu. The Data Table dialog box opens, as shown here:

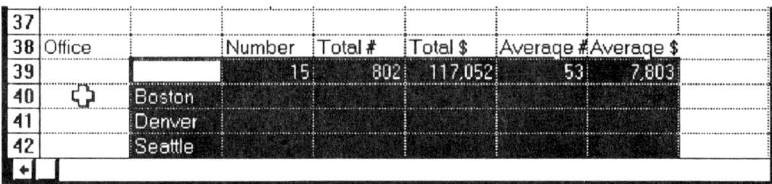

The Data Table dialog box asks you for either or both a row input cell and/or a column input cell. Since you have only one

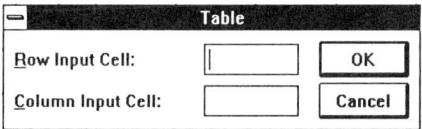

variable and it is in a column, you only need to enter a column input cell.

5. Press (TAB) to move from Row Input Cell to Column Input Cell, click on A39 (or type **$A$39**), and click on OK. The data table is then calculated, as shown here:

|    |         | Number | Total # | Total $  | Average # | Average $ |
|----|---------|--------|---------|----------|-----------|-----------|
| 37 |         |        |         |          |           |           |
| 38 | Office  |        |         |          |           |           |
| 39 |         | 15     | 802     | 117,052  | 53        | 7,803     |
| 40 | Boston  | 5      | 242     | 35319.9  | 48.4      | 7063.98   |
| 41 | Denver  | 5      | 266     | 38822.7  | 53.2      | 7764.54   |
| 42 | Seattle | 5      | 294     | 42909.3  | 58.8      | 8581.86   |

## Working with Two-Input Data Tables

The data table you just used is called a one-input data table because there is one variable (the criteria). It can have multiple formulas but only one variable. The other type of data table is a *two-input data table*. It has two variables but only one formula. In a two-input data table, one variable is in a column, as the sales offices were in the previous example, and the other variable is in a row. The formula is in the upper-left corner cell that is the intersection between the row variables and the column variables.

For an example of a two-input data table, assume you are a sales manager and want to look at the kind of money your sales people can earn with varying commission rates and varying monthly sales. The formula for this would be monthly sales times the commission rate times twelve to get annual income. The two variables are commission rates, which you want to look at from 3% through 6%, and monthly sales, which normally fall between $40,000 and $100,000. The steps to build such a table are as follows:

1. Click on the vertical scroll bar beneath the scroll box. You get a blank worksheet on your screen.

2. Click on C45, type **Commission Rate**, press (DOWN ARROW), type **Monthly Sales**, and press (ENTER).

3. Click on B48, type **3%**, press (ENTER), choose Series from the Data menu, type **.5%**, press (TAB), type **6%**, and press (ENTER). The row variables are entered.

4. Highlight B48 through H48, choose Number from the Format menu, click on the one decimal percent format you built (0.0%), and click on OK. The row variables are now formatted.

5. Click on A48, type **=e45*e46*12**, and press (DOWN ARROW) to enter the formula you want to vary.

6. Type **40,000**, press (ENTER), choose Series from the Data menu, type **10,000**, press (TAB), type **100,000**, click on Columns, and click on OK. The column variables are entered.

7. Highlight A48 through H55, choose Table from the Data menu, click on E45 for the row input cell, press (TAB), click on E46 for the column input cell, and click on OK.

Your commission table is produced, as shown in Figure 8-18. It is equivalent to doing the calculation 49 times (seven rates and

|    | A      | B     | C               | D     | E     | F     | G     | H     |
|----|--------|-------|-----------------|-------|-------|-------|-------|-------|
| 43 |        |       |                 |       |       |       |       |       |
| 44 |        |       |                 |       |       |       |       |       |
| 45 |        |       | Commission Rate |       |       |       |       |       |
| 46 |        |       | Monthly Sales   |       |       |       |       |       |
| 47 |        |       |                 |       |       |       |       |       |
| 48 | 0      | 3.0%  | 3.5%            | 4.0%  | 4.5%  | 5.0%  | 5.5%  | 6.0%  |
| 49 | 40000  | 14400 | 16800           | 19200 | 21600 | 24000 | 26400 | 28800 |
| 50 | 50000  | 18000 | 21000           | 24000 | 27000 | 30000 | 33000 | 36000 |
| 51 | 60000  | 21600 | 25200           | 28800 | 32400 | 36000 | 39600 | 43200 |
| 52 | 70000  | 25200 | 29400           | 33600 | 37800 | 42000 | 46200 | 50400 |
| 53 | 80000  | 28800 | 33600           | 38400 | 43200 | 48000 | 52800 | 57600 |
| 54 | 90000  | 32400 | 37800           | 43200 | 48600 | 54000 | 59400 | 64800 |
| 55 | 100000 | 36000 | 42000           | 48000 | 54000 | 60000 | 66000 | 72000 |

**FIGURE 8-18** Completed two-input data table

seven amounts). As you can see, a data table is a valuable analysis tool.

## USING LOOKUP FUNCTIONS

Excel has two functions that, while not database functions, are related to using databases. These are the horizontal and vertical table lookup functions HLOOKUP and VLOOKUP. The purpose of a horizontal or vertical lookup function is to be able to search a two-dimensional range to find an item based on finding a match in another item that is in the first row (horizontal lookup) or the first column (vertical lookup) and an index that tells Excel how many rows down (horizontal lookup) or across (vertical lookup) to move to find the sought after item. These functions have three arguments:

- A value to look for in the first row or column
- A range or database in which to look
- An index to determine how far down or across to look in the range to find the item sought

The formats of these functions are

HLOOKUP(*x,range,index*)
where *x* is the value to look for in the first row, and
VLOOKUP(*x,range,index*)
where *x* is the value to look for in the first column.

Use the vertical lookup function with the second database you built (April Sales) to calculate commissions earned based on the commission rates in the first database you built. The function uses the office number in each record of the second database as the value to search for in the leftmost column of the first database, which is the range of the function. An index of 5 is used since the commissions are in the fifth column. The values in the first column must be in numerical order, so the first step is to resort the first database by office number. Do that and then build the formulas with vertical lookup functions using these instructions:

1. Click on the vertical scroll bar above the scroll box until you are at the top of the worksheet and can see the first database you built.

2. Highlight A2 through E7, choose Sort from the Data menu, and click on OK to accept the defaults of sorting by rows on column A. Your database is sorted, as shown here:

|   | A | B | C | D | E | F |
|---|---|---|---|---|---|---|
| 1 | Number | Office | Manager | Quota | Commission | |
| 2 | 250 | Boston | Kaufman | 50,000 | 4.0% | |
| 3 | 255 | Atlanta | Pearson | 65,000 | 4.5% | |
| 4 | 260 | Denver | Fisher | 45,000 | 3.5% | |
| 5 | 265 | Chicago | Colby | 70,000 | 5.0% | |
| 6 | 270 | Seattle | Burke | 40,000 | 3.0% | |
| 7 | 275 | Phoenix | Shepard | 60,000 | 4.5% | |
| 8 |   |   |   |   |   |   |

3. Click on the vertical scroll bar below the scroll box and click on F22.

4. Type =e22*vlookup(a22,$a$2:$e$7,5) and press (ENTER). The formula is calculated with the result of 268.548 (4% of 6,714), as shown here:

| ormula | Format | Data | Options | Macro | Window |
|---|---|---|---|---|---|
| | =E22*VLOOKUP(A22,$A$2:$E$7,5) | | | | |

SALESAPR.XLS

| B | C | D | E | F | G |
|---|---|---|---|---|---|
| Office | Week | Sales | Amount | | Sales |
| Boston | Apr 01 | 46 | 6,714 | 268.548 | >60 |
| Boston | Apr 08 | 31 | 4,524 | | |

The lookup function took the office number, 250, in A22, searched the left column (because you used the vertical function) of the first database (A2:E7), and then, in the row in which it found 250, it went over five cells to find 4%. The 4% was then multiplied by the amount in E22. In searching for the 250 in the first database, Excel picks the first value that equals or exceeds the value for which it is searching. For that reason it is imperative that the range be sorted on the first column or row. The A2:E7 range needs to be absolute because you will be copying it down the database and you do not want it to vary as you do the A22 and E22. To complete the April Sales database, format cell F22 and copy it to the remaining entries in the database.

5. Choose Number from the Format menu, click on #,##0, and click on OK. The number is formatted with a comma and no decimal places.

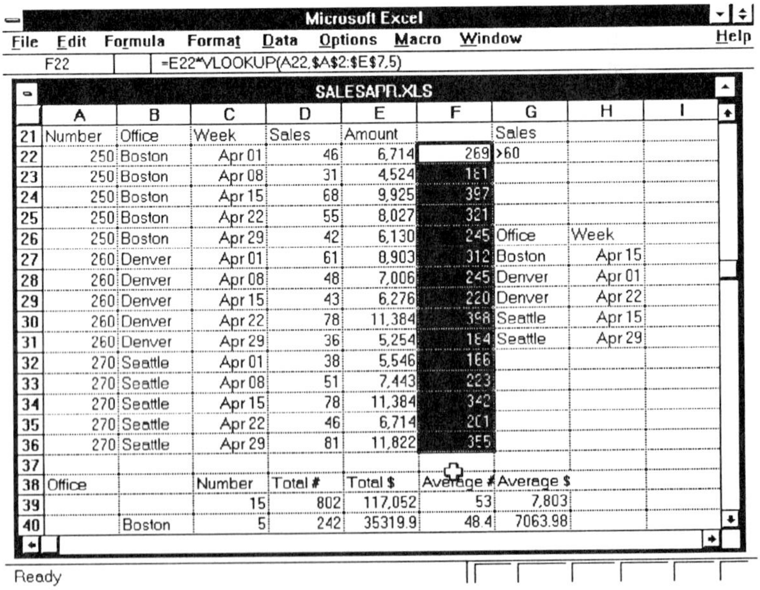

**FIGURE 8-19** Vertical lookup commission calculation

6. Highlight F22 through F36 and choose Fill Down from the Edit menu. The formula is copied down the rest of the database, as shown in Figure 8-19.

To assure yourself that the lookup function is working, check several of the numbers. For example, Denver's April 8 sales of 7,006 times 3.5% is 245, and Seattle's April 15 sales of 11,384 times 3% is 342. Remember that both the sales amount and the commission are rounded to the nearest whole number. You should find that the vertical lookup function is working perfectly.

Like several other features of Excel's database capabilities, the vertical and horizontal lookup functions are very powerful. As you can see in the example here, they allow you to combine two databases.

As a final step in this chapter, save your worksheet and leave Excel and Windows with the following instructions:

7. Choose Save from the File menu. The file is saved under its current name, replacing the version previously saved.

8. Double-click on both Excel's and the Program Manager's Control-menu box, and click on OK to leave Windows. Excel and Windows close and return you to the operating system.

# III

# ADVANCED USES OF EXCEL

Part III contains three chapters that discuss the advanced features of Excel. The pace of presentation quickens in Part III; the focus is almost entirely on advanced topics, with little or no time spent on building the worksheets used to demonstrate the topics. Of course, you are encouraged to follow along on your computer, but detailed steps for building the underlying worksheets are left to you.

Chapter 9 describes linking worksheets and using external files. Included are setting up links and transferring information among worksheets, as well as combining worksheets, exporting and importing text files, and dividing or parsing a text file. Linking worksheets is one of the more powerful features of Excel.

Chapter 10 looks at dates, functions, and macro functions. The section on functions ties together the work already done on functions in previous chapters. It provides a general discussion on using them, as well as discussion and examples of the types of functions not previously discussed. The macro section looks at macro functions in general, discusses how they are built, used, and debugged, and provides several examples.

Chapter 11 provides the *piéce de résistance*—all of the features needed to automate a sophisticated worksheet. Included are automatic loading, custom menus and dialog boxes, and updating a database from a data entry form, all operated by a set of macro functions. Chapter 11 shows you the full power of Excel.

It is not necessary for all readers to immediately read Part III. New users may want to wait until they have completed several spreadsheets of their own and know they want more of the capability of the product before reading Part III. Intermediate users probably want to continue on immediately; it is the next logical step in their Excel education. This section is what advanced users have been waiting for! At some point all readers should go through Part III; the "booster rockets" of Excel are discussed in this part. Such things as linking worksheets, functions, and macros are not as hard to use as you might think, and they significantly increase the power of Excel.

# LINKING WORKSHEETS AND USING EXTERNAL FILES

Linking Worksheets
Combining Files
Saving a Worksheet as a Text File
Importing ASCII Text Files

Establishing a link to and exchanging information between worksheets is the major topic in this chapter and a highlight of Excel. The chapter covers the process of combining several worksheets into one, including copying from one worksheet to another. Also, exporting and importing non-Excel text and number files is discussed, as is dividing or parsing a non-Excel text file.

## LINKING WORKSHEETS

If you are building a large worksheet, you can build it in two dimensions by using multiple areas on one worksheet, as shown on the left of Figure 9-1. This can be cumbersome, especially if the multiple areas are independent segments of a larger entity (as in departments, plants, or stores in a corporation). Unless each segment just fits on one screen, you have to use a combination of several keystrokes to get from one segment to another. Most importantly, if multiple people are maintaining the various portions of the large worksheet, as would be the case with multiple departments or stores in a larger corporation, you have the problem of combining their work.

Excel's answer to this is to allow multiple worksheets to be easily combined either in memory or while on disk, as the right side of Figure 9-1 shows. Each segment, such as a department, is a separate worksheet. To get from one segment to another you simply click on the next worksheet or choose it in the Window menu. Getting around and other range-oriented procedures are much easier with multiple worksheets than they are with a single large worksheet. Also, each department or other company segment can create and maintain their own worksheet, which can then be combined at the corporate level.

Multiple worksheets have a safety aspect. With a single large worksheet you have to worry about what effect inserting and deleting rows and columns will have on surrounding sections of the worksheet. With multiple worksheets you can put different sections on different sheets and forget about them as you insert and delete rows and columns in another worksheet.

The multiple worksheet structure also makes intuitive sense and simplifies the layout of almost any complex worksheet; after all, you are used to turning the pages of a book and putting new or different topics on different pages. The implementation of such a concept in a worksheet is very compelling. Build a multiple worksheet now, and see for yourself.

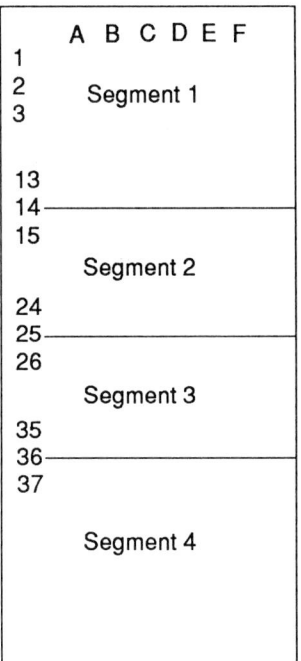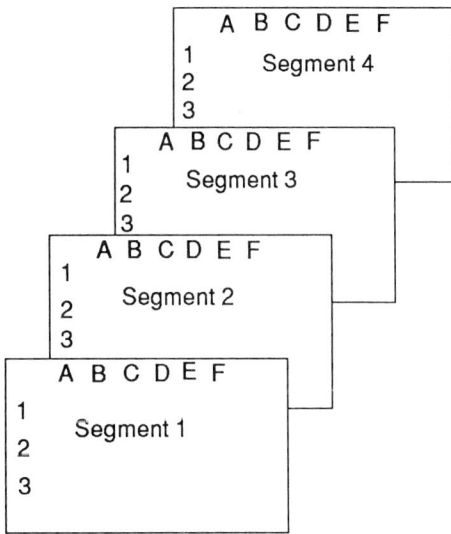

FIGURE 9-1  A single large worksheet versus multiple worksheets

## Creating Multiple Worksheets

In the examples in this chapter you use a set of simple departmental budgets for the marketing area of a corporation. Three departments—customer relations, public relations, and advertising—are summed into the total marketing budget. Each department and the total have exactly the same worksheet format. You can, therefore, build one master worksheet, copy it to the other three, and then come back and customize each of them. Prepare these worksheets now with the following instructions. Your computer should be on, Windows and Excel loaded, and you should have a blank worksheet on your screen.

1. Enter and center the titles and column headings as shown here: (column A has been widened to two normal column widths):

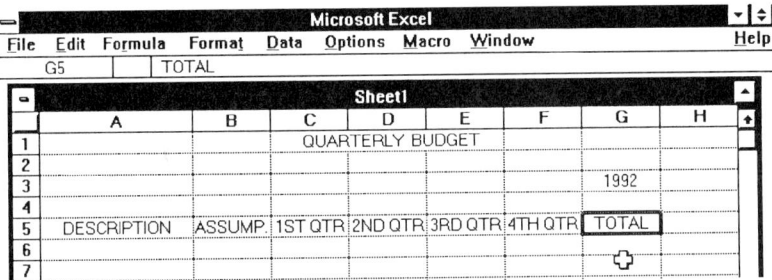

2. Add a top and bottom border in row 6, narrow that row to create a double underline, and enter the row headings as shown in Figure 9-2.

These departmental budgets are based on a head count, which varies by department, an assumption (ASSUMP.) for the average cost per head for each of the expense items, which also varies by department, and a quarterly growth percentage, which is common

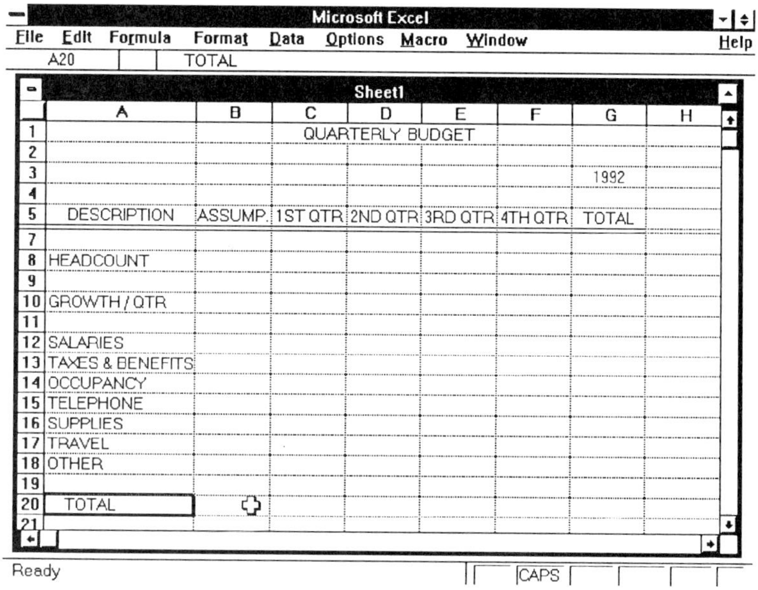

**FIGURE 9-2** Row headings and double underline

to all departments. The formula, then, for all expense items is head count times assumption times growth.

3. Enter the three growth percentages, format them with a single decimal place, and enter the first formula as shown in Figure 9-3.

In Figure 9-3 note the mixed references on all the cell addresses. These are very important since you will be copying this one formula to all the other quarters and expense items. Remember that the easiest way to get absolute and mixed references is by pressing (F4) immediately after pointing to or typing a cell address. The first time you press (F4) you get an absolute reference ($C$8), the second time you press (F4) you get a mixed reference with the row fixed (C$8), and the third time you press (F4) you get a mixed

```
                    Microsoft Excel - Sheet1
  File  Edit  Formula  Format  Data  Options  Macro  Window          Help
  C12        =C$8*$B12*(1+C$10)
        A         B      C      D      E      F      G      H
  1                         QUARTERLY BUDGET
  2
  3                                                 1992
  4
  5   DESCRIPTION  ASSUMP. 1ST QTR 2ND QTR 3RD QTR 4TH QTR  TOTAL
  7
  8   HEADCOUNT
  9
  10  GROWTH/QTR                  1.5%    3.0%    5.0%
  11
  12  SALARIES              0
  13  TAXES & BENEFITS
  14  OCCUPANCY
  15  TELEPHONE
  16  SUPPLIES
  17  TRAVEL
  18  OTHER
  19
  20  TOTAL
  21
  22
  23
  Ready                                      CAPS
```

**FIGURE 9-3** General formula and growth percentages

reference with the column fixed ($C8). You do not have to remember this because you can continue to press **F4** until you get the reference you want.

4. Select C12:F18 and choose Fill Down and Fill Right from the Edit menu to copy the formula in C12 to the other quarters and expense items.

5. Build the totals in G12:G18 and C20:F20.

6. Select B12:G20 and format it with #,##0. When you are done your master worksheet looks like Figure 9-4.

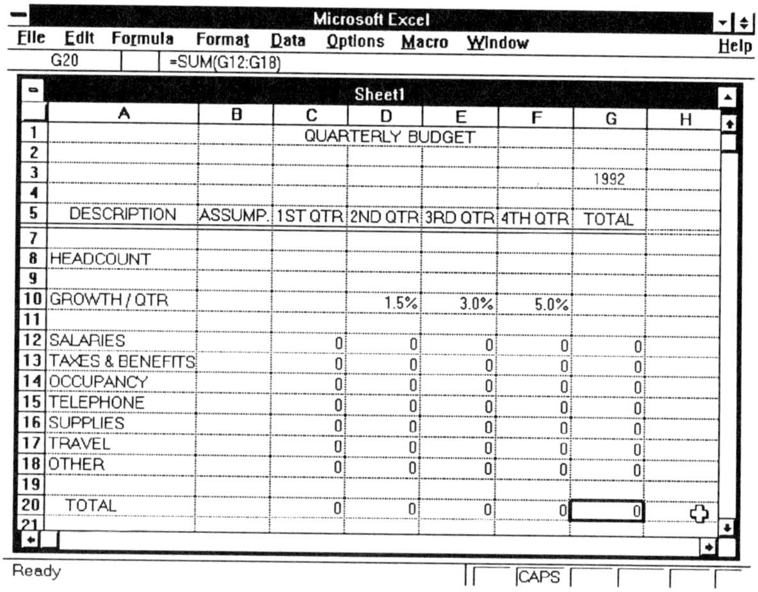

**FIGURE 9-4** Completed master worksheet

## Copying Across Worksheets

With the master worksheet complete, you can follow these steps to add the other three worksheets and copy the master worksheet to each of them.

1. Select A1:G20 and choose Copy from the Edit menu (or press (CTRL+INS)).

2. Choose New from the File menu, click on OK to select a worksheet, choose Paste from the Edit menu, widen column A to the width of two standard columns, and shorten the height of row 6 for a double underline.

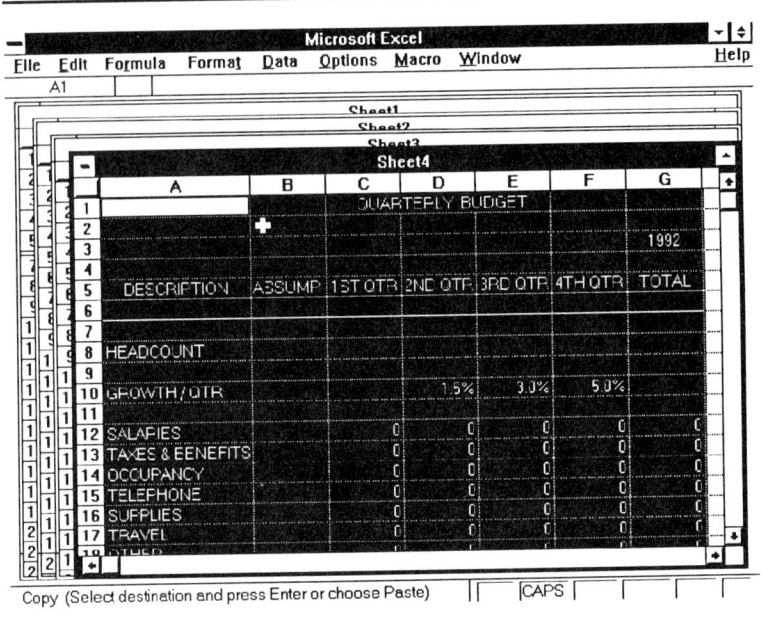

**FIGURE 9-5** Four worksheets with the base information on them

3. Repeat step 2 for a third and fourth worksheet. When you are done, your screen should look like Figure 9-5.

**HANDLING MULTIPLE WORKSHEETS** The display that you have on your screen and that is shown in Figure 9-5 is one of several ways to look at multiple worksheets. This current display is called overlapping worksheets. If you see only one window it is probably because you have maximized your view. To return to "normal"-size windows (where you can see a small amount of each window), click on the Restore option in the Control menu for the active window (not the Excel Control menu).

Remember that one way to get around with multiple worksheets is by clicking on the sheet you want to go to. The default display, shown in Figure 9-5, provides the ability to click on all the other sheets if you are looking at Sheet4, but you cannot click on any

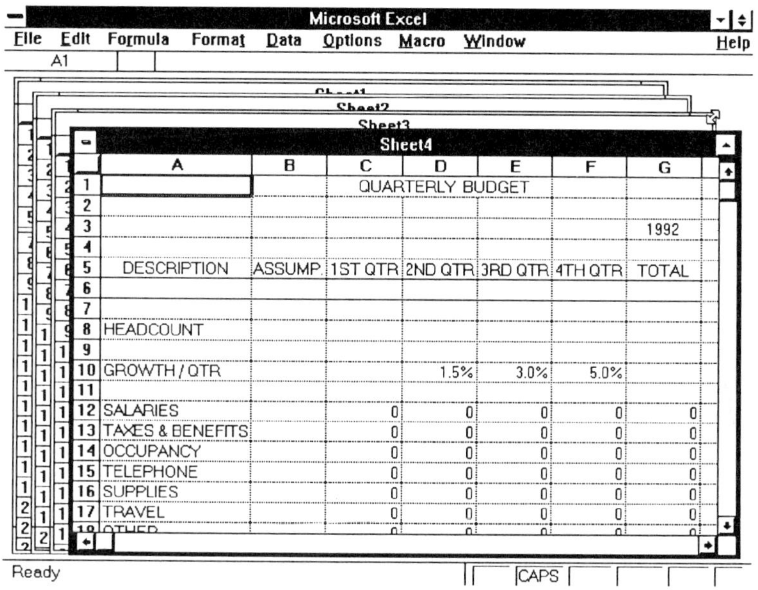

**FIGURE 9-6** Stair-stepping the right edge

other sheet if you are looking at Sheet1. The first step, then, is to pull the right edge of each worksheet to the left so they are stair-stepped in the reverse order to the left edge, as shown in Figure 9-6.

1. Drag the upper-right corner of Sheet3 to the left approximately the width of the vertical scroll bar on Sheet4. Repeat this procedure for Sheet2 and Sheet1, dragging them to the left the approximate width of the previous worksheet's scroll bar. Use the Size option on each worksheet's Control menu to do this operation with the keyboard.

Next try switching between sheets, first with the mouse and then with the Window menu.

2. Click successively on worksheets 3, 2, and 1. Notice how the sheets are now stair-stepped on the right. Had you not done step 1, you would now be looking at only Sheet1.

3. Click randomly on the various worksheets. For example, click on Sheet3, Sheet4, Sheet1, and Sheet2. After a while you can tell which is which by their heights and if they are showing on the left or right.

4. Click on the Window menu. Notice how each worksheet is listed, and the last worksheet you clicked on, the *active worksheet,* has a check mark beside it, as shown here:

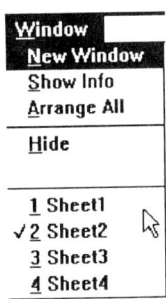

5. Choose one or two of the worksheet options from the Window menu. Notice how this method works exactly like clicking on a worksheet. The benefits of using the menu are that there is never any question which worksheet you are going to and the worksheet does not have to be visible.

All of your work so far has been with overlapping windows. Another type of window view is called a *tiled view,* which basically gives each window a small part of the screen. Look at that now.

6. Choose Arrange All from the Window menu. The windows are resized so that a portion of all the windows you have open are displayed on the screen, as shown in Figure 9-7.

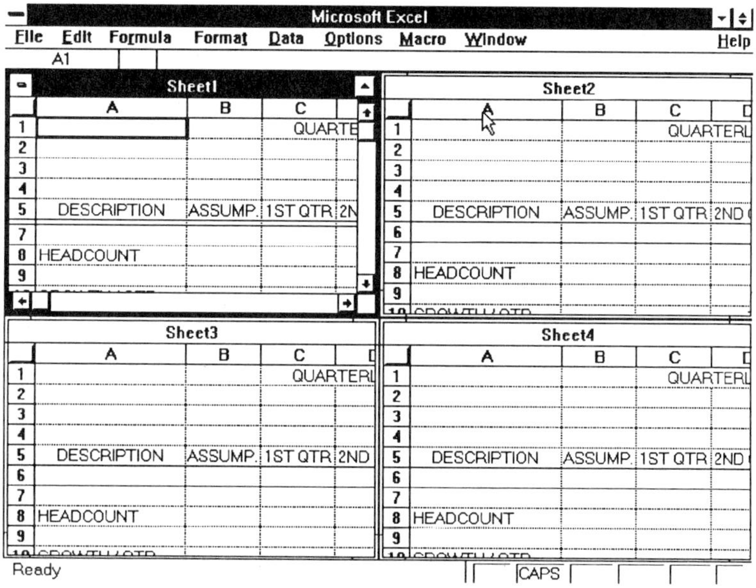

**FIGURE 9-7** Tiled view of worksheets

With the tiled view you can easily see what worksheet you want to use, and then you can click on the Maximize button to actually use the worksheet. When you restore the worksheet to its original size with the Restore option on the worksheet's Control menu, you return to the tiled view. The only disadvantage of using the tiled view is that you cannot easily get back to the overlapped view. You must manually move and size each worksheet.

**CUSTOMIZING INDIVIDUAL WORKSHEETS** Using the tiled view, customize each worksheet by following these three instructions:

1. Click on Sheet1 to make it the active sheet, and then click on its Maximize button so Sheet1 fills the Excel work area.

```
                    Microsoft Excel - Sheet1
 File  Edit  Formula  Format  Data  Options  Macro  Window              Help
 B18        125
        A        B      C      D      E      F      G      H
 1                        QUARTERLY BUDGET
 2
 3                          ADVERTISING              1992
 4
 5  DESCRIPTION  ASSUMP  1ST QTR  2ND QTR  3RD QTR  4TH QTR  TOTAL
 7
 8  HEADCOUNT            11      11      12      12
 9
10  GROWTH/QTR                   15%     3.0%    5.0%
11
12  SALARIES     7,550   83,050  84,296  93,318  95,130  355,794
13  TAXES & BENEFITS 1,095 12,042 12,223 13,531 13,794  51,590
14  OCCUPANCY     950    10,450  10,607  11,742  11,970  44,769
15  TELEPHONE     200     2,200   2,233   2,472   2,520   9,425
16  SUPPLIES      350     3,850   3,908   4,326   4,410  16,494
17  TRAVEL        250     2,750   2,791   3,090   3,150  11,781
18  OTHER         125     1,375   1,396   1,545   1,575   5,891
19
20  TOTAL               115,717 117,453 130,024 132,549 495,743
21
22
23
 Copy (Select destination and press Enter or choose Paste)    CAPS
```

**FIGURE 9-8** Head count and assumptions for Sheet1

2. Enter the title, head count, and assumptions on Sheet1, as shown in Figure 9-8. For the Taxes & Benefits assumption, enter =**14.5%\*B12** in place of the amount shown in Figure 9-8.

3. Repeat step 2 for Sheet2 and Sheet3, using Figures 9-9 and 9-10.

If your Taxes & Benefits quarterly amounts are three or four dollars different than those shown here, you missed changing the assumption to =14.5%*B12.

## Creating Linking Formulas

Sheet4 will be the total of the other three worksheets. You therefore want to replace the standard formulas in Sheet4 with formulas that

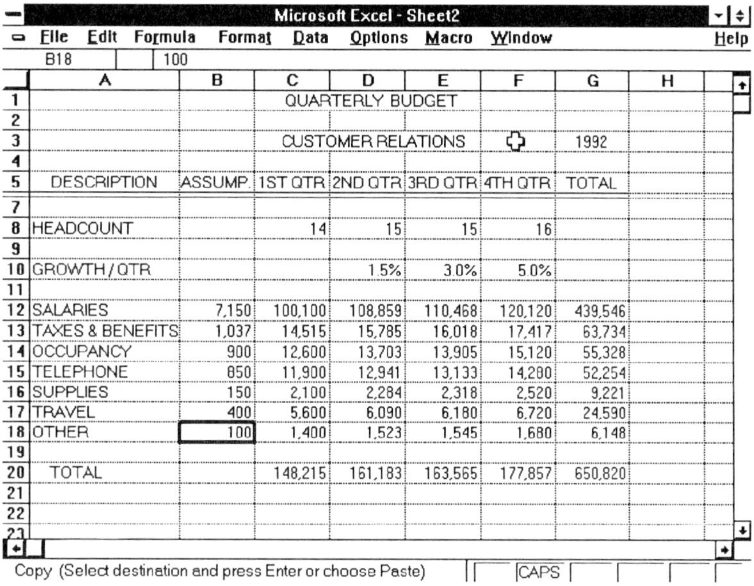


| | A | B | C | D | E | F | G | H |
|---|---|---|---|---|---|---|---|---|
| 1 | | | QUARTERLY BUDGET | | | | | |
| 2 | | | | | | | | |
| 3 | | | CUSTOMER RELATIONS | | | | 1992 | |
| 4 | | | | | | | | |
| 5 | DESCRIPTION | ASSUMP. | 1ST QTR | 2ND QTR | 3RD QTR | 4TH QTR | TOTAL | |
| 7 | | | | | | | | |
| 8 | HEADCOUNT | | 14 | 15 | 15 | 16 | | |
| 9 | | | | | | | | |
| 10 | GROWTH/QTR | | | 1.5% | 3.0% | 5.0% | | |
| 11 | | | | | | | | |
| 12 | SALARIES | 7,150 | 100,100 | 108,859 | 110,468 | 120,120 | 439,546 | |
| 13 | TAXES & BENEFITS | 1,037 | 14,515 | 15,785 | 16,018 | 17,417 | 63,734 | |
| 14 | OCCUPANCY | 900 | 12,600 | 13,703 | 13,905 | 15,120 | 55,328 | |
| 15 | TELEPHONE | 850 | 11,900 | 12,941 | 13,133 | 14,280 | 52,254 | |
| 16 | SUPPLIES | 150 | 2,100 | 2,284 | 2,318 | 2,520 | 9,221 | |
| 17 | TRAVEL | 400 | 5,600 | 6,090 | 6,180 | 6,720 | 24,590 | |
| 18 | OTHER | 100 | 1,400 | 1,523 | 1,545 | 1,680 | 6,148 | |
| 19 | | | | | | | | |
| 20 | TOTAL | | 148,215 | 161,183 | 163,565 | 177,857 | 650,820 | |
| 21 | | | | | | | | |
| 22 | | | | | | | | |
| 23 | | | | | | | | |

**FIGURE 9-9** Head count and assumptions for Sheet2

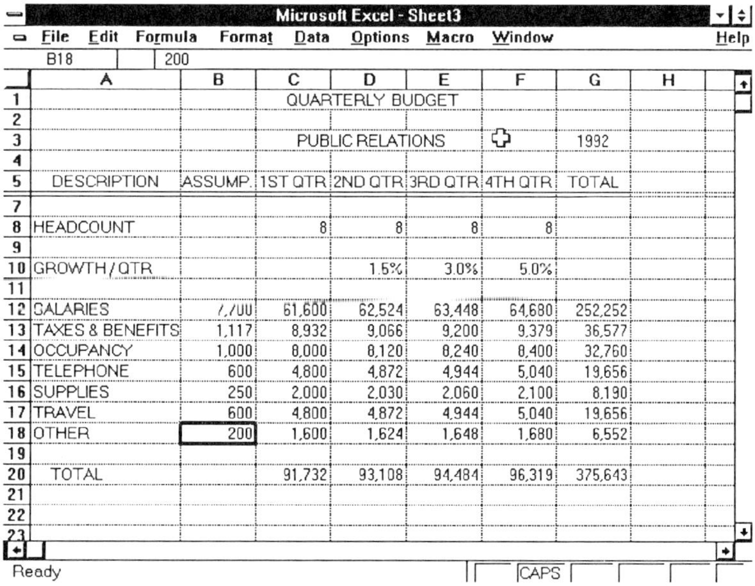


| | A | B | C | D | E | F | G | H |
|---|---|---|---|---|---|---|---|---|
| 1 | | | QUARTERLY BUDGET | | | | | |
| 2 | | | | | | | | |
| 3 | | | PUBLIC RELATIONS | | | | 1992 | |
| 4 | | | | | | | | |
| 5 | DESCRIPTION | ASSUMP. | 1ST QTR | 2ND QTR | 3RD QTR | 4TH QTR | TOTAL | |
| 7 | | | | | | | | |
| 8 | HEADCOUNT | | 8 | 8 | 8 | 8 | | |
| 9 | | | | | | | | |
| 10 | GROWTH/QTR | | | 1.5% | 3.0% | 5.0% | | |
| 11 | | | | | | | | |
| 12 | SALARIES | 7,700 | 61,600 | 62,524 | 63,448 | 64,680 | 252,252 | |
| 13 | TAXES & BENEFITS | 1,117 | 8,932 | 9,066 | 9,200 | 9,379 | 36,577 | |
| 14 | OCCUPANCY | 1,000 | 8,000 | 8,120 | 8,240 | 8,400 | 32,760 | |
| 15 | TELEPHONE | 600 | 4,800 | 4,872 | 4,944 | 5,040 | 19,656 | |
| 16 | SUPPLIES | 250 | 2,000 | 2,030 | 2,060 | 2,100 | 8,190 | |
| 17 | TRAVEL | 600 | 4,800 | 4,872 | 4,944 | 5,040 | 19,656 | |
| 18 | OTHER | 200 | 1,600 | 1,624 | 1,648 | 1,680 | 6,552 | |
| 19 | | | | | | | | |
| 20 | TOTAL | | 91,732 | 93,108 | 94,484 | 96,319 | 375,643 | |
| 21 | | | | | | | | |
| 22 | | | | | | | | |
| 23 | | | | | | | | |

**FIGURE 9-10** Head count and assumptions for Sheet3

sum the other three worksheets. The tiled view and the mouse make short work of this. Follow these steps:

1. If you are not there already, return to the tiled view so you can see all four worksheets.

2. Scroll the worksheets so that the first quarter head count is visible in each window, and click on C8 in Sheet4 to make it the active cell and worksheet, as shown in Figure 9-11.

3. Type =, double-click on C8 in Sheet1, press (F4) three times to make the reference relative, type +, double-click on C8 in Sheet2, press (F4) three times, type +, double-click on C8 in Sheet3, press (F4) three times, and press (ENTER).

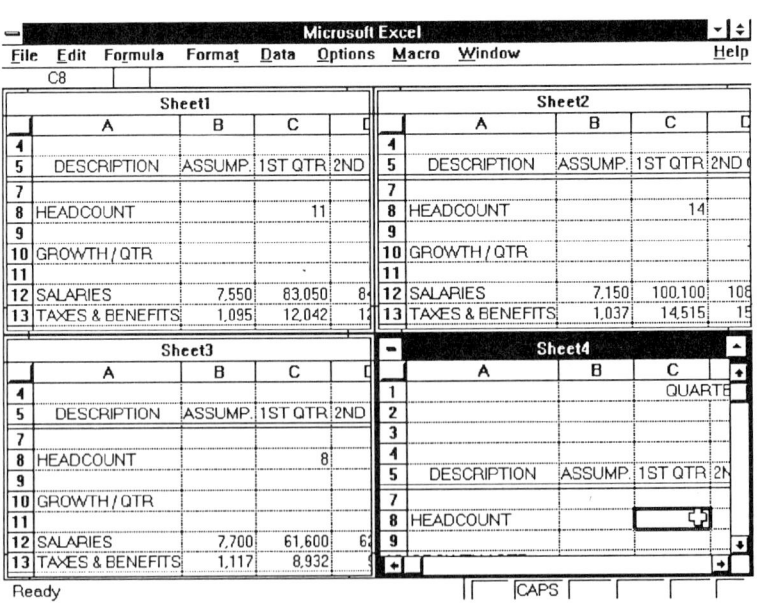

**FIGURE 9-11**   Tiled windows scrolled to show head count

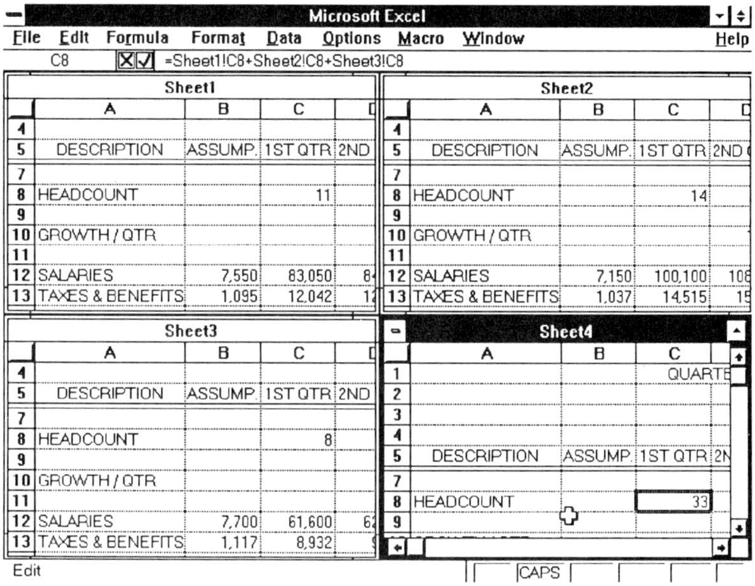

**FIGURE 9-12** External reference formula

You have created an *external reference formula,* shown in Figure 9-12. Each part of the equation references a cell in a different worksheet. This is accomplished by including the full sheet name followed by an exclamation point (!) in the reference. You need it to be relative so you can copy the same formula to the other head count and expense cells.

4. Select C8:F8 on Sheet4 and choose Fill Right from the Edit menu to copy the equation to the remaining head count cells.

5. With C8:F8 still selected, choose Copy from the Edit menu, select C12:C18 on Sheet4, and choose Paste from the Edit menu. All of the expense cells are filled with the appropriate formula, as shown in Figure 9-13.

|   | A | B | C | D | E | F | G | H |
|---|---|---|---|---|---|---|---|---|
| 1 |   |   | QUARTERLY BUDGET |   |   |   |   |   |
| 2 |   |   |   |   |   |   |   |   |
| 3 |   |   |   |   |   |   | 1992 |   |
| 4 |   |   |   |   |   |   |   |   |
| 5 | DESCRIPTION | ASSUMP. | 1ST QTR | 2ND QTR | 3RD QTR | 4TH QTR | TOTAL |   |
| 7 |   |   |   |   |   |   |   |   |
| 8 | HEADCOUNT |   | 33 | 34 | 35 | 36 |   |   |
| 9 |   |   |   |   |   |   |   |   |
| 10 | GROWTH/QTR |   |   | 1.5% | 3.0% | 5.0% |   |   |
| 11 |   |   |   |   |   |   |   |   |
| 12 | SALARIES |   | 244,750 | 255,673 | 267,234 | 279,933 | 1,047,592 |   |
| 13 | TAXES & BENEFITS |   | 35,483 | 37,073 | 38,749 | 40,590 | 151,901 |   |
| 14 | OCCUPANCY |   | 31,050 | 32,429 | 33,887 | 35,490 | 132,856 |   |
| 15 | TELEPHONE |   | 19,900 | 20,046 | 20,549 | 21,040 | 81,335 |   |
| 16 | SUPPLIES |   | 7,950 | 8,222 | 8,704 | 9,030 | 33,905 |   |
| 17 | TRAVEL |   | 13,150 | 13,753 | 14,214 | 14,910 | 56,027 |   |
| 18 | OTHER |   | 4,375 | 4,542 | 4,738 | 4,935 | 18,590 |   |
| 19 |   |   |   |   |   |   |   |   |
| 20 | TOTAL |   | 355,664 | 371,744 | 388,073 | 406,725 | 1,522,206 |   |

Cell C12: `=Sheet1!C12+Sheet2!C12+Sheet3!C12`

**FIGURE 9-13** Completed summary formulas

6. Type the title **Marketing Department** in C3 to finish the summary worksheet.

## Saving Multiple Worksheets

When you have a series of linked worksheets as you do here, it is very important that you save them in the proper sequence to maintain the linked formulas. Currently, the formulas have Sheet1, Sheet2, and so on for the filenames. If you were to save and close Sheet4 before saving Sheet1, Sheet2, and Sheet3, you lose all your references. On the other hand, if you save Sheet1, Sheet2, and Sheet3 before saving Sheet4, the worksheet references in Sheet4 automatically are replaced with the filenames. Try that next with these instructions:

## Linking Worksheets and Using External Files 347

1. Choose Restore in the Control menu to return Sheet4 to its tiled size.

2. Click on Sheet1, choose Save As from the File menu, type **c:\wi\sheet\qtrbudad,** and press (ENTER) to save Sheet1 as QTRBUDAD (your path may be different).

3. In a similar manner save Sheet2 and Sheet3 as QTRBUDCR and QTRBUDPR, respectively.

4. Click on C8 on Sheet4 and look at the formula, which is also shown in Figure 9-14.

5. Save Sheet4 as QTRBUDTO.

6. Close each sheet (double-click on the Control-menu box) in the same order (start with QTRBUDAD or what was Sheet1, and then QTRBUDTO or Sheet4 last).

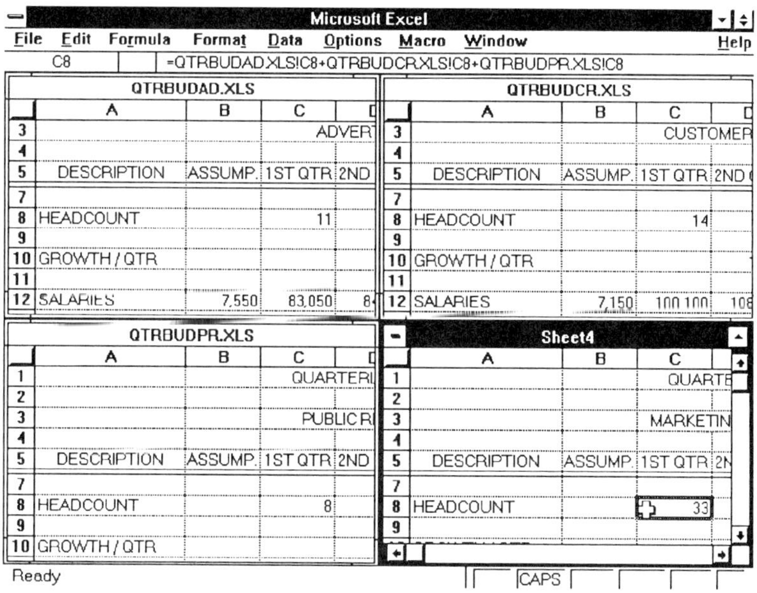

**FIGURE 9-14** External reference formula with filenames

After closing QTRBUDAD (Sheet1) notice that the head count value in QTRBUDTO (Sheet4) has become #REF!. If you look at the formula in QTRBUDTO after closing the other two worksheets you see it is still correct and now includes the full path name as well as the filename. The values on the worksheet, however, have all become #REF!. Reopen each of the files and see for yourself that everything is OK.

The external reference formulas remain OK, they just cannot get at the worksheets they reference once the worksheets have been closed. The reason for this is that Excel considers these formulas *complex* for two reasons: they reference more than one external worksheet and they are relative. Complex formulas work only if all of the worksheets being referenced are open.

If the external reference formula were considered *simple*, Excel would continue to reference it even if it were closed and stored on disk. It is, therefore, worthwhile to look at what is considered simple external references. A simple reference is

- An absolute reference

- To a cell, a range, a range name, or a constant on a single worksheet

- Not imbedded in a function

- Not a reference to a formula

One other consideration with external references is that range names are even more important than they are in other worksheet formulas. External reference formulas are not updated if you insert or delete rows or columns or move or cut cells in the worksheet being referenced. If you use a range name, the range name is adjusted for the changes to the worksheet and the external reference is correct.

## COMBINING FILES

There is at least one circumstance when complex external reference formulas cannot work: when you run out of available memory, either because of the size of the worksheet or because of a low memory system. If you cannot load all of the worksheets in memory and you must use complex formulas, you must use some other methods of combining files.

Excel provides the means to add or subtract a range on one worksheet to or from a similar range on another worksheet using the Paste Special option from the Edit menu. In other words, you can select and copy a range on one worksheet and then, through the Paste Special option, add it to a similar range on another worksheet. The important phrase is *similar range*. More accurately, the two ranges must be exactly, cell for cell, alike because one entire range is overlaid on the other. The two worksheets do have to be in memory together although you can combine six worksheets and only have 2 of them in memory at one time.

See how this works using the three worksheets created earlier in this chapter with a new total worksheet. Build the new total worksheet first with the normal Copy and Paste options and these steps:

1. Open the advertising department worksheet QTRBUDAD, select the range A1:G20, and choose Copy from the Edit menu.

2. Open a new worksheet, choose Paste from the Edit menu, widen column A and shorten row 6, delete the formulas in the range B8:F18, change the title to Combined Total, and save the new worksheet as QTRBUDCO.

You now have a blank worksheet, as shown in Figure 9-15, with the exact layout of the other three worksheets you built. You can use this new worksheet to add the other three with the Paste Special option.

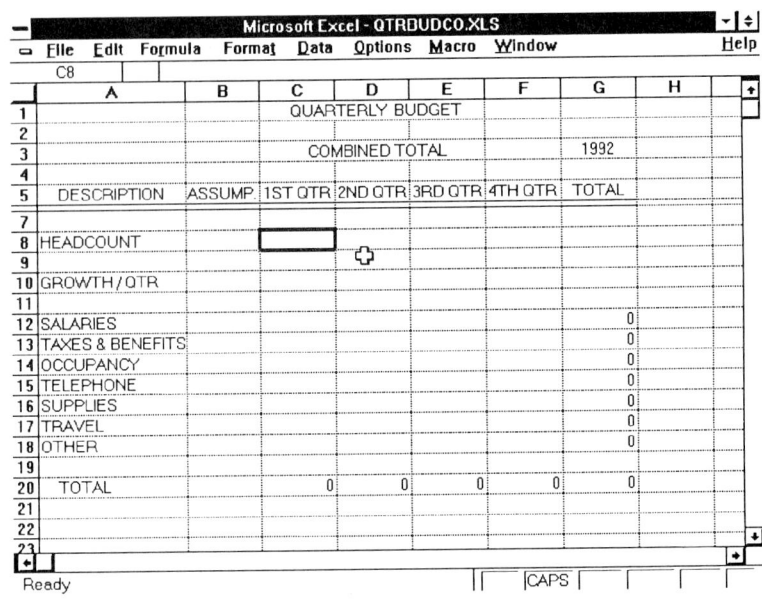

**FIGURE 9-15** New worksheet ready for adding others

3. From the Window menu, activate QTRBUDAD, select C8:F18, and choose Copy from the Edit menu.

4. Activate QTRBUDCO, select C8, and choose Paste Special from the Edit menu. The following dialog box opens:

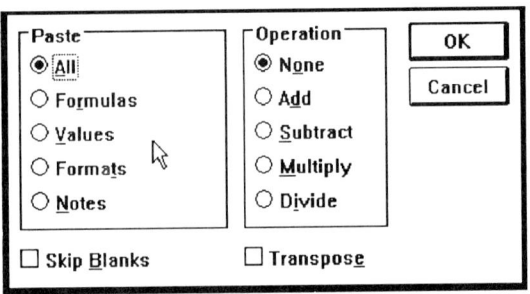

The Paste Special option allows you to paste only parts of the range you copied (the options on the left of the dialog box) and then to add, subtract, multiply, or divide the cells you copied to, from, by, or into the cells being pasted. As you are pasting you can skip blank cells in the copied range so you do not blank the contents of cells in the pasted range, and you can transpose rows and columns. In this case you want to paste only the values, and you want to add them.

5. Choose Values and Add in the dialog box and click OK. Your QTRBUDCO worksheet now looks like Figure 9-16.

6. To make this example real, close the QTRBUDAD worksheet by activating it and choosing Close from its Control menu.

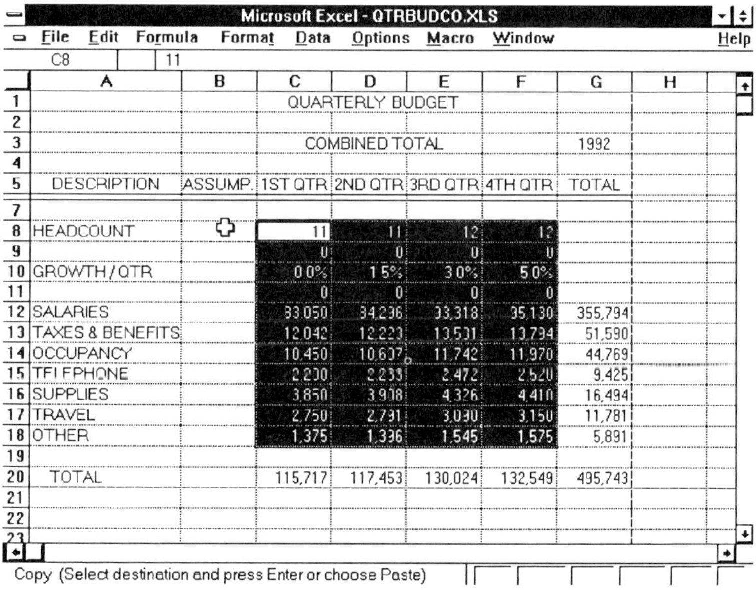

**FIGURE 9-16** Results of pasting the first worksheet

Note that you cannot close QTRBUDAD before choosing Paste Special. If you do close QTRBUDAD, Paste Special is no longer available on the Edit menu (it is dimmed).

7. Open QTRBUDCR, select C8:F18, choose Copy, activate QTRBUDCO, make sure C8 is the active cell, choose Paste Special, and then choose Values, Add, and OK. The second worksheet is added to the contents of the first.

8. Close QTRBUDCR, open QTRBUDPR, and follow the same procedure outlined in step 7.

9. Delete the range C9:F11 since it contains spurious and unnecessary information. Your final Combined Total worksheet looks like Figure 9-17.

10. Close QTRBUDPR and save QTRBUDCO a second time.

| | A | B | C | D | E | F | G | H |
|---|---|---|---|---|---|---|---|---|
| 1 | | | | QUARTERLY BUDGET | | | | |
| 2 | | | | | | | | |
| 3 | | | | COMBINED TOTAL | | | 1992 | |
| 4 | | | | | | | | |
| 5 | DESCRIPTION | ASSUMP. | 1ST QTR | 2ND QTR | 3RD QTR | 4TH QTR | TOTAL | |
| 7 | | | | | | | | |
| 8 | HEADCOUNT | | 33 | 34 | 35 | 36 | | |
| 9 | | | | | | | | |
| 10 | GROWTH/QTR | | | | | | | |
| 11 | | | | | | | | |
| 12 | SALARIES | | 244,750 | 255,679 | 267,234 | 279,930 | 1,047,592 | |
| 13 | TAXES & BENEFITS | | 35,489 | 37,073 | 38,749 | 40,590 | 151,901 | |
| 14 | OCCUPANCY | | 31,050 | 32,429 | 33,887 | 35,490 | 132,856 | |
| 15 | TELEPHONE | | 18,900 | 20,046 | 20,549 | 21,840 | 81,335 | |
| 16 | SUPPLIES | | 7,950 | 8,222 | 8,704 | 9,030 | 33,905 | |
| 17 | TRAVEL | | 13,150 | 13,753 | 14,214 | 14,910 | 56,027 | |
| 18 | OTHER | | 4,375 | 4,542 | 4,738 | 4,935 | 18,590 | |
| 19 | | | | | | | | |
| 20 | TOTAL | | 355,664 | 371,744 | 388,073 | 406,725 | 1,522,206 | |

**FIGURE 9-17** Final Combined Total worksheet

If you compare this QTRBUDCO worksheet with QTRBUDTO in Figure 9-13 (the total built with external reference formulas), you can see they are the same except for the growth percentages, which have been deleted in QTRBUDCO.

For the example in this chapter and for most of your multiple worksheet problems, the external reference formulas are a better solution than using Paste Special. Paste Special should be used only when you are memory constrained. Paste Special is easier in that you do not have to build and copy the summing formulas. Of course, the big disadvantage is that the files must have the exact same file layout. The numbers you want to add must be in the same cell positions on each worksheet.

Dates and times generally should not be combined with Paste Special; the results are not meaningful. Also, blank cells are considered to be 0 by Paste Special unless you select Skip Blanks in the Paste Special dialog box.

**Caution** The Paste Special option changes the current worksheet by copying over, adding to, or subtracting from its cells. Before using the Paste Special option, save your current worksheet and carefully position the active cell. Also, if used soon enough, Edit Undo ((ALT+BACKSPACE)) can restore the current worksheet to its contents prior to executing Paste Special.

# SAVING A WORKSHEET AS A TEXT FILE

Sometimes you want to get a range or a complete file out of Excel to use in another program. Most other programs cannot read an Excel file, but they can read a file that is written in the ASCII (American Standard Code for Information Interchange) format. Excel uses the File Save As option to accomplish this. The Save

As dialog box has an Options button. When you select this button the dialog box expands, as shown here:

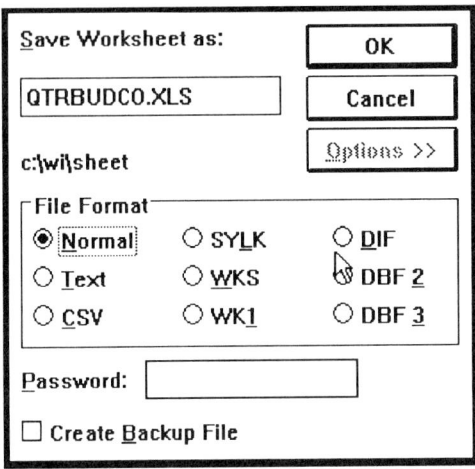

In this expanded dialog box, you get nine file formats for saving Excel worksheets. The nine file formats serve the following purposes:

| | |
|---|---|
| Normal | Saves a file in the normal Excel file format for use with the Excel program. |
| Text | Saves a file in the ASCII file format with tabs between columns and carriage returns at the end of each row. This format is primarily used to bring a worksheet into a word processing package. All formulas are replaced by their values and, if a cell has a comma or a tab in it, the cell's value is enclosed in quotation marks. |
| CSV (Comma Separated Values) | Saves a file in ASCII file format with commas between columns. Otherwise it is the same as a text file. This is primarily used by database packages. It is sometimes called an *ASCII delimited file*. |

| | |
|---|---|
| SYLK | Saves a file in the SYLK format used to transfer information among Microsoft worksheet packages including Multiplan and Excel for the Macintosh. |
| WKS | Saves a file in the Lotus WKS format used with Lotus 1-2-3 version 1A. |
| WK1 | Saves a file in the Lotus WK1 format used with Lotus 1-2-3 versions 2, 2.01, and 2.2. |
| DIF | Saves a file in the Data Interchange Format used by VisiCalc. This format does not transfer formulas, only values. |
| DBF 2 | Saves the currently defined database range in the format used by dBASE II. |
| DBF 3 | Saves the currently defined database range in the format used by dBASE III. |

For your purposes here, you want either the Text or CSV format. For use in the body of a word processed document you would use Text and then set tab stops in the word processor to recreate Excel's columns. For use in a database other than dBASE or for mail merging with word processed documents you would use CSV. Save the QTRBUDCO file in both of these formats, and then exit Excel and look at the results with these instructions. (QTRBUDCO should be displayed on your screen as the active worksheet.)

1. Choose Save As from the File menu, change the filename extension from .XLS to .TXT, and then click on Options, Text, and OK.

2. Choose Save As from the File menu, change the filename extension from .TXT to .CSV, and then click on Options, CSV, and OK.

You have now created two new files: one in the ASCII text format with the filename extension .TXT and the second in ASCII comma delimited format with the extension .CSV. Next close Excel and look at these files with Windows Write. (If you are using a runtime version of Windows, you won't be able to do this.)

3. Double-click on the Excel Control-menu box to close it.

4. Double-click on the Windows Accessories Group and then double-click again on Write to open that program. Click on the Maximize button to expand Write to full-screen size.

5. Choose Open from the File menu, change directories to \WI\ SCREEN\ (or the directory you are using for Excel files), replace the *.WRI in the filename text box with the filename QTRBUDCO.TXT, and click on OK.

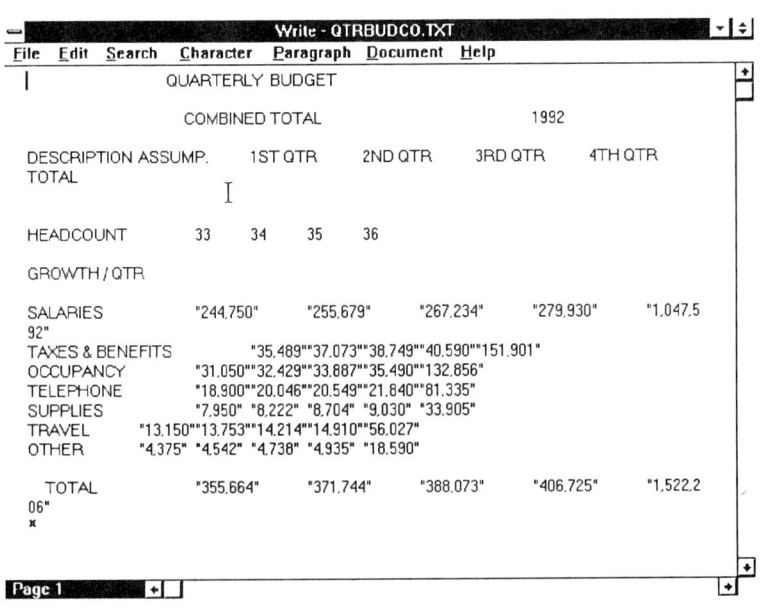

FIGURE 9-18   Quarterly Budget in Text format as displayed by Windows Write

6. Choose Convert from the dialog box that asks you if you want to convert to the Write format (although it really does not make any difference). The Quarterly Budget Combined Total Worksheet opens, as shown in Figure 9-18.

At this point the text file does not look good, but with very little work it can be markedly improved.

7. Choose Change from the Search menu, type " and click on Change All. This removes all quotation marks. Double-click on the Control-menu box of the Change dialog box to close the dialog box.

8. Choose Ruler On from the Document menu, click on the decimal tab icon (the second tab icon with the upward arrow and a period), and click in the space just below the ruler at 1.75", 2.5", 3.25", 4", 4.75", and 5.5" to set decimal tab stops at those locations. Delete one tab to the left of 1992 to bring that in line.

All of a sudden the exported worksheet looks pretty good, as shown in Figure 9-19. Additionally, since it uses tabs instead of spaces, the worksheet can be printed with a proportional spaced font and not be thrown out of alignment.

9. Choose Save As from the File menu, change the filename extension to .WRI, click on Make Backup and Text Only to turn them both off, and click on OK. The word processing file will be saved with the normal .WRI Write extension.

10. Choose Open from the File menu, type QTRBUDCO.CSV, click on OK, and click No Conversion. The second text file opens, as shown in Figure 9-20.

You can see that the CSV file has replaced tabs with commas, but otherwise it looks very similar to the text file when you originally brought it in. The big difference is that you cannot

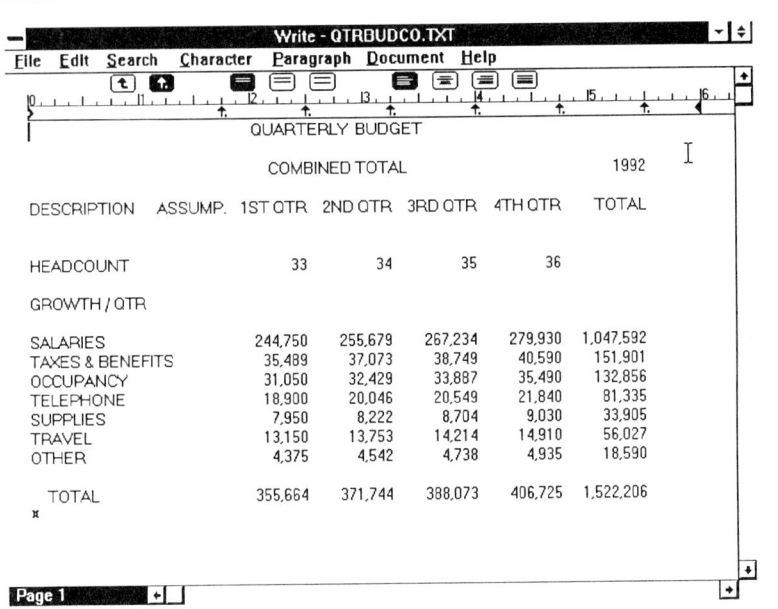

**FIGURE 9-19** Worksheet text file in Write after tabs have been inserted

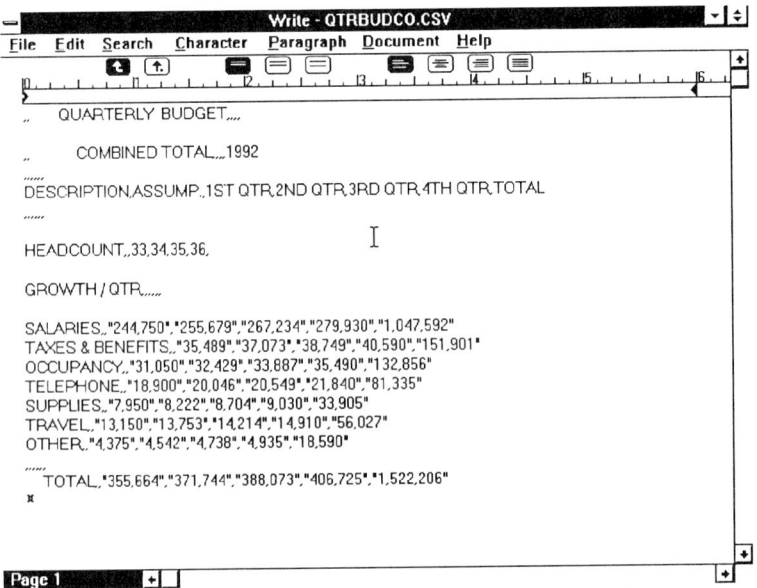

**FIGURE 9-20** CSV formatted worksheet in Write

simply set some tab stops and get a CSV file to line up properly. What you must do is replace the commas with tabs, and the comma thousands separator in a number cause a problem. In a word processing package, the CSV format is not very useful except for mail merge. The standard text format with tabs is much more useful.

# IMPORTING ASCII TEXT FILES

Just as you may need to get data out of Excel for use in other programs, you may need to get data into Excel from other programs in a format other than the Excel standard file format. The most common format is ASCII text in one of two formats: nondelimited ASCII files that are continuous text strings and delimited ASCII files. A delimited ASCII file includes delimiters, usually commas, between fields or columns and often quotation marks around text. Delimiters can also be tabs for Excel use, but most other programs recognize only commas or semicolons. Using ASCII delimited files with commas and quotation marks is the most common means of exchanging information among database programs. Many word processing programs can also read ASCII delimited files and use them with their mail merge function.

Look at how Excel brings in each of the two text files (both the .TXT and the .CSV files) as well as a nondelimited text. While you are still in Windows Write, create the nondelimited file from QTRBUDCO.CSV, which should still be on your screen.

1. Delete the first seven lines down to but not including the Headcount line (select the lines and use the Delete option on the Edit menu), delete the three lines between Headcount and Salaries, and delete the line between Other and Total as well as any leading space in front of Total.

2. Select all of the remaining text, choose Fonts from the Character menu, select Courier 10, and click on OK to change from a proportional-spaced font to a fixed-spaced font.

3. Select the full Headcount line, choose Change from the Search menu, type **,** in Find What and press the spacebar six times in Change To, and click Change Selection to replace all commas in the first line with six spaces.

4. Select the remainder of the text using the Change dialog box, which should still be open, and change ,," to two spaces. Then change all remaining commas to nothing by pressing (DEL) after highlighting the contents of the Change To text box. Change "" to two spaces, and change the remaining " to nothing.

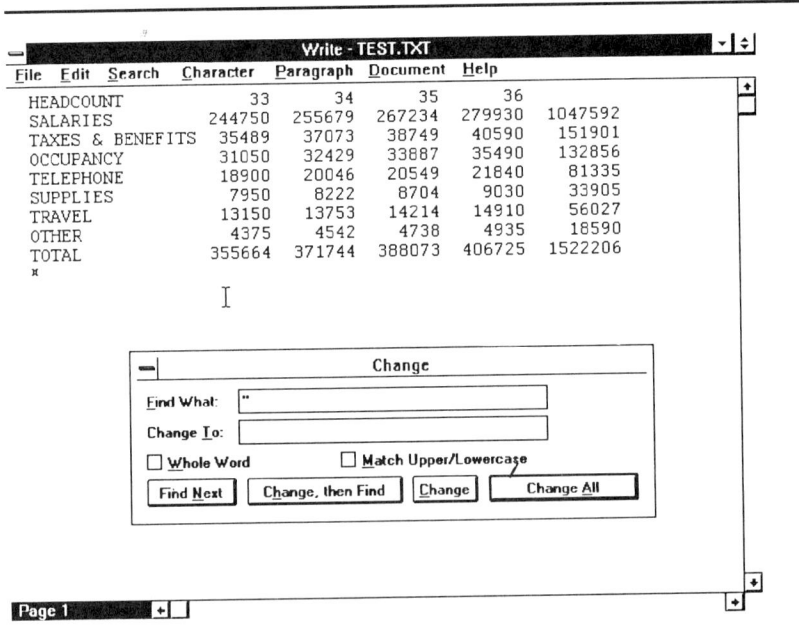

**FIGURE 9-21** Nondelimited ASCII text file in Write

5. Add and delete spaces so the numbers line up on their right as shown in Figure 9-21. Then use Save As to save the file as text only with the filename TEST.TXT.

6. Double-click on Write's Control-menu box to close it, and then double-click on the Accessories Control-menu box to reduce it to a group icon. Finally, double-click on the Excel icon to reopen Excel.

## Opening ASCII Delimited Text Files

Both the .TXT and .CSV files that you created are ASCII delimited files. The .TXT file is delimited with tabs, and the .CSV file is delimited with commas. Both files have quotes around numbers that contain comma formatting so the commas will not be treated as delimiters. Bring each of the two delimited files back into Excel and see how well they split up into rows and columns with the following steps.

1. Choose Open from the File menu, change the directory to \WI\SHEET\ (or the one you are using for this book), type **qtrbudco.txt**, and press (ENTER).

The tab delimited text file is brought in as shown in Figure 9-22. When you check individual cells, you see that everything is in place. About the only thing you lost was the comma formatting of the numbers. Had you had other text formatting, this too would have been lost.

2. Double-click on the Control-menu box to close the file called QTRBUDCO.TXT, choose Open from the File menu, type **qtrbudco.csv**, and press (ENTER).

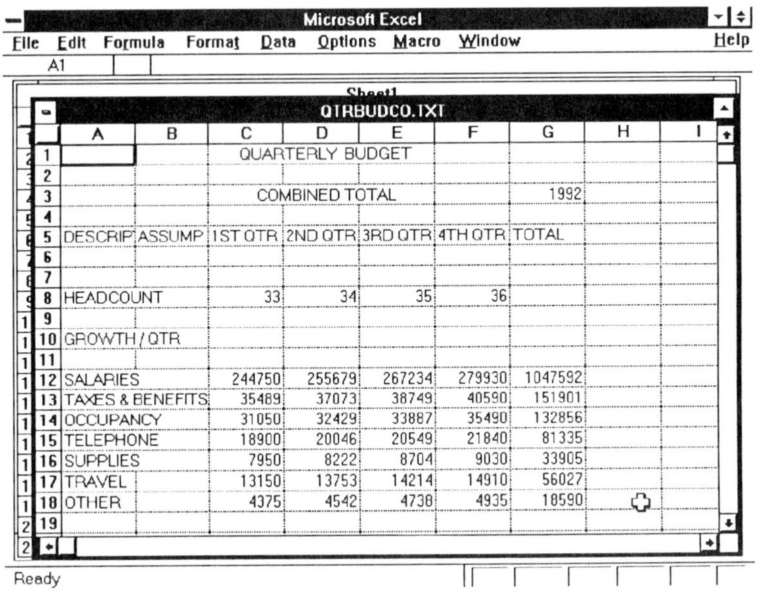

**FIGURE 9-22** Tab delimited file QTRBUDCO.TXT back in Excel

Once again the file is brought in and everything is in its correct cell, with the only loss being the comma formatting, as shown in Figure 9-23. The ease with which these files come in is not deceptive. Any ASCII delimited file will come in as easily and as well behaved. If you are using commas as delimiters, use the .CSV extension when saving the file in another application. Excel will not split the text into columns without this extension.

## Opening Nondelimited Text Files

Bringing in a nondelimited ASCII text file is a different story: Excel does not split it into columns. See for yourself by bringing in the TEST.TXT file you created in Write.

# Linking Worksheets and Using External Files 363

|  | A | B | C | D | E | F | G | H | I |
|---|---|---|---|---|---|---|---|---|---|
| 1 |  |  |  | QUARTERLY BUDGET |  |  |  |  |  |
| 2 |  |  |  |  |  |  |  |  |  |
| 3 |  |  |  | COMBINED TOTAL |  |  | 1992 |  |  |
| 4 |  |  |  |  |  |  |  |  |  |
| 5 | DESCRIP | ASSUMP | 1ST QTR | 2ND QTR | 3RD QTR | 4TH QTR | TOTAL |  |  |
| 6 |  |  |  |  |  |  |  |  |  |
| 7 |  |  |  |  |  |  |  |  |  |
| 8 | HEADCOUNT |  | 33 | 34 | 35 | 36 |  |  |  |
| 9 |  |  |  |  |  |  |  |  |  |
| 10 | GROWTH / QTR |  |  |  |  |  |  |  |  |
| 11 |  |  |  |  |  |  |  |  |  |
| 12 | SALARIES |  | 244750 | 255679 | 267234 | 279930 | 1047592 |  |  |
| 13 | TAXES & BENEFITS |  | 35489 | 37073 | 38749 | 40590 | 151901 |  |  |
| 14 | OCCUPANCY |  | 31050 | 32429 | 33887 | 35490 | 132856 |  |  |
| 15 | TELEPHONE |  | 18900 | 20046 | 20549 | 21840 | 81335 |  |  |
| 16 | SUPPLIES |  | 7950 | 8222 | 8704 | 9030 | 33905 |  |  |
| 17 | TRAVEL |  | 13150 | 13753 | 14214 | 14910 | 56027 |  |  |
| 18 | OTHER |  | 4375 | 4542 | 4730 | 4935 | 18590 |  |  |
| 19 |  |  |  |  |  |  |  |  |  |

**FIGURE 9-23** Comma delimited file QTRBUDCO.CSV back in Excel

Double-click on the Control-menu box to close the file called QTRBUDCO.CSV, choose Open from the File menu, type **test.txt**, and press (ENTER).

The file comes into Excel as shown in Figure 9-24. Each row is entirely contained in column A. Each line of text (row) in the original file produces a single long label contained in one cell. Look at several cells in column A and then in other columns.

You can see that each cell in column A contains a complete line of text. It looks like the original data, but it is all in one cell instead of occupying a row of cells. While you now have all of the information from the original file, it isn't very useful except for display. You cannot do any arithmetic on the numbers, move them, or otherwise manipulate them; they are just lines of text, all in one column. In the next section, you see how to divide these lines into discrete text and numbers.

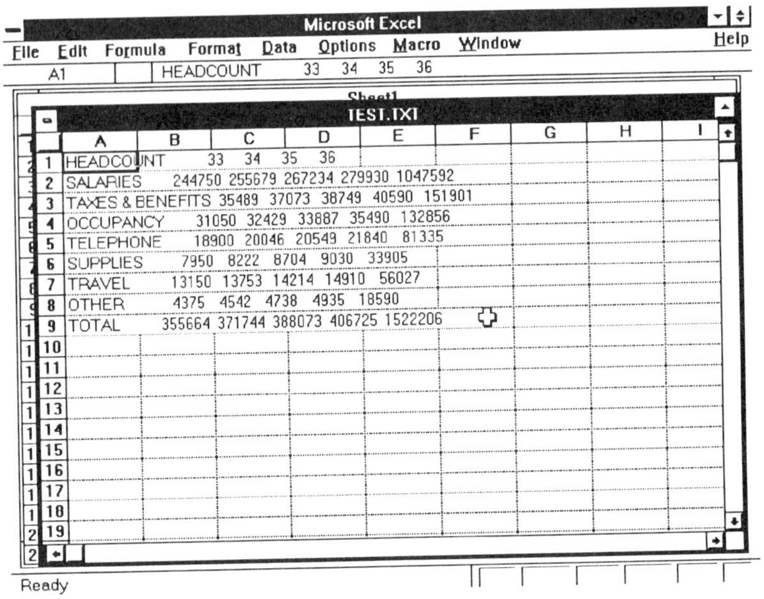

**FIGURE 9-24** Nondelimited file brought into Excel

## Parsing Nondelimited Text Files

In the previous section you imported a text file in nondelimited ASCII format. Each line of text was contained in a single cell, and the complete file was contained in a single column. To be usable, each line must be divided into text and numbers and placed into individual cells. That dividing or *parsing* of a text line is the function of the Parse option on the Data menu.

Data parsing is particularly useful if you download information from an information service such as CompuServe. For example, when you import current stock market information you get a long label containing the ticker symbol, the volume, and amounts for the high, low, close, and open prices. By itself, the information may make interesting reading, but you cannot do anything with it.

Using Data Parse, the stock market information can be divided into its components and used to update a stock portfolio.

Applying the Data Parse option is a multiple-step procedure. First you must select and reformat the information you want to parse so that it is using fixed and not proportional spacing. Then, with the Data Parse option, you must tell Excel where each column break belongs. Finally you do the actual parsing. Carry out those steps with these instructions:

1. Select A1:A9, choose Font from the Format menu, click on the Fonts command button, click on Courier, and click on OK.

By changing the font, all of the numbers line up in columns as they did in Write. The problem is everything is still in column A, as shown here:

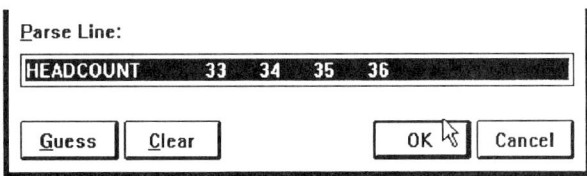

2. With A1:A9 still selected, choose Parse from the Data menu. The following Data Parse dialog box opens:

The Data Parse dialog box displays the first line you selected and asks you to identify where to break the line into columns. You identify the column breaks by entering square brackets ([ ]) for the start and end of each column. If you wish, as a start, you can have Excel guess and enter the brackets on that basis. You can also clear all of the brackets. Start out with a guess and then correct the results.

3. Click on Guess in the Data Parse dialog box. The brackets appear, as shown here:

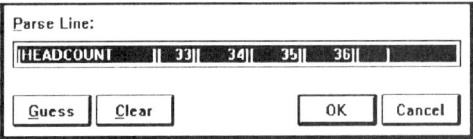

4. Click the insertion point between the opening square bracket and the "H" in HEADCOUNT. Press (RIGHT ARROW) 16 times, type ][, delete the next two square brackets, move the insertion point to just after the final closing square bracket, remove that bracket, count nine spaces after the final opening bracket, and type ]. Your dialog box looks like this:

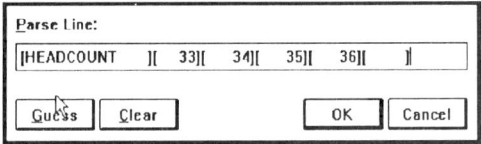

Your brackets should be set with the first interval at 16 characters, the second interval at 7 characters, the next three intervals at 8 characters each, and the final interval at 9 characters.

5. When your brackets are set, click on OK to carry out the parsing of the data. Your results should look like Figure 9-25.

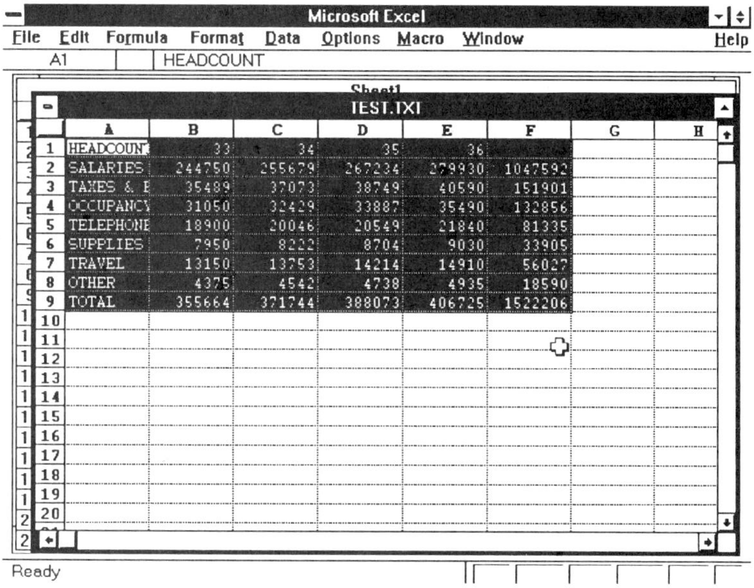

**FIGURE 9-25** Nondelimited data parsed into columns

6. Look at several individual cells to assure yourself that the text has been divided over the columns.

If for some reason your parsing did not work, you can use Edit Undo or (ALT+BACKSPACE) to return to the unparsed text strings. You can then redo the placement of the square brackets and try again.

There are two keys to making Data Parse work. First, you change the font into a fixed-spaced typeface like Courier. Second, you line the data up with spaces so that each column is defined and the same from row to row. If necessary you can break a file into several sections and parse each separately.

You can see the amount of effort required to handle a nondelimited file. Of course, sometimes there is no alternative. When possible, though, a delimited file, preferably a tab delimited file, is far superior.

7. Double-click on the TEST.TXT Control-menu box and click on No to close the worksheet without saving it.

8. Double-click on both the Excel and the Program Manager Control-menu boxes to close them.

# 10

# DATES, FUNCTIONS, AND MACROS

Using Dates and Times
Functions
Macros

This chapter brings together three subjects that do not fit easily into any other category: using dates and times, functions, and macros. All three subjects need a forum of their own, and they are the finishing touch—the "icing on the cake" that makes a good worksheet a great worksheet.

## USING DATES AND TIMES

From schedules to dates on reports and time related financial calculations, dates and times are important aspects of the problems Excel addresses. The sections that follow discuss how Excel handles dates and times internally, various ways Excel formats dates and times, and the date and time functions and arithmetic.

## Dates and Excel

Dates do not form a nice, neat, linear progression. You cannot add 12 days to April 28th and get May 10th without knowing how many days there are in April. Microsoft has solved this problem by establishing a date serial number scheme. This scheme allocates one number for every day from January 1, 1900 (date serial number 1) to December 31, 2078 (date serial number 65380). Microsoft also provides formatting and formulas to convert the date serial number to a specific calendar date. Internally Excel uses the unformatted date serial number. You can format the date serial number in several ways and get a normal-looking calendar date from a serial number. For example, when formatted with the first Excel date format, the serial number 33343 becomes 4/15/91, as shown here:

In other words, simply typing **33343**, pressing (**ENTER**), and formatting the number with Format Number m/d/yy produces the date 4/15/91. The following instructions demonstrate several other dates. Your computer should be on, Excel should be loaded, and you should have a blank worksheet on your screen.

1. Select B2:F2, choose Number from the Format menu, select the m/d/yy format, and click on OK. The range B2:F2 is formatted as m/d/yy dates.

2. Move the active cell to B2.

3. Type **33343** and press (RIGHT ARROW). The date 4/15/91 appears in B2.

4. Type **30638** and press (RIGHT ARROW). The date 11/18/83 appears in C2, as shown here:

5. Type **1**, press (RIGHT ARROW), type **65380**, and press (ENTER). The date 1/1/00 appears in D2, and E2 contains 12/31/78.

Note that when you are working in the next century, the two-digit format can be confusing. Change the format next. E2 should still be the active cell.

6. Choose Number from the Format menu, click after the last "y" in the format text box, type **yy**, and click on OK. E2 fills with #s because the date is now too big for the cell.

7. Drag on the intersection of columns E and F in the heading for about one tenth of an inch. The date 12/31/2078 appears in E2, as shown here:

|   | A | B | C | D | E | F |
|---|---|---|---|---|---|---|
| 1 |   |   |   |   |   |   |
| 2 |   | 4/15/91 | 11/18/83 |   | 1/1/00 | 12/31/2078 |
| 3 |   |   |   |   |   |   |
| 4 |   |   |   |   |   |   |

(E2: 12/31/2078)

There is one abnormality in Microsoft's date scheme. The year 1900 was not a leap year, even though the year was evenly divisible by four. Therefore, Excel assigns a date serial number to February 29, 1900. If you are generating date serial numbers between January 1, 1900, and March 1, 1900, subtract 1 from the dates produced by Excel within that period. All date serial numbers and calculated dates from March 1, 1900, onward are correct.

## Times and Excel

Microsoft has also developed a scheme for calculating time: the time is added to the date serial number as a decimal fraction of a 24-hour day. Therefore, midnight is 0.000000, noon is 0.500000, and 11:59:59 PM is 0.999988. When the decimal fractions are formatted with Excel as times, they produce normal-looking time numbers on either a 12- or 24-hour basis. The following steps show how several times are entered.

1. Select B2:E2, press (DEL), click on All, and click on OK to erase both the contents and formats of B2:E2.

2. Choose Number from the Format menu, select the first time format, h:mm AM/PM, and click on OK. The range B2:E2 is formatted with the first time format.

3. Move the active cell to B2.

4. Type **.65** and press (RIGHT ARROW). Cell B2 contains 3:36 PM, as shown here:

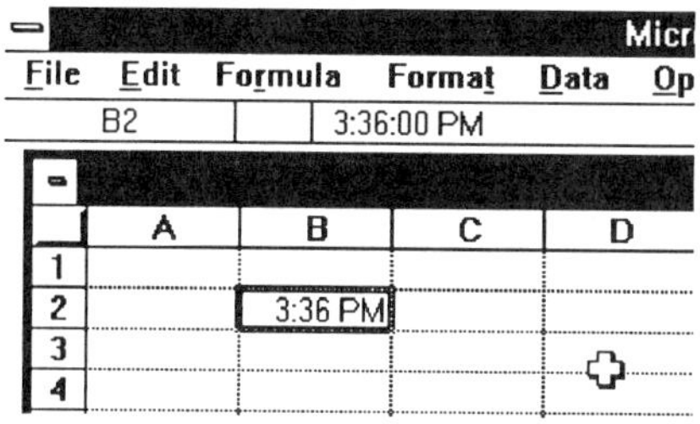

5. Type **.45** and press (RIGHT ARROW). Cell C2 contains 10:48 AM, as shown here:

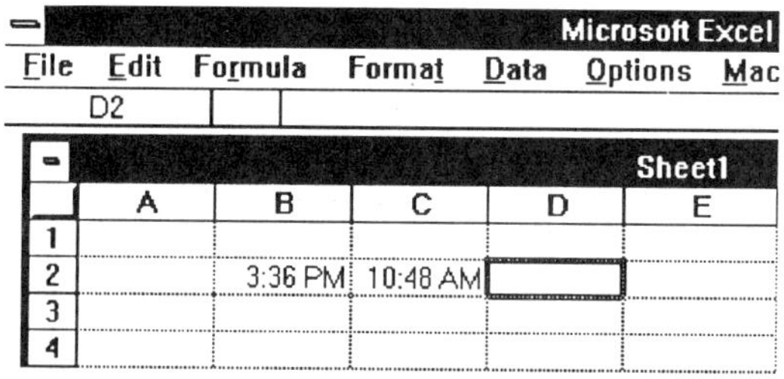

6. Type **0**, press (RIGHT ARROW), type **.9999**, and press (ENTER). Cells D2 and E2 contain 12:00 AM and 11:59 PM, as shown here:

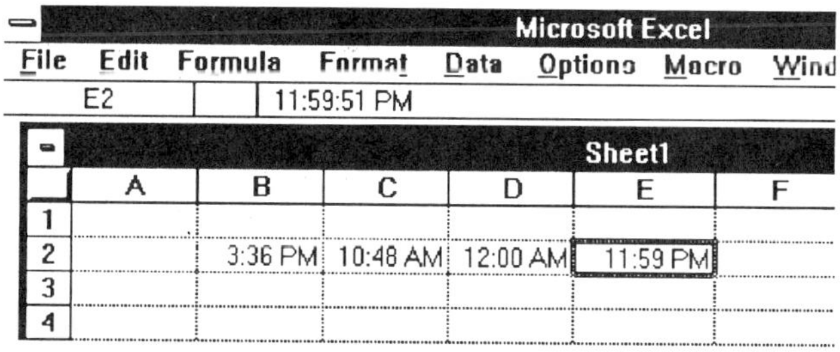

Dates and times are stored in one number. For example, 3:36 PM April 15, 1991, is stored as 33343.65. In a single cell you can display this as a date, as a time, or both, depending on the formatting.

## Formatting Dates and Times

There are four date formats, four time formats, and one combined date and time format built into Excel. The date formats use the integer part of a date serial number, and the time formats use the decimal part. The decimal part of a number is ignored by a date format, and the integer part of a number is ignored by a time format. If a date format encounters a number that is negative or greater than 65380, the cell fills with #s. If a time format encounters a negative number, the cell fills with #s.

The nine built-in date and time formats are shown in Figure 10-1. You can, of course, make your own. The components needed

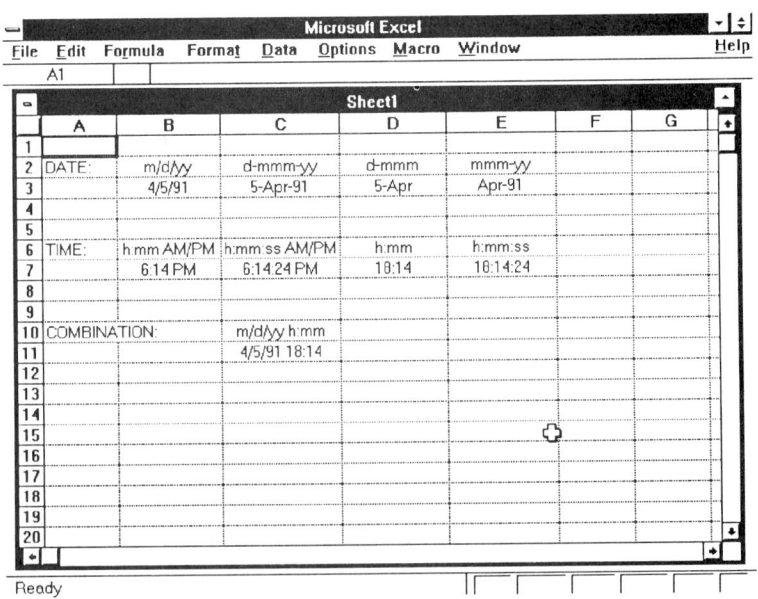

**Figure 10-1** Built-in data and time formats

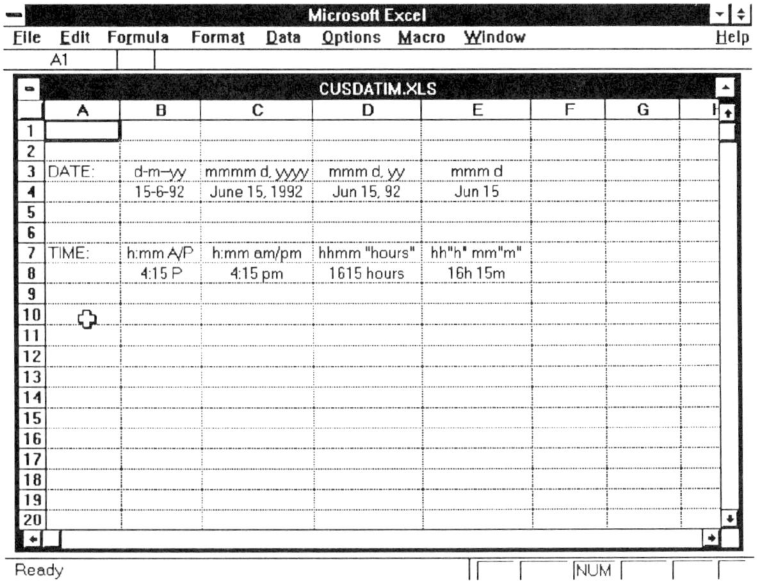

|   | A | B | C | D | E |
|---|---|---|---|---|---|
| 3 | DATE: | d-m-yy | mmmm d, yyyy | mmm d, yy | mmm d |
| 4 |  | 15-6-92 | June 15, 1992 | Jun 15, 92 | Jun 15 |
| 7 | TIME: | h:mm A/P | h:mm am/pm | hhmm "hours" | hh"h" mm"m" |
| 8 |  | 4:15 P | 4:15 pm | 1615 hours | 16h 15m |

**Figure 10-2**  Examples of custom date and time formats

to construct your own formats are shown in Chapters 6 and 12. Some examples of custom date and time formats are shown in Figure 10-2.

The choice of which format to use is one of personal taste. Some formats require wider columns than others, which may have some bearing on your decision. Also, there is no reason you cannot mix formats in a worksheet.

## Date and Time Functions

Date and time functions use the date serial number to calculate various date- and time-related numbers. There are six date and five time functions that are used in date and time arithmetic. In addition there is one function that produces the current date and/or time. Of the twelve functions, five produce a date or time serial number that

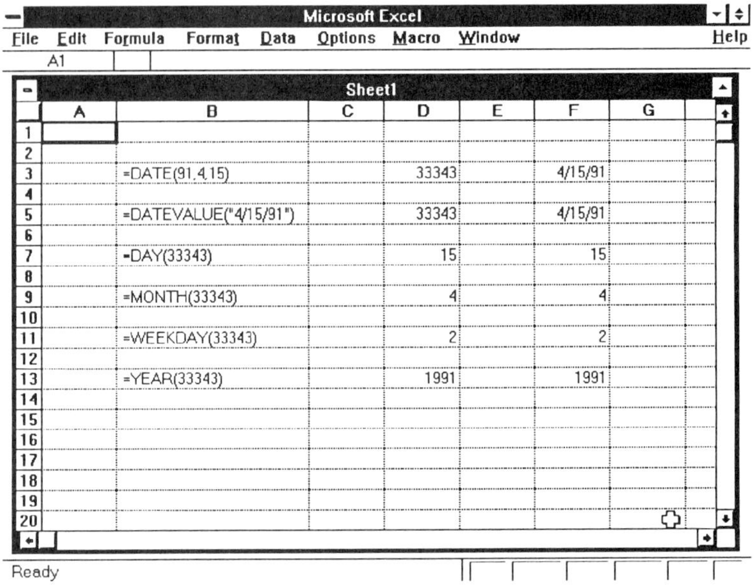

| | A | B | C | D | E | F | G |
|---|---|---|---|---|---|---|---|
| 1 | | | | | | | |
| 2 | | | | | | | |
| 3 | | =DATE(91,4,15) | | 33343 | | 4/15/91 | |
| 4 | | | | | | | |
| 5 | | =DATEVALUE("4/15/91") | | 33343 | | 4/15/91 | |
| 6 | | | | | | | |
| 7 | | =DAY(33343) | | 15 | | 15 | |
| 8 | | | | | | | |
| 9 | | =MONTH(33343) | | 4 | | 4 | |
| 10 | | | | | | | |
| 11 | | =WEEKDAY(33343) | | 2 | | 2 | |
| 12 | | | | | | | |
| 13 | | =YEAR(33343) | | 1991 | | 1991 | |

**Figure 10-3**  Date functions

must be formatted in order to be displayed properly. Any of the formats may be used with the functions.

**DATE FUNCTIONS**  The six date functions are shown in Figure 10-3. The first two produce date serial numbers, shown in the middle column of Figure 10-3, that can be formatted as dates, shown in the third column. The last four functions transform a date serial number into part of a date.

The DATE function takes three integers—one for the year, one for the month, and one for the day—and computes the date serial number. As with all functions, the three arguments (year, month, and day) can be integers that are entered directly into the function, or they can be addresses or range names that refer to cells containing or computing integers suitable for the function. DATE is used when you break out a date to sort or to use as a database criterion and you want to display the date that results from the combined pieces.

DATEVALUE converts a date in text form to a date serial number. DATEVALUE looks for text as an argument. Therefore, a date that is directly entered into the function must be enclosed in quotation marks, as shown in Figure 10-3.

The last four date functions, DAY, MONTH, WEEKDAY, and YEAR, perform the opposite function of DATE: They split out the day, month, weekday, or year from the date serial number. WEEKDAY returns an integer from 1 for Sunday to 7 for Saturday.

**TIME FUNCTIONS**  The five time functions are shown in Figure 10-4. The first two produce the date serial numbers shown in the middle column of Figure 10-4, which can be formatted as the

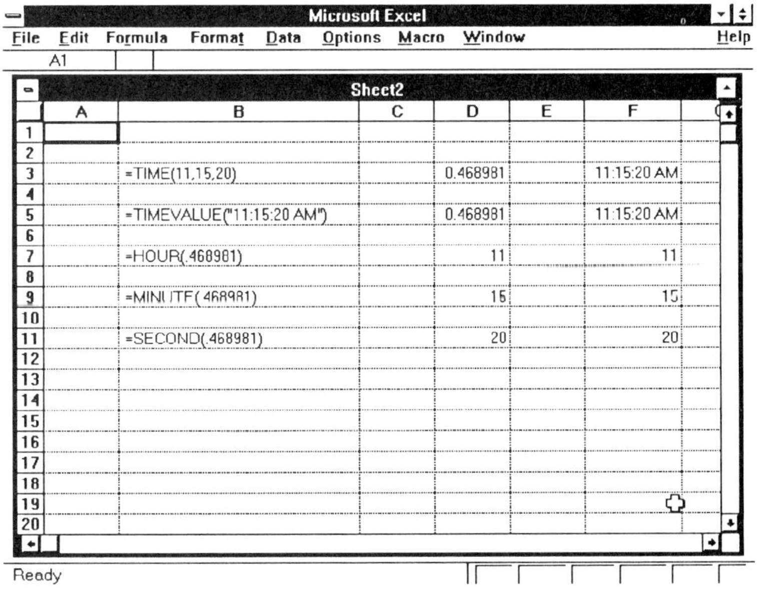

**Figure 10-4**  Time functions

times shown in the third column. The last three functions transform a time serial number into the components of time.

The TIME function uses three integers—one for hours, one for minutes, and one for seconds—to compute the time serial number. TIME is used when you break out a time for sorting or for use as a database criterion and you want to display the time that results from the combined pieces.

You use TIMEVALUE to convert a time that is entered as a label to a date serial number. TIMEVALUE looks for a label as an argument. Therefore, a time that is directly entered into the function must be enclosed in quotation marks, as shown in Figure 10-4.

The next three date functions, HOUR, MINUTE, and SECOND, perform the opposite function of TIME: They split out the hour, minute, or second from the time serial number.

**CURRENT DATE AND TIME FUNCTIONS** The function used to produce the current date and/or time is NOW. Examples of its use are shown in Figure 10-5. This function uses the internal clock-calendar in your computer to determine the current date and time. NOW produces both the integer and decimal components needed for both date and time display. If you are using the current date in a formula or with another function, use the compound function =INT(NOW( )) to use only the integer part of the current date. The decimal (time) part of NOW can cause inaccuracies in date calculations. If you simply are displaying the date, NOW by itself works. Date formats ignore the decimal part of the number.

## Entering and Generating Dates and Times

You have just seen how you can enter dates and times either by entering the date serial number (which is not very practical because you don't know what it is in most instances) or by using one of the

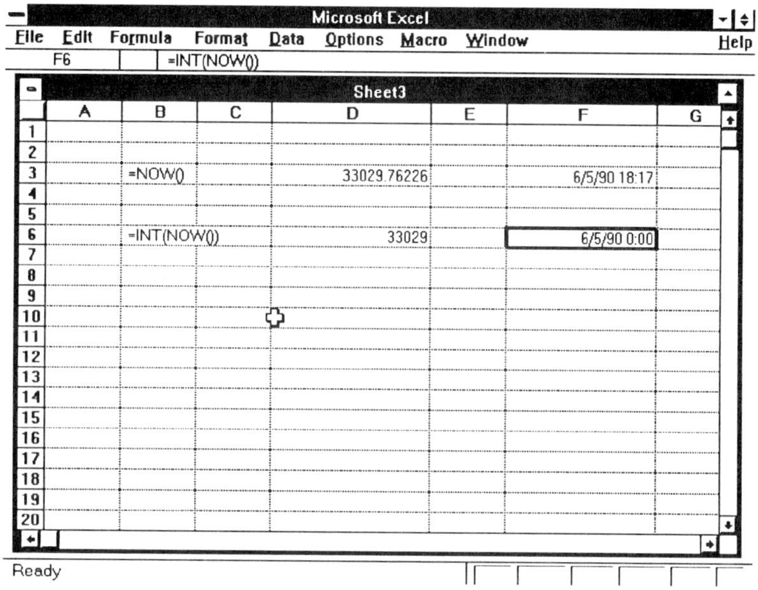

**Figure 10-5** Current date and time function

functions that convert a date or time to the date serial number. Also, you have seen how NOW generates the current date and/or time. You have two other ways to get dates and times into Excel. First, just typing a date or time on the worksheet in an Excel format produces a date or time serial number. Second, the Data Series option generates a sequence of dates or times.

**DIRECT ENTRY OF DATES AND TIMES** You can enter a date or time directly into Excel in any recognized format and get a date or time serial number. It does not have to be one of the built-in formats. When you enter a date or time, it is automatically formatted as the first date or first time format, respectively. The following instructions provide some examples of direct entry of dates and times:

1. Choose New from the File menu, and click on OK for a new worksheet.

2. Move the active cell to B3.

3. Type **4/15/91**. 4/15/91 goes in the edit area, as shown here:

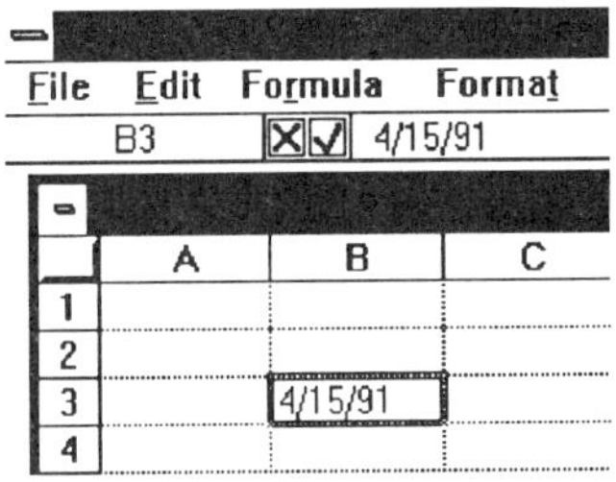

4. Press (ENTER). 4/15/91 is converted to 33343, and the cell is automatically formatted as m/d/yy, as shown here:

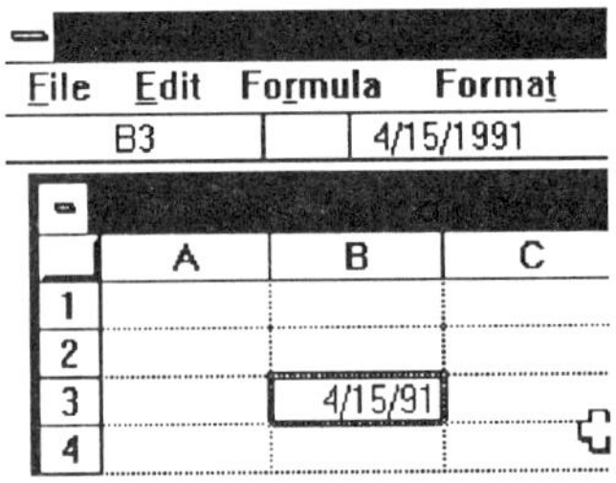

If you would like to see that 4/15/91 is in fact the date serial number 33343, reformat B3 with the General format. You might want to also do this when you get to time values.

5. Click on D3, type **4-15-91**, and press (ENTER). 4-15-91 is converted to 33343 and automatically formatted as 4/15/91 even though 4-15-91 is not a built-in format.

   If you want to enter a formula that looks like a date, you must put an equal sign in front of it.

6. Click on B5, type **3:45 PM**, and press (ENTER). 3:45 PM is converted to .65625, and the cell is automatically formatted with h:mm AM/PM.

7. Click on D5, type **3:45 p**, and press (ENTER). 3:45 p is converted to .65625, and the cell is automatically formatted as 3:45 PM even though 3:45 p is not a built-in format, as shown here:

**GENERATING A SERIES OF DATES**  In Chapter 8 you saw how you can generate dates with the Data Series option, which is a very capable and flexible tool. From any starting date to any ending date within the 178-year range of Excel's date scheme, you can generate as many dates as you can hold in the memory of your computer. If you are generating dates, you can increment them by a number of days, weekdays, months, or years.

The following steps give several examples of generating dates and times with the Data Series option:

1. Choose New from the File menu and click on OK to create a new worksheet.

2. Select B2:F13, choose number from the Format menu, select the m/d/yy date format, and click on OK to format the selected area.

3. Click on B2, type **1/31/91**, press (ENTER), select B2:B13, and choose Series from the Data menu. In the Series in and Type fields, Columns and Date should already be selected. Select Month for the unit and type **12/31/91** as the Stop value. One month is the default Step value, as shown here:

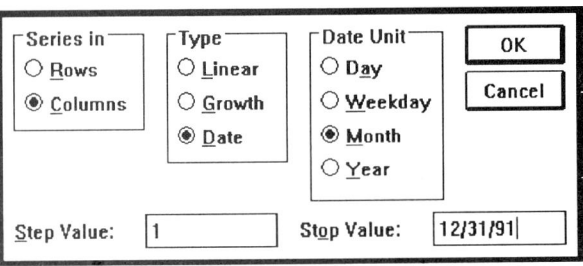

4. Press (ENTER). B2:B13 fills with a series of dates that are one month apart, from 1/31/91 through 12/31/91.

This series provides the actual month end, 1/31, 2/28, 3/31, 4/30, and so on, not just 30- or 31-day intervals. It can be a very useful capability.

5. Click on D2, type **1/31/91**, select D2:D13, choose Series from the Data menu, and type **7** for the Step value. Seven days or one week is the intended step value, as shown here:

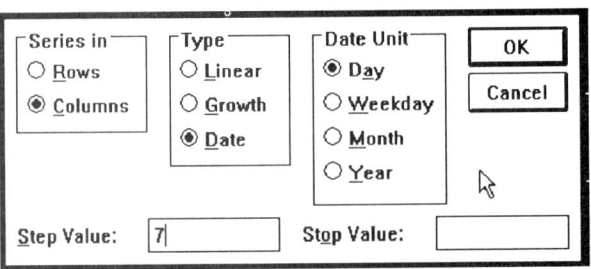

6. Press (ENTER). D2:D13 fills with a series of dates that are one week apart, from 1/31/91 through 4/18/91.

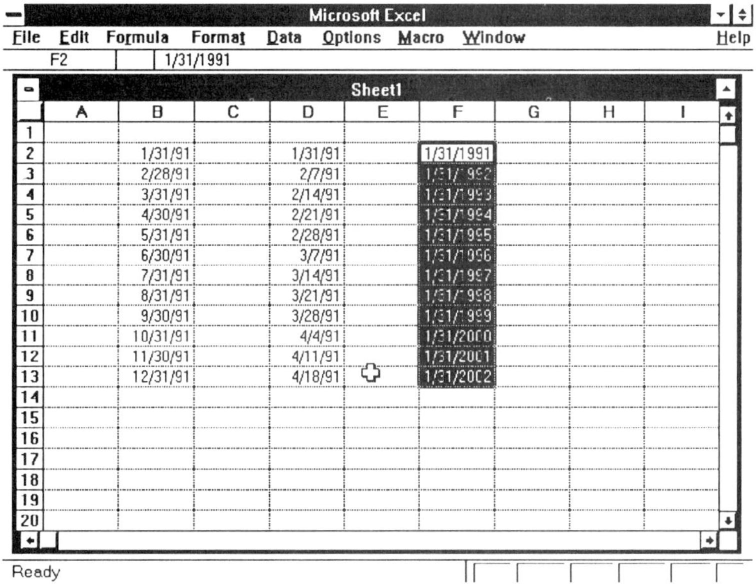

**Figure 10-6**  Date series by month, week, and year

7. Click on (F2) and do a third data series, using years as the increment from 1/31/91 to 1/31/2002. You also must reformat the column to display the dates in the next century.

When you are done, your screen should look like Figure 10-6. Column B shows a progression by month, column D shows a progression by week, and column F shows a progression by year.

**GENERATING A SERIES OF TIMES**  Generating times with Excel is not so neat as generating dates. There are no ready-made increments like hours, minutes, and seconds. When you are generating times, you must specify the increments as decimal fractions. If you want an increment of one hour, it is 1/24 or .0416666. An increment of one minute is 1/1440 or .0006944, and one second is 1/86,400 or .0000115. The next set of steps demonstrate several data series that produce times:

1. Choose New from the File menu, and click on OK to create a new worksheet.

2. Select B3:F15, choose Number from the Format menu, select h:mm:ss AM/PM, and click on OK. The selected range is formatted with the second time format.

3. Choose Column Width from the Format menu, type **12** for the new width, and click on OK. Columns B through F widen to 12 to handle the full time format.

4. Click on B3, type **11:00:00**, press (ENTER), select B3:B15, choose Series from the Data menu, type **.0000115**, and press (ENTER). B3:B15 fills with a series of times that are one second apart, from 11:00:00 through 11:00:12.

5. Click on D3, type **11:00:00**, press (ENTER), select D3:D15, choose Series from the Data menu, type **.0006944**, and press (ENTER). D3:D15 fills with a series of times that are one minute apart, from 11:00:00 through 11:12:00.

6. Click on F3, type **11:00:00**, press (ENTER), select F3:F15, choose Series from the Data menu, type **.0416666**, and press (ENTER). F3:F15 fills with a series of times that are one hour apart, from 11:00:00 AM through 11:00:00 PM.

When you are done, your screen should look like Figure 10-7. Column B shows a progression by second, column D shows a progression by minute, and column F shows a progression by hour, all formatted for a 12-hour clock.

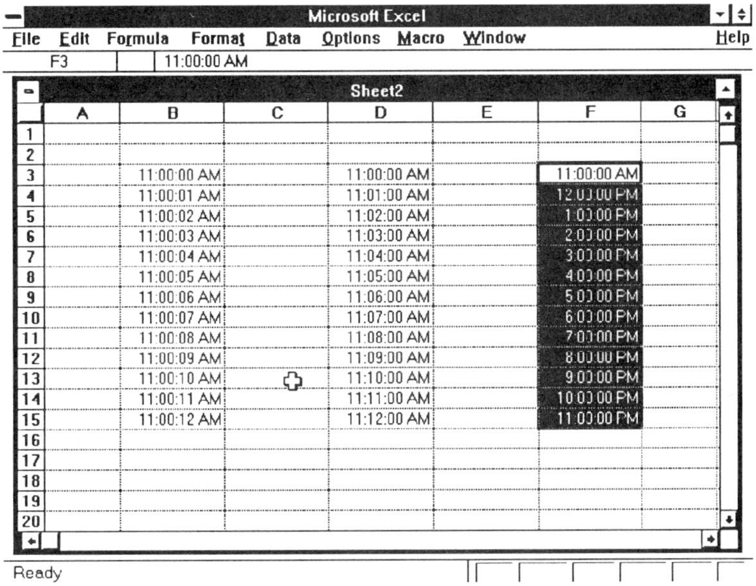

**Figure 10-7** *Time series by second, minute, and hour*

## Date and Time Arithmetic

One of the primary reasons Microsoft developed the date serial number was to allow easy date and time arithmetic. For example, you can add 1 to a date and get the day following, as shown here:

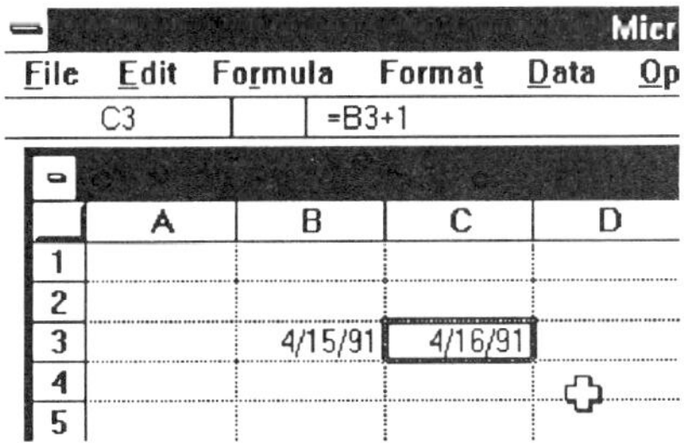

You can add 30 days and get the appropriate day in the next month:

|   | A | B | C | D | E |
|---|---|---|---|---|---|
| 1 |   |   |   |   |   |
| 2 |   |   |   |   |   |
| 3 |   | 4/15/91 | 4/16/91 | 5/15/91 |   |
| 4 |   |   |   |   |   |
| 5 |   |   |   |   |   |

D3: =B3+30

You can also subtract two dates and get the number of days between them:

|   | A | B | C | D | E | F |
|---|---|---|---|---|---|---|
| 1 |   |   |   |   |   |   |
| 2 |   |   |   |   |   |   |
| 3 |   |   | 4/15/91 | 4/16/91 | 5/15/91 | 29 |
| 4 |   |   |   |   |   |   |
| 5 |   |   |   |   |   |   |

E3: =D3-C3

The date functions are useful in date arithmetic. For example, you can use YEAR to determine the number of years between two dates, as shown here:

|   | A | B | C | D | E | F |
|---|---|---|---|---|---|---|
| 1 |   |   |   |   |   |   |
| 2 |   |   |   |   |   |   |
| 3 |   |   | 6/23/87 | 5/15/91 |   | 4 |
| 4 |   |   |   |   |   |   |
| 5 |   |   |   |   |   |   |

E3: =YEAR(C3)-YEAR(B3)

Time arithmetic is a little more complex in that you must add fractions. For example, to add one hour, you must add 1/24th, as shown here:

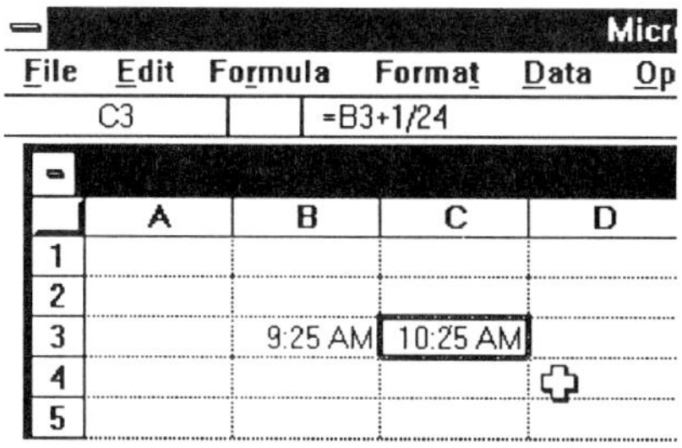

Adding ten minutes requires the fraction 10/(24*60):

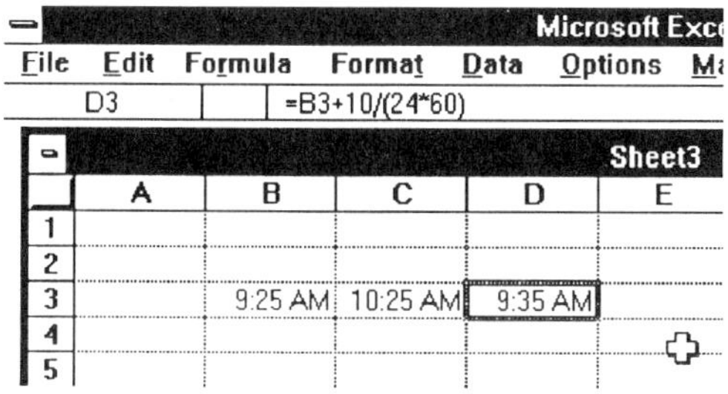

Time functions are useful in time arithmetic. For example, you can determine the number of hours between two times with two HOUR functions, as shown here:

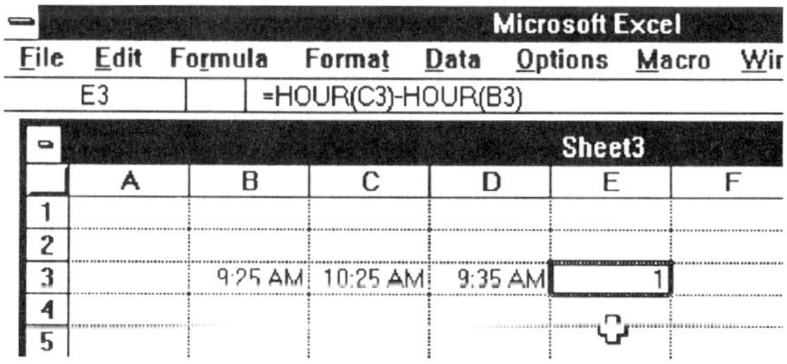

# FUNCTIONS

In earlier chapters you gained some familiarity with statistical functions, database statistical functions, and lookup functions, and you just learned about date and time functions in this chapter. Excel has five other types of functions: financial, informational, logical, mathematical, and text. These are discussed here, but first look at how functions are used and created.

## Using Functions

Functions are ready-made formulas. They perform a previously assigned task that usually involves a calculation but may also include a nonarithmetic operation. Functions always produce a result in the cell in which they are entered. For example, SUM produces a value that is the arithmetic addition of a set of numbers, and UPPER produces a text string that is all uppercase. Functions provide a faster way to accomplish many tasks. For example, using SUM (*range*) is quicker than adding each individual cell in the range if the range contains three or more cells. Functions are the only way some tasks can be accomplished. For example, NOW is the only way you can read your computer's clock-calendar with Excel.

**SPECIFYING ARGUMENTS**  Many functions require pieces of information to perform their task; for example, the range in the SUM(*range*) function. These pieces of information are called arguments. The number of arguments in a function varies between 0 and 14, and the length of arguments in a function is limited to 255 characters, including any quotation marks.

Arguments can be numbers, text, arrays, references, and logical or error values, as outlined here:

- Numbers used as arguments in a function can be numerals, numeric formulas, or addresses or range names for cells that contain numbers or numeric formulas.

- Text is any sequence of letters, numbers, spaces, or symbols. Text in a function can be literal text enclosed in quotation marks, a text formula, or an address or range name for a cell that contains literal text or a text formula.

- An array is a rectangular set of values that is treated in a special way. An array is enclosed in braces ({ }) and has a semicolon between rows. For example, the array {5,6,7;3,4,5;1,2,3} is a 3-by-3 array, with three rows that each contain three columns. Arrays used as arguments in a function can be entered directly, result from a formula that evaluates to an array, or be a set of addresses or range name for a range that contains an array or a formula that evaluates to an array. See Chapter 13 for a complete explanation of arrays.

- References can be addresses, range names, or any formula that evaluates to an address or range name.

- A logical value is either True (1) or False (0). You can enter either **True** and **False** (you may enter upper- or lowercase letters, but Excel converts them to uppercase) or the numbers **1** and **0** interchangeably. In a function, logical values may be entered directly, result from a logical formula that evaluates to either True (1) or False (0), or be in a cell referenced by an address or range name. A logical formula is one that contains one of these logical operators:

    | =  | Equal to |
    | >  | Greater than |
    | <  | Less than |
    | >= | Greater than or equal to |
    | <= | Less than or equal to |
    | <> | Not equal to |

- Error values include #DIV/0!, #N/A, #NAME?, #NULL!, #NUM!, #REF!, and #VALUE!. In a function, error values may be entered directly, result from a formula, or be contained in a cell referenced by an address or range name. A brief meaning of each of the error values is given here:

| | | |
|---|---|---|
| #DIV/0! | You tried to divide by zero | |
| #N/A | Not available | |
| #NAME? | Excel does not recognize a name | |
| #NULL! | Two ranges you expected to intersect do not | |
| #NUM! | Excel has a problem with a number | |
| #REF! | Excel cannot find a cell or range reference | |
| #VALUE! | You used the wrong type of operand or argument | |

**CREATING FUNCTIONS**   There are many different functions, but they all have the same structure, or syntax. A *syntax* is a set of rules for consistently doing something in an orderly manner—in this case, creating functions. The syntax for creating functions is as follows:

- Every function begins with the = symbol, unless it is inside a formula (that is, not the first element of the formula) or another function.

- Functions can be entered in either upper- or lowercase letters. They are displayed in uppercase by Excel. If you type a function in lowercase letters and Excel does not change it to uppercase, you know that you misspelled the function name or made some other mistake.

- Spaces cannot occur anywhere in a function, except within a literal string enclosed in quotation marks.

- The arguments of a function must be enclosed in parentheses. If one or more functions are used as arguments for other functions, the parentheses must be nested, with complete left and right sets of parentheses for each function. Even functions that do not have arguments must have a set of parentheses. For example, NOW( ).

### Dates, Functions, and Macros 391

- Two or more arguments within a function are separated by commas. You should not have more commas than there are arguments or two arguments without a comma between them.

- Blank cells that are referenced in a function are assigned the number 0.

- Functions can be used by themselves as a formula or as a part of another formula, function, or macro function.

Functions may be directly entered by typing them in a cell, following the syntax just described, or you can have Excel build the formula using the Paste Function option on the Formula menu. To do the latter, make the cell in which you want the function the active cell, and then choose Paste Function from the Formula menu. The Paste Function dialog box opens, as shown here:

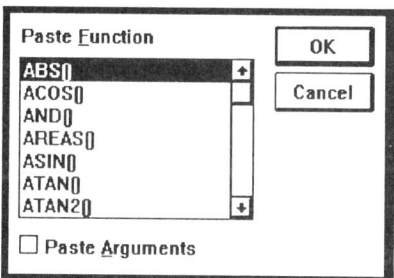

In the Paste Function dialog box, functions are listed alphabetically. You can use the scroll bar to select a function or you can type the first letter of a function to quickly jump closer to it. Click on the Paste Arguments option box, and Excel provides placeholders for the arguments to remind you what they are. If you choose to paste arguments, you must replace the placeholders with actual arguments. An example of the DDB (double declining balance) function with pasted arguments is shown here:

## Additional Functions

The next several sections of this chapter discuss the functions that have not been discussed elsewhere in the first 10 chapters. They fall into five groups: financial, informational, logical, mathematical, and text functions. Due to their number, not all of the individual functions are covered here. The following sections contain tips and suggestions for each of the five groups, along with one or two examples of functions within each group. Chapter 13 contains a detailed explanation of each function.

**FINANCIAL FUNCTIONS** Financial functions such as the following calculate amounts used in financing, budgeting, and depreciation. Optional arguments to the functions are in square brackets.

| | |
|---|---|
| FV(*interest,term, payments*[,*pv,type*]) | Returns the future value, given a series of equal payments. Optionally you can en-ter the present value and/or whether the payment is made at the end of the period (the default, *type* = 0) or at the beginning of the period (*type* = 1). |
| IRR(*range*[,*guess*]) | Returns the internal rate of return for a series of cash flows contained in the range. |
| NPV(*interest,range*) | Returns the net present number of a series of cash flows contained in the range. |

PMT(*interest,term, principal*[, *fv,type*])    Returns a payment amount for a loan, given the interest and loan term. Optionally you can enter the future value and/or whether the payment is made at the end of the period (the default, *type* = 0) or at the beginning of the period (*type* = 1).

PV(*interest,term, payments*[, *fv,type*])    Returns the present value, given a series of equal payments. Optionally you can enter the future value and/or whether the payment is made at the end of the period (the default, *type* = 0) or at the beginning of the period (*type* = 1).

SLN(*cost,salvage, life*)    Calculates depreciation expense for an asset using the straight-line depreciation method.

When you use financial functions, the term and interest rate must be in the same time units. For example, if you want a result in months, the term must be in months and the interest rate must be in months. (See the first example in the "Example" section that follows.)

The interest rate can be entered in a financial function as either a decimal (.108) or a percent (10.8%). Also, in many financial functions you must distinguish between cash outflow, which should be a negative number, and cash inflow, which should be a positive number. (See the examples that follow.)

Where a series of payments is used in a function, the payments are assumed to be equal, at regular intervals, and at the end of each period. This is known as an ordinary annuity. If you would like to change the payment to the beginning of the period, use the optional *type* argument with a value of 1.

***Examples*** To calculate the prospective monthly mortgage payment on a $140,000 home with a 30-year loan at 10.8%, use the following function:

=PMT(.108/12,30*12,140000) = -$1,312.14 / month

To calculate the annual rate of interest necessary for a $10,000 investment to grow to $24,000 over 10 years with monthly compounding, use the following function:

=RATE(10*12,0,-10000,24000)*12 = 8.79% / year

**INFORMATIONAL FUNCTIONS** Informational functions such as the following provide information about cells and areas of the worksheet, including the number of rows or columns in a range, the formatting of a cell, and whether a cell is blank, contains text, or is a logical value.

> COLUMNS(*range*) returns the number of columns in a range
> ISBLANK(*value*) returns the logical value True (1) if the value or cell is blank
> ISTEXT(*value*) returns the logical value True (1) if the value or cell is text
> ROW(*reference*) returns the row number (not the number of rows) of the first row in the reference or an array of row numbers for all of the rows in the reference

***Example*** Often it is helpful to know the column width of a cell. You can choose Column Width from the Format menu, or you can use the function CELL("width"). CELL("width") returns a value that is rounded to the nearest whole number. For example, =CELL("width") returns 8 for the standard cell width of 8.43.

**LOGICAL FUNCTIONS** Logical functions such as the following perform tests to determine if a condition is true.

AND(*condition 1,condition 2,...*) returns True (1) if all conditions or logical statements are true
IF(*condition,true-result,false-result*) evaluates an equation or condition for true or false and takes one action for a true result and another action for a false result
TRUE returns a logical True (1)

*Example* When you calculate percentages, there are situations that result in dividing by 0 and produce a #DIV/0! error. To replace a possible error with 0 in the formula =E15/C15, use the following formula in its place:

=IF(ISERR(E15/C15),0,E15/C15)

**MATHEMATICAL FUNCTIONS** Mathematical functions such as the following calculate general, matrix, and trigonometric values.

ABS(*x*) returns the absolute value of a number
ATAN(*x*) returns the arctangent of a number
MINVERSE(*array*) returns the inverse of a matrix or array
RAND( ) returns a random number between 0 and 1
ROUND(*x,n*) rounds a number off to a specific number of decimal places
SIN(*x*) returns the sine of an angle
SQRT(*x*) calculates the square root of a number

Angles used as arguments for COS, SIN, and TAN must be expressed in radians. To convert degrees to radians, multiply the degrees by PI/180. The angle that results from ACOS, ASIN, ATAN, and ATAN2 is in radians. To convert radians to degrees, multiply the radians by 180/PI.

***Example*** To calculate the length of a guy wire that is supporting a 150-foot-high antenna when the guy wire, attached to the top, makes a 55-degree angle with the ground, use the following function:

150/SIN(55*PI/180) = 183.12 feet

**TEXT FUNCTIONS** Text functions convert, parse, and manipulate text strings. Some text functions are as follows:

CHAR(*x*) returns the ASCII character corresponding to the number
EXACT(*string1,string2*) compares two text strings and returns True (1) if the two strings are the same and False (0) if they differ
LEN(*string*) returns the number of characters in a text string
MID(*string,start-number,n*) returns a certain number of characters from within a text string beginning at a specified position
PROPER(*string*) converts the first character in each word of a text string to uppercase and the rest of the characters to lowercase, as in a proper name
TEXT(*x,format*) converts a number to text with a given numeric format

The offset number used in string functions always begins at 1. The first character in a string is 1, and the last character is the length of the string. Blank cells in a string function are still considered a text string, have a length of 0, and do not return an error code.

*Example* To convert the date 4/15/91 in A1 to a text string that can be used in a title, use the following function:

=TEXT(A1,"mmmm d, yyyy")

This function returns April 15, 1991, which is text, not a value.

# MACROS

A macro is a shortcut. It is a way of accomplishing a set of Excel commands with fewer steps and a way to automate or speed up repetitive procedures. A macro is also a way to guide a less knowledgeable user through a complicated worksheet.

There are two kinds of macros in Excel. A *command macro* is a series of Excel commands, and a *function macro* is a custom function that returns a result. An example of a command macro is one that saves your worksheet, while a function macro example is one that calculates your local sales tax. You can have Excel execute a command macro by pressing two keys. A function macro is executed by putting it in a worksheet cell and recalculating the worksheet. Almost all commands that you can perform from the keyboard, the mouse, or a menu can be stored in a macro and can be activated as you choose. In addition to keyboard and menu commands, a set of *macro functions* lets you perform built-in programming functions, such as repeating a sequence or accepting input from the keyboard. With macro functions you can build custom menus and automate a worksheet. You can see that function macros, which are custom functions that return a result, and macro functions, which supply programming commands to Excel, are quite different.

Anything that you do on a repetitive basis is a candidate for a macro. Macros are stored on a separate sheet called a macro sheet.

You can create a library of macros that you can use with many worksheets, which makes macros you create even more useful.

## Macro Basics

Few Excel tasks are more repetitive than saving a file. If you take normal precautions, you save your current worksheet several times each hour. To save an existing file, you either choose Save from the File menu or press (SHIFT+F12) or (ALT+SHIFT+F2). Depending on whether you are using a mouse or the keyboard, this takes a varying number of keystrokes or mouse moves—not many, and ones that you are probably familiar with. When you repeat these actions 20 times a day, however, they begin to add up. If you could replace the actions with two keystrokes familiar to you, say (CTRL+s), it might encourage you to save your files more often. Saving an existing file, then, is a good candidate for a macro that can record and store the actual commands you use to save a file.

**RECORDING A MACRO** Built into Excel is the capability to record whatever you are doing on an Excel worksheet and storing those steps on a macro sheet. Once stored, you can "play back" the steps and repeat what you were doing. The steps that are stored on the macro sheet comprise the macro, and playing them back is called *running* the macro. You turn on the Excel macro recorder by choosing Record from the Macro menu. Do that now and record a Save macro with these instructions:

1. Choose New from the File menu and click on OK to open a new worksheet.

2. Choose Save from the File menu, type **c:\wi\sheet\macro**, and press (ENTER). Since you want to build a macro to save a worksheet that has already been saved, you must start with a worksheet that has been saved.

3. From the Macro menu choose Record. The Record Macro dialog box opens, as shown here:

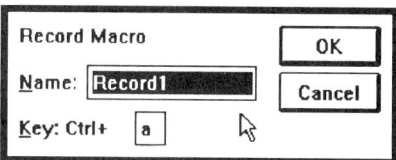

4. Type **Save.Worksheet** as the macro name, press (TAB) to move to the Key field, type **s**, and click on OK. The dialog box closes, and the Recording status indicator comes on in the Status bar.

The name of a macro can be any legitimate Excel name. It must start with a letter, can be up to 255 characters long, and can contain any combination of letters, numbers, periods, and underlines. It should not look like a reference (either D3 or R3C4) and cannot contain spaces. Since you cannot use spaces, periods or underlines are used as word separators. Periods are used in this book. An Excel name can be entered in either upper- or lowercase letters—Excel does not distinguish between the two.

The shortcut key can be any single upper- or lowercase letter. Upper- and lowercase letters are considered two different characters and will not conflict with one another. You cannot use numbers as shortcut characters.

5. Choose Save from the File menu. This is the step you want to record.

6. Choose Stop Recorder from the Macro menu. The Recording indicator disappears.

7. From the Window menu, choose Macro1. The macro sheet that was automatically created in the previous steps becomes the active sheet, as shown here:

```
       ─                                    Micr
       File  Edit  Formula  Format  Data  Op
            A1            | Save.Worksheet
       ┌──────────────────┬──────────────┐
       │        A         │      B       │
       ├──┬───────────────┼──────────────┤
       │1 │Save.Worksheet │              │
       │2 │=SAVE()        │      ✥       │
       │3 │=RETURN()      │              │
       │4 │               │              │
       │5 │               │              │
```

The macro sheet looks just like a normal worksheet except that the columns look a little wider. The macro itself is in the upper-left corner, in cells A1:A3. A1 contains the name you gave the macro. A2 and A3 are the macro functions that save the current worksheet and return control to you. Macro functions are formulas—they always begin with an equal sign (=). A macro sheet always displays formulas, not the results they produce. Displaying formulas is an option on a normal worksheet, but normally a worksheet displays the results a formula produces. You can use the Options Display option to turn off the formulas display on a macro sheet, but the resulting values are generally not informative. Here is what your Macro1 macro sheet looks like with formulas turned off:

```
       ─
       File  Edit  Formula  Format
            A2            | =SAVE()
       ┌──────────────────────────┐
       │    A    │    B    │  C   │
       ├──┬──────┼─────────┼──────┤
       │1 │Save.Worksheet  │      │
       │2 │FALSE │         │      │
       │3 │FALSE │         │      │
       │4 │      │         │      │
       │5 │      │         │      │
```

When you are displaying formulas instead of their results, everything on the worksheet is left aligned and you cannot change it with the Format alignment option. Otherwise, all formatting works on a macro sheet as it does on a worksheet.

**DOCUMENTING A MACRO**  As you create macros, you may find that after a while you forget what they do or what their shortcut keys are. Also, you may want to give one or more macros to someone else to use, and they must know what the macros do and what their shortcut keys are. For this reason you must document your macros when you create them. You can document a macro in several ways. You have used two forms of documentation already—giving the macro a descriptive name and using an obvious shortcut key. Other ways include formatting the macro name on the macro sheet so it stands out, adding one or more cell notes, and, most importantly, adding some comments, including the shortcut key, beside the macro commands. Add some comments and format the macro name with these steps:

1. With A1 as the active cell, choose Font from the Format menu, click on font number 2, which should be a bold font, and click on OK. The macro name should be made bold.

2. Click on B1, type **Saves current wksht**, press (DOWN ARROW), type **Shortcut key = s**, and press (ENTER). The upper-left corner of your macro sheet now looks like this:

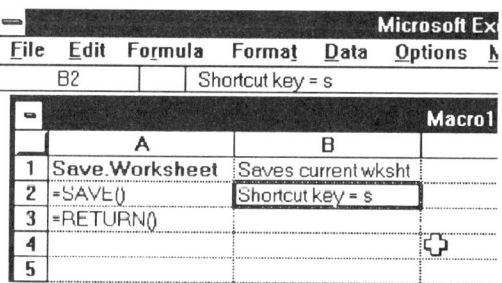

**RUNNING A MACRO**  Now that you have a finished and documented macro, you can run it in one of two ways. First and most simply, you can press (CTRL+s), the shortcut key. Second, the Run dialog box, reached by choosing Run from the Macro menu, lists all the macros available on open macro sheets, so you can select the macro you want and click on OK. Try both of these methods using the following instructions:

1. From the Windows menu, choose MACRO.XLS.

2. Press (CTRL+s). The file is saved.

If you look at the Reference area of the Formula bar or at your disk light, you will see a brief indication that the file was saved. Also, you may see the hour glass wait indicator come on briefly. Type (CTRL+s) several times until you are satisfied it is working.

3. From the Macro menu, choose Run. The Run dialog box opens, as shown here:

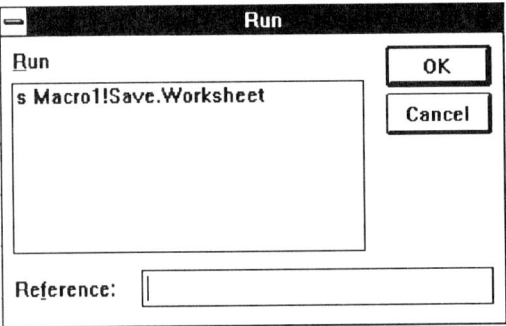

The Run dialog box lists the macro you have just created. On the left is the shortcut key followed by the name of the macro sheet and the macro name. By clicking on the entry in the list box and then on OK you can run the macro.

4. Click on the entry in the list box and on OK. Again you notice a brief flicker in the Reference area and in your disk light telling you the worksheet is saved.

The Run dialog box also serves as a reference if you should forget what the shortcut key is on a particular macro.

If you had any fears about macros, you can now set them aside. You have successfully created and run a macro!

> **Caution** Remember that File Save erases the current file on disk before replacing it with the file being saved. This means data can be lost. You may want to create a backup file through the Options command button on the Save As dialog box. This gives you the added protection of preserving the last file saved.

## Creating Additional Macros

Create several more simple and general-purpose macros. This time, however, watch the macros being built by reducing the size of the worksheet you are working on and exposing most of the macro sheet, as shown in Figure 10-8. Drag the upper-left corner of the MACRO.XLS worksheet window to reduce it to approximately the size shown in Figure 10-8. When you create a second macro, Excel places it at the top of the next available column of the current macro sheet, unless you tell Excel otherwise with the Set Recorder option in the Macro menu. Since you have used columns A and B, the next macro you create is placed in C1.

**COPY MACRO**  Another heavily used option is Copy. While it has a well-defined shortcut key built into Excel, many people find it hard to remember. Create a macro for Copy and assign it the intuitive shortcut key (CTRL+c).

1. From the Macro menu, choose Record, type **Copy.Selection**, press (TAB), type **c**, and click on OK. The Recording indicator

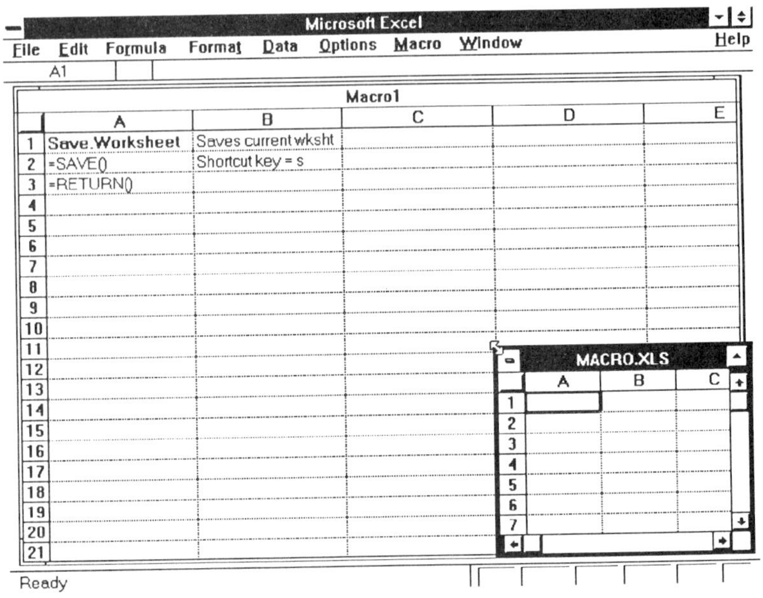

**Figure 10-8** Small worksheet set up for watching macros created

comes on in the Status bar, and the name appears in C1 on the macro sheet.

If you cannot see the Copy.Selection macro name on your macro sheet, it is because you left Excel between creating the Save macro and this macro. If you start a new session, even if you open your old macro sheet, Excel creates a new macro sheet to use for macros created in the current session, unless you tell it otherwise. (You will see how in a moment. For now, carry on creating the Copy macro even though you cannot see it.) In step 4, choose the new macro sheet from the Window menu instead of the old one.

2. Choose Copy from the Edit menu. The blinking marquee appears around A1 in MACRO.XLS. The macro function =COPY( ) appears in C2 on the macro sheet.

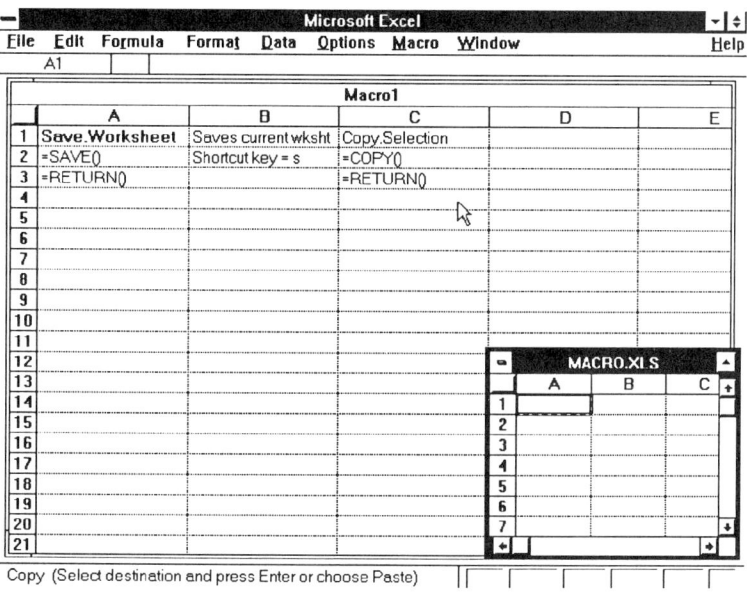

**Figure 10-9**   Copy macro added to macro sheet

3. Choose Stop Recorder from the Macro menu. The macro function =RETURN( ) appears in C3 on the macro sheet. Your screen should look like that shown in Figure 10-9.

4. Click on the macro sheet and on cell C1. From the Format menu choose Font, click on the bold font, and click on OK.

5. Click on D1, type **Copies current select**, press (DOWN ARROW), type **Shortcut key = c**, and press (ENTER). Your second macro is documented.

**SETTING A RECORDING RANGE**   Your next macro would be placed in E1, unless you tell Excel otherwise. Since that is off the screen, tell Excel you want it to begin in A5. You do that either by selecting a starting cell you want the macro to start in or by selecting a range you want the macro to occupy and then choosing the Set Recorder option from the Macro menu.

If you select a single cell in which to start the macro, Excel fills as many cells below that cell in the same column as necessary to complete the macro. If the macro reaches the bottom of the column, Excel redirects the macro to the top of the next column with a GOTO macro function, and then continues the macro in the next column. If you select a single cell and the single cell is not blank, Excel finds the last nonblank cell in the column and begins recording immediately below it. If the last nonblank cell has the RETURN( ) macro function in it, RETURN( ) is replaced by the first macro function of the new macro. In this way you can stop recording a macro and then later restart where you left off.

If you select a range in which to record a macro, the range becomes the limits within which the macro is contained. Excel starts the macro in the upper-left corner and continues to the lower-right corner, placing GOTO functions at the bottom of each column. If Excel reaches the limits of the range without completing the macro, you get a message that the range is full. Unlike selecting a single cell, if you select a range and the first cell in the range is not blank, Excel displays a message saying the range is full and cannot be set.

Set the starting cell for recording the next macro with these instructions:

1. Click on A5 of the macro sheet.

2. Choose Set Recorder from the Macro menu.

3. Choose MACRO.XLS from the Window menu to return to your worksheet.

Once you have set where you want to place your next macro, you can start the macro with either the Record or Start Recorder options on the Macro menu. Both options start in the cell you set. The principal difference is that Record is meant to start a new macro and Start Recorder is meant to be used for adding to the last macro you have entered. Start Recorder does not ask you to name or enter a shortcut key for a macro. You can use it only if you have already used Record within an Excel session (since you have most recently started Excel) or if you have used Set Recorder to establish a starting cell. If you have started a macro with Record, you can use Stop Recorder to quit macro recording and then restart with Start Recorder as if you had never quit; you need not use Set Recorder.

**FORMATTING MACRO** The custom percent format 0.0% deserves a macro for quick use. Build it next and give it the shortcut keys (CTRL+p).

1. Choose Record from the Macro menu, type **Percent.Format**, press (TAB), type **p**, and click on OK. The name appears in A5 or in the macro sheet.

2. Choose Number from the Format menu, select 0.00%, delete one decimal zero in the text box, and click on OK.

3. Choose Stop Recorder from the Macro menu to complete the macro.

4. Click on the macro sheet, click on A5, and make the name bold using Font from the Format menu. Then in B5 type **0.0% Format**, press (DOWN ARROW), type **Shortcut key = p**, and press (ENTER).

5. Widen column A by dragging on the intersection between columns A and B so you can see the full format macro function, as shown in Figure 10-10.

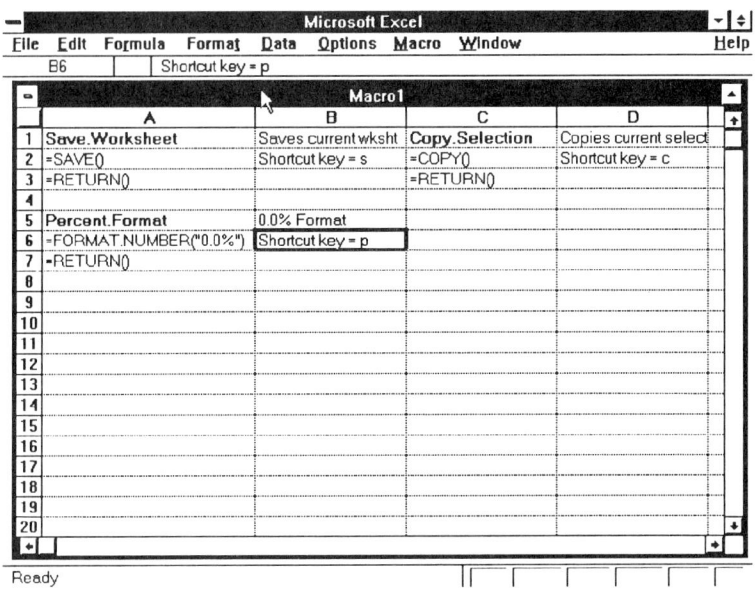

Figure 10-10    Macro sheet with Percent macro

**DATE AND TIME STAMP MACRO**   You will often want to add the date and/or time to a worksheet. Manually you must type =**NOW( )**, format the cell, and then use Copy and Paste Special to convert the function to a permanent value that does not change every time the worksheet is recalculated. It is easier to look at your watch or calendar and type the numbers as text so they do not have to be formatted. A macro takes this process down to two keystrokes that format the cell, enter the function, and convert it to a value. Create the macro following these steps:

1. Click on A9 of the macro sheet and choose Set Recorder.

2. Choose MACRO.XLS from the Window menu and click on A1 if the active cell is not already there.

3. Choose Record, type **Date.Time.Stamp**, press (TAB), type **d**, and click on OK. The name appears in A9.

4. Type =now( ) and press (ENTER).

5. Choose Number from the Format menu, select the m/d/yy h:mm format, and click on OK.

6. Widen column A of the worksheet by dragging on the intersection between columns A and B until column A is about half again larger.

7. Choose Copy from the Edit menu, choose Paste Special, click on Values and OK, and press (ESC). The =NOW( ) formula is converted to a value and the copy marquee removed.

8. Choose Stop Recorder from the Macro menu. Click on the macro sheet and document your macro as shown in Figure 10-11.

Now try out this macro.

9. Choose MACRO.XLS, click on B3, and press (CTRL+d).

The date is placed in B3 and it is formatted (although you cannot tell), but the column is not widened. Go back to the macro sheet and see why.

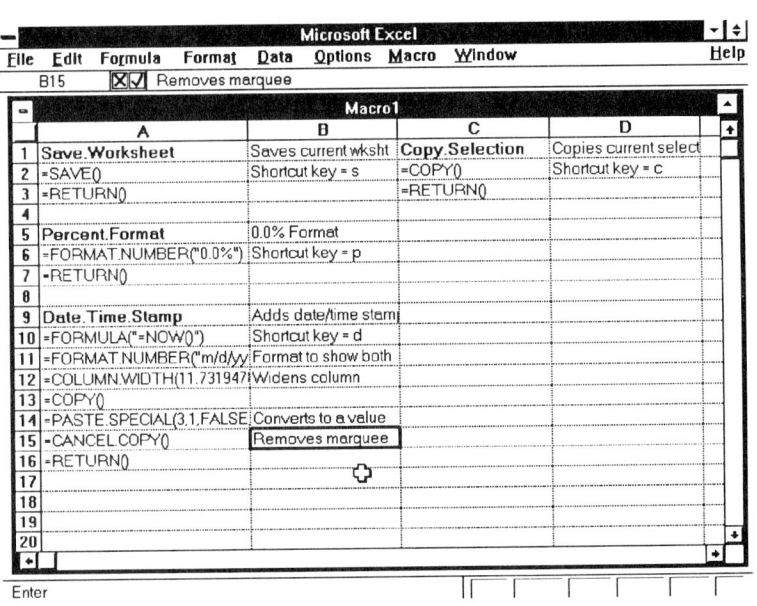

**Figure 10-11** Date/Time Stamp macro

10. Click on the macro sheet and widen column A until you can see all of the COLUMN.WIDTH macro function, as shown here:

The COLUMN.WIDTH macro function has two arguments: the width itself (your width may be different due to variation in dragging), and an optional reference. The reference shown here, C1, does not mean column C, row 1, but rather "column 1." This is the problem. To make the Date/Time Stamp macro flexible, you need to remove the column reference. Then the COLUMN.WIDTH macro function refers to the current selection, which is what you want. If your width value is a number like the one shown here, edit it also to round it to an even 11.5.

11. Click on the macro sheet and on A12. Edit A12 so that it contains =COLUMN.WIDTH(11.5).

12. Return to the MACRO.XLS worksheet and try the macro again in B5. It now works the way it should.

## Entering Macros

All the macros you have created so far have been recorded. You modified the last recorded macro to give you what you want. You can also directly type in a macro. You can use either an existing macro sheet or create a new one. You simply pick an area on the worksheet and start typing the necessary macro functions. This, of course, takes some familiarity with the macro functions and their arguments (see Chapter 14 for a complete description of all macro functions). Once you have written the macro, you can name it with the Define Name option on the Formula menu. Try that next by writing a macro to apply the #,##0 format. You can use the Percent macro as a model.

1. Click on the macro sheet and on C5. Type **Comma.Format** and press (DOWN ARROW).

2. Type **=format.number("#,##0")**, press (DOWN ARROW), type **=RETURN( )**, and press (UP ARROW) twice.

3. Choose Define Name from the Formula menu, click on Command as the macro type, press (TAB), type **f** as the shortcut key, and click on OK. (The name Comma.Format is already in the Name text box.)

4. Format the name on the macro sheet to make it bold, and enter the documentation as shown here:

| Comma.Format | #,##0 Format |
|---|---|
| =FORMAT.NUMBER("#,##0") | Shortcut key = f |
| =RETURN() | |

5. Try out the macro by returning to the MACRO.XLS worksheet, typing **62503.60**, and pressing [CTRL+f]. It works! Next press [CTRL+p], since you have not tried that macro, and format the number as a percent. It also works.

You can see that while you can type in a macro, it is much easier to use the recorder. Even if you need to do some heavy modification, building an initial structure with the recorder is a substantial benefit. It not only saves time, but also it gives you the correct macro function name and argument set. It saves you from having to either look these up or use the Paste Function option of the Formula menu.

**RULES FOR MACRO ENTRY** All parts of a macro can be typed in either upper- or lowercase. Excel converts it to uppercase if it is spelled correctly. A macro can occupy as many cells in a column as necessary. You can use both worksheet functions and macro functions. Place one function per cell. This makes the macros easier to read on the screen and easier to edit. As Excel is executing a macro and completes the instructions in one cell, it automatically goes to the cell immediately below and continues macro execution. Excel continues down a column in this manner until it reaches a terminating or redirecting macro function such as RETURN, GOTO, or HALT. During macro execution, Excel ignores a blank cell.

If a macro refers to a range, it is better to name the range than to use addresses. An address in a macro is not updated if the worksheet is changed. A range name, on the other hand, continues to track an address with changes in the worksheet. Also, if you are working with multiple files, it is a good idea to precede a range name with the filename followed by an exclamation point.

**DEBUGGING MACROS** When a macro does not behave the way you expect, you want to *debug* it, or correct it. Debugging can be as simple as correcting an obvious spelling error in a range name. In many instances, however, the error is not so obvious, as with the COLUMN.NUMBER problem in the Date/Time Stamp macro.

Debugging begins by looking carefully at what happened when the macro was run. Were there any error messages, and what did they say? What happened on the worksheet? Do you get the same result each time you run the macro?

Next, look at the macro itself. Are there any misspellings? Are there missing arguments, periods, or macro functions? If you recorded the macro, did the recorder supply some arguments you do not want? Did you use absolute addressing when you wanted relative or vice versa? Have you defined the range and macro names you are using?

Finally, go back and record the macro again to see if you get the same macro functions a second time. Carefully note all of your actions while you are recording the macro.

In most instances these steps identify the problem. If not, there is one further thing that can be done. Excel has a way of executing the macro one step at a time, pausing after each step, until you tell Excel to continue. This capability is discussed in Chapter 11.

**MACRO FUNCTIONS** A macro function, when executed, performs a predefined function that may be available from the keyboard, the menus, or the mouse. Some macro functions, however, are for purposes of further automating a process and are not available in any other form. These macro functions cause the macro to accept input from the user, wait while the user does something, make a choice among several things, or loop through a set of macro functions multiple times. These are programming macro functions, and Chapter 11 works with them extensively.

Macro functions have a common syntax that must be followed in order for Excel to understand what to do. This syntax is exactly the same as that for worksheet functions described earlier in this chapter.

## Function Macros

Function macros are custom functions you create on a macro sheet and then use on a worksheet to return a value or other result. You can distinguish function macros from command macros in two ways. First, command macros take some action like formatting, copying, or saving. Function macros take no action, but rather produce a result, like you might get from a calculation. Second, a command macro is wholly contained on the macro sheet and is executed with either the shortcut key or the Run option on the Macro menu. A function macro is created on a macro sheet, but to use it you must enter the resulting function on a worksheet.

Function macros are generally calculations you have to perform over and over. They have arguments through which you supply values and they use formulas and regular functions to calculate a result based on the values you supply. When you build a function macro, you must use three special macro functions that handle the arguments and the result. These functions, in the order in which they must be used, are as follows:

*RESULT* The RESULT function is used only if you need to change the data type of the result. The RESULT function has one argument, the data type number. If you have not used a RESULT function to change it, the result is assumed to be a number, text, or a logical value. The possible data type numbers are

1   Number
2   Text
4   Logical
8   Reference
16  Error
64  Array

Data type numbers can be added together except for the reference and array types. For example, the default of number, text, or logical is a type 7 (1+2+4).

***ARGUMENT*** You must have one ARGUMENT function for each argument in the function macro you are building. You can have up to 13 ARGUMENT functions, and they must be in the order in which they are presented in the function macro. The ARGUMENT function can have up to three arguments: a name, a data type, and a reference. You must have either a name or a reference. Whichever you specify, the other is optional. The data type is always optional. The name must be a legitimate Excel name and becomes defined by the ARGUMENT function. It can then be used by the formulas and regular functions that follow. If you do not specify a data type, Excel assumes it to be a number, text, or a logical value. If the value received by the ARGUMENT function is not a default type and you have not used the data type argument to change that, you will get a #VALUE! error. The reference argument is a cell or range reference on the macro sheet where the value received by the ARGUMENT function is placed. If you use both a name and a reference, the reference is given the name and can be referred to by it.

***RETURN*** All function macros must end with the RETURN function. The RETURN function has one argument in a function macro—the cell on the macro sheet that contains the result.

The formulas and regular functions to be used in a function macro must be placed after the last ARGUMENT function and before the RETURN function.

Function macros must be directly entered—they cannot be recorded. Build an example to see how they work. The example, call it Tax, calculates sales tax. It has two arguments: the amount on which to calculate the tax and the tax rate. Enter the tax function macro on the open macro sheet in C9.

1. Click on the macro sheet and on C9. Type **Tax** and press (ENTER). Format it as bold.

2. From the Formula menu, choose Define Name. Click on Function and OK.

3. Click on cell C10. Then type **=argument("amount",1)**, press (DOWN ARROW), and then type **=argument("rate",1)**. Now press (DOWN ARROW).

4. Type **=amount*rate**, press (DOWN ARROW), type **=return(c12)**, and press (ENTER).

5. Click on MACRO.XLS in the Window menu, and click on A5. (Drag the MACRO.XLS window to the left if you want to see the macro while you are working on the worksheet.)

6. From the Formula menu, choose Paste Function, drag the scroll box to the bottom of the scroll bar, then click on the name MACRO1.XLM!Tax( ), and click on OK. You are left with the function in the Edit area and the insertion point between the parentheses.

7. Type **100,8.1%** and press (ENTER).

The result, 8.1, appears in A5, as shown in Figure 10-12. If an argument is missing when a function macro is used, the ARGUMENT function for that argument passes a value of #N/A to the formulas and functions that follow. To allow for optional argu-

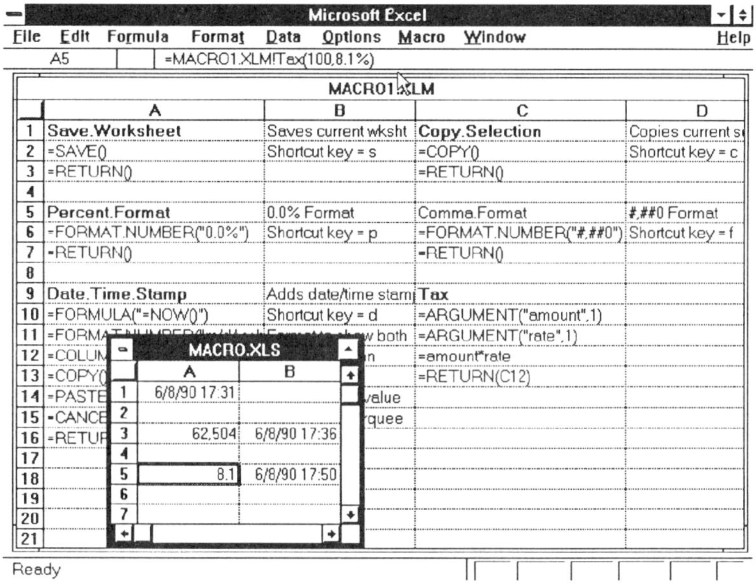

**Figure 10-12** Function macro for calculating sales tax

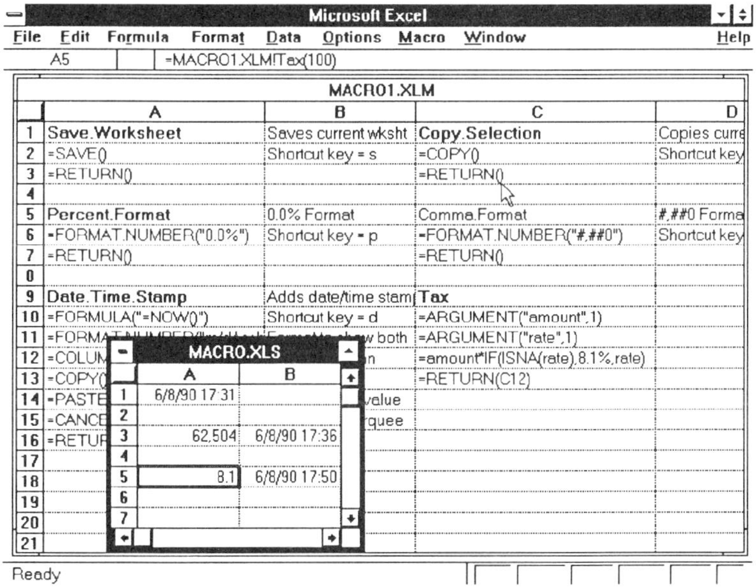

**Figure 10-13** Tax function macro with an optional argument

ments, you must trap the #N/A with an IF(ISNA( )) function. For example, if you want to make the tax rate optional in the function macro you just built, you must change the formula in C12 to =amount*IF(ISNA(rate),8.1%,rate). This way, if the rate is not entered, 8.1% would be used, as shown in Figure 10-13.

**Note** As you are going back and forth between the macro sheet and the worksheet, be aware that the worksheet is not recalculated by simply activating it. You must either make an entry to or edit a cell or choose Calculate Now from the Options menu.

Depending on who is going to use your macros, especially function macros, you must consider their error-handling capability. If you are the only one who will be using them, they can probably be fairly insensitive to errors. If novice Excel users are going to handle them, the function macros must work with many different error conditions. You are now in the position of a programmer whose hardest job probably is to figure out all the ways someone can use their program. A basic ground rule is that if it can happen, it will, and if it cannot happen, it might anyway. Chapter 11 deals entirely with writing macros to automate a worksheet so a novice can use it (and it cannot consider every possible error that could occur!).

You are left with a number of open worksheets. Only the macro sheet has potential value. Save it if you want and exit both Excel and Windows by telling Excel you do not want to save the other worksheets.

# 11

# AUTOMATING A WORKSHEET

Planning an Application
Building the Worksheet
Building the Macros
Testing and Correcting the Macros
Future Enhancements

In this chapter you will build an automated worksheet or application to be used by people who know very little about Excel. This application provides the means of entering, editing, and printing sales orders. All of these functions are complete as they might be in an actual application. At the same time there are many enhancements you can add to the application to give it more features. These enhancements are discussed at the end of the chapter.

Building the application takes several steps. The first is to plan it. You must determine what the application will do and how it will be laid out on both the macro sheet and the worksheet. The second step is to build the working part of the worksheet, the title screen, and the report range. Next you build a sophisticated dialog box that will be used for data entry. Finally you build and test the macros necessary to guide a user through the application. The macros produce a custom menu, accept data from the dialog box, update a database, and print the database.

Building an automated worksheet is a detailed process that requires concentration. The reward is to watch the worksheet operate when you get done. The results in a business can be very powerful. With applications like this you can have people who know very little about Excel doing sophisticated things with it.

The instructions in this chapter are more generalized than in previous chapters—for example, "Copy B1:G1 to B5:G5" or "Adjust the width of columns D and E to 12 characters." Also, the instructions in this chapter will use the term "enter" to mean "type something and then press (ENTER)"; previous chapters have spelled out the full procedure. It is assumed that you are familiar with such frequently used options as Copy, Paste, Insert, Delete, and Column Width. If you need help, use the bold reference in the index to find the primary discussion of a command in Chapters 1 through 11, or use the italicized reference in the index to find the command summary in Chapters 12 through 14.

## PLANNING AN APPLICATION

Planning an application entails answering five questions. First, what will the application do—what are the inputs, how is data manipulated, and what are the outputs? Second, how do these requirements translate to functions performed by Excel? Third, how will the worksheet be laid out—what functions will go where on the worksheet? Fourth, what is the logic path of operating the application—how do you logically work through all of its functions and cleanly start and stop it? And fifth, how does the logic path translate into Excel capabilities—dialog boxes, menus, and macro functions?

While all five of these steps are important, most applications built with Excel do not go through such a formal process. They generally result from the "build some, try it out, and when it works, build some more" philosophy. This chapter covers only what the application will do, how that translates to Excel, and how it is laid out on the worksheet.

## What Is It Going to Do

Before determining what an application will do, it is important to remind yourself to "keep it simple" and define the minimum set of things that you want to do. It is very easy to describe the Taj Mahal if you ignore what it will take to build it.

Here is the minimum set of things this application should do:

1. Automatically load and prepare the database worksheet

2. Accept sales orders entered with the customer name, salesperson, product description, quantity, unit price, and sales tax

3. Build a database of these items with the tax calculated and the order totaled

4. Provide for editing of the database items including changing individual fields and deleting items

5. Print the database with a heading

6. Save the worksheet and leave Excel

This translates well into Excel. You need a dialog box for entry, a database, and a print range. Excel's Set Print Area handles the selection of an output range for printing, and the Data Form option works well for editing and deleting records in the database. The result is that Excel can handle all of the requirements.

## How It Will Be Laid Out

You could lay out this application in a number of ways. You must follow only one rule: don't put anything under the database, so it can grow without interference.

The layout adopted for this example is shown in Figure 11-1. This layout includes a macro sheet and a worksheet. The macro

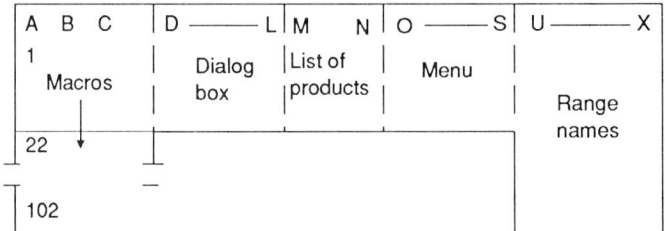

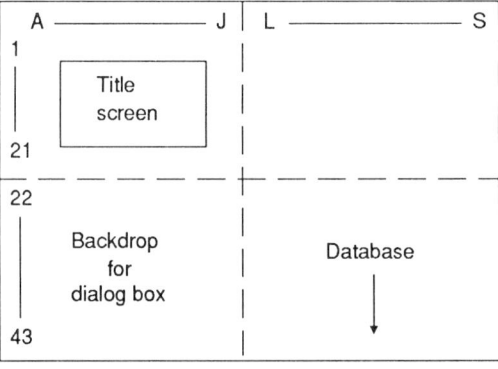

**FIGURE 11-1** Layout of the macro sheet and worksheet

sheet also contains a list of range names. The worksheet can be broken into two vertical segments. The left segment is used for two screens—one that serves as a title screen and the other that serves as a backdrop for entering the sales orders and other activities. The right segment contains the database. As you can see, the one layout rule was adhered to in forming this layout.

# BUILDING THE WORKSHEET

As with worksheets, there is no right or wrong place to start. Here, you'll start with the screens and then do the database.

## Building Screens

The order entry application you will create has two sections of the worksheet that will be used as screens—what the user will see on the screen at various times. The first of the two screens is the title screen used at startup and whenever the user completes an operation. This screen is shown in Figure 11-2 in its finished form. The other screen is really a blank screen to be used as a backdrop for other operations.

The normal frame (row and column headings, gridlines, and scroll, Formula, and Status bars) seen on an Excel screen is turned off; it has no bearing to this application. In its place you will construct a new border with Excel's Format Border option and by adjusting the column widths and row heights as shown in Figure 11-3. Your computer should be on, Excel loaded, and a blank worksheet on your screen.

1. Click on Maximize and then drag the columns and rows to the widths and heights shown in Figure 11-3. It is not necessary that they be precisely as shown since it is only a title screen.

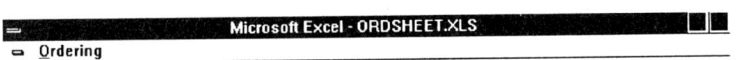
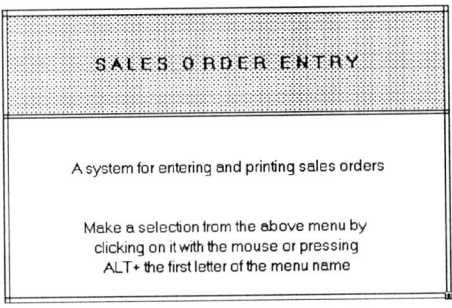

FIGURE 11-2   Title screen in its finished form

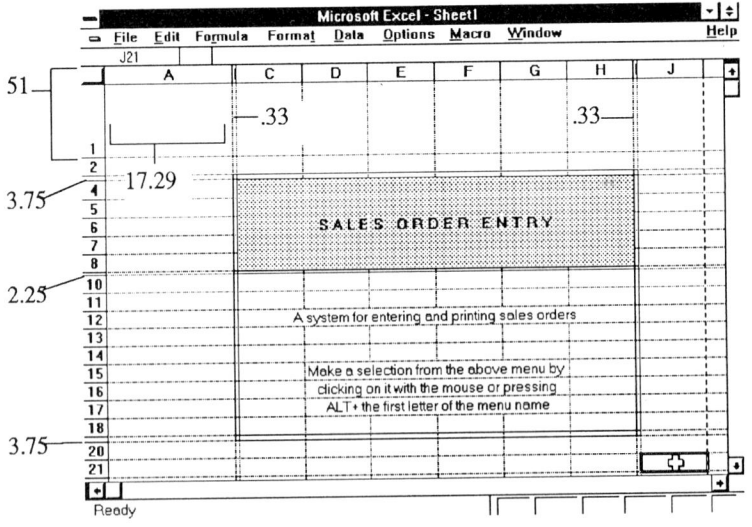

FIGURE 11-3   Column widths and row heights for title screen

The title box looks off-center in Figure 11-3 because the borders and bars are turned on.

2. Select B3:B19 and I3:I19 at the same time (by pressing **SHIFT+F8**) after the first selection), and then select Left and Right from the Format Border option.

3. Select B3:I3, B9:I9, and B19:I19 together, and then select Top and Bottom from the Format Border option. (Ignore the grayed Left and Right boxes. This is telling you that some cells you selected have Left and Right turned on.)

4. Select C4:H8, and then select Shade from the Format Border option.

5. Enter the text shown in Figure 11-3, placing it in D6, C12, and D15:D17. Make the first line bold by pressing **CTRL+2**. Add leading spaces sufficient to center each line. For the title, place one space between each character and three spaces between each word.

For the second screen there is nothing that needs to be done. The only other thing to do on the worksheet is to construct the database.

## Preparing for the Database

To prepare for the database, you need to enter a set of headings and adjust the column widths.

1. Scroll your screen so you can see L21:T42. If you cannot get a full 21 rows, make sure you have maximized the worksheet window. If you still cannot get 21 rows, make sure L21 is in the upper-left corner, and ignore the fact that you have one or two fewer rows on the bottom.

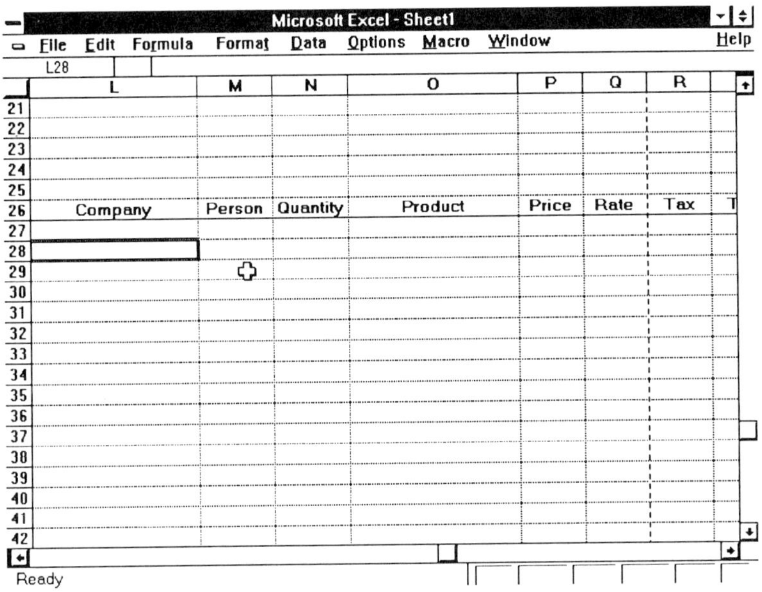

**FIGURE 11-4** Database area

You want to put the database in this location so you will not run into the short rows or narrow columns used in the title screen.

2. Widen columns L and O to 20, and narrow columns P, Q, and R to 7. Again, you can use (SHIFT+F8) to do L and O together and then do P, Q, and R together.

3. Enter the headings in row 26 that are shown in Figure 11-4, center them (Format Alignment), make them bold (Format Font 2 or (CTRL+2)), and put a bottom border under them.

Most of the remaining work involves the macro sheet, so as a final step with the worksheet, save it.

4. Choose File Save and name the file ORDSHEET.

## BUILDING THE MACROS

The next step is to automate the worksheet. This is done through a combination of recording macros and then modifying them. The macros are divided into five sections. In the first section you will build a means to prepare and control the worksheet and the screen. In the next section you will build a dialog box to accept entries for the database and then build the macros to update the database with those entries. In the third section you will record the macros to print the database, save the worksheet, and quit Excel. In the fourth section you will build macros to use Excel's Data Form to edit the database. In the final section you will build a custom menu and a macro that provides access to the rest of the macros. These macros provide the means for entering, editing, and printing data and saving and quitting the application. They also represent the five choices in the menu built in the final section.

While this may sound like a major undertaking, you will find it goes faster than you think. It is not a trivial task either. Remember that you are building a fully operable, complete application that allows a novice to do some sophisticated things with Excel. By working through this application, you should be able to build almost any application of your own.

Think of a series of interconnected macros as a logic path, a set of stepping stones with branches along the way. You start out on the path and come to a branch. You make a choice, branch off, do some task, and then return to the original path. In this application you start out with a menu that provides five choices: entering, editing, printing, saving, and quitting. You choose one, do it, and then return to the menu again to make another choice. Figure 11-5 shows a simplified logic path for the order entry application.

There are two ways to build a series of macros that represent an application: a few large macros or many small macros. Using a few large macros—for example, one macro for each item on the menu—has the benefit of clearly delineating the program flow. Many small macros, which you would combine to perform the

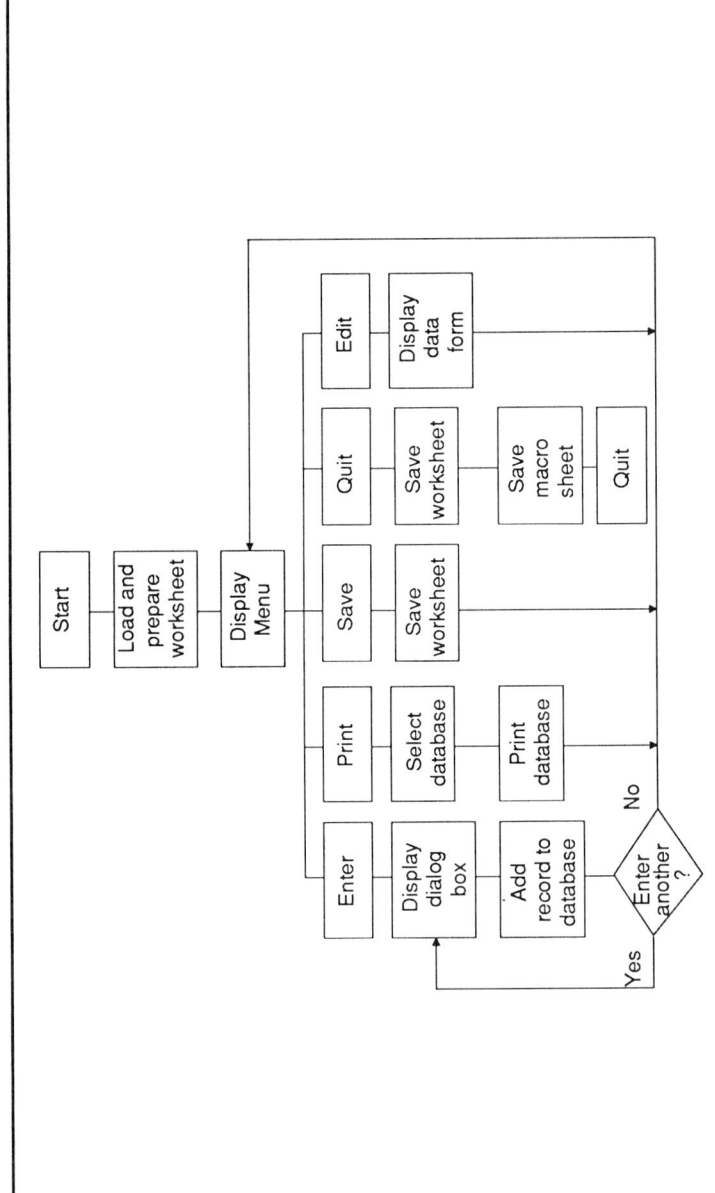

**FIGURE 11-5** Order entry logic path

menu functions, have two overpowering benefits. First, it is easier to build and test the small macros because they are small. Second, there are always small tasks that are required in several of the larger functions. By building one small macro to do these tasks and then calling these macros in each of the larger functions, you reduce repetition. Therefore, the instructions that follow have you build many small macros and then combine them to carry out the menu choices.

## Preparing and Controlling The Worksheet

Five separate macros are used to prepare and control the worksheet and the screen. The first cleans up and positions the screen. The second undoes what the first did so when you are done with the application you can return to the normal Excel environment. It is important, as you are building macros, to always have reversing macros so that when you test a macro you can undo its effects. You will see several reversing macros here.

The third macro opens the worksheet (reads it in from disk) and calls the first macro. Here you see the first of many instances of one macro calling one or more other macros. You will also get to test the first macro. The fourth and fifth macros position the screen on the title page and on a blank page, respectively.

**PREPARING THE WORKSHEET** The first macro to be created turns off the row and column headings and the gridlines, as well as the Scroll, Formula, and Status bars. It selects the area of the title page and the set print area to get rid of the dotted line that marks the print area. Record that macro now.

1. Press `CTRL+HOME` to return to the title page.

2. Create a new macro sheet, narrow column A to about half its original width, and widen column B so that only columns A, B, and C fit on the screen.

3. Click on B6 and choose Macro Set Recorder. Choose Window ORDSHEET.XLS to return to the worksheet.

4. Choose Macro Record, type **Prepare.Sheet**, and click on OK to accept the default shortcut key a.

5. Choose Options Display, select Gridlines and Row and Column Headings to turn them off, and click on OK.

6. Choose Options Workspace, select Status Bar, Scroll Bars, and Formula Bar to turn them off, and click on OK.

7. Select A1:K26 (since the rows or column headings are turned off, just drag from the upper-left corner of the worksheet to the lower-right corner). Choose Options Set Print Area. Click on the lower-right intersection of the border to park the active cell.

8. Choose Macro Stop Recorder to complete the first macro, and choose Windows Macro1 to switch to the macro sheet.

9. Type the comments shown here:

|    | A | B | C |
|----|---|---|---|
| 5  |   |   |   |
| 6  |   | Prepare.Sheet | Shortcut key = a |
| 7  |   | =DISPLAY(FALSE,FALSE,FALSE,TRUE,0) | Turn off grid & border |
| 8  |   | =WORKSPACE(FALSE,2,FALSE,FALSE,FALSE,FALSE,"/",FALSE) | Turn off bars |
| 9  |   | =SELECT("R1C1:R26C11") | Title page |
| 10 |   | =SET.PRINT.AREA() |   |
| 11 |   | =SELECT("R19C9") | Park active cell |
| 12 |   | =RETURN() |   |
| 13 |   |   |   |

If for some reason your macro is not the same as the one shown here, turn the Formula bar back on and edit your macro so it looks like the one here. When you are done, turn off your Formula bar.

**Automating a Worksheet** 431

10. Click on B14 of the macro sheet, choose Macro Set Recorder, and choose Window ORDSHEET.XLS.

If you still have a dotted line on the right side of your screen, choose File Page Setup and change the Left and Right margins to 0.5 or less until the line goes away.

**RESTORING THE WORKSHEET** Next you need a macro to restore the gridlines, headings, and bars to reverse the steps you just completed.

1. Choose Macro Record, type **Return.Sheet**, and click on OK to accept the recommended b shortcut key.

2. Choose Options Display, select Gridlines and Row and Column Headings to turn them on, and click on OK.

3. Choose Options Workspace, select Status Bar, Scroll Bars, and Formula Bar to turn them on, and click on OK.

4. Choose Macro Stop Recorder to complete the second macro, and choose Windows Macro1 to switch to the macro sheet.

5. Type the comments shown here:

| 14 | Return.Sheet | Shortcut key = b |
|---|---|---|
| 15 | =DISPLAY(FALSE,TRUE,TRUE,TRUE,0) | Turn on grid & border |
| 16 | =WORKSPACE(FALSE,2,FALSE,TRUE,TRUE,TRUE,"/",FALSE) | Turn on bars |
| 17 | =RETURN() | |

6. Click on B19 of the macro sheet, choose Macro Set Recorder, and choose Window ORDSHEET.XLS.

**OPENING THE WORKSHEET** The third macro opens the worksheet and calls the Prepare.Sheet macro.

1. If your screen has been maximized, choose Control Restore to reduce it to normal size and choose File Save and Close. That should leave you with the macro sheet as the active sheet.

2. Choose Macro Record, type **Order.Load**, and click on OK to accept the recommended shortcut key.

3. Choose File Open, type **ordsheet**, and press (ENTER) to reopen the worksheet.

4. Click on the Maximize button and press (CTRL+a) to run the Prepare.Sheet macro.

5. Choose Macro Stop Recorder to complete the macro, and choose Windows Macro1 to switch to the macro sheet.

6. Type these comments:

|    |                            |                    |
|----|----------------------------|--------------------|
| 18 |                            |                    |
| 19 | Order.Load                 | Shortcut key = c   |
| 20 | =OPEN("ordsheet.XLS")      | Load Worksheet     |
| 21 | =FULL(TRUE)                | Maximize worksheet |
| 22 | =RUN("Macro1!Prepare.Sheet") |                  |
| 23 | =RETURN()                  |                    |

7. Click on B25 of the macro sheet, choose Macro Set Recorder, and choose Window ORDSHEET.XLS.

**POSITIONING THE SCREEN** Two macros are used to position the screen. The first positions the screen on the title page and the second on the blank page underneath. Build both of these together and then modify the macro to separate them.

1. Choose Macro Record, type **Return.Home**, press (TAB), type **h** for the shortcut key, and click on OK. (The "h" was chosen for "Home," but it could be any letter not already used.)

2. Press (CTRL+HOME) and click on the lower-right intersection of the border around the title. That completes the title page positioning.

3. Turn on Scroll Lock, press (PGDN), and press (DOWN ARROW). Turn off Scroll Lock. That positions the blank page.

4. Choose Macro Stop Recorder to complete the macro, and choose Windows Macro1 to switch to the macro sheet.

You now need to split this into two macros. Additionally, your macro recorder may not have recorded (CTRL+HOME) since you immediately went to I19 (R19C9). The recorder left out what it thought was an unnecessary step since you did nothing at A1. If this happened, you need to add that step because it positions the worksheet on the screen prior to parking the active cell at I19.

5. By typing and using Cut and Paste, rearrange the Return.Home macro so that it looks like this:

| 24 | | | |
|---|---|---|---|
| 25 | Return.Home | | Shortcut key = h |
| 26 | =SELECT("R1C1") | | Go home |
| 27 | =SELECT("R19C9") | | Park active cell |
| 28 | =RETURN() | | |
| 29 | | | |
| 30 | Next.Page | | Shortcut key = n |
| 31 | =VPAGE(1) | | Down one page |
| 32 | =VLINE(1) | | Done one line |
| 33 | =RETURN() | | |

6. Select the cell that contains the Next.Page macro name (B30 in the illustration). Choose Formula Define Name, click on Command macro, press (TAB), type **n** for the shortcut key, and click on OK.

7. Click on B35 of the macro sheet (use (PGDN) if necessary), choose Macro Set Recorder, and choose Window ORD-SHEET.XLS.

You may be wondering about the R1C1 nomenclature in place of the familiar A1 nomenclature R1C1, as you probably figured out, stands for row 1, column 1. When you record a macro, this is the system used by Excel. When you write your own macros, you may also use this system, making sure the R1C1 is enclosed in quotation marks, or you may use A1 without quotation marks but preceded with an exclamation point (!). For example, =SELECT("R1C1") is the same as =SELECT(!$A$1). The R1C1 is interpreted as an absolute reference, equivalent to $A$1. If you want a relative reference, to move the active cell relative to its current position, you place [ ] around the numbers. For example =SELECT("RC[2]") moves the active cell two columns to the right, and =SELECT("R[-2]C[3]") moves the active cell up two rows and to the right three columns.

**TESTING AND DEBUGGING YOUR MACROS** You now have five macros: Prepare.Sheet, Return.Sheet, Order.Load, Return.Home, and Next.Page. Because of their small size, using the recorder to create them, and looking at the illustrations in this book, they are probably error free. You still need to prove that by trying them out. Do so now.

1. Choose File Close and click on No to not save any changes.

2. Press (CTRL+c) to execute the Order.Load macro. This macro calls the Prepare.Sheet macro, so you actually are testing two macros in one.

You should get the title screen displayed with nothing other than the Title bar and Menu bar at the top of your screen, as shown in Figure 11-6. If you did not get that, first study what you did get. Repeat the macro several times to observe what is going on. Look at any error messages. Often with macros you get an error message that tells you the line number on the macro sheet of the erroneous

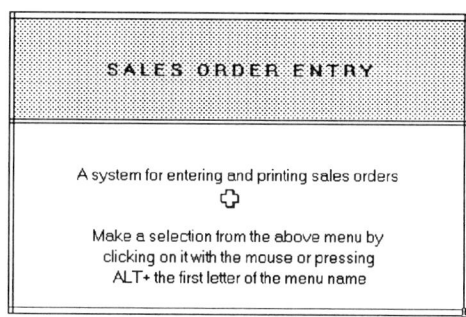

FIGURE 11-6  Title screen

macro function. If you type in macro functions, spelling errors are frequently the cause. After looking at what happens when you execute the macro, go over to the macro sheet and look carefully at the offending macro. Look at spelling, parentheses, quotation marks, and macro function arguments. Compare what you see with the illustrations shown here. These illustrations produced operating macros (really!).

3. Press (CTRL+n) to position the blank page on your screen. Except for the Title and Menu bars (and the mouse pointer) you should have a blank screen.

4. Press (CTRL+h) to position the title page on your screen.

5. Press (CTRL+b) to return to normal Excel display mode.

You should now have five proven macros. If you do not, fix them before going on.

## Building the Data Entry Tools

The data entry tools consist of a data entry dialog box and two macros—one for viewing the database and one for updating it. You also need to enter some formulas on the worksheet.

**BUILDING A DIALOG BOX** Building a dialog box is a fairly complex task. You start out with a blank rectangle on the screen and add buttons, list boxes, check boxes, text boxes, and text, and then you size and position each item. Figure 11-7 shows the completed macro sheet specification for the dialog box used in this application, shown in Figure 11-8. Thankfully, Microsoft includes

| | D | E | F | G | H | I | J | K | L |
|---|---|---|---|---|---|---|---|---|---|
| 1 | Orders.Dialog | | Key | =d | | | | | |
| 2 | =DIALOG.BOX(E6:K22) | | | | | | | | |
| 3 | =RETURN() | | | | | | | | |
| 4 | | | | | | | | | |
| 5 | Field Type | No. | X | Y | Width | Height | Text | Init/Result | Name |
| 6 | Dialog box | | 0 | 0 | 360 | 150 | | | |
| 7 | Text field | 5 | 8 | 5 | 72 | | &Company: | | |
| 8 | Text box | 6 | 8 | 20 | 192 | | | Coastal Supply | Company |
| 9 | Text field | 5 | 208 | 5 | | | &Product: | | |
| 10 | Text box (linked) | 6 | 208 | 20 | 144 | | | 9.5x13 Clasp E | Product |
| 11 | List box (linked) | 16 | 208 | 43 | 144 | 75 | ORDERS.XLMIPrc | 4 | |
| 12 | Text field | 5 | 8 | 44 | | | &Salesperson: | | |
| 13 | Text box | 6 | 8 | 59 | 96 | | | Sue | Person |
| 14 | Text field | 5 | 8 | 83 | | | &Quantity: | | |
| 15 | Number box | 8 | 8 | 98 | 96 | | | 2 | Quantity |
| 16 | Check box | 13 | 8 | 122 | | | &Taxable? | TRUE | Taxable |
| 17 | Text field | 5 | 112 | 44 | | | &Tax Rate: | | |
| 18 | Number box | 8 | 112 | 59 | 88 | | | 0.081 | Rate |
| 19 | Text field | 5 | 112 | 83 | 72 | | &Unit Price: | | |
| 20 | Number box | 8 | 112 | 98 | 88 | | | 12.95 | Price |
| 21 | OK button (default) | 1 | 208 | 122 | 64 | | Enter | | |
| 22 | Cancel button | 2 | 296 | 122 | 64 | | Cancel | | |
| 23 | | | | | | | | | |

**FIGURE 11-7** Completed dialog box specification

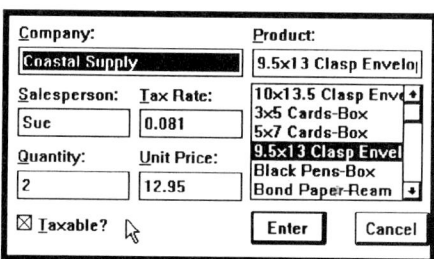

FIGURE 11-8   Working dialog box

the Dialog Editor as a separate program with Excel. The *Dialog Editor* allows you to build dialog boxes on the screen interactively by sizing and dragging the components. That way you can see what you are doing as you are doing it. Without the Dialog Editor you would have to take a stab at the specifications, execute the macro on the worksheet, observe the results, come back to the macro sheet to make a correction, and then try it again.

You load the Dialog Editor through the Control menu Run option. When started, the Dialog Editor presents a blank dialog box on the screen and its own menus. Two of the menus, File and Edit, are fairly standard, but the third menu, Item, is unique to the Dialog Editor. The Item menu, shown here, allows you to choose from among the various types of items that you can place in a dialog box.

You choose an item, and then place and size it in the blank dialog box. If there is text involved, you can type the text. After you have placed an item, or at any time, you can use the Edit menu to edit all of the specifications for the item, including its size and placement. This is really the best of both worlds. You can see on the screen how you want to size and align items, and with the Edit Info option you can see the specific coordinates to determine if items are truly lined up.

When you are done constructing a dialog box, you copy it to the Clipboard, leave the Dialog Editor, and paste the specifications for the dialog box onto the macro sheet. Therefore, begin the process of creating a dialog box by preparing the macro sheet to receive it.

1. Choose Window Macro1 to display the macro sheet. Click on the vertical scroll bar above the Scroll box until row 1 is visible. Click on the horizontal scroll bar to the right of the Scroll box and then on the right pointing scroll arrow to display the range D1:H22 (this can be a row or two less at the bottom).

2. Choose Control Run, and click on Dialog Editor and on OK to load the Dialog Editor.

3. From the Item menu choose Text and type **&Company:**. The ampersand (&) places the underline under the letter that follows the & ("C" in this case). If you want to include an ampersand in the text, enter two of them.

4. Choose Item Edit Box and click on OK to accept the default Text Box. A text box appears under Company. Drag the right edge of the text box to the right about three quarters of an inch.

5. Choose Item Text and type **&Salesperson:**.

6. Choose Item Edit Box and click on OK to accept the default Text Box. A text box appears under Salesperson. Drag the right edge of the box to the left about three quarters of an inch.

7. Choose Item Text and type **&Quantity:**.

8. Choose Item Edit Box and click on Number and on OK to create a number box. A number box appears under Quantity. Drag the right edge of the box to the left about three quarters of an inch.

9. Choose Item Button, and click on Check Box and on OK.

10. Choose Edit Info, type **&Taxable?** in the Text text box and **True** in the Init/Result text box, as shown here:

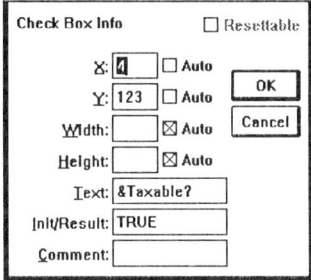

The Init/Result field contains the initial value and the result of anything entered in the dialog box. Your x and y coordinates may be different than what is shown here. Ignore that for the moment; you will do a final alignment later.

11. Click on OK to close the Edit Info dialog box and then drag the bottom edge of your dialog box down about one quarter of an inch and drag the left and right edges outward about half an inch each. See Figures 11-8 and 11-9 for correct sizing. Do not

worry about absolute precision. It is not important and you will do some correcting later on the macro sheet.

12. Choose Item Text and type **&Product:**. Drag this text to the upper-right.

13. Choose Item List Box, and click on Linked and on OK. If necessary, drag the text and list box up under the Product text.

A linked list box is one in which the selected item in the list appears in the text box. On a pure list box you can only select items on the list. With a linked list, you can enter an item not on the list by typing it into the text box.

14. Choose Item Text and type **&Tax Rate:**. Drag it into place opposite Salesperson.

15. Choose Item Edit Box, and click on Number and on OK to create a number Box. A number box appears under Tax Rate (if not, drag it there). Drag the right edge of the box to the left about one inch—so the right edge lines up with the Company text box.

16. Choose Item Text and type **&Unit Price:**. Drag it opposite Quantity.

17. Choose Item Edit Box, and click on Number and on OK to create a number Box. A number box appears under Unit Price (if not, drag it there). Drag the right edge of the box to the left about one inch—so the right edge lines up with the Company text box.

18. Choose Item Button and click on OK to produce an OK command button that is the default. Type **Enter** and drag the button under the left edge of the list box.

You can have several OK buttons, each with a label different than OK on them. One of the buttons is considered the default and activates when you press (**ENTER**)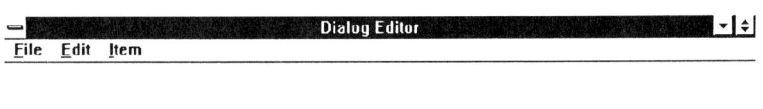. All OK or Cancel buttons close the dialog box. The OK buttons use the information entered into the dialog box to update the Init/Result area in the macro sheet. The Cancel buttons do not update the Init/Result area.

19. Choose Item Button, and click on Cancel and on OK to produce a Cancel command button. Drag the button under the right edge of the list box.

20. Align each item in the dialog box so that it looks approximately like Figure 11-9. Again, it is not important to have the dialog box be an exact duplicate of the one shown here.

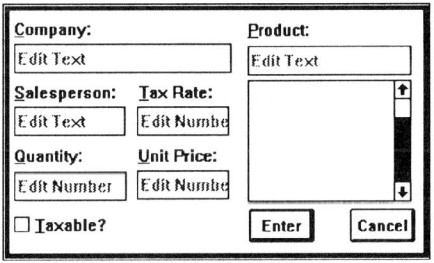

**FIGURE 11-9**  Finished dialog box in the Dialog Editor

| | D | E | F | G | H | I | J | K | L |
|---|---|---|---|---|---|---|---|---|---|
| 3 | | | | | | | | | |
| 4 | | | | | | | | | |
| 5 | Field Type | No. | X | Y | Width | Height | Text | Init/Result | Name |
| 6 | | | 0 | 0 | 360 | 150 | | | |
| 7 | | 5 | 8 | 5 | 72 | | &Company: | | |
| 8 | | 6 | 8 | 20 | 192 | | | | |
| 9 | | 5 | 8 | 44 | | | &Salesperson: | | |
| 10 | | 6 | 8 | 59 | 96 | | | | |
| 11 | | 5 | 8 | 83 | | | &Quantity: | | |
| 12 | | 8 | 8 | 98 | 104 | | | | |
| 13 | | 13 | 8 | 122 | | | &Taxable? | TRUE | |
| 14 | | 5 | 208 | 5 | | | &Product: | | |
| 15 | | 6 | 208 | 20 | 144 | | | | |
| 16 | | 16 | 208 | 43 | 144 | 75 | | | |
| 17 | | 5 | 112 | 44 | | | &Tax Rate: | | |
| 18 | | 8 | 112 | 59 | 88 | | | | |
| 19 | | 5 | 112 | 83 | | | &Unit Price: | | |
| 20 | | 8 | 112 | 98 | 88 | | | | |
| 21 | | 1 | 208 | 122 | 64 | | Enter | | |
| 22 | | 2 | 296 | 122 | 64 | | Cancel | | |
| 23 | | | | | | | | | |
| 24 | | | | | | | | | |

**FIGURE 11-10** Dialog box settings with headings

21. Choose Edit Copy to copy the dialog box specifications to the Clipboard.

22. Minimize the Dialog Editor. Click on E6 on the macro sheet and choose Edit Paste. The specifications appear on the macro sheet.

23. Narrow the columns and add the column headings shown in Figure 11-10.

**DIALOG BOX SETTINGS** There are eight columns in a dialog box's specifications (columns E through L in Figure 11-10). The first contains a number that specifies the type of item in the dialog box (see the list that follows). The second and third columns are the x and y coordinates on which the upper-left corner of each item is located. The fourth and fifth columns are the height and width of each item. You can get the position of the lower-right corner of each item by adding the width to the x coordinate and the height to the y coordinate. Measurement starts in the upper-left corner of the dialog box. The sixth column contains any text associated with the item. The character preceded by an ampersand (&) has an underline placed beneath it. In the case of a list box, the text column eventually contains the reference to the list that is used in the box. The Init/Result column contains either initial values or the results of using the dialog box. This is the column that contains the data that will be used to update the database. The final column is meant for comments and notes, but in this application it is used for the range name.

The meaning of the type numbers in the first column are as follows:

| | | | |
|---|---|---|---|
| 1 | Default OK button | 12 | Option button |
| 2 | Normal Cancel button | 13 | Check box |
| 3 | Normal OK button | 14 | Group box |
| 4 | Default Cancel button | 15 | List box |
| 5 | Text | 16 | Linked list box |
| 6 | Text box | 17 | Icon |
| 7 | Integer box | 18 | Linked File list box |
| 8 | Number box | 19 | Linked drive and directory list box |
| 9 | Formula box | | |
| 10 | Reference box | 20 | Directory text |
| 11 | Option button group | | |

The first row contains the specifications for the dialog box itself. From then on, most items take two lines—one for the text label and the second for the text edit box. The order in which items are listed is the order in which they will be addressed. It is the order in which you would proceed if you pressed (TAB) on each field. There is one change to this order that is worthwhile—to move the product text, text box, and list box (three rows) up under the company text box. Move the product rows and enter the field types and range names next.

1. Insert 3 rows above the salesperson text. Remember to insert across all seven columns that are being used, but not across the the columns to the left that contain the macros.

2. Cut and paste the three product rows to the newly created rows, and delete the original product rows.

3. Enter the field types in column D and the range names in column L, as shown in Figure 11-11.

4. Select K8:L20, choose Formula Create Names, click on Right Column and on OK. The names to the right of the Init/Result

| | D | E | F | G | H | I | J | K | L |
|---|---|---|---|---|---|---|---|---|---|
| 3 | | | | | | | | | |
| 4 | | | | | | | | | |
| 5 | Field Type | No. | X | Y | Width | Height | Text | Init/Result | Name |
| 6 | Dialog box | | 0 | 0 | 360 | 150 | | | |
| 7 | Text field | 5 | 8 | 5 | 72 | | &Company: | | |
| 8 | Text box | 6 | 8 | 20 | 192 | | | | Company |
| 9 | Text field | 5 | 208 | 5 | | | &Product | | |
| 10 | Text box (linked) | 6 | 208 | 20 | 144 | | | | Product |
| 11 | List box (linked) | 16 | 208 | 43 | 144 | 75 | | | |
| 12 | Text field | 5 | 8 | 44 | | | &Salesperson: | | |
| 13 | Text box | 6 | 8 | 59 | 96 | | | | Person |
| 14 | Text field | 5 | 8 | 83 | | | &Quantity: | | |
| 15 | Number box | 8 | 8 | 98 | 96 | | | | Quantity |
| 16 | Check box | 13 | 8 | 122 | | | &Taxable? | TRUE | Taxable |
| 17 | Text field | 5 | 112 | 44 | | | &Tax Rate: | | |
| 18 | Number box | 8 | 112 | 59 | 88 | | | | Rate |
| 19 | Text field | 5 | 112 | 83 | 72 | | &Unit Price: | | |
| 20 | Number box | 8 | 112 | 98 | 88 | | | | Price |
| 21 | OK button (default) | 1 | 208 | 122 | 64 | | Enter | | |
| 22 | Cancel button | 2 | 296 | 122 | 64 | | Cancel | | |

**FIGURE 11-11** Items and range names on dialog specification

| | I | J | K | L | M | N |
|---|---|---|---|---|---|---|
| | | | | | Red Pens-Box | |
| 5 | Height | Text | Init/Result | Name | Products | |
| 6 | 150 | | | | 10x13.5 Clasp Envelope | |
| 7 | | &Company: | | | 3x5 Cards-Box | |
| 8 | | | | Company | 5x7 Cards-Box | |
| 9 | | &Product: | | | 9.5x13 Clasp Envelope | |
| 10 | | | | Product | Black Pens-Box | |
| 11 | 75 | | | | Bond Paper-Ream | |
| 12 | | &Salesperson: | | | Copy Paper-Case | |
| 13 | | | | Person | Copy Paper-Ream | |
| 14 | | &Quantity: | | | HB Lead-Box | |
| 15 | | | | Quantity | Mechanical Pencil | |
| 16 | | &Taxable? | TRUE | Taxable | No. 10 Envelopes | |
| 17 | | &Tax Rate: | | | No. 2 Pencils-Box | |
| 18 | | | | Rate | Red Pens-Box | |
| 19 | | &Unit Price: | | | | |
| 20 | | | | Price | | |
| 21 | | Enter | | | | |
| 22 | | Cancel | | | | |

**FIGURE 11-12** Product list

column name some of the cells in the Init/Result column. For example, K8 is named Company and K13 is named Person.

5. Scroll the screen to the right, click on M5, type **Products**, press (DOWN ARROW), and continue to type the list of products shown in Figure 11-12. This is the list of products that will be displayed in the list box in the dialog box.

6. Select the full list, choose Formula Define Names, and click on OK to accept the defaults presented and name the list Products.

7. Click on J11 (the text field for the product list box) and enter **Orders.XLM!Products** to tie the new list to the list box in the dialog box.

This completes the dialog box specifications. Now you need only create a small enabling macro and try out your dialog box.

8. Scroll your screen so D1 is visible, click on D1, and type these three macro lines and their associated documentation:

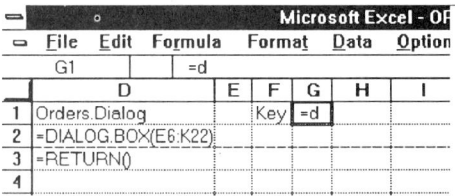

9. Select the macro name (Orders.Dialog), choose Formula Define Name, click on Command, press (TAB), type **d**, and click on OK.

10. Save the macro sheet with the name ORDERS.XLM.

Next try the dialog box and see what happens.

11. Press (CTRL+d). The dialog box should open as shown here:

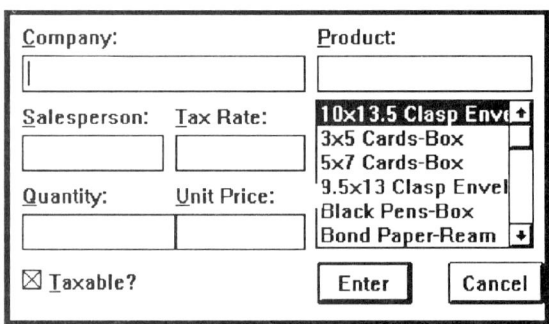

Your dialog box may have a few small glitches, as does this one. The quantity number box is too large and the unit price label is too large. Fix those and any other problems your dialog box may have, and then try entering some data.

12. Click on Cancel to close the dialog box, and then change the width of the quantity number box (H15) to 96, like the Salesperson text box width.

13. Add a width to the Unit price text field by clicking on it (H19), typing **72**, and pressing (ENTER).

14. Press (CTRL+d). The dialog box opens again with your corrections, as shown here:

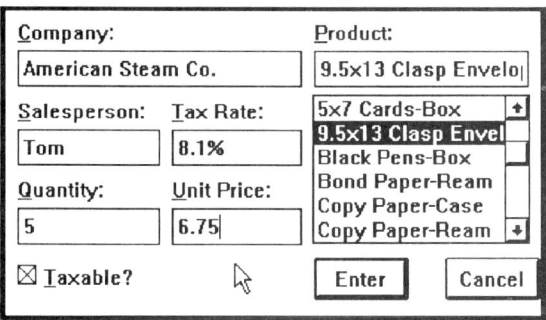

15. Enter some data as shown in the previous illustration and press (ENTER). The data you entered in the dialog box will then be transferred to the macro sheet (column K) as you can see in Figure 11-13.

That completes the dialog box. You are now ready to build the macros that will take data placed in column K of the macro sheet and update the database on the worksheet.

**UPDATING THE DATABASE** You need to build two macros: one that allows you to view the database, and one that does the actual updating. Start by viewing the database.

| | D | E | F | G | H | I | J | K | L | |
|---|---|---|---|---|---|---|---|---|---|---|
| 1 | Orders.Dialog | | Key | =d | | | | | | |
| 2 | =DIALOG.BOX(E6:K22) | | | | | | | | | |
| 3 | =RETURN() | | | | | | | | | |
| 4 | | | | | | | | | | |
| 5 | Field Type | No. | X | Y | Width | Height | Text | Init/Result | Name | Pro |
| 6 | Dialog box | | 0 | 0 | 360 | 150 | | | | 10x |
| 7 | Text field | 5 | 8 | 5 | 72 | | &Company: | | | 3x5 |
| 8 | Text box | 6 | 8 | 20 | 192 | | | American Ste | Company | 5x7 |
| 9 | Text field | 5 | 208 | 5 | | | &Product | | | 9.5x |
| 10 | Text box (linked) | 6 | 208 | 20 | 144 | | | 9.5x13 Clasp E | Product | Bla |
| 11 | List box (linked) | 16 | 208 | 43 | 144 | 75 | ORDERS.XLM!Pi | 4 | | Bor |
| 12 | Text field | 5 | 8 | 44 | | | &Salesperson: | | | Cop |
| 13 | Text box | 6 | 8 | 59 | 96 | | | Tom | Person | Cop |
| 14 | Text field | 5 | 8 | 83 | | | &Quantity: | | | HB |
| 15 | Number box | 8 | 8 | 98 | 96 | | | 5 | Quantity | Me |
| 16 | Check box | 13 | 8 | 122 | | | &Taxable? | TRUE | Taxable | No. |
| 17 | Text field | 5 | 112 | 44 | | | &Tax Rate: | | | No. |
| 18 | Number box | 8 | 112 | 59 | 88 | | | 0.081 | Rate | Red |
| 19 | Text field | 5 | 112 | 83 | 72 | | &Unit Price: | | | |
| 20 | Number box | 8 | 112 | 98 | 88 | | | 6.75 | Price | |
| 21 | OK button (default) | 1 | 208 | 122 | 64 | | Enter | | | |
| 22 | Cancel button | 2 | 296 | 122 | 64 | | Cancel | | | |

**FIGURE 11-13**  Data transferred from the dialog box

1. Scroll the macro sheet so you can see B35. Click on B35, choose Macro Set Recorder, and choose Window ORDSHEET.XLS.

2. Choose Macro Record, type **View.Database**, press (TAB), type **v** for the shortcut key, and click on OK.

3. Press (CTRL+a) to prepare the worksheet.

4. Turn on Scroll Lock, press (CTRL+PGDN) and (RIGHT ARROW) to move horizontally, and press (PGDN) to move vertically. Turn off Scroll Lock.

5. Click on the Company name heading on the worksheet. Choose Macro Stop Recorder. Choose Window ORDERS.XLM.

6. Document your new macro as shown here:

| 34 | | |
|---|---|---|
| 35 | View.Database | Shortcut key = v |
| 36 | =RUN("ORDERS.XLM!Prepare.Sheet") | Prepare worksheet |
| 37 | =HPAGE(1) | Position worksheet |
| 38 | =HLINE(1) | |
| 39 | =VPAGE(1) | |
| 40 | =SELECT("R26C12") | Upper corner of DB |
| 41 | =RETURN() | |
| 42 | | |

7 Click on B43, choose Macro Set Recorder, and choose Window ORDSHEET.XLS.

The next step is to build the formulas for transferring the orders from the macro sheet to the worksheet.

8. Press (CTRL+b) to return to the normal Excel screen. Scroll the screen so you can see and click on L22.

9. Beginning in L22, type the external reference formulas to match the field names in row 26. The first is **=ORDERS.XLM!Company**. Repeat this process for the Person, Quantity, Product, Price, and Rate fields.

10. For Tax (R22), enter the formula

    =if(orders.xlm!taxable=true,n22*p22*q22,0)

    and for Total (S22) enter

    =n22*p22+r22

The first formula calculates the tax by multiplying the quantity (N22) times the price (P22) times the tax rate (Q22), if the sale is taxable, or returns 0 if the sale is not taxable. The second formula calculates the Total Sale by multiplying the quantity (N22) times the price (P22) and adding the tax (R22).

11. Format the quantity (N22) with #,##0; format price (P22), tax (R22), and total (S22) with #,##0.00; and format rate (Q22) with the custom format 0.0%.

12. Select L22:S22, choose Edit copy, select L27:L28, choose Edit Paste Special, click on Values, and click on OK. You now have the beginnings of the database.

13. Select L26:S30 (be sure to include the two blank lines—one is mandatory and the second is insurance so you can add records to the database and maintain the Database range), and choose Data Set Database to establish the database range. Your screen should look like the one shown in Figure 11-14.

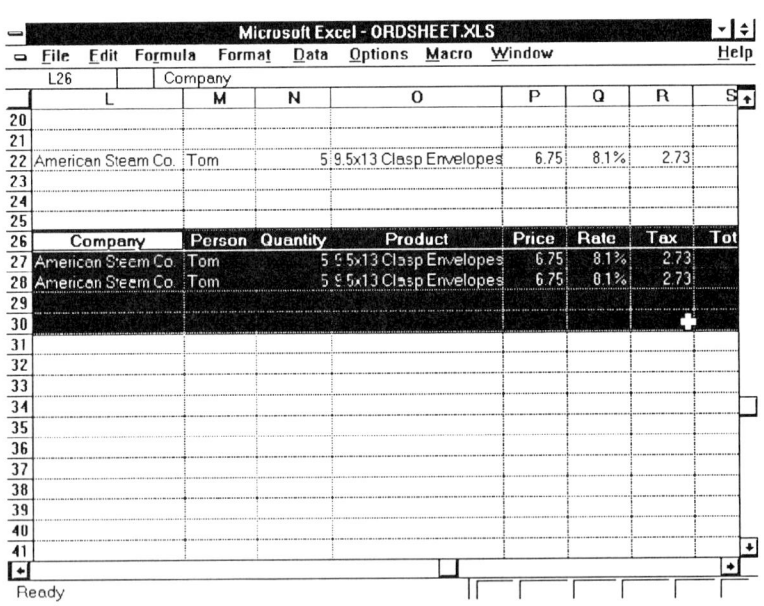

**FIGURE 11-14** Database range

You are now ready to build the macro that updates the database.

1. Choose Macro Record, type **Add.Record**, press (TAB), type **r** for the shortcut key, and click on OK.

2. Press (CTRL+v) to execute the View.Database macro.

3. Press (CTRL+DOWN ARROW) and then (DOWN ARROW) again, and press (SHIFT+RIGHT ARROW) seven times. You have now selected the first blank line under the last record in the database. Pressing (CTRL+DOWN ARROW) is an important step because it gets you to the bottom of a database of any length.

4. Choose Edit Insert, make sure Shift Cells Down is selected, and click on OK.

5. Choose Formula Goto, type **l21**, and click on OK. Select the full database record you are creating in L22 (Company name) through S22 (Total sale).

6. Choose Edit Copy, click on Company in the heading (that is, cell L26), press (CTRL+DOWN ARROW) and (DOWN ARROW) again. Choose Edit Paste Special, click on Values, and click on OK.

7. Press (CTRL+h) to return to the title screen and (CTRL+n) to display the blank screen.

8. Choose Macro Stop Recorder and choose Window OR-DERS.XLM. Your Add.Record macro should look like the one shown in Figure 11-15.

This macro has two problems as it is recorded. Notice that the fourth line (row 46), =SELECT("R29C12:R29C19), and the eleventh line (row 53), =SELECT("R29C12"), are absolute references.

| | A | B | C |
|---|---|---|---|
| 36 | | =RUN("ORDERS.XLM!Prepare.Sheet") | Prepare worksheet |
| 37 | | =HPAGE(1) | Position worksheet |
| 38 | | =HLINE(1) | |
| 39 | | =VPAGE(1) | |
| 40 | | =SELECT("R26C12") | Upper corner of DB |
| 41 | | =RETURN() | |
| 42 | | | |
| 43 | | Add.Record | |
| 44 | | =RUN("ORDERS.XLM!View.Database") | |
| 45 | | =SELECT.END(4) | |
| 46 | | =SELECT("R29C12:R29C19") | |
| 47 | | =INSERT(2) | |
| 48 | | =FORMULA.GOTO("R21C12") | |
| 49 | | =SELECT("R22C12:R22C19") | |
| 50 | | =COPY() | |
| 51 | | =SELECT("R26C12") | |
| 52 | | =SELECT.END(4) | |
| 53 | | =SELECT("R29C12") | |
| 54 | | =PASTE.SPECIAL(3,1,FALSE,FALSE) | |
| 55 | | =CANCEL.COPY() | |
| 56 | | =RUN("ORDERS.XLM!Return.Home") | |
| 57 | | =RUN("ORDERS.XLM!Next.Page") | |
| 58 | | =RETURN() | |
| 59 | | | |
| 60 | | | |

**FIGURE 11-15** Add.Record macro as recorded

These work only once; the next time you use the macro to add a record, it copies over the record you just added. The references need to be changed to be relative to the current active cell. You will recall that this means the commands should be =SELECT ("R[1]C:R[1]C[7]") and =SELECT("R[1]C").

9. Change lines four and eleven (rows 46 and 53) to =SELECT("R[1]C:R[1]C[7]") and =SELECT("R[1]C"), respectively, and add the comments shown in Figure 11-16. (You need to turn on the Formula bar by choosing Options Workspace and clicking on Formula Bar.)

10. Click on B60 (scroll the screen if necessary), choose Macro Set Recorder, and choose Window ORDSHEET.XLS. Also, if you

| | A | B | C |
|---|---|---|---|
| 37 | | =HPAGE(1) | Position worksheet |
| 38 | | =HLINE(1) | |
| 39 | | =VPAGE(1) | |
| 40 | | =SELECT("R26C12") | Upper corner of DB |
| 41 | | =RETURN() | |
| 42 | | | |
| 43 | | Add.Record | Shortcut key = r |
| 44 | | =RUN("ORDERS.XLM!View.Database") | Upper left corner |
| 45 | | =SELECT.END(4) | Bottom of database |
| 46 | | =SELECT("R[1]C:R[1]C[7]") | First blank line |
| 47 | | =INSERT(2) | Insert new row |
| 48 | | =FORMULA.GOTO("R21C12") | |
| 49 | | =SELECT("R22C12:R22C19") | Record to be added |
| 50 | | =COPY() | |
| 51 | | =SELECT("R26C12") | Upper left corner |
| 52 | | =SELECT.END(4) | Bottom of database |
| 53 | | =SELECT("R[1]C") | First blank line |
| 54 | | =PASTE.SPECIAL(3,1,FALSE,FALSE) | Paste values |
| 55 | | =CANCEL.COPY() | |
| 56 | | =RUN("ORDERS.XLM!Return.Home") | |
| 57 | | =RUN("ORDERS.XLM!Next.Page") | |
| 58 | | =RETURN() | |
| 59 | | | |
| 60 | | | |

**FIGURE 11-16** Corrected Add.Record macro

have not already, choose Options Workspace and turn off the Formula bar.

## Using Data Form for Editing

With a database in place, you now need to be able to edit and delete records. Excel has a built-in capability for this in the Data Form option. Build a macro to use this feature next.

1. Choose Macro Record, type **Edit.It**, press (TAB), type **e** (e may already be the default), and click on OK.

2. Press (CTRL+h) and (CTRL+n) to assure that the worksheet is positioned correctly.

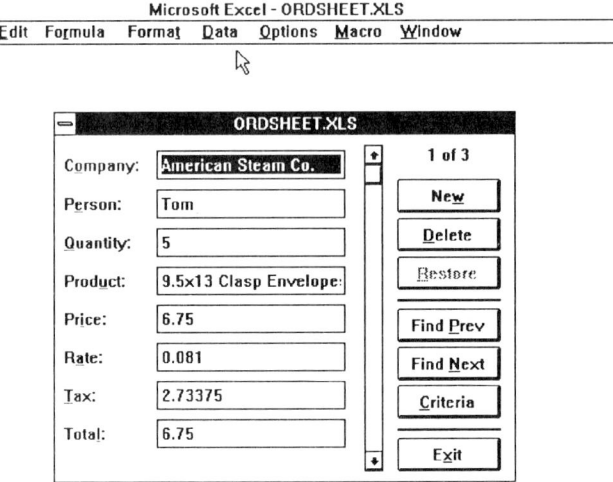

**FIGURE 11-17** Excel's data form

3. Choose Data Form. Excel's data form is displayed, as shown in Figure 11-17.

   With the data form you can edit individual fields of a record, add and delete records, and find records based on criteria you enter. Yes, you could have used this in place of the dialog box you built, but then you would not have had such an excellent opportunity to build a dialog box.

4. Click on the scroll bar to go from record to record, or use the Find buttons.

5. Click on Exit to leave the data form, and press (CTRL+h) to display the title screen.

6. Choose Macro Stop Recorder and Window ORDERS.XLM. The Edit.It macro is shown here. Add the comments shown.

| | | |
|---|---|---|
| Edit.It | | Shortcut key = e |
| =RUN("ORDERS.XLM!Return.Home") | | |
| =RUN("ORDERS.XLM!Next.Page") | | |
| =DATA.FORM() | | Display the data |
| =RUN("ORDERS.XLM!Return.Home") | | |
| =RETURN() | | |

7. Click on B67 (scroll the screen if necessary), choose Macro Set Recorder, and choose Window ORDSHEET.XLS.

## Printing, Saving, and Quitting

You next need to be able to print and save your worksheet and leave Excel. Build macros for those purposes now.

**BUILDING A PRINTING MACRO** The printing macro is actually two macros: one to select and set the print area and the other to do the printing. Build both of these next.

1. Choose Macro Record, type **Select.Database**, press (TAB), type **f** (if necessary) for the shortcut key, and click on OK.

2. Press (CTRL+v) to execute the View.Database macro.

3. Press (SHIFT+CTRL+RIGHT ARROW) and (SHIFT+CTRL+DOWN ARROW) to select the database.

4. Choose Options Set Print Area to define the print area.

5. Choose Macro Stop Recorder and Window ORDERS.XLM.

6. Change the third line to read

   =SELECT("ORDSHEET.XLS!DATABASE")

and add the comments shown here:

| bb | | |
|----|---|---|
| 67 | Select.Database | Shortcut key = f |
| 68 | =RUN("ORDERS.XLM!View.Database") | |
| 69 | =SELECT("ORDSHEET.XLS!DATABASE") | |
| 70 | =SET.PRINT.AREA() | |
| 71 | =RETURN() | |
| 72 | | |

7. Click on B74 (scroll the screen if necessary), choose Macro Set Recorder, and choose Window ORDSHEET.XLS.

8. Choose Macro Record, type **Print.It**, press (TAB), type **p** for the shortcut key, and click on OK.

9. Choose File Page Setup; type **&l&d&cORDERS&rPage &p** for the header; press (TAB), (DEL) to remove the footer, and (TAB); set the margins as Left 0.5, Right 0.5, Top 1, Bottom 0.5; turn off the row and column headings; and click on OK.

10. Press (CTRL+f) to the set the print range, choose File Print, and click on OK in the Print dialog box. Figure 11-18 shows the result.

11. Press (CTRL+h) to return to the title page.

12. Choose Macro Stop Recorder and Window ORDERS.XLM.

13. Enter the comments shown here:

| 73 | | |
|----|---|---|
| 74 | Print.It | Shortcut key = p |
| 75 | =PAGE.SETUP("&l&d&cORDERS&rPage &p","",0.05,0.5,1,0.5,FALSE,T | header & margins |
| 76 | =RUN("ORDERS.XLM!Select.Database") | |
| 77 | =PRINT(1,,1,FALSE,FALSE,1) | |
| 78 | =RUN("ORDERS.XLM!Return.Home") | |
| 79 | =RETURN() | |
| 80 | | |

14. Click on B81 (scroll the screen if necessary) and choose Macro Set Recorder.

| 7/12/90 | | | ORDERS | | | | Page 1 |
|---|---|---|---|---|---|---|---|
| Company | Person | Quantity | Product | Price | Rate | Tax | Total |
| American Steam Co. | Tom | 5 | 9.5x13 Clasp Envelopes | 6.75 | 8.1% | 2.73 | 36.48 |
| American Steam Co. | Tom | 5 | 9.5x13 Clasp Envelopes | 6.75 | 8.1% | 2.73 | 36.48 |
| Micro Corp | Tom | 5 | Copy Paper-Ream | 6.75 | 8.1% | 2.73 | 36.48 |
| Micro Corp | Tom | 7 | Bond Paper-Ream | 12.95 | 8.1% | 7.34 | 97.99 |
| Coastal Supply | Sue | 3 | 5x7 Cards-Box | 4.60 | 8.1% | 1.12 | 14.92 |
| Coastal Supply | Sue | 2 | 9.5x13 Clasp Envelopes | 12.95 | 8.1% | 2.10 | 28.00 |

**FIGURE 11-18**  Printed database

**SAVING AND QUITTING**  The saving and quitting macros are trivial by comparison to what you have already done. Build them here.

1. Save the macro sheet, choose Window ORDSHEET.XLS, and save the worksheet. Now if something goes wrong, you do not lose anything.

2. Choose Macro Record, type **Save.It**, press (TAB), type **s**, and click on OK.

3. Press (CTRL+h) to ensure you are on the title screen and choose File Save.

4. Choose Macro Stop Recorder and Window ORDERS.XLM.

5. Click on B86 (scroll the screen if necessary), choose Macro Set Recorder, and choose Window ORDSHEET.XLS.

6. Choose Macro Record, type **Quit.It**, press (TAB), type **q**, and click on OK.

7. Press (CTRL+b) to return to the normal Excel display, and press (CTRL+s) to save the worksheet.

8. Choose File Close and then File Save to save the macro sheet.

9. Choose Macro Stop Recorder.

One macro function needs to be added to the Quit.It macro: QUIT( ). This is the function you use to actually leave Excel.

10. Move the last =RETURN( ) down one row and enter =QUIT( ).

11. Add the comments shown in Figure 11-19.

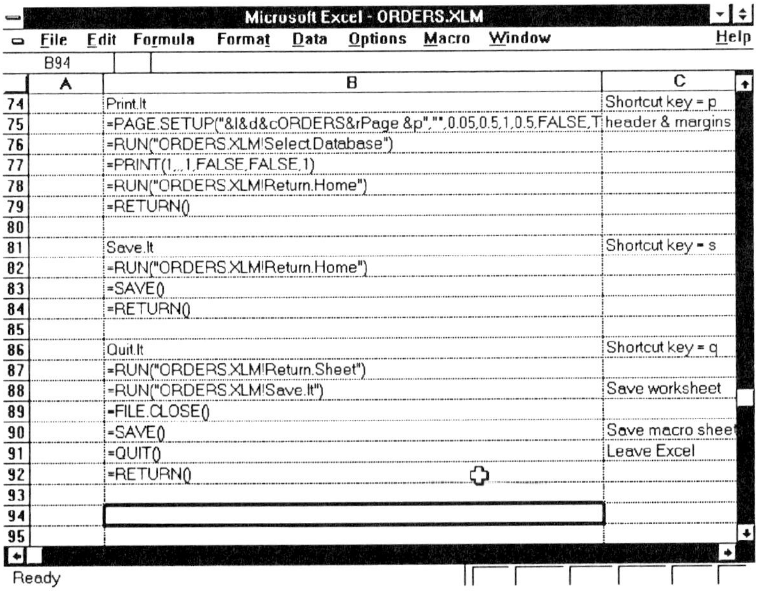

| Row | A | B | C |
|---|---|---|---|
| 74 | Print.It | | Shortcut key = p |
| 75 | | =PAGE.SETUP("&l&d&cORDERS&rPage &p","",0.05,0.5,1,0.5,FALSE,T | header & margins |
| 76 | | =RUN("ORDERS.XLM!SelectDatabase") | |
| 77 | | =PRINT(1,,1,FALSE,FALSE,1) | |
| 78 | | =RUN("ORDERS.XLM!Return.Home") | |
| 79 | | =RETURN() | |
| 80 | | | |
| 81 | Save.It | | Shortcut key = s |
| 82 | | =RUN("ORDERS.XLM!Return.Home") | |
| 83 | | =SAVE() | |
| 84 | | =RETURN() | |
| 85 | | | |
| 86 | Quit.It | | Shortcut key = q |
| 87 | | =RUN("ORDERS.XLM!Return.Sheet") | |
| 88 | | =RUN("ORDERS.XLM!Save.It") | Save worksheet |
| 89 | | =FILE.CLOSE() | |
| 90 | | =SAVE() | Save macro sheet |
| 91 | | =QUIT() | Leave Excel |
| 92 | | =RETURN() | |

**FIGURE 11-19** Save and Quit macros

12. Click on B94 (scroll the screen if necessary) and choose Macro Set Recorder.

## Building and Using a Menu

To tie together all of the macros you have built into a system with a menu, you need three macros and the menu specifications. One of the macros displays the menu, the second automatically loads the worksheet, and the third is used to combine the data entry and update functions. You also need a macro to return to normal Excel menus. Build these items next beginning with the menu.

1. Scroll the macro sheet so O1:S22 is displayed.

2. Adjust the column width and type in the macros and text shown in Figure 11-20.

|    | O | P | Q | R | S |
|----|---|---|---|---|---|
| 1  |   |   |   | Display.Menu | Shortcut key = m |
| 2  |   |   |   | =ADD.BAR() |   |
| 3  |   |   |   | =ADD.MENU(R2,O14:S21) | new bar in O14:S21 |
| 4  |   |   |   | =SHOW.BAR(R2) |   |
| 5  |   |   |   | =RETURN() |   |
| 6  |   |   |   |   |   |
| 7  |   |   |   | Excel.Menu | Shortcut key = l |
| 8  |   |   |   | =SHOW.BAR(1) | Display full menus |
| 9  |   |   |   | =RETURN() |   |
| 10 |   |   |   |   |   |
| 11 |   |   |   |   |   |
| 12 |   |   |   |   |   |
| 13 |   |   |   |   |   |
| 14 | &Ordering |   |   |   |   |
| 15 | &Order Entry | Orders.xlm!Enter.It |   | Enters a new order |   |
| 16 | - |   |   |   |   |
| 17 | &Print Database | Orders.xlm!Print.It |   | Prints the list of orders |   |
| 18 | &Save Database | Orders.xlm!Save.It |   | Saves the Oders database |   |
| 19 | &Quit Ordering | Orders.xlm!Quit.It |   | Saves database and Quits Excel |   |
| 20 | - |   |   |   |   |
| 21 | &Edit Database | Orders.xlm!Edit.It |   | Edits database with Excel Form |   |

**FIGURE 11-20** Menu specifications and macros

The lower part of the five columns, beginning in row 14, is the menu specification. The first column contains the menu name in O14. The & says to place an underline under the following letter. The remaining items in column O are the options on the menu, again with underlined letters specified. Column P contains the macros that are called when you choose a menu option, column Q is not used, column R contains the comments that are displayed in the Status bar, and column S may contain calls to custom help messages.

The Display.Menu macro creates a new menu bar in R2, adds a new menu to the Menu bar defined in R2, based on the specification in O14:S21, and shows the Menu bar defined in R2. The Excel.Menu macro returns you to the full Excel Menu bar. The SHOW.BAR (1) argument stands for full menus. The other alternatives are

- 2  Full Chart menus
- 3  Nil menus (File only)
- 4  Info menus
- 5  Short menus
- 6  Short Chart menus

3. Click on R1, choose Formula Define name, click on Command, type **m** for the shortcut key, and click on OK. Also click on R7, choose Formula Define name, click on Command, type **l** for the shortcut key, and click on OK.

4. Scroll back to A1 on the macro sheet and enter the Auto_Open macro shown here:

| | A | B | C |
|---|---|---|---|
| 1 | | Start.It | Shortcut key = o |
| 2 | Auto_Open | =RUN("ORDERS.XLM!Order.load") | |
| 3 | | =RUN("ORDERS.XLM!Display.Menu") | |
| 4 | | =RETURN() | |
| 5 | | | |

The Auto_Open macro automatically loads the worksheet when you load the macro sheet. That is why the macro sheet has the name ORDERS while the worksheet has the harder to remember name.

5. Use Formula Define Name to define the macro name Start.It with the shortcut key o for open. Also use Formula Create Names Left after selecting A1:B3 to define Auto_Open.

6. Insert a new row across the three columns, A17:C17, and type **=show.bar(1)** in B17. With this added macro function, the Excel menus are restored with the Return.Sheet macro.

The final step is to tie the dialog box together with the Add.Record macro and an IF function to see if the user wants to enter additional records.

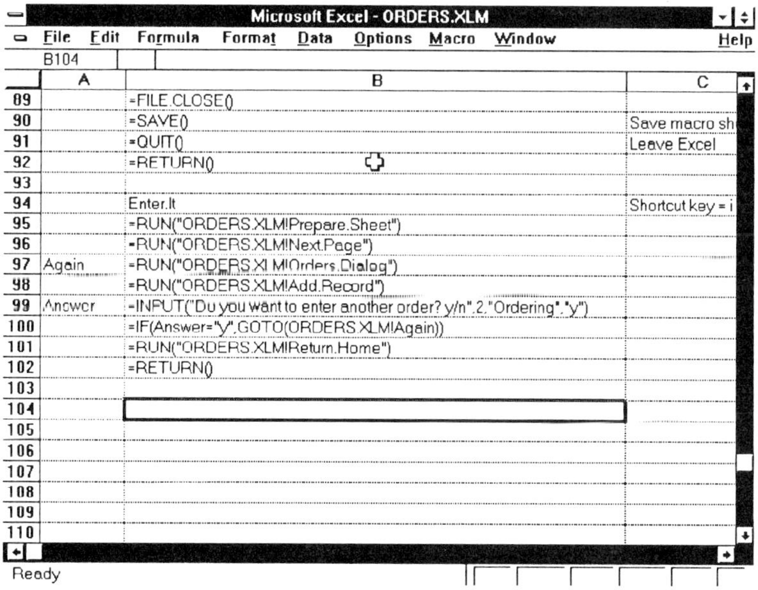

Microsoft Excel - ORDERS.XLM
File Edit Formula Format Data Options Macro Window Help
B104
A B C
89 =FILE.CLOSE()
90 =SAVE() Save macro sh
91 =QUIT() Leave Excel
92 =RETURN()
93
94 Enter.It Shortcut key = i
95 =RUN("ORDERS.XLM!Prepare.Sheet")
96 =RUN("ORDERS.XLM!Next.Page")
97 Again =RUN("ORDERS.XLM!Orders.Dialog")
98 =RUN("ORDERS.XLM!Add.Record")
99 Answer =INPUT("Do you want to enter another order? y/n",2,"Ordering","y")
100 =IF(Answer="y",GOTO(ORDERS.XLM!Again))
101 =RUN("ORDERS.XLM!Return.Home")
102 =RETURN()
103
104
105
106
107
108
109
110
Ready


**FIGURE 11-21** Enter.It macro

7. Type the macro functions shown in Figure 11-21. Define the macro name and type the comment. Also select A97:B99 and use Formula Create Names Left to define the two names there.

The Enter.It macro uses the INPUT and IF macro functions to determine if you want to continue to enter orders. The INPUT function, which displays a small dialog box, has this format:

INPUT(*prompt,type[,title,default,x,y]* )

*Title, default,* and *X* and *Y* are optional. *Prompt* is text that is displayed in the dialog box. *Type* is the data type, which has these possible values:

| | |
|---|---|
| 0 | Formula |
| 1 | Number |
| 2 | Text |
| 4 | Logical |
| 8 | Reference |
| 16 | Error |
| 64 | Array |

You can sum the types. The default, for example is 7, which is the sum of Formula, Number, Text, and Logical. The title is displayed at the top of the dialog box, the default is a proposed response to the question being asked, and the x and y coordinates are for positioning the dialog box.

The IF macro function has a format similar to a normal IF function:

IF(*condition,true response[ , false response]*)

*Condition* is a logical statement that evaluates to either True or False. If the condition is True then *true response* is returned;

otherwise, *false response* is returned. With a macro function, responses may be GOTO functions, as in the Enter.It macro.

# TESTING AND CORRECTING THE MACROS

The normal testing process is primarily one of trying out the macros and seeing what happens. Then, based on what you have seen, you can make the necessary corrections. To speed up that process, print out your macros and the range names, and then compare the results to Figures 11-22 and 11-23. Sometimes "desk checking" like this can eliminate the majority of errors, which are usually typographical, before you ever run the macros.

Use these instructions to print out the macros and the range names:

1. Select A1:C102, choose Options Set Print Area, and choose File Print. The result is shown in Figure 11-22.

2. Scroll your macro sheet so T1:X22 is visible. Click on U2, choose Formula Paste name, and then select Paste List.

3. Type the headings and narrow the columns, as shown in Figure 11-23.

4. Select T1:Y31, choose Options Set Print Area, choose File Print, and click on OK. The range names are printed.

5. Compare your printouts to Figures 11-22 and 11-23 and make the necessary corrections.

## Working Through the Application

The next step is to execute each part of the macro and see what happens. Use these steps for that purpose.

|     | A         | B                                                        | C                        |
| --- | --------- | -------------------------------------------------------- | ------------------------ |
| 1   |           | Start.It                                                 | Shortcut key = o         |
| 2   | Auto_Open | =RUN("ORDERS.XLM!Order.load")                            |                          |
| 3   |           | =RUN("ORDERS.XLM!Display.Menu")                          |                          |
| 4   |           | =RETURN()                                                |                          |
| 5   |           |                                                          |                          |
| 6   |           | Prepare.Sheet                                            | Shortcut key = a         |
| 7   |           | =DISPLAY(FALSE,FALSE,FALSE,TRUE,0)                       | Turn off grid & border   |
| 8   |           | =WORKSPACE(FALSE,2,FALSE,FALSE,FALSE,FALSE,"/",FALSE)    | Turn off bars            |
| 9   |           | =SELECT("R1C1:R26C11")                                   | Title page               |
| 10  |           | =SET.PRINT.AREA()                                        |                          |
| 11  |           | =SELECT("R19C9")                                         | Park active cell         |
| 12  |           | =RETURN()                                                |                          |
| 13  |           |                                                          |                          |
| 14  |           | Return.Sheet                                             | Shortcut key = b         |
| 15  |           | =DISPLAY(FALSE,TRUE,TRUE,TRUE,0)                         | Turn on grid & border    |
| 16  |           | =WORKSPACE(FALSE,2,FALSE,TRUE,TRUE,TRUE,"/",FALSE)       | Turn on bars             |
| 17  |           | =SHOW.BAR(1)                                             |                          |
| 18  |           | =RETURN()                                                |                          |
| 19  |           |                                                          |                          |
| 20  |           | Order.Load                                               | Shortcut key = c         |
| 21  |           | =OPEN("ordsheet.XLS")                                    | Load Worksheet           |
| 22  |           | =FULL(TRUE)                                              | Maximize worksheet       |
| 23  |           | =RUN("Orders.XLM!Prepare.Sheet")                         |                          |
| 24  |           | =RETURN()                                                |                          |
| 25  |           |                                                          |                          |
| 26  |           | Return.Home                                              | Shortcut key = h         |
| 27  |           | =SELECT("R1C1")                                          | Go home                  |
| 28  |           | =SELECT("R19C9")                                         | Park active cell         |
| 29  |           | =RETURN()                                                |                          |
| 30  |           |                                                          |                          |
| 31  |           | Next.Page                                                | Shortcut key = n         |
| 32  |           | =VPAGE(1)                                                | Down one page            |
| 33  |           | =VLINE(1)                                                | Done one line            |
| 34  |           | =RETURN()                                                |                          |
| 35  |           |                                                          |                          |
| 36  |           | View.Database                                            | Shortcut key = v         |
| 37  |           | =RUN("ORDERS.XLM!Prepare.Sheet")                         | Prepare worksheet        |
| 38  |           | =HPAGE(1)                                                | Position worksheet       |
| 39  |           | =HLINE(1)                                                |                          |
| 40  |           | =VPAGE(1)                                                |                          |
| 41  |           | =SELECT("R26C12")                                        | Upper corner of DB       |
| 42  |           | =RETURN()                                                |                          |
| 43  |           |                                                          |                          |
| 44  |           | Add.Record                                               | Shortcut key = r         |
| 45  |           | =RUN("ORDERS.XLM!View.Database")                         | Upper left corner        |
| 46  |           | =SELECT.END(4)                                           | Bottom of database       |
| 47  |           | =SELECT("R[1]C:R[1]C[7]")                                | First blank line         |
| 48  |           | =INSERT(2)                                               | Insert new row           |
| 49  |           | =FORMULA.GOTO("R21C12")                                  |                          |
| 50  |           | =SELECT("R22C12:R22C19")                                 | Record to be added       |
| 51  |           | =COPY()                                                  |                          |
| 52  |           | =SELECT("R26C12")                                        | Upper left corner        |
| 53  |           | =SELECT.END(4)                                           | Bottom of database       |
| 54  |           | =SELECT("R[1]C")                                         | First blank line         |
| 55  |           | =PASTE.SPECIAL(3,1,FALSE,FALSE)                          | Paste values             |
| 56  |           | =CANCEL.COPY()                                           |                          |
| 57  |           | =RUN("ORDERS.XLM!Return.Home")                           |                          |
| 58  |           | =RUN("ORDERS.XLM!Next.Page")                             |                          |

**FIGURE 11-22** Macro listing

| | A | B | C |
|---|---|---|---|
| 59 | | =RETURN() | |
| 60 | | | |
| 61 | | Edit.It | Shortcut key = e |
| 62 | | =RUN("ORDERS.XLM!Return.Home") | |
| 63 | | =RUN("ORDERS.XLM!Next.Page") | |
| 64 | | =DATA.FORM() | Display the data form |
| 65 | | =RUN("ORDERS.XLM!Return.Home") | |
| 66 | | =RETURN() | |
| 67 | | | |
| 68 | | Select.Database | Shortcut key = f |
| 69 | | =RUN("ORDERS.XLM!View.Database") | |
| 70 | | =SELECT("ORDSHEET.XLS!DATABASE") | |
| 71 | | =SET.PRINT.AREA() | |
| 72 | | =RETURN() | |
| 73 | | | |
| 74 | | Print.It | Shortcut key = p |
| 75 | | =PAGE.SETUP("&l&d&cORDERS&rPage &p","",0.05,0.5,1,0.5,FALSE,TRUE | header & margins |
| 76 | | =RUN("ORDERS.XLM!Select.Database") | |
| 77 | | =PRINT(1,,,1,FALSE,FALSE,1) | |
| 78 | | =RUN("ORDERS.XLM!Return.Home") | |
| 79 | | =RETURN() | |
| 80 | | | |
| 81 | | Save.It | Shortcut key = s |
| 82 | | =RUN("ORDERS.XLM!Return.Home") | |
| 83 | | =SAVE() | |
| 84 | | =RETURN() | |
| 85 | | | |
| 86 | | Quit.It | Shortcut key = q |
| 87 | | =RUN("ORDERS.XLM!Return.Sheet") | |
| 88 | | =RUN("ORDERS.XLM!Save.It") | Save worksheet |
| 89 | | =FILE.CLOSE() | |
| 90 | | =SAVE() | Save macro sheet |
| 91 | | =QUIT() | Leave Excel |
| 92 | | =RETURN() | |
| 93 | | | |
| 94 | | Enter.It | Shortcut key = i |
| 95 | | =RUN("ORDERS.XLM!Prepare.Sheet") | |
| 96 | | =RUN("ORDERS.XLM!Next.Page") | |
| 97 | Again | =RUN("ORDERS.XLM!Orders.Dialog") | |
| 98 | | =RUN("ORDERS.XLM!Add.Record") | |
| 99 | Answer | =INPUT("Do you want to enter another order? y/n",2,"Ordering","y") | |
| 100 | | =IF(Answer="y",GOTO(ORDERS.XLM!Again)) | |
| 101 | | =RUN("ORDERS.XLM!Return.Home") | |
| 102 | | =RETURN() | |

**FIGURE 11-22** Macro listing (*continued*)

|  | U | V | W | X |
|---|---|---|---|---|
| 1 | Range Name | Range | 2 = Macro | Key |
| 2 | Add.Record | = $B$44 | 2 | r |
| 3 | Again | = $B$97 | 0 | |
| 4 | Answer | = $B$99 | 0 | |
| 5 | Auto_Open | = $B$2 | 0 | |
| 6 | Company | = $K$8 | 0 | |
| 7 | Display.Menu | = $R$1 | 2 | m |
| 8 | Edit.It | = $B$61 | 2 | e |
| 9 | Enter.It | = $B$94 | 2 | i |
| 10 | Excel.Menu | = $R$7 | 2 | l |
| 11 | Next.Page | = $B$31 | 2 | n |
| 12 | Order.Load | = $B$20 | 2 | c |
| 13 | Orders.Dialog | = $D$1 | 2 | d |
| 14 | Person | = $K$13 | 0 | |
| 15 | Prepare.Sheet | = $B$6 | 2 | a |
| 16 | Price | = $K$20 | 0 | |
| 17 | Print.It | = $B$74 | 2 | p |
| 18 | Print_Area | = $A$1:$C$102 | 0 | |
| 19 | Product | = $K$10 | 0 | |
| 20 | Products | = $M$6:$M$18 | 0 | |
| 21 | Quantity | = $K$15 | 0 | |
| 22 | Quit.It | = $B$86 | 2 | q |
| 23 | Rate | = $K$18 | 0 | |
| 24 | Recorder | = $B$94:$B$16384 | 0 | |
| 25 | Return.Home | = $B$26 | 2 | h |
| 26 | Return.Sheet | = $B$14 | 2 | b |
| 27 | Save.It | = $B$81 | 2 | s |
| 28 | Select.Database | = $B$68 | 2 | f |
| 29 | Start.It | = $B$1 | 2 | o |
| 30 | Taxable | = $K$16 | 0 | |
| 31 | View.Database | = $B$36 | 2 | v |
| 32 | | | | |

**FIGURE 11-23**  List of range names

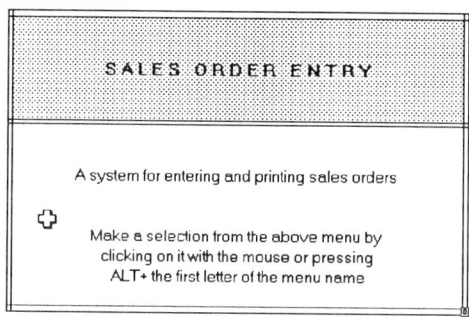

**FIGURE 11-24**   Title screen with menu

1. Save and close both the worksheet and the macro sheet. Choose File Open, select ORDERS.XLM, and click on OK. The macro begins by displaying the title screen with the single Ordering menu, as shown in Figure 11-24.

2. Select the menu, and it should open as shown here:

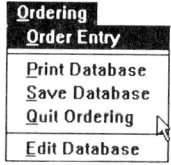

3. Choose Order Entry. The dialog box shown in Figure 11-25 opens.

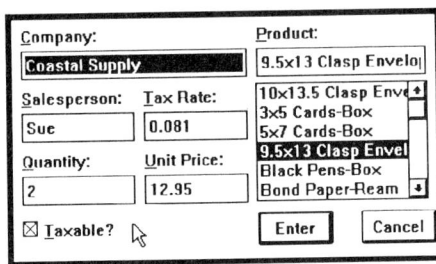

**FIGURE 11-25** Open dialog box

4. Enter a record. What you put in the fields does not matter. Use (TAB) to go from field to field and (ENTER) to complete the entry.

When you press (ENTER) (or click on the Enter command button) you should see the database being updated. Then the second dialog box, shown in Figure 11-26, opens, asking if you want to enter another record.

5. Click on OK to accept the y default, and enter another item. Follow the same procedure outlined in step 4. When you get to the "Do you want to enter another order?" prompt, answer **n**.

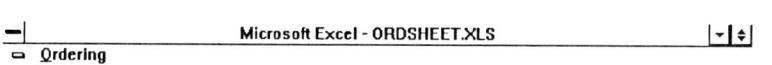

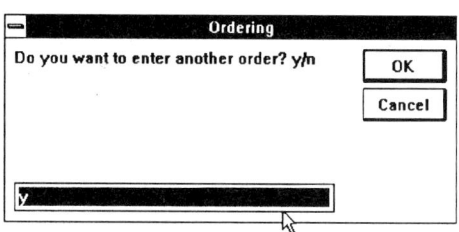

FIGURE 11-26   Question dialog box

6. Choose Edit from the menu and try out the various options on Excel's Data Form.

7. Choose Print. The output you get should be similar to that shown in Figure 11-18.

8. Choose Save. You should see some indication of that worksheet being saved.

9. Finally, choose Quit. You should be returned to Windows.

If your macros did not execute perfectly the first time, take heart—it happens to almost everybody. Observe what is not working right. Compare your printed list of macros with the ones presented here. Within a few iterations of trying the macros and making changes, you should get them to operate properly.

# FUTURE ENHANCEMENTS

A large number of improvements can be made to enhance this application.

One easy enhancement is to stop the screen flashing during macro execution by inserting ECHO(FALSE) macro functions at the start of the Prepare.Sheet, Add.Record, and Print.It macros and then an ECHO(TRUE) at the end of each of those macros. This prevents Excel from updating the screen during those macros.

Another enhancement would be to sort the orders by customer and prepare statements from the results. Also, by sorting on the product you can look at sales by product.

One enhancement that should have been in the original product is to add a date field to both the database and the data entry dialog box. Should you want to do this, you can paste the dialog box specifications back into the Dialog Editor, make the changes, and then paste it back on the macro sheet.

You now have an exceptionally powerful tool at your disposal. You can make of it just about whatever you wish.

# IV

# COMMAND REFERENCE

Part IV provides a complete command reference for Excel. Over three chapters it lists in alphabetical order and provides a description for every menu option, worksheet function, and macro function. Part IV is not meant to be read. Rather it is a quick and handy reference for looking up how a particular menu option or function works.

# 12

# MENU COMMANDS

Chart
Data
Edit
File
Format
Formula
Gallery
Help
Info
Macro
Options
Window

The primary means of telling Excel what you want to do is a menu. To make a choice from a menu, you first select the menu and then choose the option that meets your needs. The second bar from the top of the Excel window is the Menu bar. To select a menu you can click on it with the mouse or use one of several keyboard techniques. The keyboard techniques include pressing (ALT), typing / (slash), pressing (F10) and then typing the underlined letter in the menu name, or using the direction keys to move the highlight to the menu name and pressing (ENTER).

Once you have opened a menu, you can choose one of its options in one of three ways: click on the option with the mouse, type the underlined letter in its name, or move the highlight to it with the direction keys and press (ENTER). If an option is already highlighted, as New is in the File menu, you can select it simply by pressing (ENTER).

The Status bar at the bottom of the screen indicates what action the highlighted menu option performs.

The Menu bar that appears depends on the active document. If the active document is a chart, menus pertaining to charts appear in the Menu bar. If the active document is a worksheet, menus pertaining to worksheets appear in the Menu bar.

The balance of this chapter describes all of Excel's menu options, which are listed in alphabetical order. Use this chapter as a quick and easy reference. The full option including the menu name was used for sorting. For example, File Print is under File, and found between File Page Setup and File Printer Setup. All options begin with and are listed under one of the 12 Excel menus: Chart, Data, Edit, File, Format, Formula, Gallery, Help, Info, Options, Macro, and Window.

To help you use this menu option reference, the page number in the index that refers to the option listing in this chapter is italicized.

# CHART

The Chart menu appears on the Menu bar only if the active document is a chart. The Chart menu contains options that allow you to change the appearance of your chart, including adding text and titles to many chart elements, adding arrows and gridlines, and adding legends. You also can turn one or both of the axes on or off, change the type of gridlines used, and change the chart into a combination chart by placing half of the data series in an overlay that can be a different chart type. From the Chart menu you also can select the active chart or the plot area on the active chart for various formatting functions, protect the chart with a password, recalculate the underlying worksheet and redraw the chart, and change to short or long menus.

## Chart Add Arrow

The Chart Add Arrow option allows you to add an arrow to your chart. Once you add the arrow, you can move and size it with the Format Move or Format Size option or with the mouse. You also can change its appearance with the Format Patterns option.

## Chart Add Legend

The Chart Add Legend option allows you to add a legend to your chart. If you included series names when you selected the area to be charted on your worksheet, the series names automatically are used for the legend. Once you have added a legend by choosing the Chart Add Legend option, you can format the legend using the Format Patterns, Font, and Legend options.

Once you choose the Add Legend option, the Delete Legend option appears in its place on the Chart menu.

## Chart Add Overlay

The Chart Add Overlay option appears on the Chart menu only if the Full Menus option is activated. The Add Overlay option allows you to create an overlay chart for your existing chart. If you have an odd number of series, there is one more series on the main chart than on the overlay. If you have an even number of series, there is the same number of series on the main chart and on the overlay. If you want to control this default distribution of series, see the Format Overlay option. The overlay chart is created as a line chart. To change it to another type of chart, use the Format Overlay option.

## Chart Attach Text

The Chart Attach Text option allows you to attach text such as titles for the chart, value axis, category axis, series, or data point. Once you choose the Chart Attach Text option, a dialog box appears with the following options, so you can choose where you want the text attached.

| | |
|---|---|
| Chart Title | Attach a title to the chart |
| Value Axis | Attach a title to the value or Y-axis |
| Category Axis | Attach a title to the category or X-axis |
| Series Or Data Point | Attach a title to a series or data point |

Once you choose where you want your title and press the OK button, you have the opportunity to type in the title you want. Once you've typed in your title, press (ENTER).

## Chart Axes

The Chart Axes option allows you to make the axes on your chart visible or invisible. Once you choose the Chart Axes option, a dialog box appears that allows you to turn on or off the category or X-axis and the value or Y-axis for both the main chart and the overlay chart.

## Chart Calculate Now

**SHORTCUT** `F9`

The Chart Calculate Now option recalculates all open documents and redraws all open charts according to the options that you set in the Options Calculation dialog box. The Options Calculation option appears on the Options menu, which appears on the Menu bar when the active document is a worksheet. You use the Chart Calculate Now option if you have set the calculation to manual in the Options Calculation dialog box, and you want to recalculate and redraw your chart.

## Chart Delete Arrow

The Chart Delete Arrow option allows you to remove a selected arrow from your chart. This option appears only if you have an arrow selected. Otherwise the Chart Add Arrow option appears on the Chart menu in its place.

## Chart Delete Legend

The Chart Delete Legend option appears on the Chart menu only if you have a legend on your chart. If you do not have a legend, the option Chart Add Legend appears on the Chart menu instead. The Chart Delete Legend option removes the legend from your chart.

## Chart Delete Overlay

The Chart Delete Overlay option appears on the Chart menu only if the Full Menus option is activated and only if you have an overlay on your active chart. If you do not have an overlay, the option Chart Add Overlay appears on the menu instead. The Chart Delete Overlay option deletes the overlay and puts all the series from the overlay chart onto the main chart.

## Chart Full Menus

The Chart Full Menus option allows you to turn the Full Menus option on, so all menus appear with all their options. The Chart Full Menus option appears on the Chart menu only if the Short Menus option is activated. If you have full menus, then the option appears as Chart Short Menus instead.

## Chart Gridlines

The Chart Gridlines option allows you to control whether the gridlines on your chart are visible or invisible. Once you choose the Chart Gridlines option, a dialog box appears, allowing you to turn on or off major and minor gridlines for both the value axis and the category axis.

## Chart Protect Document

The Chart Protect Document option allows you to protect your chart from modifications. Once you choose this option, a dialog box appears in which you can type a password and choose if you want the contents, the window, or both protected. The contents refers to all aspects of the chart— series, formatting, and so on. The window refers to the window the chart appears in. If you protect the window, you cannot move, size, or hide the window. Once you choose OK in this dialog box, you cannot change what you have protected without the password you typed. If you want to unprotect the chart using the Chart Unprotect Document option, you must have the password you typed here.

## Chart Select Chart

The Chart Select Chart option selects the entire active chart. You then can use the following options to change the chart:

| | |
|---|---|
| Edit Clear | Clear the formats and/or data series |
| Edit Copy | Copy the formats and/or data series |
| Format Overlay | Change the chart type and formats |
| Format Font | Change the font used for the text for the entire chart |
| Format Main Chart | Change the chart type and formats |
| Format Patterns | Change the borders, background, or foreground |

## Chart Select Plot Area

The Chart Select Plot Area selects an area within the axis on your chart so you can format it using the Format Patterns option.

## Chart Short Menus

The Chart Short Menus option appears on the Chart menu only if the Full Menus option is activated. Once you choose the Chart Short Menus option, all the menus are shortened. Short menus have the most frequently used options on them, while full menus have all options on them. Once you choose the Chart Short Menus option, the option Chart Full Menus appears on the chart menu in its place.

## Chart Unprotect Document

The Chart Unprotect Document option appears on the Chart menu only if the Full Menus option is activated. The Chart Unprotect

Document allows you to unprotect a document you password-protected with the Chart Protect Document option. You must remember the password you used when you protected the document, or you cannot unprotect it. Once you choose the Chart Unprotect Document option, a dialog box appears in which you must type the password and choose OK. The option Chart Protect Document then appears on the Chart menu in place of Chart Unprotect Document.

# DATA

The Data menu contains options for setting up and manipulating a database. The Data menu is used with databases to define them; to determine selection criteria; to find, extract, or delete selected records based on the criteria; to view and maintain them as a form instead of a table; and to sort them. The Data menu is also used to fill a range of cells with a series of numbers or dates, to create a table, and to divide a text string into individual cells (Parse).

## Data Delete

Data Delete appears on the Data menu only if the Full Menus selection is activated. To delete records from the database, you must first define the criteria using the Set Criteria option. Data Delete permanently deletes any records in the database that match the criteria you set.

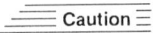 You cannot undo Data Delete with the Edit Undo option. Make sure you want to delete the records before you choose this option. It is a good idea to save the worksheet immediately before selecting this option so you can recover it if you make an error. Also, do not include blank rows in the criteria range unless you want to delete all records in the database.

## Data Exit Find

**SHORTCUT** (ESC)

Choosing the Data Exit Find option causes you to exit from the Data Find option. Data Exit Find appears on the menu only after you have chosen the Data Find option. Other ways of exiting from Data Find include choosing another option, editing a cell, selecting (clicking on) a cell outside the database, or pressing (ESC). Once you choose the Data Exit Find option, the Data Find option once again appears on the menu. Choosing the Data Find option again finds the next occurrence of a record in the database that matches the criteria defined in the Set Criteria option. For more information, see "Data Find."

## Data Extract

Data extract copies database records that match the criteria specified using the Set Criteria option and places them in the extract range. Before you choose the Data Extract option, you must select the extract range. The easiest way is to select a range that contains only the field names of the data you will extract. When you choose the Data Extract option, Excel puts the extracted data in the cells immediately below the field names and clears all the cells below the extracted data to the bottom of the worksheet. You can also select an extract range that contains field names and cells that will contain the extracted data. All the cells in the extract range are replaced with extracted data. If your extract range is too small, Excel gives you a message. At that time you can redefine the extract range and choose the Data Extract option again.

After you choose the Data Extract option, a dialog box appears that allows you to decide if you want to exclude duplicate records. If you do, choose the Unique Records Only option.

> **Caution:** You cannot undo the Data Extract option with the Edit Undo option. Another thing to be aware of is that if a cell in a record you are extracting contains a formula, the extracted record contains the value of the cell, not the formula.

## Data Find

Data Find selects the first record in the database that matches the criteria defined using the Data Set Criteria option. The first matching record is highlighted and the scroll bars become striped. As you scroll down the database, Excel selects only the records that match the defined criteria.

To exit from Data Find, choose the Data Exit Find option. Data Exit Find appears on the menu only after you have chosen the Data Find option. Other ways of exiting from Data Find include choosing another option, editing a cell, selecting a cell outside the database, or pressing (ESC). Once you choose the Data Exit Find option or exit in another way from Data Find, the Data Find option once again appears on the menu.

If you want to search backward through the database rather than forward, hold down (SHIFT) when you choose the Data Find option.

## Data Form

The Data Form option displays the currently defined database as a form in a dialog box. Each of the field names in your database appears on the left side of the dialog box, next to its own field. On the right side of the dialog box are options that you can choose: New, Delete, Restore, Find Prev, Find Next, Criteria, and Exit. You can add new records to your database by choosing the New option and then filling in the blank fields. You can find records by setting the criteria with the Criteria option and then choosing the Find option. These options are *not* the same as the Set Criteria, Data Find, Data Delete, and Data Extract options. If you set your criteria using the Criteria option in the dialog box, it does not change the criteria you defined using the Set Criteria option.

The dialog box also contains a scroll bar that allows you to move up and down the database with your mouse. Here is a summary of ways to move around the database with your mouse:

| | |
|---|---|
| Click in a field | Select a field |
| Click on the down arrow at the bottom of the scroll bar | Go to the same field in the next record |
| Click on the up arrow at the bottom of the scroll bar | Go to the same field in the previous record |
| Click on the scroll bar below the scroll box | Go to the same field 10 records forward |
| Click on the scroll bar above the scroll box | Go to the same field 10 records back |
| Drag the scroll box to the bottom of the scroll bar | Go to a new record at the end of the database |
| Drag the scroll box to the top of the scroll bar | Go to the first record in the database |

You can also use the keyboard to move around the database:

| | |
|---|---|
| `TAB` | Go to the next field in the current record |
| `ENTER` | Go to the first field in the next record |
| `SHIFT+TAB` | Go to the previous field in the current record |
| `SHIFT+ENTER` | Go to the first field in the previous record |
| `UP ARROW` | Go to the same field in the previous record |
| `DOWN ARROW` | Go to the same field in the next record |
| `PG UP` | Go to the same field 10 records back |
| `PGDN` | Go to the same field 10 records forward |
| `CTRL+PGUP` | Go to the first record in the database |
| `CTRL+PGDN` | Go to a new record at the end of the database |

Here is a summary of all the items in the dialog box:

***Record Indicator*** The Record Indicator is located at the upper-right corner of the dialog box. It tells you which record of the database you are in. For example, if the record indicator displays "2 of 15," you know you are in the second record of a database 15 records long. The total number of records indicates how many nonblank records there are in the database.

***Delete*** The Delete option deletes whatever record is currently being displayed in the dialog box and moves subsequent records up to fill in the space.

***Criteria*** The Criteria option is not the same as the Data Set Criteria option. The Criteria option allows you to define criteria to be used to find records within the Data Form environment.

***Exit*** The Exit option exits you from the Data Form option.

***Find Next*** The Find Next option finds the next instance in the database that matches the criteria you set using the Criteria option (the Criteria option in the dialog box, *not* the Data Set Criteria option).

***Find Prev*** The Find Prev option finds the previous instance in the database that matches the criteria you set using the Criteria option (the Criteria option in the dialog box, *not* the Data Set Criteria option).

***Form*** The Form option appears in the dialog box only after you choose the Criteria option. Choosing the Form option returns you to the regular dialog box.

***Restore*** The Restore option allows you to undo changes that you made to a record. To undo edits you made to a record, you must choose the Restore option before you go on to a new record.

## Data Parse

The Data Parse option appears on the Data menu only if the Full Menus option has been activated. The Data Parse option is usually used after you import data to Excel from another application. Sometimes each record of the imported data is put into one cell. You want to spread the data from that cell over many cells, so each field appears in its own cell. This is done using Data Parse.

After you import the data, select the parse range. The range can only be one column wide and as many rows as you want. Then select the Data Parse option. A dialog box appears with Parse Line, Guess, and Clear options. The Parse Line box displays the contents of the first cell in your parse range. You can type brackets in the box to indicate where you want the cell divisions to be. The Guess option tells Excel to guess where the cell divisions should be. The Clear option clears previously set brackets so you can try again. It may take several tries to get the data parsed the way you want it.

## Data Series

The Data Series option appears on the Data menu only if the Full Menus option is activated. The Data Series option fills in the range you specified with incremental values. The first cell in the range must contain the starting value. For example, if you select part of a column and the first cell in the selection contains 10, you can use the Data Series option to fill in the rest of the selection with 11, 12, 13, 14, and so on.

After you choose the Data Series option, a dialog box appears with the following options:

***Series in***   You can decide if you want the series to be filled in by row or by column. If you choose Series In Rows, Excel fills in the series starting at the upper-left corner of the selection and fills row by row. If you choose Series in Columns, Excel fills in the series starting at the upper-left corner of the selection and fills column by column.

***Type***   The Type option in the dialog box allows you to decide how the series is incremented. Your choices are

| | |
|---|---|
| Date | Uses date calculations to figure out the incremental values |
| Growth | Multiplies the value in each cell by the step value to get the value of the next cell |
| Linear | Adds the step value to the value in each cell to get the value of the next cell |

***Date Unit***   The Data Unit option is accessible only if you have set Type to Date. Date Unit allows you to select the unit the date will be incremented by: Day, Weekday, Month, or Year.

***Step Value***   Use Step Value to set the amount by which you want to increment each value in the series. If you want to decrement the series, use a negative number.

***Stop Value***   Use Stop Value to set the last value in the series. Data Series stops filling in values when it gets to the end of the range or to the stop value.

## Data Set Criteria

The Data Set Criteria option sets the criteria range, which is used to select records using the Data Find, Data Extract, and Data Delete options.

The criteria range is usually on the same worksheet as the database, but is outside the database range. Since you could use it often, place the criteria range where it is convenient (to the side or on the top of the database). The first row of the criteria range must contain field names that match one or more of the field names in the database. You must have one or more rows beneath the first row to put the criteria in. Once you have set up and selected your criteria range, choose the Data Set Criteria option.

After you have defined your criteria range using the Data Set Criteria option, you can change the criteria as much as you want. You do not have to redefine the range every time you change the criteria.

Excel creates a name for the criteria range—CRITERIA; the name and range can be accessed, changed, and deleted using the Formula Define Names option.

## Data Set Database

The Data Set Database option allows you to define a range as a database. The first row in your range must contain your field names, and the rows beneath it contain data. You can use the Data Set Database option on an existing worksheet with data already filled in, or use it before you enter any data. Be sure to include a few blank lines at the bottom of the database range. Excel creates a name for the database—DATABASE; the name and range can be accessed, changed, and deleted using the Formula Define Names option.

## Data Sort

The Data Sort option sorts the data in the range you selected. After you select the range you want to sort and choose the Data Sort option, a dialog box appears. The dialog box allows you to decide if you want the selection sorted by rows or columns and to define sort keys. Sort keys tell Excel which column you want to sort by if you are sorting by rows, and which row you want to sort by if you are sorting by columns. The 1st Key setting is the most important, then the 2nd Key, and then the 3rd Key. Each sort key box allows you to decide if you want to sort in Ascending or Descending order.

The Ascending sequence in which Excel sorts is as follows:

1. Numbers from the largest negative number to the largest positive number

2. Text, ignoring capitalization, and including numbers entered as text, in this sequence: space ! " # $ % & ' ( ) *+, - . / 0 1 2 3 4 5 6 7 8 9 : ; < = > ? @ a b c d e f g h i j k l m n o p q r s t u v w x y z [ \ ] ^ _ ` { | } ~ ¢ ¥ ±

3. Logical values, False first and then True

4. Error values

5. Blank cells

The descending order is the reverse of this order, except blank cells are always sorted last.

# EDIT

The Edit menu contains options that enable you to edit your document. You use the Edit menu to copy, move, and clear the contents of a cell or range of cells; to undo or repeat the last thing you did; and to insert and delete rows and columns.

## Edit Copy

**SHORTCUT** `CTRL+INS`

**WORKSHEET** The Edit Copy option defines your selection so that you can paste it with the Edit Paste or Edit Paste Special option. Edit Copy followed by Edit Paste or Edit Paste Special allows the copying of text, numbers, and formulas from one location in a file to another location on a worksheet in memory. The copy selection can be a single cell, a range in the current worksheet, a range in another worksheet, or characters from the Formula bar.

To copy cells, you must first select the range you want to copy. The selection must be a rectangular area. Then choose Edit Copy. Excel outlines the selection with a marquee. After selecting the cells to be copied, you need to paste them into the new area. For additional information, see Edit Paste and Edit Paste Special.

**CHART** You can copy characters from the Formula bar or a whole chart to another chart. To copy one chart to another, the chart you want to copy from must be active. Choose the Edit Copy option. Activate the chart you want to copy to, and select Edit Paste or Edit Paste Special. For more information, see Edit Paste or Edit Paste Special.

## Edit Copy Picture

The Edit Copy Picture option allows you to copy a pictorial representation of your current selection into the Excel Clipboard. The option only appears on the Edit menu if you hold down `SHIFT` as you select the menu. The Edit Copy Picture option appears instead of the Edit Copy option.

Once you have the pictorial representation of part of a worksheet or a chart in the Clipboard, you can paste it into a document created by a word processor.

## Edit Cut

### SHORTCUT (SHIFT+DEL)

**WORKSHEET** The Edit Cut option allows you to define your selection so you can move it with the Edit Paste or Edit Paste Special option. Edit Cut followed by Edit Paste or Edit Paste Special allows you to move text, numbers, and formulas from one location in a file to another location on a worksheet in memory. The cut selection can be a single cell, a range in the current worksheet, a range in another worksheet, or characters from the Formula bar.

To cut cells, you must first select the range you want to cut; the selection must be a rectangular area. Then choose Edit Cut. After selecting the cells to be moved, you need to paste them into the new area. For additional information, see Edit Paste and Edit Paste Special.

**CHART** The Edit Cut option works only on characters in the Formula bar when your active document is a chart.

## Edit Delete

### SHORTCUT (CTRL+-)

The Edit Delete option allows you to remove the cells in your selection from the worksheet. The cells adjacent to the deleted area will move over to fill in the space. If you delete an entire row or rows, Excel shifts up the cells below the deleted area. If you delete an entire column or columns, Excel shifts left the cells to the right of the deleted area. If you delete a selected region smaller than a whole row or column, Excel asks you in a dialog box if you want to shift the remaining cells up or left.

 If you want to clear cells rather than shift them, use the Edit Clear option.

## Edit Fill Down

**SHORTCUT** (CTRL+X)

The Edit Fill Down option allows you to copy the contents and formats from the top row in a selection to the remaining cells in the selection below it. If there is data or formatting in the selection already, it is replaced by the formatting and data from the top row.

## Edit Fill Left

The Edit Fill Left option appears on the Edit menu only if you hold down (SHIFT) when you activate the menu. Edit Fill Left allows you to copy the contents and formats from the right column in a selection to the cells in the selection to the left of it. If there is data or formatting in the selection already, it is replaced by the data and formatting from the rightmost column in the selection.

## Edit Fill Right

Edit Fill Right allows you to copy the contents and formats from the left column in a selection to the cells in the selection to the right of it. If there is data or formatting in the selection already, it is replaced by the data and formatting from the leftmost column in the selection.

## Edit Fill Up

The Edit Fill Up option appears on the Edit menu only if you hold down (SHIFT) when you activate the menu. The Edit Fill Up option allows you to copy the contents and formats from the bottom row in a selection to the cells in the selection above it. If there is data or formatting in the selection already, it is replaced by the data and formatting from the bottom row.

## Edit Insert

### SHORTCUT (CTRL++)

The Edit Insert option allows you to insert a blank cell or range of cells into the selected area. The selected cells are shifted to accommodate the new cells. If whole rows are selected, Excel automatically moves the selected rows down to make room for the new rows. Similarly, if whole columns are selected, Excel automatically moves the selected columns to the right to make room for the new columns. If a range smaller than whole rows or columns is selected, Excel asks you in a dialog box if you want to shift the selected cells to the right or down.

## Edit Paste

### SHORTCUT (SHIFT+INS)

**WORKSHEET** The Edit Paste option allows you to paste a group of cells that you have selected and defined (using Edit Cut or Edit Copy) to a new location. Edit Paste pastes all cell properties. If you want to paste only certain cell properties—for example, contents or formatting—use Edit Paste Special. You also can use Edit Paste to paste characters cut from the Formula bar.

Once you have selected the cells and activated the marquee with Edit Cut or Edit Paste, you need to select the place that you want to move the group of cells to. You can simply go to the upper-left cell of the location where you want to put the cells. Excel fills down and right to match the size of the cut or copy region. Alternatively you can select a region that is exactly the same size as the region that you defined using Edit Cut or Edit Copy.

If you defined your region using Edit Copy, you can make multiple copies in one of two ways. If you want to make multiple copies simultaneously, choose all the areas to which you want to paste using a multiple selection. Alternatively, you can just continue to select paste areas and choose the Edit Paste option until you have copied the cells everywhere you want them. You do not need to redefine the area each time with Edit Copy.

*Note* You cannot make multiple copies of a region defined with Edit Cut.

*Caution* Edit Paste overwrites existing data, formulas, and formatting on the worksheet. Be sure that enough space exists in the range you are copying to.

**CHART** The Edit Paste option allows you to copy from a worksheet to a chart, or from a chart to another chart. When the copied area is from a worksheet, Excel creates a data series out of the cells and pastes them into the active chart. You can also paste copied or cut characters from the Formula bar.

When you are copying from one chart to another chart, Excel adds the data series to any data series already on the active chart, but replaces the formatting with the formatting from the copied chart. If you want to paste only certain attributes of the chart, use the Edit Paste Special option.

## Edit Paste Link

The Edit Paste Link option appears on the Edit menu only if you have the Full Menus option activated. The Edit Paste Link option allows you to copy data into the cells in the current selection and establish a link with the origin of the data. The link causes your worksheet to change when the source data changes. The source of the data can be an Excel worksheet or another application.

To use Edit Paste Link you must first select and copy the source data. Then activate the cell or cells that you want to paste to, and choose Edit Paste Link. If your copy area is more than one cell and your paste selection is one cell, Excel fills down and right to match the size of the copy area. Any data and formatting in that area is lost, so make sure you have enough room to paste the whole selection.

## Edit Paste Special

**WORKSHEET** The Edit Paste Special option allows you to paste certain attributes from a copied selection to your current selection. You can paste formatting without pasting any data, for example. You can also combine values from the paste area with values from the copy area.

To use Edit Paste Special you first must use Edit Copy to copy a selection of cells. Then select the place where you want to paste the cells and choose Edit Paste Special. A dialog box appears, allowing you to choose which attributes of the copied cells you would like pasted into the new area. You can also choose a mathematical function, which combines the values of the cells from the copied area with the values in the paste area (assuming that there is data in the paste area).

**CHART** To paste from another chart, select and copy the chart using Edit Copy, and then activate or create a chart and choose

Edit Paste Special. A dialog box appears from which you can choose the attributes of the copied chart that you would like to place in the active chart.

To paste from a worksheet, select and copy the cells using Edit Copy, and then activate or create a chart and choose Edit Paste Special. Excel displays a dialog box, allowing you to choose how you want to add the data from the worksheet to the chart.

## Edit Repeat

**SHORTCUT** (ALT+ENTER)

The Edit Repeat option allows you to repeat the last option you took (including options) if possible. It can be used for repeating formatting in different groups of cells.

## Edit Undo

**SHORTCUT** (ALT+BACKSPACE)

The Edit Undo option allows you to reverse the last option you took, if possible. You can only undo the last option or the last cell entry you typed.

# FILE

The File menu provides the means of creating new worksheets, charts, and macro sheets; opening existing worksheets, charts, and macro sheets stored on disk; and closing, saving, and deleting worksheets, charts, and macro sheets. The File menu also allows you to set up the page you will print, set up your printer, print a worksheet or chart, and exit Excel.

## File Close

The File Close option allows you to close the active document. If the document contains changes that have not been saved, Excel asks you if you want to save the changes.

## File Close All

The File Close All option only appears on the File menu when you hold down (SHIFT) when you activate the menu. Close All closes all of the windows on your screen. If any of the documents have open unsaved changes, Excel asks if you want to save the changes for each document.

## File Delete

The File Delete option appears on the File menu only if the Full Menus option is activated. The File Delete option deletes a file on disk from the current directory. When you choose the File Delete option, a dialog box appears. Select the file you want to delete from the Files list box, and then choose OK. Before finally deleting a file, Excel asks you to confirm. Answering No cancels the deletion; answering Yes completes the deletion. Repeat these steps to delete more files. The entry in the File Name box determines which files are listed in the Files box. For example, *.* shows all files in the directory; *.XLM shows all files with the .XLM extension. If the current directory is not the directory you want, type in the desired directory in the File Name box; for example, C:\DATA\*.XLS.

*Caution:* Make sure you want to delete a file before doing it. Once a file is deleted, it is gone.

## File Exit

Choose File Exit to exit from Microsoft Excel. If you have any open documents containing unsaved changes, Excel asks you if you want to save the changes or not. You can choose Yes to save, No to ignore changes, or Cancel to cancel the File Exit option.

## File Links

File Links appears on the File menu only if the Full Menus option is activated. The File Links option causes Excel to open all supporting documents to the active document. You can also change links to a document with this option. The dialog box also allows you to mark the linked files as read only.

## File New

**SHORTCUT** `SHIFT+F11` (worksheet), `F11` (chart), `CTRL+F11` (macro)

The File New option opens a new document in a new window. When you choose the File New option, Excel asks you if you want to open a new worksheet, chart, or macro sheet. If you want to create a new chart, you must first select the cells you want to chart on a worksheet, choose File New, and then choose Chart in the dialog box. Excel automatically plots the contents of the selected cells onto the new chart.

## File Open

The File Open option allows you to open an existing document from disk. When you choose the File Open option, a dialog box appears. Select the file you want to open from the Files list box, and then choose OK. The entry in the File Name box determines which files are listed in the Files list box. For example, *.* shows all files in the directory; *.XLM shows all files that have the .XLM extension. If the current directory is not the directory you want, type in the desired directory in the File Name box; for example, C:\DATA\*.XLS. You can set files to read only by checking the Read Only option in the dialog box.

## File Page Setup

**WORKSHEET** The File Page Setup option allows you to change the appearance of the printed document. When you choose the File Page Setup option, a dialog box appears that allows you to set the header, footer, and margins and choose if you want gridlines or row and column headings printed on the document. Here is a table of header and footer codes that control how the header and footer look on the printed page:

| Code | Description |
| --- | --- |
| &B | Print the left, center, or right part of the header or footer in bold |
| &C | Center the text that follows |
| &D | Print the current date |
| &F | Print the name of the document |
| &I | Print the left, center, or right part of the header or footer in italic |
| &L | Left justify the text that follows |
| &P | Print the page numbers |
| &P+NUMBER | Add the number to the page number and print it |
| &P-NUMBER | Subtract the number from the page number and print it |
| &R | Right justify the characters that follow |
| &T | Print the current time |
| && | Print an ampersand |

**CHART** If you are in a chart when you choose File Page Setup, a different dialog box appears. This dialog box allows you to determine the printed size of the current chart. You can print it the same size as the screen, fit it on the page while retaining the same proportion as appears on the screen, or print it to fit on the page as large as possible.

## File Print

**SHORTCUT** (SHIFT+F12)

**WORKSHEET** File Print prints the active document. The page settings associated with the document are used to format the output (see File Page Setup). File Print prints the entire worksheet, unless you set a different print area with the Options Set Print Area option. When you choose the File Print option, a dialog box appears in which you can set how many copies you want printed and the pages you want printed and choose options such as draft quality and preview. The preview option allows you to look at the document on the screen the way it will appear on paper.

**CHART** File Print prints the active chart. The size of the printed chart is determined by the File Page Setup dialog box settings.

## File Printer Setup

File Printer Setup allows you to tell Excel which printer you will use. You must choose the File Printer Setup option the first time you use a printer, when you change printers, or when you want to change the settings of your printer. If you want to install a new printer or change the printer port, you must use the Windows Control Panel.

## File Save

**SHORTCUT** (SHIFT+F12)
File Save saves the current file to disk in a worksheet format with an .XLS extension, unless another extension is designated. The first time you save a file, Excel asks you for a filename. Every time you choose File Save thereafter, you cannot enter another filename. If you want to save the file under a different name, you must use the File Save As option.

## File Save As

**SHORTCUT** (F12)
File Save As allows you to save a new document or save an existing document under a different name. If the document already has a name, the name appears in the dialog box. You can keep that name by choosing OK. If you want to save the document under another name, type the name in the dialog box. It is not necessary to type the extension (for example, .XLS). You can choose the Options option in the dialog box to choose the file format, create a password for the file, or create a backup file.

## File Save Workspace

The File Save Workspace option appears on the menu only if the Full Menu option is activated. The File Save Workspace option saves a group of windows and documents under one name. Typically this is used to save all the documents and windows that you have open. It is useful when you are working on a project in which you have a number of files open. Before you end your Excel session, you can save the workspace file. The next time you start working in Excel, you can open the workspace file, which opens all the files you had open when you saved the workspace. Workspace files have an .XLW extension.

> **Caution:** The workspace file contains a list of the documents open when you chose the Save Workspace option. It does not contain the actual documents. *Do not* delete the individual files just because you saved them with the Save Workspace option.

## File Unhide Window

The Unhide Window option appears on the File menu only when there are no open, unhidden windows in the workspace. When you choose the Unhide Window option, a list of windows you have previously hidden appears in a dialog box. Choose the file you would like to unhide, and then choose OK. If the hidden file is password protected, you are asked for the password before the window is unhidden. You can cancel the option by clicking the Cancel button.

# FORMAT

The Format menu allows you to determine how a cell entry looks. If it contains a number, you can format it as dollars or percents, with or without commas, and with the number of decimal places you desire. For both text and numbers, you can left, right, or center align them; place a border around or shade them; protect a cell from being overwritten; and determine a cell's width and height. Finally, you can justify text in a range of cells. In Chart mode you can format various parts of either the main or overlay chart.

## Format Alignment

The Format Alignment option aligns selected cells. After you choose the Format Alignment option, a dialog box appears from which you can choose the alignment you want:

| | |
|---|---|
| Center | Centers the cell contents |
| Fill | Fills the entire cell with the contents of the cell. For example, if the cell contains an asterisk, and you choose the Format Alignment Fill option, the entire cell will be filled with asterisks |
| General | Right aligns numbers, left aligns text, and centers errors and logical values. This is the Excel default alignment |
| Left | Left aligns cell contents |
| Right | Right aligns cell contents |

## Format Border

The Format Border option places a border around the selection, or shades the selection, or both. After you choose the Format Border option, a dialog box appears from which you can choose the following options:

| | |
|---|---|
| Bottom | Places a solid border on the bottom side of every cell in the selection |
| Left | Places a solid border on the left side of every cell in the selection |
| Outline | Places a solid border around the entire selection |
| Right | Places a solid border on the right side of every cell in the selection |
| Shade | Shades every cell in the selection |

Top                        Places a solid border on the top side of every cell in the selection

If you want to put a border around every cell in the selection, choose the Left, Right, Top, and Bottom options. If you want to put a border around the entire selection, choose the Outline option.

## Format Cell Protection

The Format Cell Protection option appears on the Format menu only if the Full Menus option is activated. You can use the Format Cell Protection option to select cells that you do not want to be able to edit. You can also use the Format Cell Protection option to hide the formulas within cells.

Format Cell Protection is the first of a two-part protection scheme built into Excel. The second part is Options Protect Document. First identify the cells to be locked or unlocked with Format Cell Protection. Then with Options Protect Document you turn on or off total document protection. If a cell is locked, you cannot write to it after you use Options Protect Document. By default all cells start out locked. You therefore must unlock those cells to which you want to be able to write after choosing Options Project Document.

After you choose the Format Cell Protection option, a dialog box appears with two options: Locked and Hidden.

**LOCKED**  The Locked option unlocks the selected range if the current status is Locked or relocks it if the status is Not Locked. The default is for a cell to be locked.

**HIDDEN**  The Hidden option hides the formulas within the range if they are currently not hidden and unhides them if they are currently hidden. The default is for formulas not to be hidden.

## Format Column Width

The Format Column Width option sets the width of the column or columns that are selected. You need to have only one cell in the column selected to set the width for the entire column. The default column width for Excel is 8.43.

You can also change the column width using the mouse. First select all the columns you want to format. Then point to the line between the column headings to the right of one of the columns you want to format. You will see the icon change to a double-headed arrow. Press the mouse button and drag to the width you want and let go. All selected columns are set to the new width.

## Format Font

The Format Font option allows you to choose the fonts you want for the document you are working on. The dialog box that appears when you select Format Font is different for charts and worksheets.

**WORKSHEET** The Format Font option changes the font for the selected cells. You can change the font for the entire worksheet. After choosing the Format Font option, a dialog box appears with four fonts to choose from. When you select a font, the row height adjusts to accommodate the font if the row height is not big enough.

You can have only four fonts on your worksheet at once. If you choose the Fonts>> button, the dialog box enlarges. In addition to the four fonts in the Fonts box, the dialog box has the following options:

*Font*  The Font box has a list of fonts you can choose from.

*Printer Fonts*  If the Printer Fonts box is turned on, the fonts that appear in the Fonts box are printer fonts. If the Printer Fonts box is turned off, the fonts that appear in the Fonts box are screen fonts.

***Replace***  Replace replaces the font selected in the Fonts box at the top of the dialog box with the font, size, and style you select from the list.

***Size***  The sizes available for the font highlighted in the Font list box appear in the Size box. You can choose any of the sizes for your font.

***Style***  You can choose any of the styles for the selected font. The styles you can choose from are Bold, Italic, Underline, and Strikeout.

**CHART**  To change fonts on your chart, select the text you want to format with a new font, and choose the Format Font option. If you want to change the font for the entire chart, use the Chart Select Chart option, and then choose the Format Font option. If you have not selected the text to format yet, the Format Font option is grayed on the Format menu. Once you choose the Format Font option, a dialog box appears that has the following options:

***Background***  The Background option controls the background behind the text and offers the following choices:

| | |
|---|---|
| Automatic | Excel automatically sets the background |
| Transparent | Sets the background area to transparent, so you can see what is behind the text |
| White Out | Sets the background area to whatever background color or pattern you are using in your chart |

***Color***  The Color option allows you to select the color of the text. It can be automatically set by Excel by choosing the Automatic option, or you can select one of the colors in the box. The colors you can select and the box to choose to select that color are summarized here:

| Color | Box to Choose |
|---|---|
| White | White box |
| Black | Black box |
| Red | R |
| Green | G |
| Blue | B |
| Yellow | Y |
| Magenta | M |
| Cyan | C |

*Font*   The Font box has a list of fonts you can choose from.

*Patterns*   Any changes you made in the Format Font box are carried out, and the Format Patterns dialog box is displayed. For more information, see Format Patterns.

*Printer Fonts*   If the Printer Fonts box is turned on, the fonts that appear in the Fonts box are printer fonts. If the Printer Fonts box is turned off, the fonts that appear in the Fonts box are screen fonts.

*Size*   The sizes available for the font highlighted in the Font list box appear in the Size box. You can choose any of these sizes for your font.

*Style*   You can choose any of the styles for your font. The styles you can choose from are Bold, Italic, Underline, and Strikeout.

*Text*   Any changes you made in the Format Font box are carried out, and the Format Text dialog box is displayed. For more information, see Format Text.

## Format Justify

The Format Justify option appears on the Format menu only if the Full Menus option is activated. The Format Justify option justifies the text in the leftmost column of a selection. The left column in the selection must contain text only. The text in the left column is treated as a single string and distributed from the top cell in the column in such a way that each successive cell in the column is filled with text. Blank cells in the column are interpreted as paragraph separators. Every paragraph is justified separately.

## Format Legend

The Format Legend option appears on the Format menu only when the active document is a chart. The Format Legend option allows you to choose where the legend will appear on your chart. To add a legend, you must use the Chart Add Legend option. When you choose the Format Legend option, a dialog box appears with the following options:

***Font*** Any changes you make in the Format Legend box are carried out, and the Format Font dialog box is displayed. For more information, see "Format Font."

***Type*** The following options in the Type box allow you to choose the location of the legend:

| | |
|---|---|
| Bottom | Places the legend horizontally at the bottom of the chart |
| Corner | Places the legend vertically in the upper-right corner of the chart |
| Top | Places the legend horizontally at the top of the chart |
| Vertical | Places the legend vertically at the right side of the chart |

*Patterns* Any changes you make in the Format Legend box are carried out, and the Format Patterns dialog box is displayed. For more information, see "Format Patterns."

## Format Main Chart

The Format Main Chart option appears only if the active document is a chart. The option allows you to set the main chart's formats and type. When you select the Format Main Chart option, a dialog box appears. All available options appear in the dialog box. Options that are not currently relevant appear gray in the dialog box. The dialog box has two main boxes, Type and Format.

*Type* The Type box allows you to choose the type of chart you want. The options are Area, Bar, Column, Line, Pie, and Scatter.

*Format* The format box allows you to set the formatting options for the main chart.

| | |
|---|---|
| Stacked | Choosing this option causes the series within a category to appear on top of another. |
| Vary by Categories | This option is only relevant if there is a single series on the chart. Excel gives each data point a different pattern or color. |
| Drop Lines | This option causes Excel to put lines on the chart from the highest value in each category to the category axis. |
| 100% | Each category is shown as a percentage. All the categories added together equal 100%. Absolute values do not appear on the chart. |

| | |
|---|---|
| Overlapped | This option determines if the markers in a cluster overlap or not. If it is turned on, they overlap by the amount indicated in the % Overlap box. |
| Hi-Lo Lines | This option causes Excel to extend lines from the highest to the lowest point in each category. |
| % Overlap | The % Overlap option allows you to choose the percentage of the width of a column or bar that the different bars or columns within a cluster overlap, if the Overlapped option is selected. If the Overlapped option is not selected, then the % Overlap sets the distance between bars or columns within a cluster. |
| % Cluster Spacing | This option allows you to determine the distance between clusters. The percentage is the percentage of the width of a column or bar. |
| Angle of First Pie Slice | This option is only relevant if you have a Pie chart. It allows you to choose the angle of the first edge of the first slice. The angle is measured clockwise from the Y-axis (vertical axis). |

## Format Move

The Format Move option appears on the Format menu only if the active document is a chart. The option allows you to move a selected chart object with the keyboard. After you select the object, choose the Format Move option, use the direction keys to move the object where you want it, and then press (ENTER).

## Format Number

The Format Number option allows you to format selected cells with regard to how numbers appear in those cells. After selecting the cells you want to format, choose the Format Number option. A dialog box appears that allows you to choose from the Excel built-in number formats in the Format Number box, or allows you to create your own format in the Format box. You can also delete formats from the Format Number box that you previously created.

*Format Number* The Format Number box is where Excel displays all the built-in number formats and any custom formats you have created. The default format is General. The following table shows how the built-in formats display a number or a date. The formats appear in the same order they do in the dialog box.

|  | *Numbers You Enter:* | | |
|---|---|---|---|
| **Format** | **8000** | **-8** | **.8** |
| General | 8000 | -8 | 0.8 |
| 0 | 8000 | -8 | 1 |
| 0.00 | 8000.00 | -8.00 | 0.80 |
| #,##0 | 8,000 | -8 | 1 |
| #,##0.00 | 8,000.00 | -8.00 | 0.80 |
| $#,##0;($#,##0) | $8,000 | ($8) | $1 |
| $#,##0;[RED]($#,##0) | $8,000 | ($8)* | $1 |
| $#,##0.00;($#,##0.00) | $8,000.00 | $(8.00) | $0.80 |
| $#,##0.00;[RED]($#,##0.00) | $8,000.00 | ($8.00)* | $0.80 |
| 0% | 800000% - | 800% | 80% |
| 0.00% | 800000.00% | -800.00% | 80.00% |
| 0.00E+00 | 8.00E+03 - | 8.00E+00 | 8.00E-01 |

*Displayed or printed in red if equipment supports it.

| Format | Date You Type:<br>7/6/91 |
|---|---|
| m/d/yy | 7/6/91 |
| d-mmm-yy | 6-Jul-91 |
| d-mmm | 6-Jul |
| mmm-yy | Jul-91 |

| Format | Time You Type:<br>7:45:36 PM |
|---|---|
| h:mm AM/PM | 7:45 PM |
| h:mm:ss AM/PM | 7:45:36 PM |
| h:mm | 19:45 |
| h:mm:ss | 19:45:36 |

| Format | Date and Time You Type:<br>7/6/91 7:45 PM |
|---|---|
| m/d/yy h:mm | 7/6/91 19:45 |

***Format*** The Format box is where you can create custom formats. A format consists of up to four parts separated by semicolons. The first part is for positive numbers, the second for negative numbers, the third for zero values, and the fourth for text. If you want to exclude certain types of numbers from being displayed, do not put any formatting between the semicolons. For example, if you do not want negative numbers displayed, you can create a format like #,##0;;0.00, which displays positive numbers in one format, does not display negative numbers, and displays zero values in a different format. You can use the following formatting symbols when creating your own formats:

| Symbol | Usage |
|---|---|
| 0 | Specifies the number of decimal places to the right of the decimal point and the minimum digits to the left of the decimal point. For example, with the built-in format 0.00 you always have two decimal places to the right of the decimal point and at least one digit to the left of the decimal point. With the 0.00 format, the following numbers are formatted as shown: |

| Entry | Display |
|---|---|
| .456 | 0.46 |
| 45 | 45.00 |

| Symbol | Usage |
|---|---|
| # | Specifies the number of optional digits on either side of the decimal point. For example, in the built-in format #,##0 the # is used to provide the optional digits surrounding the comma used as a thousands separator. These will be blank if there are not enough digits to fill the number of places. You want the first place to be a 0 and not a # so you will get at least a 0 printed if you have fraction too small to round to 1. With the #,##0 format, the following entries are formatted as shown: |

| Entry | Display |
|---|---|
| 46.67 | 47 |
| 12345 | 12,345 |

Specifies position of the decimal point.

| | |
|---|---|
| , | Specifies that the thousands separator is a comma if a comma is surrounded by 0's or #'s. |
| ; | Separates sections of a format. There can be up to four sections. The first, or leftmost, specifies how to format positive numbers, the second section specifies how to format negative numbers, the third specifies how to format zero, and the fourth section specifies how to handle text. All numbers are handled the same if there is only one section. With two sections, positive and zero values are formatted with the first, and negative numbers are formatted with the second. Text is not given special treatment with only three sections. An example of how to use the semicolon is shown with the next set of symbols. |
| $+- () : space | Specifies a literal character to be displayed. For example, with the built-in format $#,##0;($#,##0) you have a $ to the left of the leftmost number and ( ) around negative numbers. With the $#,##0 ;($#,##0) format, the following numbers are formatted as shown: |

| Entry | Display |
|---|---|
| -45.67 | ($46) |
| 1234 | $1,234 |

If ( ) are specified for negative numbers, positive numbers are shifted one position to the left so that negative numbers will line up.

| | |
|---|---|
| "text" | Specifies that whatever is between the " " is displayed. For example, $#,##0"DB" ;$#,##0" CR";0 indicates a DB is placed after positive |

numbers, a CR is placed after negative numbers, and a 0 appears for zero values.

\    Specifies that the character following the \ is displayed. This is the same as enclosing a single character in " ".

@    Specifies where any text in a cell is placed in a format. For example, with 0.00 ;@ all numbers are formatted with 0.00 and any text appearing in the cell should also be displayed (0.00 by itself does the same thing).

*    Specifies that the character following the * is repeated to fill any unused space in the cell. For example, $**#,##0 places a $ in the leftmost position in a cell, fills any intervening space with *, and right-aligns the number in the cell as usual. With the $**#,##0 format, the following numbers are formatted as shown:

| Entry | Display |
|-------|---------|
| 45    | $*******45 |
| 1234  | $***1,234 |

%    Specifies that a number is multiplied by 100 and a % placed to the right. For example, the built-in format 0.00% multiplies the number by 100 and places a % after it. With the 0.00% format, the following numbers are formatted as shown:

| Entry  | Display |
|--------|---------|
| .07    | 7.00%   |
| .4575  | 45.75%  |
| -0.067 | -6.70%  |

| E+ E- e+ e- | Specifies that the scientific format is used with either E or e. If a - is specified, only negative numbers have a sign. With +, both positive and negative numbers have a sign. For example, the built-in format 0.00E+00 uses the scientific format with a capital E and both plus and minus signs. With the 0.00E+00 format, the following numbers are formatted as shown: |

| Entry | Display |
|---|---|
| 4567 | 4.57E+03 |
| -12345 | -1.23E+04 |
| .0045 | 4.50E-03 |

| m mm mmm mmmm | Specifies that a month is displayed as a number without a leading zero (m) or with a leading zero (mm), as a three-letter abbreviation (mmm), or as a full name. If m or mm follows h or hh, it specifies minutes rather than a month. |
| d dd ddd dddd | Specifies that a day is displayed as a number without a leading zero (d) or with a leading zero (dd), as a three-letter abbreviation (ddd), or as a full name. |
| yy yyyy | Specifies that a year is displayed as either a two- (yy) or four-digit number (yyyy). |
| h hh | Specifies that an hour is displayed as either a number without a leading zero (h) or a number with a leading zero (hh). |
| m mm | Specifies that a minute is displayed as either a number without a leading zero (m) or a number with a leading zero (mm). If the m or mm do not appear after an h or hh, the month is displayed. |

| s ss | Specifies that a second is displayed as either a number without a leading zero (s) or a number with a leading zero (ss). |
| AM/PM am/pm A/P a/p | Specifies that time should be displayed using a 12-hour clock with AM, am, A, or a before noon and PM, pm, P, or p from noon to midnight. |
| [color] | Specifies that the characters in the cell are displayed in a color. The colors available are black, white, red, green, blue, yellow, magenta, and cyan. |

When you have a fixed number of decimal places, the decimal digits are rounded to fit the format. Also, if you have blank format sections (semicolons with nothing between them), it means that type of number is not displayed. For example 0.00;;;@ displays and formats positive numbers and text, but does not display negative numbers and zero values.

## Format Overlay

The Format Overlay option appears on the Format menu only if the active document is a chart and the Full Menus option is activated. The Format Overlay option allows you to format overlays you have created with Chart Add Overlay. After you choose the Format Overlay option, a dialog box appears that contains a Type box, a Format box, a First Series in Overlay Chart box, and an Automatic Series Distribution box.

***Type*** The Type box allows you to choose the type of chart you want. The choices are Area, Bar, Column, Combination, Line, Pie, or Scatter.

***Format*** The format box allows you to set the following formatting options for the main chart:

| | |
|---|---|
| Stacked | Causes the series within a category to appear on top of another. |
| Vary by Categories | Only relevant if there is a single series on the chart. Excel gives each data point a different pattern or color. |
| Drop Lines | Causes Excel to put lines on the chart from the highest value in each category to the category axis. |
| 100% | Each category is shown as a percentage. All the categories added together equal 100%. Absolute values do not appear on the chart. |
| Overlapped | Determines if the markers in a cluster overlap or not. If it is turned on, they overlap by the amount indicated in the % Overlap box. |
| Hi-Lo Lines | Causes Excel to extend lines from the highest to the lowest point in each category. |
| % Overlap | Allows you to choose the percentage of the width of a column or bar that the different bars or columns within a cluster overlap, if the Overlapped option is selected. If the Overlapped option is not selected, then the % Overlap sets the distance between bars or columns within a cluster. |
| % Cluster Spacing | Allows you to determine the distance between clusters. The percentage is the percentage of the width of a column or bar. |
| Angle of First Pie Slice | Only relevant if you have a Pie chart. It allows you to choose the angle of the first edge of the first slice. The angle is measured clockwise from the Y-axis (vertical axis). |

***First Series in Overlay Chart*** The number you put in this box tells Excel which series you want plotted on the overlay chart. If you have 4 series and you put a 2 in the First Series in Overlay

Chart, series 1 appears on the main chart and series 2, 3, and 4 appear on the overlay chart.

***Automatic Series Distribution*** If this box is turned on, Excel automatically distributes the series between the main chart and the overlay chart for you.

## Format Patterns

The Format Patterns option appears on the Format menu only if the active document is a chart. The option allows you to change the pattern on an object or objects selected on your chart. For example, if your chart is a Bar chart, you can select a series and use Format Patterns to cause the bars to appear striped, checked, or dotted. After you select your objects and choose the Format Patterns option, a dialog box appears containing only those options that apply to the objects you selected. The following options may appear in your dialog box:

| | |
|---|---|
| Invisible | Selected objects do not appear on the chart. |
| Automatic | Excel picks a pattern or color for each series for you. |
| Apply To All | Excel applies the choices you make to all data points on the chart. |
| Invert If Negative | Excel inverts the pattern for negative values. |
| Pattern | Allows you to pick a pattern for the objects you selected. |
| Color | Allows you to pick a color for the objects you selected. |

| **Color** | **Box to Choose** |
|---|---|
| White | White box |
| Black | Black box |

|  |  |
|---|---|
| Red | R |
| Green | G |
| Blue | B |
| Yellow | Y |
| Magenta | M |
| Cyan | C |

Weight — Allows you to control the width of a selected line, border, arrow, or axis.

Style — Allows you to control the style of a selected line, border, arrow, or axis if one of those objects is selected. The Style box is also used to control the markers if your chart is a Line chart.

Shadow — Allows you to shade the bottom and right sides of the selected chart, text, or legend.

Tick Mark Type — Allows you to change the tick marks on your axes. You can choose from these mark types:

| | |
|---|---|
| Invisible | Tick marks don't appear on the chart |
| Inside | Tick marks appear on the inside of the axes |
| Outside | Tick marks appear on the outside of the axes |
| Cross | Tick marks appear across the axes line |

Tick Labels — Allows you to decide where you want the tick labels to appear. Your choices are:

| | |
|---|---|
| None | Removes all tick labels |
| Low | Tick labels appear at the low end of the chart axis |
| High | Tick labels appear at the high end of the chart axis |
| Next To Axis | The default setting; tick labels appear next to the chart axis |

| | |
|---|---|
| Arrowhead | Allows you to control the appearance of arrows on your chart. |
| Font | Any changes you made in the Format Patterns box are carried out, and the Format Font dialog box is displayed. For more information, see "Format Font." |
| Legend | Any changes you made in the Format Patterns box are carried out, and the Format Legend dialog box is displayed. For more information, see "Format Legend." |
| Scale | Any changes you made in the Format Patterns box are carried out, and the Format Scale dialog box is displayed. For more information, see "Format Scale." |
| Text | Any changes you made in the Format Patterns box are carried out, and the Format Text dialog box is displayed. For more information, see "Format Text." |

## Format Row Height

The Format Row Height option sets the height of the row or rows that are selected. You need to have only one cell in the row selected in order to set the height for the entire row. The default row height for Excel is 13.

You can also change the row height using the mouse. First select all the rows you want to format. Then point to the line between the row headings on the bottom of one of the rows you want to format. The icon changes to a double-headed arrow. Click the mouse, drag to the height you want, and let go. All selected rows are set to the new height.

## Format Scale

The Format Scale option appears on the Format menu only if the active document is a chart. The option allows you to control the appearance of the axes on your chart. You must first select an axis to format, and then select the Format Scale option. The dialog box that appears varies depending on whether you selected the category axis or the value axis.

*Category Axis*   If you select the category axis before you choose the Format Scale option, the Category Axis Scale dialog box appears with the following options:

| | |
|---|---|
| Value Axis Crosses At Category Number | Allows you to select the value on the category axis where you want the value axis to cross. The default value for this option is 1. |
| Number Of Categories Between Tick Labels | Allows you to decide how many categories you want between tick labels. The default value for this option is 1, which puts a tick label at every category. If you want a tick label between every other category, type 2 in this box. |
| Number Of Categories Between Tick Marks | Allows you to decide how many categories you want between tick marks. The default value for this option is 1, which puts a tick mark at every category. If you want a tick mark between every other category, type 2 in this box. |
| Value Axis Crosses Between Categories | If this option is turned on, Excel crosses the axis between categories. |
| Categories In Reverse Order | If this option is turned on, the categories are shown right to left rather than left to right. |

| | |
|---|---|
| Value Axis Crosses At Maximum Category | If this option is turned on, the value axis crosses the category axis at the maximum category. |
| Patterns | Any changes you made in the Format Scale box are carried out, and the Format Patterns dialog box is displayed. For more information, see "Format Patterns." |
| Font | Any changes you made in the Format Scale box are carried out, and the Format Font dialog box is displayed. For more information, see "Format Font." |

*Value Axis*   If you select the value axis before you choose the Format Scale option, the Value Axis Scale dialog box appears with the following options:

| | |
|---|---|
| Minimum | When the Automatic box is turned on, the lowest value in any series in the chart is included. If it is not turned on, you can type a value in the box on the right side to tell Excel what you want the minimum value on your chart to be. |
| Maximum | When the Automatic box is turned on, the highest value in any series in the chart is included. If it is not turned on, you can type a value in the box on the right side to tell Excel what you want the maximum value on your chart to be. |
| Major Unit | When the Automatic box is turned on, Excel figures out the distance between the major tick marks for you. If you do not have the Automatic box turned on, you can type a number in the box on the right to tell Excel the distance you want between the major tick marks. |

| | |
|---|---|
| Minor Unit | When the Automatic box is turned on, Excel figures out the distance between the minor tick marks for you. If you do not have the Automatic box turned on, you can type a number in the box on the right to tell Excel the distance you want between the minor tick marks. |
| Category Axis Crosses At | When the Automatic box is turned on, Excel crosses the value axis at zero. If you want the category axis to cross the value axis at some other value, type the value in the box to the right and turn the Automatic box off. |
| Logarithmic Scale | Tells Excel you want to use a logarithmic scale for your chart. |
| Values In Reverse Order | If this option is turned on, you are telling Excel you want values to appear in ascending order from top to bottom. |
| Category Axis Crosses At Maximum Value | If this option is turned on, Excel crosses the category axis and the value axis at the maximum value on the value axis. |
| Value Axis Crosses At Maximum Category | If this option is turned on, the value axis crosses the category axis at the maximum category. This option is relevant only if the chart you are working on is a scatter chart. |
| Patterns | Any changes you made in the Format Scale box are carried out, and the Format Patterns dialog box is displayed. For more information, see "Format Patterns." |
| Font | Any changes you made in the Format Scale box are carried out, and the Format Font dialog box is displayed. For more information, see "Format Font." |

## Format Size

The Format Size option appears on the Format menu only if the active document is a chart. The option allows you to resize a selected chart object using the keyboard. After selecting the chart object and choosing the Format Size option, use the direction keys to size the object, and then press (ENTER).

## Format Text

The Format Text option appears on the Format menu only if the active document is a chart. The option allows you to format selected text. After you select the text you want to format and choose the Format Text option, a dialog box appears with the following options:

| | |
|---|---|
| Text Alignment | Allows you to decide if you want horizontal text aligned to the left, center, or right and vertical text aligned to the top, center, or bottom. |
| Vertical Text | When turned on, Excel stacks the selected text vertically. |
| Automatic Text | When turned on, Excel restores any edited text to the text originally created with Attach Text. |
| Automatic Size | If text border sizes have been changed, turning this box on restores the box to its original size. |
| Patterns | Any changes you made in the Format Text box are carried out, and the Format Patterns dialog box is displayed. For more information, see "Format Patterns." |
| Font | Any changes you made in the Format Text box are carried out, and the Format Font dialog box is displayed. For more information, see "Format Font." |

# FORMULA

The Formula menu is used to build and maintain formulas on the worksheet. This includes creating, using, and deleting range names; adding functions; and switching between absolute and relative references. You can also add notes to cells, go to a particular cell, select cells based on their contents, search and replace text, and select cells of a specified type.

## Formula Apply Names

The Formula Apply Names option allows you to replace cell references with meaningful names in selected formulas on your worksheet. You must select a region in which you want to apply names to your formulas. If you choose the Formula Apply Names option and only one cell is selected, names will be applied to all formulas on the worksheet.

After you select the Formula Apply Names option, a dialog box appears that allows you to select which of the names that you defined with the Formula Define Name option you want applied to the formulas in your selected range. The options available in the dialog box are described here:

*Apply Names*   Allows you to select the names that you want to apply to the formulas in the selected range. You can select as many names as you want. Use the direction keys while holding down the (CTRL) key, and press the spacebar to select or remove a name. Alternatively, hold down (SHIFT) while clicking the mouse on the names you want.

*Ignore Relative/Absolute*   With this box turned off, Excel replaces only absolute cell references with absolute names, relative cell references with relative names, and mixed cell references with mixed names. If the box is turned on, Excel replaces cell references with names despite their type.

***Use Row And Column Names*** With this box turned off, Excel replaces cell references with names only if an exact match can be found. If this box is turned on, Excel tries to replace the cell references with exact names, but if it cannot find a match, it looks for a name defined for the range that contains the cell in question and uses the name it finds in the formula.

If you click the Options button, three more options appear in the dialog box:

***Omit Column Name If Same Column*** If this box is turned on and if the cell in question is in a row-oriented named range, Excel uses the row-oriented named range even if there is a column-oriented name for the same cell. If this box is turned off, Excel replaces cell references with both the column and row name, if both names are defined.

***Omit Row Name If Same Row*** If this box is turned on and if the cell in question is in a column-oriented named range, Excel uses the column-oriented named range even if there is a row-oriented name for the same cell. If this box is turned off, Excel replaces cell references with both the row and column name, if both names are defined.

***Name Order*** Allows you to choose which name you want to come first if the cell is in both a row-oriented named range and a column-oriented named range.

## Formula Create Names

**SHORTCUT** `CTRL+SHIFT+F3`

The Formula Create Names option appears on the Formula menu only if the Full Menus option is activated. This option allows you to define many names at once. You must select a range of cells with names included on one edge of the range. Choose the Formula Create Names option and a dialog box appears allowing you to tell Excel where the names are in your selection. You can put the names along more than one edge in your selection.

| | |
|---|---|
| Top Row | The names are in the top row. Each cell in the top row names the cell below it. |
| Left Column | The names are in the left column. Each cell in the left column names the cell to the right of it. |
| Bottom Row | The names are in the bottom row. Each cell in the bottom row names the cell above it. |
| Right Column | The names are in the right column. Each cell in the right column names the cell to the left of it. |

## Formula Define Names

**SHORTCUT** (CTRL+F3)

The Formula Define Names option allows you to create a name for a cell or a range of cells, a multiple selection, a value, or a formula. You can also delete names that Excel creates automatically when executing other options. For example, if you create a print area with the Set Print Area option, Excel creates a named print range. You can delete that print range using the Formula Define Names option.

**WORKSHEET** If you select a range before you choose the Formula Define Names option, the range you selected automatically appears in the Refers To box inside the dialog box. If you do not select a range before you choose the Formula Define Names option, you can type in a range or formula in the Refers To box. There are four objects in the Define Names dialog box:

***Names In Sheet*** Lists all the names that are defined for the worksheet. If you want to delete a name or change the name it refers to, you can select the name with the mouse or the arrow keys and delete or modify it.

***Name*** Excel proposes a name if possible for the range that you selected before choosing the Formula Define Names command. If the active cell in the selected range contains a name, it proposes that name as the name for the selected range. If you did not select a range or Excel cannot find a name to propose, you can type a name in this box. You also can select a name from the Names in Sheet box, and it will appear in the Name box.

***Refers To*** Contains the selected range if you selected a range before choosing the Formula Define Names command. If you did not select a range, you can type in a range, a formula, a value, or another name. The name in the Name box is the name for what appears or what you put in the Refers To box.

***Delete*** Deletes the selected name from the Names In Sheet box. If you delete a name that appears in formulas on your worksheet, the #NAME? error message appears in the formula.

**MACRO SHEET** If you select the Formula Define Names option when the active document is a macro sheet, the dialog box has an option in addition to all the options just described for the worksheet.

Macro            Allows you to define the type of macro on your macro sheet. There are three options—Function, Command, and None. If you choose the Command option, you also can type a shortcut key using any alphabetic character. To run a macro using the shortcut key, hold down `CTRL` and press the shortcut key.

## Formula Find

**SHORTCUT** `F7`

The Formula Find option allows you to search the selected cells or the entire worksheet for occurrences of text or numbers. If you select cells before you choose the Formula Find option, Excel searches only the selected cells. If you do not select a range before choosing the Formula Find option, Excel searches the entire worksheet. Once you select the Formula Find option, a dialog box appears with the following options:

Find What           Allows you to type the text that you want to search for. You can type **#REF!** and **#NAME?** to find error messages.

Look In             Allows you to choose which cells in the selected range you want to search. You can choose Formulas, Values, or Notes.

Look At            Allows you to decide if you want the text you typed in the Find What box to be matched with the whole number or text in the cell, or part of the number or text in the cell.

Look By            Allows you to decide if you want the search done by rows or columns.

## Formula Goto

**SHORTCUT** `F5`

The Formula Goto option allows you to quickly select a named area or cell. When you choose the Formula Goto option, a dialog box appears. After you choose OK, Excel remembers where you were before, so if you choose Formula Goto again, your previous selection appears in the Reference box automatically. This makes it convenient to go back and forth between two parts of your worksheet.

Goto
: Lists all of the defined names on your worksheet. If you select one of these names and choose OK, the area associated with the defined name is selected on your worksheet.

Reference
: You can type a cell reference or a name in this box and choose OK, and Excel goes to the area or cell you specified.

## Formula Note

**SHORTCUT** `SHIFT+F2`

The Formula Note option allows you to add a note to a cell. The note does not actually appear on the worksheet, but you can print the notes with the worksheets or you can look at notes with the Window Show Info option. The Formula Note option gives you a way of documenting your worksheet. Once you choose the Formula Note option, a dialog box appears with the following options:

Cell
: Allows you to type in a cell reference for which you want to enter a note. If you want to modify

| | |
|---|---|
| | or delete an existing note, you can select a note from the Notes In Sheet box, and the cell reference automatically appears in the Cell box. |
| Notes In Sheet | Allows you to select existing notes so you can modify or delete them. |
| Note | This is where you enter a new note or where the note appears when you select an existing note. |
| Add | If you choose the Add button, the text in the Note box is added to the cell in the Cell box. |
| Delete | If you choose the Delete button, the note selected in the Notes In Sheet box is deleted. |

## Formula Paste Function

### SHORTCUT (SHIFT+F3)

The Formula Paste Function option allows you to paste an Excel built-in function into the Formula bar. If the Formula bar is active when you choose the option, the function is pasted in at the insertion point. If the Formula bar is not active, Excel activates it and pastes the function there. Once you choose the Formula Paste Function option, a dialog box with these two options appears:

| | |
|---|---|
| Paste Function | Lists all of Excel's built-in functions for you to choose from. It also lists any function macros you have created on any open macro sheets. To choose a function, select it and choose the OK button. |
| Paste Arguments | If you turn this box on, descriptions of the arguments are pasted with the function. If the function has more than one argument profile, another dialog box appears where you can choose which one you want. |

## Formula Paste Name

**SHORTCUT** F3

**WORKSHEET** The Formula Paste Name option allows you to paste names that you have previously defined with the Formula Define Names or the Formula Create Names option into the formula bar. You can also paste a list of all defined names onto your worksheet. Once you choose the Formula Paste Name option, a dialog box appears containing the following options:

Paste Name — Lists all defined names for your worksheet. You can choose one of these names to paste by selecting it and then clicking the OK button.

Paste List — The Paste List option tells Excel you want to paste all defined names and what they refer to on your worksheet. The paste region is two columns wide and starts from the active cell. If you have data in the paste region, it is wiped out. If you make a mistake, choose the Edit Undo command immediately.

**MACRO SHEET** If the active document is a macro sheet, the Paste List option behaves differently. Everything else works the same.

Paste List — Tells Excel you want to paste all defined names and what they refer to on your worksheet. The paste region is four columns wide and starts from the active cell. The first column contains the name, the second contains what the name refers to, the third column contains a 1 if the name is for a function macro and a 2 if the name is for a command macro, and the fourth column contains the shortcut key if there is one. If you have data in the paste region, it is wiped out. If you make a mistake, choose the Edit Undo command immediately.

## Formula Reference

### SHORTCUT F4

The Formula Reference option allows you to convert the cell reference in the formula bar to a different kind of cell reference. The cell reference that you want to convert can either be selected, or you can place the insertion point inside or to the right of it. The following table shows how the cell reference changes each time you press F4 or choose the menu option:

| Before | After |
|--------|-------|
| A1     | $A$1  |
| $A$1   | A$1   |
| A$1    | $A1   |
| $A1    | A1    |

## Formula Replace

The Formula Replace option appears on the Formula menu only if the Full Menus option is activated. The Formula Replace option allows you to search for and replace characters with new characters. If you have selected a range, Excel searches for and replaces characters within that range. If you do not select a range before choosing the Formula Replace option, Excel searches for and replaces characters over the whole worksheet. Once you choose the Formula Replace option, a dialog box appears with the following options:

| | |
|---|---|
| Replace | You can type the text you want to replace in the Replace box. If you have done a search using Formula Find, Excel automatically places the searched-for text in the Replace box. You can choose to accept the characters Excel placed in the box for you, or you can type in other characters. You can use the Excel wildcards ? (for any single character) and * (for any number of characters) in the Replace box. |
| With | Type in the characters you want to use as a replacement in this box. |
| Look At | This box allows you to decide if you want the text you typed in the Replace box to be matched with the whole number or text in the cell or part of the number or text in the cell. |
| Look By | This box allows you to decide if you want the search done by rows or columns. |
| Replace All | This option tells Excel to replace all occurrences of the characters in the Replace box with the characters in the With box. |
| Find Next | This option tells Excel to find the next occurrence of the characters in the Replace box. If you want to find the previous occurrence, hold down (SHIFT) while you choose the Find Next option. |
| Replace | This option tells Excel to replace the characters in the Replace box with the characters in the With box if the current cell contains the characters in the Replace box. Excel then searches for the next occurrence of the characters in the Replace box. |

# Formula Select Special

The Formula Select Special option appears on the Formula menu only if the Full Menus option is activated. The Formula Select Special option allows you to select cells with particular characteristics. You define the characteristics by which you want to select in the dialog box that appears after you choose the Formula Select Special option. If you select a range before choosing the Formula Select Special option, Excel selects only within that range. If you select only one cell before choosing the option, Excel selects from the entire worksheet. The options in the dialog box are described here:

*Notes*  Causes Excel to make a multiple selection of all the cells that have a note attached.

*Constants*  Causes Excel to make a multiple selection of all the cells that contain a constant. You use the four boxes under the Formulas option to choose the kinds of constants you want to select.

| Numbers | Constant numbers |
| Text | Constant text |
| Logicals | True and False entered as constants rather than the result of an evaluation |
| Errors | Errors entered as constants rather than the result of an evaluation |

*Formulas*  Causes Excel to make a multiple selection of all the cells that contain a formula. You use the four boxes under the Formulas option to choose the kinds of formulas you want to select.

| | |
|---|---|
| Numbers | Selects cells that have formulas that evaluate to numbers |
| Text | Selects cells that have formulas that evaluate to text |
| Logicals | Selects cells that have formulas that evaluate to True or False |
| Errors | Selects cells that have formulas that produce errors |

***Blanks*** Causes Excel to make a multiple selection of all the cells that contain a blank.

***Current Region*** Causes Excel to make a selection around the active cell.

***Current Array*** If the active cell belongs to an array, this option causes the entire array to be selected.

***Row Differences*** Causes Excel to compare the cell in the same column as the active cell with all the other cells in its row, and then to select cells that are different from the comparison cell.

***Column Differences*** Causes Excel to compare the cell in the same row as the active cell with all the other cells in its column, and then to select cells that are different from the comparison cell.

***Precedents*** Causes Excel to make a multiple selection of all the cells that the formulas in the original selection refer to.

***Dependents*** Causes Excel to make a multiple selection of all the cells that are referred to by formulas in the original selection.

***Direct Only*** A supplement to the Precedents and Dependents options. This option causes Excel to make a multiple selection of all the cells that the formulas in the original selection refer to directly if the Precedents option is on. The Direct Only option causes Excel to make a multiple selection of all the cells that are referred to directly by formulas in the original selection if the Dependents option is on.

*All Levels*   A supplement to the Precedents and Dependents options. This option causes Excel to make a multiple selection of all the cells that the formulas in the original selection refer to directly or indirectly if the Precedents option is on. This option causes Excel to make a multiple selection of all the cells that are referred to directly or indirectly by formulas in the original selection if the Dependents option is on.

# GALLERY

The Gallery menu appears on the menu bar only if the active document is a chart. This menu allows you to choose the format of the active chart. All options on the menu (except Preferred and Set Preferred) work in the same way. When you select the option, a dialog box appears with a pictorial representation of each option for that type of chart. The Next and Previous buttons allow you to display the Gallery dialog box for the next or previous options on the Gallery menu. To choose a type of chart, click on the picture of it and click OK. If you have an overlay chart, hold down (SHIFT) while clicking the OK button to preserve the overlay.

## Gallery Area

The Gallery Area option allows you to set Area as the format for the active chart. When you choose the Gallery Area option from the menu, a dialog box appears that contains pictorial representations of all the different kinds of Area charts available. To set your format, choose one of the Area chart options, and then click OK.

If you have an overlay chart and want to preserve the overlay, hold down (SHIFT) while you click the OK button. The choices in the Area dialog box are as follows:

| | |
|---|---|
| Area | 1. Simple Area chart |
| | 2. 100% Area chart |
| | 3. Area chart with drop lines |
| | 4. Area chart with gridlines |
| | 5. Area chart with the areas labeled |
| Next | Allows you to display the dialog box for the next chart type on the Gallery menu |
| Previous | Allows you to display the dialog box for the previous chart type on the Gallery menu |

## Gallery Bar

The Gallery Bar option allows you to set Bar as the format for the active chart. When you choose the Gallery Bar option from the menu, a dialog box appears that contains pictorial representations of all the different kinds of Bar charts available. To set your format, choose one of the Bar chart options, and then choose OK. If you have an overlay chart and want to preserve the overlay, hold down (SHIFT) while you click the OK button. The choices in the Bar dialog box are as follows:

| | |
|---|---|
| Bar | 1. Simple Bar chart |
| | 2. Bar chart for a singe series with varied patterns |
| | 3. Stacked Bar chart |
| | 4. Overlapped Bar chart |
| | 5. 100% Stacked Bar chart |
| | 6. Bar chart with vertical gridlines |
| | 7. Bar chart with value labels |

| | |
|---|---|
| Next | Allows you to display the dialog box for the next chart type on the Gallery menu |
| Previous | Allows you to display the dialog box for the previous chart type on the Gallery menu |

## Gallery Column

The Gallery Column option allows you to set Column as the format for the active chart. When you choose the Gallery Column option from the menu, a dialog box appears that contains pictorial representations of all the different kinds of Column charts available. To set your format, choose one of the column chart options, and then click OK. If you have an overlay chart and want to preserve the overlay, hold down (SHIFT) while you click the OK button. The choices in the Column dialog box are as follows:

| | |
|---|---|
| Column | 1. Simple Column chart |
| | 2. Column chart for a single series with varied patterns |
| | 3. Stacked Column chart |
| | 4. Overlapped Column chart |
| | 5. 100% Stacked Column chart |
| | 6. Column chart with horizontal gridlines |
| | 7. Column chart with value labels |
| | 8. Column chart with no space between columns |
| Next | Allows you to display the dialog box for the next chart type on the Gallery menu |
| Previous | Allows you to display the dialog box for the previous chart type on the Gallery menu |

## Gallery Combination

The Gallery Combination option allows you to set Combination as the format for the active chart. The Gallery Combination option allows you to create an overlay chart. If there are an odd number of series, there will be one more series in the main chart than in the overlay chart. If there are an even number of series, there will be the same number of series in the main chart as in the overlay chart. If you want to control this default distribution of series, see the Format Overlay option. When you choose the Gallery Combination option from the menu, a dialog box appears that contains pictorial representations of all the different kinds of Combination charts available. To set your format, choose one of the Combination chart options, and then click OK. If you have an overlay chart and want to preserve the overlay, hold down (SHIFT) while you click the OK button. The choices in the Combination dialog box are as follows:

| | |
|---|---|
| Combination | 1. Column main chart and Line overlay chart |
| | 2. Column main chart and Line overlay chart with separate scales |
| | 3. Line main chart and Line overlay chart with separate scales |
| | 4. Area main chart and Column overlay chart |
| | 5. Bar main chart and Line overlay chart with high, low, and closing series for use with stock market applications |
| Next | Allows you to display the dialog box for the next chart type on the Gallery menu |
| Previous | Allows you to display the dialog box for the previous chart type on the Gallery menu |

## Gallery Line

The Gallery Line option allows you to set Line as the format for the active chart. When you choose the Gallery Line option from the menu, a dialog box appears that contains pictorial representations of all the different kinds of Line charts available. To set your format, choose one of the Line chart options, and then click OK. If you have an overlay chart and want to preserve the overlay, hold down (SHIFT) while you click the OK button. The choices in the Line dialog box are as follows:

| | |
|---|---|
| Line | 1. Chart with lines and markers |
| | 2. Chart with lines only |
| | 3. Chart with markers only |
| | 4. Chart with lines, markers, and horizontal gridlines |
| | 5. Chart with lines, markers, and horizontal and vertical gridlines |
| | 6. Chart with lines, markers, and logarithmic scaled gridlines |
| | 7. High-low-close chart with markers and high-low lines |
| | 8. Chart for stock quotes with high-low lines and close markers |
| Next | Allows you to display the dialog box for the next chart type on the Gallery menu |
| Previous | Allows you to display the dialog box for the previous chart type on the Gallery menu |

## Gallery Pie

The Gallery Pie option allows you to set Pie as the format for the active chart. When you choose the Gallery Pie option from the menu, a dialog box appears that contains pictorial representations of all the different kinds of Pie charts available. To set your format, choose one of the Pie chart options, and then click OK. If you have an overlay chart and want to preserve the overlay, hold down (SHIFT) while you click the OK button. The choices in the Pie dialog box are as follows:

| | |
|---|---|
| Pie | 1. Simple Pie chart |
| | 2. Pie chart with the same pattern on every wedge and each wedge labeled with categories |
| | 3. Pie chart with the first wedge exploded |
| | 4. Pie chart with all wedges exploded |
| | 5. Pie chart with category labels |
| | 6. Pie chart with value labels as percentages |
| Next | Allows you to display the dialog box for the next chart type on the Gallery menu |
| Previous | Allows you to display the dialog box for the previous chart type on the Gallery menu |

## Gallery Preferred

The Gallery Preferred option appears on the Gallery menu only if the Full Menus option is activated. The Gallery Preferred option allows you to set the active chart format to the format you set with the Gallery Set Preferred option. Excel's default preferred format is format 1 of Gallery Column.

## Gallery Scatter

The Gallery Scatter option allows you to set Scatter as the format for the active chart. When you choose the Gallery Scatter option from the menu, a dialog box appears that contains pictorial representations of all the different kinds of Scatter charts available. To set your format, choose one of the Scatter chart options, and then click OK. If you have an overlay chart and want to preserve the overlay, hold down (SHIFT) while you click the OK button. The choices in the Scatter dialog box are as follows:

| | |
|---|---|
| Scatter | 1. Scatter chart with markers only |
| | 2. Scatter chart with markers connected with lines |

|  | 3. Scatter chart with markers and both horizontal and vertical gridlines |
|---|---|
|  | 4. Scatter chart with markers and horizontal gridlines |
|  | 5. Scatter chart with markers and logarithmic gridlines |
| Next | Allows you to display the dialog box for the next chart type on the Gallery menu |
| Previous | Allows you to display the dialog box for the previous chart type on the Gallery menu |

## Gallery Set Preferred

The Gallery Set Preferred option appears on the Gallery menu only if the Full Menus option is activated. Gallery Set Preferred allows you to change the default chart, which is the chart format that Excel always uses when you choose the File New Chart option. To change the preferred chart format, change the active chart to the format you want to be the default, and then choose the Gallery Set Preferred option. The next time you open a new chart or choose the Gallery Preferred option, the chart is automatically set to the format you set using the Set Preferred option.

If you want your preferred chart formatting preserved, you can use the File Save Workspace option. The next time you use Excel, you can open the workspace file, and your preferred chart formatting is restored to its previous setting.

# HELP

The Help menu provides access to the help system. This can begin with an index of help topics, a list of keys on the keyboard, or Lotus 1-2-3 or Multiplan equivalent commands. The Help menu also provides access to a tutorial either directly or through the Excel Feature Guide. Finally, the Help menu provides information about the version of Excel you are using and the amount of memory available.

## Help About

The Help About option gives you information about Excel and hardware resources such as how much conventional memory you have available, how much expanded memory you have available, if you have a math coprocessor, and which version of Excel you are running.

## Help Feature Guide

The Help Feature Guide option allows you to start the Excel Feature Guide. The Feature Guide is an on-line reference that explains various features of Excel and gives you an opportunity to practice using the features in a guided environment. The seven parts of the Feature Guide are listed here:

| | |
|---|---|
| 1. What's In The Feature Guide | Tells you how to move around the Feature Guide. |
| 2. Basic Mechanics | Gives descriptions of and opportunities to practice basic Excel skills, such as moving around, using menus, editing, copying, saving, and printing. |
| 3. Multiple Windows | Describes how to use multiple windows, including splitting and freezing, and offers opportunities for guided practice of these options. |
| 4. Worksheet Formatting | Instructs you on how to do formatting, and includes guided practices. |
| 5. Charts | Shows you how to create and customize a chart and gives you an opportunity to practice these options in a guided environment. |

|                        |                                                    |
|------------------------|----------------------------------------------------|
| 6. Macros              | Teaches you how to use Excel's macro capabilities. Guided practice sessions are available to help you learn how to record, use, write, and edit macros. |
| 7. Auditing and Documenting | Helps you learn how to define and apply names to your worksheet. It also shows you how to use notes. Guided practice sessions are available. |

## Help Index

The Help Index option tells Excel to display the Excel help index. You can use the index to find help on any option or function. If you want to get help on any topic listed in the help index, simply select that topic and press (ENTER).

## Help Keyboard

The Help Keyboard option displays help on the keys you can use with Excel. If help is already open, the help window is activated and keyboard help is displayed in the window. If help is not open, Excel opens a help window and displays the keyboard help in that window.

## Help Lotus 123

The Help Lotus 123 option allows you to type a Lotus 1-2-3 command into a dialog box, and Excel tells you the equivalent Excel option, if any.

## Help Multiplan

The Help Multiplan option allows you to type a Multiplan command into a dialog box, and Excel tells you the equivalent Excel option, if any.

## Help Tutorial

The Help Tutorial option starts the Excel tutorial. The tutorial gives you an overview of Excel and a chance to practice using Excel in a guided environment. If you have documents open when you start the tutorial, Excel saves them for you, and when you exit the tutorial, your workspace is restored for you. You can start and stop the tutorial at any time. You need not go all the way through the tutorial after you start it. The following six modules are in the tutorial:

| | |
|---|---|
| 1. How To Use This Tutorial | Tells you how to use the Excel tutorial. |
| 2. Introduction | Explains the key features of Excel, and how to use on-line help. |
| 3. Worksheets | Helps you learn how to create, format, edit, print, and save worksheets and teaches you how to use functions. |
| 4. Charts | Introduces Excel charts, and shows you how to create, format, edit, print, and save charts. |
| 5. Databases | Introduces Excel databases and teaches you how to set up and use a database. |
| 6. Macros | Explains the Excel macros basics, and shows you how to record, run, and edit macros. |

## INFO

The Info menu appears as part of a new Menu bar if you choose Show Info from the Windows menu (it is the only unique menu on that Menu bar). The Info menu lets you toggle (turn on or off) nine types of information that can be displayed in the Info window. These nine types of information are the options on the menu:

| | |
|---|---|
| Cell | Displays the address of the active cell, which is displayed in the Info window. Default is on. |
| Dependents | Displays the list of cells whose formulas refer to the active cell. Default is off. |
| Format | Displays the format characteristics of the active cell, including alignment, borders, font, number format, and shading. Default is off. |
| Formula | Displays the contents of the active cell as it is displayed in the Edit area of the Formula bar. Default is on. |
| Precedents | Displayed the list of cells referred to by formulas in the active cell. Default is off. |
| Protection | Displays the protection status of the active cell, telling you if the cell is locked or the formula is hidden. Default is off. |
| Names | Displays the list of range names that include the active cell. Default is off. |
| Note | Displays the contents of a note attached to the active cell. Default is on. |
| Value | Displays the contents of the active cell as it is displayed in the cell itself. Default is off. |

# MACRO

The Macro menu allows you to record functions on the macro sheet as you carry out commands on a regular worksheet, to run macros once they have been recorded or written, and to set several options for recording macros.

## Macro Absolute Record

The Macro Absolute Record option appears on the Macro menu only if the Full Menus option is activated. The Macro Absolute Record option allows you to tell Excel to record your macro using absolute cell references. After choosing this option you can go ahead and record. This menu option changes to Macro Relative Record as soon as you choose Macro Absolute Record.

## Macro Record

The Macro Record option turns on the macro recorder. It records your following actions so you can repeat them later. Your actions are recorded on a macro sheet. If no macro sheet is open, Excel opens one for you. The Excel macro recording function works like a tape recorder. You turn the recorder on, do the actions that you want recorded, turn the recorder off, and play it back with the Macro Run option. Once you choose the Macro Record option, a dialog box appears with the following options:

| | |
|---|---|
| Name | Allows you to type in a name for your macro. If you do not type in a name, Excel names the macro for you. |
| Key | Allows you to define a shortcut key. You start the macro by holding down (CTRL) and pressing the shortcut key. You can use any upper- or lowercase letter. |

After you type in the name and the shortcut key, click the OK button. Everything you do from now on is recorded, until you turn the recorder off. When you want to stop recording, choose Macro Stop Recorder, which appears on the menu only after you choose the Macro Record option.

## Macro Relative Record

The Macro Relative Record option appears on the Macro menu only if the Full Menus option is activated. The Macro Relative Record option allows you to tell Excel to record your macro using relative cell references. After choosing this option you can go ahead and record. This menu option changes to Macro Absolute Record as soon as you choose the Macro Relative Record option.

## Macro Run

The Macro Run option allows you to run a macro from any open macro sheet. Once you choose the Macro Run option, a dialog box appears with the following options:

Run  Lists all the available macros. Macros are available if they are on open macro sheets and they are named. Each named macro appears in the Run box in the format *Filename*.XLM!*Macro.Name*. Select the macro you want to run, and click the OK button.

Reference  Allows you to type the name of the macro you want to run yourself. If you chose a macro from the Run box, the name automatically appears in the Reference box.

## Macro Set Recorder

The Macro Set Recorder option appears on the Macro menu only if the Full Menus option is activated. The Macro Set Recorder option allows you to tell Excel where on the macro sheet you want the next macro you record to be placed. If you select a range before you choose the Macro Set Recorder option, Excel starts recording your macro in the upper-left corner, goes down the column to the end, and then goes to the top of the next column, and so on. If you select only a cell, Excel uses that cell as the start cell and records the macro down in the same column.

### Macro Start Recorder

The Macro Start Recorder option appears on the Macro menu only if the Full Menus option is activated. The Macro Start Recorder option allows you to record your subsequent actions on a macro sheet. You must first use the Macro Set Recorder option to set the macro range or have used the Macro Record previously. Once the Macro Start Recorder option has been chosen, the Macro Stop Recorder option appears on the menu in its place. You can use the Macro Start Recorder and Macro Stop Recorder options to pause while you are recording a macro.

### Macro Stop Recorder

Macro Stop Recorder stops a macro recording that you started with either Macro Record or Macro Start Record. The Macro Stop Recorder option appears on the menu after you start recording a macro in place of the Macro Start Recorder option.

## OPTIONS

The Options menu is the catch-all menu for options that do not fit in any other menu. It provides the means of specifying the areas of the worksheet to be printed and to identify repeated titles on a printout. The Options menu also allows you to set manual page breaks, to determine how your screen will look, to freeze columns on the left and rows on the top of a worksheet, and to protect a document (worksheet, chart, or macro sheet) or window from being overwritten. Additionally, you can use the Options menu to set how Excel calculates a worksheet; force the recalculation of a worksheet at any time; change overall defaults like the display of the Status bar, scroll bars, and Formula bar; and change the type of menus.

## Options Calculate Document

**SHORTCUT** (SHIFT+F9)

The Options Calculate Document option appears on the Options menu only if you hold down (SHIFT) when you choose the Options menu. The Options Calculate Document option allows you to calculate the active worksheet, chart, or macro sheet. The calculations are done according to the settings in the Update Remote Reference and Precision As Displayed options in the Options Calculation dialog box. Excel normally does calculations on your document automatically. If you set the calculation to Manual in the Options Calculation dialog box, you must tell Excel to calculate the document using the Options Calculate Document option or the Options Calculate Now option.

## Options Calculate Now

**SHORTCUT** (F9)

The Options Calculate Now option allows you to calculate all open documents. The Options Calculate Now option also allows you to calculate a formula in the Formula bar and replace it with the result. To calculate formulas in all the open documents, simply choose the Options Calculate Now option, making sure the Formula bar is not active. To calculate a formula in the Formula bar, choose the

Options Calculate Now option while the Formula bar is active and the formula in the Formula bar begins with an equal sign.

## Options Calculation

The Options Calculation option lets you control the calculation and recalculation of open documents. This is the option you choose if you want to turn automatic recalculation off. When you choose the Options Calculation option, a dialog box appears. The dialog box has three sections, each with several options, as described here:

*Calculation*   There are three options within the Calculation box:

| | |
|---|---|
| Automatic | The default setting for Excel. Every time a change is made to your document that requires recalculation, it is done automatically. |
| Automatic Except Tables | This option tells Excel to recalculate everything automatically except formulas within tables. When you want to calculate the tables, use the Options Calculate Now option or the Options Calculate Document option. |
| Manual | This option tells Excel you do not want to recalculate your documents until you explicitly tell it to with the Options Calculate Now option or the Options Calculate Document option. |

*Iteration*   Turn this box on to control the number of iterations Excel does on a recalculation. You can specify the maximum number of iterations in the Maximum Iterations box. Alternatively, you can put a value in the Maximum Change box to tell Excel to iterate until the maximum change in any value is less than the number you specify. If the Iterations box is turned off, Excel's defaults are 100 iterations and a maximum value of 0.001.

***Maximum Iterations*** In this box you can specify the maximum number of iterations Excel does when recalculating a document, if the Iterations box is turned on. If the Iterations box is turned off, Excel's defaults are 100 iterations and a maximum value of 0.001.

***Maximum Change*** In this box you can specify the number that Excel stops iterating when all values change less than that amount, when the Iterations box is turned on. If the Iterations box is turned off, Excel's defaults are 100 iterations and a maximum value of 0.001.

***Update Remote References*** When this box is turned on, formulas with remote references are updated every time the document is recalculated. When the box is turned off, formulas with remote references are not updated each time the document is recalculated.

***Precision As Displayed*** If this box is turned on, Excel stores the calculated values in cells exactly as displayed. If this box is turned off, Excel stores the calculated values in cells with a precision of 15 digits. If you recalculate your worksheet with the Precision As Displayed box turned on and then turn the box off, your values will not be restored to a full precision of 15 digits.

***1904 Date System*** This box causes dates to be calculated using the 1904 system if turned on, and the 1900 system if turned off. Dates are stored in Excel as serial numbers, and a serial number of 1 will produce a date of 1/1/1900 in the 1900 system, and a date of 1/1/1904 in the 1904 system. The usual format is 1900, but if you imported a file from another application, and your dates are off by four years, turn the 1904 Date System box on.

# Options Display

The Options Display option allows you to change the active worksheet's display. Once you choose the Options Display option, a dialog box appears that you can use to set the alternatives for the display. The options in the dialog box are described here:

***Formulas*** If the Formulas box is turned on, cells with formulas in them display the formulas rather than the values to which the formulas evaluate. If the Formulas box is turned off, values are displayed rather than formulas.

***Gridlines*** If the Gridlines box is turned on, gridlines are displayed on your worksheet. If the Gridlines box is turned off, gridlines are not displayed on your worksheet.

***Row & Column Headings*** If the Row & Column Headings box is turned on, row and column headings are displayed on your worksheet. If the Row & Column Headings box is turned off, row and column headings are not displayed on your worksheet.

***Zero Values*** If the Zero Values box is turned on, zero values are displayed on your worksheet. If the Zero Values box is turned off, zero values are not displayed on your worksheet, and blank cells are displayed in their place.

***Gridline & Heading Color*** This box allows you to choose the colors you want your gridlines and headings to be. You can set the box to Automatic or choose one of the following colors:

| **Color** | **Box to Choose** |
| --- | --- |
| White | White box |
| Black | Black box |
| Red | R |
| Green | G |
| Blue | B |

Yellow      Y
Magenta     M
Cyan        C

## Options Freeze Panes

The Options Freeze Panes option appears on the Options menu only if the Full Menus option is activated. The Options Freeze Panes option allows you to tell Excel not to scroll parts of your worksheet when you have used the Control Split option to split your worksheet. If you have a vertical split, the pane or panes to the left of the split do not scroll horizontally. If you have a horizontal split, the pane or panes above the split do not scroll vertically.

## Options Full Menus

The Options Full Menus option tells Excel to display all the menus with all options available. Once you choose the Options Full Menus option, the Short Menus option appears in its place on the Options menu.

## Options Protect Document

The Options Protect Document option appears on the Options menu only if the Full Menus option is activated. The Options Protect Document option allows you to prevent alterations to be made on your worksheet. You can set cell protection options with the Format Cell Protection option. If you turn off the Gridlines option with the Options Display option, all protected cells appear underlined. After you choose the Protect Document option, a dialog box appears with the following options:

| | |
|---|---|
| Password | Allows you to enter a password for your document. If you protect your document with a password, do not forget your password. There is no way to find out what your password is if you forget it and no way to access your document without it. |
| Contents | If you turn the Contents option on, everything in your worksheet is protected except the windows. You cannot change the formatting or contents of any cells that have been locked. |
| Windows | If you turn the Windows option on, you cannot change the worksheet's window. You can only close a window that has been protected with the File Close option. |

## Options Remove Page Break

The Options Remove Page Break option appears on the Options menu only if the Full Menus option is activated. The Options Remove Page Break option allows you to move page breaks that you set with the Options Set Page Break option. It will not remove automatic page breaks. The Options Set Page Break option appears on the Options menu only if the active cell is directly above or to the right of a manual page break set with the Option Set Page Break option. If the active cell is not directly above or to the right of a manual page break, the option Set Page Break appears on the Options menu instead of the Remove Page Break option.

## Options Set Page Break

The Options Set Page Break option appears on the Options menu only if the Full Menus option is activated. The Set Page Break option allows you to manually set page breaks. The active cell determines where the page break appears; it is to the left of and above the active cell. You can remove manual page breaks only with the Remove Page Breaks option.

## Options Set Print Area

The Options Set Print Area option allows you to select only part of your worksheet to print. You can select one block or use (SHIFT+F8) to make a multiple selection. Multiple selections are printed one section at a time. If you want to delete your Print Area, you must delete the named object Print_Area with the Formula Define Names Delete option. If you do not set a print area, the entire worksheet is printed. If you use print titles in conjunction with a print area, make sure that your print titles selection does not overlap your print area selection. If they do overlap, your print titles will be printed twice, once as the print titles and once as the print area.

## Options Set Print Titles

The Options Set Print Titles option appears on the Options menu only if the Full Menus option is activated. Set Print Titles allows you to set selected columns and/or rows to be printed on every page of your printed document. For example, if you have column headings in row 1, you could select row 1 and choose the Set Print Titles option. Even if your worksheet is many pages long, at the top of every page the column headings in row 1 are printed. Row headings work the same way. You can think of row and column headings that you define as a custom version of Excel's row numbers and column letters.

When you select a print titles area, you must select the entire row or column. You can have more than one row or column in the print titles area, but they must be together on the worksheet. If you want to select both rows and columns as the print titles area, use (SHIFT+F8) to make a multiple selection. If you want to delete the print titles area that you set with Set Print Titles, you must delete it with the Formula Define Names Delete option.

If you use print titles in conjunction with a print area, make sure that your print titles selection does not overlap your print area selection. If they do overlap, your print titles will be printed twice, once as the print titles and once as the print area.

## Options Short Menus

The Options Short Menus option tells Excel to display the menus with the most frequently used options only. Once you choose the Short Menus option, the Full Menus option appears in its place on the Options menu.

## Options Unfreeze Panes

The Options Unfreeze Panes option appears on the Options menu only if the Full Menus option is activated and only after you choose the Freeze Panes option. The Options Unfreeze Panes option tells Excel to unfreeze panes you froze with the Options Freeze Panes option. Once you choose the Unfreeze Panes option, the Freeze Panes option appears once again on the Options menu.

## Options Unprotect Document

The Options Unprotect Document option appears on the Options menu only if the Full Menus option is activated. This option allows you to unprotect a document that you protected with the Options Protect Document option. Once you choose the Options Unprotect Document option, a dialog box appears asking for the password you created. You must remember your password to unprotect your document.

## Options Workspace

The Options Workspace option appears on the Options menu only if the Full Menus option is activated. The Options Workspace option allows you to set various options that apply to your entire Excel session. Once you choose the Options Workspace option, a dialog box appears with the following options:

Fixed Decimal   If the Fixed Decimal box is turned on, Excel uses the number you put in the Places box to automatically place a decimal place in a number for you.

Places   If the Fixed Decimal box is turned on, Excel uses the number you put in the Places box to automatically place a decimal place in a number for you. If you type **2** in the Places box and then type the number **300**, 3.00 is entered in the cell. If you type **-2** in the Places box and then type the number **300**, 30,000 appears in the cell. Only numbers that you enter without a decimal are affected. If you type **3.9**, 3.9 appears in the cell.

R1C1   If this box is turned on, cell references are displayed in the format R1C1. If this box is turned off, cell references are displayed in the format A1. The cell B5 in format A1 appears as $B$5. In R1C1 format, B5 appears as R2C5. Notice that both rows and columns are numbered.

Status Bar   If the Status Bar box is turned on, the Status bar is displayed. If the Status Bar box is turned off, the Status bar is not displayed.

Scroll Bars   If the Scroll Bars box is turned on, scroll bars appear on your worksheets. Scroll bars allow

| | |
|---|---|
| Formula Bar | you to move around your worksheet quickly with a mouse. If the Scroll Bars box is turned off, you will be able to see more of your worksheets.<br>If the Formula Bar box is turned on, the Formula bar is displayed. If the Formula Bar box is turned off, the Formula bar is not displayed, even when you are entering or editing a formula. |
| Alternate Menu Key | This box allows you to enter a character you can use to access the menu. Normally you access the menu with ALT or the slash key. If you want to access the menu with something other than the slash key, type it in this box. |
| Ignore Remote Requests | If this box is turned on, Excel ignores Dynamic Data Exchange (DDE) requests from other Windows application. If you want to link an Excel document with another window's application, this box should be turned off. |

# WINDOW

The Window menu allows you to open another window on the same worksheet, to look at information behind the current active cell, to arrange all open windows so they can be seen on the screen, to hide or unhide a window, and to choose among open windows.

## To Activate a Window

The menu does not have an Activate Window option. Instead, each window you have open is listed. Choose the window that you want to activate from the list of names.

## Window Arrange All

The Window Arrange All option rearranges all your open windows so they appear on your screen in a nonoverlapping manner. The space on the screen is divided as evenly as possible between the windows. This option is especially useful when you have several open windows overlapping and you "lose track" of a window. This option makes all your windows appear on the screen at once. You can then resize and move the windows where you want them.

## Window Hide

The Window Hide option appears on the Window menu only when the Full Menus option is activated. The Window Hide option hides the active window. The document in the window is still open, and you can reference it the same way you reference any other open document. If it is a protected document (see "Options Protect Document"), you are asked for a password when you hide it and again when you unhide it.

## Window More Windows

The Window More Windows option appears on the Window menu only if you have more than nine open windows. If you have more than nine windows open and you choose the More Windows option, a dialog box appears that lists all of the windows you have open. You can select one of the windows, and choose OK, and Excel activates that window.

## Window New Window

The Window New Window option allows you to create an additional window for the active document. The two windows are completely independent of each other. With two windows in the same document, you can see two different areas of your spreadsheet at once.

## Window Show Document

**SHORTCUT** `CTRL+F2`

The Window Show Document option appears on the Window menu only when the Full Menus option is activated and the Info window is the active window. The Window Show Document option allows you to return to the active document.

## Window Show Info

**SHORTCUT** `CTRL+F2`

Window Show Info appears on the Window menu only when the Full Menus option is activated and the active document is a worksheet or macro sheet. The Info window shows the following information about the active document:

| | |
|---|---|
| Cell | The active cell |
| Formula | The formula in the active cell |
| Value | The value the active cell evaluates to |
| Format | The format of the active cell |
| Protect | The cell protection status of the active cell |
| Names | The names defined for the active cell |
| Precedents | The cells that the formula in this cell refers to |
| Dependents | The cells that refer to the active cell |
| Note | The note attached to the cell |

You can control which of these items the Info window displays by using the Info menu options. The Info menu appears only if the Full Menus option is activated.

## Window Unhide

The Window Unhide option appears on the Window menu only if the Full Menus option is activated. The Window Unhide option allows you to unhide a hidden window. If you have only one window hidden when you choose the Window Unhide option, Excel simply unhides it. If you have more than one window hidden when you choose the Window Unhide option, Excel displays a dialog box that allows you to select the window you want to unhide.

# 13

# FUNCTIONS

Arrays
Summary of Functions by Type
Alphabetical List of Functions

Functions are predefined formulas that considerably extend the power of Excel. With them you can perform with one command many calculations that would otherwise require a complex formula or not be possible at all in Excel.

This chapter provides two lists of functions. The first is a brief summary that lists the functions by type: database, financial, information, logical, lookup, mathematical, matrix, statistical, text, time and date, and trigonometric. The second list is alphabetic and describes each function in more detail. It displays the arguments required by the function and gives a short example. First, a brief discussion of arrays is necessary.

## ARRAYS

Several functions have arrays as arguments and/or return arrays as their results. An *array* is nothing more than a range—a rectangular set of cells on a worksheet. An array is displayed in braces ({ }); for example, {A1:C6} is an array. As long as an array is used only as an argument in a function, it is no different from a range. It behaves and should be handled exactly like a range, and it is normally called a range in this book. When a function returns an array it is called an *array function,* and it is treated differently from other functions.

Since an array function returns an array, it fills several cells, not just one as do other functions. Therefore, before entering an array function, you must select or highlight a range of cells to be used for the result of the function. Also, you must tell Excel that it is working with an array. You do this by pressing (CTRL+SHIFT+ENTER) instead of (ENTER) after you complete typing the function. When you press (CTRL+SHIFT+ENTER), Excel places braces around the function or formula and you will see them in the edit area of the Formula bar when you highlight any one of the cells used by the array function. You cannot type the braces; they must be placed there by Excel. If you edit an array formula, the braces disappear. After editing, you must again press (CTRL+SHIFT+ENTER) to tell Excel it is working with an array.

As an example of an array function, look at how the COLUMN function is entered. The COLUMN function returns an array that contains the column numbers in a range. Therefore, the formula =COLUMN(A1:C3) returns the horizontal array {1,2,3}. Since there are three elements in the resulting array you need to highlight three cells in a row prior to entering the formula. Do that and enter the formula:

Highlight A1:C1, type =**column(a1:c3)**, and then press (CTRL+SHIFT+ENTER). The number 1 appears in A1, 2 in B1, and 3 in C1, representing the column numbers of the columns in the range A1:C3.

# SUMMARY OF FUNCTIONS BY TYPE

The following list summarizes the functions by type. A more complete description of each function is given in the alphabetic list of functions that follows this summary.

## Database Functions

**DAVERAGE**  Based on criteria, returns an average of the values in a field of a database table.

**DCOUNT**  Based on criteria, returns a count of the number of cells containing numbers in a field of a database table.

**DCOUNTA**  Based on criteria, returns a count of the number of nonblank cells in a field of a database table.

**DMAX**  Based on criteria, returns the largest value found in a field of a database table.

**DMIN**  Based on criteria, returns the smallest value found in a field of a database table.

**DPRODUCT**  Based on criteria, returns the product of the values in a field of a database.

**DSTDEV** Based on criteria, calculates the sample standard deviation of values in a field of a database table. More accurate than DSTDEVP with small tables.

**DSTDEVP** Based on criteria, calculates the population standard deviation of all the values in a field of a database table. More accurate than DSTDEV with large tables.

**DSUM** Based on criteria, adds values in a field of a database table.

**DVAR** Based on criteria, returns the sample variance of values in a field of a database table. More accurate than DVARP when the number of items is small.

**DVARP** Based on criteria, returns the population variance of values in a field of a database table. More accurate than DVAR when the number of items is large.

## Financial Functions

**DDB** Returns the depreciation expense for an asset using the double declining balance method.

**FV** Returns the future value of a series of equal payments.

**IPMT** Returns the interest payment amount for a loan, given the interest and loan term.

**IRR** Returns the internal rate of return for a series of cash flows.

**MIRR** Returns the modified internal rate of return for a series of cash flows.

**NPER** Returns the number of payments for a loan or investment.

**NPV** Returns the net present value of a series of cash flows.

**PMT** Returns a payment amount for a loan, given the interest and loan term.

**PPMT** Returns a principle payment amount for a loan, given the period, interest rate, present value, and loan term.

**PV** Returns the present value of a series of equal payments.

**RATE** Returns the interest rate generated on an investment.

**SLN** Returns the depreciation expense for an asset using the straight-line depreciation method.

**SYD** Returns the depreciation expense for an asset using the sum-of-the-year's-digits depreciation method.

## Information Functions

**AREAS** Returns the number of selections (areas) in a multiple selection.

**CELL** Returns information about a cell.

**COLUMN** Returns an array of column numbers in a given range.

**COLUMNS**   Returns the number of columns contained in a given range.

**INDIRECT**   Returns the contents of a cell from its reference.

**ISBLANK**   Returns a logical True value for a blank value or a logical False value for anything other than a blank value.

**ISERR**   Returns a logical True value for an error value other than the value #N/A or a logical False value for the value #N/A or anything other than an error value.

**ISERROR**   Returns a logical True value for any error value or a logical False value for anything other than any error value.

**ISLOGICAL**   Return a logical True value for a logical value, or a logical False value for anything other than a logical value.

**ISNA**   Returns a logical True value for the value #N/A or a logical False value for any value other than #N/A.

**ISNONTEXT**   Returns a logical True value if a cell contains anything but text; returns a logical False value if the cell contains text.

**ISNUMBER**   Returns a logical True value if a cell contains a number; returns a logical False value if the cell contains anything but a number.

**ISREF**   Returns a logical True value if a cell contains a reference; returns a logical False value if the cell contains anything but a reference.

**ISTEXT**  Returns a logical True value if a cell contains text; returns a logical False value if the cell contains anything but text.

**N**  Returns the value of the first cell in a range. If the cell contains anything but a number or a logical True value, N returns 0.

**NA**  This returns a value of #N/A to designate that data is not available.

**ROW**  Returns an array of row numbers in a given range.

**ROWS**  Returns the number of rows contained in a given range.

**T**  Returns the text in the first cell in a range. If the cell contains anything but text, T returns the empty string ("").

**TYPE**  Returns the type of the argument.

## Logical Functions

**AND**  Returns True if all arguments evaluate to logical True values.

**FALSE**  Returns a logical False value.

**IF**  Evaluates a condition or equation for true or false, and returns one value for a true condition and another value for a false condition.

**NOT**  Returns a logical True value if the argument evaluates to a logical False value.

**OR** Returns a logical True value if any argument evaluates to a logical True value.

**TRUE** Returns a logical True value.

## Lookup Functions

**CHOOSE** Searches for a value or string in a group of values or strings.

**HLOOKUP** Returns the contents of a specified cell from a horizontal lookup table.

**INDEX** Returns the value of a specified cell from a two- or three-dimensional lookup table.

**LOOKUP** Returns the contents of a specified cell from a lookup table.

**MATCH** Returns the index of a specified cell from a lookup table.

**VLOOKUP** Returns the contents of a specified cell from a vertical lookup table.

## Mathematical Functions

**ABS** Returns the absolute value of a value.

**EXP** Raises the constant e to a specific power.

**FACT** Returns the factorial of a value.

**INT** Returns the integer portion of a value.

**LN** Returns the natural (base e) logarithm of a number.

**LOG** Calculates the logarithm of a value to a specified base.

**LOG10** Calculates the base 10 logarithm of a value.

**MOD** Returns the modulus (the remainder) of a division.

**PI** Returns the value $\pi$ (3.1415926535...).

**PRODUCT** Returns the product of the arguments.

**RAND** Returns a random number between 0 and 1.

**ROUND** Rounds a number to a specific number of decimal places.

**SIGN** Returns the sign of a value.

**SQRT** Calculates the square root of a value.

**TRUNC** Returns the integer part of a value.

## Matrix Functions

**MDETERM** Returns the determinant of an array.

**MINVERSE**  Returns the inverse of an array.

**MMULT**  Returns the product of two arrays.

**TRANSPOSE**  Returns the transposition of an array.

## Statistical Functions

**AVERAGE**  Returns the average of a range of values.

**COUNT**  Returns the number of cells containing numbers in a range.

**COUNTA**  Returns the number of non-blank cells in a range.

**GROWTH**  Returns the values on an exponential growth trend.

**LINEST**  Returns the parameters of a linear trend.

**LOGEST**  Returns the parameters of an exponential trend.

**MAX**  Returns the maximum value in a range of values.

**MIN**  Returns the minimum value in a range of values.

**STDEV**  Returns the sample standard deviation for a range of values.

**STDEVP**  Returns the population standard deviation of a range of values.

**SUM**  Returns the sum for a range of cells.

**TREND**  Returns the values on a linear trend.

**VAR**  Returns the sample variance for a range of values.

**VARP**  Returns the population variance of a range of values.

## Text Functions

**CHAR**  Returns the ASCII (American Standard Code for Information Interchange) character that corresponds to a given code.

**CLEAN**  Returns the text string with all nonprintable characters removed.

**CODE**  Examines the first character in a text string and returns the ASCII code corresponding to it.

**DOLLAR**  Returns a text string of a given number in currency format.

**EXACT**  Compares two text strings and returns True if the two are the same and False if they differ.

**FIND**  Searches for a text string within a text string, starting at an offset, and returns the position number of the first occurrence of the first string in the second.

**FIXED**  Returns a text string that is the number argument rounded.

**LEFT**  Returns the number of designated characters positioned at the beginning of the text string.

**LEN**  Returns the number of characters in a text string.

**LOWER**  Converts uppercase letters in a text string to lowercase.

**MID**  Returns the number of characters at a specified position in a text string.

**PROPER**  Converts the first character in each word to uppercase and the rest of the characters to lowercase, as in a proper name.

**REPLACE**  Replaces a given number of characters in one text string, beginning at an offset, with the characters from another text string.

**REPT**  Repeats or copies a text string a specified number of times.

**RIGHT**  Returns the designated number of characters positioned at the end of a text string.

**SEARCH**  Searches for a text string within a text string and returns the position number of the first occurrence of the first string in the second.

**SUBSTITUTE**  Replaces a given number of characters in one text string with the characters from another text string.

**TEXT**  Converts a value to a text string using the format given.

**TRIM**  Removes consecutive, leading, and trailing spaces from a text string.

**UPPER**  Converts all lowercase letters in a text string to uppercase.

**VALUE**  Makes a value out of a text string that looks like a number.

## Time and Date Functions

**DATE**  Returns the date serial number for a set of year, month, and day values.

**DATEVALUE**  Calculates the date serial number for a text string that looks like a date.

**DAY**  Returns the day of the month—a number from 1 to 31—from a date serial number.

**HOUR**  Returns the hour from a time serial number. The hour can be a number from 0 (midnight) to 23 (11:00 PM).

**MINUTE**  Returns the minutes from a time serial number. The resulting minute can be a number from 0 to 59.

**MONTH**  Returns the month of the year—a number from 1 to 12—from a date serial number.

**NOW**  Returns the serial number for the current time and date.

**SECOND** Returns the second in a time serial number. The second returned can be a number from 0 to 59.

**TIME** Returns the time serial number for a given hour, minutes, and seconds.

**TIMEVALUE** Returns the time serial number for a text string that looks like a time.

**WEEKDAY** Returns the day of the week corresponding to the given serial number.

**YEAR** Returns the year—a number from 1900 to 2078—from a date serial number.

## Trigonometric Functions

**ACOS** Returns the arccosine of a value.

**ASIN** Returns the arcsine of a value.

**ATAN** Returns the arctangent of a value.

**ATAN2** Returns the four-quadrant arctangent of a value.

**COS** Returns the cosine of an angle.

**SIN** Returns the sine of an angle.

**TAN** Returns the tangent of an angle.

# ALPHABETICAL LIST OF FUNCTIONS

This section provides an alphabetical list of all Excel functions. It includes the arguments required for each function, a description, and an example.

## ABS(x)

Returns the positive absolute value of x.

*Example*   =ABS(-2400) returns the value 2400.

## ACOS(x)

Returns the arccosine in radians of a value between -1 and 1 (radians times 180/PI( ) equals degrees).

*Example*   =ACOS(.5) returns the arccosine of .5—1.047 radians or 60 degrees.

## AND(x1,x2,...xn)

Returns True if all arguments evaluate to logical True values. If any argument evaluates to a logical False, returns a False value. This function can have up to 14 arguments. If any of the arguments are references, they should refer to cells or arrays that contain logical values. If there are no logical values specified, this function returns the error message #VALUE!.

*Example*   =AND(E4>200) returns True if the cell E4 contains a value greater than 200; otherwise it returns False.

## AREAS(x)

Returns the number of selection (areas) in the argument. The argument x can be a reference to a single or multiple selection.

***Example*** =AREAS(Inventory) returns 2 if the name Inventory refers to the multiple selection A1:B200,F1:G200.

## ASIN(x)

Returns the arcsine in radians of a value between -1 and 1 (radians times 180/PI( ) equals degrees).

***Example*** =ASIN(.5) returns the arcsine of .5—.523 radians or 30 degrees.

## ATAN(x)

Returns the arctangent in radians of a value (radians times 180/PI( ) equals degrees).

***Example*** =ATAN(.5) returns the arctangent of .5—.463 radians or 26.6 degrees.

## ATAN2(x-coordinate-of-an-angle, y-coordinate-of-an-angle)

Returns the four-quadrant arctangent in radians of an angle, given the x and y coordinates of the angle (radians time 180/PI( ) equals degrees).

***Example*** =ATAN2(-.5,.5) returns the four-quadrant arctangent of the angle whose *x* and *y* coordinates are -.5 and .5, respectively—2.356 radians or 135 degrees.

## AVERAGE(*range1,range2,...rangen*)

Returns the average of all the values in the listed ranges. There is a limit of 14 arguments.

***Example*** =AVG(H15:H35) returns the average of the values in cells H15 to H35.

## CELL(*attribute,[range]*)

Examines the first cell in a range and returns information based on the attribute specified. If the range argument is omitted, the current selection is considered to be the range. The following attributes can be used:

| | |
|---|---|
| "address" | The absolute cell address |
| "col" | The column number |
| "contents" | The contents of the cell |
| "format" | The cell format: |
| | C0 for Currency, 0 digits to right of decimal |
| | C2 for Currency, 2 digits to right of decimal |
| | F0 for Fixed, 0 digits to right of decimal |
| | F2 for Fixed, 2 digits to right of decimal |
| | G for General, a label, or a blank cell |
| | P0 for Percent, 0 digits to right of decimal |
| | P2 for Percent, 2 digits to right of decimal |
| | S2 for Scientific, 2 digits to right of decimal |

| | |
|---|---|
| | D1 for date in dd-mmm-yy format |
| | D2 for date in dd-mmm format |
| | D3 for date in mmm-yy format |
| | D4 for date in mm/dd/yy or dd/mm/yy h:mm format |
| | D6 for time in hh:mm:ss am/pm format |
| | D7 for time in hh:mm am/pm format |
| | D8 for time in hh:mm:ss format |
| | D9 for time in hh:mm format |
| "prefix" | The label prefix: |
| | ' if left-aligned label |
| | " if right-aligned label |
| | ^ if centered label |
| | Blank if empty or a value |
| "protect" | The protection status: |
| | 1 if the cell is protected |
| | 0 if the cell is unprotected |
| "row" | The row number |
| "type" | The type of data that the cell contains: |
| | b if blank |
| | v if a value or formula |
| | l if a label or text |
| "width" | The column width |

*Example* =IF(CELL("format",G25)=d1,0,1) returns 0 if cell G25 contains a date format; otherwise it returns 1.

## CHAR(*ASCII-code*)

Returns the character matching the ASCII (American Standard Code for Information Interchange) code.

*Example* =CHAR(171) produces the one-half symbol (½).

## CHOOSE(*offset,list*)

Returns a value or a text string from a position in a list that is offset by the value specified. The offset can be any value from 1 to the number of items in the list. The number 1 retrieves the contents of the first item, and *n*, where *n* is the number of items in the list, retrieves the contents of the last item.

*Example* =CHOOSE(3,"Jan","Feb","Mar","Apr","May") returns the string value "Mar".

## CLEAN(*string*)

Returns the text string with all nonprintable characters removed.

*Example* =CLEAN(A1) returns the string in cell A1 with all nonprintable characters removed.

## CODE(*string*)

Returns the ASCII (American Standard Code for Information Interchange) code that is represented by the first character in the text string. The string can be a literal string, a formula or function that equates to a string, or a reference to a cell containing a string or label.

*Example* =CODE("abc") returns the value 97, which corresponds to the lowercase letter "a."

## COLUMN(*range*)

Returns a horizontal array of the column numbers (*not* the number of columns) in a range. If you press (ENTER) after entering this function, you get the column number of the first column in the range. If you press (CTRL+SHIFT+ENTER) after entering this function, you get a horizontal array of all of the columns in the range.

*Example*  =COLUMN(A2:D3) returns 1 if you press (ENTER) or {1,2,3,4} if you press (CTRL+SHIFT+ENTER) after highlighting a row of four cells.

## COLUMNS(*range*)

Returns the number of columns in a range.

*Example*  =COLUMN(A1:B20) returns 2.

## COS(*x*)

Returns the cosine of an angle for a number measured in radians. (Degrees times PI( )/180 equals radians.)

*Example*  =COS(H15) returns the cosine of the number, measured in radians, contained in H15.

## COUNT(*range1,range2,...rangen*)

Returns the number of cells containing numbers in the ranges listed. Cells containing text, logical values, empty cells, or error values are ignored.

*Example* =COUNT(H15:H27) counts the number of cells containing numbers in the range H15 to H27.

## COUNTA(*range1,range2,...rangen*)

Returns the number of nonblank cells in the ranges listed. Cells containing text, values (including 0), or errors are considered nonblank.

*Example* =COUNTA(H15:H27) counts the number of nonblank cells in the range H15 to H27.

## DATE(*year,month,day*)

Returns the date serial number for a given year, month, and day value. The date serial number (a number between 1 and 65380) may be stored in a cell and formatted as a date (1/1/1900 through 12/31/2078).

*Example* =DATE(90,4,5) returns the value 32968, which can be formatted as 4/5/1990.

## DATEVALUE(*string*)

Returns the date serial number for a text string that look like a date. This is used to convert dates entered as labels, or dates from other applications, into date serial numbers that Excel can use in calculations.

*Example* =DATEVALUE("6/7/90") returns the value 33031.

## DAVERAGE(*input-range, field,criteria-range*)

Based on criteria contained in the criteria range, DAVERAGE searches the input range for all records matching the criteria. When it finds the matching records, it returns an average of the values in the designated field of those records.

*Example* =DAVERAGE(INPUT,"DOLLARS",CRIT-RANGE), based on the criteria in CRIT-RANGE, searches the INPUT database for selected customers and returns an average of the values in the DOLLARS field for matching records.

## DAY(*date-serial-number*)

From a date serial number, a value from 1 to 31 is returned representing the day of the month.

*Example* =DAY(NOW( )) returns the day of the month for the current date.

## DCOUNT(*input-range, [field],criteria-range*)

Searches the input range for a match to the criteria as contained in a criteria range, and then returns a count of the number of cells that contain numbers in the named field. The field argument is optional. If no field argument is included, DCOUNT returns the number of database records that match the criteria as contained in a criteria range.

*Example* =DCOUNT(INPUT,"DOLLARS",CRIT-RANGE) searches the INPUT database for selected customers as defined in CRIT-RANGE, and returns a count of customers that contain numbers in the DOLLARS field.

## DCOUNTA(*input-range, [field],criteria-range*)

Searches the input range for a match to the criteria as contained in a criteria range, and then returns a count of the number of nonblank cells in the named field. The field argument is optional. If no field argument is included, DCOUNTA returns the number of nonblank database records that match the criteria as contained in a criteria range.

*Example* =DCOUNTA(INPUT,"DOLLARS",CRIT-RANGE) searches the INPUT database for selected customers, as defined in CRIT-RANGE, and returns a count of customers that contain nonblank cells in the DOLLARS field.

## DDB(*cost,salvage,life,period*)

Returns the depreciation for a specific period using the double declining balance method of depreciation.

*Example* =DDB(57000,12000,5,2) returns the depreciation of $13,680 for the second year of something that cost $57,000, has a salvage value of $12,000, and has a 5-year life.

## DMAX(*input-range,field, criteria-range*)

Searches the input range for all matches to the criteria as defined in the criteria range, and then returns the largest value in the named field.

*Example* =DMAX(INPUT,"COST",CRIT-RANGE) searches the INPUT database for the matching records defined in CRIT-RANGE. Then it returns the largest value in the COST field.

## DMIN(*input-range,field, criteria-range*)

Searches the input range for all matches to the criteria defined in the criteria range, and then returns the smallest value found in the named field.

*Example* =DMIN(INPUT,"COST",CRIT-RANGE) searches INPUT for the matching records defined in CRIT-RANGE, and then returns the smallest value found in the COST field.

## DOLLAR(*number,[digits]*)

Rounds *number* to the number of digits to the right of the decimal place specified by *digits*, and returns the rounded number as text in the currency format $#,##0.00;($#,##0.00). If *digits* is omitted, the default value is 2 digits.

*Example*   =DOLLAR(5.00234,2) returns the text string "$5.00".

## DPRODUCT(*input-range, field,criteria-range*)

Searches the input range for all matches to the criteria defined in the criteria range, and then returns the product of the values found in the named field.

*Example*   =DPRODUCT(DATABASE,"COST",CRITERIA) returns the product of the costs in the database that satisfy the criteria.

## DSTDEV(*input-range,field, criteria-range*)

Searches the input range for all matches to the criteria defined in the criteria range, and then calculates the sample standard deviation of values in the named field. DSTDEV is more accurate than DSTDEVP with a small database.

*Example*   =DSTDEVP(INPUT,"INCOME",CRIT-RANGE) searches the INPUT database for matching records as defined in

CRIT-RANGE. Then it calculates the estimated standard deviation of a sample of values in the INCOME field.

## DSTDEVP(*input-range, field,criteria-range*)

Searches the input range for all matches to the criteria defined in the criteria range, and then calculates the population standard deviation of all the values in the named field. DSTDEVP is more accurate than DSTDEV with a large database.

*Example* =DSTDEVP(INPUT,"INCOME",CRIT-RANGE) searches the INPUT database for matching records as defined in CRIT-RANGE, and then calculates the population standard deviation of all of the values in the INCOME field.

## DSUM(*input-range,field, criteria-range*)

Searches the input range for all values matching the criteria defined in the criteria range, and then sums the values in the named field.

*Example* =DSUM(INPUT,"SALESAMT",CRIT-RANGE) searches the INPUT database for records matching the one defined in CRIT-RANGE. Then it adds the values in the SALESAMT field to calculate the total.

## DVAR(*input-range,field, criteria-range*)

Searches the input range for values matching those defined in the criteria range, and then returns the estimated variance of a sample of values in the named field. The results are more accurate than DVARP with small databases.

*Example*  =DVAR(INPUT,"POP",CRIT-RANGE) searches the INPUT database for the values defined in CRIT-RANGE. When matches are found, it calculates the variance of a sample of the POP field.

## DVARP(*input-range,field, criteria-range*)

Searches the input-range for values matching those defined in the criteria range, and then returns the population variance of all the values in the named field. The result is more accurate than DVAR with large databases.

*Example*  =DVARP(INPUT,"POP",CRIT-RANGE) searches the INPUT database for the values defined in CRIT-RANGE. When matches are found, it calculates the variance for the entire POP field.

## EXACT(*string1,string2*)

Returns a True condition if *string1* and *string2* are exactly the same; otherwise it returns a False condition. The text strings can be literal strings, formulas that equate to strings, or references to cells containing strings.

*Example*  =EXACT(A5,"April") compares the contents of A5 with the string "April" and returns True or False depending on the match. "APRIL" or "april" would both result in a False condition.

## EXP(x)

Returns the value e (which is approximately 2.718282) raised to the power of $x$.

*Example* =EXP(2) raises the value of e to the second power. This equals 7.389.

## FACT(x)

Returns the factorial of the argument $x$. The formula for the factorial of $x$ is:

$$FACT(x) = x * (x-1) * (x-2) * ... * 1$$

*Examples* =FACT(4) = 4*3*2*1 = 24, and =FACT(3.2) = 3*2*1 = 6 (non-integers are truncated).

## FALSE( )

Returns the logical False value.

*Example* =IF(B6=FALSE,.15,0) tests cell B6 for a False condition. If B6 is blank or zero, the value .15 is returned; otherwise 0 is returned.

## FIND(search-string,string, [start-position])

Beginning at the *start-position* of a string, FIND searches the *string* for a match to the *search-string* and returns the position of the match. The search string and string can be literals, formulas that equate to strings, or references to cells containing strings. The search is case-sensitive and cannot find letters when the case is not identical. If *start-position* is omitted, the default value is 1.

*Example*   =FIND("x","Excel") results in a value of 2.

## FIXED(*number,[digits]*)

Returns *number* as text, rounded to the number of digits to the right of the decimal given by *digits*, if *digits* is positive. If you give a negative number for *digits*, *number* is rounded to the left of the decimal point. The *digits* argument is optional; if you omit it, the default value for *digits* is 2.

*Examples*   =FIXED(456.76834,2) returns "456.77", and =FIXED(456325.76,-2) returns "456,300".

## FV(*interest,number-of-periods, payment,[present-value],[type]*)

Returns the future value of an investment consisting of a series of equal payments made for a term at a fixed interest rate. The interest rate and payment must be on the same basis; for example, if the interest rate is in months, the payment must be per month. If the optional arguments *present-value* and *type* are omitted, the default value for both arguments is 0. When *type* is 0, the payment is due at the end of the period. When *type* is 1, the payment is due at the beginning of the period.

*Example*   =FV(.1,15,-1500) calculates the future value of $47,658.72 for a series of $1500 annual payments invested at 10% per year for 15 years.

## GROWTH(y-array,[x-array], [new-x-array])

Returns an array that describes an exponential curve fit to the data stored in *y-array*, and optionally *x-array*. If *x-array* is omitted, it is assumed it is {1, 2, ...}. If *new-x-array* is omitted, it is assumed to be the same as *x-array*. You must enter GROWTH as an array formula by pressing (CTRL+SHIFT+ENTER), or (CTRL+SHIFT) plus a mouse click. Before entering the function you must highlight the number of cells in the resulting array. The array returned by GROWTH describes the exponential curve with coordinates. If you want an exponential curve array described by a y-intercept and a slope, use LOGEST.

***Example*** Given the array

|   | A | B |
|---|---|---|
| 1 | MON | 300 |
| 2 | TUE | 310 |
| 3 | WED | 340 |
| 4 | THU | 350 |
| 5 | FRI | 380 |

=GROWTH(B1:B5) returns the array {297.3, 315.5, 334.8, 355.3, 377.0} if you highlight C1:C5 prior to entering the function and press (CTRL+SHIFT+ENTER) after typing it.

## HLOOKUP(x,range,row)

Returns an entry from a two-dimensional horizontal lookup table. Excel searches the top row of a range for the largest value that is less than or equal to *x* and then in that column retrieves the contents of a second cell, which is in the specified row. A horizontal lookup table is a range of cells in which the ascending overall values are in a row. This is an example of a horizontal lookup table:

| EMPLOYEES | 1985 | 1990 | 1995 |
|-----------|--------|--------|--------|
| Smith | 20,000 | 30,000 | 40,000 |
| Jones | 18,000 | 36,000 | 54,000 |

If the value of *x* is not exactly equal to a value in the top row of the lookup range, HLOOKUP finds the closest value that is not larger than *x*. *Row* is the number of the row where the value is to be retrieved. The first (top) row is 1.

*Example* =HLOOKUP(1990,SALARIES,2) searches for 1990 in the first row of the SALARIES range (SALARIES is the table immediately above) and returns the value that is in row 2: 30,000.

## HOUR(*time-serial-number*)

Returns the hour from a time serial number. The hour can be a number from 0 (midnight) to 23 (11:00 PM).

*Examples* =HOUR(NOW( )) returns the current hour, while HOUR(.5) returns 12 (noon).

## IF(*condition,true-value, [false-value]*)

Evaluates a condition or equation for true or false and returns one value for a true condition and another value for a false condition. The false value argument is optional.

*Example* =IF(PMT>5000,.05,.025) determines if PMT is greater than 5000. If the condition is true (PMT is greater than 5000), the value 5% is returned. Otherwise a value of 2.5% is returned.

## INDEX(range(s),row, column,[area])

Searches a specified range and returns the value that is in the specified row and column. The first row is row 1 and the first column is column 1. If you have multiple ranges (C1:D5,E8:G9,F4:H8 for example), *area* specifies which range to use. In the example, area 1 would be C1:D5 and area 3 would be F4:H8. You use INDEX instead of HLOOKUP or VLOOKUP when you wish to search for a value by means of its placement in a range, rather than looking for another value it is associated with.

*Example* =INDEX((A1:F18,A20:F38),13,4,2) returns the value from the range of cells A20:F38 in cell D33 (fourth column, thirteenth row, and second area or range).

## INDIRECT(cell-reference, [reference-type])

Returns the contents of the cell that *cell-reference* refers to. If the cell reference is not valid, Excel returns the error value #REF!. If *reference-type* is omitted, the cell reference is assumed to be in the A1 format. If *reference-type* is included, it is expected to be either True or False. If it is True, the cell reference is assumed to be in the A1 format. If it is False, the cell reference is assumed to be in the R1C1 format.

*Example* =INDIRECT(E3) returns 5 if E3 contains the cell reference B3 as a text entry and the cell B3 contains the number 5.

## INT(x)

Returns *x* rounded to the nearest integer.

*Example* =INT(5.357) returns the value 5.

## IPMT(*interest,period,number-of-periods, present-value,[future-value],[type]*)

Returns the interest payment amount for a loan, given the interest and the loan term. *Future-value* is an optional argument. If it is omitted, it is assumed that the future value of a loan is $0. If it is included, it is the balance that you wish to obtain after the last payment is made. *Type* is also an optional argument. When *type* is 0, payments are due at the end of the period. When *type* is 1, payments are due at the beginning of the period. If the *type* argument is omitted, it is assumed to be 0.

*Example* =IPMT(0.12,4,4,9000) returns -$317.48.

## IRR(*range,[estimated-rate-of-return]*)

Returns the internal rate of return for a series of cash flows contained in the range. The *estimated-rate-of-return* argument, if omitted, is assumed to be 10%. *Estimated-rate-of-return* usually is not necessary, as the default argument is sufficient. If you get a #NUM! error, you may need to use or modify *estimated-rate-of-return*. The first cell usually contains a negative number for the initial investment or outflow of cash; positive numbers are inflows. The internal rate of return is the interest rate that gives a series of cash flows a net present value of zero.

*Example* =IRR(A2:A10,.08) estimates the internal rate of return for the cash flows that are contained in cells A2 to A10. It uses 8% as the beginning estimated rate of return.

## ISBLANK(x)

Evaluates a location for a blank cell and returns True if it contains a blank cell, or returns False if it does not contain a blank cell.

***Example*** =ISBLANK(B3) evaluates the contents of B3 for a blank cell. If a blank cell is found, True is returned; otherwise False is returned.

## ISERR(x)

Returns True if $x$ contains an Excel error value except #N/A, or False for an error value of #N/A or anything other than another Excel error value.

***Example*** =IF(ISERR(B15),0,B26) checks B15 for an error condition. If an error condition exists other than #N/A, ISERR returns a True and IF returns 0. Otherwise the formula returns the value in B26.

## ISERROR(x)

Returns True if $x$ contains any Excel error value or False for anything other than any Excel error value.

***Example*** =IF(ISERROR(B15/B25),0,B15/B25) checks a division of B15 by B25 for any Excel error condition. If an error condition exists (possibly indicating division by 0), the calculation returns 0. Otherwise the formula returns the result of the division.

## ISLOGICAL(x)

Evaluates a location, string, condition, or value for a logical value—True (1) or False (0)—and returns True if a cell contains a logical value or False if the cell does not contain a logical value.

*Example* =ISLOGICAL(B6) returns True if B6 contains a logical value or returns False for any other values.

## ISNA(x)

Returns True if $x$ contains an #N/A value or False for anything other than an #N/A value.

*Example* =ISNA(F2) returns True if F2 contains #N/A; otherwise it returns False.

## ISNONTEXT(x)

Evaluates a location, string, value, or condition for a text string and returns True if it is not a text string or False if it is a text string.

*Example* =ISNONTEXT(NAME) evaluates the contents of NAME for a text string. If a text string is found, False is returned; otherwise True is returned.

## ISNUMBER(x)

Evaluates a location, string, condition, or value for a number and returns True if it is a number or is blank, or returns False if it is anything else.

*Example* =ISNUMBER(B6) returns True if B6 contains a value or blanks and returns False for any other values.

## ISREF(*x*)

Evaluates a location, string, value, or condition for a reference and returns True if it is a reference or False if it is not a reference.

*Example* =ISREF(NAME) evaluates NAME to see if it is a range name. If it is a range name, True is returned; otherwise False is returned.

## ISTEXT(*x*)

Evaluates a location, string, value, or condition for a text string and returns True if it is or contains a text string, or returns FALSE if it is not or does not contain a text string.

*Example* =ISTEXT(NAME) evaluates the contents of NAME for a text string. If a text string is found, True is returned; otherwise False is returned.

## LEFT(*string,[x]*)

Returns the leftmost number of characters specified by *x* that are contained in the text string. The string can be a literal, a reference to a cell containing a string, or a formula that equates to a string. The *x* argument is optional. If omitted, the default value is 1.

*Example* =LEFT(G8,10) returns the first 10 characters in the string contained in G8.

## LEN(*string*)

Returns the number of characters in the specified text string. The string can be a literal, a reference to a cell containing a string, or a formula that equates to a string.

*Example* =LEN(B8&C8) returns the number of characters in cells B8 and C8.

## LINEST(*y-array,[x-array]*)

Returns an array that describes a straight-line fit to the data stored in *y-array,* and optionally *x-array*. If the *x-array* argument is omitted, it is assumed that it is {1, 2, ...}. You must enter LINEST as an array formula by pressing (CTRL+SHIFT+ENTER) or (CTRL+SHIFT) plus a mouse click. The array returned by LINEST describes the straight-line fit with a y-intercept and a slope. If you want a straight-line array described by coordinates, use TREND.

*Example* Given the array

|   | A | B |
|---|---|---|
| 1 | MON | 300 |
| 2 | TUE | 310 |
| 3 | WED | 340 |
| 4 | THU | 350 |
| 5 | FRI | 380 |

=LINEST(B1:B5) returns the array {20, 276}, where 20 is the slope of the line and 276 is the y-intercept.

## LN(*x*)

Returns the natural logarithm to the base e of a value.

*Example* =LN(B9) returns the natural logarithm of the number contained in B9.

## LOG(x,[base])

Returns the logarithm to the optionally given base of a value. If the base argument is omitted, the default value is 10.

*Example* =LOG(H15,8) returns the base 8 logarithm of the value contained in H15.

## LOG10(x)

Returns the common (base 10) logarithm of a value.

*Example* =LOG10(H15) returns the common logarithm of the value contained in H15.

## LOGEST(y-array,[x-array])

Returns an array that describes an exponential curve fit to the data stored in *y-array,* and optionally *x-array*. If the *x-array* argument is omitted, it is assumed that it is {1, 2, ...}. You must enter LOGEST as an array formula by first highlighting two empty cells where you want the results, typing the function, and then pressing CTRL+SHIFT+ENTER or CTRL+SHIFT plus a mouse click. The array returned by LOGEST describes the exponential curve fit as a y-intercept and a slope. If you want a straight-line array described by coordinates, use GROWTH.

***Example*** Given the array

|   | A | B |
|---|---|---|
| 1 | MON | 300 |
| 2 | TUE | 310 |
| 3 | WED | 340 |
| 4 | THU | 350 |
| 5 | FRI | 380 |

=LOGEST(B1:B5) returns the array {1.06, 280.13}.

# LOOKUP(*x,lookup-range, [return-range]*)

Returns an entry from an array. If the array contains only one column or row, you may want to specify *return-range*. Excel searches through the first column or row of the array and looks for the value $x$. If the value of $x$ is not exactly equal to a value in the top row or column of the lookup range, LOOKUP finds the closest value that is not larger than $x$.

If your range is more than one column or row, Excel determines the orientation of the array by comparing the width to the height of the array. If the array is wider than it is tall or is square, LOOKUP searches for $x$ in the top row and returns the contents of the corresponding cell in the bottom row. If the array is taller than it is wide, LOOKUP searches for $x$ in the left column and returns the contents of the corresponding cell in the rightmost column.

If your array contains only one column or row, LOOKUP returns the contents of the corresponding cell from the return range. Do not specify the return range unless your array is one-dimensional.

*Example* Given the array

|   | A | B |
|---|---|---|
| 1 | MILEAGE | MODEL |
| 2 | 12 | Comet |
| 3 | 22 | Excelerator |
| 4 | 38 | Orbiter |
| 5 | 57 | Economatic |
| 6 | 120 | Magic |

=LOOKUP(28,A2:A6,B2:B6) returns "Excelerator".
=LOOKUP(28,A2:B6) also returns "Excelerator". Notice that you can use either method in this case because the example array only has a lookup column and a return column.

## LOWER(*string*)

Converts all characters in the specified string to lowercase letters.

*Example* =LOWER("STANDARD") converts "STANDARD" to "standard".

## MATCH(*x,range,[type]*)

Returns the relative position of an entry in the range that matches *x* according to *type*. The following table summarizes the possible types:

| Type | Returns Relative Position for | Order of Range Array |
|---|---|---|
| 1 | Largest value <= x | Ascending order |
| -1 | Smallest value >= x | Descending order |
| 0 | Value = x | Any order |

***Example*** Given the array

|   | A | B |
|---|---|---|
| 1 | WEIGHT | ANIMAL |
| 2 | 1 | Parrot |
| 3 | 15 | Cat |
| 4 | 18 | Monkey |
| 5 | 27 | Goat |
| 6 | 35 | Dog |

MATCH(20,A2:A7,1) returns 3, the relative position of the largest value $\leq 20$. Notice the array is in ascending order.

Given the array

|   | A | B |
|---|---|---|
| 1 | WEIGHT | ANIMAL |
| 2 | 35 | Dog |
| 3 | 27 | Goat |
| 4 | 18 | Monkey |
| 5 | 15 | Cat |
| 6 | 1 | Parrot |

=MATCH(20,A2:A7,-1) returns 2, the relative position of the smallest value $\geq 20$. Notice the array is in descending order.

=MATCH("mon*",B2:B7,0) returns 3, the relative position of Monkey. Notice that Excel wildcards can be used, and MATCH is case-insensitive. (Wildcards are used to represent unknown characters. The wildcard * represents any number of characters, and ? represents one character.)

## MAX(*list*)

Returns the largest number in the specified list, which can be a list of numbers, formulas, or references to ranges of cells containing numbers or formulas.

*Example* =MAX(87,A8,B9:B11) returns the largest number between 87 and the numbers contained in A8 or the range B9 to B11.

## MDETERM(*numeric-square-array*)

Returns the matrix determinant of *numeric-square-array*. If the array is not square, does not contain numbers, or is empty, MDETERM returns an error #VALUE!.

*Example*   Given the array

|   | A | B | C |
|---|---|---|---|
| 1 | 1 | 2 | 3 |
| 2 | 3 | 0 | 1 |
| 3 | 2 | 1 | 0 |

=MDETERM(A1:C3) returns 12.

## MID(*string,offset-number, number-of- characters*)

Returns the specified number of characters in the middle of a text string, beginning with the character at *offset-number*. The string can be a literal, a reference to a cell containing a string, or a formula that equates to a string.

*Example* =MID(H15,FIND(" ",H15)+1,LEN(H15)-FIND(" ",H15)) separates the first and last names in the string in H15. The first FIND function returns the position of the first space in the string and adds 1 to it to identify the start of the second word—the *offset-number*. The LEN function returns the number of characters in the string and subtracts the number of characters to the first space. This results in the MID function returning the characters in the string that follow the space—normally the last name.

## MIN(*list*)

Returns the smallest number in the list. The list can contain numbers, formulas, or references to cells containing numbers or formulas.

***Example*** =MIN(A7,H19,50) compares the numbers contained in cells A7 and H19 and the number 50 and returns the smallest of them.

## MINUTE(*time-serial-number*)

Returns the minutes from a time serial number. The resulting minute is an integer from 0 to 59.

***Example*** The function =MINUTE(NOW( )) returns the current minute of the day.

## MINVERSE(*numeric-square-array*)

Returns the matrix inverse of *numeric-square-array*. The inverse of an array is an array. You must highlight an array (range) of equal size in which you want the result placed and then press CTRL+SHIFT+ENTER after typing the function.

***Example*** Given the array

|   | A | B | C |
|---|---|---|---|
| 1 | 1 | 2 | 3 |
| 2 | 3 | 0 | 1 |
| 3 | 2 | 1 | 0 |

=MINVERSE(A1:C3) returns the following array (if you highlight D1:F3 before typing the formula):

|   | D | E | F |
|---|---|---|---|
| 1 | -0.08333 | 0.25 | 0.16667 |
| 2 | 0.16667 | -0.5 | 0.666667 |
| 3 | 0.25 | 0.25 | 0.5 |

This can also be displayed as: {-0.08333, 0.25, 0.16667; 0.16667, -0.5, 0.666667; 0.25, 0.25, 0.5}.

If you do not highlight an array before typing the function, the cell that the formula is entered into contains -0.08333. If you check the type, you see that it is an array (=TYPE(MINVERSE(A1:C3)) returns 64, the array type). If you want to see specific elements in the array, use the INDEX function (=INDEX(MINVERSE(A1:C3),2,2) returns -0.5).

## MIRR(range,investment-rate,interest)

Returns the modified internal rate of return for a series of cash flows contained in the array range. The cost of the investment (*investment-rate*) and the interest received on the reinvestment of cash (*interest*) are both considered when calculating the modified internal rate of return. The first cell usually contains a negative number for the initial investment or outflow of cash; positive numbers are in-flows. The internal rate of return is the interest rate that gives a series of cash flows a net present value of zero.

*Example* =MIRR(A2:A10,10%,13%) estimates the modified internal rate of return for the cash flows that are contained in cells A2 to A10. It uses 10% as the investment rate and 13% as the interest rate.

## MMULT(range1,range2)

Returns the product resulting from the matrix multiplication of two ranges of numbers. The ranges must be arrays of the same size and shape, and the result is an array of the same size and shape. You must highlight a range of the correct size for the result, enter the function, and press CTRL+SHIFT+ENTER.

*Example* Given the array

|   | A | B | C | D |
|---|---|---|---|---|
| 1 | 3 | 2 | 2 | 3 |
| 2 | 1 | 2 | 3 | 4 |

=MMULT(A1:B2,C1:D2) multiplies the two matrices defined by the two ranges. If you were to select E1:F2 to contain the result, it would contain:

|   | E  | F  |
|---|----|----|
| 1 | 12 | 17 |
| 2 | 8  | 11 |

## MOD(x,y)

This function returns the modulus or remainder of the value $x$ that is divided by $y$.

*Example* =MOD(5,2) returns the value 1.

## MONTH(date-serial-number)

Returns the month of the year, an integer from 1 to 12, from a date serial number.

*Example* =MONTH(NOW( )) returns the month of the year for the current date.

## N(*range*)

Returns the value of the first cell in the specified range. If the cell contains a value, that value is returned. If the cell contains a logical True, 1 is returned. If the cell contains anything else, 0 is returned. This function can be used to check for numeric data.

*Example* =N(C5:C5) returns the value contained in C5, 1 if C5 contains a logical True, or 0 if the cell is empty or contains a label.

## NA( )

Returns the value #N/A, which means "not available."

*Example* =NA( ) returns the value #N/A.

## NOT(*x*)

Returns the opposite of *x*, where *x* must evaluate to a logical True or a logical False.

*Examples* =NOT(FALSE) returns True, and =NOT(3 = 3) returns False.

## NOW( )

Returns the current date or time serial number. The date appears as the integer portion and the time as the decimal portion. The NOW( ) result can be formatted as a time, a date, or both with the

Excel date and time formatting options. Regardless of how it is displayed, the serial number is available for calculations. NOW( ) recalculates each time the formulas in the worksheet are recalculated.

*Example*  =NOW( ) returns 33468.99126 if it is 11:47 PM on August 18, 1991.

## NPER(*interest,payment,present-value, [future- value],[type]* )

Returns the number of periods for an investment, given the payment amount and the interest rate. *Future-value* is an optional argument. If it is omitted it is assumed that the future value is $0. If it is included it is the balance that you wish to obtain after the last payment is made. *Type* is an optional argument. When *type* is 0, payments are due at the end of the period; when *type* is 1, payments are due at the beginning of the period. If the *type* argument is omitted, it is assumed to be 0.

*Example*  =NPER(1.8%,-180,-1000,55500) returns 100. The interest rate is 1.8% per month, the payments are $180, the present value is $1000 (the cost of the investment), and the future value is $55,500.

## NPV(*interest,range*)

Returns the net present value of a series of cash flows contained in *range,* discounted at the given interest rate.

*Example*  =NPV(.08,C15:C25) returns the net present value of the cash flows contained in cells C15 through C25 and discounted at 8%.

## OR(x1,x2,...xn)

Returns the logical OR of the arguments *x1* through *xn,* which all must evaluate to logical values. If any of the arguments evaluates to True, OR returns True. If all the arguments evaluate to False, OR returns False.

*Example*  =OR(1=2,3=3,5=10) returns True.

## PI( )

Returns the value $\pi$, which is approximately 3.1415926535..., the ratio of the circumference of a circle to its diameter.

*Example*  =PI( )*8^2 returns 201.06, which is the area of a circle whose radius is 8.

## PMT(*interest,number-of-periods, present- value,[future-value],[type]* )

Returns the payment amount for a loan given the interest and the loan term. *Future-value* is an optional argument. If it is omitted it is assumed that the future value of a loan is $0. If it is included it is the balance that you wish to obtain after the last payment is made. *Type* is an optional argument. When *type* is 0, payments are due at the end of the period. When *type* is 1, payments are due at the beginning of the period. If the *type* argument is omitted it is assumed to be 0.

*Examples*  =PMT(10%/12,12,0,9000) returns -$716.24, and =PMT(10%/12,48,9000) returns -$228.26.

## PPMT(*interest,period,number-of-periods, present-value,[future-value],[type]*)

Returns the principle payment amount for a loan given the period, interest rate, present value, and the loan term. *Future-value* is an optional argument. If it is omitted it is assumed that the future value of a loan is $0. If it is included it is the balance that you wish to obtain after the last payment is made. *Type* is an optional argument. When *type* is 0, payments are due at the end of the period. When *type* is 1, payments are due at the beginning of the period. If the *type* argument is omitted, it is assumed to be 0.

*Example*   =PPMT(10%/12,1,48,9000) returns -$153.26.

## PRODUCT(*x1,x2,...xn*)

Returns the product of the arguments *x1* through *xn*. Arguments can be anything but errors or text that cannot be translated into numbers. There can be up to 14 arguments. Each of the arguments can also be a range of cells on the worksheet.

*Example*   =PRODUCT(1,4,6,2) returns 48. If the numbers (1, 4, 6, 2) are in cells A1 through D1, then =PRODUCT(A1:D1) also returns 48.

## PROPER(*string*)

Converts the first letter of all words in a text string to uppercase and the remaining letters to lowercase, as in a proper name.

*Example*   =PROPER("the little RED HEN") converts the string to "The Little Red Hen".

## PV(*interest,number-of-periods, payment,[future-value],[type]*)

Returns the present value of a series of equal payments for a specified term and interest rate. The number of periods and interest rate must be expressed in the same time units (months, years, etc). *Future-value* is an optional argument. If it is omitted it is assumed that the future value of a loan is $0. If it is included it is the balance that you wish to obtain after the last payment is made. *Type* is an optional argument. When *type* is 0, payments are due at the end of the period. When *type* is 1, payments are due at the beginning of the period. If the *type* argument is omitted, it is assumed to be 0.

*Example*  =PV(.065/12,120,1000) returns the present value of $88,068.50 for $1000 invested monthly for 10 years at a 6.5% annual interest rate.

## RAND( )

Generates a random number between 0 and 1. If you want a two-digit random number, multiply by 100 (=RAND( )*100); for a three-digit random number, multiply by 1000.

*Example*  =RAND( ) returns a random number between 0 and 1.

## RATE(*number-of-periods,payment, present-value,[future-value],[type],[guess]*)

Returns the interest rate given equal payments for a specified number of periods and the present value. *Future-value* is an optional argument. If it is omitted it is assumed that the future value is $0. If it is included it is the balance that you wish to obtain after the last payment is made. *Type* is an optional argument. When *type* is 0, payments are due at the end of the period. When *type* is 1, payments are due at the beginning of the period. If the *type* argument is omitted, it is assumed to be 0. *Guess* is also an optional argument, with a default value of 10%.

*Example*   =RATE(120,-300,20000)*12 returns the annual interest rate of 13.12%.

## REPLACE (*original-string,offset-number, number-of-characters,new-string*)

Replaces the specified number of characters in the original text string, beginning with the offset number, with the new string. Either string can be a literal, a reference to a cell containing text, or a formula that equates to a string. The offset number is the offset from the beginning of the original string at which the replacement is to take place.

If *number-of-characters* is the same as the number of characters in the original string, the original string is replaced with the new string. If *offset-number* is greater than *number-of-characters* in the original string, the new string is appended to it. If *number-of-characters* is 0, the new string is inserted in the original string. If the new string contains no characters, the original string is deleted.

*Example*   =REPLACE("Income Statement",17,0,", as of April, 1990") appends the new string onto the original string, resulting in "Income Statement, as of April, 1990".

## REPT(*string,number-of-times*)

Repeats or duplicates a string the specified number of times. The string can be a literal, a reference to a cell containing a label, or a formula that equates to a string.

*Example*   =REPT("-",20) prints 20 hyphens.

## RIGHT(*string, [number-of-characters]*)

Returns the rightmost specified number of characters in a string. The string can be a literal, a reference to a cell containing a label, or a formula that equates to a string. If *number-of-characters* is 0, no characters are returned. If *number-of-characters* is greater than the number in *string*, the entire string is returned. The *number-of-characters* argument is optional, with a default value of 1.

*Example*  The function =RIGHT("The Month of January",7) returns "January".

## ROUND(*value,number-of-decimal-places*)

Rounds a value to the specified number of decimal places.

*Example*  =ROUND(536.8175,3) returns 536.818.

## ROW(*range*)

Returns a vertical array of the row numbers (*not* the number of rows) in *range*. You must highlight a range large enough to receive the resulting array prior to entering the function, and then press (CTRL+SHIFT+ENTER) instead of (ENTER) after typing the function.

*Example*  =ROW(A1:A4) will return the array {1,2,3,4}. If you highlight A1:A4 prior to entering the function and then press (CTRL+SHIFT+ENTER), you have 1 in cell A1, 2 in A2, 3 in A3, and 4 in A4.

## ROWS(*range*)

Returns the number of rows in a range.

*Example*   =ROWS(A1:A18) returns the number 18.

## SEARCH(*search-string,string, [start-position]*)

Beginning at the starting position of a text string, SEARCH searches the string for a match to the search string and returns the position where the match is found. The *search-string* and *string* arguments can be literals, formulas that equate to strings, or references to cells containing strings. The search is case-insensitive and finds letters when the case is not identical. The *start-position* argument is optional, with a default value of 1.

*Example*   =SEARCH("no",A6,6) results in the value 8 in the string "yes no no yes no" in cell A6.

## SECOND(*time-serial-number*)

Returns the seconds in a time serial number. The resulting second is an integer from 0 to 59.

*Example*   =SECOND(NOW( )) returns the current seconds.

## SIGN(*x*)

Returns 1 if $x$ is a positive number, returns -1 if $x$ is negative, and returns 0 if $x$ is zero.

*Examples* =SIGN(5) returns 1, =SIGN(-5) returns -1, and =SIGN(0) returns 0.

## SIN(*x*)

Calculates the sine of an angle measured in radians. (Degrees times PI( )/180 equals radians.)

*Example* =SIN(B18) calculates the sine of the radian value in cell B18.

## SLN(*cost,salvage,life*)

Returns the depreciation expense of an asset for a period using the straight-line depreciation method. Enter the cost of the asset, its expected salvage value, and the expected asset life.

*Example* =SLN(5000,300,10) returns the annual depreciation expense of $470 for a machine that costs $5000 and is expected to be worth $300 in 10 years.

## SQRT(*x*)

Returns the square root of a positive value.

*Example* =SQRT(B55) returns the square root of the value in cell B55.

## STDEV(*list*)

Returns the sample standard deviation of the values itemized in the list. The list can contain any combination of numbers, formulas, or references to cells containing numbers or formulas. Use

STDEVP when the number of items in the list is large; use STDEV when the number is small.

*Example*  =STDEV(A14:A20) returns the sample standard deviation of the values contained in the range A14 to A20.

## STDEVP(*list*)

Returns the population standard deviation of the values itemized in the list. The list can contain any combination of numbers, formulas, or references to cells containing numbers or formulas. Use STDEVP when the number of items in the list is large; use STDEV when the number is small.

*Example*  =STDEVP(A14:H120) returns the population standard deviation of the values contained in the range A14 to H120.

## SUBSTITUTE (*original-string,old-sub-string, new-sub-string,[instance-number]*)

Replaces the text string specified by *old-sub-string* with the string specified by *new-sub-string* in the *original-string*. The string specifications can be literals, references to a cell containing a string, or formulas that equate to a string. The optional *instance-number* argument allows you to specify which instance of *old-sub-string* you want to replace with *new-sub-string*.

*Example*  =SUBSTITUTE("Income Statement","Statement","Projection") returns "Income Projection".

## SUM(*range1,range2,...rangen*)

Returns the sum of the values contained in the range(s).

*Example* =SUM(A1:A5,C6:C18) returns the sum of the values in the range A1 through A5 and C6 through C18.

## SYD(*cost,salvage,life,period*)

Returns the depreciation expense for a given period of an asset using the sum-of-the-year's-digits depreciation method. Enter the cost of the asset, its expected salvage value and expected life, and the period for which the depreciation is to be calculated.

*Example* =SYD(5000,300,10,5) returns the depreciation expense of $512.73 for the fifth year for a machine that costs $5000 and is expected to have a salvage value of $300 at the end of a 10 year life using the sum of the year's digits method.

## T(*x*)

Returns *x* as text if *x* is text or refers to text; otherwise returns the empty string. This function is not necessary in Excel, because Excel functions requiring a text string automatically convert a number to an empty string. Therefore the T function is only used for compatibility with other programs.

*Example* =T("January") returns "January", and =T(1234) returns "".

## TAN(*x*)

Returns the tangent of a value measured in radians. (Degrees times PI( )/180 equals radians.)

*Example* =TAN(H28) returns the tangent of the angle in H28.

## TEXT(*x,format*)

Returns *x* as text in the Excel format specified by the *format* argument.

*Example* =TEXT(5.458,"$0.00") returns "$5.46".

## TIME(*hour,minutes,seconds*)

Returns the time serial number for the stated hour, minutes, and seconds. The hour can be a number from 1 to 23; minutes from 0 to 59; and seconds from 0 to 59.

*Example* =The function TIME(15,15,0) calculates the time serial number of .6354167 for 3:15 PM.

## TIMEVALUE(*string*)

Returns the time serial number for a string of characters that is in an Excel time format. The string can be a reference to a cell containing a label, a string of characters, or a formula that results in a string. This function is used to convert labels or data from another application to a time serial number that can be used in calculations.

*Example* =TIMEVALUE("10:15 AM") returns the time serial number of .427083.

## TRANSPOSE(*array*)

Returns the transposition of *array*. To transpose an array, the first row of the given array is the first column of the resulting array, the second row becomes the second column, and so on. Since the result is an array, you must highlight a range of the correct size to hold the results, enter the formula, and then press `CTRL+SHIFT+ENTER`.

***Example*** =TRANSPOSE(1,4,6;2,3,7) returns {1, 2; 4, 3; 6, 7}. Looking at this in array form, if the original array is

|   | A | B | C |
|---|---|---|---|
| 1 | 1 | 4 | 6 |
| 2 | 2 | 3 | 7 |

and you highlight D1:E3, type =**TRANSPOSE(A1:C2)**, and press `CTRL+SHIFT+ENTER`, D1:E3 has

|   | D | E |
|---|---|---|
| 1 | 1 | 2 |
| 2 | 4 | 3 |
| 3 | 6 | 7 |

## TREND(*y-array,[x-array], [new-x-array]*)

Returns an array that describes a straight-line fit to the data stored in *y-array*, and optionally *x-array*. If the *x-array* argument is omitted, it is assumed to be {1, 2, ...}. If the *new-x-array* argument is omitted, it is assumed to be the same as the *x-array* argument. You must enter TREND as an array formula by first highlighting a range large enough to hold the resulting array, typing the formula, and finally pressing `CTRL+SHIFT+ENTER`, or `CTRL+SHIFT` plus a mouse click. The array returned by TREND describes the straight-line fit with coordinates. If you want a straight line array described by a y-intercept and a slope, use LINEST.

***Example*** Given the array

|   | A | B |
|---|---|---|
| 1 | MON | 300 |
| 2 | TUE | 310 |
| 3 | WED | 340 |
| 4 | THU | 350 |
| 5 | FRI | 380 |

=TREND(B1:B5) returns the array {296, 316, 336, 356, 376}.

## TRIM(*string*)

Returns the string with all the spaces removed, except one space between each word.

*Example* =TRIM("Stars   and   Stripes") returns "Stars and Stripes".

## TRUE( )

Returns the logical value True.

*Example* =IF(NAME="Smith",TRUE,FALSE) returns True if the NAME range contains Smith; otherwise it returns False.

## TRUNC(*x*)

Returns the number *x*, with all digits to the right of the decimal place removed.

*Example* =TRUNC(4.567) returns 4.

## TYPE(x)

Returns the type of the argument *x*. The table below summarizes the possible return types:

| Return Type | x |
|---|---|
| 1 | Number |
| 2 | Text |
| 4 | Logical |
| 16 | Error |
| 64 | Array |

*Example* =TYPE(ROW(A1:C3)) returns 64 because row is an array function.

## UPPER(*string*)

Returns the string in all uppercase letters.

*Example* =UPPER("January") returns "JANUARY".

## VALUE(*string*)

Returns the text string as a number, if possible. If it is not possible to convert the string to a number, VALUE returns the error #VALUE!

*Example* =VALUE("$5,480.00") returns 5480.

## VAR(*list*)

Returns the sample variance of the values itemized in the list. The list can contain any combination of numbers, formulas, or references to cells containing numbers or formulas. Use VARP when the number of items in the list is large; use VAR when the number is small.

*Example* =VAR(A14:A20) returns the sample variance of the values contained in the range A14 through A20.

## VARP(*list*)

Returns the population variance of the values itemized in the list. The list can contain any combination of numbers, formulas, or references to cells containing numbers or formulas. Use VARP when the number of items in the list is large; use VAR when the number is small.

*Example* =VARP(A14:H120) returns the population variance of the values contained in the range A14 through H120.

## VLOOKUP(*x,range,column*)

Returns an entry from a two-dimensional vertical lookup table. Excel searches the left column of *range* for the largest value that is less than or equal to *x* and then in that row, retrieves the contents of a second cell, which is in *column*. A vertical lookup table is a range of cells in which the ascending overall values are in a column. This table, called SALES, is an example of a vertical lookup table:

| YEARS | STOREA  | STOREB  | STOREC  |
|-------|---------|---------|---------|
| 1985  | 100,000 | 50,000  | 80,000  |
| 1990  | 200,000 | 150,000 | 160,000 |
| 1995  | 300,000 | 250,000 | 320,000 |

If the value of *x* is not exactly equal to a value in the left column, VLOOKUP finds the closest value that is not larger than *x*. *Column* is the number of the column where the value is to be retrieved. The first (leftmost) column is 1.

*Example* =VLOOKUP(1990,SALES,3) searches for the value 1990 in the first column of the SALES range and returns the value that is in column 3: 150,000.

## WEEKDAY(*date-serial-number*)

Returns the day of the week corresponding to a date serial number. The day of the week is given as a number from 1 to 7 for Sunday to Saturday.

*Example* =WEEKDAY(DATE(90,4,5)) returns 5, which is Thursday.

## YEAR(*date-serial-number*)

Returns the year, a number from 1900 to 2078, from a date serial number.

*Example* =YEAR(NOW( )) returns the four-digit year for today's date.

# 14

# MACRO FUNCTIONS

Macro functions are predefined advanced commands that considerably extend the power of Excel. With them you can perform operations that you are not able to do any other way.

This chapter lists the macro functions available in Excel alphabetically by name. Following each name is a brief description of what the macro function does.

Some of the macro functions have two versions that are identical except that the function name is followed by a question mark in one version. The second version automatically brings up a dialog box. The arguments for the function are usually optional and are used as default values in the dialog box. The version of the function without the question mark does not normally bring up a dialog box, and in most cases the arguments are mandatory.

All the regular functions are available to you when you are writing macros and can be used exactly the same way when you are using them in formulas. See Chapter 13 for complete descriptions of the regular Excel functions.

All of the menu options are available to you as macro functions. They are listed here, but you should refer to Chapter 12 for a complete description of what they do.

Arguments enclosed in square brackets ([ ]) are optional.

## A1.R1C1(*x*)

Same as the Options Workspace option (see Chapter 12 for a complete description). If *x* is True the A1 style is used, and if *x* is False the R1C1 style is used.

## ABSREF(*relative-reference, cell-reference*)

Returns the absolute cell reference for the range calculated with respect to the cell reference argument. The relative reference (in R1C1 style), given as a string, is turned into an A1 style reference with respect to the cell reference argument.

*Example*   ABSREF("R[1]C[1]",A1) returns B2.

## ACTIVATE(*window-name, [pane-number]*)

Same as the Window Activate Window option (see Chapter 12 for a complete description). The *window-name* argument is the name of the window you want to activate. The optional *pane-number* argument allows you to specify which pane you want activated if there is more than one pane in the window.

## ACTIVATE.NEXT( )

Selects the next window. Same as pressing `CTRL + F6`.

## ACTIVATE.PREV( )

Selects the previous window. Same as pressing `CTRL + SHIFT + F6`.

## ACTIVE.CELL( )

Returns the contents of the active cell in the current selection.

***Examples*** ACTIVE.CELL( ) returns the contents of the active cell, and REFTEXT(ACTIVE.CELL( )) returns the external cell reference of the active cell.

## ADD.ARROW( )

Same as the Chart Add Arrow option (see Chapter 12 for a complete description).

## ADD.BAR( )

Adds a menu bar to the menu system and returns the menu bar's ID number. If there are already 15 menu bars, ADD.BAR returns the error #VALUE!. To display the bar that you added, use SHOW.BAR.

## ADD.COMMAND(*bar-number, menu,command-ref*)

Adds a command to a menu. *Bar-number* is the number of the menu bar you want to add the command to. The *menu* argument is the menu that you want to add the command to and can be a name or the number of the menu. *Command-ref* is a reference to a macro sheet where the new command is stored.

## ADD.MENU(*bar-number,menu*)

Adds a menu to a menu bar. *Bar-number* is the number of the menu bar that you want to add the menu to. The *menu* argument is a reference to a macro sheet where the new menu is stored. ADD.MENU adds the new menu and returns the position of the new menu.

## ADD.OVERLAY( )

Same as the Chart Add Overlay option (see Chapter 12 for a complete description).

## ALERT(*message,type*)

Returns a dialog box. The *message* is displayed in the dialog box. The *type* controls the type of dialog box displayed. Type 1 displays a choice dialog box with OK and CANCEL buttons. Type 2 displays an information dialog box with an OK button. Type 3 displays an error dialog box with an OK button.

*Example* ALERT("Are you ready to continue?",1) displays a dialog box with the message "Are you ready to continue?", an OK button, and a CANCEL button.

## ALIGNMENT(*type-number*) or ALIGNMENT?(*[type-number]*)

Same as the Format Alignment option (see Chapter 12 for a complete description). *Type-number* is the type of the alignment given as one of the following numbers. In the dialog box version (with the question mark), *type-number,* if included, is the default value for the dialog box that appears.

1. General
2. Left
3. Center
4. Right
5. Fill

## APP.ACTIVATE(*[title],[pause]*)

Activates an application. *Title* is the name of the application you want to activate. If *title* is omitted, the default title is Microsoft Excel. *Pause* must be a logical value. If *pause* is True or is omitted, APP.ACTIVATE waits until Excel is activated before activating the application. If pause is False, APP.ACTIVATE activates the application right away.

## APP.MAXIMIZE( )

Same as the Control Maximize option.

## APP.MOVE(*horizontal,vertical*) or
## APP.MOVE?(*[horizontal],[vertical]*)

Same as the Control Move option.

## APP.RESTORE( )

Same as the Control Restore option.

## APP.SIZE(*width,height*) or
## APP.SIZE?(*[width],[height]*)

Same as the Control Size option.

## APPLY.NAMES(*name-array,ignore,row-col, omit-column,omit-row,order,append*) or
## APPLY.NAMES?(*[name-array], [ignore],[row-col],[omit-column], [omit-row],[order],[append]*)

Same as the Formula Apply Names option (see Chapter 12 for a complete description). *Name-array* contains the name(s) to apply. The arguments *ignore, row-col, omit-column,* and *omit-row* correspond to check boxes in the Formula Apply Names dialog box. *Append* must be logical. If append is True, APPLY.NAMES applies names to names defined by Formula Define Name or Formula Create Names. If append is False, APPLY.NAMES applies names to names in *name-array*. In the dialog box version (with the question mark), all arguments are optional. If they are included, they are used as defaults for the dialog box that appears.

## ARGUMENT(*name,[type]*) or
## ARGUMENT(*[name],[type],reference*)

Used in a function macro to declare an argument. *Name* is the name of the argument, and *type* is one of the following types of argument. *Reference* is the reference to the argument.

| | | | |
|---|---|---|---|
| 1 | Number | 8 | Reference |
| 2 | Text | 16 | Error |
| 4 | Logical | 64 | Array |

## ARRANGE.ALL( )

Same as the Window Arrange All option (see Chapter 12 for a complete description).

## ATTACH.TEXT(*attach,[series],[point]*)

Same as the Chart Attach Text option (see Chapter 12 for a complete description). The *attach* option allows you to define where you want to attach the text using one of the following numbers:

1. Title
2. Value axis
3. Category axis
4. Series or data point

You also can specify a series or data point to attach text to.

**AXES([main-category],[main-value], [overlay- category],[overlay-value] ) or AXES?([main-category], [main-value],[overlay-category], [overlay-value] )**

Same as the Chart Axes option (see Chapter 12 for a complete description). The arguments correspond to the check boxes in the Axes dialog box. In the dialog box version (with the question mark), if the arguments are included, they are the defaults for the dialog box that appears.

**BEEP(x)**

Causes a beep in the tone specified by x, which must be between 1 and 4.

**BORDER(outline,left,right,top, bottom,shade) or BORDER?([outline],[left],[right], [top],[bottom],[shade] )**

Same as the Format Border option (see Chapter 12 for a complete description). The arguments correspond to the check boxes in the Format Border dialog box. In the dialog box version (with the question mark), if the arguments are included, they are used as defaults for the dialog box that appears.

**BREAK( )**

Causes a break in a loop. Execution continues with the code following the loop code.

## CALCULATE.DOCUMENT( )

Same as the Options Calculate Document option if the current document is a worksheet, or Chart Calculate Document if the current document is a chart (see Chapter 12 for a complete description).

## CALCULATE.NOW( )

Same as the Options Calculate Now option if the current document is a worksheet, or Chart Calculate Now if the current document is a chart (see Chapter 12 for a complete description).

## CALCULATION(*type,iteration, max-iterations,max-change, remote-ref,precision,date-system*) or CALCULATION?(*[type],[iteration], [max-iterations],[max- change], [remote-ref],[precision],[date-system]*)

Same as the Options Calculation option (see Chapter 12 for a complete description). In the dialog box version (with the question mark), the arguments, if included, are used as default values for the dialog box that appears.

## CALL(*reg-result,[argument-list]*)

Returns a procedure from the Windows dynamic library. CALL requires that you do a REGISTER macro first. *Reg-result* references the result of the REGISTER macro, and *argument-list* is passed to the procedure.

 CALL should be used only by accomplished programmers. Used incorrectly, CALL could cause errors in your system with the possible loss of data.

## CALLER( )

Returns a reference to the function macro that called the function macro currently running. If the currently running macro is not a function macro but a command macro, CALLER returns the error #REF!.

## CANCEL.COPY( )

Same as pressing the (ESC) key to cancel the copy marquee. (See Chapter 12 for a complete description of copying.)

## CANCEL.KEY(*escape, [macro-reference]*)

Causes the (ESC) key to be disabled if the escape argument is False. If the escape argument is True, the (ESC) key is enabled. If the escape argument is True and a macro reference is included, the macro referred to by *macro-reference* is started when the (ESC) key is pressed.

## CELL.PROTECTION(*[locked],[hidden]*) or CELL.PROTECTION?(*[locked],[hidden]*)

Same as the Format Cell Protection option (see Chapter 12 for a complete description). The arguments correspond to the check boxes in the Format Cell Protection dialog box. In the dialog box version (with the question mark), the arguments, if included, are used as default values for the dialog box that appears.

## CHANGE.LINK(*old-link-doc-name, new-link-doc-name*) or
## CHANGE.LINK?(*[old-link-doc-name], [new-link-doc-name]*)

Same as the File Links option (see Chapter 12 for a complete description). In the dialog box version (with the question mark), the arguments, if included, are used as default values for the dialog box that appears.

## CHECK.COMMAND(*bar,menu, command,check*)

Causes a check to be placed or removed from beside an option in a menu. *Bar* is the number of the menu bar, *menu* is the name or number of the menu, and *command* is the name or number of the command where you want to place or remove a check. If *check* is True, a check is placed beside the command. If *check* is False, a check is removed from beside the command.

## CLEAR(*x*) or
## CLEAR?( *[x]* )

Same as the Edit Clear option (see Chapter 12 for a complete description). The argument *x* controls what aspects of the range to clear and is one of the following numbers:

1. All
2. Formats
3. Formulas
4. Notes

The default value for *x* is 3, which is used if *x* is omitted. In the dialog box version (with the question mark), if the argument *x* is included, it is used as the default value for the dialog box that appears.

## CLOSE([x])

Same as the File Close option (see Chapter 12 for a complete description). The argument $x$ is a logical value that tells CLOSE what to do with unsaved changes. If $x$ is True, the changes are saved. If $x$ is False, the changes are not saved. If $x$ is omitted, a dialog box appears allowing you to choose if you want changes saved or not.

## CLOSE.ALL( )

Same as the File Close All option (see Chapter 12 for a complete description).

## COLUMN.WIDTH(*width,[range]*) or COLUMN.WIDTH?(*[width],[range]*)

Same as the Format Column Width option (see Chapter 12 for a complete description). *Width* is given as a number. The unit of *width* is the width of one character of the primary font for the current document. The primary font is the font that appears first in the Format Font dialog box. Range, if omitted, is assumed to be the current selection. In the dialog box version (with the question mark), the arguments, if included, are used as default values for the dialog box that appears.

## COMBINATION(*format*) or
## COMBINATION?(*[format]*)

Same as the Gallery Combination option (see Chapter 12 for a complete description). *Format* must be a number corresponding to gallery format. In the dialog box version (with the question mark), the argument, if included, is used as a default value for the dialog box that appears.

## COPY( )

Same as the Edit Copy option (see Chapter 12 for a complete description).

## COPY.CHART(*display*) or
## COPY.CHART?(*[display]*)

Same as the Edit Copy Chart option in Excel for the Apple Macintosh and Edit Copy Picture in Excel for Windows. If *display* is 1, the chart is copied as it is shown on the screen. If *display* is 2, the chart is copied as it is when it is printed. In the dialog box version (with the question mark), if the display option is included it is used as a default value for the dialog box that appears.

## COPY.PICTURE(*appearance,size*)

Same as the Edit Copy Picture option (see Chapter 12 for a complete description). The *appearance* and *size* arguments must be either 1 or 2. If the argument is given as 1, the picture is copied as it appears on the screen. If the argument is given as 2, the picture is copied as it appears when it is printed.

## CREATE.NAMES(*top-row,left-col, bottom-row,right-col*) or CREATE.NAMES?(*[top-row], [left-col],[bottom-row],[right-col]*)

Same as the Formula Create Names option (see Chapter 12 for a complete description). The arguments correspond to the check boxes in the Create Names dialog box. In the dialog box version (with the question mark), if the arguments are included, they are used as default values in the dialog box.

## CUT( )

Same as the Edit Cut option (see Chapter 12 for a complete description).

## DATA.DELETE( ) or DATA.DELETE?( )

Same as the Data Delete option (see Chapter 12 for a complete description). The dialog box version of the DATA.DELETE function (with the question mark) displays a warning dialog box that alerts the user that deleting data is permanent. The version without the question mark does not display the warning.

## DATA.FIND(*x*)

Same as the Data Find option if *x* is True and the Data Exit Find option if *x* is False. See Chapter 12 for a complete description of these options.

## DATA.FIND.NEXT( )

Same as pressing the (DOWN ARROW) key after choosing the Data Find option (see Chapter 12 for a complete description).

## DATA.FIND.PREV( )

Same as pressing the (UP ARROW) key after choosing the Data Find option (see Chapter 12 for a complete description).

## DATA.FORM( )

Same as the Data Form option (see Chapter 12 for a complete description).

## DATA.SERIES(*row-col,series, date,step,stop*) or DATA.SERIES?(*[row-col], [series],[date],[step],[stop]*)

Same as the Data Series option (see Chapter 12 for a complete description). The *row-col* argument must be either 1 (for rows) or

2 (for columns). The *series* option must be 1, 2, or 3. If *series* is 1, it is a linear type series. If *series* is 2, it is a growth type series. If *series* is 3, it is a date type series. The *date* argument must be 1 (day), 2 (weekday), 3 (month), or 4 (year). In the dialog box version (with the question mark), the arguments, if included, are used as default values for the dialog box that appears.

## DEFINE.NAME(*name,reference, [type],[shortcut]*) or DEFINE.NAME?(*[name], [reference],[type],[shortcut]*)

Same as the Formula Define Name option (see Chapter 12 for a complete description). *Reference* is assumed to be the current selection if it is omitted. If included, *reference* can be text, a value, a formula, a cell reference, or a range. The *type* and *shortcut* arguments are used only if the item being named is a macro. If *type* is 1, the macro is a function macro. If *type* is 2, the macro is a command macro. If *type* is 3, the item is not a macro. The default value for *type* is 3. The *shortcut* argument specifies the shortcut key for a macro. In the dialog box version (with the question mark), the arguments, if included, are used as default values for the dialog box that appears.

## DELETE.ARROW( )

Same as the Chart Delete Arrow option (see Chapter 12 for a complete description).

## DELETE.BAR(*x*)

Causes the menu bar specified by *x* to be deleted. The menu bar must have previously been added with the ADD.BAR function.

## DELETE.COMMAND(*bar-number, menu,command*)

Deletes a command from a menu. *Bar-number* is the number of the menu bar you want to delete the command from. The *menu* argument is the menu that you want to delete the command from. *Menu* can be a name or the number of the menu. *Command* is the name or the number of the command you want to delete.

## DELETE.FORMAT(*string*)

Same as deleting a format specified by the string argument with the Format Number option (see Chapter 12 for a complete description of this function).

## DELETE.MENU(*bar-number,menu*)

Deletes a menu from a menu bar. The *bar-number* is the number of the menu bar that you want to delete the menu from. The *menu* argument is the name or number of the menu that you want to delete. After you delete the menu, all the menus to the right of the deleted menu are shifted one position, so that their numbers are decreased by 1.

## DELETE.NAME(*name*)

Same as deleting a previously defined name with the Formula Define Name option (see Chapter 12 for a complete description).

## DELETE.OVERLAY( )

Same as the Chart Delete Overlay option (see Chapter 12 for a complete description).

## DEREF(*reference*)

Returns the value of the cell or range of cells referred to by *reference*. If *reference* refers to a range, then the value returned is an array.

## DIALOG.BOX(*reference*)

Causes the dialog box described in the area of a macro sheet given by the *reference* argument to be displayed. If *reference* is invalid, DIALOG.BOX returns the error #VALUE!. The reference area must, at a minimum, be two rows tall and must be seven columns wide. (See Chapter 11 for more information.)

## DIRECTORY(*path*)

Causes the current directory to be set to the directory that is specified by *path*.

*Example*  DIRECTORY("C:\data") causes the current directory to be set to C:\DATA.

## DISABLE.INPUT(*logical*)

Causes all input to be prevented if the logical value is True. If the logical value is False, input is enabled again.

## DISPLAY(*[formula],[gridlines], [headings],[zero],[color]*)

Same as the Options Display option (see Chapter 12 for a complete description). If an argument or arguments are omitted, their status is unchanged. The *color* argument is a number from 0 to 8, corresponding to the available colors shown in the Options Display dialog box.

## DISPLAY(cell,formula,value,format, protection,names, precedents, dependents,note)

Same as the Info menu. Each argument corresponds to an option on the Info menu. If an argument or arguments are omitted, their status is unchanged. All arguments except *precedents* and *dependents* must be either True, False, or omitted. If an argument is True, it is the same as enabling that option on the Info menu. The *precedents* and *dependents* arguments can be either 0, 1, or 2. If the argument is 0, no levels are listed. If the argument is 1, direct references are listed. If the argument is 2, all reference levels are listed.

## DOCUMENTS( )

Returns an array containing the names of all open documents in alphabetical order.

## ECHO(x)

Causes screen updating to be disabled if $x$ is False. Causes screen updating to be enabled if $x$ is True.

## EDIT.DELETE(x) or EDIT.DELETE?(x)

Same as the Edit Delete option (see Chapter 12 for more information). If $x$ is 1, cells are shifted left. If $x$ is 2, cells are shifted up. In the dialog box version (with the question mark), if the argument $x$

is included its value is used as the default for the dialog box that appears.

## ENABLE.COMMAND(*bar-number, menu-ref,command,enable*)

Enables a command on a menu if the *enable* argument is True. Disables a command on a menu if the *enable* argument is False. *Bar-number* is the number of the menu bar on which you want to enable or disable the command. The *menu-ref* argument is the menu on which you want to enable or disable the command. *Menu-ref* can be a name or the number of the menu. *Command* is the name or the number of the command you want to enable or disable.

## ERROR(*enable,[macro]*)

Turns error checking on if *enable* is True, and turns error checking off if *enable* is False. If *enable* is True and a macro reference is included, control is given to the macro specified by the *macro* argument. This allows you to customize error handling.

## EXEC(*name,[window]*)

Causes the program given by the *name* argument to start running. The *window* argument must be a 1, 2, or 3. If the argument is 1, the program is started in a normal window. If the argument is 2, the program is started in a minimized window. If the argument is 3, the program is started in a maximized window. If the EXEC function cannot start the program, an error value of #VALUE! is returned. If EXEC is successful, the ID number of the started program is returned.

## EXECUTE(*channel,string*)

Executes the command(s) specified by the *string* in the application connected to the given *channel*. If the channel number is not valid, EXECUTE returns a #VALUE! error. If the application connected to the given channel is unavailable, EXECUTE returns an #N/A! error. If the (ESC) key is pressed before the application has a chance to answer, EXECUTE returns a #DIV/0! error. If the request is refused by the application, EXECUTE returns a #REF! error.

## EXTRACT(*unique*) or EXTRACT?(*[unique]*)

Same as the Data Extract option (see Chapter 12 for a complete description). If *unique* is True, the unique check box is turned on. If *unique* is False, the unique check box is turned off. In the dialog box version (with the question mark), if the *unique* argument is included, the value is used as a default for the dialog box that appears.

## FCLOSE(*x*)

Causes a file opened with the FOPEN function to be closed. The argument *x* is the file number returned by FOPEN. If *x* is not a valid file number, FCLOSE returns the error #VALUE!.

## FILE.CLOSE( )

Same as the File Close option (see Chapter 12 for more information on this function).

## FILE.DELETE(*name*) or
## FILE.DELETE?(*[name]*)

Same as the File Delete option (see Chapter 12 for more information). The *name* argument is a text string that is the name of the document you want to delete. In the non-dialog box version (without the question mark), if the name is invalid FILE.DELETE displays a dialog box asking for a valid filename. In the dialog box version (with the question mark), you can use Excel wildcards in the *name* argument to show only certain files in the dialog box that appears.

## FILES(*[directory]*)

Returns an array containing the filenames of the files in the specified directory.

## FILL.DOWN( )

Same as the Edit Fill Down option (see Chapter 12 for more information).

## FILL.LEFT( )

Same as the Edit Fill Left option (see Chapter 12 for more information).

## FILL.RIGHT( )

Same as the Edit Fill Right option (see Chapter 12 for more information).

## FILL.UP( )

Same as the Edit Fill Up option (see Chapter 12 for more information on this function).

## FOPEN(*name-string,access-type*)

Causes the file specified by *name-string* to be opened, and an ID number to be returned. If the name is not valid, FOPEN returns an #N/A! error. The *access-type* argument must be 1, 2, or 3. If *access-type* is 1, the file is given a read/write status. If *access-type* is 2, the file is give a read only status. If *access-type* is 3, a new file is opened and given read/write status.

## FOR(*counter,start,end,step*)

Begins a FOR-NEXT loop that continues until *counter* reaches the *end* value, or until the (ESC) key is pressed. The *start* value is initially added to the counter and, on each iteration of the loop, the *step* value is added to the *counter*. The loop begins with the function immediately following FOR and extends to NEXT. When *counter* exceeds *end*, execution continues with the function immediately following NEXT.

## FORMAT.FONT(*name,size,bold, italic,underline,strikeout*) or FORMAT.FONT?(*[name],[size], [bold],[italic],[underline],[strikeout]*)

Same as the Format Font option if the current document is a worksheet or macro sheet (see Chapter 12 for more information).

The arguments correspond to the options in the Format Font dialog box. *Size* is the size of the font in points. *Bold, italic, underline,* and *strikeout* must be True to turn the option on and False to turn the option off. In the dialog box version (with the question mark), the arguments, if included, are the default values for the dialog box that appears.

## FORMAT.FONT(*color, background,apply-all,font-name,size, bold, italic,underline,strikeout* ) or FORMAT.FONT?(*[color], [background],[apply-all],[font-name],[size], [bold],[italic],[underline],[strikeout]*)

Same as the Format Font option if the current document is a chart (see Chapter 12 for more information). The arguments correspond to the options in the Format Font dialog box. *Color* is a number from 0 through 8 corresponding to the nine color choices in the Format Font dialog box. *Background* is 1 (automatic), 2 (transparent), or 3 (white out). *Apply-all* corresponds to the Apply All check box. *Font-name* is the name of the font. *Size* is the size of the font in points. *Bold, italic, underline,* and *strikeout* correspond to check boxes with the same name. A logical value of True turns the check box on, and a value of False turns the check box off. In the dialog box version (with the question mark), the arguments, if included, are the default values for the dialog box that appears.

## FORMAT.LEGEND(*position*) or FORMAT.LEGEND?(*[position]*)

Same as the Format Legend option (see Chapter 12 for more information). The *position* argument can be any of the following numbers:

1 Bottom
2 Corner
3 Top
4 Vertical

In the dialog box version (with the question mark), the argument, if included, is a default value for the dialog box that appears.

## FORMAT.MOVE(*x,y*) or FORMAT.MOVE?(*[x],[y]*)

Same as the Format Move option (see Chapter 12 for more information). The units for the arguments *x* and *y* are points. *X* and *y* are measured from the lower-left corner of the window. In the dialog box version (with the question mark), the arguments, if included, are default values for the dialog box that appears.

## FORMAT.NUMBER(*string*) or FORMAT.NUMBER?(*[string]*)

Same as the Format Number option (see Chapter 12 for more information). The argument *string* is the format for the number given as a text string such as "$#,##0". In the dialog box version (with the question mark), the argument, if included, is a default for the dialog box that appears.

## FORMAT.SIZE(*width,height*) or FORMAT.SIZE?(*[width],[height]*)

Same as the Format Size option (see Chapter 12 for more information). *Width* and *height* are numbers whose units are points. In the dialog box version (with the question mark), the arguments, if included, are default values for the dialog box that appears.

## FORMAT.TEXT(horizontal-alignment, vertical-alignment,vertical-text,automatic-text,automatic-size,show-key,show-value) or FORMAT.TEXT?([horizontal-alignment], [vertical-alignment],[vertical-text], [automatic-text],[automatic-size], [show-key],[show-value] )

Same as the Format Text option (see Chapter 12 for more information). *Horizontal-alignment* and *vertical-alignment* can be 1 (top), 2 (center), or 3 (right). The rest of the options correspond to check boxes with the same name. A value of True turns the check box on; a value of False turns the check box off. In the dialog box version (with the question mark), the arguments, if included, are default values for the dialog box that appears.

## FORMULA(*formula-string,reference*)

Causes the formula given in the *formula-string* argument to be entered into the cell designated by the *reference* argument if the current document is a worksheet. If the current document is a chart, then *formula-string* is entered in the current selection. The current selection determines how the formula string is treated in a chart.

## FORMULA.ARRAY (*formula-string,reference*)

This is the same as entering an array formula and then pressing `CTRL + SHIFT + ENTER`.

## FORMULA.FILL
## (*formula-string,[reference]*)

Same as entering a formula and pressing (CTRL + ENTER). The formula in the *formula-string* argument is entered into the cell or cells specified by the *reference* argument. If *reference* is omitted the formula is entered into the cells in the current selection.

## FORMULA.FIND(*string,in,at,by,dir*) or
## FORMULA.FIND?(*[string],[in],[at],[by],[dir]*)

Same as the Formula Find option (see Chapter 12 for more information). *String* specifies the search text string. The arguments *in, at, by,* and *dir* are defined as follows:

| In | At | By | Dir |
|---|---|---|---|
| 1  Formulas | 1  Whole | 1  Rows | 1  Next |
| 2  Values | 2  Part | 2  Columns | 2  Previous |
| 3  Notes | | | |

In the dialog box version (with the question mark), the arguments, if included, are default values for the dialog box that appears.

## FORMULA.FIND.NEXT( )

Same as pressing the (F7) key (see Formula Find in Chapter 12 for more information).

## FORMULA.FIND.PREV( )

Same as pressing the SHIFT + F7 keys (see Formula Find in Chapter 12 for more information).

## FORMULA.GOTO(*reference*) or FORMULA.GOTO?(*[reference]*)

Same as the Formula Goto option (see Chapter 12 for more information). The dialog box version (with the question mark) of the FORMULA.GOTO function has an optional *reference* argument. If *reference* is omitted, FORMULA.GOTO? goes to the cells that were active before the FORMULA.GOTO? function was executed.

## FORMULA.REPLACE(*search-string, replace-string,[at],[by],[which-cells]*) or FORMULA.REPLACE?(*[search-string], [replace-string],[at],[by],[which-cells]*)

Same as the Formula Replace option (see Chapter 12 for more information). The arguments *at* and *by* are defined as follows:

| At | | By | |
|---|---|---|---|
| 1 | Whole | 1 | Rows |
| 2 | Part | 2 | Columns |

The *which-cells* argument is a logical value that is True if you want to replace only the current cell and False if you want to replace the whole selection or the whole document (if the current selection is a cell). In the dialog box version (with the question mark), the arguments, if included, are default values for the dialog box that appears.

## FPOS(*file,[position]*)

Positions the file opened with the FOPEN function, specified by the file number given by the FOPEN function. If the *position* argument is not given, it is assumed to be the current position.

## FREAD(*file,number-of-characters*)

Reads the *number-of-characters* given in *file*. *File* must be a file opened with the FOPEN function and specified by the file number returned by FOPEN. If the file number is not valid, FREAD returns a #VALUE! error. If FREAD cannot read the specified *number-of-characters*, FREAD returns an #N/A! error.

## FREADLN(*file*)

Reads from the current position to the end of the line from *file*. *File* must be a file opened with the FOPEN function and specified by the file number returned by FOPEN. If the file number is not valid, FREADNL returns a #VALUE! error. If FREADLN cannot read the specified value, FREADLN returns an #N/A! error.

## FREEZE.PANES(*x*)

Same as the Options Freeze Panes option if *x* is True. Same as the Options Unfreeze Panes option if *x* is False (see Chapter 12 for more information).

## FSIZE(*file*)

Returns the size of *file*. The size is measured in number of characters. *File* must have been opened with the FOPEN function and be specified with the number that FOPEN returns. If the file number is not valid, FSIZE returns a #VALUE! error.

## FULL(x)

Same as maximizing the active window by pressing (CTRL + F10), if *x* is True. Same as restoring the active window by pressing (CTRL + F5), if *x* is False.

## FWRITE(*file,string*)

Causes the *string* to be written into the file at the current position. *File* must be a file opened with the FOPEN function and specified by the number returned by FOPEN. If the file number is not valid, FWRITE returns a #VALUE! error. If FWRITE is unable to write to the file, WRITE returns an #N/A! error.

## FWRITELN(*file,string*)

Causes *string*, followed by a linefeed, to be written into *file* at the current position. *File* must be a file opened with the FOPEN function and specified by the number returned by FOPEN. If the file number is not valid, FWRITELN returns a #VALUE! error. If FWRITELN is unable to write to the file, WRITELN returns an #N/A! error.

## GALLERY.AREA(*format, [cancel-overlay]*) or GALLERY.AREA?(*[format],[cancel-overlay]*)

Same as the Gallery Area option (see Chapter 12 for more information). *Format* is the number of the format in the gallery. If *cancel-overlay* is True, the overlay chart is deleted. If *cancel-overlay* is False, the format is applied to whichever chart contains the current selection. The default value for *cancel-overlay* is False. In the dialog box version (with the question mark), the arguments, if included, are default values for the dialog box that appears.

## GALLERY.BAR(*format*, [*cancel-overlay*]) or GALLERY.BAR?([*format*], [*cancel-overlay*])

Same as the Gallery Bar option (see Chapter 12 for more information). *Format* is the number of the format in the gallery. If *cancel-overlay* is True, the overlay chart is deleted. If *cancel-overlay* is False, the format is applied to whichever chart contains the current selection. The default value for *cancel-overlay* is False. In the dialog box version (with the question mark), the arguments, if included, are default values for the dialog box that appears.

## GALLERY.COLUMN(*format*, [*cancel-overlay*]) or GALLERY.COLUMN?([*format*], [*cancel-overlay*])

Same as the Gallery Column option (see Chapter 12 for more information). *Format* is the number of the format in the gallery. If *cancel-overlay* is True, the overlay chart is deleted. If *cancel-overlay* is False, the format is applied to whichever chart contains the current selection. The default value for *cancel-overlay* is False. In the dialog box version (with the question mark), the arguments, if included, are default values for the dialog box that appears.

## GALLERY.LINE(*format, [cancel-overlay]*) or GALLERY.LINE?(*[format], [cancel-overlay]*)

Same as the Gallery Line option (see Chapter 12 for more information). *Format* is the number of the format in the gallery. If *cancel-overlay* is True, the overlay chart is deleted. If *cancel-overlay* is False, the format is applied to whichever chart contains the current selection. The default value for *cancel-overlay* is False. In the dialog box version (with the question mark), the arguments, if included, are default values for the dialog box that appears.

## GALLERY.PIE(*format, [cancel-overlay]*) or GALLERY.PIE?(*[format], [cancel-overlay]*)

Same as the Gallery Pie option (see Chapter 12 for more information). *Format* is the number of the format in the gallery. If *cancel-overlay* is True, the overlay chart is deleted. If *cancel-overlay* is False, the format is applied to whichever chart contains the current selection. The default value for *cancel-overlay* is False. In the dialog box version (with the question mark), the arguments, if included, are default values for the dialog box that appears.

## GALLERY.SCATTER(*format, [cancel-overlay]*) or GALLERY.SCATTER?(*[format], [cancel-overlay]*)

Same as the Gallery Scatter option (see Chapter 12 for more information). *Format* is the number of the format in the gallery. If *cancel-overlay* is True, the overlay chart is deleted. If *cancel-overlay* is False, the format is applied to whichever chart contains the current selection. The default value for *cancel-overlay* is False. In the dialog box version (with the question mark), the arguments, if included, are default values for the dialog box that appears.

## GET.BAR( )

Returns the number representing the current menu bar.

## GET.CELL(*type,[reference]*)

Returns information about a cell given as a cell reference. If *reference* is a range, the information is given about the upper-left cell in the range. If *reference* is missing, the default is the active selection. The *type* argument allows you to specify the type of information you would like returned about the cell. *Type* can be any of the following:

1. Returns the reference of the top left cell, as text
2. Returns thg top row
3. Returns the left column

4 Returns the type of the cell
5 Returns the contents of the cell
6 Returns the formula in the cell, as text
7 Returns the format of the cell, as text
8 Returns the alignment of the cell
   1 General
   2 Left
   3 Center
   4 Right
   5 Fill
9 Returns True if cell has a left border; otherwise returns False
10 Returns True if cell has a right border; otherwise returns False
11 Returns True if cell has a top border; otherwise returns False
12 Returns True if cell has a bottom border; otherwise returns False
13 Returns True if the cell is shaded; otherwise returns False
14 Returns True if the cell is locked; otherwise returns False
15 Returns True if the cell is hidden; otherwise returns False
16 Returns the width of the cell, in characters
17 Returns the height of the cell, in points
18 Returns the name of the font used in the cell, as text
19 Returns the font size, in points
20 Returns True if the cell is bold; otherwise returns False
21 Returns True if the cell is italic; otherwise returns False
22 Returns True if the cell is underlined; otherwise returns False
23 Returns True if the cell is overstruck; otherwise returns False

# GET.CHART.ITEM
# (*horizontal-vertical,[point],[item]*)

Returns the position of a chart item. If you want the horizontal position, set the *horizontal-vertical* argument to 1. If you want the vertical position, set the *horizontal-vertical* argument to 2. The *point* argument defines what part of the item you would like the position of. If the item is a point, set the *point* argument to 1. If the item is a non-data line, set the *point* argument to 1 for lower-left and 2 for upper-right. If the item is an arrow, set the *point* argument to 1 for the base of the arrow and 2 for the head of the arrow. If the item is an area, use the following values for the point argument:

1. Upper-left
2. Upper-middle
3. Upper-right
4. Middle-right
5. Lower-right
6. Lower-middle
7. Lower-left
8. Middle-left

If the item is a pie section, use the following values for the point argument:

1. Outer-counterclockwise point
2. Outer-center point
3. Outer-clockwise point
4. Mid-clockwise point
5. Center point
6. Mid-counterclockwise point

The *item* argument allows you to select an item. If the argument is omitted, it is assumed to be the current item selected.

## GET.DEF(*definition-string,[document]*)

Returns a name that is defined for *definition-string* in *document*. If *definition-string* is a cell reference, it should be given in R1C1 style. If more than one name is defined for *definition-string,* the first name is returned.

## GET.DOCUMENT(*type,[name]*)

Returns information about a document. The *type* argument controls what information about the document is returned. Types 1 through 8 are general information, types 9 through 12 differ depending on the kind of document, and types 13 through 26 apply to worksheets and macros.

1. Returns the document name as text.
2. Returns the path of the document as text. If the document is unsaved, GET.DOCUMENT returns an #N/A! error.
3. Returns the document type:
   1. Worksheet
   2. Chart
   3. Macro
   4. Info
4. Returns True if there are unsaved changes in the document; otherwise returns False.
5. Returns True if the document is read only; otherwise returns False.
6. Returns True if the document is protected; otherwise returns False.
7. Returns True if the document contents are protected; otherwise returns False.

8   Returns True if the document windows are protected; otherwise returns False.
9   If the document is a chart, returns the chart type:
    1   Area        4   Line
    2   Bar         5   Pie
    3   Column      6   Scatter
9   Returns the number of the first unempty row, if the document is a worksheet or a macro.
10  If the document is a chart, returns the overlay chart type, or #N/A! if there is no overlay chart.
    1   Area        4   Line
    2   Bar         5   Pie
    3   Column      6   Scatter
10  Returns the number of the last unempty row, if the document is a worksheet or a macro.
11  Returns the number of series there are in the main chart, if the document is a chart.
11  Returns the number of the first unempty column, if the document is a worksheet or a macro.
12  Returns the number of series there are in the overlay chart, if the document is a chart.
12  Returns the number of the last unempty column, if the document is a worksheet or a macro.
13  Returns the number of windows there are for the document.
14  Returns the calculation type:
    1   Automatic
    2   Automatic, except tables
    3   Manual
15  Returns True if iteration is turned on; otherwise returns False.
16  Returns the maximum number of iterations.
17  Returns the maximum change between iterations.
18  Returns True if remote reference updating is turned on; otherwise returns False.

19   Returns True if document is set to Precision As Displayed; otherwise returns False.

20   Returns True if 1904 date system is enabled; otherwise returns False.

21   Returns the four fonts for the document in an array.

22   Returns the sizes of the four fonts for the document in an array.

23   Returns a logical array indicating which of the four fonts are bold.

24   Returns a logical array indicating which of the four fonts are italic.

25   Returns a logical array indicating which of the four fonts are underlined.

26   Returns a logical array indicating which of the four fonts are overstruck.

## GET.FORMULA(*reference*)

Returns the contents of the cell, as text, referred to by *reference*, as it appears in the Formula bar. If the reference is a range, GET.FORMULA returns the contents of the upper-left cell, as text, in the range as it appears in the Formula bar.

## GET.NAME(*name*)

Returns what *name* refers to. If *name* is given as a reference, it should be in R1C1 style.

## GET.NOTE(*reference, [start],[length]* )

Returns the note attached to the cell referred to by *reference*, starting at *start* and of the length given by *length*. If *start* is omitted, the default value is 1. If *length* is omitted, the default value is the length of the note or 255, whichever is less.

## GET.WINDOW(*type, [window-name]*)

Returns information about the window referred to by *window-name*. The *type* argument allows you to determine the type of information that is returned. Types 1 through 7 are general information, types 8 through 12 apply to worksheets and macros, and types 13 through 19 return horizontal arrays.

| | |
|---|---|
| 1 | Returns the name of the document in the window, as text |
| 2 | Returns the number of the window |
| 3 | Returns the horizontal position measured in points from the left edge of the screen |
| 4 | Returns the vertical position measured in points from the top of the screen |
| 5 | Returns the width of the window, in points |
| 6 | Returns the height of the window, in points |
| 7 | Returns True if the window is hidden; otherwise returns False |
| 8 | Returns True if formulas are displayed; otherwise returns False |
| 9 | Returns True if gridlines are displayed; otherwise returns False |
| 10 | Returns True if row and column headings are displayed; otherwise returns False |
| 11 | Returns True if zeros are displayed; otherwise returns False |
| 12 | Returns the color of the gridlines and headings as a number from 0 through 8, as shown in the Options Display dialog box (0 is Automatic) |

13  Returns the left column of every window pane as a horizontal array
14  Returns the top row of every window pane as a horizontal array
15  Returns the number of columns in every window pane as a horizontal array
16  Returns the number of rows in every window pane as a horizontal array
17  Returns the number of the active pane (1 is upper-left or upper, 2 is upper-right or right, 3 is lower-left or lower, 4 is lower-right)
18  Returns the logical value True if the window is split vertically; otherwise returns False
19  Returns the logical value True if the window is split horizontally; otherwise returns False

## GET.WORKSPACE(*type*)

Returns information about the workspace, where *type* controls the information that is returned; as outlined here:

1  Returns the name of the environment, as text
2  Returns the version of Microsoft Excel that you are running
3  Returns the number of decimals if autodecimal is turned on; otherwise returns 0
4  Returns True if the workspace is in R1C1 mode; otherwise returns False
5  Returns True if the scroll bars are displayed; otherwise returns False
6  Returns True if the status bar is displayed; otherwise returns False
7  Returns True if the formula bar is displayed; otherwise returns False

8   Returns True if remote requests are allowed; otherwise returns False
9   Returns either the alternate menu key or the #N/A! error if there is no alternate menu key set
10  Returns the mode of the workspace:
    0   No mode
    1   Data find mode
    2   Copy mode
    3   Cut mode
11  Returns the horizontal position of the Excel window measured from the left edge of the screen, in points
12  Returns the vertical position of the Excel window measured from the top edge of the screen, in points
13  Returns the width of the workspace, in points
14  Returns the height of the workspace, in points
15  Returns a number that indicates the status of the Excel workspace:
    1   Regular
    2   Minimized
    3   Maximized
16  Returns the amount of free memory, in kilobytes
17  Returns the total amount of memory available, in kilobytes
18  Returns True if you have a math coprocessor; otherwise returns False
19  Returns True if you have a mouse; otherwise returns False

## GOTO(*reference*)

Moves the current cell on a macro sheet to the cell referred to by *reference*. Usually *reference* is a cell, but if it is a range, the current cell is the upper-left cell in the range. GOTO is used to control the execution flow of a macro.

## GRIDLINES(*category-major-gridlines, category- minor-gridlines,value-major-gridlines,value-minor-gridlines*) or GRIDLINES?(*[category-major-gridlines], [category-minor- gridlines],[value-major-gridlines],[value-minor-gridlines]*)

Same as the Chart Gridlines option (see Chapter 12 for more information). The arguments correspond to check boxes in the dialog box. In the dialog box version (with the question mark) the arguments, if included, are default settings for the dialog box.

## HALT( )

Causes all macros to stop execution.

## HELP(*[topic]*)

Causes help to be displayed on the specified topic. *Topic* is a reference to a range in a custom help file. If no *topic* argument is given, HELP displays the help index.

## HIDE( )

Same as the Window Hide option (see Chapter 12 for more information).

## HLINE(*number-of-columns*)

Same as scrolling by column. *Number-of- columns* controls how many columns to scroll past. Positive numbers scroll to the right; negative numbers scroll to the left.

## HPAGE(*number-of-windows*)

Same as scrolling horizontally by window. *Number-of-windows* controls how many windows to scroll past. Positive numbers scroll to the right; negative numbers scroll to the left.

## HSCROLL(*scroll-to,[logical]*)

Same as scrolling horizontally. If the *logical* argument is True, then HSCROLL scrolls to the column given as the *scroll-to* argument. If *logical* is False or not present, then *scroll-to* should be given as a fraction between 0 and 1. If *scroll-to* is 0, HSCROLL scrolls to the left edge of the current document. If *scroll-to* is 1, HSCROLL scrolls to the right edge of the current document. Any fraction in between 0 and 1 causes HSCROLL to scroll to the appropriate column (there are 256 possible columns, so 23/256 would scroll to column 23).

## INITIATE(*application,topic*)

Causes a dynamic data exchange (DDE) channel to be opened between Excel and the specified application, and returns the channel number. *Topic* can be something specific to the application, or simply "System," or the name of a document. To use INITIATE you must have the full version of Windows (version 2.0 or later).

## INPUT(*prompt,type,[title], [default],[horizontal],[vertical]*)

Causes an input dialog box to be displayed. The *prompt, title,* and *default* arguments are text strings. The default *title* is "Input." The *type* argument can be one of the following:

| | |
|---|---|
| 1 Formula | 8 Reference |
| 2 Number | 16 Error |
| 3 Text | 64 Array |
| 4 Logical | |

The *horizontal* and *vertical* arguments are given in points from the edge of the workspace. The dialog box is centered if these arguments are not present.

## INSERT(*direction*) or INSERT?(*[direction]*)

Same as the Edit Insert option (see Chapter 12 for more information). If *direction* is 1, cells are shifted right. If *direction* is 2, cells are shifted down. In the dialog box version (with the question mark) the argument, if included, is a default for the dialog box that appears.

## JUSTIFY( )

Same as the Format Justify option (see Chapter 12 for more information).

## LEGEND(*logical*)

Same as the Chart Add Legend option if the *logical* argument is True. Same as the Chart Delete Legend option if the *logical* argument is False. (See Chapter 12 for more information.)

## LINKS(*name*)

Returns an array of names of all external links to the document named. If there are no external references, LINKS returns an #N/A! error.

## LIST.NAMES( )

Same as selecting the Formula Paste Name option, and then choosing the Paste List button (see Chapter 12 for more information).

## MAIN.CHART(type,stacked,100%, vary-by-cat,overlapped,drop-lines, hi-lo-lines,overlap%,cluster%,pie-angle) or MAIN.CHART?([type],[stacked],[100%], [vary-by-cat],[overlapped],[drop-lines], [hi-lo-lines],[overlap%],[cluster%],[pie-angle] )

Same as the Formula Main Chart option (see Chapter 12 for more information). The *type* argument can have the following values:

1. Area
2. Bar
3. Column
4. Line
5. Pie
6. Scatter

The *stacked, 100%, vary-by-cat, overlapped, drop-lines,* and *hi-lo-lines* arguments are check boxes. If the argument is True, the check box is checked. *Overlap%, cluster%,* and *pie-angle* are numbers. If an argument does not apply to a type of chart, it is ignored. In the dialog box version (with the question mark), the arguments, if included, are default values for the dialog box that appears.

## MAIN.CHART.TYPE(type)

This is the same as the Excel for the Apple Macintosh function MAIN.CHART(*type*). This macro function is included for compatibility.

## MESSAGE(*logical,[message-string]*)

Causes a message string to be displayed in the message area of the Status bar, if the *logical* argument is True. Causes the status bar to show regular command help messages, if the *logical* argument is False.

## MOVE(*horizontal,vertical, [window-name]*)

Same as the Control Move option. Causes the specified window (or the current window if the *window-name* argument is omitted) to be moved so that its upper-left corner is positioned according to the horizontal and vertical arguments (measured in points).

## NAMES(*[document]*)

Returns an array containing all the names defined for *document*. If *document* is not specified, NAMES returns an array of names defined for the active document.

## NEW(*file-type*) or NEW?(*[file-type]*)

Same as the File New option (see Chapter 12 for more information). In the dialog box version (with the question mark), if the *file-type* argument is included, it is used as a default value for the dialog box that appears. Listed here are the different file type options:

1. Worksheet
2. Chart
3. Macro

## NEW.WINDOW( )

Same as the Window New Window option (see Chapter 12 for more information).

## NEXT( )

Terminates a FOR-NEXT loop or a WHILE-NEXT loop. See the FOR macro function description.

## NOTE(*[new-string],[reference], [start],[length]* )

Causes a note to be modified for a cell referred to by *reference*. *New-string* replaces the number of characters in the existing note specified by *length*, starting at the character specified by *start*. The defaults for the arguments are listed here:

| | |
|---|---|
| *new-string* | "" |
| *reference* | Active cell |
| *start* | 1 |
| *length* | Length of *new-string* or 255, whichever is less |

## OFFSET(*reference,row-offset, column-offset,[height],[width]* )

Returns a reference offset from the specified reference. The *row-offset* and *column-offset* arguments are used to find the upper-left corner of the reference to be returned. OFFSET returns a reference *width* wide and *height* tall. If the *width* and *height* arguments are not given, the default value for each argument is 1.

***Example***   OFFSET(A1,2,2,2,2) returns C3:D4.

## ON.DATA(*document,[macro]*)

Causes *macro* to start whenever the remotely referenced *document* receives data from another application, if the *macro* argument is included. Causes ON.DATA to be turned off if the *macro* argument is not included.

## ON.KEY(*key,macro*)

Causes *macro* to be started whenever *key* (or a key combination) is pressed. *Key* (or a key combination) must be given as a text string. If you want to use a nonalphanumeric key, place the name of the key inside braces or curly brackets. Listed here are some special codes for keys that are coded with characters other than their key names:

| Key | Code |
|---|---|
| ALT | % |
| CTRL | ^ |
| DOWN ARROW | {DOWN} |
| ENTER | ~ OR {ENTER} |
| ESCAPE | {ESC} OR {ESCAPE} |
| LEFT ARROW | {LEFT} |
| PGDN | {PGDN} |
| PGUP | {PGUP} |
| PRTSC | {PRTSC} |
| RIGHT ARROW | {RIGHT} |
| SHIFT | + |
| UP ARROW | {UP} |

If you want to enter a %, ^, ~, or + meaning the key itself, enclose the symbol in braces.

***Example*** ON.KEY("+{PGUP}","REC.XLM!MonthEnd") starts MonthEnd when the (SHIFT + PGUP) keys are pressed.

## ON.TIME(*time,macro,[wait],[logical]*)

Causes *macro* to start at the specified time, if the *logical* argument is True. Causes previous requests to start *macro* at the specified time to be ignored if the *logical* argument is False. If the *logical* argument is omitted, the default value is True. The *time* argument can be just a time, or a date and a time. If it is just a time, the macro runs every day at the same time. If Excel cannot start the macro at the specified time, it keeps trying for the amount of time specified by *wait*. The default value for *wait* is the maximum time.

## ON.WINDOW(*[window-name],macro*)

Causes *macro* to start whenever the window specified by *window-name* is activated. Both arguments must be given as strings. If *window-name* is not given, the macro is started whenever any window is activated.

## OPEN(*file,links,read-only*) or OPEN?(*[file],[links],[read-only]*)

Same as the File Open option (see Chapter 12 for more information). The *file* argument must be given as a text string. In the dialog box version (with the question mark), the *file* argument can contain Excel wildcards, so you can control the files listed in the dialog box that appears. The *links* argument can be one of the following numbers:

0   Do not update references
1   Update external references only
2   Update remote references only
3   Update external and remote references

The *read-only* argument corresponds to the read-only check box. Set *read-only* to True to turn the check box on and to False to turn the check box off.

## OPEN.LINKS(*document-list, [read-only]*) or OPEN.LINKS?(*[document-list], [read-only]*)

Same as the File Links option. *Document-list* must be a list of text strings that are document names, references, or arrays that contain names or references. In the dialog box version (with the question mark), they are listed in the dialog box that appears. The *read-only* argument corresponds to the read-only check box in the File Links dialog box. In the dialog box version, if a value is given for the *read-only* argument, it is the default for the dialog box that appears.

*Example*   OPEN LINKS(LINKS( )) opens the files that are linked to the current document.

## OVERLAY(*type,stacked,100%, vary-by- cat,overlapped,drop-lines, hi-lo-lines,overlap%,cluster%,pie-angle*) or OVERLAY?([*type*],[*stacked*],[*100%*], [*vary-by-cat*],[*overlapped*],[*drop-lines*], [*hi-lo- lines*],[*overlap%*],[*cluster%*],[*pie-angle*] )

Same as the Format Overlay option (see Chapter 12 for more information). The *type* argument can have the following values:

1 Area        4 Line
2 Bar         5 Pie
3 Column      6 Scatter

The *stacked, 100%, vary-by-cat, overlapped, drop-lines,* and *hi-lo-lines* arguments correspond to check boxes. If one or more of these arguments are True, those check boxes are checked. The *overlap%, cluster%,* and *pie-angle* arguments are numbers. Arguments that do not apply to a particular chart type are ignored for that type.

## OVERLAY.CHART.TYPE(*type*)

Same as the Excel for the Apple Macintosh function OVERLAY(type-1). This macro function is included for compatibility. Same as DELETE.OVERLAY if the *type* argument is 0.

**PAGE.SETUP(***header,footer,l-margin, r-margin,top-margin,bottom-margin, headings,gridlines***)** or
**PAGE.SETUP?(***[header],[footer], [l-margin],[r-margin],[top-margin], [bottom-margin],[headings],[gridlines]***)**

> Same as the File Page Setup option, if the active document is a worksheet or macro sheet (see Chapter 12 for more information). The *header* and *footer* arguments should be given as text strings. The margin arguments should be given as numbers. The *headings* and *gridlines* arguments correspond to check boxes, and if they are True the box is checked. In the dialog box version (with the question mark), the arguments, if included, are default values for the dialog box that appears.

**PAGE.SETUP(***header,footer,l-margin, r-margin,top-margin,bottom-margin,size***)** or
**PAGE.SETUP?(***[header],[footer], [l-margin],[r-margin],[top-margin], [bottom-margin],[size]***)**

> Same as the File Page Setup option, if the active document is a chart (see Chapter 12 for more information). The *header* and *footer* arguments should be given as text strings. The margin arguments should be given as numbers. The *size* argument can have any of the following values:

1  Screen size
2  Fit to page
3  Full page

In the dialog box version (with the question mark), the arguments, if included, are default values for the dialog box that appears.

## PARSE(*string*) or PARSE?(*[string]*)

Same as the Data Parse option where the text string is the parse line (see Chapter 12 for more information). In the dialog box version (with the question mark), the argument, if included, is a default value for the dialog box that appears.

## PASTE( )

Same as the Edit Paste option (see Chapter 12 for more information on this function).

## PASTE.LINK( )

Same as the Edit Paste Link option (see Chapter 12 for more information).

## PASTE.SPECIAL(attribute,operation, skip-blanks,transpose) or PASTE.SPECIAL?([attribute],[operation], [skip-blanks],[transpose])

Same as the Edit Paste Special option, if you are pasting into a worksheet or a macro sheet (see Chapter 12 for more information). In the dialog box version (with the question mark), the arguments, if included, are default values for the dialog box that appears. The *attribute* argument allows you to choose which of the following attributes you want to paste:

1. All
2. Formulas
3. Values
4. Formats
5. Notes

The *operation* argument allows you to choose which of the following operations you would like to perform on the paste range:

1. None
2. Add
3. Subtract
4. Multiply
5. Divide

The *skip-blanks* and the *transpose* arguments correspond to check boxes with the same name.

## PASTE.SPECIAL(*orientation,series, categories,apply-to-all*) or PASTE.SPECIAL?(*[orientation], [series],[categories],[apply-to-all]*)

Same as the Edit Paste Special option, if you are pasting from a worksheet into a chart (see Chapter 12 for more information). In the dialog box version (with the question mark), the arguments, if included, are default values for the dialog box that appears. The *orientation* argument allows you to tell PASTE.SPECIAL if the values are in rows (1) or columns (2). The remaining arguments correspond to the check boxes in the Paste Special dialog box.

## PASTE.SPECIAL(*attribute*) or PASTE.SPECIAL?(*[attribute]*)

Same as the Edit Paste Special option, if you are pasting from a worksheet or macro onto a chart (see Chapter 12 for more information). In the dialog box version (with the question mark), the arguments, if included, are default settings for the dialog box that appears. The *attribute* argument allows you to choose which of the following attributes you want to paste:

1. All
2. Formats
3. Formulas

## PATTERNS(*auto-border,border-style, border-color,border-weight, shadow,auto-area,pattern,foreground, background,apply-to-all*)

Same as the Format Patterns option, if the current selection is a chart or part of a chart, such as a plot area, legend, label, or bar (see Chapter 12 for more information). The *border-style, border-color, border-weight, shadow, pattern, foreground, background,* and *apply-to-all* arguments correspond to settings in the Format Patterns dialog box. The *auto-border* and the *auto-area* arguments can have the following values:

- 0   Set by the user
- 1   Set automatically
- 2   Invisible

## PATTERNS(*auto-line,line-style, line-color,line-weight,major-ticks, minor-ticks,tick-labels*)

Same as the Format Patterns option, if the current selection is an axis (see Chapter 12 for more information). The *line-style, line-color,* and *line-weight* arguments correspond to settings in the Format Patterns dialog box. The *auto-line* argument can have the following values:

- 0   Set by the user
- 1   Set automatically
- 2   Invisible

The *major-ticks* and *minor-ticks* arguments can have the following values:

1 Invisible
2 Inside
3 Outside
4 Cross

The *tick-labels* argument can have the following values:

1 None
2 Low
3 High
4 Next to the axis

## PATTERNS(*auto-line,line-style, line-color,line-weight*)

Same as the Format Patterns option, if the current selection is a line (see Chapter 12 for more information). The *line-style, line-color,* and *line-weight* arguments correspond to settings in the Format Patterns dialog box. The *auto-line* argument can have the following values:

0 Set by the user
1 Set automatically
2 Invisible

## PATTERNS(*auto-line,line-style,line-color, line-weight,auto-marker,marker-style, foreground,background,apply-to-all*)

Same as the Format Patterns option, if the current selection is a data line (see Chapter 12 for more information). The *line-style, line-color, line-weight, marker-style, foreground, background,* and *apply-to-all* arguments correspond to settings in the Format

Patterns dialog box. The *auto-line* argument can have the following values:

- 0    Set by the user
- 1    Set automatically
- 2    Invisible

The *auto-marker* argument can have the following values:

- 0    Set by the user
- 1    Set automatically
- 2    Invisible

## PATTERNS(*auto-line,line-style,line-color, line-weight,arrowhead-width, arrowhead-length,arrowhead-type*)

Same as the Format Patterns option, if the current selection is an arrow (see Chapter 12 for more information). The *line-style, line-color,* and *line-weight* arguments correspond to settings in the Format Patterns dialog box. The *auto-line* argument can have the following values:

- 0    Set by the user
- 1    Set automatically
- 2    Invisible

The *arrowhead-width* argument can have the following values:

- 1    Narrow
- 2    Medium
- 3    Wide

The *arrowhead-length* argument can have the following values:

1  Short
2  Medium
3  Long

The *arrowhead-type* argument can have the following values:

1  None
2  Open
3  Closed

## POKE(*channel,item-name, document*)

Causes the data in the specified document to be sent to the named item in the application connected to the specified channel. The channel must have been opened by the INITIATE function. If the channel number is not valid, POKE returns a #VALUE! error. If the user presses the (ESC) key before the application answers, POKE returns a #DIV/0! error. If the application refuses POKE's request, POKE returns a #REF! error.

## PRECISION(*logical*)

Same as the Options Calculation option and turning the Precision as Displayed check box off, if the logical argument is True. Same as the Options Calculation option and turning the Precision as Displayed check box on, if the logical argument is False (see Chapter 12 for more information).

## PREFERRED( )

Same as the Gallery Preferred option (see Chapter 12 for more information).

## PRINT(*all-or-part,first-page,last- page, number-of-copies,draft-quality, preview,attributes*) or PRINT?(*[all-or-part],[first-page], [last-page],[number-of- copies], [draft-quality],[preview],[attributes]*)

Same as the File Print option (see Chapter 12 for more information). In the dialog box version (with the question mark), the arguments, if included, are default values for the dialog box that appears. The *all-or-part* argument can be either 1 (print all) or 2 (print part). If the *all-or-part* argument is 1, the *first-page* and *last-page* arguments are ignored. The *number-of-copies, draft-quality,* and *preview* arguments correspond to arguments in the File Print dialog box. The *attributes* argument (only applicable if the document is a worksheet or macro sheet) can have the following values:

1 Worksheet or macro sheet
2 Notes
3 Both

## PRINTER.SETUP(*printer-name*) or PRINTER.SETUP?(*[printer-name]*)

Same as the File Printer Setup option (see Chapter 12 for more information). The *printer-name* argument should be entered as a string precisely as it appears in the File Printer Setup dialog box.

In the dialog box version (with the question mark), the argument, if included, is the default value for the dialog box that appears.

## PROTECT.DOCUMENT (*contents,windows*) or PROTECT.DOCUMENT? (*[contents],[windows]*)

Same as the Options Protect Document option, if the active document is a worksheet or macro sheet and one or both of the arguments is True. Same as the Chart Protect Document option, if the active document is a chart and one or both of the arguments is True. Same as the Options Unprotect Document option, if the active document is a worksheet or macro sheet and both of the arguments are False. Same as the Chart Unprotect Document option, if the active document is a chart and both of the arguments are False. The arguments correspond to the check boxes in the dialog box (see Chapter 12 for more information). In the dialog box version (with the question mark), the arguments, if included, are default values for the dialog box that appears.

## QUIT( )

Same as the File Exit option (see Chapter 12 for more information).

## REFTEXT(*reference,[style]*)

Returns the reference as text in A1 style if the *style* argument is True, and R1C1 style if the *style* argument is False. The default value for *style* is False.

## REGISTER(*library, procedure,arg-code*)

Returns a string that is used by CALL. CALL and REGISTER should be used only by experts. Used incorrectly, CALL or REGISTER could cause errors in your system.

## RELREF(*reference,with-respect-to*)

Returns an R1C1-style relative reference as a text string, given *reference* and a *with-respect-to* argument that is the upper-left corner to which the reference is relative.

*Example*   RELREF(B2,A1) returns "R[1]C[1]"

## REMOVE.PAGE.BREAK( )

Same as the Options Remove Page Break option (see Chapter 12 for more information).

## RENAME.COMMAND(*bar-number, menu- ref,command,name-string*)

Renames a command on a menu with the name specified by *name-string*. *Bar-number* is the number of the menu bar where the command is that you want to rename. The *menu-ref* argument is the menu where the command is that you want to rename and can be the name or the number of the menu. *Command* is the name or the number of the command you want to rename.

## REPLACE.FONT(*font,font-name, size,bold,italic,underlined,strikeout*)

Same as the Format Font option (see Chapter 12 for more information). The arguments correspond to options in the Format Font dialog box.

## REQUEST(*channel,item*)

Returns an array containing information obtained by requesting the item from the application connected to the specified channel. The *item* argument must be a text string. The channel must have been opened by the INITIATE function. If the channel number is not valid, REQUEST returns a #VALUE! error. If the user presses the (ESC) key before the application answers, REQUEST returns a #DIV/0! error. If the application refuses REQUEST's request, REQUEST returns a #REF! error. If the application is busy, REQUEST returns an #N/A! error. You must have the full version of Windows (2.0 or higher) to use this function.

## RESTART(*[stack-level]*)

Causes the number of return addresses specified by *stack-level* to be removed from the stack. If the *stack-level* argument is omitted, the default value is all the addresses on the stack.

## RESULT(*type*)

Defines the type of result that a macro returns. *Type* can be any of the following values:

| | | | |
|---|---|---|---|
| 1 | Number | 8 | Reference |
| 2 | Text | 16 | Error |
| 4 | Logical | 64 | Array |
| 7 | Number, text, or logical | | |

The default value for *type* is 7.

## RETURN(*[value]*)

Returns the value given in the *value* argument and stops running the macro returning control to whatever started the macro. The *value* argument is not given if the macro is a command macro.

## ROW.HEIGHT(*height,[reference], [default-height]*) or ROW.HEIGHT?(*[height], [reference],[default-height]*)

Same as the Format Row Height option (see Chapter 12 for more information). If the *reference* argument is omitted, the default is the current selection. In the dialog box version (with the question mark), the arguments are default settings for the dialog box that appears.

## RUN(*reference*) or RUN?(*[reference]*)

Same as the Macro Run option (see Chapter 12 for more information). The *reference* argument, if given, should be a text string.

## SAVE( )

This is the same as the File Save option (see Chapter 12 for more information).

## SAVE.AS(*name,type, password,backup-logical*) or SAVE.AS?(*[name],[type], [password],[backup-logical]*)

Same as the File Save As option (see Chapter 12 for more information). In the dialog box version (with the question mark), the arguments, if included, are default values for the dialog box that appears. The arguments correspond to options in the File Save As dialog box. The *type* argument can be any of the following values:

| | | | |
|---|---|---|---|
| 1 | Normal | 6 | CSV |
| 2 | SYLK | 7 | DBF2 |
| 3 | Text | 8 | DBF3 |
| 4 | WKS | 9 | DIF |
| 5 | WK1 | | |

## SAVE.WORKSPACE(*[name]*) or SAVE.WORKSPACE?(*[name]*)

Same as the File Save Workspace option (see Chapter 12 for more information). *Name* should be given as a text string. The default for the *name* argument is RESUME.XLW. In the dialog box version (with the question mark), the argument, if included, is used as a default value for the dialog box that appears.

## SCALE(*cross-at,categories-per-tick-labels,categories-per-ticks, cross-between,reverse-order, cross-at-max-category*)

Same as the Format Scale option, if the selected item is a category axis and the chart is not a scatter chart (see Chapter 12 for more information). *Cross-at, categories-per-tick-labels,* and *categories-per-ticks* should be given as numbers appropriate for each argument. *Cross-between, reverse-order,* and *cross-at-max- category* correspond to check boxes in the Format Scale dialog box.

## SCALE(*minimum,maximum,major-unit, minor-unit,axis-cross,log-scale, reverse-order,cross-at-max-category*)

Same as the Format Scale option, if the selected item is a value axis or if the chart is a scatter chart (see Chapter 12 for more information). *Minimum, maximum, major-unit, minor-unit,* and *axis-cross* correspond to settings in the Format Scale dialog box. They can be set to True to cause the default settings to be activated, or they can be numbers. *Log-scale, reverse- order,* and *cross-at-max-category* correspond to check boxes in the Format Scale dialog box.

## SELECT(*[range],active-cell*)

Same as selecting a cell or range on a worksheet or macro. *Active-cell* must be within the range. If range is omitted, *active-cell* should be given as a relative cell reference.

***Example*** SELECT(,"R[1]C[1]") causes the active cell to move down one row and over one column from the current active cell.

## SELECT(*code*)

Same as selecting an item on a chart. *Code* can be any of the following strings:

| | |
|---|---|
| "Arrow *n*" | Selects the *n*th arrow |
| "Axis 1" | Selects the main chart's value axis |
| "Axis 2" | Selects the main chart's category axis |
| "Axis 3" | Selects the overlay chart's value axis |
| "Axis 4" | Selects the overlay chart's category axis |
| "Chart" | Selects the whole chart |
| "Dropline 1" | Selects the droplines for the main chart |
| "Dropline 2" | Selects the droplines for the overlay chart |
| "Gridline 1" | Selects the major gridlines for the value axis |
| "Gridline 2" | Selects the minor gridlines for the value axis |
| "Gridline 3" | Selects the major gridlines for the category axis |
| "Gridline 4" | Selects the minor gridlines for the category axis |
| "Hiloline 1" | Selects the hi-lo lines for the main chart |
| "Hiloline 2" | Selects the hi-lo lines for the overlay chart |
| "Legend" | Selects the legend |
| "Plot" | Selects the plot area |
| "S*n*P*m*" | Selects the data corresponding to series *n* and data point *m* |
| "Text Axis 1" | Selects the main chart value axis label |
| "Text Axis 2" | Selects the main chart category axis label |
| "Text *n*" | Selects the *n*th floating text item |
| "Text S*n*" | Selects the text attached to series *n* |
| "Text S*n*P*m*" | Selects the text attached to series *n* and point *m* |
| "Title" | Selects the chart title |

## SELECT.CHART( )

Same as the SELECT("Chart") function. Also the same as the Chart Select Chart option (see Chapter 12 for more information).

## SELECT.END(*direction*)

This is the same as pressing `CTRL + LEFT ARROW` if *direction* is 1. Same as pressing `CTRL + RIGHT ARROW` if *direction* is 2. Same as pressing `CTRL + UP ARROW` if *direction* is 3. Same as pressing `CTRL + DOWN ARROW` if *direction* is 4.

## SELECT.LAST.CELL( )

Causes the last cell in the worksheet to be selected.

## SELECT.PLOT.AREA( )

Same as the Chart Select Plot Area option (see Chapter 12 for more information). Also the same as the SELECT("Plot") function.

## SELECT.SPECIAL(*attributes, [type],[levels]*)

Same as the Formula Select Special option (see Chapter 12 for more information). The *attributes* argument can have any of the following values:

| | | | |
|---|---|---|---|
| 1 | Notes | 6 | Present array |
| 2 | Constants | 7 | Row differences |
| 3 | Formulas | 8 | Column differences |
| 4 | Blanks | 9 | Precedents |
| 5 | Present range | 10 | Dependents |

If *attributes* is set to constants (2) or formulas (3), you can set the *type* argument to numbers (1), text (2), logicals (3), or errors (16) to control which constants or formulas are selected. The *levels* argument can be set to either 1 (direct) or 2 (all).

## SELECTION( )

Returns the current selection's value. If SELECTION is used with REFTEXT, the current selection's external reference is returned.

**EXAMPLE**  REFTEXT(SELECTION( )) returns the current selection's external cell reference as text.

## SEND.KEYS(*string,[logical]*)

Sends *string* to the active application as virtual keystrokes. If you want to use a nonalphanumeric key, place the name of the key inside braces or curly brackets. Listed here are some special codes for keys that are coded with characters other than their key names. If the logical value is True, Excel waits for the string to be processed as keystrokes before going on. If the logical value is False, Excel continues without waiting.

| Key | Code |
|---|---|
| ALT | % |
| CTRL | ^ |
| DOWN ARROW | {DOWN} |
| ENTER | ~ OR {ENTER} |
| ESC | {ESC} OR {ESCAPE} |
| LEFT ARROW | {LEFT} |
| PGDN | {PGDN} |
| PGUP | {PGUP} |
| PRTSC | {PRTSC} |
| RIGHT ARROW | {RIGHT} |
| SHIFT | + |
| UP ARROW | {UP} |

If you want to send a %, ^, ~, or + meaning the key itself, enclose the symbol in braces.

## SET.CRITERIA( )

Same as the Data Set Criteria option (see Chapter 12 for more information).

## SET.DATABASE( )

Same as the Data Set Database option (see Chapter 12 for more information).

## SET.NAME(*name,[refers-to]*)

Causes *name* to be set to the value or reference specified by *refers-to,* if that argument is included. If the *refers-to* argument is omitted, the name is deleted.

***Example***   SET.NAME("cost",1000) sets the name cost to be the value 1000.

## SET.PAGE.BREAK( )

Same as the Options Set Page Break option (see Chapter 12 for more information).

## SET.PREFERRED( )

Same as the Gallery Set Preferred option (see Chapter 12 for more information).

## SET.PRINT.AREA( )

Same as the Options Set Print Area option (see Chapter 12 for more information).

## SET.PRINT.TITLES( )

Same as the Options Set Print Titles option (see Chapter 12 for more information).

## SET.VALUE(*reference,values*)

Sets the value in the cell or cells referred to by the *reference* argument to the value specified by the *values* argument. If there is already a formula in the cell or cells, the formula is not changed. If *reference* is a range, *values* must be a range of the same size.

## SHORT.MENUS(*logical*)

Same as the Options Short Menus option, if the logical value is True. Same as the Options Full Menus option, if the logical value is False (see Chapter 12 for more information).

## SHOW.ACTIVE.CELL( )

Same as pressing CTRL + BACKSPACE. Adjusts the window so that the active cell is visible.

## SHOW.BAR(*bar-ID*)

Causes the menu bar specified by *bar-ID* to be displayed. *Bar-ID* must be either a number of a built-in menu bar or a number that is returned by ADD.BAR if the bar you want to show is a custom menu bar. If the menu bar you want to show is a built-in menu bar, use one of the following numbers for *bar-ID*:

1. A full menu bar for a worksheet or macro sheet
2. A full menu bar for a chart
3. A menu if there is no window active
4. An Info window menu
5. A short menu bar for a worksheet or macro sheet
6. A short menu bar for a chart

## SHOW.CLIPBOARD( )

Same as choosing the Control Run option and then choosing Clipboard.

## SHOW.INFO(*logical*)

Causes the Info window to be activated if the logical argument is True. Causes the document linked to the Info window to be activated if the logical argument is False.

## SIZE(*window-width,window-height, [window-name]*)

Same as the Control Size option. Causes the window specified by *window-name* to be sized according the *window-width* and *window-height* arguments, given in points. If the *window-name* argument is omitted, the default is the current window.

## SORT(*sort-by,primary-key,primary-order, [secondary-key],[secondary-order], [third-key],[third-order]*) or SORT?(*[sort-by],[primary-key], [primary-order],[secondary-key], [secondary-order],[third-key],[third-order]*)

Same as the Data Sort option (see Chapter 12 for more information). The *sort-by* argument should be 1 if you want to sort by rows or 2 if you want to sort by columns. *Primary-order, secondary-order,* and *third-order* arguments should be 1 for ascending and 2 for descending. The *primary-key, secondary-key,* and *third-key* arguments should be references to the rows or columns you want to sort. In the dialog box version (with the question mark), the arguments, if included, are default values for the dialog box that appears.

## SPLIT(*horizontal,vertical*)

Same as the Control Split option. The *horizontal* and *vertical* arguments are measured in rows and columns and tell SPLIT where to split the window.

## STEP( )

Causes the Single Step dialog box to appear, allowing you to step through the macro, halt the macro, or continue executing the macro.

## STYLE(*bold-font,italic-font*) or
## STYLE?(*[bold-font],[italic-font]*)

Causes the current selection to be formatted with the available bold font if the *bold-font* argument is True, and formatted with the available italic font if the *italic-font* argument is True. In the dialog box version (with the question mark), the arguments, if included, are default values for the dialog box that appears.

## TABLE(*[row],[column]*) or
## TABLE?(*[row],[column]*)

Same as the Data Table option (see Chapter 12 for more information). The *row* and *column* arguments should be references to the row and column inputs. If only one of the arguments is given, TABLE creates a one-input table. In the dialog box version (with the question mark), the arguments, if included, are default values for the dialog box that appears.

## TERMINATE(*channel*)

Causes the channel (previously opened with the INITIATE function) to be closed. TERMINATE returns a #VALUE! error if it cannot close the channel. You must have the full version of Windows (2.0 or higher) to use this function.

## TEXTREF(*reference-string,[style]*)

Converts *reference-string* into an A1-style reference. If *style* is True, *reference-string* is in A1-style. If *style* is False or not present, *reference-string* is in R1C1-style.

## UNDO( )

Same as the Edit Undo option (see Chapter 12 for more information).

## UNHIDE(*window-name*)

Same as the Window Unhide option (see Chapter 12 for more information).

## UNLOCKED.NEXT( )

Same as pressing (TAB) to move to the next unlocked cell.

## UNLOCKED.PREV( )

This is the same as pressing (SHIFT + TAB) to move to the previous unlocked cell.

## VLINE(*x*)

Same as scrolling *x* number of rows in the currently active window. If *x* is a negative number, VLINE scrolls up. If *x* is a positive number, VLINE scrolls down.

## VPAGE(x)

Same as scrolling $x$ number of pages vertically in the currently active window. If $x$ is a negative number, VLINE scrolls up. If $x$ is a positive number, VLINE scrolls down.

## VSCROLL(scroll-to, logical)

Same as scrolling to the row given by the *scroll-to* argument if the *logical* argument is True. If the *logical* argument is False, the *scroll-to* argument should be given as a fraction between 0 and 1. If *scroll-to* is 0, VSCROLL scrolls to the top edge. If *scroll-to* is 1, VSCROLL scrolls to the bottom edge. Any fraction between 0 and 1 causes VSCROLL to scroll to the appropriate row.

## WAIT(x)

Stops the executing of a macro for $x$ length of time. The argument x should be given as a time serial number. Press (ESC) to resume execution before the specified time is up.

## WHILE(logical)

Starts a WHILE-NEXT loop. The loop is executed until the *logical* argument is False. The loop begins with the function immediately following WHILE and extends to NEXT. When *logical* is False, execution continues with the function immediately following NEXT.

## WINDOWS( )

Returns an array that contains the names of all windows open on your screen, in layered level order. The top window comes first, the bottom window comes last.

**WORKSPACE(*fixed-decimals,auto-decimals, r1c1,scroll-bars,formula-bar,status-bar, alt-menu- key,ignore-remote-requests*) or WORKSPACE?(*[fixed-decimals], [auto-decimals],[r1c1],[scroll- bars], [formula-bar],[status-bar],[alt-menu-key], [ignore-remote-requests]* )**

Same as the Options Workspace option (see Chapter 12 for more information). The arguments correspond to options in the Options Workspace dialog box. In the dialog box version (with the question mark), the arguments, if included, are default values for the dialog box that appears.

# INSTALLING WINDOWS AND EXCEL

What Equipment Do You Need?
What Equipment Do You Have?
Preparing to Store Data
Running Setup
Starting Windows and Excel
Leaving Excel and Windows

There are many combinations of computers, disks, displays, and printers with which Windows and Excel can operate. As a result, providing installation instructions might have become a complex process were it not for the Setup programs that come with both Windows and Excel. These programs do most of the work for you. You have only to determine what equipment you have and then run the Setup programs, answering the questions they ask you.

This appendix describes what equipment you need, how to determine what equipment you have, and how to start and use both

Windows and Excel Setup programs. In addition, it discusses how you prepare to store the data you create with Excel and how to leave Windows and Excel.

This appendix is written for Windows 3 and Excel 2.1C. While most of what is said here may be true for other versions of either product, you need to be on the lookout for differences. Also, it is possible to run Excel "by itself" using a runtime version of Windows 2—you cannot use Windows itself, only Excel. Without Windows you cannot run multiple programs and you cannot transfer information using the Clipboard.

## WHAT EQUIPMENT DO YOU NEED?

Windows and Excel run on IBM PC, AT, and PS/2 computers and compatibles. Windows 3 can run in three modes, and each mode has different hardware requirements. You should use the most capable mode you can with the hardware you have available. The three modes and their requirements are as follows:

*386 enhanced mode* Requires an Intel 80386 or higher processor and 2MB (megabytes, or millions of characters) or more of memory—(640KB (kilobytes, or thousands of characters) of *conventional memory* and at least 1024KB of *extended memory* (see discussion on memory later in this appendix). 386 enhanced mode makes use of the 80386's virtual memory capability to use the disk as additional memory. Also, 386 enhanced mode allows you to run multiple non-Windows applications at one time—a process called multitasking—as well as multitask Windows applications. 386 enhanced mode is the most capable of the operating modes.

*Standard mode* Requires an Intel 80286 or higher processor and 1MB or more of memory (640KB of conventional memory and at least 256KB of extended memory). Standard mode allows you to use extended memory and switch among non-Windows applications as well as multitask Windows applications. Standard mode is the normal operating mode.

***Real mode*** Requires an Intel 8086, 8088, or higher processor and 640KB of conventional memory. Real mode allows you to use the least amount of memory and provides the most compatibility with previous versions of Windows.

Other system requirements for Windows and for Excel are as follows:

| | |
|---|---|
| Disk | Windows and Excel require a hard disk and a floppy disk. You can use any kind of floppy disk, 5 1/4- or 3 1/2-inch, 360KB to 1.44MB. For Windows 3 you need at least 6MB of free hard disk space, and for Excel you need at least 3MB more. You should also leave 2MB of disk space to swap sections of memory. To be comfortable, you should have 12MB for Windows and Excel. |
| Display | Windows and Excel require a graphics display and display adapter. It is recommended that you use VGA, EGA, or Hercules adapters and displays over the original CGA due to the latter's low resolution. Many other displays are supported by Windows and Excel. |
| Printer | A printer is not necessary for Windows and Excel to run, but of course you cannot print without one. Windows and Excel can use almost any printer. Among the printers supported by Windows and |

|  |  |
|---|---|
|  | Excel are the IBM Proprinter, IBM Graphics printer, Epson FX 80, HP LaserJet, Apple LaserWriter, and any printer compatible with these. |
| Operating system | Windows 3 and Excel 2.1C require MS DOS or PC DOS versions 3.1 and above. |
| Mouse | A mouse is not required for either Windows or Excel, but it is very strongly recommended. Either a Microsoft mouse or any compatible pointing device can be used. |
| Network | Windows and Excel will run on the major local area networks including 3Com 3+ and EtherSeries, AT&T Starlan, IBM PC Network, IBM Token Ring Network, Novell NetWare, and Ungermann-Bass/One. |
| Math coprocessor | A math coprocessor speeds up calculating your worksheets, but it is not required. The type of coprocessor you need depends on the type and speed of processor you have: a 20 MHZ 80386 processor requires a 20 MHZ 80387 coprocessor, a 12 MHZ 80286 processor requires a 12 MHZ 80287 coprocessor, and so on. |
| Other | To use the Windows communications software, you need a Hayes-compatible modem. Plotters compatible with an HP 7470A are supported by Excel. |

# WHAT EQUIPMENT DO YOU HAVE?

When you install Windows and Excel, you have to tell the Setup program on which of your hard disk drives you want to install

1. Amount of memory by type:  Conventional memory: _____
                               Extended memory:     _____
                               Expanded memory:     _____
2. On which disk drive and directory will Windows be installed? _____
3. On which disk drive and directory will Excel be installed? _____
4. What kind of computer and processor are you using? _____
5. What is the layout of your keyboard? _____
6. What kind of display adapter do you have? _____
7. What kind of printer do you have? _____
8. To which computer port is your printer attached? _____
9. What fonts are available for your printer _____
10. In which country are you using Windows and Excel? _____
11. What version of DOS are you using? _____
12. What kind of network are you connected to? _____
13. Will you be using a mouse with Windows and Excel? _____
14. Do you know the contents of your CONFIG.SYS? _____
15. Do you know the contents of your AUTOEXEC.BAT? _____

**TABLE A-1**  Microsoft Windows 3.0 and Excel 2.1C Installation Questions

Windows and Excel, what kind of display and printer you have, and answer several related questions. You must determine the answers to these questions, shown in Table A-1, before running Setup.

If you can fill in Table A-1 without further information, then do so and skip to "Preparing to Store Data." If you need further information, read the following sections. If you still cannot fill in the blanks, you may need to talk to the dealer from whom you purchased your computer or call Microsoft Product Support (206-454-2030).

As you install Windows and Excel, suggested answers are provided for many of the above questions. If you think you know the answers, you might try the installation and see if the Setup programs agree with you. The very worst that can happen is that

Windows and Excel will not run and you have to redo the installation.

## Memory

There are three kinds of memory: conventional memory, extended memory, and expanded memory.

- *Conventional* memory, which is in all machines, is the first 640KB of memory and is sometimes called *base memory*. DOS permanently uses some of this memory, as do most memory-resident utilities you load. All applications, including Windows, also need some conventional memory.

- *Extended* memory is available on 80286, 80386, and 80486 computers. All memory beyond 640KB can be extended memory on these computers. An extended memory manager, such as Windows HIMEM.SYS, is needed to manage extended memory so two programs do not try to use the same extended memory at the same time. Some applications, such as Standard and 386 enhanced mode Windows, can directly use extended memory with equal ease and speed to conventional memory.

- *Expanded* memory is available on most computers through an expansion memory board or, in some cases, on the motherboard. Memory beyond 640KB can be expanded memory, but an expanded memory manager is required. Expanded memory is indirectly accessed through a small amount of memory between 640KB and 1MB. Due to this and a heavy reliance on its management software, expanded memory is slower and more cumbersome to use than extended memory. Among the several versions of expanded memory, the most recent is Lotus-Intel-Microsoft Expanded Memory Specifications (LIM EMS) 4.0.

You need to determine how much of each of these types of memory you have. This is normally done with a utility program that came with your memory expansion board or with your computer. For Windows 3 and Excel, you should configure your memory to all extended memory beyond 640KB. If you need expanded memory for another program, use the minimum possible and configure the rest as extended. You need at least 256KB extended memory for standard mode Windows and at least 1MB for 386 enhanced mode Windows.

## Disk Drives

Windows and Excel require hard disks to store your programs and your data. If you have only one hard disk drive, it is your logical choice. If you have multiple hard disk drives, you should choose the one with the most available space. The easiest way to find out how much space is left on your hard disk is to type **dir**. You can change disk drives by typing the drive letter followed by a colon (**c:**, for example). To comfortably run Windows and Excel you need 12MB of disk space and you should have at least 1MB to store data files. All of this space can be either in one disk drive or spread over two or more. From a space management standpoint, it is probably easier if it is in one drive, although there might be some slight gain in efficiency if you place the programs on one drive and the data on another.

## Disk Directories

Since a hard disk can store so much information, they should be divided into *directories*. Directories are artificial areas of unspecified size that contain files or subdirectories. With directories and subdirectories you can create a tree structure consisting of several

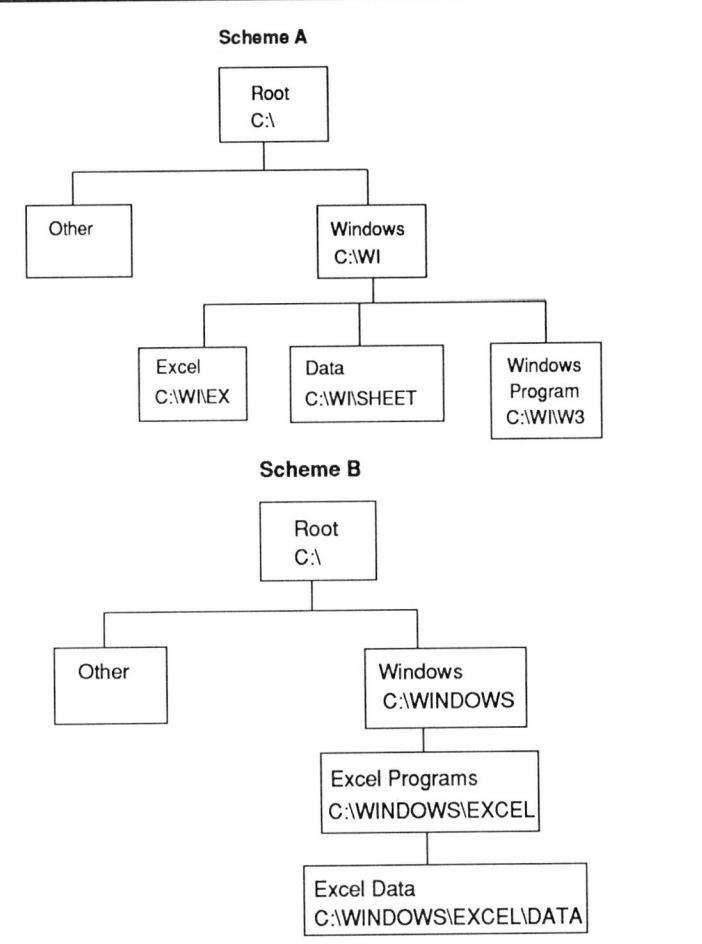

**FIGURE A-1** Directory schemes

levels. The highest level is called the *root directory*. Every hard disk has a root directory. There are many directory/subdirectory schemes that you can use to contain your Windows programs, Excel programs, and Excel data. Figure A-1 shows two such schemes. The directory scheme used in this book is labeled Scheme A in Figure A-1. There is no need to use this scheme; you will just have to remember to change the instructions for storing data when they are given.

## Displays

The choice of display is really a choice based on your *display adapter*—the card or module in your computer to which your display is connected. The Setup program tries to determine what your display adapter is and will list its name as an option. You can accept that option or you can change to another. It is very likely that the display adapter found by Setup is the correct one for your computer. Unless you are certain you want to use a different display adapter, accept the option highlighted by Setup; you can always come back and change it later.

There are four primary choices and a number of variations for display adapters. The four primary choices are Color Graphics Adapter (CGA), Hercules or Monochrome Graphics Adapter (MGA), Enhanced Graphics Adapter (EGA), and Video Graphics Array (VGA). Most computers have a display adapter compatible with one of these. If the option highlighted by Setup does not work, you cannot find a recognizable alternative in the list of options presented by Setup, and none of the primary choices seem to work, look at the manuals that came with your computer. If you still cannot determine which adapter is right for your computer, contact the dealer from whom you purchased the computer or Microsoft Product Support.

## Printers

The Setup program for Windows presents over 150 printer models from which you can choose. With so many choices, it is very likely that you will find your printer on the list. If you cannot find your printer, check your printer's manual to see if it emulates another printer. Some good bets are Diablo 630, Epson FX-80, HP Laser-

Jet, IBM Graphics printer, IBM Proprinter, or one of the Postscript printers. If you cannot find a printer your printer emulates, select Generic/Text Only to use temporarily and contact Microsoft Product Support. They can probably send you a disk with the program or a driver for your printer.

You need to tell Windows to which port on your computer your printer is connected. There are two kinds of ports: serial and parallel. If you have a choice, use parallel—it is both faster and simpler. Parallel ports are labeled LPT1, LPT2, and so on. Serial ports are labeled COM1, COM2, and so on. If you do not know which port to use, try LPT1 first, then COM1, LPT2, and finally COM2. One of these four ports is probably the one you need.

## Changing CONFIG.SYS

CONFIG.SYS is a file that, if present, is automatically referenced when you start your computer. It contains a series of parameters that tells DOS how to structure itself and what utility programs to load. Of special importance to Windows are two parameters in CONFIG.SYS that tell the operating system how many files can be open at any one time and how many buffers to set up to hold file data. Windows and Excel require that 30 files be open at once and that you have 10 or 20 buffers.

In addition to the files and buffers parameters, you need to load one or more Windows utility programs with the CONFIG.SYS file. In all cases you should load the disk-caching utility SMARTDRV.SYS. This utility significantly speeds up getting information from the disk. Also, if you use SMARTDRV.SYS, you can set your buffers to 10 and save conventional memory. If you are using an 80286 or above, you need the extended memory manager HIMEM.SYS. If you need to run a program in expanded memory, you can use the utility program EMM386.SYS to convert extended memory into expanded memory on 80386 computers. If you are using an EGA display adapter and want to run non-Windows applications with Windows in real or standard mode, you should load the EGA.SYS utility.

Therefore, you must have a CONFIG.SYS file and it should contain the following statements:

FILES=30 (or some number greater than 30)
BUFFERS=10 (or 20 without SMARTDRV.SYS)
DEVICE=HIMEM.SYS (if you have extended memory)
DEVICE=SMARTDRV.SYS (must come after HIMEM.SYS)

**Note** SMARTDRV.SYS has two parameters after it that specify the normal cache size and the minimum cache size. For example, a CONFIG.SYS statement might be

DEVICE=SMARTDRV.SYS 1024 256

where the normal cache size is 1024 and the minimum cache size is 256. When Windows starts in standard or 386 enhanced mode and SMARTDRV.SYS is using extended memory, it reduces SMARTDRV.SYS to the minimum value.

When you run Windows Setup to install Windows, you are asked if you want Setup to check and add to or correct your CONFIG.SYS file. If you say yes, all these statements are added or adjusted as necessary to produce the correct CONFIG.SYS file for your system.

## Changing AUTOEXEC.BAT

AUTOEXEC.BAT is a special *batch file* that is run immediately after the CONFIG.SYS file whenever you start your computer. A batch file contains a series of normal DOS commands that are run when you execute the file that contains them. An AUTOEXEC.BAT file is normally used to establish the default path with a DOS PATH command, to configure the DOS prompt with a

PROMPT command, and to run various memory-resident or other programs that you want run when you start your system.

For Windows and Excel, you should include the Windows directory in your PATH statement and, if you plan to do most of your work under Windows, you may want to load Windows from your AUTOEXEC.BAT file. Windows and Excel occasionally write a temporary file that is later erased. Sometimes, due to a power interruption or similar incident, these files do not get erased. It is, therefore, a good idea to place these temporary files in their own directory. You can do that with the AUTOEXEC.BAT file.

Your AUTOEXEC.BAT file might contain the following statements (without the parenthetical comments):

```
PROMPT $P$G (makes your DOS prompt C:\ >)
PATH C:\WINDOWS;C\DOS (sets your default path)
SET TEMP=C:\TEMP
WIN (loads Windows)
```

These statements assume that Windows is in the C:\WINDOWS directory, DOS is in the C:\DOS directory, and you have created a directory C:\TEMP that stores temporary files.

The Windows Setup program asks you if you want to modify your AUTOEXEC.BAT file. If you say yes, your Windows directory is added to your path statement, and WIN is added to the end of AUTOEXEC.BAT to load windows.

## PREPARING TO STORE DATA

When you use Excel, you will create documents that you will want to come back and use again at a later time. To preserve this data, you store it in files on a disk. The files are preserved when you turn the computer off. The programs that comprise Excel are also stored in files on a disk.

With a hard-disk-based system, you also have a floppy disk drive. Therefore, you can store the data on either floppy or hard disks. From the standpoints of both speed and ease of use, it is best to store data, in addition to the programs, on your hard disk. Since hard disks store so much information, they should be divided into directories, which are arbitrarily named areas that you establish for particular purposes. To prepare to store the data you create with Excel, you should create one or more directories.

## Creating Directories On a Hard Disk

To store the program files on a hard disk, the Windows and Excel Setup programs automatically create directories for you or use directories you create or already have. The default name for the Windows directory is \WINDOWS and for Excel it is \EXCEL, but you can name them anything you like and still use the Setup program to create them.

If you want to use existing Windows and Excel directories, you can do so without concern. If you want to create your own directories to hold the Windows and Excel program files, use these instructions. Your computer should be turned on and you should be at an operating system prompt such as C or C:\>.

1. Type **cd\** and press (ENTER) to make sure you are in the root directory.

2. Type **md\wi** and press (ENTER) to create a directory named WI.

3. Type **cd\wi** and press (ENTER) to change to the new WI directory.

4. Type **md w3**, press (ENTER), type **md ex**, press (ENTER), type **md sheet**, and press (ENTER) to create three subdirectories under the \WI directory to hold Windows, Excel, and the Excel data files you'll create in this book, respectively.

The above instructions follow the directory Scheme A on Figure A-1. If you want to use another scheme or name your directories something else, replace Scheme A and its directory names with the scheme and names you want to use. A directory name can be from one to eight characters long and can include all the letters, numbers, and special characters on your keyboard *except* the following:

. " / \ [ ] : | + = ; , * ?

You may want to create one or two other directories to hold other data files. If you do, use separate data directories, rather than using the Windows or Excel program directories, for two reasons. First, when you get an update to Windows or Excel you will want to remove the old program files and replace them with new ones. The easiest way to do this is to delete the entire contents of the directory. If there are files you want to keep there, you cannot do that. Second, if you want to do some file maintenance with DOS, the number of program files will make looking for data files more difficult than if they had their own directory.

5. Type **md** *name* and press (ENTER) for each directory you want to create, where *name* is the directory name you want to use. For example, type **md data** and press (ENTER) to create a subdirectory named DATA under the \WI directory.

## RUNNING SETUP

Running the Windows and Excel Setup programs is very simple. As a matter of fact, you do it with only four instructions each (assuming your computer is turned on and you are at a DOS prompt—C> or C:\ >):

1. Place the Windows Setup disk in drive A or any other floppy disk drive you have and close the door.

2. Type **a:** and press (ENTER) to make drive A current. (If you are using a different drive, type that drive letter in place of A.)

3. Type **setup** and press (ENTER) to start the Setup program.

4. Follow the instructions on the screen.

If you created the directories previously recommended, you must type **c:\wi\w3** when asked for the directory in which to install Windows.

Check the list of system components against the table you prepared earlier. If there are discrepancies, check your table, use (UP ARROW) or (DOWN ARROW) to move the highlight to the item that is wrong, press (ENTER), and then select the alternative you want from the options presented.

You can install as many printers as you have available, but the first one you choose will be the default—the one automatically used unless you instruct otherwise. When you have selected a printer (by placing the mouse pointer on it and pressing the left mouse button or pressing (ALT+L) and using (DOWN ARROW) to move the highlight to it), click on the Install button or press (ALT+I), click on Configure or press (ALT+C), click on the computer port to use (LPT1, COM1, and so on) or use (DOWN ARROW) to move the highlight to it, and click on OK or press (ENTER) to complete installing the first printer. Repeat the process for each printer you want to install. Be sure to configure each printer by specifying the port to use. On some printers—laser printers in particular—you also must set them up. To do that, choose Setup from the Configure window (click on Setup or press (ALT+S)). When you are done installing all the printers you have, click on OK or press (ENTER).

Near the end of running Setup, you are asked if you want to search your hard disk for applications to run under Windows. Since you have not installed Excel yet, click on Cancel or press (ESC) to not do this at this time.

With the answers in the equipment table and only minimal use of your intuition, you should be able to successfully install Windows. If you have problems, press the (F1) function key for help screens about what you are doing at the moment.

When you have successfully completed installing Windows, repeat the procedure with Excel.

1. Place the Excel Setup disk in drive A or any other floppy disk drive you have and close the door.

2. Type **a:** and press (ENTER) to make drive A current (if you are using a different drive, type that drive letter in place of A).

3. Type **setup** and press (ENTER) to start the Setup program.

4. Follow the instructions on the screen.

If you created the directories previously recommended, you must type **c:\wi\ex** when asked for the directory in which to install Excel.

## STARTING WINDOWS AND EXCEL

If you allowed Setup to completely modify your AUTOEXEC.BAT file, Windows automatically loads every time you reboot your computer. In any case, you need to reboot your computer to pick up the changes made to your CONFIG.SYS file. Do that now. If you also modified your AUTOEXEC.BAT file, windows will load. If you did not let Setup modify your AUTOEXEC.BAT file, you must change your path to include the Windows directory and then load Windows. Use these instructions if you did not modify your AUTOEXEC.BAT file (you should be at a DOS prompt):

1. Type **c:**, press (ENTER), type **cd\**, and press (ENTER) to make sure you are on your C hard disk drive and in your root directory. If Windows is installed on a drive other than C, use the drive letter for the drive on which it is installed.

2. Type **path c:\wi\w3;c:\dos;c:\** and press (ENTER) to establish the path to use for running Windows. If your Windows directory name is something other than \WI\W3, enter that directory name in place of \WI\W3. If your DOS directory is something other than \DOS, use that directory name.

3. Type **win** and press (ENTER) to load Windows.

When Windows is loaded, the screen shown in Figure A-2 appears.

The initial screen shows the Main group of Windows system applications under the Program Manager. Your first task is to identify the application programs, such as Excel, that you want to run under Windows.

4. Double-click (click twice in rapid succession) on the Windows Setup icon in the Main group window (or use the arrow keys to move the highlight to the Windows Setup icon and press (ENTER)).

5. Click on Options at the top of the Windows Setup window or press (ALT+O). The Options menu opens.

6. Click on Set Up Applications, or type **S** to choose Set Up Applications from the menu.

7. Click on OK or press (ENTER) to search all drives for applications to run under Windows. The search begins, and you will see a thermometer bar telling you how far along you are.

When the search is complete, you get a window with a list on the left and an empty box on the right, as shown in Figure A-3. You need to select the applications you want to run under Windows from the list on the left. You can choose Add All, but that is not recommended because you would probably add more programs you do not want to use under Windows than programs you do. Therefore, you must look down the list and select only those programs you are sure you want to run under Windows—be sure to include Excel. Non-Windows applications such as 1-2-3 and WordPerfect can run under Windows 3, so you may want to include some of these applications. This is especially true if you

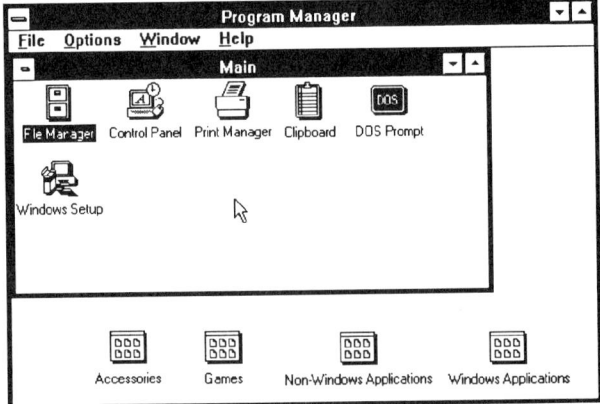

**FIGURE A-2** Initial Windows screen

can use 386 enhanced mode, because with this you can run multiple non-Windows applications and switch among them.

8. Click on the programs you want in the list on the left, clicking on the downward pointing arrow on the right of the list to see more of the list. With the keyboard, use (DOWN ARROW) to move the selection box to the programs you want to run under Windows and press the spacebar to select them.

9. When you have selected all of the programs you want to run under Windows, click on Add or press (ALT+A). You will see the programs appear in the box on the right.

10. When the process is complete, click on OK or press (ENTER) to close the Set Up Applications window. The Windows Setup window reappears.

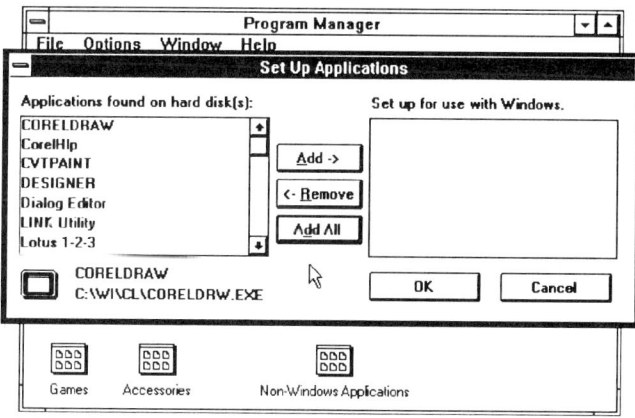

FIGURE A-3   Set Up Applications window

11. Move the mouse pointer to the small horizontal bar in the upper-left corner of the Windows Setup window, and press the left mouse button twice in rapid succession (double-click). From the keyboard, press (ALT) and the spacebar to open the Windows Setup Control menu. Type C to close the window. The Main group window reappears.

To load Excel, you must close the Main group window and open the Windows Applications group window.

12. Again, double-click on the small horizontal bar in the upper-left corner of the Main group window or press (ALT) and the spacebar and then (RIGHT ARROW) to open the Main group's Control menu in the upper-left corner of the Main group window. Type C to close the window.

13. Double-click on the Windows Applications icon at the bottom of the window, or press (CTRL+F6) to move the highlight to the Windows Applications icon and press (ENTER). The Windows Applications window opens, as shown in Figure A-4.

14. Double-click on the Excel icon, or press (LEFT ARROW) or (RIGHT ARROW) to move the highlight to it and press (ENTER). Excel is loaded, as shown in Figure A-5.

## LEAVING EXCEL AND WINDOWS

When you wish to leave Excel and return to the DOS prompt, do so with this instruction:

1. Double-click on the bar in the upper-left corner of the Excel window (not the Sheet1 window), or press (ALT) and the spacebar and type C. You leave Excel and return to Windows.

Installing Windows and Excel 725

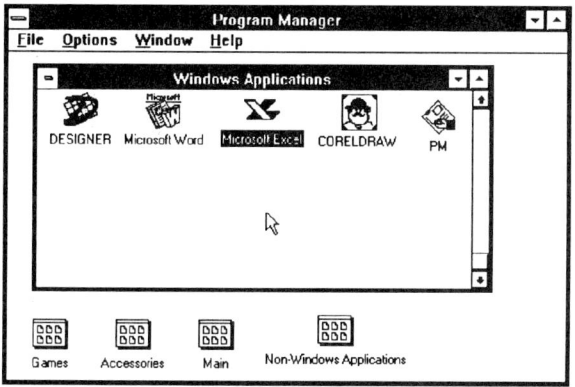

**FIGURE A-4**   Windows Applications window

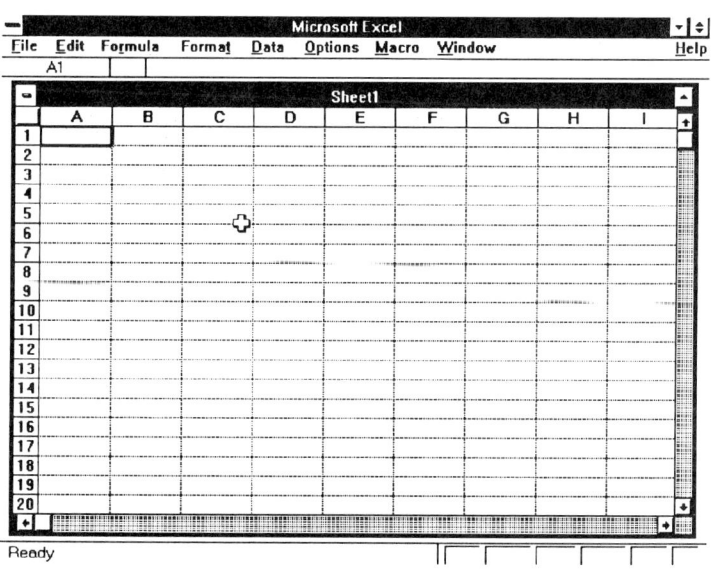

**FIGURE A-5**   Excel as it is originally loaded

2. Double-click on the bar in the upper-left corner of the Program Manager window (not the Windows Applications window), or press (ALT) and the spacebar and type **C**.

3. You are asked if you want to end your Windows session. Click on OK or press (ENTER). You are returned to DOS.

# INDEX

A1, 434
A1.R1C1 macro function, 628
ABS mathematical function, 572, 579
Absolute addressing, 156, 159-161
Absolute value, 572, 579
ABSREF macro function, 628
ACOS trigonometric function, 578, 579
ACTIVATE macro function, 628-629
Activate Window option, 560
ACTIVE.CELL macro function, 629
Active window, 9, 79, (illus., 80)
ADD macro functions, 629-630
Add option, 351
Addresses, 54-57
ALERT macro function, 630
Alignment
    cell, 502
    option, 105
    text, 104-105
    text in chart, 524
ALIGNMENT macro function, 631
Ampersand, printing of, 498
AND logical function, 571, 579
Applications
    entry order of, (illus., 428)
    layout for, 422-423
    planning, 420-423
    starting, 20-25
    using main group, 37-45
    window set-up, (illus., 723)
APP macro functions, 631-632
APPLY.NAMES macro function, 632
Arccosine, 578, 579
Area charts, 238, (illus., 239)
Area icon, defined, 9
AREAS information function, 569, 580
ARGUMENT macro function, 415, 633
Arguments
    pasting, 531
    specified for functions, 388-390
ARRANGE.ALL macro function, 633

Array, 566-567, 594
    selecting cells as part of, 536
    function, 566
    transposition, 574, 621-622
Arrows, 475, 477, 520, 642
ASCII
    code, 583
    comma delimited format, 356
    comma delimited text file, (illus., 363)
    delimited files, 359, 361-362
    files, 359
    nondelimited text files, 362-368,
    reading with File Save as option, 353-354
    text files, 361-368
    text format, 355-356
    text function, 582
ASIN trigonometric function, 578, 580
Assumptions
    adding, 226
    use of for formulas, 157-159
ATTACH.TEXT macro function, 633
ATAN trigonometric function, 578, 580
ATAN2 trigonometric function, 578, 580-581
Automatic page breaks, 556
Automatic series distribution box, 518
Automatic sizing, of borders, 524
Automatic text, 524
AUTOEXEC.BAT, changing the, 715-716
Average, database, 567, 586
AVERAGE statistical function, 574, 581
AXES macro function, 634
Axis, 476, 523
Background option, in chart font, 505
Bar charts, 239-242, 538, (illus., 240)
    sales by quarter with, (illus., 75)
Bars, delete, 642
Batch file, 715
BEEP macro function, 634
Blank cells, displayed for zero values, 554
Blank value, 570, 598
Blanks, selecting cells containing, 536

727

Bold font, 505
BORDER macro function, 634
Borders
    creating double-line, (illus., 145)
    dialog box, (illus., 29)
    horizontal, (illus., 146)
    placing, 143-146
    selecting, 502
    vertical, (illus., 146)
BREAK macro function, 634
Buttons, minimize and maximize, 8
CALCULATE macro functions, 635
Calculation
    active worksheet, 551
    automatic, 552
    controlling, 552
    macro function, 635
    options, 552
Calculator, 7
    fixing, 112-113
Calendar, 7
CALL macro function, 635
CALLER macro function, 636
CANCEL macro functions, 636
Card file, 7
Cascading menus, defined, 26
Category axis, 231
Category Axis Scale dialog box, 521-522
Cell, 55
    information from a, 569, 581-582
    moving to next, 113
    value of first, 571, 610
CELL information function, 569, 581-582
CELL.PROTECTION macro function, 636
Cell references
    converting, 533
    recording macros using, 548
    replacing absolute, 525-526
Cells, 54-57
    adding notes to, 207-208
    comparing, 536
    counting number of in database field, 567, 587
    deleting in worksheet, 491
    moving single, 92-93
Centering text, 498
Change All option, 357
CHANGE.LINK macro function, 637
Change option, 357
Changes, in information entered, 113-120
CHAR text function, 575, 582
Characters
    literal, 513
    repeating, 514
    search and replace of, 533-534

Chart Add Arrow options, 475
Chart Add Legend option, 475, 507
Chart Add Overlay option, 475-476
Chart Attach Text option, 476
Chart Axes option, 476
Chart Calculate Now option, 477
Chart Delete options, 477-479
Chart Full Menus option, 478
Chart Gridlines option, 478
Chart menu, 232-236, 474-480
Chart options, 236, (listed, 236, 479)
Chart Protect Document option, 478
Chart Select Chart option, 479
Chart Select Plot Area option, 479
Chart Short Menus option, 479
Chart Unprotect Document option, 479-480
Charts, 73-76, 237-238. *See also* Customizing
    area, 238
    bar, 239-242
    building, 230-236
    changing, 254-255
    column, 242
    combination, 243-244
    components, 51
    copying, 489
    copying data from worksheet, 250-251
    customizing, 231-236
    data range, (illus., 232)
    determining printed size of, 499
    elements, 236
    line, 244-246, 251-268
    opening new, 253, 497
    pie, 246-248, 269-278
    preferred types of, 233, 234
    producing, 229-281
    recalculating and redrawing, 477
    scatter, 248-251
    selecting, 238-251
    stacked column, 278-281
    types, 75, 230-231, 233
CHECK.COMMAND macro function, 637
CHOOSE lookup function, 572, 583
CLEAN text function, 575, 583
Clear dialog box, options for, 173
CLEAR macro function, 637-638
Clear option, in Data Parse, 485
Clipboard, 6
    copying picture into, 489-490
Clock, 7, 20-24
Clock Window Open, (illus., 21)
CLOSE macro functions, 638
Closing
    files, 496
    line charts, 268

Closing, *continued*
    pie charts, 276-278
    stacked column charts, 279-281
Cluster overlap, 517
Cluster spacing, 509, 517
Clustered bar chart, 240
CODE text function, 575, 583
Colors
    changing, 274-276
    choosing for gridlines and headings, 554-555
    selecting text, 505-506, (listed, 506)
    specifying for cells, 516
Column charts, 242-243, 539, (illus., 254)
    titles, legends and notes, (illus., 256)
Column headings, printing, 557
COLUMN information function, 569, 583-584
Column numbers, returning array of, 569, 584
Column width
    adjusting, 204-206
    changing with mouse, 504
    default, 504
    macro, 410-411
    setting, 504
    worksheet, 108-109
COLUMN.WIDTH macro function, 638
Columnar formulas, 154-157
    finishing, 154-155
Columns, 71
    deleting, 176-177, 204
    deleting in worksheet, 490-491
    for worksheets, 79-80
    inserting, 176-177
    resizing, (illus., 207)
    sorting by, 488
    widening, (illus., 196)
    worksheet, 53-54
COLUMNS information function, 570, 584
Combination charts, 243-244, 540, (illus., 244)
COMBINATION macro function, 639
Command macro, 433
Commands, 60-65
    delete, 643
    direct mouse, 63
    keyboard, 64
    menu, 61
Commas, replacing with tabs, 359
CompuServe, 364
CONFIG.SYS, 714-715
Constants, selecting cells containing, 535
Contents, width for worksheet, 108-109
Contents option, protecting worksheet with, 556
Control menu, 8, 33-37
Control panel, 39
    installing new printer on, 499

Control Split option, 555
Copies, making multiple, 493
Copy
    edit, 489
    option, 167, 304
    range combinations, 167-168, (illus., 168)
COPY macro functions, 403-405, 639-640
Copying
    between charts with Edit Paste option, 493
    charts, 489
    for worksheet, 167-168, 491-492
    types of, 167
    worksheets, 489
Corrections, worksheet, 177-178
COS trigonometric function, 578, 584
CREATE.NAMES macro function, 640
Criteria option, 483-484
Criteria range, 302
CSV file, 359, 361
Custom formats, 511
Customizing charts, 232-236
CUT macro function, 640
Cutting, 490
Data
    commands, 72
    storing, 716-718
    not available, 571, 610
Data Delete option, 480
Data entry tools, building, 436-453
Data Exit Find option, 481
Data Extract, 309, 311, 481-482
Data Find option, 307, 481, 482
Data form, (illus., 453)
Data Form option, 482-485
Data menu, 84, 290, 480-501
Data Parse, 366, 367
Data Parse option, 365, 485
Data points, 230, 231
Data series, 230, 231, 287, (illus., 298)
Data Series option, 252-253, 285-287, 296, 485-486
Data Set Criteria option, 482, 487
Data Set Database option, 302
Data Sort, 289, 291
Data Sort option, 488
Data table, 319-321
    input cell in, 321
    one-input, 320
    two-input, 322-324
Database, 70-73, (exercises, 425-427, 448-451)
    analyzing information from, 312-324
    ascending and descending sort order in, 293
    building, 283-289, 301
    changing criteria, (illus., 320)
    completing data entry in, 299

Database, *continued*
    components, 51
    criteria range, 304-307
    dates in, (illus., 300)
    dates reformatted in, (illus., 299)
    DCOUNT completed in, (illus., 318)
    defining a, 302-303
    defining an extract range in, 309-310
    entering data, 296-299, (exercise, 297-298)
    entering field names in, 284-285
    entering records in, 288-289
    extract range selected in, (illus., 310)
    extracting selected records in, 311-312
    field, 284, 313, 314
    field names, 284
    finding selected records in, 307-309
    formatting, (illus., 290)
    functions, 313, 324-327, (summary, 567-568)
    identifying sort key in, 292-293
    numbering with a data series in, 285-287
    parts, (illus., 72)
    printed, (illus., 457)
    range, 302, 313, 314-316, (illus., 450)
    range names, 315
    record, 284-285
    resorting, 294-295
    selecting information from, 296-312
    selecting sort range in, 290-291
    selection criteria for, 303-307
    sort key in, 292
    sorting, 289-295, (illus., 292)
    specifying criteria, 303-307
    statistical functions, 313-324, (illus., 319)
    two-input data table in, (illus., 323)
    uses, 71-73, 301-312
    using Data Find in, (illus., 309)
    vertical lookup in, (illus., 326)
DATA macro functions, 640-642
Date, 369-372, 380-381
    arithmetic, 385-387
    automatic formatting of, 380
    calculating with 1904 system, 553
    entry, 378-381
    format, 511
    formatting, 371, 374-375
    functions, 375-377, 378, (illus., 376)
    generating, 381-383
    printing current, 498
    selecting, 486
Date and time formats, (illus., 374, 375)
Date and time functions, (illus., 379)
Date serial number, 374, 375, 377, 378, 585
Date series, (illus., 383)
Date stamp macro, 408-411
DATE time and date function, 577, 585
Date Unit option, in Data Series dialog box, 486
DATEVALUE time and date function, 377, 577, 586
Date/Time Stamp macro, (illus., 410)
DAVERAGE database function, 567, 586
Day, specifying, 515
DAY time and date function, 577, 586
DCOUNT database function, 567, 587
DCOUNTA database function, 567, 587
DDB financial function, 568, 588
DDE (Dynamic Data Exchange), 560
Debugging macros, 413
Decimal digits, 112-113, 516
Decimal places, setting, 512
Decimals, rounding of, 573, 616
Defaults, setting with control panel, 38-41
DEFINE.NAME macro function, 642
Define Names dialog box, 527-529
Delete
    file, 496
    in worksheet, 490-491
Delete option, in Data Form dialog box, 484
DELETE macro functions, 642-643
Dependents option, in Formula Select Special, 536
Depreciation
    double declining balance, 568, 588
    straight-line, 569, 618
DEREF macro function, 644
Detail formatting, 196-202
Dialog box, 27-31, 86-87, (illus., 436, 437)
    building, 438-442
    components, 30-31
    data transferred from, (illus., 448)
    Edit Info, 439
    File Open, (illus., 28)
    in Dialog Editor, (illus., 441)
    macro function, 644
    open, (illus., 468)
    printer setup, (illus., 29)
    product list for, (illus., 445)
    question, (illus., 469)
    settings, 444-447, (illus., 442)
    summary of contents of, 484-485
Dialog Editor, 437
Dialog specifications, names on, (illus., 444)
Direct mouse commands, 63
Direction keys, 64-65, 92-96
Directories, hard disk, 127-128, 717-718
    creating with File Manager, 41-45
DIRECTORY macro function, 644
Directory tree, 41-42, (illus., 42)
DISABLE.INPUT macro function, 644
Disk directories, 711-713
Display, 713

Display, *continued*
    changing worksheet, 553-554
Display adaptors, 713
DISPLAY macro function, 644-645
DMAX database function, 567, 588
DMIN database function, 567, 588
Document
    active, 562-563
    closing, 496
    opening existing, 497-498
    printing name of, 498
    protecting, 555-556
    returning to active, 562
    unprotect in Chart, 479-480
DOCUMENTS macro function, 645
DOLLAR function, 589
Dollar signs, adding, 200-201
Double declining balance method, 568, 588
DPRODUCT database function, 567, 589
DSTDEV database function, 568, 589-590
DSTDEVP database function, 568, 590
DSUM database function, 568, 590
DVAR database function, 568, 590-591
DVARP database function, 568, 591
Dynamic Data Exchange (DDE), 560
ECHO macro function, 645
Edit area, 88
Edit Clear option, in Chart Select Chart, 479
Edit Copy option, 299, 451, 479, 489
Edit Copy Picture option, 489-490
Edit Cut option, 490
Edit Delete option, 490-491
Edit Fill Down option, 491
Edit Fill Left option, 491
Edit Fill Right option, 491
Edit Fill Up option, 492
Edit Insert option, 492
Edit keys, described, 117-118
Edit menu, 82, 488-495
    pasting options, 121-123
    results of choosing Fill Down, (illus., 124)
Edit Paste Link option, 494
Edit Paste option, 489, 492-493
Edit Paste Special option, 489, 493, 494-495
Edit Repeat option, 495
Edit Undo option, 495
EDIT.DELETE macro function, 645-646
Editing, 115-117
    correcting errors, 139-141
    formula, 161-165
    insert mode, 116
    macro, 453-455
    overtype mode, 116
    Undo for removal and restoring in, 115

Editing, *continued*
    with Data Form, 453-455
    with mouse, 118-120
ENABLE.COMMAND macro function, 646
ERROR macro function, 646
Error value, 570, 598
EXACT text function, 575, 591
Excel
    installing, 720
    loading, (illus., 725)
    Setup Disk, 720
EXEC macro function, 646
EXECUTE macro function, 647
Exit
    from Data Find option, 481, 482
    from Excel, 497
Exit Find option, 308
Exit option, 484
EXP mathematics function, 572, 592
External reference formula, 345, 348, 353
External references, 348
EXTRACT macro function, 647
Extract range, 302, 481
FACT mathematics function, 573, 592
Factorial, 573, 592
FALSE logical function, 571, 592
FCLOSE macro function, 647
Field names, 71, 487
Fields, 70-71
File Close All option, 496
File Close option, 496
File Delete option, 496
File Exit option, 497
File formats, 354-355
File Links option, 497
File Manager, (illus., 42)
File menu, 82, 495-501
File New option, 497
File Open dialog box, (illus., 28)
File Open option, 497-498
File Page Setup option, 456, 498-499
File Print option, 499
File Printer Setup option, 499
File Save option, 426, 500
File Save As option, 500
File Save Workspace option, 500-501
File Unhide Window option, 501
FILE.CLOSE macro function, 647
FILE.DELETE macro function, 648
Filename, selecting, 500
Files, 124-129
    combining, 349-353
    linking, 66-68, 497
FILES macro function, 648

Fill Down option, 336
FILL macro functions, 648
Fill Right option, 336
Financial functions, 392-393, (listed, 392-393)
    summary of, 568-569
Financial plan, (illus., 54)
FIND text function, 575, 592-593
Find Next option, in Data Form dialog box, 484
Find Prev option, in Data Form dialog box, 484
Fixed Decimal box, 559
FIXED text function, 575, 593
Font box, 504, 506
Font list box, 505
Font options, defined, 236
Fonts, 504-506
    dialog box, (illus., 87)
Footers, 213
    controlling, 498
FOPEN macro function, 649
FOR macro function, 649
Form option, in Data Form dialog box, 484
Format, 194-196
    default, 510
    percentage, 197-199
Format Alignment option, 502
Format Border option, 423-425, 502-503
Format box, for main chart, 508-509
Format box, in Format Overlay option, 516-517
Format Cell Protection option, 503
Format Column Width option, 504
Format Font dialog box, 507, 522, 523, 524
Format Font option, 479, 504-506
Format Justify option, 507
Format Legend option, 507-508
FORMAT macro functions, 649-651
Format Main Chart option, 479, 508-509
Format menu, 83, 235-236, 501-524
    options, (listed, 501-524)
Format Move option, 509
Format Number option, 510-516
Format Overlay option, 479, 516-518
Format Patterns dialog box, 506, 523
Format Patterns option, 479, 518-520
Format Row Height option, 520
Format Scale dialog box, 520
Format Scale option, 521-523
Format Size option, 524
Format symbols, (listed, 189-194)
Format Text dialog box, 506, 520
Format Text option, 524
Formatting, 185-196
    database, 288-289
    macro, 407
    symbols, 512-516

Formula Apply Names option, 525-526
Formula bar, 87-89
    box, 560
    calculating formulas in, 551-552
    pasting built-in function into, 531
Formula building, 151-154
Formula Create Names option, 526-527
Formula Define Names option, 306, 433, 460, 527
Formula Define Names Delete option, 557
Formula Find option, 529
Formula Goto option, 451, 530
FORMULA macro functions, 652-654
Formula menu, 83, 525-537
Formula Note option, 530-531
Formula Paste Function option, 531
Formula Paste Name option, 532-533
Formula Reference option, 533
Formula Replace option, 533-534
Formula Select Special option, 535-537
Formulas, 57-60
    box, 554
    building columnar, 150-155
    copying, 155-157
    copying a column of, 166-167, (illus., 157)
    copying a row of, 170-172
    creating linking, 344-346
    editing, 161-165
    entering for worksheet, 147-167
    moving for layout changes, 203
    relative addressing, 156
    selecting cells containing, 535-536
    using assumptions in, 157-159
FPOS macro function, 655
FREAD macro function, 655
FREADLN macro function, 655
Freeze Panes option, 558
FREEZE.PANES macro function, 655
FSIZE macro function, 655
FULL macro function, 656
Function keys, 64, 96-102
    shortcuts, 99
Function macros, 414-416
Functions, 57-60, 387-397, 565-626
    as a formula, 391
    blank cells and, 391
    case sensitivity of, 390
    creating, 390-391
    error values in, 389-390
    financial, 392-394
    HLOOKUP, 324-327
    IF (ISNAC), 418
    logical, 395
    logical value, 389
    Lookup, 324-327

Functions, *continued*
    macro, 65
    mathematical, 395-396
    numbers as arguments in, 388
    parentheses and, 390
    pasting into formula bar, 531
    spaces in, 390
    string, 396
    sum (range), 388
    syntax for creating, 390-391
    text, 388, 396-397
    VLOOKUP, 324-327
    with = symbol, 390
    with specifying arguments, 388
Future value, determining, 568, 593
FV financial function, 568, 593
FWRITE macro function, 656
FWRITELN macro function, 656
Gallery Area option, 537-538
Gallery Bar option, 538-539
Gallery Column option, 539
Gallery Combination function, 539-540
Gallery Line option, 540-541
GALLERY macro functions, 656-658
Gallery menu, 232-234, 537-543
Gallery Pie option, 541-542
Gallery Preferred option, 542
    default of, 542
Gallery Scatter option, 542-543
Gallery Set Preferred option, 543
General format, 194-195
GET macro functions, 659-667
Glossary terms, explanation of, 68
GOTO macro function, 406, 667
Gridline and Heading Color box, 554-555
Gridlines
    box, 554
    chart, 478
    display, 554
    turning on and off, 478
GRIDLINES macro function, 668
Grabber hand, defined, 68
GROWTH function, 594
Growth percentages formatted, (illus., 198)
Guess option, 366
    in Data Parse, 485
HALT macro function, 668
Headers, 213
    centering, 201-202
    controlling, 498
Headings
    codes for with functions listed, 213-214
    completed column of, (illus., 143)
    entering for a page, 213-215

Headings, *continued*
    entering row of, 142-143
    placing of for worksheet, 138-143
Height, 520
Help, 45-49, 68-70
Help About option, 544
Help Feature Guide option, 544-545
Help Index option, 545
Help Keyboard option, 545
Help Lotus 1-2-3 option, 545
HELP macro function, 668
Help menu, 543-546
Help Multiplan option, 545
Help Tutorial option, 546
Help window, for Edit Copy command, (illus., 69)
Hidden option, in format cell protection, 503
Hidden window, unhiding, 563
HIDE macro function, 668
Hiding windows, 561
High-low-close charts, 245
HLINE macro function, 668
HLOOKUP function, 324-327, 572, 594-595
Horizontal array, 566
Horizontal lookup table, 572, 594-595
Hour, specifying, 515
HOUR time and date function, 577, 595
HPAGE macro function, 669
HSCROLL macro function, 669
Icons, 9
    moved, (illus., 13)
IF logical function, 571, 595
IF macro function, 462
Index
    help, 97, 545
    windows help, 47-48
INDEX lookup function, 572, 596
INDIRECT information function, 570, 596
Individual column width, adjusting, 204-206
Info menu, 546-547
Information, editing, 103-131
Informational functions, 394
INITIATE macro function, 669
Init/Result field, 439
INPUT macro function, 669-670
INSERT macro function, 670
Inserting, new columns or rows in worksheet, 492
INT mathematic function, 573, 596-597
Interest payments, determining, 568, 597
Interest rate, determining, 569, 614-615
Internal rate of return, determining, 568, 597
IPMT financial function, 568, 597
IRR financial function, 568, 597
ISBLANK information function, 570, 598
ISERR information function, 570, 598

ISLOGICAL information function, 570, 599
ISNA information function, 570, 599
ISNONTEXT information function, 570, 599
ISNUMBER information function, 570, 599
ISREF information function, 570, 600
ISTEXT information function, 571, 600
Italic typeface, 498, 505
Item button option, 439
Item edit box, 439
Item List Box option, 440
Item Text option, 440
Iteration box, 552
Iterations, 552-553
Jump terms, defined, 68
Justification, 498, 507
JUSTIFY macro function, 670
Keyboard, 31-37, 62, 91-102
    divisions, 91
    help, 545
    indicators for status bar, 90-91
    menu choices from, 474
    moving through database from, 483
    using to control menu options, 34-37
Keys, shortcut, 65
Labels, 138-141
Layout, changing, 202-210
Leaving Excel, 281
LEFT text functions, 576, 600
Legend, 520
    adding to chart, 475
    creating, 257-258
    deleting from chart, 477
    marker, (illus., 260)
    placing in chart, 507-508
LEGEND macro function, 670
LEN text function, 576, 601
Line chart, 476
Line charts, 244-246, 258, 261, 540-541,
    adding annotation for, 256-266
    changing type for, 254-256
    closing, 268
    creating, 251-268
    edited with series formula, 258-261
    formatting text in, 264-266
    highlighting data series ranges in, 252-253
    pattern dialog box for, (illus., 266)
    placing titles and text in, 261-264
    plotting with, 251-253
    saving and printing, 267-268
    selecting ranges in, 251-253
    shadow bordering of, (illus., 267)
    title of worksheets, (illus., 263)
    unattached texts for, 257
    with stock market charts, 245-246

LINEST function, 601
Linked files, 497
LINKS macro function, 670
List, paste, 532
LIST.NAMES macro function, 671
Literal, defined, 57
LN mathematics function, 573, 601
Loans
    calculating payment amount of, 569, 612
    principle payment amount of, 569, 613
Locked option, in format cell protection, 503
LOG mathematics function, 573, 602
LOG10 mathematics function, 573, 602
Logarithmic scale, 523
LOGEST function, 602-603
Logical formulas, defined, 57
Logical functions, 395, 571-572
Logical value, 570, 599
LOOKUP function, 572, 603-604
Lookup functions, 324-327, (exercise, 325-327)
Loops, 649, 673
Lotus 1-2-3, help option for, 545
Lowercase letters, 604. *See also* Case sensitivity
LOWER text function, 576, 604
Macro Absolute Record option, 548
Macro, 398-403
    column width, 410-411
    command, 414
    corrected Add.Record, (illus., 453)
    copy, 403-405, (illus., 405)
    date and time stamp, 408-411
Macro functions, 65, 397, 400, 413-414
    condition statement for, 462
    Enter.It, (illus., 461)
    GOTO, 406
    return, 406
    terminating, 412
Macro listing, (illus., 464-465)
Macro menu, 85, 547-550
Macro name, formatting, 401
Macro Record option, 431, 548
Macro Relative Record option, 549
Macro Run option, 549
Macro Set Recorder option, 430, 549-550
Macro sheet, 65, 400, (illus., 422)
    Formula Define Names option in, 528-529
    Paste List option in, 532-533
Macro Start Recorder option, 550
Macro Stop Recorder option, 430, 548, 550
Macros, 61, 397-418
    building, 427-463
    building a dialog box with, 436-442
    building printing, 455-457
    creating, 403-411, (illus., 404)

Macros, *continued*
    debugging, 413, 434, 463-470
    dialog box setting for, 442-447
    documenting, 400-401
    entering, 411-414, (exercise, 411-412)
    executing, (exercise, 467-470)
    formatting, 407
    opening worksheets with, 431-432
    positioning screens with, 432-434
    preparing worksheets with, 429-436
    printing, (exercise, 463)
    recording, 398-400, 548-550
    recording using absolute cell references, 548
    restoring worksheets with, 431-432
    running, 398, 401-403, (exercise, 402)
    saving and quitting, 457-459, (illus., 458)
    setting a recording range with, 405-407
    updating the database with, 447-453
Main application group, 37-45
MAIN macro functions, 671
Manual page breaks, 557. *See also* Page breaks
Margins, (illus., 216)
    changing, 498
    setting for page, 215-217
MATCH lookup function, 572, 604-605
Math coprocessor, 544
Mathematical functions, 395-396, (listed, 395)
    choosing in Edit Paste Special option, 494
Matrix functions, summary of, 573-574
MAX function, 605-606
MDETERM matrix function, 573, 606
Memory, 710
    information on available, 544
Menu bar, 8, 81-87, 473, 474
    alternatives, 460
Menu commands, 473-563
Menu data, 84
Menu file, 82
    File Manager's, (illus., 44)
    options, 26
Menu format, 83
Menu formula, 83
Menu options, 474
Menu system, using, (exercise, 121)
Menus, 25-31, 78-91, 120-124
    building, 459-463, (exercise, 459)
    cascading, 26
    display, 558
    edit, 82
    Excel, (listed, 474)
    full in chart, 479
    macro, 85
    options, 25-26, 84-85
    short in chart, 479

Menus, *continued*
    window, 85-86
Message area, 89-90
MESSAGE macro function, 672
Message string, 672
MID text function, 576, 606-607
MIN function, 607
MINUTE time and date function, 577, 607
Minutes, specifying, 515
MINVERSE matrix function, 574, 607-608
MIRR financial function, 569, 608
Mixed addresses, 156, 161
MMULT matrix function, 574, 609
MOD mathematics function, 573, 609
Modifications, worksheet, 226
Modified internal rate of return, determining, 569, 608
Modulus, 573, 609
MONTH time and date function, 577, 609-610
Months, specifying, 515
Mouse, 10-14, 62, 344, 473
MOVE macro function, 672
Moving chart objects with keyboard, 509
Multiplan, help option for, 545
Multiple files, 66-68
N information function, 571, 610
NA information function, 571, 610
Name file, 500
Name window, 675
Named area, selection of in Formula Goto option, 530
Names, 526-532
NAMES macro function, 672
Negative numbers, 514
Net present value, calculating, 569, 611
New charts, creating, 253
NEW macro functions, 672-673
NEXT macro function, 673
NOT logical function, 571, 610
NOTE macro function, 673
Notepad, 7, 22
Notes, 530-535
NOW time and date function, 378, 379, 577, 610-611
NPER financial function, 569, 611
NPV financial function, 569, 611
Number formats, built-in, 510-511
Numbers
    cell, 55
    editing and completing column, 148-150
    entering columns of, 148-150
    entering worksheet, 104-113, 147-167, (exercise, 109-111)
Numeric formulas, 57
Numeric keyboard, 111-112
OFFSET macro function, 673
ON macro functions, 674-675

100 percent Bar chart, 242
OPEN macro function, 675-676
Options Calculate Document option, 551
Options Calculate Now option, 551-552
Options Calculation dialog box, 477, 551
Options Calculation option, 552-553
Options option, choosing file format with, 500
Options Display option, 400, 553-555
Options Freeze Panes option, 555
Options Full Menus option, 555
Options, menu, 474, 475-563
Options menu, 84-85, 550-560
Options Protect Document option, 503, 555-556
Options Remove Page Break option, 556
Options Set Page Break option, 556-557
Options Set Print Area option, 455, 557
Options Set Print Titles option, 557-558
Options Short Menus option, 558
Options Unfreeze Panes option, 558
Options Unprotect Document option, 558
Options Workspace option, 559-560
OR logical function, 572, 612
Order Entry option, 467
Order of calculation, 58-59
Outlining, cell, 502
Overall column width format, 195-196
Overall format, (illus., 188)
Overall number format, 186-189
Overlap box, 509, 517
Overlapping windows, rearranging, 561
Overlay chart, 477-478, 517-518
OVERLAY macro functions, 677
Overlays
    adding to chart, 475-476
    creating chart, 540
    formatting, 516-518
    preserving, 538
Page breaks, 688
    setting and removing, 556-557
    setting manual, 550
Page numbers, printing, 498
Page setup, 212-217
    changing, 498-499
PAGE.SETUP macro function, 678
Paintbrush, 7, 23
Panes, 66
    unfreezing, 558
Paragraph separators, 507
Paragraphs, justified, 507
Parameters, setting, 311-217
Parse Line box, 485
PARSE macro function, 679
Parse range, selecting, 485
Parsing nondelimited text files, 364-368

Password, 480, 500, 556, 558
    for chart protection, 478
    in hiding windows, 561
Paste arguments option box, 391
Paste function dialog box, 391
Paste function option, 391
PASTE macro function, 679
Paste Special
    command, 225-226
    option, 349, 351, 352, 353
PASTE macro functions, 679-681
Pasting, 492-495
    options in Edit Menu, (exercise, 121-123)
Pattern options, 236
Patterns
    changing, 274-276
    changing in Format Legend box, 508
    choosing chart, 506
    dialog box, (illus., 266, 276)
    format, 518-520, 522
    format in Chart Select Chart, 479
PATTERNS macro function, 682-685
Payments, determining number of, 569, 611
Percentage format, creating, 197-199
Percentage growth formula, 170
Phone list, worksheet, (illus., 70)
Pi, 573, 612
Picture, copying, 489-490
Pie charts, 246-248, 541-542, (illus., 74)
    adding percentages to, (exercise, 270)
    adding refinements in, 273-277
    adding titles in, 271-273, (exercise, 271-272)
    angle of first slice in, 509, 517
    changing color of, 274-276
    changing patterns of, 274-276
    closing, 276-278
    creating, 269-278
    editing labels in, (illus., 247)
    exploding a wedge in, 276, (exercise, 276)
    patterns dialog box for, (illus., 276)
    printing, 276-278
    saving, 276-278
    selecting, 269-271
    slices, 248
PIF Editor, 7
PMT financial function, 569, 612
Point, data, 476
POKE macro function, 685
Port, changing printer, 499
PPMT financial function, 569, 613
Precedents option, in Formula Select Special, 536
Precision As Displayed box, 553
PRECISION macro function, 685
PREFERRED macro function, 686

Present value of payments, determining, 569, 614
Preview, zoomed, (illus., 220)
Print area, setting, 557
Print dialog box, (illus., 219)
PRINT macro function, 686
Print option, 218
Print Range, 211-212
Print titles, overlapping, 557
Printer Fonts box, 504
Printer Setup dialog box, (illus., 29)
PRINTER.SETUP macro function, 686-687
Printers, 222-223, 713-714
    changing, 499
    installing new, 499
    ports, 714
    problems with, 223
    setting up, 499
Printing
    charts same size as screen, 499
    files, 499
    line charts, 267-268
    macro, 455-457, (exercise, 455-456)
    multiple copies, 499
    page, 217-222
    pie charts, 276-278
    quality of, 499
    saving and quitting, 455-459
    stacked column charts, 279-281
PRODUCT mathematics function, 573, 613
Program Manager Help, index to, (illus., 46)
Prompt command, 716
PROPER text function, 576, 613
PROTECT.DOCUMENT macro function, 687
Protection
    chart, 478
    document, 555-556
    format cell, 503
PV financial function, 569, 614
Quit, 227-228
    Excel, 102, 129-131
RAND mathematics function, 573, 614
Random number, 573, 614
Ranges, 54-57, (illus., 171)
    clearing, 172-174
    defined for standard charts, 230-231
    defining as a database, 487
    erasing, 208-209
    filling in with Data Series option, 485-486
    formatted, (illus., 187)
    highlighted, (illus., 64)
    names, 56, (listed, 466), (exercise, 316)
    names proposed by Excel for, 528
    number of rows in, 571, 617
    setting criteria, 487

Ranges, *continued*
    similar, 349
RATE financial function, 569, 614-615
Ready mode, defined, 89-90
Real mode, 707-708
Record Indicator, in Data Form dialog box, 484
Recorder, 7
    macro, 548
Records, 71
    adding new to database, 482
    defined, 70
    deleting from database, 480
Reference area, for formula bar, 87
References, 335
REFTEXT macro function, 687
    using with SELECTION macro function, 695
REGISTER macro function, 688
Relative addressing, 156
RELREF macro function, 688
Remote references, updating, 553
REMOVE.PAGE.BREAK macro function, 688
RENAME.COMMAND macro function, 688
Repeat, edit, 495
Replace, character, 533-534
REPLACE text function, 576, 615
REPLACE.FONT macro function, 689
REPT text function, 576, 615
REQUEST macro function, 689
RESTART macro function, 689
Restore
    button, 15
    option, 338
    option in Data Form dialog box, 485
RESULT macro function, 414-415, 689-690
RETURN macro function, 415-416, 690
Reverse order, 521, 523
RIGHT text function, 576, 616
R1C1, 434, 559
ROUND mathematic function, 573, 616
Row and Column Headings box, 554
Row headings, printing, 557
Row labels, completing, (illus., 140)
ROW macro function, 571, 616
Row numbers, array of, 571, 616
ROW.HEIGHT macro function, 690
Rows, 53-54, 71
    comparing cells in, 536
    deleting, 175-176, 490-491
    inserting, 174-177
    setting height of, 520
    sorting by, 488
    worksheet, 79-80
ROWS information function, 571, 617
Ruler On option, 357

Run dialog box, 401, 402, 403
RUN macro option, 690
Sample standard deviation, 568, 589
Save As dialog box, 354-355
SAVE macro functions, 691, (exercise, 398-399)
Saving, 227-228
    and quitting in worksheet, 178-181
    and quitting macros, (exercise, 457-459)
    line charts, 267-268
    pie charts, 276-278
    stacked column charts, 279-281
SCALE macro function, 692
Scale option, 236
Scatter charts, 248-251, 542-543, (illus., 249)
Scientific format, 515
Screens, 78-91
    blank worksheet, (illus., 78)
    moving single, 93
    positioning of, 432-433
    widths and heights for title, (illus., 424)
Scroll arrows, 18
Scroll bars, 18-20, 559-560
Scrolling, 18, 555
Search
    backward in database, 482
    character, 533-534
    in Formula Find option, 529
    menu, 357
    string and value, 572, 583
SEARCH text function, 576, 617
SECOND time and date function, 578, 617
Seconds, specifying, 516
SELECT macro functions, 692-694
SELECTION macro function, 695
SEND.KEYS macro function, 695-696
Series
    automatic distribution of, 518
Series formula, 258-261
Series names, adding, 475
Set Criteria option, 303
SET macro functions, 696-697
Set Recorder option, 406, 407
Shade option, 425
Shading, cell, 502
Shadow, 519
Shortcut keys, 27, 65
SHORT.MENUS macro function, 697
SHOW macro functions, 698
Show Info option, 546
SIGN mathematic function, 573, 617
SIN trigonometric function, 579, 618
Size, font in chart, 506
Size box, font, 505
SIZE macro function, 699

Sizing, chart with keyboard, 524
Skip-blanks, 680
Slash key, 560
SLN financial function, 569, 618
SORT macro function, 699
Sort order, 293
Sorting, 488
Source data, copying, 494
SPLIT macro function, 699
SQRT mathematic function, 573, 618
Stacked bar chart, 240
Stacked column chart, 278-281
Stacked line chart, 238
Standard charts, 230-231
Standard deviation, 568, 589-590, 619
Standard mode, 706-707
Start Recorder option, 407
Statistical functions, 313-319, 574-575
Status bar, 89-91, 474, 559
STDEV function, 618
STDEVP function, 619
STEP macro function, 700
Step Value option, in Data Series dialog box, 486
Stock market charts, 245-246, (illus., 246)
Stop Recorder option, 405
Stop Value option, in Data Series dialog box, 486
Straight-line depreciation method, 569, 618
Strikeout font, 505
String, duplicating, 615
String function, 396
STYLE macro function, 700
Styles, font in chart, 506
SUBSTITUTE text function, 576, 619
SUM formula, (illus., 153)
SUM function, 619-620
Sum-of-the-year's-digits depreciation, 569, 620
SYD financial function, 569, 620
Symbols, formatting, 512-516
T information function, 571, 620
TABLE macro function, 700
Tabs, replaced with commas, 357, 359
TAN trigonometric function, 578, 620
Templates, making, 224-228
TERMINATE macro function, 700
Text
    alignment, 104-105
    attaching to chart, 476
    entering for worksheet, 104-113
    entries, (illus., 108)
Text file
    delimited, 361-362
    importing, (exercise, 359-361)
    nondelimited, 359, 362-368
    opening, (exercise, 361)

Text file, *continued*
    opening nondelimited ASCII, 362-364
    parsing, (exercise, 365-368)
    tab delimited, 361
    saving a worksheet as, 353-359
Text formatting, in line charts, 264-266
Text formula, defined, 57
Text functions, 396, (listed, 396-397)
    summary of, 575-577
Text, line chart, 261-264
Text string, returning, 575, 583, 676
TEXT text function, 576, 621
Text, typing, (exercise, 105-108)
Text, vertical alignment of in chart, 524
TEXTTREF macro function, 701
Tick labels, 519, 521
Tick Mark Type, changing, 519, 341, 344
Time
    arithmetic, 385-387
    automatic formatting of, 381
    calculating, 372-374, (exercise, 372-373)
    entry, 378-381
    format, 511
    formatting, 374-375
    functions, 375-378, (illus., 377)
    generating, 383-385, (exercise, 384)
    printing current, 498
Time and date functions, summary of, 577-578
Time stamp macro, 408-411
TIME time and date function, 578, 621
TIMEVALUE time and date function, 378, 578, 621
Tiled view, 340-341
Title
    centering, 141-142
    chart, 476
    recentering, 206-207
Title bar, defined, 8
Title screen, (illus., 435)
    with menu, (illus., 467)
Titles
    changing, 224-225
    deleting, 558
    in line charts, 261-264
    placing of for worksheet, 138-143
Totals and percents, (illus., 172)
TRANSPOSE matrix function, 574, 621-622
Transposition, array, 574, 621-622
TREND function, 622-623
Trigonometric functions, summary of, 578
TRIM text function, 577, 623
TRUE logical function, 572, 623
TRUNC mathematic function, 573, 623
Tutorial, 543, 546
Type box, 507, 516

TYPE information function, 571, 624
Type option, in Data Series dialog box, 486
Underlining, 505
Undo, edit, 495
UNDO macro function, 701
Undo option, 115, 209-210
UNHIDE macro function, 701
Unhide Window option, 501
Unique Record Only option, 481
UNLOCKED macro functions, 701
Unprotect document, 558
Uppercase letters, 613, 624. *See also* case sensitivity
UPPER text function, 577, 624
Value axis, 231
Value Axis Scale dialog box, 522
VALUE text function, 577, 624
Values, adding in database, 568, 590
Values option, 351
VAR function, 624-625
Variance, 568, 590, 624
VARP function, 625
Version, information about Excel, 544
Vertical lookup table, 572, 625-626
Visual interface, defined, 6
VLINE macro function, 701
VLOOKUP function, 324-327, 572, 625-626
VPAGE macro function, 702
VSCROLL macro function, 702
WAIT macro function, 702
WEEKDAY time and date function, 578, 626
WHILE macro function, 702
Wildcard characters, 125
Window accessories, 14, 20
Window Arrange All option, 561
Window Hide option, 561
Window menu, 85-86, 546, 560-563
Window More Windows option, 561
Window ORDSHEET.XLS, 430
Window New Window option, 561-562
Window Show Document option, 562
Window Show Info option, 562-563
Window tools, (listed, 7)
Window Unhide option, 563
WINDOWS macro function, 702
Windows option, 556
Windows, 14, 5-50, (exercise, 717-718)
    activating, 560
    application, 14-15, (illus., 25, 725)
    bars in, 80-91
    changing AUTOEXEC.BAT in, 715-716
    changing CONFIG.SYS in, 714-715
    closing, 496
    directories, 717-718
    equipment required for, 706

Windows, *continued*
    help for Edit Copy command, (illus., 69)
    help index, (illus., 47)
    installing, 705-726, (table, 709)
    leaving, 49-50, 724-726, (exercise, 724-726)
    memory required for, 710-711
    multiple, 544
    network, 708
    notepad, (illus., 22)
    overlapping, 338, 561
    Paintbrush, (illus., 23)
    printers for, 707-708, 713-714
    Program Manager, (illus., 36, 49)
    setup programs, 718-720, (exercise, 719)
    shrunken accessories, (illus., 17)
    starting, 9, 720-724, (exercise, 721-722)
    tiled-view, 340-341
    worksheet, 65-66, (illus., 66)
    write, 359
Window-sizing, (exercise, 16-18)
Worksheets, 53-70, (illus., 53, 178)
    adding to, (illus., 350)
    automating, 419, 420
    building, 349, 423-426
    changing, 339-340
    chart menus for, 232
    column width of, 108-109
    combining files, 349-353, (exercise, 349-352)
    completing, 169-181
    components of, 51
    copying, 167-168, 489
    copying between, 337-342, (exercise, 337-338)
    correcting, 177-178
    creating, 135-181
    creating linking formulas for, 342-346
    creating multiple, 334-337
    CSV formatted, (illus., 358)
    customizing, 341, (exercise, 341-342)
    dragging, 339
    entering formulas in, 147-167

Worksheets, *continued*
    entering numbers in, 147-167
    erasing, (illus., 210)
    file formats, 354-355
    headings for, 138-143
    importing ASCII text files in, 359-368
    labels, 138-143
    layout changes, 202-210, (illus., 137)
    linking, 332-348
    loading, 184-185
    macros, 429-431
    multiple, 252, 332, 338-341
    opening, (exercise, 432)
    overlapping, 338
    placing borders in, 143-146
    planning, 136-138
    preparing databases for, 425-426
    printing, 211-224, (illus., 180, 222)
    recalculating with Options menu, 551
    restoring, 431-432, (exercise, 431)
    row headings, (illus., 335)
    saving, 146-147, 178-181, 224
    saving multiple, 346-348, (illus., 333)
    titles for, 138-143
    typing on, 104-113
    values, 348
    windows, 65-66, 79-80
    with stair-stepping, (illus., 339)
    with summary formulas, (illus., 346)
Workspace, 8
Workspace file, 500-501
WORKSPACE macro function, 703
Write, word processing program, 7
Write formula, converting the, 357
X-axis, turning off in chart, 476
XY charts, (illus., 249)
Y-axis, turning off in chart, 476
Year, specifying, 515
YEAR time and date function, 578, 626
Zero Values box, 554

# EXCEL 2.1 COMMAND CARD

## Shortcut Keys

| OPTION | SHORTCUT KEY |
|---|---|
| Absolute/mixed/relative | F4 |
| Add to current selection | SHIFT + F8 |
| Calculate active document | SHIFT + F9 |
| Calculate all documents | F9 or CTRL + = |
| Cancel | ESC |
| Clear | DEL |
| Clear formula | CTRL + DEL |
| Close active application | ALT + F4 |
| Close active document | CTRL + F4 |
| Copy | CTRL + INSERT |
| Create names | CTRL + SHIFT + F3 |
| Cut | SHIFT + DELETE |
| Define names | CTRL + F3 |
| Delete cells | CTRL + - |
| Delete contents (Clear) | DEL |
| Exit find | ESC |
| Extend selection | F8 |
| Fill down | CTRL + < or CTRL + SHIFT + , |
| Fill right | CTRL + > or CTRL + SHIFT + . |

| OPTION | SHORTCUT KEY |
|---|---|
| Find dialog box | SHIFT + F5 |
| Find next | F7 |
| Find previous | SHIFT + F7 |
| Font 1 | CTRL + 1 |
| Font 2 | CTRL + 2 |
| Font 3 | CTRL + 3 |
| Font 4 | CTRL + 4 |
| Format 2 decimal places | CTRL + ! or CTRL + SHIFT + 1 |
| Format date | CTRL + # or CTRL + SHIFT + 3 |
| Format dollars | CTRL + $ or CTRL + SHIFT + 4 |
| Format general | CTRL + ~ or CTRL + SHIFT + ` |
| Format percent | CTRL + % or CTRL + SHIFT + 5 |
| Format scientific | CTRL + ^ or CTRL + SHIFT + 6 |
| Format time | CTRL + @ or CTRL + SHIFT + 2 |
| Formula/value display | CTRL + ' |
| Goto | F5 |
| Help in context | SHIFT + F1 |
| Help index | F1 |
| Insert cells | CTRL + + or CTRL + SHIFT + = |

©Martin S. Matthews and Carole B. Matthews

Excel 2.1 Made Easy

| OPTION | SHORTCUT KEY |
|---|---|
| Insert date while editing | CTRL + ; |
| Insert formula above | CTRL + ' |
| Insert time while editing | CTRL + : or CTRL + SHIFT + ; |
| Insert value above | CTRL + " or CTRL + SHIFT + ' |
| Maximize application window | ALT + F10 (runtime Windows only) |
| Maximize/redstore document window | CTRL + F10 |
| Menu | F10 |
| Minimize application window | ALT + F9 (runtime Windows only) |
| Move application window | ALT + F7 (runtime Windows only) |
| Move document window | CTRL + F7 |
| New chart | F11 or ALT + F1 |
| New macro | CTRL + F11 or ALT + CTRL + F1 |
| New worksheet | SHIFT + F11 or ALT + SHIFT + F1 |
| Next pane | F6 |
| Next window | CTRL + F6 |
| Note entry, edit | SHIFT + F2 |
| Open file | CTRL + F12 or ALT + CTRL + F2 |

| OPTION | SHORTCUT KEY |
|---|---|
| Paste | SHIFT + INSERT |
| Paste function | SHIFT + F3 |
| Paste name | F3 |
| Previous pane | SHIFT + F6 |
| Previous window | CTRL + SHIFT + F6 |
| Print selection | ALT + CTRL + SHIFT + F2 |
| Repeat | ALT + ENTER |
| Save | SHIFT + F12 or ALT + SHIFT + F2 |
| Save as | F12 or ALT + F2 |
| Select column | CTRL + SPACEBAR |
| Select region | CTRL + * or CTRL + SHIFT + 8 |
| Select row | SHIFT + SPACEBAR |
| Show document/info | CTRL + F2 |
| Size application window | ALT + F8 (runtime Windows only) |
| Size document window | CTRL + F8 |
| Undo | ALT + BACKSPACE |